rendering of the Bible from the original languages, crafted to present its tone, rhythm, events, and ideas in everyday language.

Dalton - I wanted to send you a copy of Preston Bible. I sent one like this. It is just the New Testament and the book of Psalms & Proverbs - thought it would be easier to understand.

Love
Grammy

New Testament with Psalms and Proverbs

EUGENE H. PETERSON

The **MESSAGE**

NUMBERED EDITION

The Bible in Contemporary Language

NAVPRESS

NavPress is the publishing ministry of The Navigators, an international Christian organization and leader in personal spiritual development. NavPress is committed to helping people grow spiritually and enjoy lives of meaning and hope through personal and group resources that are biblically rooted, culturally relevant, and highly practical.

**For a free catalog go to www.NavPress.com
or call 1.800.366.7788 in the United States or 1.800.839.4769 in Canada.**

THE MESSAGE: The Bible in Contemporary Language
Copyright © 2002 by Eugene H. Peterson. All rights reserved.
THE MESSAGE Numbered Edition copyright © 2005

Version 2.0

www.messagebible.com.

Creative Team: Kent Wilson, Arvid Wallen, Pat Reinheimer, Darla Hightower, Cara Iverson, and Kathy Mosier

ISBN 1-60006-135-4

Bible, English. Message. 2002.
    The message : the Bible in contemporary language / Eugene H. Peterson.
        p. cm.
    ISBN 1-60006-135-4
    I. Peterson, Eugene H., 1932- II. Title.

BS195 .M47 2002
220.5'209--dc21

2002024653

Published in association with the literary agency of Alive Communications, Inc.,
7680 Goddard St., Suite 200, Colorado Springs, CO 80920.

Printed in the United States of America

3 4 5 6 7 8 9 10 11 12 13 14 15 16 17 / 15 14 13 12 11 10 09

NEW TESTAMENT

TO THE READER

If there is anything distinctive about *The Message*, perhaps it is because the text is shaped by the hand of a working pastor. For most of my adult life I have been given a primary responsibility for getting the message of the Bible into the lives of the men and women with whom I worked. I did it from pulpit and lectern, in home Bible studies and at mountain retreats, through conversations in hospitals and nursing homes, over coffee in kitchens and while strolling on an ocean beach. *The Message* grew from the soil of forty years of pastoral work.

As I worked at this task, this Word of God, which forms and transforms human lives, did form and transform human lives. Planted in the soil of my congregation and community the seed words of the Bible germinated and grew and matured. When it came time to do the work that is now *The Message*, I often felt that I was walking through an orchard at harvest time, plucking fully formed apples and peaches and plums from laden branches. There's hardly a page in the Bible I did not see lived in some way or other by the men and women, saints and sinners, to whom I was pastor—and then verified in my nation and culture.

I didn't start out as a pastor. I began my vocational life as a teacher and for several years taught the biblical languages of Hebrew and Greek in a theological seminary. I expected to live the rest of my life as a professor and scholar, teaching and writing and studying. But then my life took a sudden vocational turn to pastoring in a congregation.

I was now plunged into quite a different world. The first noticeable difference was that nobody seemed to care much about the Bible, which so recently people had been paying me to teach them. Many of the people I worked with now knew virtually nothing about it, had never read it, and weren't interested in learning. Many others had spent years reading it but for them it had gone flat through familiarity, reduced to clichés. Bored, they dropped it. And there weren't many people in between. Very few were interested in what I considered my primary work, getting the words of the Bible into their heads and hearts, getting the message lived. They found newspapers and magazines, videos and pulp fiction more to their taste.

Meanwhile I had taken on as my life work the responsibility of getting these very people to listen, really listen, to the message in this book.

I knew I had my work cut out for me.

I lived in two language worlds, the world of the Bible and the world of Today. I had always assumed they were the same world. But these people didn't see it that way. So out of necessity I became a "translator" (although I wouldn't have called it that then), daily standing on the border between two worlds, getting the language of the Bible that God uses to create and save us, heal and bless us, judge and rule over us, into the language of Today that we use to gossip and tell stories, give directions and do business, sing songs and talk to our children.

And all the time those old biblical languages, those powerful and vivid Hebrew and Greek originals, kept working their way underground in my speech, giving energy and sharpness to words and phrases, expanding the imagination of the people with whom I was working to hear the language of the Bible in the language of Today and the language of Today in the language of the Bible.

I did that for thirty years in one congregation. And then one day (it was April 30, 1990) I got a letter from an editor asking me to work on a new version of the Bible along the lines of what I had been doing as a pastor. I agreed. The next ten years was harvest time. *The Message* is the result.

The Message is a reading Bible. It is not intended to replace the excellent study Bibles that are available. My intent here (as it was earlier in my congregation and community) is simply to get people reading it who don't know that the Bible is read-able at all, at least by them, and to get people who long ago lost interest in the Bible to read it again. But I haven't tried to make it easy—there is much in the Bible that is hard to understand. So at some point along the way, soon or late, it will be important to get a standard study Bible to facilitate further study. Meanwhile, read in order to live, praying as you read, "God, let it be with me just as you say."

— EUGENE H. PETERSON

THE MESSAGE

Reading is the first thing, just reading the Bible. As we read we enter a new world of words and find ourselves in on a conversation in which God has the first and last words. We soon realize that we are included in the conversation. We didn't expect this. But this is precisely what generation after generation of Bible readers do find: The Bible is not only written about us but to us. In these pages we become insiders to a conversation in which God uses words to form and bless us, to teach and guide us, to forgive and save us.

We aren't used to this. We are used to reading books that explain things, or tell us what to do, or inspire or entertain us. But this is different. This is a world of revelation: God revealing to people just like us—men and women created in God's image—how God works and what is going on in this world in which we find ourselves. At the same time that God reveals all this, God draws us in by invitation and command to participate in God's working life. We gradually (or suddenly) realize that we are insiders in the most significant action of our time as God establishes his grand rule of love and justice on this earth (as it is in heaven). "Revelation" means that we are reading something we couldn't have guessed or figured out on our own. Revelation is what makes the Bible unique.

And so just reading this Bible, *The Message*, and listening to what we read, is the first thing. There will be time enough for study later on. But first, it is important simply to read, leisurely and thoughtfully. We need to get a feel for the way these stories and songs, these prayers and conversations, these sermons and visions, invite us into this large, large world in which the invisible God is behind and involved in everything visible and illuminates what it means to live here—really live, not just get across the street. As we read, and the longer we read, we begin to "get it"—we are in conversation with God. We find ourselves listening and answering in matters that most concern us: who we are, where we came from, where we are going, what makes us tick, the texture of the world and the communities we live in, and—most of all—the incredible love of God among us, doing for us what we cannot do for ourselves.

Through reading the Bible, we see that there is far more to the world, more to us, more to what we see and more to what we don't see—more to everything!—than we had ever dreamed, and that this "more" has to do with God.

This is new for many of us, a different sort of book—a book that reads us even as we read it. We are used to picking up and reading books for what we can get out of them: information we can use, inspiration to energize us, instructions on how to do something or other, entertainment to while away a rainy day, wisdom that will guide us into living better. These things can and do take place when reading the Bible, but the Bible is given to us in the first place simply to invite us to make ourselves at home in the world of God, God's word and world, and become familiar with the way God speaks and the ways in which we answer him with our lives.

❊

Our reading turns up some surprises. The biggest surprise for many is how accessible this book is to those who simply open it up and read it. Virtually anyone can read this Bible with understanding. The reason that new translations are made every couple of generations or so is to keep the language of the Bible current with the common speech we use, the very language in which it was first written. We don't have to be smart or well-educated to understand it, for it is written in the words and sentences we hear in the marketplace, on school playgrounds, and around the dinner table. Because the Bible is so famous and revered, many assume that we need experts to explain and interpret it for us—and, of course, there are some things that need to be explained. But the first men and women who listened to these words now written in our Bibles were ordinary, everyday, working-class people. One of the greatest of the early translators of the Bible into English, William Tyndale, said that he was translating so that "the boy that driveth the plough" would be able to read the Scriptures.

One well-educated African man, who later became one of the most influential Bible teachers in our history (Augustine), was greatly offended when he first read the Bible. Instead of a book cultivated and polished in the literary style he admired so much, he found it full of homespun, earthy stories of plain, unimportant people. He read it in a Latin translation full of slang and jargon. He took one look at what he considered the "unspiritual" quality of so many of its characters and the everydayness of Jesus, and contemptuously abandoned it. It was years before he realized that God had not taken the form of a sophisticated intellectual to teach us about highbrow heavenly culture so we could appreciate the finer things of God. When he saw that God entered our lives as a Jewish servant in order to save us from our sins, he started reading the Book gratefully and believingly.

Some are also surprised that Bible reading does not introduce us to a "nicer" world. This biblical world is decidedly not an ideal world, the kind we see advertised in travel posters. Suffering and injustice and ugliness are not purged from the world in which God works and loves and saves. Nothing is glossed over. God works patiently and deeply, but often in hidden ways, in the mess of our humanity and history. Ours is not a neat and tidy world in which we are assured that we can get everything under our control. This takes considerable getting used to—there is mystery everywhere. The Bible does not give us a predictable cause-effect world in which we can plan our careers and secure our futures.

It is not a dream world in which everything works out according to our adolescent expectations—there is pain and poverty and abuse at which we cry out in indignation, "You can't let this happen!" For most of us it takes years and years and years to exchange our dream world for this real world of grace and mercy, sacrifice and love, freedom and joy—the God-saved world.

Yet another surprise is that the Bible does not flatter us. It is not trying to sell us anything that promises to make life easier. It doesn't offer secrets to what we often think of as prosperity or pleasure or high adventure. The reality that comes into focus as we read the Bible has to do with what God is doing in a saving love that includes us and everything we do. This is quite different from what our sin-stunted and culture-cluttered minds imagined. But our Bible reading does not give us access to a mail-order catalog of idols from which we can pick and choose to satisfy our fantasies. The Bible begins with God speaking creation and us into being. It continues with God entering into personalized and complex relationships with us, helping and blessing us, teaching and training us, correcting and disciplining us, loving and saving us. This is not an escape from reality but a plunge into more reality—a sacrificial but altogether better life all the way.

God doesn't force any of this on us: God's word is personal address, inviting, commanding, challenging, rebuking, judging, comforting, directing—but not forcing. Not coercing. We are given space and freedom to answer, to enter the conversation. For more than anything else the Bible invites our participation in the work and language of God.

As we read, we find that there is a connection between the Word Read and the Word Lived. Everything in this book is live-able. Many of us find that the most important question we ask as we read is not "What does it mean?" but "How can I live it?" So we read personally, not impersonally. We read in order to live our true selves, not just get information that we can use to raise our standard of living. Bible reading is a means of listening to and obeying God, not gathering religious data by which we can be our own gods.

You are going to hear stories in this Book that will take you out of your preoccupation with yourself and into the spacious freedom in which God is working the world's salvation. You are going to come across words and sentences that stab you awake to a beauty and hope that will connect you with your real life.

Be sure to answer.

EUGENE H. PETERSON is a pastor, scholar, writer, and poet. After teaching at a seminary and then giving nearly thirty years to church ministry in the Baltimore area, he created *The Message* — a vibrant Bible paraphrase that connects with today's readers like no other.

It took Peterson a full ten years to complete. He worked from the original Greek and Hebrew texts to guarantee authenticity. At the same time, his ear was always tuned to the cadence and energy of contemporary English.

Eugene and his wife, Jan, now live in his native Montana. They are the parents of three and the grandparents of six.

TRANSLATION CONSULTANTS

Peterson's work has been thoroughly reviewed by the following team of recognized Old and New Testament scholars, who ensured that it is accurate as well as faithful to the original languages.

NEW TESTAMENT TEAM
William W. Klein, *Denver Seminary* (chair)
Darrell L. Bock, *Dallas Theological Seminary*
Donald A. Hagner, *Fuller Theological Seminary*
Moisés Silva, *Gordon-Conwell Theological Seminary*
Rodney A. Whitacre, *Trinity Episcopal School for Ministry*

THE NEW TESTAMENT

THE NEW TESTAMENT

The arrival of Jesus signaled the beginning of a new era. God entered history in a personal way, and made it unmistakably clear that he is on our side, doing everything possible to save us. It was all presented and worked out in the life, death, and resurrection of Jesus. It was, and is, hard to believe — seemingly too good to be true.

But one by one, men and women did believe it, believed Jesus was God alive among them and for them. Soon they would realize that he also lived in them. To their great surprise they found themselves living in a world where God called all the shots — had the first word on everything; had the last word on everything. That meant that everything, quite literally every thing, had to be re-centered, re-imagined, and re-thought.

They went at it with immense gusto. They told stories of Jesus and arranged his teachings in memorable form. They wrote letters. They sang songs. They prayed. One of them wrote an extraordinary poem based on holy visions. There was no apparent organization to any of this; it was all more or less spontaneous and, to the eye of the casual observer, haphazard. Over the course of about fifty years, these writings added up to what would later be compiled by the followers of Jesus and designated "The New Testament."

Three kinds of writing — eyewitness stories, personal letters, and a visionary poem — make up the book. Five stories, twenty one letters, one poem.

In the course of this writing and reading, collecting and arranging, with no one apparently in charge, the early Christians, whose lives were being changed and shaped by what they were reading, arrived at the conviction that there was, in fact, someone in charge — God's Holy Spirit was behind and in it all. In retrospect, they could see that it was not at all random or haphazard, that every word worked with every other word, and that all the separate documents worked in intricate harmony. There was nothing accidental in any of this, nothing merely circumstantial. They were bold to call what had been written "God's Word," and trusted their lives to it. They accepted its authority over their lives. Most of its readers since have been similarly convinced.

A striking feature in all this writing is that it was done in the street language of the day, the idiom of the playground and marketplace. In the Greek-speaking world of that day, there were two levels of language: formal and informal. Formal language was used to write philosophy and history, government decrees and epic poetry. If someone were to sit down and consciously write for posterity, it would of course be written in this formal language with its learned vocabulary and precise diction. But if the writing was routine — shopping lists, family letters, bills, and receipts — it was written in the common, informal idiom of everyday speech, street language.

And this is the language used throughout the New Testament. Some people are taken aback by this, supposing that language dealing with a holy God and holy things should be elevated — stately and ceremonial. But one good look at Jesus — his preference for down-to-earth stories and easy association with common people — gets rid of that supposition. For Jesus is the descent of God to our lives, just as they are, not the ascent of our lives to God, hoping he might approve when he sees how hard we try.

And that is why the followers of Jesus in their witness and preaching, translating and teaching, have always done their best to get the Message — the "good news" — into the language of whatever streets they happen to be living on. In order to understand the Message right, the language must be right — not a refined language that appeals to our aspirations after the best but a rough and earthy language that reveals God's presence and action where we least expect it, catching us when we are up to our elbows in the soiled ordinariness of our lives and God is the furthest thing from our minds.

This version of the New Testament in a contemporary idiom keeps the language of the Message current and fresh and understandable in the same language in which we do our shopping, talk with our friends, worry about world affairs, and teach our children their table manners. The goal is not to render a word-for-word conversion of Greek into English, but rather to convert the tone, the rhythm, the events, the ideas, into the way we actually think and speak.

In the midst of doing this work, I realized that this is exactly what I have been doing all my vocational life. For thirty-five years as a pastor I stood at the border between two languages, biblical Greek and everyday English, acting as a translator, providing the right phrases, getting the right words so that the men and women to whom I was pastor could find their way around and get along in this world where God has spoken so decisively and clearly in Jesus. I did it from the pulpit and in the kitchen, in hospitals and restaurants, on parking lots and at picnics, always looking for an English way to make the biblical text relevant to the conditions of the people.

MATTHEW

The story of Jesus doesn't begin with Jesus. God had been at work for a long time. Salvation, which is the main business of Jesus, is an old business. Jesus is the coming together in final form of themes and energies and movements that had been set in motion before the foundation of the world.

Matthew opens the New Testament by setting the local story of Jesus in its world historical context. He makes sure that as we read his account of the birth, life, death, and resurrection of Jesus, we see the connections with everything that has gone before. "Fulfilled" is one of Matthew's characteristic verbs: such and such happened "that it might be *fulfilled.*" Jesus is unique, but he is not odd.

Better yet, Matthew tells the story in such a way that not only is everything previous to us completed in Jesus; *we* are completed in Jesus. Every day we wake up in the middle of something that is already going on, that has been going on for a long time: genealogy and geology, history and culture, the cosmos — God. We are neither accidental nor incidental to the story. We get orientation, briefing, background, reassurance.

Matthew provides the comprehensive context by which we see all God's creation and salvation completed in Jesus, and all the parts of our lives — work, family, friends, memories, dreams — also completed in Jesus. Lacking such a context, we are in danger of seeing Jesus as a mere diversion from the concerns announced in the newspapers. Nothing could be further from the truth.

MATTHEW

1 The family tree of Jesus Christ, David's son, Abraham's son:

2-6 Abraham had Isaac,
Isaac had Jacob,
Jacob had Judah and his brothers,
Judah had Perez and Zerah (the mother was Tamar),
Perez had Hezron,
Hezron had Aram,
Aram had Amminadab,
Amminadab had Nahshon,
Nahshon had Salmon,
Salmon had Boaz (his mother was Rahab),
Boaz had Obed (Ruth was the mother),
Obed had Jesse,
Jesse had David,
    and David became king.

6-11 David had Solomon (Uriah's wife was the mother),
Solomon had Rehoboam,
Rehoboam had Abijah,
Abijah had Asa,
Asa had Jehoshaphat,
Jehoshaphat had Joram,
Joram had Uzziah,
Uzziah had Jotham,
Jotham had Ahaz,
Ahaz had Hezekiah,
Hezekiah had Manasseh,
Manasseh had Amon,
Amon had Josiah,
Josiah had Jehoiachin and his brothers,
    and then the people were taken into the Babylonian exile.

12-16 When the Babylonian exile ended,
Jeconiah had Shealtiel,
Shealtiel had Zerubbabel,
Zerubbabel had Abiud,
Abiud had Eliakim,
Eliakim had Azor,
Azor had Zadok,
Zadok had Achim,
Achim had Eliud,
Eliud had Eleazar,
Eleazar had Matthan,
Matthan had Jacob,
Jacob had Joseph, Mary's husband,
    the Mary who gave birth to Jesus,
    the Jesus who was called Christ.

17   There were fourteen generations from Abraham to David,
        another fourteen from David to the Babylonian exile,
        and yet another fourteen from the Babylonian exile to Christ.

THE BIRTH OF JESUS

18-19   The birth of Jesus took place like this. His mother, Mary, was engaged to be married to Joseph. Before they came to the marriage bed, Joseph discovered she was pregnant. (It was by the Holy Spirit, but he didn't know that.) Joseph, chagrined but noble, determined to take care of things quietly so Mary would not be disgraced.

20-23   While he was trying to figure a way out, he had a dream. God's angel spoke in the dream: "Joseph, son of David, don't hesitate to get married. Mary's pregnancy is Spirit-conceived. God's Holy Spirit has made her pregnant. She will bring a son to birth, and when she does, you, Joseph, will name him Jesus — 'God saves' — because he will save his people from their sins." This would bring the prophet's embryonic sermon to full term:

    Watch for this — a virgin will get pregnant and bear a son;
    They will name him Immanuel (Hebrew for "God is with us").

24-25   Then Joseph woke up. He did exactly what God's angel commanded in the dream: He married Mary. But he did not consummate the marriage until she had the baby. He named the baby Jesus.

SCHOLARS FROM THE EAST

1-2   2 After Jesus was born in Bethlehem village, Judah territory — this was during Herod's kingship — a band of scholars arrived in Jerusalem from the East. They asked around, "Where can we find and pay homage to the newborn King of the Jews? We observed a star in the eastern sky that signaled his birth. We're on pilgrimage to worship him."

3-4   When word of their inquiry got to Herod, he was terrified — and not Herod alone, but most of Jerusalem as well. Herod lost no time. He gathered all the high priests and religion scholars in the city together and asked, "Where is the Messiah supposed to be born?"

5-6   They told him, "Bethlehem, Judah territory. The prophet Micah wrote it plainly:

    It's you, Bethlehem, in Judah's land,
        no longer bringing up the rear.
    From you will come the leader
        who will shepherd-rule my people, my Israel."

7-8   Herod then arranged a secret meeting with the scholars from the East. Pretending to be as devout as they were, he got them to tell him exactly when the birth-announcement star appeared. Then he told them the prophecy about Bethlehem, and said, "Go find this child. Leave no stone unturned. As soon as you find him, send word and I'll join you at once in your worship."

9-10   Instructed by the king, they set off. Then the star appeared again, the same star they had seen in the eastern skies. It led them on until it hovered over the place of the child. They could hardly contain themselves: They were in the right place! They had arrived at the right time!

11   They entered the house and saw the child in the arms of Mary, his mother. Overcome, they kneeled and worshiped him. Then they opened their luggage and presented gifts: gold, frankincense, myrrh.

12   In a dream, they were warned not to report back to Herod. So they worked out another route, left the territory without being seen, and returned to their own country.

13   After the scholars were gone, God's angel showed up again in Joseph's dream and commanded, "Get up. Take the child and his mother and flee to Egypt. Stay until further notice. Herod is on the hunt for this child, and wants to kill him."

14-15   Joseph obeyed. He got up, took the child and his mother under cover of darkness. They were out of town and well on their way by daylight. They lived in Egypt until Herod's death. This Egyptian exile fulfilled what Hosea had preached: "I called my son out of Egypt."

16-18   Herod, when he realized that the scholars had tricked him, flew into a rage. He commanded the murder of every little boy two years old and under who lived in Bethlehem and its surrounding hills. (He determined that age from information he'd gotten from the scholars.) That's when Jeremiah's sermon was fulfilled:

> A sound was heard in Ramah,
>   weeping and much lament.
> Rachel weeping for her children,
>   Rachel refusing all solace,
> Her children gone,
>   dead and buried.

19-20   Later, when Herod died, God's angel appeared in a dream to Joseph in Egypt: "Up, take the child and his mother and return to Israel. All those out to murder the child are dead."

21-23   Joseph obeyed. He got up, took the child and his mother, and reentered Israel. When he heard, though, that Archelaus had succeeded his father, Herod, as king in Judea, he was afraid to go there. But then Joseph was directed in a dream to go to the hills of Galilee. On arrival, he settled in the village of Nazareth. This move was a fulfillment of the prophetic words, "He shall be called a Nazarene."

THUNDER IN THE DESERT!

1-2   While Jesus was living in the Galilean hills, John, called "the Baptizer," was preaching in the desert country of Judea. His message was simple and austere, like his desert surroundings: "Change your life. God's kingdom is here."

3   John and his message were authorized by Isaiah's prophecy:

> Thunder in the desert!
> Prepare for God's arrival!
> Make the road smooth and straight!

4-6   John dressed in a camel-hair habit tied at the waist by a leather strap. He lived on a diet of locusts and wild field honey. People poured out of Jerusalem, Judea, and the Jordanian countryside to hear and see him in action. There at the Jordan River those who came to confess their sins were baptized into a changed life.

1-10 When John realized that a lot of Pharisees and Sadducees were showing up for a baptismal experience because it was becoming the popular thing to do, he exploded: "Brood of snakes! What do you think you're doing slithering down here to the river? Do you think a little water on your snakeskins is going to make any difference? It's your life that must change, not your skin! And don't think you can pull rank by claiming Abraham as father. Being a descendant of Abraham is neither here nor there. Descendants of Abraham are a dime a dozen. What counts is your life. Is it green and blossoming? Because if it's deadwood, it goes on the fire.

11-12 "I'm baptizing you here in the river, turning your old life in for a kingdom life. The real action comes next: The main character in this drama — compared to him I'm a mere stagehand — will ignite the kingdom life within you, a fire within you, the Holy Spirit within you, changing you from the inside out. He's going to clean house — make a clean sweep of your lives. He'll place everything true in its proper place before God; everything false he'll put out with the trash to be burned."

13-14 Jesus then appeared, arriving at the Jordan River from Galilee. He wanted John to baptize him. John objected, "I'm the one who needs to be baptized, not *you!*"

15 But Jesus insisted. "Do it. God's work, putting things right all these centuries, is coming together right now in this baptism." So John did it.

16-17 The moment Jesus came up out of the baptismal waters, the skies opened up and he saw God's Spirit — it looked like a dove — descending and landing on him. And along with the Spirit, a voice: "This is my Son, chosen and marked by my love, delight of my life."

THE TEST

1-3 **4** Next Jesus was taken into the wild by the Spirit for the Test. The Devil was ready to give it. Jesus prepared for the Test by fasting forty days and forty nights. That left him, of course, in a state of extreme hunger, which the Devil took advantage of in the first test: "Since you are God's Son, speak the word that will turn these stones into loaves of bread."

4 Jesus answered by quoting Deuteronomy: "It takes more than bread to stay alive. It takes a steady stream of words from God's mouth."

5-6 For the second test the Devil took him to the Holy City. He sat him on top of the Temple and said, "Since you are God's Son, jump." The Devil goaded him by quoting Psalm 91: "He has placed you in the care of angels. They will catch you so that you won't so much as stub your toe on a stone."

7 Jesus countered with another citation from Deuteronomy: "Don't you dare test the Lord your God."

8-9 For the third test, the Devil took him to the peak of a huge mountain. He gestured expansively, pointing out all the earth's kingdoms, how glorious they all were. Then he said, "They're yours — lock, stock, and barrel. Just go down on your knees and worship me, and they're yours."

10 Jesus' refusal was curt: "Beat it, Satan!" He backed his rebuke with a third quotation from Deuteronomy: "Worship the Lord your God, and only him. Serve him with absolute single-heartedness."

11   The Test was over. The Devil left. And in his place, angels! Angels came and took care of Jesus' needs.

TEACHING AND HEALING

12-17   When Jesus got word that John had been arrested, he returned to Galilee. He moved from his hometown, Nazareth, to the lakeside village Capernaum, nestled at the base of the Zebulun and Naphtali hills. This move completed Isaiah's sermon:

Land of Zebulun, land of Naphtali,
   road to the sea, over Jordan,
   Galilee, crossroads for the nations.
People sitting out their lives in the dark
   saw a huge light;
Sitting in that dark, dark country of death,
   they watched the sun come up.

This Isaiah-prophesied sermon came to life in Galilee the moment Jesus started preaching. He picked up where John left off: "Change your life. God's kingdom is here."

18-20   Walking along the beach of Lake Galilee, Jesus saw two brothers: Simon (later called Peter) and Andrew. They were fishing, throwing their nets into the lake. It was their regular work. Jesus said to them, "Come with me. I'll make a new kind of fisherman out of you. I'll show you how to catch men and women instead of perch and bass." They didn't ask questions, but simply dropped their nets and followed.

21-22   A short distance down the beach they came upon another pair of brothers, James and John, Zebedee's sons. These two were sitting in a boat with their father, Zebedee, mending their fishnets. Jesus made the same offer to them, and they were just as quick to follow, abandoning boat and father.

23-25   From there he went all over Galilee. He used synagogues for meeting places and taught people the truth of God. God's kingdom was his theme — that beginning right now they were under God's government, a good government! He also healed people of their diseases and of the bad effects of their bad lives. Word got around the entire Roman province of Syria. People brought anybody with an ailment, whether mental, emotional, or physical. Jesus healed them, one and all. More and more people came, the momentum gathering. Besides those from Galilee, crowds came from the "Ten Towns" across the lake, others up from Jerusalem and Judea, still others from across the Jordan.

YOU'RE BLESSED

1-2   5 When Jesus saw his ministry drawing huge crowds, he climbed a hillside. Those who were apprenticed to him, the committed, climbed with him. Arriving at a quiet place, he sat down and taught his climbing companions. This is what he said:

3   "You're blessed when you're at the end of your rope. With less of you there is more of God and his rule.

4   "You're blessed when you feel you've lost what is most dear to you. Only

then can you be embraced by the One most dear to you.

5 "You're blessed when you're content with just who you are—no more, no less. That's the moment you find yourselves proud owners of everything that can't be bought.

6 "You're blessed when you've worked up a good appetite for God. He's food and drink in the best meal you'll ever eat.

7 "You're blessed when you care. At the moment of being 'care-full,' you find yourselves cared for.

8 "You're blessed when you get your inside world—your mind and heart—put right. Then you can see God in the outside world.

9 "You're blessed when you can show people how to cooperate instead of compete or fight. That's when you discover who you really are, and your place in God's family.

10 "You're blessed when your commitment to God provokes persecution. The persecution drives you even deeper into God's kingdom.

11-12 "Not only that—count yourselves blessed every time people put you down or throw you out or speak lies about you to discredit me. What it means is that the truth is too close for comfort and they are uncomfortable. You can be glad when that happens—give a cheer, even!—for though they don't like it, I do! And all heaven applauds. And know that you are in good company. My prophets and witnesses have always gotten into this kind of trouble.

SALT AND LIGHT

13 "Let me tell you why you are here. You're here to be salt-seasoning that brings out the God-flavors of this earth. If you lose your saltiness, how will people taste godliness? You've lost your usefulness and will end up in the garbage.

14-16 "Here's another way to put it: You're here to be light, bringing out the God-colors in the world. God is not a secret to be kept. We're going public with this, as public as a city on a hill. If I make you light-bearers, you don't think I'm going to hide you under a bucket, do you? I'm putting you on a light stand. Now that I've put you there on a hilltop, on a light stand—shine! Keep open house; be generous with your lives. By opening up to others, you'll prompt people to open up with God, this generous Father in heaven.

COMPLETING GOD'S LAW

17-18 "Don't suppose for a minute that I have come to demolish the Scriptures—either God's Law or the Prophets. I'm not here to demolish but to complete. I am going to put it all together, pull it all together in a vast panorama. God's Law is more real and lasting than the stars in the sky and the ground at your feet. Long after stars burn out and earth wears out, God's Law will be alive and working.

19-20 "Trivialize even the smallest item in God's Law and you will only have trivialized yourself. But take it seriously, show the way for others, and you will find honor in the kingdom. Unless you do far better than the Pharisees in the matters of right living, you won't know the first thing about entering the kingdom.

MURDER

21-22 "You're familiar with the command to the ancients, 'Do not murder.' I'm telling you that anyone who is so much as angry with a brother or sister is guilty of murder. Carelessly call a brother 'idiot!' and you just might find yourself hauled into court. Thoughtlessly yell 'stupid!' at a sister and you are on the brink of hellfire. The simple moral fact is that words kill.

23-24 "This is how I want you to conduct yourself in these matters. If you enter your place of worship and, about to make an offering, you suddenly remember a grudge a friend has against you, abandon your offering, leave immediately, go to this friend and make things right. Then and only then, come back and work things out with God.

25-26 "Or say you're out on the street and an old enemy accosts you. Don't lose a minute. Make the first move; make things right with him. After all, if you leave the first move to him, knowing his track record, you're likely to end up in court, maybe even jail. If that happens, you won't get out without a stiff fine.

ADULTERY AND DIVORCE

27-28 "You know the next commandment pretty well, too: 'Don't go to bed with another's spouse.' But don't think you've preserved your virtue simply by staying out of bed. Your *heart* can be corrupted by lust even quicker than your *body*. Those leering looks you think nobody notices—they also corrupt.

29-30 "Let's not pretend this is easier than it really is. If you want to live a morally pure life, here's what you have to do: You have to blind your right eye the moment you catch it in a lustful leer. You have to choose to live one-eyed or else be dumped on a moral trash pile. And you have to chop off your right hand the moment you notice it raised threateningly. Better a bloody stump than your entire being discarded for good in the dump.

31-32 "Remember the Scripture that says, 'Whoever divorces his wife, let him do it legally, giving her divorce papers and her legal rights'? Too many of you are using that as a cover for selfishness and whim, pretending to be righteous just because you are 'legal.' Please, no more pretending. If you divorce your wife, you're responsible for making her an adulteress (unless she has already made herself that by sexual promiscuity). And if you marry such a divorced adulteress, you're automatically an adulterer yourself. You can't use legal cover to mask a moral failure.

EMPTY PROMISES

33-37 "And don't say anything you don't mean. This counsel is embedded deep in our traditions. You only make things worse when you lay down a smoke screen of pious talk, saying, 'I'll pray for you,' and never doing it, or saying, 'God be with you,' and not meaning it. You don't make your words true by embellishing them with religious lace. In making your speech sound more religious, it becomes less true. Just say 'yes' and 'no.' When you manipulate words to get your own way, you go wrong.

LOVE YOUR ENEMIES

38-42 "Here's another old saying that deserves a second look: 'Eye for eye, tooth for tooth.' Is that going to get us anywhere? Here's what I propose: 'Don't hit back at all.' If someone strikes you, stand there and take it. If someone drags you into court and sues for the shirt off your back, giftwrap your best coat and make a present of it. And if someone takes unfair advantage of you, use the occasion to practice the servant life. No more tit-for-tat stuff. Live generously.

43-47 "You're familiar with the old written law, 'Love your friend,' and its un-written companion, 'Hate your enemy.' I'm challenging that. I'm telling you to love your enemies. Let them bring out the best in you, not the worst. When someone gives you a hard time, respond with the energies of prayer, for then you are working out of your true selves, your God-created selves. This is what God does. He gives his best — the sun to warm and the rain to nourish — to everyone, regardless: the good and bad, the nice and nasty. If all you do is love the lovable, do you expect a bonus? Anybody can do that. If you simply say hello to those who greet you, do you expect a medal? Any run-of-the-mill sinner does that.

48 "In a word, what I'm saying is, *Grow up.* You're kingdom subjects. Now live like it. Live out your God-created identity. Live generously and gra-ciously toward others, the way God lives toward you."

THE WORLD IS NOT A STAGE

1 6 "Be especially careful when you are trying to be good so that you don't make a performance out of it. It might be good theater, but the God who made you won't be applauding.

2-4 "When you do something for someone else, don't call attention to yourself. You've seen them in action, I'm sure — 'playactors' I call them — treating prayer meeting and street corner alike as a stage, acting com-passionate as long as someone is watching, playing to the crowds. They get applause, true, but that's all they get. When you help someone out, don't think about how it looks. Just do it — quietly and unobtrusively. That is the way your God, who conceived you in love, working behind the scenes, helps you out.

PRAY WITH SIMPLICITY

5 "And when you come before God, don't turn that into a theatrical pro-duction either. All these people making a regular show out of their prayers, hoping for stardom! Do you think God sits in a box seat?

6 "Here's what I want you to do: Find a quiet, secluded place so you won't be tempted to role-play before God. Just be there as simply and honestly as you can manage. The focus will shift from you to God, and you will begin to sense his grace.

7-13 "The world is full of so-called prayer warriors who are prayer ignorant. They're full of formulas and programs and advice, peddling techniques for getting what you want from God. Don't fall for that nonsense. This is your Father you are dealing with, and he knows better than you what you need. With a God like this loving you, you can pray very simply. Like this:

Our Father in heaven,
Reveal who you are.
Set the world right;
Do what's best —
    as above, so below.
Keep us alive with three square meals.
Keep us forgiven with you and forgiving others.
Keep us safe from ourselves and the Devil.
You're in charge!
You can do anything you want!

You're ablaze in beauty!
Yes. Yes. Yes.

14-15 "In prayer there is a connection between what God does and what you do. You can't get forgiveness from God, for instance, without also forgiving others. If you refuse to do your part, you cut yourself off from God's part.

16-18 "When you practice some appetite-denying discipline to better concentrate on God, don't make a production out of it. It might turn you into a small-time celebrity but it won't make you a saint. If you 'go into training' inwardly, act normal outwardly. Shampoo and comb your hair, brush your teeth, wash your face. God doesn't require attention-getting devices. He won't overlook what you are doing; he'll reward you well.

A LIFE OF GOD-WORSHIP

19-21 "Don't hoard treasure down here where it gets eaten by moths and corroded by rust or — worse! — stolen by burglars. Stockpile treasure in heaven, where it's safe from moth and rust and burglars. It's obvious, isn't it? The place where your treasure is, is the place you will most want to be, and end up being.

22-23 "Your eyes are windows into your body. If you open your eyes wide in wonder and belief, your body fills up with light. If you live squinty-eyed in greed and distrust, your body is a dank cellar. If you pull the blinds on your windows, what a dark life you will have!

24 "You can't worship two gods at once. Loving one god, you'll end up hating the other. Adoration of one feeds contempt for the other. You can't worship God and Money both.

25-26 "If you decide for God, living a life of God-worship, it follows that you don't fuss about what's on the table at mealtimes or whether the clothes in your closet are in fashion. There is far more to your life than the food you put in your stomach, more to your outer appearance than the clothes you hang on your body. Look at the birds, free and unfettered, not tied down to a job description, careless in the care of God. And you count far more to him than birds.

27-29 "Has anyone by fussing in front of the mirror ever gotten taller by so much as an inch? All this time and money wasted on fashion — do you think it makes that much difference? Instead of looking at the fashions, walk out into the fields and look at the wildflowers. They never primp or shop, but have you ever seen color and design quite like it? The ten best-dressed men and women in the country look shabby alongside them.

30-33 "If God gives such attention to the appearance of wildflowers — most of which are never even seen — don't you think he'll attend to you, take pride in you, do his best for you? What I'm trying to do here is to get you to relax, to not be so preoccupied with *getting,* so you can respond to God's *giving.* People who don't know God and the way he works fuss over these things, but you know both God and how he works. Steep your life in God-reality, God-initiative, God-provisions. Don't worry about missing out. You'll find all your everyday human concerns will be met.

34 "Give your entire attention to what God is doing right now, and don't get worked up about what may or may not happen tomorrow. God will help you deal with whatever hard things come up when the time comes.

A Simple Guide for Behavior

1-5   7 "Don't pick on people, jump on their failures, criticize their faults — unless, of course, you want the same treatment. That critical spirit has a way of boomeranging. It's easy to see a smudge on your neighbor's face and be oblivious to the ugly sneer on your own. Do you have the nerve to say, 'Let me wash your face for you,' when your own face is distorted by contempt? It's this whole traveling road-show mentality all over again, playing a holier-than-thou part instead of just living your part. Wipe that ugly sneer off your own face, and you might be fit to offer a washcloth to your neighbor.

6   "Don't be flip with the sacred. Banter and silliness give no honor to God. Don't reduce holy mysteries to slogans. In trying to be relevant, you're only being cute and inviting sacrilege.

7-11   "Don't bargain with God. Be direct. Ask for what you need. This isn't a cat-and-mouse, hide-and-seek game we're in. If your child asks for bread, do you trick him with sawdust? If he asks for fish, do you scare him with a live snake on his plate? As bad as you are, you wouldn't think of such a thing. You're at least decent to your own children. So don't you think the God who conceived you in love will be even better?

12   "Here is a simple, rule-of-thumb guide for behavior: Ask yourself what you want people to do for you, then grab the initiative and do it for *them*. Add up God's Law and Prophets and this is what you get.

Being and Doing

13-14   "Don't look for shortcuts to God. The market is flooded with surefire, easygoing formulas for a successful life that can be practiced in your spare time. Don't fall for that stuff, even though crowds of people do. The way to life — to God! — is vigorous and requires total attention.

15-20   "Be wary of false preachers who smile a lot, dripping with practiced sincerity. Chances are they are out to rip you off some way or other. Don't be impressed with charisma; look for character. Who preachers *are* is the main thing, not what they say. A genuine leader will never exploit your emotions or your pocketbook. These diseased trees with their bad apples are going to be chopped down and burned.

21-23   "Knowing the correct password — saying 'Master, Master,' for instance — isn't going to get you anywhere with me. What is required is serious obedience — *doing* what my Father wills. I can see it now — at the Final Judgment thousands strutting up to me and saying, 'Master, we preached the Message, we bashed the demons, our God-sponsored projects had everyone talking.' And do you know what I am going to say? 'You missed the boat. All you did was use me to make yourselves important. You don't impress me one bit. You're out of here.'

24-25   "These words I speak to you are not incidental additions to your life, homeowner improvements to your standard of living. They are foundational words, words to build a life on. If you work these words into your life, you are like a smart carpenter who built his house on solid rock. Rain poured down, the river flooded, a tornado hit — but nothing moved that house. It was fixed to the rock.

26-27   "But if you just use my words in Bible studies and don't work them into your life, you are like a stupid carpenter who built his house on the sandy beach. When a storm rolled in and the waves came up, it collapsed like a house of cards."

28-29 When Jesus concluded his address, the crowd burst into applause. They had never heard teaching like this. It was apparent that he was living everything he was saying — quite a contrast to their religion teachers! This was the best teaching they had ever heard.

HE CARRIED OUR DISEASES

1-2 Jesus came down the mountain with the cheers of the crowd still ringing in his ears. Then a leper appeared and went to his knees before Jesus, praying, "Master, if you want to, you can heal my body."

3-4 Jesus reached out and touched him, saying, "I want to. Be clean." Then and there, all signs of the leprosy were gone. Jesus said, "Don't talk about this all over town. Just quietly present your healed body to the priest, along with the appropriate expressions of thanks to God. Your cleansed and grateful life, not your words, will bear witness to what I have done."

5-6 As Jesus entered the village of Capernaum, a Roman captain came up in a panic and said, "Master, my servant is sick. He can't walk. He's in terrible pain."

7 Jesus said, "I'll come and heal him."

8-9 "Oh, no," said the captain. "I don't want to put you to all that trouble. Just give the order and my servant will be fine. I'm a man who takes orders and gives orders. I tell one soldier, 'Go,' and he goes; to another, 'Come,' and he comes; to my slave, 'Do this,' and he does it."

10-12 Taken aback, Jesus said, "I've yet to come across this kind of simple trust in Israel, the very people who are supposed to know all about God and how he works. This man is the vanguard of many outsiders who will soon be coming from all directions — streaming in from the east, pouring in from the west, sitting down at God's kingdom banquet alongside Abraham, Isaac, and Jacob. Then those who grew up 'in the faith' but had no faith will find themselves out in the cold, outsiders to grace and wondering what happened."

13 Then Jesus turned to the captain and said, "Go. What you believed could happen has happened." At that moment his servant became well.

14-15 By this time they were in front of Peter's house. On entering, Jesus found Peter's mother-in-law sick in bed, burning up with fever. He touched her hand and the fever was gone. No sooner was she up on her feet than she was fixing dinner for him.

16-17 That evening a lot of demon-afflicted people were brought to him. He relieved the inwardly tormented. He cured the bodily ill. He fulfilled Isaiah's well-known sermon:

He took our illnesses,
He carried our diseases.

YOUR BUSINESS IS LIFE, NOT DEATH

18-19 When Jesus saw that a curious crowd was growing by the minute, he told his disciples to get him out of there to the other side of the lake. As they left, a religion scholar asked if he could go along. "I'll go with you, wherever," he said.

20 Jesus was curt: "Are you ready to rough it? We're not staying in the best inns, you know."

21 Another follower said, "Master, excuse me for a couple of days, please. I have my father's funeral to take care of."

22 Jesus refused. "First things first. Your business is life, not death. Follow me. Pursue life."

23-25 Then he got in the boat, his disciples with him. The next thing they knew, they were in a severe storm. Waves were crashing into the boat — and he was sound asleep! They roused him, pleading, "Master, save us! We're going down!"

26 Jesus reprimanded them. "Why are you such cowards, such faint-hearts?" Then he stood up and told the wind to be silent, the sea to quiet down: "Silence!" The sea became smooth as glass.

27 The men rubbed their eyes, astonished. "What's going on here? Wind and sea come to heel at his command!"

THE MADMEN AND THE PIGS

28-31 They landed in the country of the Gadarenes and were met by two mad-men, victims of demons, coming out of the cemetery. The men had terror-ized the region for so long that no one considered it safe to walk down that stretch of road anymore. Seeing Jesus, the madmen screamed out, "What business do you have giving us a hard time? You're the Son of God! You weren't supposed to show up here yet!" Off in the distance a herd of pigs was browsing and rooting. The evil spirits begged Jesus, "If you kick us out of these men, let us live in the pigs."

32-34 Jesus said, "Go ahead, but get out of here!" Crazed, the pigs stampeded over a cliff into the sea and drowned. Scared to death, the swineherds bolted. They told everyone back in town what had happened to the madmen and the pigs. Those who heard about it were angry about the drowned pigs. A mob formed and demanded that Jesus get out and not come back.

WHO NEEDS A DOCTOR?

1-3 Back in the boat, Jesus and the disciples recrossed the sea to Jesus' hometown. They were hardly out of the boat when some men carried a paraplegic on a stretcher and set him down in front of them. Jesus, impressed by their bold belief, said to the paraplegic, "Cheer up, son. I forgive your sins." Some religion scholars whispered, "Why, that's blasphemy!"

4-8 Jesus knew what they were thinking, and said, "Why this gossipy whispering? Which do you think is simpler: to say, 'I forgive your sins,' or, 'Get up and walk'? Well, just so it's clear that I'm the Son of Man and authorized to do either, or both. . . ." At this he turned to the paraplegic and said, "Get up. Take your bed and go home." And the man did it. The crowd was awestruck, amazed and pleased that God had authorized Jesus to work among them this way.

9 Passing along, Jesus saw a man at his work collecting taxes. His name was Matthew. Jesus said, "Come along with me." Matthew stood up and followed him.

10-11 Later when Jesus was eating supper at Matthew's house with his close followers, a lot of disreputable characters came and joined them. When the Pharisees saw him keeping this kind of company, they had a fit, and lit into Jesus' followers. "What kind of example is this from your Teacher, acting cozy with crooks and riffraff?"

12-13   Jesus, overhearing, shot back, "Who needs a doctor: the healthy or the sick? Go figure out what this Scripture means: 'I'm after mercy, not religion.' I'm here to invite outsiders, not coddle insiders."

KINGDOM COME

14   A little later John's followers approached, asking, "Why is it that we and the Pharisees rigorously discipline body and spirit by fasting, but your followers don't?"

15   Jesus told them, "When you're celebrating a wedding, you don't skimp on the cake and wine. You feast. Later you may need to pull in your belt, but not now. No one throws cold water on a friendly bonfire. This is Kingdom Come!"

16-17   He went on, "No one cuts up a fine silk scarf to patch old work clothes; you want fabrics that match. And you don't put your wine in cracked bottles."

JUST A TOUCH

18-19   As he finished saying this, a local official appeared, bowed politely, and said, "My daughter has just now died. If you come and touch her, she will live." Jesus got up and went with him, his disciples following along.

20-22   Just then a woman who had hemorrhaged for twelve years slipped in from behind and lightly touched his robe. She was thinking to herself, "If I can just put a finger on his robe, I'll get well." Jesus turned—caught her at it. Then he reassured her: "Courage, daughter. You took a risk of faith, and now you're well." The woman was well from then on.

23-26   By now they had arrived at the house of the town official, and pushed their way through the gossips looking for a story and the neighbors bringing in casseroles. Jesus was abrupt: "Clear out! This girl isn't dead. She's sleeping." They told him he didn't know what he was talking about. But when Jesus had gotten rid of the crowd, he went in, took the girl's hand, and pulled her to her feet—alive. The news was soon out, and traveled throughout the region.

BECOME WHAT YOU BELIEVE

27-28   As Jesus left the house, he was followed by two blind men crying out, "Mercy, Son of David! Mercy on us!" When Jesus got home, the blind men went in with him. Jesus said to them, "Do you really believe I can do this?" They said, "Why, yes, Master!"

29-31   He touched their eyes and said, "Become what you believe." It happened. They saw. Then Jesus became very stern. "Don't let a soul know how this happened." But they were hardly out the door before they started blabbing it to everyone they met.

32-33   Right after that, as the blind men were leaving, a man who had been struck speechless by an evil spirit was brought to Jesus. As soon as Jesus threw the evil tormenting spirit out, the man talked away just as if he'd been talking all his life. The people were up on their feet applauding: "There's never been anything like this in Israel!"

34   The Pharisees were left sputtering, "Hocus-pocus. It's nothing but hocus-pocus. He's probably made a pact with the Devil."

35-38   Then Jesus made a circuit of all the towns and villages. He taught in their meeting places, reported kingdom news, and healed their diseased bodies, healed their bruised and hurt lives. When he looked out over the crowds, his heart broke. So confused and aimless they were, like sheep with no shepherd. "What a huge harvest!" he said to his disciples. "How few workers! On your knees and pray for harvest hands!"

THE TWELVE HARVEST HANDS

1-4 10 The prayer was no sooner prayed than it was answered. Jesus called twelve of his followers and sent them into the ripe fields. He gave them power to kick out the evil spirits and to tenderly care for the bruised and hurt lives. This is the list of the twelve he sent:

Simon (they called him Peter, or "Rock"),
Andrew, his brother,
James, Zebedee's son,
John, his brother,
Philip,
Bartholomew,
Thomas,
Matthew, the tax man,
James, son of Alphaeus,
Thaddaeus,
Simon, the Canaanite,
Judas Iscariot (who later turned on him).

5-8 Jesus sent his twelve harvest hands out with this charge: "Don't begin by traveling to some far-off place to convert unbelievers. And don't try to be dramatic by tackling some public enemy. Go to the lost, confused people right here in the neighborhood. Tell them that the kingdom is here. Bring health to the sick. Raise the dead. Touch the untouchables. Kick out the demons. You have been treated generously, so live generously.

9-10 "Don't think you have to put on a fund-raising campaign before you start. You don't need a lot of equipment. *You* are the equipment, and all you need to keep that going is three meals a day. Travel light.

11 "When you enter a town or village, don't insist on staying in a luxury inn. Get a modest place with some modest people, and be content there until you leave.

12-15 "When you knock on a door, be courteous in your greeting. If they welcome you, be gentle in your conversation. If they don't welcome you, quietly withdraw. Don't make a scene. Shrug your shoulders and be on your way. You can be sure that on Judgment Day they'll be mighty sorry—but it's no concern of yours now.

16 "Stay alert. This is hazardous work I'm assigning you. You're going to be like sheep running through a wolf pack, so don't call attention to yourselves. Be as cunning as a snake, inoffensive as a dove.

17-20 "Don't be naive. Some people will impugn your motives, others will smear your reputation—just because you believe in me. Don't be upset when they haul you before the civil authorities. Without knowing it, they've done you—and me—a favor, given you a platform for preaching the kingdom news! And don't worry about what you'll say or how you'll say it. The right words will be there; the Spirit of your Father will supply the words.

21-23 "When people realize it is the living God you are presenting and not some idol that makes them feel good, they are going to turn on you, even people in your own family. There is a great irony here: proclaiming so much love, experiencing so much hate! But don't quit. Don't cave in. It is all well worth it in the end. It is not success you are after in such times but survival. Be survivors! Before you've run out of options, the Son of Man will have arrived.

24-25 "A student doesn't get a better desk than her teacher. A laborer doesn't make more money than his boss. Be content—pleased, even—when you, my students, my harvest hands, get the same treatment I get. If they call me, the Master, 'Dungface,' what can the workers expect?

26-27 "Don't be intimidated. Eventually everything is going to be out in the open, and everyone will know how things really are. So don't hesitate to go public now.

28 "Don't be bluffed into silence by the threats of bullies. There's nothing they can do to your soul, your core being. Save your fear for God, who holds your entire life—body and soul—in his hands.

FORGET ABOUT YOURSELF

29-31 "What's the price of a pet canary? Some loose change, right? And God cares what happens to it even more than you do. He pays even greater attention to you, down to the last detail—even numbering the hairs on your head! So don't be intimidated by all this bully talk. You're worth more than a million canaries.

32-33 "Stand up for me against world opinion and I'll stand up for you before my Father in heaven. If you turn tail and run, do you think I'll cover for you?

34-37 "Don't think I've come to make life cozy. I've come to cut—make a sharp knife-cut between son and father, daughter and mother, bride and mother-in-law—cut through these cozy domestic arrangements and free you for God. Well-meaning family members can be your worst enemies. If you prefer father or mother over me, you don't deserve me. If you prefer son or daughter over me, you don't deserve me.

38-39 "If you don't go all the way with me, through thick and thin, you don't deserve me. If your first concern is to look after yourself, you'll never find yourself. But if you forget about yourself and look to me, you'll find both yourself and me.

40-42 "We are intimately linked in this harvest work. Anyone who accepts what you do, accepts me, the One who sent you. Anyone who accepts what I do accepts my Father, who sent me. Accepting a messenger of God is as good as being God's messenger. Accepting someone's help is as good as giving someone help. This is a large work I've called you into, but don't be overwhelmed by it. It's best to start small. Give a cool cup of water to someone who is thirsty, for instance. The smallest act of giving or receiving makes you a true apprentice. You won't lose out on a thing."

JOHN THE BAPTIZER

1 **11** When Jesus finished placing this charge before his twelve disciples, he went on to teach and preach in their villages.

2-3 John, meanwhile, had been locked up in prison. When he got wind of what Jesus was doing, he sent his own disciples to ask, "Are you the

One we've been expecting, or are we still waiting?"

4-6 Jesus told them, "Go back and tell John what's going on:

> The blind see,
> The lame walk,
> Lepers are cleansed,
> The deaf hear,
> The dead are raised,
> The wretched of the earth learn that God is on their side.

"Is this what you were expecting? Then count yourselves most blessed!"

7-10 When John's disciples left to report, Jesus started talking to the crowd about John. "What did you expect when you went out to see him in the wild? A weekend camper? Hardly. What then? A sheik in silk pajamas? Not in the wilderness, not by a long shot. What then? A prophet? That's right, a prophet! Probably the best prophet you'll ever hear. He is the prophet that Malachi announced when he wrote, 'I'm sending my prophet ahead of you, to make the road smooth for you.'

11-14 "Let me tell you what's going on here: No one in history surpasses John the Baptizer; but in the kingdom he prepared you for, the lowliest person is ahead of him. For a long time now people have tried to force themselves into God's kingdom. But if you read the books of the Prophets and God's Law closely, you will see them culminate in John, teaming up with him in preparing the way for the Messiah of the kingdom. Looked at in this way, John is the 'Elijah' you've all been expecting to arrive and introduce the Messiah.

15 "Are you listening to me? Really listening?

16-19 "How can I account for this generation? The people have been like spoiled children whining to their parents, 'We wanted to skip rope, and you were always too tired; we wanted to talk, but you were always too busy.' John came fasting and they called him crazy. I came feasting and they called me a lush, a friend of the riffraff. Opinion polls don't count for much, do they? The proof of the pudding is in the eating."

THE UNFORCED RHYTHMS OF GRACE

20 Next Jesus let fly on the cities where he had worked the hardest but whose people had responded the least, shrugging their shoulders and going their own way.

21-24 "Doom to you, Chorazin! Doom, Bethsaida! If Tyre and Sidon had seen half of the powerful miracles you have seen, they would have been on their knees in a minute. At Judgment Day they'll get off easy compared to you. And Capernaum! With all your peacock strutting, you are going to end up in the abyss. If the people of Sodom had had your chances, the city would still be around. At Judgment Day they'll get off easy compared to you."

25-26 Abruptly Jesus broke into prayer: "Thank you, Father, Lord of heaven and earth. You've concealed your ways from sophisticates and know-it-alls, but spelled them out clearly to ordinary people. Yes, Father, that's the way you like to work."

27 Jesus resumed talking to the people, but now tenderly. "The Father has given me all these things to do and say. This is a unique Father-Son

operation, coming out of Father and Son intimacies and knowledge. No one knows the Son the way the Father does, nor the Father the way the Son does. But I'm not keeping it to myself; I'm ready to go over it line by line with anyone willing to listen.

28-30   "Are you tired? Worn out? Burned out on religion? Come to me. Get away with me and you'll recover your life. I'll show you how to take a real rest. Walk with me and work with me—watch how I do it. Learn the unforced rhythms of grace. I won't lay anything heavy or ill-fitting on you. Keep company with me and you'll learn to live freely and lightly."

IN CHARGE OF THE SABBATH

1-2   12 One Sabbath, Jesus was strolling with his disciples through a field of ripe grain. Hungry, the disciples were pulling off the heads of grain and munching on them. Some Pharisees reported them to Jesus: "Your disciples are breaking the Sabbath rules!"

3-5   Jesus said, "Really? Didn't you ever read what David and his companions did when they were hungry, how they entered the sanctuary and ate fresh bread off the altar, bread that no one but priests were allowed to eat? And didn't you ever read in God's Law that priests carrying out their Temple duties break Sabbath rules all the time and it's not held against them?

6-8   "There is far more at stake here than religion. If you had any idea what this Scripture meant—'I prefer a flexible heart to an inflexible ritual'—you wouldn't be nitpicking like this. The Son of Man is no lackey to the Sabbath; he's in charge."

9-10   When Jesus left the field, he entered their meeting place. There was a man there with a crippled hand. They said to Jesus, "Is it legal to heal on the Sabbath?" They were baiting him.

11-14   He replied, "Is there a person here who, finding one of your lambs fallen into a ravine, wouldn't, even though it was a Sabbath, pull it out? Surely kindness to people is as legal as kindness to animals!" Then he said to the man, "Hold out your hand." He held it out and it was healed. The Pharisees walked out furious, sputtering about how they were going to ruin Jesus.

IN CHARGE OF EVERYTHING

15-21   Jesus, knowing they were out to get him, moved on. A lot of people followed him, and he healed them all. He also cautioned them to keep it quiet, following guidelines set down by Isaiah:

Look well at my handpicked servant;
     I love him so much, take such delight in him.
I've placed my Spirit on him;
     he'll decree justice to the nations.
But he won't yell, won't raise his voice;
     there'll be no commotion in the streets.
He won't walk over anyone's feelings,
     won't push you into a corner.
Before you know it, his justice will triumph;
     the mere sound of his name will signal hope, even
          among far-off unbelievers.

No Neutral Ground

22-23 Next a poor demon-afflicted wretch, both blind and deaf, was set down before him. Jesus healed him, gave him his sight and hearing. The people who saw it were impressed — "This has to be the Son of David!"

24 But the Pharisees, when they heard the report, were cynical. "Black magic," they said. "Some devil trick he's pulled from his sleeve."

25-27 Jesus confronted their slander. "A judge who gives opposite verdicts on the same person cancels himself out; a family that's in a constant squabble disintegrates; if Satan banishes Satan, is there any Satan left? If you're slinging devil mud at me, calling me a devil kicking out devils, doesn't the same mud stick to your own exorcists?

28-29 "But if it's by *God's* power that I am sending the evil spirits packing, then God's kingdom is here for sure. How in the world do you think it's possible in broad daylight to enter the house of an awake, able-bodied man and walk off with his possessions unless you tie him up first? Tie him up, though, and you can clean him out.

30 "This is war, and there is no neutral ground. If you're not on my side, you're the enemy; if you're not helping, you're making things worse.

31-32 "There's nothing done or said that can't be forgiven. But if you deliberately persist in your slanders against God's Spirit, you are repudiating the very One who forgives. If you reject the Son of Man out of some misunderstanding, the Holy Spirit can forgive you, but when you reject the Holy Spirit, you're sawing off the branch on which you're sitting, severing by your own perversity all connection with the One who forgives.

33 "If you grow a healthy tree, you'll pick healthy fruit. If you grow a diseased tree, you'll pick worm-eaten fruit. The fruit tells you about the tree.

34-37 "You have minds like a snake pit! How do you suppose what you say is worth anything when you are so foul-minded? It's your heart, not the dictionary, that gives meaning to your words. A good person produces good deeds and words season after season. An evil person is a blight on the orchard. Let me tell you something: Every one of these careless words is going to come back to haunt you. There will be a time of Reckoning. Words are powerful; take them seriously. Words can be your salvation. Words can also be your damnation."

Jonah-Evidence

38 Later a few religion scholars and Pharisees got on him. "Teacher, we want to see your credentials. Give us some hard evidence that God is in this. How about a miracle?"

39-40 Jesus said, "You're looking for proof, but you're looking for the wrong kind. All you want is something to titillate your curiosity, satisfy your lust for miracles. The only proof you're going to get is what looks like the absence of proof: Jonah-evidence. Like Jonah, three days and nights in the fish's belly, the Son of Man will be gone three days and nights in a deep grave.

41-42 "On Judgment Day, the Ninevites will stand up and give evidence that will condemn this generation, because when Jonah preached to them they changed their lives. A far greater preacher than Jonah is here, and you squabble about 'proofs.' On Judgment Day, the Queen of Sheba will come forward and bring evidence that will condemn this generation, because she traveled from a far corner of the earth to listen to wise Solomon. Wisdom far greater than Solomon's is right in front of you, and you quibble over 'evidence.'

43-45 "When a defiling evil spirit is expelled from someone, it drifts along through the desert looking for an oasis, some unsuspecting soul it can bedevil. When it doesn't find anyone, it says, 'I'll go back to my old haunt.' On return it finds the person spotlessly clean, but vacant. It then runs out and rounds up seven other spirits more evil than itself and they all move in, whooping it up. That person ends up far worse off than if he'd never gotten cleaned up in the first place.

"That's what this generation is like: You may think you have cleaned out the junk from your lives and gotten ready for God, but you weren't hospitable to my kingdom message, and now all the devils are moving back in."

Obedience Is Thicker than Blood

46-47 While he was still talking to the crowd, his mother and brothers showed up. They were outside trying to get a message to him. Someone told Jesus, "Your mother and brothers are out here, wanting to speak with you."

48-50 Jesus didn't respond directly, but said, "Who do you think my mother and brothers are?" He then stretched out his hand toward his disciples. "Look closely. These are my mother and brothers. Obedience is thicker than blood. The person who obeys my heavenly Father's will is my brother and sister and mother."

A Harvest Story

1-3 **13** At about that same time Jesus left the house and sat on the beach. In no time at all a crowd gathered along the shoreline, forcing him to get into a boat. Using the boat as a pulpit, he addressed his congregation, telling stories.

3-8 "What do you make of this? A farmer planted seed. As he scattered the seed, some of it fell on the road, and birds ate it. Some fell in the gravel; it sprouted quickly but didn't put down roots, so when the sun came up it withered just as quickly. Some fell in the weeds; as it came up, it was strangled by the weeds. Some fell on good earth, and produced a harvest beyond his wildest dreams.

9 "Are you listening to this? Really listening?"

Why Tell Stories?

10 The disciples came up and asked, "Why do you tell stories?"

11-15 He replied, "You've been given insight into God's kingdom. You know how it works. Not everybody has this gift, this insight; it hasn't been given to them. Whenever someone has a ready heart for this, the insights and understandings flow freely. But if there is no readiness, any trace of receptivity soon disappears. That's why I tell stories: to create readiness, to nudge the people toward receptive insight. In their present state they can stare till doomsday and not see it, listen till they're blue in the face and not get it. I don't want Isaiah's forecast repeated all over again:

Your ears are open but you don't hear a thing.
Your eyes are awake but you don't see a thing.
The people are blockheads!
They stick their fingers in their ears

so they won't have to listen;
They screw their eyes shut
  so they won't have to look,
  so they won't have to deal with me face-to-face
  and let me heal them.

¹⁶⁻¹⁷ "But you have God-blessed eyes — eyes that see! And God-blessed ears — ears that hear! A lot of people, prophets and humble believers among them, would have given anything to see what you are seeing, to hear what you are hearing, but never had the chance.

THE MEANING OF THE HARVEST STORY

¹⁸⁻¹⁹ "Study this story of the farmer planting seed. When anyone hears news of the kingdom and doesn't take it in, it just remains on the surface, and so the Evil One comes along and plucks it right out of that person's heart. This is the seed the farmer scatters on the road.

²⁰⁻²¹ "The seed cast in the gravel — this is the person who hears and instantly responds with enthusiasm. But there is no soil of character, and so when the emotions wear off and some difficulty arrives, there is nothing to show for it.

²² "The seed cast in the weeds is the person who hears the kingdom news, but weeds of worry and illusions about getting more and wanting everything under the sun strangle what was heard, and nothing comes of it.

²³ "The seed cast on good earth is the person who hears and takes in the News, and then produces a harvest beyond his wildest dreams."

²⁴⁻²⁶ He told another story. "God's kingdom is like a farmer who planted good seed in his field. That night, while his hired men were asleep, his enemy sowed thistles all through the wheat and slipped away before dawn. When the first green shoots appeared and the grain began to form, the thistles showed up, too.

²⁷ "The farmhands came to the farmer and said, 'Master, that was clean seed you planted, wasn't it? Where did these thistles come from?'

²⁸ "He answered, 'Some enemy did this.'

"The farmhands asked, 'Should we weed out the thistles?'

²⁹⁻³⁰ "He said, 'No, if you weed the thistles, you'll pull up the wheat, too. Let them grow together until harvest time. Then I'll instruct the harvesters to pull up the thistles and tie them in bundles for the fire, then gather the wheat and put it in the barn.'"

³¹⁻³² Another story. "God's kingdom is like a pine nut that a farmer plants. It is quite small as seeds go, but in the course of years it grows into a huge pine tree, and eagles build nests in it."

³³ Another story. "God's kingdom is like yeast that a woman works into the dough for dozens of loaves of barley bread — and waits while the dough rises."

³⁴⁻³⁵ All Jesus did that day was tell stories — a long storytelling afternoon. His storytelling fulfilled the prophecy:

I will open my mouth and tell stories;
I will bring out into the open
  things hidden since the world's first day.

THE CURTAIN OF HISTORY

36 Jesus dismissed the congregation and went into the house. His disciples came in and said, "Explain to us that story of the thistles in the field."

37-39 So he explained. "The farmer who sows the pure seed is the Son of Man. The field is the world, the pure seeds are subjects of the kingdom, the thistles are subjects of the Devil, and the enemy who sows them is the Devil. The harvest is the end of the age, the curtain of history. The harvest hands are angels.

40-43 "The picture of thistles pulled up and burned is a scene from the final act. The Son of Man will send his angels, weed out the thistles from his kingdom, pitch them in the trash, and be done with them. They are going to complain to high heaven, but nobody is going to listen. At the same time, ripe, holy lives will mature and adorn the kingdom of their Father.

"Are you listening to this? Really listening?

44 "God's kingdom is like a treasure hidden in a field for years and then accidentally found by a trespasser. The finder is ecstatic — what a find! — and proceeds to sell everything he owns to raise money and buy that field.

45-46 "Or, God's kingdom is like a jewel merchant on the hunt for excellent pearls. Finding one that is flawless, he immediately sells everything and buys it.

47-50 "Or, God's kingdom is like a fishnet cast into the sea, catching all kinds of fish. When it is full, it is hauled onto the beach. The good fish are picked out and put in a tub; those unfit to eat are thrown away. That's how it will be when the curtain comes down on history. The angels will come and cull the bad fish and throw them in the garbage. There will be a lot of desperate complaining, but it won't do any good."

51 Jesus asked, "Are you starting to get a handle on all this?"

They answered, "Yes."

52 He said, "Then you see how every student well-trained in God's kingdom is like the owner of a general store who can put his hands on anything you need, old or new, exactly when you need it."

53-57 When Jesus finished telling these stories, he left there, returned to his hometown, and gave a lecture in the meetinghouse. He made a real hit, impressing everyone. "We had no idea he was this good!" they said. "How did he get so wise, get such ability?" But in the next breath they were cutting him down: "We've known him since he was a kid; he's the carpenter's son. We know his mother, Mary. We know his brothers James and Joseph, Simon and Judas. All his sisters live here. Who does he think he is?" They got their noses all out of joint.

58 But Jesus said, "A prophet is taken for granted in his hometown and his family." He didn't do many miracles there because of their hostile indifference.

THE DEATH OF JOHN

1-2 **14** At about this time, Herod, the regional ruler, heard what was being said about Jesus. He said to his servants, "This has to be John the Baptizer come back from the dead. That's why he's able to work miracles!"

3-5 Herod had arrested John, put him in chains, and sent him to prison to placate Herodias, his brother Philip's wife. John had provoked Herod by naming his relationship with Herodias "adultery." Herod wanted to kill him, but he was afraid because so many people revered John as a prophet of God.

6-12 But at his birthday celebration, he got his chance. Herodias's daughter provided the entertainment, dancing for the guests. She swept Herod away. In his drunken enthusiasm, he promised her on oath anything she wanted. Already coached by her mother, she was ready: "Give me, served up on a platter, the head of John the Baptizer." That sobered the king up fast. Unwilling to lose face with his guests, he did it — ordered John's head cut off and presented to the girl on a platter. She in turn gave it to her mother. Later, John's disciples got the body, gave it a reverent burial, and reported to Jesus.

Supper for Five Thousand

13-14 When Jesus got the news, he slipped away by boat to an out-of-the-way place by himself. But unsuccessfully — someone saw him and the word got around. Soon a lot of people from the nearby villages walked around the lake to where he was. When he saw them coming, he was overcome with pity and healed their sick.

15 Toward evening the disciples approached him. "We're out in the country and it's getting late. Dismiss the people so they can go to the villages and get some supper."

16 But Jesus said, "There is no need to dismiss them. You give them supper."

17 "All we have are five loaves of bread and two fish," they said.

18-21 Jesus said, "Bring them here." Then he had the people sit on the grass. He took the five loaves and two fish, lifted his face to heaven in prayer, blessed, broke, and gave the bread to the disciples. The disciples then gave the food to the congregation. They all ate their fill. They gathered twelve baskets of leftovers. About five thousand were fed.

Walking on the Water

22-23 As soon as the meal was finished, he insisted that the disciples get in the boat and go on ahead to the other side while he dismissed the people. With the crowd dispersed, he climbed the mountain so he could be by himself and pray. He stayed there alone, late into the night.

24-26 Meanwhile, the boat was far out to sea when the wind came up against them and they were battered by the waves. At about four o'clock in the morning, Jesus came toward them walking on the water. They were scared out of their wits. "A ghost!" they said, crying out in terror.

27 But Jesus was quick to comfort them. "Courage, it's me. Don't be afraid."

28 Peter, suddenly bold, said, "Master, if it's really you, call me to come to you on the water."

29-30 He said, "Come ahead."

Jumping out of the boat, Peter walked on the water to Jesus. But when he looked down at the waves churning beneath his feet, he lost his nerve and started to sink. He cried, "Master, save me!"

31 Jesus didn't hesitate. He reached down and grabbed his hand. Then he said, "Faint-heart, what got into you?"

32-33 The two of them climbed into the boat, and the wind died down. The disciples in the boat, having watched the whole thing, worshiped Jesus, saying, "This is it! You are God's Son for sure!"

34-36 On return, they beached the boat at Gennesaret. When the people got wind that he was back, they sent out word through the neighborhood and rounded up all the sick, who asked for permission to touch the edge of his coat. And whoever touched him was healed.

WHAT POLLUTES YOUR LIFE

1-2   **15** After that, Pharisees and religion scholars came to Jesus all the way from Jerusalem, criticizing, "Why do your disciples play fast and loose with the rules?"

3-9   But Jesus put it right back on them. "Why do you use your rules to play fast and loose with God's commands? God clearly says, 'Respect your father and mother,' and, 'Anyone denouncing father or mother should be killed.' But you weasel around that by saying, 'Whoever wants to, can say to father and mother, What I owed to you I've given to God.' That can hardly be called respecting a parent. You cancel God's command by your rules. Frauds! Isaiah's prophecy of you hit the bull's-eye:

These people make a big show of saying the right thing,
    but their heart isn't in it.
They act like they're worshiping me,
    but they don't mean it.
They just use me as a cover
    for teaching whatever suits their fancy."

10-11   He then called the crowd together and said, "Listen, and take this to heart. It's not what you swallow that pollutes your life, but what you vomit up."

12   Later his disciples came and told him, "Did you know how upset the Pharisees were when they heard what you said?"

13-14   Jesus shrugged it off. "Every tree that wasn't planted by my Father in heaven will be pulled up by its roots. Forget them. They are blind men leading blind men. When a blind man leads a blind man, they both end up in the ditch."

15   Peter said, "I don't get it. Put it in plain language."

16-20   Jesus replied, "You, too? Are you being willfully stupid? Don't you know that anything that is swallowed works its way through the intestines and is finally defecated? But what comes out of the mouth gets its start in the heart. It's from the heart that we vomit up evil arguments, murders, adulteries, fornications, thefts, lies, and cussing. That's what pollutes. Eating or not eating certain foods, washing or not washing your hands — that's neither here nor there."

HEALING THE PEOPLE

21-22   From there Jesus took a trip to Tyre and Sidon. They had hardly arrived when a Canaanite woman came down from the hills and pleaded, "Mercy, Master, Son of David! My daughter is cruelly afflicted by an evil spirit."

23   Jesus ignored her. The disciples came and complained, "Now she's bothering us. Would you please take care of her? She's driving us crazy."

24   Jesus refused, telling them, "I've got my hands full dealing with the lost sheep of Israel."

25   Then the woman came back to Jesus, went to her knees, and begged. "Master, help me."

26   He said, "It's not right to take bread out of children's mouths and throw it to dogs."

27   She was quick: "You're right, Master, but beggar dogs do get scraps from the master's table."

28   Jesus gave in. "Oh, woman, your faith is something else. What you want is what you get!" Right then her daughter became well.

29-31   After Jesus returned, he walked along Lake Galilee and then climbed a mountain and took his place, ready to receive visitors. They came, tons of them, bringing along the paraplegic, the blind, the maimed, the mute — all sorts of people in need — and more or less threw them down at Jesus' feet to see what he would do with them. He healed them. When the people saw the mutes speaking, the maimed healthy, the paraplegics walking around, the blind looking around, they were astonished and let everyone know that God was blazingly alive among them.

32   But Jesus wasn't finished with them. He called his disciples and said, "I hurt for these people. For three days now they've been with me, and now they have nothing to eat. I can't send them away without a meal — they'd probably collapse on the road."

33   His disciples said, "But where in this deserted place are you going to dig up enough food for a meal?"

34-39   Jesus asked, "How much bread do you have?"

"Seven loaves," they said, "plus a few fish." At that, Jesus directed the people to sit down. He took the seven loaves and the fish. After giving thanks, he divided it up and gave it to the people. Everyone ate. They had all they wanted. It took seven large baskets to collect the leftovers. Over four thousand people ate their fill at that meal. After Jesus sent them away, he climbed in the boat and crossed over to the Magadan hills.

SOME BAD YEAST

1-4   **16** Some Pharisees and Sadducees were on him again, pressing him to prove himself to them. He told them, "You have a saying that goes, 'Red sky at night, sailor's delight; red sky at morning, sailors take warning.' You find it easy enough to forecast the weather — why can't you read the signs of the times? An evil and wanton generation is always wanting signs and wonders. The only sign you'll get is the Jonah sign." Then he turned on his heel and walked away.

5-6   On their way to the other side of the lake, the disciples discovered they had forgotten to bring along bread. In the meantime, Jesus said to them, "Keep a sharp eye out for Pharisee-Sadducee yeast."

7-12   Thinking he was scolding them for forgetting bread, they discussed in whispers what to do. Jesus knew what they were doing and said, "Why all these worried whispers about forgetting the bread? Runt believers! Haven't you caught on yet? Don't you remember the five loaves of bread and the five thousand people, and how many baskets of fragments you picked up? Or the seven loaves that fed four thousand, and how many baskets of leftovers you collected? Haven't you realized yet that bread isn't the problem? The problem is yeast, Pharisee-Sadducee yeast." Then they got it: that he wasn't concerned about eating, but teaching — the Pharisee-Sadducee kind of teaching.

SON OF MAN, SON OF GOD

13   When Jesus arrived in the villages of Caesarea Philippi, he asked his disciples, "What are people saying about who the Son of Man is?"

14   They replied, "Some think he is John the Baptizer, some say Elijah, some Jeremiah or one of the other prophets."

15   He pressed them, "And how about you? Who do you say I am?"

16   Simon Peter said, "You're the Christ, the Messiah, the Son of the living God."

17-18   Jesus came back, "God bless you, Simon, son of Jonah! You didn't get that answer out of books or from teachers. My Father in heaven, God himself, let you in on this secret of who I really am. And now I'm going to tell you who you are, *really* are. You are Peter, a rock. This is the rock on which I will put together my church, a church so expansive with energy that not even the gates of hell will be able to keep it out.

19   "And that's not all. You will have complete and free access to God's kingdom, keys to open any and every door: no more barriers between heaven and earth, earth and heaven. A yes on earth is yes in heaven. A no on earth is no in heaven."

20   He swore the disciples to secrecy. He made them promise they would tell no one that he was the Messiah.

YOU'RE NOT IN THE DRIVER'S SEAT

21-22   Then Jesus made it clear to his disciples that it was now necessary for him to go to Jerusalem, submit to an ordeal of suffering at the hands of the religious leaders, be killed, and then on the third day be raised up alive. Peter took him in hand, protesting, "Impossible, Master! That can never be!"

23   But Jesus didn't swerve. "Peter, get out of my way. Satan, get lost. You have no idea how God works."

24-26   Then Jesus went to work on his disciples. "Anyone who intends to come with me has to let me lead. You're not in the driver's seat; *I* am. Don't run from suffering; embrace it. Follow me and I'll show you how. Self-help is no help at all. Self-sacrifice is the way, my way, to finding yourself, your true self. What kind of deal is it to get everything you want but lose yourself? What could you ever trade your soul for?

27-28   "Don't be in such a hurry to go into business for yourself. Before you know it the Son of Man will arrive with all the splendor of his Father, accompanied by an army of angels. You'll get everything you have coming to you, a personal gift. This isn't pie in the sky by and by. Some of you standing here are going to see it take place, see the Son of Man in kingdom glory."

SUNLIGHT POURED FROM HIS FACE

1-3   **17** Six days later, three of them saw that glory. Jesus took Peter and the brothers, James and John, and led them up a high mountain. His appearance changed from the inside out, right before their eyes. Sunlight poured from his face. His clothes were filled with light. Then they realized that Moses and Elijah were also there in deep conversation with him.

4   Peter broke in, "Master, this is a great moment! What would you think if I built three memorials here on the mountain—one for you, one for Moses, one for Elijah?"

5   While he was going on like this, babbling, a light-radiant cloud enveloped them, and sounding from deep in the cloud a voice: "This is my Son, marked by my love, focus of my delight. Listen to him."

6-8   When the disciples heard it, they fell flat on their faces, scared to death. But Jesus came over and touched them. "Don't be afraid." When they opened their eyes and looked around all they saw was Jesus, only Jesus.

9   Coming down the mountain, Jesus swore them to secrecy. "Don't breathe a word of what you've seen. After the Son of Man is raised from the dead, you are free to talk."

10   The disciples, meanwhile, were asking questions. "Why do the religion scholars say that Elijah has to come first?"

11-13   Jesus answered, "Elijah does come and get everything ready. I'm telling you, Elijah has already come but they didn't know him when they saw him. They treated him like dirt, the same way they are about to treat the Son of Man." That's when the disciples realized that all along he had been talking about John the Baptizer.

With a Mere Kernel of Faith

14-16   At the bottom of the mountain, they were met by a crowd of waiting people. As they approached, a man came out of the crowd and fell to his knees begging, "Master, have mercy on my son. He goes out of his mind and suffers terribly, falling into seizures. Frequently he is pitched into the fire, other times into the river. I brought him to your disciples, but they could do nothing for him."

17-18   Jesus said, "What a generation! No sense of God! No focus to your lives! How many times do I have to go over these things? How much longer do I have to put up with this? Bring the boy here." He ordered the afflicting demon out — and it was out, gone. From that moment on the boy was well.

19   When the disciples had Jesus off to themselves, they asked, "Why couldn't we throw it out?"

20   "Because you're not yet taking *God* seriously," said Jesus. "The simple truth is that if you had a mere kernel of faith, a poppy seed, say, you would tell this mountain, 'Move!' and it would move. There is nothing you wouldn't be able to tackle."

22-23   As they were regrouping in Galilee, Jesus told them, "The Son of Man is about to be betrayed to some people who want nothing to do with God. They will murder him — and three days later he will be raised alive." The disciples felt terrible.

24   When they arrived at Capernaum, the tax men came to Peter and asked, "Does your teacher pay taxes?"

25   Peter said, "Of course."

But as soon as they were in the house, Jesus confronted him. "Simon, what do you think? When a king levies taxes, who pays — his children or his subjects?"

26-27   He answered, "His subjects."

Jesus said, "Then the children get off free, right? But so we don't upset them needlessly, go down to the lake, cast a hook, and pull in the first fish that bites. Open its mouth and you'll find a coin. Take it and give it to the tax men. It will be enough for both of us."

WHOEVER BECOMES SIMPLE AGAIN

1

18

At about the same time, the disciples came to Jesus asking, "Who gets the highest rank in God's kingdom?"

2-5 For an answer Jesus called over a child, whom he stood in the middle of the room, and said, "I'm telling you, once and for all, that unless you return to square one and start over like children, you're not even going to get a look at the kingdom, let alone get in. Whoever becomes simple and elemental again, like this child, will rank high in God's kingdom. What's more, when you receive the childlike on my account, it's the same as receiving me.

6-7 "But if you give them a hard time, bullying or taking advantage of their simple trust, you'll soon wish you hadn't. You'd be better off dropped in the middle of the lake with a millstone around your neck. Doom to the world for giving these God-believing children a hard time! Hard times are inevitable, but you don't have to make it worse — and it's doomsday to you if you do.

8-9 "If your hand or your foot gets in the way of God, chop it off and throw it away. You're better off maimed or lame and alive than the proud owners of two hands and two feet, godless in a furnace of eternal fire. And if your eye distracts you from God, pull it out and throw it away. You're better off one-eyed and alive than exercising your twenty-twenty vision from inside the fire of hell.

10 "Watch that you don't treat a single one of these childlike believers arrogantly. You realize, don't you, that their personal angels are constantly in touch with my Father in heaven?

WORK IT OUT BETWEEN YOU

12-14 "Look at it this way. If someone has a hundred sheep and one of them wanders off, doesn't he leave the ninety-nine and go after the one? And if he finds it, doesn't he make far more over it than over the ninety-nine who stay put? Your Father in heaven feels the same way. He doesn't want to lose even one of these simple believers.

15-17 "If a fellow believer hurts you, go and tell him — work it out between the two of you. If he listens, you've made a friend. If he won't listen, take one or two others along so that the presence of witnesses will keep things honest, and try again. If he still won't listen, tell the church. If he won't listen to the church, you'll have to start over from scratch, confront him with the need for repentance, and offer again God's forgiving love.

18-20 "Take this most seriously: A yes on earth is yes in heaven; a no on earth is no in heaven. What you say to one another is eternal. I mean this. When two of you get together on anything at all on earth and make a prayer of it, my Father in heaven goes into action. And when two or three of you are together because of me, you can be sure that I'll be there."

A STORY ABOUT FORGIVENESS

21 At that point Peter got up the nerve to ask, "Master, how many times do I forgive a brother or sister who hurts me? Seven?"

22 Jesus replied, "Seven! Hardly. Try seventy times seven.

23-25 "The kingdom of God is like a king who decided to square accounts with his servants. As he got under way, one servant was brought before him who had run up a debt of a hundred thousand dollars. He couldn't pay up, so the king ordered the man, along with his wife, children, and goods, to be auctioned off at the slave market.

26-27 "The poor wretch threw himself at the king's feet and begged, 'Give me a chance and I'll pay it all back.' Touched by his plea, the king let him off, erasing the debt.

28 "The servant was no sooner out of the room when he came upon one of his fellow servants who owed him ten dollars. He seized him by the throat and demanded, 'Pay up. Now!'

29-31 "The poor wretch threw himself down and begged, 'Give me a chance and I'll pay it all back.' But he wouldn't do it. He had him arrested and put in jail until the debt was paid. When the other servants saw this going on, they were outraged and brought a detailed report to the king.

32-35 "The king summoned the man and said, 'You evil servant! I forgave your entire debt when you begged me for mercy. Shouldn't you be compelled to be merciful to your fellow servant who asked for mercy?' The king was furious and put the screws to the man until he paid back his entire debt. And that's exactly what my Father in heaven is going to do to each one of you who doesn't forgive unconditionally anyone who asks for mercy."

DIVORCE

1-2 **19** When Jesus had completed these teachings, he left Galilee and crossed the region of Judea on the other side of the Jordan. Great crowds followed him there, and he healed them.

3 One day the Pharisees were badgering him: "Is it legal for a man to divorce his wife for any reason?"

4-6 He answered, "Haven't you read in your Bible that the Creator originally made man and woman for each other, male and female? And because of this, a man leaves father and mother and is firmly bonded to his wife, becoming one flesh — no longer two bodies but one. Because God created this organic union of the two sexes, no one should desecrate his art by cutting them apart."

7 They shot back in rebuttal, "If that's so, why did Moses give instructions for divorce papers and divorce procedures?"

8-9 Jesus said, "Moses provided for divorce as a concession to your hard heartedness, but it is not part of God's original plan. I'm holding you to the original plan, and holding you liable for adultery if you divorce your faithful wife and then marry someone else. I make an exception in cases where the spouse has committed adultery."

10 Jesus' disciples objected, "If those are the terms of marriage, we're stuck. Why get married?"

11-12 But Jesus said, "Not everyone is mature enough to live a married life. It requires a certain aptitude and grace. Marriage isn't for everyone. Some, from birth seemingly, never give marriage a thought. Others never get asked — or accepted. And some decide not to get married for kingdom reasons. But if you're capable of growing into the largeness of marriage, do it."

TO ENTER GOD'S KINGDOM

13-15 One day children were brought to Jesus in the hope that he would lay hands on them and pray over them. The disciples shooed them off. But Jesus intervened: "Let the children alone, don't prevent them from coming to me. God's kingdom is made up of people like these." After laying hands on them, he left.

16   Another day, a man stopped Jesus and asked, "Teacher, what good thing must I do to get eternal life?"

17   Jesus said, "Why do you question me about what's good? *God* is the One who is good. If you want to enter the life of God, just do what he tells you."

18-19   The man asked, "What in particular?"

Jesus said, "Don't murder, don't commit adultery, don't steal, don't lie, honor your father and mother, and love your neighbor as you do yourself."

20   The young man said, "I've done all that. What's left?"

21   "If you want to give it all you've got," Jesus replied, "go sell your possessions; give everything to the poor. All your wealth will then be in heaven. Then come follow me."

22   That was the last thing the young man expected to hear. And so, crestfallen, he walked away. He was holding on tight to a lot of things, and he couldn't bear to let go.

23-24   As he watched him go, Jesus told his disciples, "Do you have any idea how difficult it is for the rich to enter God's kingdom? Let me tell you, it's easier to gallop a camel through a needle's eye than for the rich to enter God's kingdom."

25   The disciples were staggered. "Then who has any chance at all?"

26   Jesus looked hard at them and said, "No chance at all if you think you can pull it off yourself. Every chance in the world if you trust God to do it."

27   Then Peter chimed in, "We left everything and followed you. What do we get out of it?"

28-30   Jesus replied, "Yes, you have followed me. In the re-creation of the world, when the Son of Man will rule gloriously, you who have followed me will also rule, starting with the twelve tribes of Israel. And not only you, but anyone who sacrifices home, family, fields — whatever — because of me will get it all back a hundred times over, not to mention the considerable bonus of eternal life. This is the Great Reversal: many of the first ending up last, and the last first."

A Story About Workers

1-2   **20** "God's kingdom is like an estate manager who went out early in the morning to hire workers for his vineyard. They agreed on a wage of a dollar a day, and went to work.

3-5   "Later, about nine o'clock, the manager saw some other men hanging around the town square unemployed. He told them to go to work in his vineyard and he would pay them a fair wage. They went.

5-6   "He did the same thing at noon, and again at three o'clock. At five o'clock he went back and found still others standing around. He said, 'Why are you standing around all day doing nothing?'

7   "They said, 'Because no one hired us.'

"He told them to go to work in his vineyard.

8   "When the day's work was over, the owner of the vineyard instructed his foreman, 'Call the workers in and pay them their wages. Start with the last hired and go on to the first.'

9-12   "Those hired at five o'clock came up and were each given a dollar. When those who were hired first saw that, they assumed they would get far more. But they got the same, each of them one dollar. Taking the dollar, they groused angrily to the manager, 'These last workers put in only one easy hour, and you just made them equal to us, who slaved all day under a scorching sun.'

13-15 "He replied to the one speaking for the rest, 'Friend, I haven't been unfair. We agreed on the wage of a dollar, didn't we? So take it and go. I decided to give to the one who came last the same as you. Can't I do what I want with my own money? Are you going to get stingy because I am generous?'

16 "Here it is again, the Great Reversal: many of the first ending up last, and the last first."

To Drink from the Cup

17-19 Jesus, now well on the way up to Jerusalem, took the Twelve off to the side of the road and said, "Listen to me carefully. We are on our way up to Jerusalem. When we get there, the Son of Man will be betrayed to the religious leaders and scholars. They will sentence him to death. They will then hand him over to the Romans for mockery and torture and crucifixion. On the third day he will be raised up alive."

20 It was about that time that the mother of the Zebedee brothers came with her two sons and knelt before Jesus with a request.

21 "What do you want?" Jesus asked.

She said, "Give your word that these two sons of mine will be awarded the highest places of honor in your kingdom, one at your right hand, one at your left hand."

22 Jesus responded, "You have no idea what you're asking." And he said to James and John, "Are you capable of drinking the cup that I'm about to drink?"

They said, "Sure, why not?"

23 Jesus said, "Come to think of it, you *are* going to drink my cup. But as to awarding places of honor, that's not my business. My Father is taking care of that."

24-28 When the ten others heard about this, they lost their tempers, thoroughly disgusted with the two brothers. So Jesus got them together to settle things down. He said, "You've observed how godless rulers throw their weight around, how quickly a little power goes to their heads. It's not going to be that way with you. Whoever wants to be great must become a servant. Whoever wants to be first among you must be your slave. That is what the Son of Man has done: He came to serve, not be served—and then to give away his life in exchange for the many who are held hostage."

29-31 As they were leaving Jericho, a huge crowd followed. Suddenly they came upon two blind men sitting alongside the road. When they heard it was Jesus passing, they cried out, "Master, have mercy on us! Mercy, Son of David!" The crowd tried to hush them up, but they got all the louder, crying, "Master, have mercy on us! Mercy, Son of David!"

32 Jesus stopped and called over, "What do you want from me?"

33 They said, "Master, we want our eyes opened. We want to see!"

34 Deeply moved, Jesus touched their eyes. They had their sight back that very instant, and joined the procession.

1-3 2 1 When they neared Jerusalem, having arrived at Bethphage on Mount Olives, Jesus sent two disciples with these instructions: "Go over to the village across from you. You'll find a donkey tethered there, her colt with her. Untie her and bring them to me. If anyone asks what you're doing, say, 'The Master needs them!' He will send them with you."

4-5 This is the full story of what was sketched earlier by the prophet:

Tell Zion's daughter,
"Look, your king's on his way,
    poised and ready, mounted
On a donkey, on a colt,
    foal of a pack animal."

6-9 The disciples went and did exactly what Jesus told them to do. They led the donkey and colt out, laid some of their clothes on them, and Jesus mounted. Nearly all the people in the crowd threw their garments down on the road, giving him a royal welcome. Others cut branches from the trees and threw them down as a welcome mat. Crowds went ahead and crowds followed, all of them calling out, "Hosanna to David's son!" "Blessed is he who comes in God's name!" "Hosanna in highest heaven!"

10 As he made his entrance into Jerusalem, the whole city was shaken. Unnerved, people were asking, "What's going on here? Who is this?"

11 The parade crowd answered, "This is the prophet Jesus, the one from Nazareth in Galilee."

HE KICKED OVER THE TABLES

12-14 Jesus went straight to the Temple and threw out everyone who had set up shop, buying and selling. He kicked over the tables of loan sharks and the stalls of dove merchants. He quoted this text:

My house was designated a house of prayer;
You have made it a hangout for thieves.

Now there was room for the blind and crippled to get in. They came to Jesus and he healed them.

15-16 When the religious leaders saw the outrageous things he was doing, and heard all the children running and shouting through the Temple, "Hosanna to David's Son!" they were up in arms and took him to task. "Do you hear what these children are saying?"

Jesus said, "Yes, I hear them. And haven't you read in God's Word, 'From the mouths of children and babies I'll furnish a place of praise'?"

17 Fed up, Jesus turned on his heel and left the city for Bethany, where he spent the night.

THE WITHERED FIG TREE

18-20 Early the next morning Jesus was returning to the city. He was hungry. Seeing a lone fig tree alongside the road, he approached it anticipating a breakfast of figs. When he got to the tree, there was nothing but fig leaves.

He said, "No more figs from this tree — ever!" The fig tree withered on the spot, a dry stick. The disciples saw it happen. They rubbed their eyes, saying, "Did we really see this? A leafy tree one minute, a dry stick the next?"

21-22   But Jesus was matter-of-fact: "Yes — and if you embrace this kingdom life and don't doubt God, you'll not only do minor feats like I did to the fig tree, but also triumph over huge obstacles. This mountain, for instance, you'll tell, 'Go jump in the lake,' and it will jump. Absolutely everything, ranging from small to large, as you make it a part of your believing prayer, gets included as you lay hold of God."

TRUE AUTHORITY

23   Then he was back in the Temple, teaching. The high priests and leaders of the people came up and demanded, "Show us your credentials. Who authorized you to teach here?"

24-25   Jesus responded, "First let me ask you a question. You answer my question and I'll answer yours. About the baptism of John — who authorized it: heaven or humans?"

25-27   They were on the spot and knew it. They pulled back into a huddle and whispered, "If we say 'heaven,' he'll ask us why we didn't believe him; if we say 'humans,' we're up against it with the people because they all hold John up as a prophet." They decided to concede that round to Jesus. "We don't know," they answered.

Jesus said, "Then neither will I answer your question.

THE STORY OF TWO SONS

28   "Tell me what you think of this story: A man had two sons. He went up to the first and said, 'Son, go out for the day and work in the vineyard.'

29   "The son answered, 'I don't want to.' Later on he thought better of it and went.

30   "The father gave the same command to the second son. He answered, 'Sure, glad to.' But he never went.

31-32   "Which of the two sons did what the father asked?"

They said, "The first."

Jesus said, "Yes, and I tell you that crooks and whores are going to precede you into God's kingdom. John came to you showing you the right road. You turned up your noses at him, but the crooks and whores believed him. Even when you saw their changed lives, you didn't care enough to change and believe him.

THE STORY OF THE GREEDY FARMHANDS

33-34   "Here's another story. Listen closely. There was once a man, a wealthy farmer, who planted a vineyard. He fenced it, dug a winepress, put up a watchtower, then turned it over to the farmhands and went off on a trip. When it was time to harvest the grapes, he sent his servants back to collect his profits.

35-37   "The farmhands grabbed the first servant and beat him up. The next one they murdered. They threw stones at the third but he got away. The owner tried again, sending more servants. They got the same treatment. The owner was at the end of his rope. He decided to send his son. 'Surely,' he thought, 'they will respect my son.'

38-39   "But when the farmhands saw the son arrive, they rubbed their hands in greed. 'This is the heir! Let's kill him and have it all for ourselves.' They grabbed him, threw him out, and killed him.

40 "Now, when the owner of the vineyard arrives home from his trip, what do you think he will do to the farmhands?"

41 "He'll kill them—a rotten bunch, and good riddance," they answered. "Then he'll assign the vineyard to farmhands who will hand over the profits when it's time."

42-44 Jesus said, "Right—and you can read it for yourselves in your Bibles:

The stone the masons threw out
  is now the cornerstone.
This is God's work;
  we rub our eyes, we can hardly believe it!

"This is the way it is with you. God's kingdom will be taken back from you and handed over to a people who will live out a kingdom life. Whoever stumbles on this Stone gets shattered; whoever the Stone falls on gets smashed."

45-46 When the religious leaders heard this story, they knew it was aimed at them. They wanted to arrest Jesus and put him in jail, but, intimidated by public opinion, they held back. Most people held him to be a prophet of God.

THE STORY OF THE WEDDING BANQUET

1-3 **22** Jesus responded by telling still more stories. "God's kingdom," he said, "is like a king who threw a wedding banquet for his son. He sent out servants to call in all the invited guests. And they wouldn't come!

4 "He sent out another round of servants, instructing them to tell the guests, 'Look, everything is on the table, the prime rib is ready for carving. Come to the feast!'

5-7 "They only shrugged their shoulders and went off, one to weed his garden, another to work in his shop. The rest, with nothing better to do, beat up on the messengers and then killed them. The king was outraged and sent his soldiers to destroy those thugs and level their city.

8-10 "Then he told his servants, 'We have a wedding banquet all prepared but no guests. The ones I invited weren't up to it. Go out into the busiest intersections in town and invite anyone you find to the banquet.' The servants went out on the streets and rounded up everyone they laid eyes on, good and bad, regardless. And so the banquet was on—every place filled.

11-13 "When the king entered and looked over the scene, he spotted a man who wasn't properly dressed. He said to him, 'Friend, how dare you come in here looking like that!' The man was speechless. Then the king told his servants, 'Get him out of here—fast. Tie him up and ship him to hell. And make sure he doesn't get back in.'

14 "That's what I mean when I say, 'Many get invited; only a few make it.'"

PAYING TAXES

15-17 That's when the Pharisees plotted a way to trap him into saying something damaging. They sent their disciples, with a few of Herod's followers mixed in, to ask, "Teacher, we know you have integrity, teach the way of God accurately, are indifferent to popular opinion, and don't pander to your students. So tell us honestly: Is it right to pay taxes to Caesar or not?"

18-19 Jesus knew they were up to no good. He said, "Why are you playing these games with me? Why are you trying to trap me? Do you have a coin? Let me see it." They handed him a silver piece.

20 "This engraving — who does it look like? And whose name is on it?"

21 They said, "Caesar."

"Then give Caesar what is his, and give God what is his."

22 The Pharisees were speechless. They went off shaking their heads.

MARRIAGE AND RESURRECTION

23-28 That same day, Sadducees approached him. This is the party that denies any possibility of resurrection. They asked, "Teacher, Moses said that if a man dies childless, his brother is obligated to marry his widow and get her with child. Here's a case where there were seven brothers. The first brother married and died, leaving no child, and his wife passed to his brother. The second brother also left her childless, then the third — and on and on, all seven. Eventually the wife died. Now here's our question: At the resurrection, whose wife is she? She was a wife to each of them."

29-33 Jesus answered, "You're off base on two counts: You don't know your Bibles, and you don't know how God works. At the resurrection we're beyond marriage. As with the angels, all our ecstasies and intimacies then will be with God. And regarding your speculation on whether the dead are raised or not, don't you read your Bibles? The grammar is clear: God says, 'I am — not *was* — the God of Abraham, the God of Isaac, the God of Jacob.' The living God defines himself not as the God of dead men, but of the *living*." Hearing this exchange the crowd was much impressed.

THE MOST IMPORTANT COMMAND

34-36 When the Pharisees heard how he had bested the Sadducees, they gathered their forces for an assault. One of their religion scholars spoke for them, posing a question they hoped would show him up: "Teacher, which command in God's Law is the most important?"

37-40 Jesus said, "'Love the Lord your God with all your passion and prayer and intelligence.' This is the most important, the first on any list. But there is a second to set alongside it: 'Love others as well as you love yourself.' These two commands are pegs; everything in God's Law and the Prophets hangs from them."

DAVID'S SON AND MASTER

41-42 As the Pharisees were regrouping, Jesus caught them off balance with his own test question: "What do you think about the Christ? Whose son is he?" They said, "David's son."

43-45 Jesus replied, "Well, if the Christ is David's son, how do you explain that David, under inspiration, named Christ his 'Master'?

God said to my Master,
"Sit here at my right hand
until I make your enemies your footstool."

"Now if David calls him 'Master,' how can he at the same time be his son?"

46 That stumped them, literalists that they were. Unwilling to risk losing face again in one of these public verbal exchanges, they quit asking questions for good.

RELIGIOUS FASHION SHOWS

1-3 23 Now Jesus turned to address his disciples, along with the crowd that had gathered with them. "The religion scholars and Pharisees are competent teachers in God's Law. You won't go wrong in following their teachings on Moses. But be careful about following *them*. They talk a good line, but they don't live it. They don't take it into their hearts and live it out in their behavior. It's all spit-and-polish veneer.

4-7 "Instead of giving you God's Law as food and drink by which you can banquet on God, they package it in bundles of rules, loading you down like pack animals. They seem to take pleasure in watching you stagger under these loads, and wouldn't think of lifting a finger to help. Their lives are perpetual fashion shows, embroidered prayer shawls one day and flowery prayers the next. They love to sit at the head table at church dinners, basking in the most prominent positions, preening in the radiance of public flattery, receiving honorary degrees, and getting called 'Doctor' and 'Reverend.'

8-10 "Don't let people do that to *you*, put you on a pedestal like that. You all have a single Teacher, and you are all classmates. Don't set people up as experts over your life, letting them tell you what to do. Save that authority for God; let *him* tell you what to do. No one else should carry the title of 'Father'; you have only one Father, and he's in heaven. And don't let people maneuver you into taking charge of them. There is only one Life-Leader for you and them — Christ.

11-12 "Do you want to stand out? Then step down. Be a servant. If you puff yourself up, you'll get the wind knocked out of you. But if you're content to simply be yourself, your life will count for plenty.

FRAUDS!

13 "I've had it with you! You're hopeless, you religion scholars, you Pharisees! Frauds! Your lives are roadblocks to God's kingdom. You refuse to enter, and won't let anyone else in either.

15 "You're hopeless, you religion scholars and Pharisees! Frauds! You go halfway around the world to make a convert, but once you get him you make him into a replica of yourselves, double-damned.

16-22 "You're hopeless! What arrogant stupidity! You say, 'If someone makes a promise with his fingers crossed, that's nothing; but if he swears with his hand on the Bible, that's serious.' What ignorance! Does the leather on the Bible carry more weight than the skin on your hands? And what about this piece of trivia: 'If you shake hands on a promise, that's nothing; but if you raise your hand that God is your witness, that's serious'? What ridiculous hairsplitting! What difference does it make whether you shake hands or raise hands? A promise is a promise. What difference does it make if you make your promise inside or outside a house of worship? A promise is a promise. God is present, watching and holding you to account regardless.

23-24 "You're hopeless, you religion scholars and Pharisees! Frauds! You keep meticulous account books, tithing on every nickel and dime you get, but on the meat of God's Law, things like fairness and compassion and commitment — the absolute basics! — you carelessly take it or leave it. Careful bookkeeping is commendable, but the basics are required. Do you have any idea how silly you look, writing a life story that's wrong from start to finish, nitpicking over commas and semicolons?

25-26 "You're hopeless, you religion scholars and Pharisees! Frauds! You burnish the surface of your cups and bowls so they sparkle in the sun, while the insides are maggoty with your greed and gluttony. Stupid Pharisee! Scour the insides, and then the gleaming surface will mean something.

27-28 "You're hopeless, you religion scholars and Pharisees! Frauds! You're like manicured grave plots, grass clipped and the flowers bright, but six feet down it's all rotting bones and worm-eaten flesh. People look at you and think you're saints, but beneath the skin you're total frauds.

29-32 "You're hopeless, you religion scholars and Pharisees! Frauds! You build granite tombs for your prophets and marble monuments for your saints. And you say that if you had lived in the days of your ancestors, no blood would have been on your hands. You protest too much! You're cut from the same cloth as those murderers, and daily add to the death count.

33-34 "Snakes! Reptilian sneaks! Do you think you can worm your way out of this? Never have to pay the piper? It's on account of people like you that I send prophets and wise guides and scholars generation after generation — and generation after generation you treat them like dirt, greeting them with lynch mobs, hounding them with abuse.

35-36 "You can't squirm out of this: Every drop of righteous blood ever spilled on this earth, beginning with the blood of that good man Abel right down to the blood of Zechariah, Barachiah's son, whom you murdered at his prayers, is on your head. All this, I'm telling you, is coming down on you, on your generation.

37-39 "Jerusalem! Jerusalem! Murderer of prophets! Killer of the ones who brought you God's news! How often I've ached to embrace your children, the way a hen gathers her chicks under her wings, and you wouldn't let me. And now you're so desolate, nothing but a ghost town. What is there left to say? Only this: I'm out of here soon. The next time you see me you'll say, 'Oh, God has blessed him! He's come, bringing God's rule!'"

ROUTINE HISTORY

1-2 Jesus then left the Temple. As he walked away, his disciples pointed out how very impressive the Temple architecture was. Jesus said, "You're not impressed by all this sheer *size*, are you? The truth of the matter is that there's not a stone in that building that is not going to end up in a pile of rubble."

3 Later as he was sitting on Mount Olives, his disciples approached and asked him, "Tell us, when are these things going to happen? What will be the sign of your coming, that the time's up?"

4-8 Jesus said, "Watch out for doomsday deceivers. Many leaders are going to show up with forged identities, claiming, 'I am Christ, the Messiah.' They will deceive a lot of people. When reports come in of wars and rumored wars, keep your head and don't panic. This is routine history; this is no sign of the end. Nation will fight nation and ruler fight ruler, over and over. Famines and earthquakes will occur in various places. This is nothing compared to what is coming.

9-10   "They are going to throw you to the wolves and kill you, everyone hating you because you carry my name. And then, going from bad to worse, it will be dog-eat-dog, everyone at each other's throat, everyone hating each other.

11-12   "In the confusion, lying preachers will come forward and deceive a lot of people. For many others, the overwhelming spread of evil will do them in — nothing left of their love but a mound of ashes.

13-14   "Staying with it — that's what God requires. Stay with it to the end. You won't be sorry, and you'll be saved. All during this time, the good news — the Message of the kingdom — will be preached all over the world, a witness staked out in every country. And then the end will come.

THE MONSTER OF DESECRATION

15-20   "But be ready to run for it when you see the monster of desecration set up in the Temple sanctuary. The prophet Daniel described this. If you've read Daniel, you'll know what I'm talking about. If you're living in Judea at the time, run for the hills; if you're working in the yard, don't return to the house to get anything; if you're out in the field, don't go back and get your coat. Pregnant and nursing mothers will have it especially hard. Hope and pray this won't happen during the winter or on a Sabbath.

21-22   "This is going to be trouble on a scale beyond what the world has ever seen, or will see again. If these days of trouble were left to run their course, nobody would make it. But on account of God's chosen people, the trouble will be cut short.

THE ARRIVAL OF THE SON OF MAN

23-25   "If anyone tries to flag you down, calling out, 'Here's the Messiah!' or points, 'There he is!' don't fall for it. Fake Messiahs and lying preachers are going to pop up everywhere. Their impressive credentials and dazzling performances will pull the wool over the eyes of even those who ought to know better. But I've given you fair warning.

26-28   "So if they say, 'Run to the country and see him arrive!' or, 'Quick, get downtown, see him come!' don't give them the time of day. The Arrival of the Son of Man isn't something you go to see. He comes like swift lightning to you! Whenever you see crowds gathering, think of carrion vultures circling, moving in, hovering over a rotting carcass. You can be quite sure that it's not the living Son of Man pulling in those crowds.

29   "Following those hard times,

Sun will fade out,
    moon cloud over,
Stars fall out of the sky,
    cosmic powers tremble.

30-31   "Then, the Arrival of the Son of Man! It will fill the skies — no one will miss it. Unready people all over the world, outsiders to the splendor and power, will raise a huge lament as they watch the Son of Man blazing out of heaven. At that same moment, he'll dispatch his angels with a trumpet-blast summons, pulling in God's chosen from the four winds, from pole to pole.

32-35   "Take a lesson from the fig tree. From the moment you notice its buds form, the merest hint of green, you know summer's just around the corner. So it is with you: When you see all these things, you'll know he's at the door. Don't take this lightly. I'm not just saying this for some future generation, but for all of you. This age continues until all these things take place. Sky and earth will wear out; my words won't wear out.

36 "But the exact day and hour? No one knows that, not even heaven's angels, not even the Son. Only the Father knows.

37-39 "The Arrival of the Son of Man will take place in times like Noah's. Before the great flood everyone was carrying on as usual, having a good time right up to the day Noah boarded the ark. They knew nothing—until the flood hit and swept everything away.

39-44 "The Son of Man's Arrival will be like that: Two men will be working in the field—one will be taken, one left behind; two women will be grinding at the mill—one will be taken, one left behind. So stay awake, alert. You have no idea what day your Master will show up. But you do know this: You know that if the homeowner had known what time of night the burglar would arrive, he would have been there with his dogs to prevent the break-in. Be vigilant just like that. You have no idea when the Son of Man is going to show up.

45-47 "Who here qualifies for the job of overseeing the kitchen? A person the Master can depend on to feed the workers on time each day. Someone the Master can drop in on unannounced and always find him doing his job. A God-blessed man or woman, I tell you. It won't be long before the Master will put this person in charge of the whole operation.

48-51 "But if that person only looks out for himself, and the minute the Master is away does what he pleases—abusing the help and throwing drunken parties for his friends—the Master is going to show up when he least expects it and make hash of him. He'll end up in the dump with the hypocrites, out in the cold shivering, teeth chattering."

THE STORY OF THE VIRGINS

1-5 **25** "God's kingdom is like ten young virgins who took oil lamps and went out to greet the bridegroom. Five were silly and five were smart. The silly virgins took lamps, but no extra oil. The smart virgins took jars of oil to feed their lamps. The bridegroom didn't show up when they expected him, and they all fell asleep.

6 "In the middle of the night someone yelled out, 'He's here! The bridegroom's here! Go out and greet him!'

7-8 "The ten virgins got up and got their lamps ready. The silly virgins said to the smart ones, 'Our lamps are going out; lend us some of your oil.'

9 "They answered, 'There might not be enough to go around; go buy your own.'

10 "They did, but while they were out buying oil, the bridegroom arrived. When everyone who was there to greet him had gone into the wedding feast, the door was locked.

11 "Much later, the other virgins, the silly ones, showed up and knocked on the door, saying, 'Master, we're here. Let us in.'

12 "He answered, 'Do I know you? I don't think I know you.'

13 "So stay alert. You have no idea when he might arrive.

The Story About Investment

14-18   "It's also like a man going off on an extended trip. He called his servants together and delegated responsibilities. To one he gave five thousand dollars, to another two thousand, to a third one thousand, depending on their abilities. Then he left. Right off, the first servant went to work and doubled his master's investment. The second did the same. But the man with the single thousand dug a hole and carefully buried his master's money.

19-21   "After a long absence, the master of those three servants came back and settled up with them. The one given five thousand dollars showed him how he had doubled his investment. His master commended him: 'Good work! You did your job well. From now on be my partner.'

22-23   "The servant with the two thousand showed how he also had doubled his master's investment. His master commended him: 'Good work! You did your job well. From now on be my partner.'

24-25   "The servant given one thousand said, 'Master, I know you have high standards and hate careless ways, that you demand the best and make no allowances for error. I was afraid I might disappoint you, so I found a good hiding place and secured your money. Here it is, safe and sound down to the last cent.'

26-27   "The master was furious. 'That's a terrible way to live! It's criminal to live cautiously like that! If you knew I was after the best, why did you do less than the least? The least you could have done would have been to invest the sum with the bankers, where at least I would have gotten a little interest.

28-30   "'Take the thousand and give it to the one who risked the most. And get rid of this "play-it-safe" who won't go out on a limb. Throw him out into utter darkness.'

The Sheep and the Goats

31-33   "When he finally arrives, blazing in beauty and all his angels with him, the Son of Man will take his place on his glorious throne. Then all the nations will be arranged before him and he will sort the people out, much as a shepherd sorts out sheep and goats, putting sheep to his right and goats to his left.

34-36   "Then the King will say to those on his right, 'Enter, you who are blessed by my Father! Take what's coming to you in this kingdom. It's been ready for you since the world's foundation. And here's why:

> I was hungry and you fed me,
> I was thirsty and you gave me a drink,
> I was homeless and you gave me a room,
> I was shivering and you gave me clothes,
> I was sick and you stopped to visit,
> I was in prison and you came to me.'

37-40   "Then those 'sheep' are going to say, 'Master, what are you talking about? When did we ever see you hungry and feed you, thirsty and give you a drink? And when did we ever see you sick or in prison and come to you?' Then the King will say, 'I'm telling the solemn truth: Whenever you did one of these things to someone overlooked or ignored, that was me — you did it to me.'

41-43 "Then he will turn to the 'goats,' the ones on his left, and say, 'Get out, worthless goats! You're good for nothing but the fires of hell. And why? Because—

> I was hungry and you gave me no meal,
> I was thirsty and you gave me no drink,
> I was homeless and you gave me no bed,
> I was shivering and you gave me no clothes,
> Sick and in prison, and you never visited.'

44 "Then those 'goats' are going to say, 'Master, what are you talking about? When did we ever see you hungry or thirsty or homeless or shivering or sick or in prison and didn't help?'

45 "He will answer them, 'I'm telling the solemn truth: Whenever you failed to do one of these things to someone who was being overlooked or ignored, that was me—you failed to do it to me.'

46 "Then those 'goats' will be herded to their eternal doom, but the 'sheep' to their eternal reward."

ANOINTED FOR BURIAL

1-2 26 When Jesus finished saying these things, he told his disciples, "You know that Passover comes in two days. That's when the Son of Man will be betrayed and handed over for crucifixion."

3-5 At that very moment, the party of high priests and religious leaders was meeting in the chambers of the Chief Priest named Caiaphas, conspiring to seize Jesus by stealth and kill him. They agreed that it should not be done during Passover Week. "We don't want a riot on our hands," they said.

6-9 When Jesus was at Bethany, a guest of Simon the Leper, a woman came up to him as he was eating dinner and anointed him with a bottle of very expensive perfume. When the disciples saw what was happening, they were furious. "That's criminal! This could have been sold for a lot and the money handed out to the poor."

10-13 When Jesus realized what was going on, he intervened. "Why are you giving this woman a hard time? She has just done something wonderfully significant for me. You will have the poor with you every day for the rest of your lives, but not me. When she poured this perfume on my body, what she really did was anoint me for burial. You can be sure that wherever in the whole world the Message is preached, what she has just done is going to be remembered and admired."

14-16 That is when one of the Twelve, the one named Judas Iscariot, went to the cabal of high priests and said, "What will you give me if I hand him over to you?" They settled on thirty silver pieces. He began looking for just the right moment to hand him over.

THE TRAITOR

17 On the first of the Days of Unleavened Bread, the disciples came to Jesus and said, "Where do you want us to prepare your Passover meal?"

18-19 He said, "Enter the city. Go up to a certain man and say, 'The Teacher says, My time is near. I and my disciples plan to celebrate the Passover meal at your house.'" The disciples followed Jesus' instructions to the letter, and prepared the Passover meal.

20-21   After sunset, he and the Twelve were sitting around the table. During the meal, he said, "I have something hard but important to say to you: One of you is going to hand me over to the conspirators."

22   They were stunned, and then began to ask, one after another, "It isn't me, is it, Master?"

23-24   Jesus answered, "The one who hands me over is someone I eat with daily, one who passes me food at the table. In one sense the Son of Man is entering into a way of treachery well-marked by the Scriptures — no surprises here. In another sense that man who turns him in, turns traitor to the Son of Man — better never to have been born than do this!"

25   Then Judas, already turned traitor, said, "It isn't me, is it, Rabbi?"
Jesus said, "Don't play games with me, Judas."

THE BREAD AND THE CUP

26-29 During the meal, Jesus took and blessed the bread, broke it, and gave it to his disciples:

> Take, eat.
> This is my body.

Taking the cup and thanking God, he gave it to them:

> Drink this, all of you.
> This is my blood,
> God's new covenant poured out for many people
>   for the forgiveness of sins.

"I'll not be drinking wine from this cup again until that new day when I'll drink with you in the kingdom of my Father."

30   They sang a hymn and went directly to Mount Olives.

GETHSEMANE

31-32 Then Jesus told them, "Before the night's over, you're going to fall to pieces because of what happens to me. There is a Scripture that says,

> I'll strike the shepherd;
> helter-skelter the sheep will be scattered.

But after I am raised up, I, your Shepherd, will go ahead of you, leading the way to Galilee."

33   Peter broke in, "Even if everyone else falls to pieces on account of you, I won't."

34   "Don't be so sure," Jesus said. "This very night, before the rooster crows up the dawn, you will deny me three times."

35   Peter protested, "Even if I had to die with you, I would never deny you." All the others said the same thing.

36-38   Then Jesus went with them to a garden called Gethsemane and told his disciples, "Stay here while I go over there and pray." Taking along Peter and the two sons of Zebedee, he plunged into an agonizing sorrow. Then he said, "This sorrow is crushing my life out. Stay here and keep vigil with me."

39 Going a little ahead, he fell on his face, praying, "My Father, if there is any way, get me out of this. But please, not what I want. You, what do *you* want?"

40-41 When he came back to his disciples, he found them sound asleep. He said to Peter, "Can't you stick it out with me a single hour? Stay alert; be in prayer so you don't wander into temptation without even knowing you're in danger. There is a part of you that is eager, ready for anything in God. But there's another part that's as lazy as an old dog sleeping by the fire."

42 He then left them a second time. Again he prayed, "My Father, if there is no other way than this, drinking this cup to the dregs, I'm ready. Do it your way."

43-44 When he came back, he again found them sound asleep. They simply couldn't keep their eyes open. This time he let them sleep on, and went back a third time to pray, going over the same ground one last time.

45-46 When he came back the next time, he said, "Are you going to sleep on and make a night of it? My time is up, the Son of Man is about to be handed over to the hands of sinners. Get up! Let's get going! My betrayer is here."

WITH SWORDS AND CLUBS

47-49 The words were barely out of his mouth when Judas (the one from the Twelve) showed up, and with him a gang from the high priests and religious leaders brandishing swords and clubs. The betrayer had worked out a sign with them: "The one I kiss, that's the one — seize him." He went straight to Jesus, greeted him, "How are you, Rabbi?" and kissed him.

50-51 Jesus said, "Friend, why this charade?"

Then they came on him — grabbed him and roughed him up. One of those with Jesus pulled his sword and, taking a swing at the Chief Priest's servant, cut off his ear.

52-54 Jesus said, "Put your sword back where it belongs. All who use swords are destroyed by swords. Don't you realize that I am able right now to call to my Father, and twelve companies — more, if I want them — of fighting angels would be here, battle-ready? But if I did that, how would the Scriptures come true that say this is the way it has to be?"

55-56 Then Jesus addressed the mob: "What is this — coming out after me with swords and clubs as if I were a dangerous criminal? Day after day I have been sitting in the Temple teaching, and you never so much as lifted a hand against me. You've done it this way to confirm and fulfill the prophetic writings."

Then all the disciples cut and ran.

FALSE CHARGES

57-58 The gang that had seized Jesus led him before Caiaphas the Chief Priest, where the religion scholars and leaders had assembled. Peter followed at a safe distance until they got to the Chief Priest's courtyard. Then he slipped in and mingled with the servants, watching to see how things would turn out.

59-60 The high priests, conspiring with the Jewish Council, tried to cook up charges against Jesus in order to sentence him to death. But even though many stepped up, making up one false accusation after another, nothing was believable.

60-61 Finally two men came forward with this: "He said, 'I can tear down this Temple of God and after three days rebuild it.' "

62 The Chief Priest stood up and said, "What do you have to say to the accusation?"

63 Jesus kept silent.

Then the Chief Priest said, "I command you by the authority of the living God to say if you are the Messiah, the Son of God."

64 Jesus was curt: "You yourself said it. And that's not all. Soon you'll see it for yourself:

The Son of Man seated at the right hand of the Mighty One,
Arriving on the clouds of heaven."

65-66 At that, the Chief Priest lost his temper, ripping his robes, yelling, "He blasphemed! Why do we need witnesses to accuse him? You all heard him blaspheme! Are you going to stand for such blasphemy?"

They all said, "Death! That seals his death sentence."

67-68 Then they were spitting in his face and banging him around. They jeered as they slapped him: "Prophesy, Messiah: Who hit you that time?"

DENIAL IN THE COURTYARD

69 All this time, Peter was sitting out in the courtyard. One servant girl came up to him and said, "You were with Jesus the Galilean."

70 In front of everybody there, he denied it. "I don't know what you're talking about."

71 As he moved over toward the gate, someone else said to the people there, "This man was with Jesus the Nazarene."

72 Again he denied it, salting his denial with an oath: "I swear, I never laid eyes on the man."

73 Shortly after that, some bystanders approached Peter. "You've got to be one of them. Your accent gives you away."

74-75 Then he got really nervous and swore. "I don't know the man!"

Just then a rooster crowed. Peter remembered what Jesus had said: "Before the rooster crows, you will deny me three times." He went out and cried and cried and cried.

THIRTY SILVER COINS

1-2 *27* In the first light of dawn, all the high priests and religious leaders met and put the finishing touches on their plot to kill Jesus. Then they tied him up and paraded him to Pilate, the governor.

3-4 Judas, the one who betrayed him, realized that Jesus was doomed. Overcome with remorse, he gave back the thirty silver coins to the high priests, saying, "I've sinned. I've betrayed an innocent man."

They said, "What do we care? That's *your* problem!"

5 Judas threw the silver coins into the Temple and left. Then he went out and hung himself.

6-10 The high priests picked up the silver pieces, but then didn't know what to do with them. "It wouldn't be right to give this—a payment for murder!—as an offering in the Temple." They decided to get rid of it by buying the "Potter's Field" and use it as a burial place for the homeless. That's how the field got called "Murder Meadow," a name that has stuck to this day. Then Jeremiah's words became history:

They took the thirty silver pieces,
The price of the one priced by some sons of Israel,
And they purchased the potter's field.

And so they unwittingly followed the divine instructions to the letter.

PILATE

11 Jesus was placed before the governor, who questioned him: "Are you the 'King of the Jews'?"

Jesus said, "If you say so."

12-14 But when the accusations rained down hot and heavy from the high priests and religious leaders, he said nothing. Pilate asked him, "Do you hear that long list of accusations? Aren't you going to say something?" Jesus kept silence—not a word from his mouth. The governor was impressed, really impressed.

15-18 It was an old custom during the Feast for the governor to pardon a single prisoner named by the crowd. At the time, they had the infamous Jesus Barabbas in prison. With the crowd before him, Pilate said, "Which prisoner do you want me to pardon: Jesus Barabbas, or Jesus the so-called Christ?" He knew it was through sheer spite that they had turned Jesus over to him.

19 While court was still in session, Pilate's wife sent him a message: "Don't get mixed up in judging this noble man. I've just been through a long and troubled night because of a dream about him."

20 Meanwhile, the high priests and religious leaders had talked the crowd into asking for the pardon of Barabbas and the execution of Jesus.

21 The governor asked, "Which of the two do you want me to pardon?"

They said, "Barabbas!"

22 "Then what do I do with Jesus, the so-called Christ?"

They all shouted, "Nail him to a cross!"

23 He objected, "But for what crime?"

But they yelled all the louder, "Nail him to a cross!"

24 When Pilate saw that he was getting nowhere and that a riot was imminent, he took a basin of water and washed his hands in full sight of the crowd, saying, "I'm washing my hands of responsibility for this man's death. From now on, it's in your hands. You're judge and jury."

25 The crowd answered, "We'll take the blame, we and our children after us."

26 Then he pardoned Barabbas. But he had Jesus whipped, and then handed over for crucifixion.

THE CRUCIFIXION

27-31 The soldiers assigned to the governor took Jesus into the governor's palace and got the entire brigade together for some fun. They stripped him and dressed him in a red toga. They plaited a crown from branches of a thornbush and set it on his head. They put a stick in his right hand for a scepter. Then they knelt before him in mocking reverence: "Bravo, King of the Jews!" they said. "Bravo!" Then they spit on him and hit him on the head with the stick. When they had had their fun, they took off the toga and put his own clothes back on him. Then they proceeded out to the crucifixion.

32-34 Along the way they came on a man from Cyrene named Simon and made him carry Jesus' cross. Arriving at Golgotha, the place they call "Skull

Hill," they offered him a mild painkiller (a mixture of wine and myrrh), but when he tasted it he wouldn't drink it.

35-40   After they had finished nailing him to the cross and were waiting for him to die, they whiled away the time by throwing dice for his clothes. Above his head they had posted the criminal charge against him: THIS IS JESUS, THE KING OF THE JEWS. Along with him, they also crucified two criminals, one to his right, the other to his left. People passing along the road jeered, shaking their heads in mock lament: "You bragged that you could tear down the Temple and then rebuild it in three days — so show us your stuff! Save yourself! If you're really God's Son, come down from that cross!"

41-44   The high priests, along with the religion scholars and leaders, were right there mixing it up with the rest of them, having a great time poking fun at him: "He saved others — he can't save himself! King of Israel, is he? Then let him get down from that cross. We'll *all* become believers then! He was so sure of God — well, let him rescue his 'Son' now — if he wants him! He did claim to be God's Son, didn't he?" Even the two criminals crucified next to him joined in the mockery.

45-46   From noon to three, the whole earth was dark. Around mid-afternoon Jesus groaned out of the depths, crying loudly, "*Eli, Eli, lama sabachthani?*" which means, "My God, my God, why have you abandoned me?"

47-49   Some bystanders who heard him said, "He's calling for Elijah." One of them ran and got a sponge soaked in sour wine and lifted it on a stick so he could drink. The others joked, "Don't be in such a hurry. Let's see if Elijah comes and saves him."

50   But Jesus, again crying out loudly, breathed his last.

51-53   At that moment, the Temple curtain was ripped in two, top to bottom. There was an earthquake, and rocks were split in pieces. What's more, tombs were opened up, and many bodies of believers asleep in their graves were raised. (After Jesus' resurrection, they left the tombs, entered the holy city, and appeared to many.)

54   The captain of the guard and those with him, when they saw the earthquake and everything else that was happening, were scared to death. They said, "This has to be the Son of God!"

55-56   There were also quite a few women watching from a distance, women who had followed Jesus from Galilee in order to serve him. Among them were Mary Magdalene, Mary the mother of James and Joseph, and the mother of the Zebedee brothers.

THE TOMB

57-61   Late in the afternoon a wealthy man from Arimathea, a disciple of Jesus, arrived. His name was Joseph. He went to Pilate and asked for Jesus' body. Pilate granted his request. Joseph took the body and wrapped it in clean linens, put it in his own tomb, a new tomb only recently cut into the rock, and rolled a large stone across the entrance. Then he went off. But Mary Magdalene and the other Mary stayed, sitting in plain view of the tomb.

62-64   After sundown, the high priests and Pharisees arranged a meeting with Pilate. They said, "Sir, we just remembered that that liar announced while he was still alive, 'After three days I will be raised.' We've got to get that tomb sealed until the third day. There's a good chance his disciples will come and steal the corpse and then go around saying, 'He's risen from the dead.' Then we'll be worse off than before, the final deceit surpassing the first."

65-66 Pilate told them, "You will have a guard. Go ahead and secure it the best you can." So they went out and secured the tomb, sealing the stone and posting guards.

RISEN FROM THE DEAD

1-4 28 After the Sabbath, as the first light of the new week dawned, Mary Magdalene and the other Mary came to keep vigil at the tomb. Suddenly the earth reeled and rocked under their feet as God's angel came down from heaven, came right up to where they were standing. He rolled back the stone and then sat on it. Shafts of lightning blazed from him. His garments shimmered snow-white. The guards at the tomb were scared to death. They were so frightened, they couldn't move.

5-6 The angel spoke to the women: "There is nothing to fear here. I know you're looking for Jesus, the One they nailed to the cross. He is not here. He was raised, just as he said. Come and look at the place where he was placed.

7 "Now, get on your way quickly and tell his disciples, 'He is risen from the dead. He is going on ahead of you to Galilee. You will see him there.' That's the message."

8-10 The women, deep in wonder and full of joy, lost no time in leaving the tomb. They ran to tell the disciples. Then Jesus met them, stopping them in their tracks. "Good morning!" he said. They fell to their knees, embraced his feet, and worshiped him. Jesus said, "You're holding on to me for dear life! Don't be frightened like that. Go tell my brothers that they are to go to Galilee, and that I'll meet them there."

11-15 Meanwhile, the guards had scattered, but a few of them went into the city and told the high priests everything that had happened. They called a meeting of the religious leaders and came up with a plan: They took a large sum of money and gave it to the soldiers, bribing them to say, "His disciples came in the night and stole the body while we were sleeping." They assured them, "If the governor hears about your sleeping on duty, we will make sure you don't get blamed." The soldiers took the bribe and did as they were told. That story, cooked up in the Jewish High Council, is still going around.

16-17 Meanwhile, the eleven disciples were on their way to Galilee, headed for the mountain Jesus had set for their reunion. The moment they saw him they worshiped him. Some, though, held back, not sure about *worship*, about risking themselves totally.

18-20 Jesus, undeterred, went right ahead and gave his charge: "God authorized and commanded me to commission you: Go out and train everyone you meet, far and near, in this way of life, marking them by baptism in the threefold name: Father, Son, and Holy Spirit. Then instruct them in the practice of all I have commanded you. I'll be with you as you do this, day after day after day, right up to the end of the age."

MARK

Mark wastes no time in getting down to business — a single-sentence introduction, and not a digression to be found from beginning to end. An event has taken place that radically changes the way we look at and experience the world, and he can't wait to tell us about it. There's an air of breathless excitement in nearly every sentence he writes. The sooner we get the message, the better off we'll be, for the message is good, incredibly good: God is here, and he's on our side.

The bare announcement that God exists doesn't particularly qualify as news. Most people in most centuries have believed in the existence of God or gods. It may well be, in fact, that human beings in aggregate and through the centuries have given more attention and concern to divinity than to all their other concerns put together — food, housing, clothing, pleasure, work, family, whatever.

But that God is here right now, and on our side, actively seeking to help us in the way we most need help — *this* qualifies as news. For, common as belief in God is, there is also an enormous amount of guesswork and gossip surrounding the subject, which results in runaway superstition, anxiety, and exploitation. So Mark, understandably, is in a hurry to tell us what happened in the birth, life, death, and resurrection of Jesus — the Event that reveals the truth of God to us, so that we can live in reality and not illusion. He doesn't want us to waste a minute of these precious lives of ours ignorant of this most practical of all matters — that God is passionate to save us.

MARK

JOHN THE BAPTIZER

1-3 The good news of Jesus Christ—the Message!—begins here, following to the letter the scroll of the prophet Isaiah.

Watch closely: I'm sending my preacher ahead of you;
He'll make the road smooth for you.
Thunder in the desert!
Prepare for God's arrival!
Make the road smooth and straight!

4-6 John the Baptizer appeared in the wild, preaching a baptism of life-change that leads to forgiveness of sins. People thronged to him from Judea and Jerusalem and, as they confessed their sins, were baptized by him in the Jordan River into a changed life. John wore a camel-hair habit, tied at the waist with a leather belt. He ate locusts and wild field honey.

7-8 As he preached he said, "The real action comes next: The star in this drama, to whom I'm a mere stagehand, will change your life. I'm baptizing you here in the river, turning your old life in for a kingdom life. His baptism—a holy baptism by the Holy Spirit—will change you from the inside out."

9-11 At this time, Jesus came from Nazareth in Galilee and was baptized by John in the Jordan. The moment he came out of the water, he saw the sky split open and God's Spirit, looking like a dove, come down on him. Along with the Spirit, a voice: "You are my Son, chosen and marked by my love, pride of my life."

GOD'S KINGDOM IS HERE

12-13 At once, this same Spirit pushed Jesus out into the wild. For forty wilderness days and nights he was tested by Satan. Wild animals were his companions, and angels took care of him.

14-15 After John was arrested, Jesus went to Galilee preaching the Message of God: "Time's up! God's kingdom is here. Change your life and believe the Message."

16-18 Passing along the beach of Lake Galilee, he saw Simon and his brother Andrew net-fishing. Fishing was their regular work. Jesus said to them, "Come with me. I'll make a new kind of fisherman out of you. I'll show you how to catch men and women instead of perch and bass." They didn't ask questions. They dropped their nets and followed.

19-20 A dozen yards or so down the beach, he saw the brothers James and John, Zebedee's sons. They were in the boat, mending their fishnets. Right off, he made the same offer. Immediately, they left their father Zebedee, the boat, and the hired hands, and followed.

CONFIDENT TEACHING

21-22 Then they entered Capernaum. When the Sabbath arrived, Jesus lost no time in getting to the meeting place. He spent the day there teaching. They were surprised at his teaching — so forthright, so confident — not quibbling and quoting like the religion scholars.

23-24 Suddenly, while still in the meeting place, he was interrupted by a man who was deeply disturbed and yelling out, "What business do you have here with us, Jesus? Nazarene! I know what you're up to! You're the Holy One of God, and you've come to destroy us!"

25-26 Jesus shut him up: "Quiet! Get out of him!" The afflicting spirit threw the man into spasms, protesting loudly — and got out.

27-28 Everyone there was incredulous, buzzing with curiosity. "What's going on here? A new teaching that does what it says? He shuts up defiling, demonic spirits and sends them packing!" News of this traveled fast and was soon all over Galilee.

29-31 Directly on leaving the meeting place, they came to Simon and Andrew's house, accompanied by James and John. Simon's mother-in-law was sick in bed, burning up with fever. They told Jesus. He went to her, took her hand, and raised her up. No sooner had the fever left than she was up fixing dinner for them.

32-34 That evening, after the sun was down, they brought sick and evil-afflicted people to him, the whole city lined up at his door! He cured their sick bodies and tormented spirits. Because the demons knew his true identity, he didn't let them say a word.

The Leper

35-37 While it was still night, way before dawn, he got up and went out to a secluded spot and prayed. Simon and those with him went looking for him. They found him and said, "Everybody's looking for you."

38-39 Jesus said, "Let's go to the rest of the villages so I can preach there also. This is why I've come." He went to their meeting places all through Galilee, preaching and throwing out the demons.

40 A leper came to him, begging on his knees, "If you want to, you can cleanse me."

41-45 Deeply moved, Jesus put out his hand, touched him, and said, "I want to. Be clean." Then and there the leprosy was gone, his skin smooth and healthy. Jesus dismissed him with strict orders: "Say nothing to anyone. Take the offering for cleansing that Moses prescribed and present yourself to the priest. This will validate your healing to the people." But as soon as the man was out of earshot, he told everyone he met what had happened, spreading the news all over town. So Jesus kept to out-of-the-way places, no longer able to move freely in and out of the city. But people found him, and came from all over.

A Paraplegic

1-5 After a few days, Jesus returned to Capernaum, and word got around that he was back home. A crowd gathered, jamming the entrance so no one could get in or out. He was teaching the Word. They brought a paraplegic to him, carried by four men. When they weren't able to get in because of the crowd, they removed part of the roof and lowered the paraplegic on his stretcher. Impressed by their bold belief, Jesus said to the paraplegic, "Son, I forgive your sins."

6-7 Some religion scholars sitting there started whispering among themselves, "He can't talk that way! That's blasphemy! God and only God can forgive sins."

8-12 Jesus knew right away what they were thinking, and said, "Why are you so skeptical? Which is simpler: to say to the paraplegic, 'I forgive your sins,' or say, 'Get up, take your stretcher, and start walking'? Well, just so it's clear that I'm the Son of Man and authorized to do either, or both . . ." (he looked now at the paraplegic), "Get up. Pick up your stretcher and go home." And the man did it—got up, grabbed his stretcher, and walked out, with everyone there watching him. They rubbed their eyes, incredulous—and then praised God, saying, "We've never seen anything like this!"

THE TAX COLLECTOR

13-14 Then Jesus went again to walk alongside the lake. Again a crowd came to him, and he taught them. Strolling along, he saw Levi, son of Alphaeus, at his work collecting taxes. Jesus said, "Come along with me." He came.

15-16 Later Jesus and his disciples were at home having supper with a collection of disreputable guests. Unlikely as it seems, more than a few of them had become followers. The religion scholars and Pharisees saw him keeping this kind of company and lit into his disciples: "What kind of example is this, acting cozy with the riffraff?"

17 Jesus, overhearing, shot back, "Who needs a doctor: the healthy or the sick? I'm here inviting the sin-sick, not the spiritually-fit."

FEASTING OR FASTING?

18 The disciples of John and the disciples of the Pharisees made a practice of fasting. Some people confronted Jesus: "Why do the followers of John and the Pharisees take on the discipline of fasting, but your followers don't?"

19-20 Jesus said, "When you're celebrating a wedding, you don't skimp on the cake and wine. You feast. Later you may need to pull in your belt, but not now. As long as the bride and groom are with you, you have a good time. No one throws cold water on a friendly bonfire. This is Kingdom Come!"

21-22 He went on, "No one cuts up a fine silk scarf to patch old work clothes; you want fabrics that match. And you don't put your wine in cracked bottles."

23-24 One Sabbath day he was walking through a field of ripe grain. As his disciples made a path, they pulled off heads of grain. The Pharisees told on them to Jesus: "Look, your disciples are breaking Sabbath rules!"

25-28 Jesus said, "Really? Haven't you ever read what David did when he was hungry, along with those who were with him? How he entered the sanctuary and ate fresh bread off the altar, with the Chief Priest Abiathar right there watching—holy bread that no one but priests were allowed to eat—and handed it out to his companions?" Then Jesus said, "The Sabbath was made to serve us; we weren't made to serve the Sabbath. The Son of Man is no lackey to the Sabbath. He's in charge!"

DOING GOOD ON THE SABBATH

1-3 3 Then he went back in the meeting place where he found a man with a crippled hand. The Pharisees had their eyes on Jesus to see if he would heal him, hoping to catch him in a Sabbath infraction. He said to the man with the crippled hand, "Stand here where we can see you."

4 Then he spoke to the people: "What kind of action suits the Sabbath best? Doing good or doing evil? Helping people or leaving them helpless?" No one said a word.

5-6 He looked them in the eye, one after another, angry now, furious at their hard-nosed religion. He said to the man, "Hold out your hand." He held it out—it was as good as new! The Pharisees got out as fast as they could, sputtering about how they would join forces with Herod's followers and ruin him.

THE TWELVE APOSTLES

7-10 Jesus went off with his disciples to the sea to get away. But a huge crowd from Galilee trailed after them—also from Judea, Jerusalem, Idumea, across the Jordan, and around Tyre and Sidon—swarms of people who had heard the reports and had come to see for themselves. He told his disciples to get a boat ready so he wouldn't be trampled by the crowd. He had healed many people, and now everyone who had something wrong was pushing and shoving to get near and touch him.

11-12 Evil spirits, when they recognized him, fell down and cried out, "You are the Son of God!" But Jesus would have none of it. He shut them up, forbidding them to identify him in public.

13-19 He climbed a mountain and invited those he wanted with him. They climbed together. He settled on twelve, and designated them apostles. The plan was that they would be with him, and he would send them out to proclaim the Word and give them authority to banish demons. These are the Twelve:

> Simon (Jesus later named him Peter, meaning "Rock"),
> James, son of Zebedee,
> John, brother of James (Jesus nicknamed the Zebedee
>   brothers Boanerges, meaning "Sons of Thunder"),
> Andrew,
> Philip,
> Bartholomew,
> Matthew,
> Thomas,
> James, son of Alphaeus,
> Thaddaeus,
> Simon the Canaanite,
> Judas Iscariot (who betrayed him).

SATAN FIGHTING SATAN?

20-21 Jesus came home and, as usual, a crowd gathered—so many making demands on him that there wasn't even time to eat. His friends heard what was going on and went to rescue him, by force if necessary. They suspected he was getting carried away with himself.

22-27 The religion scholars from Jerusalem came down spreading rumors that he was working black magic, using devil tricks to impress them with spiritual power. Jesus confronted their slander with a story: "Does it make sense to send a devil to catch a devil, to use Satan to get rid of Satan? A constantly squabbling family disintegrates. If Satan were fighting Satan, there soon wouldn't be any Satan left. Do you think it's possible in broad daylight to enter the house of an awake, able-bodied man, and walk off with his possessions unless you tie him up first? Tie him up, though, and you can clean him out.

28-30   "Listen to this carefully. I'm warning you. There's nothing done or said that can't be forgiven. But if you persist in your slanders against God's Holy Spirit, you are repudiating the very One who forgives, sawing off the branch on which you're sitting, severing by your own perversity all connection with the One who forgives." He gave this warning because they were accusing him of being in league with Evil.

JESUS' MOTHER AND BROTHERS

31-32   Just then his mother and brothers showed up. Standing outside, they relayed a message that they wanted a word with him. He was surrounded by the crowd when he was given the message, "Your mother and brothers and sisters are outside looking for you."

33-35   Jesus responded, "Who do you think are my mother and brothers?" Looking around, taking in everyone seated around him, he said, "Right here, right in front of you — my mother and my brothers. Obedience is thicker than blood. The person who obeys God's will is my brother and sister and mother."

THE STORY OF THE SCATTERED SEED

1-2   He went back to teaching by the sea. A crowd built up to such a great size that he had to get into an offshore boat, using the boat as a pulpit as the people pushed to the water's edge. He taught by using stories, many stories.

3-8   "Listen. What do you make of this? A farmer planted seed. As he scattered the seed, some of it fell on the road and birds ate it. Some fell in the gravel; it sprouted quickly but didn't put down roots, so when the sun came up it withered just as quickly. Some fell in the weeds; as it came up, it was strangled among the weeds and nothing came of it. Some fell on good earth and came up with a flourish, producing a harvest exceeding his wildest dreams.

9   "Are you listening to this? Really listening?"

10-12   When they were off by themselves, those who were close to him, along with the Twelve, asked about the stories. He told them, "You've been given insight into God's kingdom — you know how it works. But to those who can't see it yet, everything comes in stories, creating readiness, nudging them toward receptive insight. These are people —

Whose eyes are open but don't see a thing,
Whose ears are open but don't understand a word,
Who avoid making an about-face and getting forgiven."

13   He continued, "Do you see how this story works? All my stories work this way.

14-15   "The farmer plants the Word. Some people are like the seed that falls on the hardened soil of the road. No sooner do they hear the Word than Satan snatches away what has been planted in them.

16-17   "And some are like the seed that lands in the gravel. When they first hear the Word, they respond with great enthusiasm. But there is such shallow soil of character that when the emotions wear off and some difficulty arrives, there is nothing to show for it.

18-19   "The seed cast in the weeds represents the ones who hear the kingdom news but are overwhelmed with worries about all the things they have to do and all the things they want to get. The stress strangles what they heard, and nothing comes of it.

20   "But the seed planted in the good earth represents those who hear the Word, embrace it, and produce a harvest beyond their wildest dreams."

GIVING, NOT GETTING

21-22   Jesus went on: "Does anyone bring a lamp home and put it under a washtub or beneath the bed? Don't you put it up on a table or on the mantel? We're not keeping secrets, we're telling them; we're not hiding things, we're bringing them out into the open.

23   "Are you listening to this? Really listening?

24-25   "Listen carefully to what I am saying—and be wary of the shrewd advice that tells you how to get ahead in the world on your own. Giving, not getting, is the way. Generosity begets generosity. Stinginess impoverishes."

NEVER WITHOUT A STORY

26-29   Then Jesus said, "God's kingdom is like seed thrown on a field by a man who then goes to bed and forgets about it. The seed sprouts and grows—he has no idea how it happens. The earth does it all without his help: first a green stem of grass, then a bud, then the ripened grain. When the grain is fully formed, he reaps—harvest time!

30-32   "How can we picture God's kingdom? What kind of story can we use? It's like a pine nut. When it lands on the ground it is quite small as seeds go, yet once it is planted it grows into a huge pine tree with thick branches. Eagles nest in it."

33-34   With many stories like these, he presented his message to them, fitting the stories to their experience and maturity. He was never without a story when he spoke. When he was alone with his disciples, he went over everything, sorting out the tangles, untying the knots.

THE WIND RAN OUT OF BREATH

35-38   Late that day he said to them, "Let's go across to the other side." They took him in the boat as he was. Other boats came along. A huge storm came up. Waves poured into the boat, threatening to sink it. And Jesus was in the stern, head on a pillow, sleeping! They roused him, saying, "Teacher, is it nothing to you that we're going down?"

39-40   Awake now, he told the wind to pipe down and said to the sea, "Quiet! Settle down!" The wind ran out of breath; the sea became smooth as glass. Jesus reprimanded the disciples: "Why are you such cowards? Don't you have any faith at all?"

41   They were in absolute awe, staggered. "Who is this, anyway?" they asked. "Wind and sea at his beck and call!"

THE MADMAN

1-5   **5** They arrived on the other side of the sea in the country of the Gerasenes. As Jesus got out of the boat, a madman from the cemetery came up to him. He lived there among the tombs and graves. No one could restrain him—he couldn't be chained, couldn't be tied down. He had been tied up many times with chains and ropes, but he broke the chains, snapped the ropes. No one was strong enough to tame him. Night and day he roamed through the graves and the hills, screaming out and slashing himself with sharp stones.

6-8 When he saw Jesus a long way off, he ran and bowed in worship before him — then bellowed in protest, "What business do you have, Jesus, Son of the High God, messing with me? I swear to God, don't give me a hard time!" (Jesus had just commanded the tormenting evil spirit, "Out! Get out of the man!")

9-10 Jesus asked him, "Tell me your name."

He replied, "My name is Mob. I'm a rioting mob." Then he desperately begged Jesus not to banish them from the country.

11-13 A large herd of pigs was browsing and rooting on a nearby hill. The demons begged him, "Send us to the pigs so we can live in them." Jesus gave the order. But it was even worse for the pigs than for the man. Crazed, they stampeded over a cliff into the sea and drowned.

14-15 Those tending the pigs, scared to death, bolted and told their story in town and country. Everyone wanted to see what had happened. They came up to Jesus and saw the madman sitting there wearing decent clothes and making sense, no longer a walking madhouse of a man.

16-17 Those who had seen it told the others what had happened to the demon-possessed man and the pigs. At first they were in awe — and then they were upset, upset over the drowned pigs. They demanded that Jesus leave and not come back.

18-20 As Jesus was getting into the boat, the demon-delivered man begged to go along, but he wouldn't let him. Jesus said, "Go home to your own people. Tell them your story — what the Master did, how he had mercy on you." The man went back and began to preach in the Ten Towns area about what Jesus had done for him. He was the talk of the town.

A RISK OF FAITH

21-24 After Jesus crossed over by boat, a large crowd met him at the seaside. One of the meeting-place leaders named Jairus came. When he saw Jesus, he fell to his knees, beside himself as he begged, "My dear daughter is at death's door. Come and lay hands on her so she will get well and live." Jesus went with him, the whole crowd tagging along, pushing and jostling him.

25-29 A woman who had suffered a condition of hemorrhaging for twelve years — a long succession of physicians had treated her, and treated her badly, taking all her money and leaving her worse off than before — had heard about Jesus. She slipped in from behind and touched his robe. She was thinking to herself, "If I can put a finger on his robe, I can get well." The moment she did it, the flow of blood dried up. She could feel the change and knew her plague was over and done with.

30 At the same moment, Jesus felt energy discharging from him. He turned around to the crowd and asked, "Who touched my robe?"

31 His disciples said, "What are you talking about? With this crowd pushing and jostling you, you're asking, 'Who touched me?' Dozens have touched you!"

32-33 But he went on asking, looking around to see who had done it. The woman, knowing what had happened, knowing she was the one, stepped up in fear and trembling, knelt before him, and gave him the whole story.

34 Jesus said to her, "Daughter, you took a risk of faith, and now you're healed and whole. Live well, live blessed! Be healed of your plague."

꙳

35   While he was still talking, some people came from the leader's house and told him, "Your daughter is dead. Why bother the Teacher any more?"

36   Jesus overheard what they were talking about and said to the leader, "Don't listen to them; just trust me."

37-40   He permitted no one to go in with him except Peter, James, and John. They entered the leader's house and pushed their way through the gossips looking for a story and neighbors bringing in casseroles. Jesus was abrupt: "Why all this busybody grief and gossip? This child isn't dead; she's sleeping." Provoked to sarcasm, they told him he didn't know what he was talking about.

40-43   But when he had sent them all out, he took the child's father and mother, along with his companions, and entered the child's room. He clasped the girl's hand and said, *"Talitha koum,"* which means, "Little girl, get up." At that, she was up and walking around! This girl was twelve years of age. They, of course, were all beside themselves with joy. He gave them strict orders that no one was to know what had taken place in that room. Then he said, "Give her something to eat."

Just a Carpenter

1-2   He left there and returned to his hometown. His disciples came along. On the Sabbath, he gave a lecture in the meeting place. He made a real hit, impressing everyone. "We had no idea he was this good!" they said. "How did he get so wise all of a sudden, get such ability?"

3   But in the next breath they were cutting him down: "He's just a carpenter—Mary's boy. We've known him since he was a kid. We know his brothers, James, Justus, Jude, and Simon, and his sisters. Who does he think he is?" They tripped over what little they knew about him and fell, sprawling. And they never got any further.

4-6   Jesus told them, "A prophet has little honor in his hometown, among his relatives, on the streets he played in as a child." Jesus wasn't able to do much of anything there—he laid hands on a few sick people and healed them, that's all. He couldn't get over their stubbornness. He left and made a circuit of the other villages, teaching.

The Twelve

7-8   Jesus called the Twelve to him, and sent them out in pairs. He gave them authority and power to deal with the evil opposition. He sent them off with these instructions:

8-9   "Don't think you need a lot of extra equipment for this. *You* are the equipment. No special appeals for funds. Keep it simple.

10   "And no luxury inns. Get a modest place and be content there until you leave.

11   "If you're not welcomed, not listened to, quietly withdraw. Don't make a scene. Shrug your shoulders and be on your way."

12-13   Then they were on the road. They preached with joyful urgency that life can be radically different; right and left they sent the demons packing; they brought wellness to the sick, anointing their bodies, healing their spirits.

THE DEATH OF JOHN

14 King Herod heard of all this, for by this time the name of Jesus was on everyone's lips. He said, "This has to be John the Baptizer come back from the dead — that's why he's able to work miracles!"

15 Others said, "No, it's Elijah."

Others said, "He's a prophet, just like one of the old-time prophets."

16 But Herod wouldn't budge: "It's John, sure enough. I cut off his head, and now he's back, alive."

17-20 Herod was the one who had ordered the arrest of John, put him in chains, and sent him to prison at the nagging of Herodias, his brother Philip's wife. For John had provoked Herod by naming his relationship with Herodias "adultery." Herodias, smoldering with hate, wanted to kill him, but didn't dare because Herod was in awe of John. Convinced that he was a holy man, he gave him special treatment. Whenever he listened to him he was miserable with guilt — and yet he couldn't stay away. Something in John kept pulling him back.

21-22 But a portentous day arrived when Herod threw a birthday party, inviting all the brass and bluebloods in Galilee. Herodias's daughter entered the banquet hall and danced for the guests. She dazzled Herod and the guests.

22-23 The king said to the girl, "Ask me anything. I'll give you anything you want." Carried away, he kept on, "I swear, I'll split my kingdom with you if you say so!"

24 She went back to her mother and said, "What should I ask for?"

"Ask for the head of John the Baptizer."

25 Excited, she ran back to the king and said, "I want the head of John the Baptizer served up on a platter. And I want it now!"

26-29 That sobered the king up fast. But unwilling to lose face with his guests, he caved in and let her have her wish. The king sent the executioner off to the prison with orders to bring back John's head. He went, cut off John's head, brought it back on a platter, and presented it to the girl, who gave it to her mother. When John's disciples heard about this, they came and got the body and gave it a decent burial.

SUPPER FOR FIVE THOUSAND

30-31 The apostles then rendezvoused with Jesus and reported on all that they had done and taught. Jesus said, "Come off by yourselves; let's take a break and get a little rest." For there was constant coming and going. They didn't even have time to eat.

32-34 So they got in the boat and went off to a remote place by themselves. Someone saw them going and the word got around. From the surrounding towns people went out on foot, running, and got there ahead of them. When Jesus arrived, he saw this huge crowd. At the sight of them, his heart broke — like sheep with no shepherd they were. He went right to work teaching them.

35-36 When his disciples thought this had gone on long enough — it was now quite late in the day — they interrupted: "We are a long way out in the country, and it's very late. Pronounce a benediction and send these folks off so they can get some supper."

37 Jesus said, "You do it. Fix supper for them."

They replied, "Are you serious? You want us to go spend a fortune on food for their supper?"

38   But he was quite serious. "How many loaves of bread do you have? Take an inventory."

That didn't take long. "Five," they said, "plus two fish."

39-44   Jesus got them all to sit down in groups of fifty or a hundred—they looked like a patchwork quilt of wildflowers spread out on the green grass! He took the five loaves and two fish, lifted his face to heaven in prayer, blessed, broke, and gave the bread to the disciples, and the disciples in turn gave it to the people. He did the same with the fish. They all ate their fill. The disciples gathered twelve baskets of leftovers. More than five thousand were at the supper.

WALKING ON THE SEA

45-46   As soon as the meal was finished, Jesus insisted that the disciples get in the boat and go on ahead across to Bethsaida while he dismissed the congregation. After sending them off, he climbed a mountain to pray.

47-49   Late at night, the boat was far out at sea; Jesus was still by himself on land. He could see his men struggling with the oars, the wind having come up against them. At about four o'clock in the morning, Jesus came toward them, walking on the sea. He intended to go right by them. But when they saw him walking on the sea, they thought it was a ghost and screamed, scared out of their wits.

50-52   Jesus was quick to comfort them: "Courage! It's me. Don't be afraid." As soon as he climbed into the boat, the wind died down. They were stunned, shaking their heads, wondering what was going on. They didn't understand what he had done at the supper. None of this had yet penetrated their hearts.

53-56   They beached the boat at Gennesaret and tied up at the landing. As soon as they got out of the boat, word got around fast. People ran this way and that, bringing their sick on stretchers to where they heard he was. Wherever he went, village or town or country crossroads, they brought their sick to the marketplace and begged him to let them touch the edge of his coat—that's all. And whoever touched him became well.

THE SOURCE OF YOUR POLLUTION

1-4   The Pharisees, along with some religion scholars who had come from Jerusalem, gathered around him. They noticed that some of his disciples weren't being careful with ritual washings before meals. The Pharisees—Jews in general, in fact—would never eat a meal without going through the motions of a ritual hand-washing, with an especially vigorous scrubbing if they had just come from the market (to say nothing of the scourings they'd give jugs and pots and pans).

5   The Pharisees and religion scholars asked, "Why do your disciples flout the rules, showing up at meals without washing their hands?"

6-8   Jesus answered, "Isaiah was right about frauds like you, hit the bull's-eye in fact:

These people make a big show of saying the right thing,
      but their heart isn't in it.
They act like they are worshiping me,
      but they don't mean it.

> They just use me as a cover
>> for teaching whatever suits their fancy,
> Ditching God's command
>> and taking up the latest fads."

9-13 He went on, "Well, good for you. You get rid of God's command so you won't be inconvenienced in following the religious fashions! Moses said, 'Respect your father and mother,' and, 'Anyone denouncing father or mother should be killed.' But you weasel out of that by saying that it's perfectly acceptable to say to father or mother, 'Gift! What I owed you I've given as a gift to God,' thus relieving yourselves of obligation to father or mother. You scratch out God's Word and scrawl a whim in its place. You do a lot of things like this."

14-15 Jesus called the crowd together again and said, "Listen now, all of you — take this to heart. It's not what you swallow that pollutes your life; it's what you vomit — that's the real pollution."

17 When he was back home after being with the crowd, his disciples said, "We don't get it. Put it in plain language."

18-19 Jesus said, "Are you being willfully stupid? Don't you see that what you swallow can't contaminate you? It doesn't enter your heart but your stomach, works its way through the intestines, and is finally flushed." (That took care of dietary quibbling; Jesus was saying that *all* foods are fit to eat.)

20-23 He went on: "It's what comes out of a person that pollutes: obscenities, lusts, thefts, murders, adulteries, greed, depravity, deceptive dealings, carousing, mean looks, slander, arrogance, foolishness — all these are vomit from the heart. *There* is the source of your pollution."

24-26 From there Jesus set out for the vicinity of Tyre. He entered a house there where he didn't think he would be found, but he couldn't escape notice. He was barely inside when a woman who had a disturbed daughter heard where he was. She came and knelt at his feet, begging for help. The woman was Greek, Syro-Phoenician by birth. She asked him to cure her daughter.

27 He said, "Stand in line and take your turn. The children get fed first. If there's any left over, the dogs get it."

28 She said, "Of course, Master. But don't dogs under the table get scraps dropped by the children?"

29-30 Jesus was impressed. "You're right! On your way! Your daughter is no longer disturbed. The demonic affliction is gone." She went home and found her daughter relaxed on the bed, the torment gone for good.

31-35 Then he left the region of Tyre, went through Sidon back to Galilee Lake and over to the district of the Ten Towns. Some people brought a man who could neither hear nor speak and asked Jesus to lay a healing hand on him. He took the man off by himself, put his fingers in the man's ears and some spit on the man's tongue. Then Jesus looked up in prayer, groaned mightily, and commanded, "*Ephphatha!* — Open up!" And it happened. The man's hearing was clear and his speech plain — just like that.

36-37 Jesus urged them to keep it quiet, but they talked it up all the more, beside themselves with excitement. "He's done it all and done it well. He gives hearing to the deaf, speech to the speechless."

A MEAL FOR FOUR THOUSAND

1-3 **8** At about this same time he again found himself with a hungry crowd on his hands. He called his disciples together and said, "This crowd is breaking my heart. They have stuck with me for three days, and now they have nothing to eat. If I send them home hungry, they'll faint along the way — some of them have come a long distance."

4 His disciples responded, "What do you expect us to do about it? Buy food out here in the desert?"

5 He asked, "How much bread do you have?"

"Seven loaves," they said.

6-10 So Jesus told the crowd to sit down on the ground. After giving thanks, he took the seven bread loaves, broke them into pieces, and gave them to his disciples so they could hand them out to the crowd. They also had a few fish. He pronounced a blessing over the fish and told his disciples to hand them out as well. The crowd ate its fill. Seven sacks of leftovers were collected. There were well over four thousand at the meal. Then he sent them home. He himself went straight to the boat with his disciples and set out for Dalmanoutha.

11-12 When they arrived, the Pharisees came out and started in on him, badgering him to prove himself, pushing him up against the wall. Provoked, he said, "Why does this generation clamor for miraculous guarantees? If I have anything to say about it, you'll not get so much as a hint of a guarantee."

CONTAMINATING YEAST

13-15 He then left them, got back in the boat, and headed for the other side. But the disciples forgot to pack a lunch. Except for a single loaf of bread, there wasn't a crumb in the boat. Jesus warned, "Be very careful. Keep a sharp eye out for the contaminating yeast of Pharisees and the followers of Herod."

16-19 Meanwhile, the disciples were finding fault with each other because they had forgotten to bring bread. Jesus overheard and said, "Why are you fussing because you forgot bread? Don't you see the point of all this? Don't you get it at all? Remember the five loaves I broke for the five thousand? How many baskets of leftovers did you pick up?"

They said, "Twelve."

20 "And the seven loaves for the four thousand — how many bags full of leftovers did you get?"

"Seven."

21 He said, "Do you still not get it?"

22-23 They arrived at Bethsaida. Some people brought a sightless man and begged Jesus to give him a healing touch. Taking him by the hand, he led him out of the village. He put spit in the man's eyes, laid hands on him, and asked, "Do you see anything?"

24-26 He looked up. "I see men. They look like walking trees." So Jesus laid hands on his eyes again. The man looked hard and realized that he had recovered perfect sight, saw everything in bright, twenty-twenty focus. Jesus sent him straight home, telling him, "Don't enter the village."

THE MESSIAH

27 Jesus and his disciples headed out for the villages around Caesarea Philippi. As they walked, he asked, "Who do the people say I am?"

28   "Some say 'John the Baptizer,'" they said. "Others say 'Elijah.' Still others say 'one of the prophets.'"

29   He then asked, "And you—what are you saying about me? Who am I?"
Peter gave the answer: "You are the Christ, the Messiah."

30-32   Jesus warned them to keep it quiet, not to breathe a word of it to anyone. He then began explaining things to them: "It is necessary that the Son of Man proceed to an ordeal of suffering, be tried and found guilty by the elders, high priests, and religion scholars, be killed, and after three days rise up alive." He said this simply and clearly so they couldn't miss it.

32-33   But Peter grabbed him in protest. Turning and seeing his disciples wavering, wondering what to believe, Jesus confronted Peter. "Peter, get out of my way! Satan, get lost! You have no idea how God works."

34-37   Calling the crowd to join his disciples, he said, "Anyone who intends to come with me has to let me lead. You're not in the driver's seat; *I* am. Don't run from suffering; embrace it. Follow me and I'll show you how. Self-help is no help at all. Self-sacrifice is the way, my way, to saving yourself, your true self. What good would it do to get everything you want and lose you, the real you? What could you ever trade your soul for?

38   "If any of you are embarrassed over me and the way I'm leading you when you get around your fickle and unfocused friends, know that you'll be an even greater embarrassment to the Son of Man when he arrives in all the splendor of God, his Father, with an army of the holy angels."

1   9 Then he drove it home by saying, "This isn't pie in the sky by and by. Some of you who are standing here are going to see it happen, see the kingdom of God arrive in full force."

IN A LIGHT-RADIANT CLOUD

2-4   Six days later, three of them *did* see it. Jesus took Peter, James, and John and led them up a high mountain. His appearance changed from the inside out, right before their eyes. His clothes shimmered, glistening white, whiter than any bleach could make them. Elijah, along with Moses, came into view, in deep conversation with Jesus.

5-6   Peter interrupted, "Rabbi, this is a great moment! Let's build three memorials— one for you, one for Moses, one for Elijah." He blurted this out without thinking, stunned as they all were by what they were seeing.

7   Just then a light-radiant cloud enveloped them, and from deep in the cloud, a voice: "This is my Son, marked by my love. Listen to him."

8   The next minute the disciples were looking around, rubbing their eyes, seeing nothing but Jesus, only Jesus.

9-10   Coming down the mountain, Jesus swore them to secrecy. "Don't tell a soul what you saw. After the Son of Man rises from the dead, you're free to talk." They puzzled over that, wondering what on earth "rising from the dead" meant.

11   Meanwhile they were asking, "Why do the religion scholars say that Elijah has to come first?"

12-13   Jesus replied, "Elijah does come first and get everything ready for the coming of the Son of Man. They treated this Elijah like dirt, much like they will treat the Son of Man, who will, according to Scripture, suffer terribly and be kicked around contemptibly."

14-16 When they came back down the mountain to the other disciples, they saw a huge crowd around them, and the religion scholars cross-examining them. As soon as the people in the crowd saw Jesus, admiring excitement stirred them. They ran and greeted him. He asked, "What's going on? What's all the commotion?"

17-18 A man out of the crowd answered, "Teacher, I brought my mute son, made speechless by a demon, to you. Whenever it seizes him, it throws him to the ground. He foams at the mouth, grinds his teeth, and goes stiff as a board. I told your disciples, hoping they could deliver him, but they couldn't."

19-20 Jesus said, "What a generation! No sense of God! How many times do I have to go over these things? How much longer do I have to put up with this? Bring the boy here." They brought him. When the demon saw Jesus, it threw the boy into a seizure, causing him to writhe on the ground and foam at the mouth.

21-22 He asked the boy's father, "How long has this been going on?"

"Ever since he was a little boy. Many times it pitches him into fire or the river to do away with him. If you can do anything, do it. Have a heart and help us!"

23 Jesus said, "If? There are no 'ifs' among believers. Anything can happen."

24 No sooner were the words out of his mouth than the father cried, "Then I believe. Help me with my doubts!"

25-27 Seeing that the crowd was forming fast, Jesus gave the vile spirit its marching orders: "Dumb and deaf spirit, I command you — Out of him, and stay out!" Screaming, and with much thrashing about, it left. The boy was pale as a corpse, so people started saying, "He's dead." But Jesus, taking his hand, raised him. The boy stood up.

28 After arriving back home, his disciples cornered Jesus and asked, "Why couldn't we throw the demon out?"

29 He answered, "There is no way to get rid of this kind of demon except by prayer."

30-32 Leaving there, they went through Galilee. He didn't want anyone to know their whereabouts, for he wanted to teach his disciples. He told them, "The Son of Man is about to be betrayed to some people who want nothing to do with God. They will murder him. Three days after his murder, he will rise, alive." They didn't know what he was talking about, but were afraid to ask him about it.

SO YOU WANT FIRST PLACE?

33 They came to Capernaum. When he was safe at home, he asked them, "What were you discussing on the road?"

34 The silence was deafening — they had been arguing with one another over who among them was greatest.

35 He sat down and summoned the Twelve. "So you want first place? Then take the last place. Be the servant of all."

36-37 He put a child in the middle of the room. Then, cradling the little one in his arms, he said, "Whoever embraces one of these children as I do embraces me, and far more than me — God who sent me."

38   John spoke up, "Teacher, we saw a man using your name to expel demons and we stopped him because he wasn't in our group."

39-41   Jesus wasn't pleased. "Don't stop him. No one can use my name to do something good and powerful, and in the next breath cut me down. If he's not an enemy, he's an ally. Why, anyone by just giving you a cup of water in my name is on our side. Count on it that God will notice.

42   "On the other hand, if you give one of these simple, childlike believers a hard time, bullying or taking advantage of their simple trust, you'll soon wish you hadn't. You'd be better off dropped in the middle of the lake with a millstone around your neck.

43-48   "If your hand or your foot gets in God's way, chop it off and throw it away. You're better off maimed or lame and alive than the proud owner of two hands and two feet, godless in a furnace of eternal fire. And if your eye distracts you from God, pull it out and throw it away. You're better off one-eyed and alive than exercising your twenty-twenty vision from inside the fire of hell.

49-50   "Everyone's going through a refining fire sooner or later, but you'll be well-preserved, protected from the *eternal* flames. Be preservatives yourselves. Preserve the peace."

DIVORCE

1-2   **10** From there he went to the area of Judea across the Jordan. A crowd of people, as was so often the case, went along, and he, as he so often did, taught them. Pharisees came up, intending to give him a hard time. They asked, "Is it legal for a man to divorce his wife?"

3   Jesus said, "What did Moses command?"

4   They answered, "Moses gave permission to fill out a certificate of dismissal and divorce her."

5-9   Jesus said, "Moses wrote this command only as a concession to your hardhearted ways. In the original creation, God made male and female to be together. Because of this, a man leaves father and mother, and in marriage he becomes one flesh with a woman — no longer two individuals, but forming a new unity. Because God created this organic union of the two sexes, no one should desecrate his art by cutting them apart."

10-12   When they were back home, the disciples brought it up again. Jesus gave it to them straight: "A man who divorces his wife so he can marry someone else commits adultery against her. And a woman who divorces her husband so she can marry someone else commits adultery."

13-16   The people brought children to Jesus, hoping he might touch them. The disciples shooed them off. But Jesus was irate and let them know it: "Don't push these children away. Don't ever get between them and me. These children are at the very center of life in the kingdom. Mark this: Unless you accept God's kingdom in the simplicity of a child, you'll never get in." Then, gathering the children up in his arms, he laid his hands of blessing on them.

To Enter God's Kingdom

17   As he went out into the street, a man came running up, greeted him with great reverence, and asked, "Good Teacher, what must I do to get eternal life?"

18-19   Jesus said, "Why are you calling me good? No one is good, only God. You know the commandments: Don't murder, don't commit adultery, don't steal, don't lie, don't cheat, honor your father and mother."

20   He said, "Teacher, I have — from my youth — kept them all!"

21   Jesus looked him hard in the eye — and loved him! He said, "There's one thing left: Go sell whatever you own and give it to the poor. All your wealth will then be heavenly wealth. And come follow me."

22   The man's face clouded over. This was the last thing he expected to hear, and he walked off with a heavy heart. He was holding on tight to a lot of things, and not about to let go.

23-25   Looking at his disciples, Jesus said, "Do you have any idea how difficult it is for people who 'have it all' to enter God's kingdom?" The disciples couldn't believe what they were hearing, but Jesus kept on: "You can't imagine how difficult. I'd say it's easier for a camel to go through a needle's eye than for the rich to get into God's kingdom."

26   *That* set the disciples back on their heels. "Then who has any chance at all?" they asked.

27   Jesus was blunt: "No chance at all if you think you can pull it off by yourself. Every chance in the world if you let God do it."

28   Peter tried another angle: "We left everything and followed you."

29-31   Jesus said, "Mark my words, no one who sacrifices house, brothers, sisters, mother, father, children, land — whatever — because of me and the Message will lose out. They'll get it all back, but multiplied many times in homes, brothers, sisters, mothers, children, and land — but also in troubles. And then the bonus of eternal life! This is once again the Great Reversal: Many who are first will end up last, and the last first."

32-34   Back on the road, they set out for Jerusalem. Jesus had a head start on them, and they were following, puzzled and not just a little afraid. He took the Twelve and began again to go over what to expect next. "Listen to me carefully. We're on our way up to Jerusalem. When we get there, the Son of Man will be betrayed to the religious leaders and scholars. They will sentence him to death. Then they will hand him over to the Romans, who will mock and spit on him, give him the third degree, and kill him. After three days he will rise alive."

The Highest Places of Honor

35   James and John, Zebedee's sons, came up to him. "Teacher, we have something we want you to do for us."

36   "What is it? I'll see what I can do."

37   "Arrange it," they said, "so that we will be awarded the highest places of honor in your glory — one of us at your right, the other at your left."

38   Jesus said, "You have no idea what you're asking. Are you capable of drinking the cup I drink, of being baptized in the baptism I'm about to be plunged into?"

39-40   "Sure," they said. "Why not?"

Jesus said, "Come to think of it, you *will* drink the cup I drink, and be baptized in my baptism. But as to awarding places of honor, that's not my business. There are other arrangements for that."

41-45 When the other ten heard of this conversation, they lost their tempers with James and John. Jesus got them together to settle things down. "You've observed how godless rulers throw their weight around," he said, "and when people get a little power how quickly it goes to their heads. It's not going to be that way with you. Whoever wants to be great must become a servant. Whoever wants to be first among you must be your slave. That is what the Son of Man has done: He came to serve, not to be served — and then to give away his life in exchange for many who are held hostage."

46-48 They spent some time in Jericho. As Jesus was leaving town, trailed by his disciples and a parade of people, a blind beggar by the name of Bartimaeus, son of Timaeus, was sitting alongside the road. When he heard that Jesus the Nazarene was passing by, he began to cry out, "Son of David, Jesus! Mercy, have mercy on me!" Many tried to hush him up, but he yelled all the louder, "Son of David! Mercy, have mercy on me!"

49-50 Jesus stopped in his tracks. "Call him over."

They called him. "It's your lucky day! Get up! He's calling you to come!" Throwing off his coat, he was on his feet at once and came to Jesus.

51 Jesus said, "What can I do for you?"

The blind man said, "Rabbi, I want to see."

52 "On your way," said Jesus. "Your faith has saved and healed you."

In that very instant he recovered his sight and followed Jesus down the road.

Entering Jerusalem on a Colt

1-3 **11** When they were nearing Jerusalem, at Bethphage and Bethany on Mount Olives, he sent off two of the disciples with instructions: "Go to the village across from you. As soon as you enter, you'll find a colt tethered, one that has never yet been ridden. Untie it and bring it. If anyone asks, 'What are you doing?' say, 'The Master needs him, and will return him right away.'"

4-7 They went and found a colt tied to a door at the street corner and untied it. Some of those standing there said, "What are you doing untying that colt?" The disciples replied exactly as Jesus had instructed them, and the people let them alone. They brought the colt to Jesus, spread their coats on it, and he mounted.

8-10 The people gave him a wonderful welcome, some throwing their coats on the street, others spreading out rushes they had cut in the fields. Running ahead and following after, they were calling out,

Hosanna!
Blessed is he who comes in God's name!
Blessed the coming kingdom of our father David!
Hosanna in highest heaven!

11 He entered Jerusalem, then entered the Temple. He looked around, taking it all in. But by now it was late, so he went back to Bethany with the Twelve.

THE CURSED FIG TREE

12-14 As they left Bethany the next day, he was hungry. Off in the distance he saw a fig tree in full leaf. He came up to it expecting to find something for breakfast, but found nothing but fig leaves. (It wasn't yet the season for figs.) He addressed the tree: "No one is going to eat fruit from you again — ever!" And his disciples overheard him.

15-17 They arrived at Jerusalem. Immediately on entering the Temple Jesus started throwing out everyone who had set up shop there, buying and selling. He kicked over the tables of the bankers and the stalls of the pigeon merchants. He didn't let anyone even carry a basket through the Temple. And then he taught them, quoting this text:

My house was designated a house of prayer for the nations;
You've turned it into a hangout for thieves.

18 The high priests and religion scholars heard what was going on and plotted how they might get rid of him. They panicked, for the entire crowd was carried away by his teaching.

19 At evening, Jesus and his disciples left the city.

20-21 In the morning, walking along the road, they saw the fig tree, shriveled to a dry stick. Peter, remembering what had happened the previous day, said to him, "Rabbi, look — the fig tree you cursed is shriveled up!"

22-25 Jesus was matter-of-fact: "Embrace this God-life. Really embrace it, and nothing will be too much for you. This mountain, for instance: Just say, 'Go jump in the lake' — no shuffling or shilly-shallying — and it's as good as done. That's why I urge you to pray for absolutely everything, ranging from small to large. Include everything as you embrace this God-life, and you'll get God's everything. And when you assume the posture of prayer, remember that it's not all *asking*. If you have anything against someone, *forgive* — only then will your heavenly Father be inclined to also wipe your slate clean of sins."

HIS CREDENTIALS

27-28 Then when they were back in Jerusalem once again, as they were walking through the Temple, the high priests, religion scholars, and leaders came up and demanded, "Show us your credentials. Who authorized you to speak and act like this?"

29-30 Jesus responded, "First let me ask you a question. Answer my question and then I'll present my credentials. About the baptism of John — who authorized it: heaven or humans? Tell me."

31-33 They were on the spot, and knew it. They pulled back into a huddle and whispered, "If we say 'heaven,' he'll ask us why we didn't believe John; if we say 'humans,' we'll be up against it with the people because they all hold John up as a prophet." They decided to concede that round to Jesus. "We don't know," they said.

Jesus replied, "Then I won't answer your question either."

THE STORY ABOUT A VINEYARD

1-2 12 Then Jesus started telling them stories. "A man planted a vineyard. He fenced it, dug a winepress, erected a watchtower, turned it over to the farmhands, and went off on a trip. At the time for harvest, he sent a servant back to the farmhands to collect his profits.

3-5   "They grabbed him, beat him up, and sent him off empty-handed. So he sent another servant. That one they tarred and feathered. He sent another and that one they killed. And on and on, many others. Some they beat up, some they killed.

6   "Finally there was only one left: a beloved son. In a last-ditch effort, he sent him, thinking, 'Surely they will respect my son.'

7-8   "But those farmhands saw their chance. They rubbed their hands together in greed and said, 'This is the heir! Let's kill him and have it all for ourselves.' They grabbed him, killed him, and threw him over the fence.

9-11   "What do you think the owner of the vineyard will do? Right. He'll come and clean house. Then he'll assign the care of the vineyard to others. Read it for yourselves in Scripture:

> That stone the masons threw out
>   is now the cornerstone!
> This is God's work;
>   we rub our eyes — we can hardly believe it!"

12   They wanted to lynch him then and there but, intimidated by public opinion, held back. They knew the story was about them. They got away from there as fast as they could.

PAYING TAXES TO CAESAR

13-14   They sent some Pharisees and followers of Herod to bait him, hoping to catch him saying something incriminating. They came up and said, "Teacher, we know you have integrity, that you are indifferent to public opinion, don't pander to your students, and teach the way of God accurately. Tell us: Is it lawful to pay taxes to Caesar or not?"

15-16   He knew it was a trick question, and said, "Why are you playing these games with me? Bring me a coin and let me look at it." They handed him one.

"This engraving — who does it look like? And whose name is on it?"

"Caesar," they said.

17   Jesus said, "Give Caesar what is his, and give God what is his."

Their mouths hung open, speechless.

OUR INTIMACIES WILL BE WITH GOD

18-23   Some Sadducees, the party that denies any possibility of resurrection, came up and asked, "Teacher, Moses wrote that if a man dies and leaves a wife but no child, his brother is obligated to marry the widow and have children. Well, there once were seven brothers. The first took a wife. He died childless. The second married her. He died, and still no child. The same with the third. All seven took their turn, but no child. Finally the wife died. When they are raised at the resurrection, whose wife is she? All seven were her husband."

24-27   Jesus said, "You're way off base, and here's why: One, you don't know your Bibles; two, you don't know how God works. After the dead are raised up, we're past the marriage business. As it is with angels now, all our ecstasies and intimacies then will be with God. And regarding the dead, whether or not they are raised, don't you ever read the Bible? How God at the bush said to Moses, 'I am — not *was* — the God of Abraham, the God of Isaac, and the God of Jacob'? The living God is God of the *living*, not the dead. You're way, way off base."

The Most Important Commandment

28 One of the religion scholars came up. Hearing the lively exchanges of question and answer and seeing how sharp Jesus was in his answers, he put in his question: "Which is most important of all the commandments?"

29-31 Jesus said, "The first in importance is, 'Listen, Israel: The Lord your God is one; so love the Lord God with all your passion and prayer and intelligence and energy.' And here is the second: 'Love others as well as you love yourself.' There is no other commandment that ranks with these."

32-33 The religion scholar said, "A wonderful answer, Teacher! So lucid and accurate — that God is one and there is no other. And loving him with all passion and intelligence and energy, and loving others as well as you love yourself. Why, that's better than all offerings and sacrifices put together!"

34 When Jesus realized how insightful he was, he said, "You're almost there, right on the border of God's kingdom."

After that, no one else dared ask a question.

35-37 While he was teaching in the Temple, Jesus asked, "How is it that the religion scholars say that the Messiah is David's 'son,' when we all know that David, inspired by the Holy Spirit, said,

God said to my Master,
  "Sit here at my right hand
  until I put your enemies under your feet."

"David here designates the Messiah 'my Master' — so how can the Messiah also be his 'son'?"

The large crowd was delighted with what they heard.

38-40 He continued teaching. "Watch out for the religion scholars. They love to walk around in academic gowns, preening in the radiance of public flattery, basking in prominent positions, sitting at the head table at every church function. And all the time they are exploiting the weak and helpless. The longer their prayers, the worse they get. But they'll pay for it in the end."

41-44 Sitting across from the offering box, he was observing how the crowd tossed money in for the collection. Many of the rich were making large contributions. One poor widow came up and put in two small coins — a measly two cents. Jesus called his disciples over and said, "The truth is that this poor widow gave more to the collection than all the others put together. All the others gave what they'll never miss; she gave extravagantly what she couldn't afford — she gave her all."

Doomsday Deceivers

1 **13** As he walked away from the Temple, one of his disciples said, "Teacher, look at that stonework! Those buildings!"

2 Jesus said, "You're impressed by this grandiose architecture?

There's not a stone in the whole works that is not going to end up in a heap of rubble."

3-4 Later, as he was sitting on Mount Olives in full view of the Temple, Peter, James, John, and Andrew got him off by himself and asked, "Tell us, when is this going to happen? What sign will we get that things are coming to a head?"

5-8 Jesus began, "Watch out for doomsday deceivers. Many leaders are going to show up with forged identities claiming, 'I'm the One.' They will deceive a lot of people. When you hear of wars and rumored wars, keep your head and don't panic. This is routine history, and no sign of the end. Nation will fight nation and ruler fight ruler, over and over. Earthquakes will occur in various places. There will be famines. But these things are nothing compared to what's coming.

9-10 "And watch out! They're going to drag you into court. And then it will go from bad to worse, dog-eat-dog, everyone at your throat because you carry my name. You're placed there as sentinels to truth. The Message has to be preached all across the world.

11 "When they bring you, betrayed, into court, don't worry about what you'll say. When the time comes, say what's on your heart — the Holy Spirit will make his witness in and through you.

12-13 "It's going to be brother killing brother, father killing child, children killing parents. There's no telling who will hate you because of me.

"Stay with it — that's what is required. Stay with it to the end. You won't be sorry; you'll be saved.

RUN FOR THE HILLS

14-18 "But be ready to run for it when you see the monster of desecration set up where it should *never* be. You who can read, make sure you understand what I'm talking about. If you're living in Judea at the time, run for the hills; if you're working in the yard, don't go back to the house to get anything; if you're out in the field, don't go back to get your coat. Pregnant and nursing mothers will have it especially hard. Hope and pray this won't happen in the middle of winter.

19-20 "These are going to be hard days — nothing like it from the time God made the world right up to the present. And there'll be nothing like it again. If he let the days of trouble run their course, nobody would make it. But because of God's chosen people, those he personally chose, he has already intervened.

NO ONE KNOWS THE DAY OR HOUR

21-23 "If anyone tries to flag you down, calling out, 'Here's the Messiah!' or points, 'There he is!' don't fall for it. Fake Messiahs and lying preachers are going to pop up everywhere. Their impressive credentials and dazzling performances will pull the wool over the eyes of even those who ought to know better. So watch out. I've given you fair warning.

24-25 "Following those hard times,

Sun will fade out,
    moon cloud over,
Stars fall out of the sky,
    cosmic powers tremble.

26-27   "And then they'll see the Son of Man enter in grand style, his Arrival filling the sky — no one will miss it! He'll dispatch the angels; they will pull in the chosen from the four winds, from pole to pole.

28-31   "Take a lesson from the fig tree. From the moment you notice its buds form, the merest hint of green, you know summer's just around the corner. And so it is with you. When you see all these things, you know he is at the door. Don't take this lightly. I'm not just saying this for some future generation, but for this one, too — these things will happen. Sky and earth will wear out; my words won't wear out.

32-37   "But the exact day and hour? No one knows that, not even heaven's angels, not even the Son. Only the Father. So keep a sharp lookout, for you don't know the timetable. It's like a man who takes a trip, leaving home and putting his servants in charge, each assigned a task, and commanding the gatekeeper to stand watch. So, stay at your post, watching. You have no idea when the homeowner is returning, whether evening, midnight, cockcrow, or morning. You don't want him showing up unannounced, with you asleep on the job. I say it to you, and I'm saying it to all: Stay at your post. Keep watch."

ANOINTING HIS HEAD

1-2   **14** In only two days the eight-day Festival of Passover and the Feast of Unleavened Bread would begin. The high priests and religion scholars were looking for a way they could seize Jesus by stealth and kill him. They agreed that it should not be done during Passover Week. "We don't want the crowds up in arms," they said.

3-5   Jesus was at Bethany, a guest of Simon the Leper. While he was eating dinner, a woman came up carrying a bottle of very expensive perfume. Opening the bottle, she poured it on his head. Some of the guests became furious among themselves. "That's criminal! A sheer waste! This perfume could have been sold for well over a year's wages and handed out to the poor." They swelled up in anger, nearly bursting with indignation over her.

6-9   But Jesus said, "Let her alone. Why are you giving her a hard time? She has just done something wonderfully significant for me. You will have the poor with you every day for the rest of your lives. Whenever you feel like it, you can do something for them. Not so with me. She did what she could when she could — she pre-anointed my body for burial. And you can be sure that wherever in the whole world the Message is preached, what she just did is going to be talked about admiringly."

10-11   Judas Iscariot, one of the Twelve, went to the cabal of high priests, determined to betray him. They couldn't believe their ears, and promised to pay him well. He started looking for just the right moment to hand him over.

TRAITOR TO THE SON OF MAN

12   On the first of the Days of Unleavened Bread, the day they prepare the Passover sacrifice, his disciples asked him, "Where do you want us to go and make preparations so you can eat the Passover meal?"

13-15   He directed two of his disciples, "Go into the city. A man carrying a water jug will meet you. Follow him. Ask the owner of whichever house he enters, 'The Teacher wants to know, Where is my guest room where I can eat the Passover meal with my disciples?' He will show you a spacious second-story room, swept and ready. Prepare for us there."

16 The disciples left, came to the city, found everything just as he had told them, and prepared the Passover meal.

17-18 After sunset he came with the Twelve. As they were at the supper table eating, Jesus said, "I have something hard but important to say to you: One of you is going to hand me over to the conspirators, one who at this moment is eating with me."

19 Stunned, they started asking, one after another, "It isn't me, is it?"

20-21 He said, "It's one of the Twelve, one who eats with me out of the same bowl. In one sense, it turns out that the Son of Man is entering into a way of treachery well-marked by the Scriptures — no surprises here. In another sense, the man who turns him in, turns traitor to the Son of Man — better never to have been born than do this!"

"THIS IS MY BODY"

22 In the course of their meal, having taken and blessed the bread, he broke it and gave it to them. Then he said,

Take, this is my body.

23-24 Taking the chalice, he gave it to them, thanking God, and they all drank from it. He said,

This is my blood,
God's new covenant,
Poured out for many people.

25 "I'll not be drinking wine again until the new day when I drink it in the kingdom of God."

26 They sang a hymn and then went directly to Mount Olives.

27-28 Jesus told them, "You're all going to feel that your world is falling apart and that it's my fault. There's a Scripture that says,

I will strike the shepherd;
The sheep will go helter-skelter.

"But after I am raised up, I will go ahead of you, leading the way to Galilee."

29 Peter blurted out, "Even if everyone else is ashamed of you when things fall to pieces, I won't be."

30 Jesus said, "Don't be so sure. Today, this very night in fact, before the rooster crows twice, you will deny me three times."

31 He blustered in protest, "Even if I have to die with you, I will never deny you." All the others said the same thing.

GETHSEMANE

32-34 They came to an area called Gethsemane. Jesus told his disciples, "Sit here while I pray." He took Peter, James, and John with him. He plunged into a sinkhole of dreadful agony. He told them, "I feel bad enough right now to die. Stay here and keep vigil with me."

35-36   Going a little ahead, he fell to the ground and prayed for a way out: "Papa, Father, you can — can't you? — get me out of this. Take this cup away from me. But please, not what I want — what do *you* want?"

37-38   He came back and found them sound asleep. He said to Peter, "Simon, you went to sleep on me? Can't you stick it out with me a single hour? Stay alert, be in prayer, so you don't enter the danger zone without even knowing it. Don't be naive. Part of you is eager, ready for anything in God; but another part is as lazy as an old dog sleeping by the fire."

39-40   He then went back and prayed the same prayer. Returning, he again found them sound asleep. They simply couldn't keep their eyes open, and they didn't have a plausible excuse.

41-42   He came back a third time and said, "Are you going to sleep all night? No — you've slept long enough. Time's up. The Son of Man is about to be betrayed into the hands of sinners. Get up. Let's get going. My betrayer has arrived."

A GANG OF RUFFIANS

43-47   No sooner were the words out of his mouth when Judas, the one out of the Twelve, showed up, and with him a gang of ruffians, sent by the high priests, religion scholars, and leaders, brandishing swords and clubs. The betrayer had worked out a signal with them: "The one I kiss, that's the one — seize him. Make sure he doesn't get away." He went straight to Jesus and said, "Rabbi!" and kissed him. The others then grabbed him and roughed him up. One of the men standing there unsheathed his sword, swung, and came down on the Chief Priest's servant, lopping off the man's ear.

48-50   Jesus said to them, "What is this, coming after me with swords and clubs as if I were a dangerous criminal? Day after day I've been sitting in the Temple teaching, and you never so much as lifted a hand against me. What you in fact have done is confirm the prophetic writings." All the disciples cut and ran.

51-52   A young man was following along. All he had on was a bedsheet. Some of the men grabbed him but he got away, running off naked, leaving them holding the sheet.

CONDEMNED TO DEATH

53-54   They led Jesus to the Chief Priest, where the high priests, religious leaders, and scholars had gathered together. Peter followed at a safe distance until they got to the Chief Priest's courtyard, where he mingled with the servants and warmed himself at the fire.

55-59   The high priests conspiring with the Jewish Council looked high and low for evidence against Jesus by which they could sentence him to death. They found nothing. Plenty of people were willing to bring in false charges, but nothing added up, and they ended up canceling each other out. Then a few of them stood up and lied: "We heard him say, 'I am going to tear down this Temple, built by hard labor, and in three days build another without lifting a hand.'" But even they couldn't agree exactly.

60-61   In the middle of this, the Chief Priest stood up and asked Jesus, "What do you have to say to the accusation?" Jesus was silent. He said nothing.

The Chief Priest tried again, this time asking, "Are you the Messiah, the Son of the Blessed?"

62 Jesus said, "Yes, I am, and you'll see it yourself:

> The Son of Man seated
> At the right hand of the Mighty One,
> Arriving on the clouds of heaven."

63-64 The Chief Priest lost his temper. Ripping his clothes, he yelled, "Did you hear that? After that do we need witnesses? You heard the blasphemy. Are you going to stand for it?"

They condemned him, one and all. The sentence: death.

65 Some of them started spitting at him. They blindfolded his eyes, then hit him, saying, "Who hit you? Prophesy!" The guards, punching and slapping, took him away.

THE ROOSTER CROWED

66-67 While all this was going on, Peter was down in the courtyard. One of the Chief Priest's servant girls came in and, seeing Peter warming himself there, looked hard at him and said, "You were with the Nazarene, Jesus."

68 He denied it: "I don't know what you're talking about." He went out on the porch. A rooster crowed.

69-70 The girl spotted him and began telling the people standing around, "He's one of them." He denied it again.

After a little while, the bystanders brought it up again. "You've *got* to be one of them. You've got 'Galilean' written all over you."

71-72 Now Peter got really nervous and swore, "I never laid eyes on this man you're talking about." Just then the rooster crowed a second time. Peter remembered how Jesus had said, "Before a rooster crows twice, you'll deny me three times." He collapsed in tears.

STANDING BEFORE PILATE

1 **15** At dawn's first light, the high priests, with the religious leaders and scholars, arranged a conference with the entire Jewish Council. After tying Jesus securely, they took him out and presented him to Pilate.

2-3 Pilate asked him, "Are you the 'King of the Jews'?"

He answered, "If you say so." The high priests let loose a barrage of accusations.

4-5 Pilate asked again, "Aren't you going to answer anything? That's quite a list of accusations." Still, he said nothing. Pilate was impressed, really impressed.

6-10 It was a custom at the Feast to release a prisoner, anyone the people asked for. There was one prisoner called Barabbas, locked up with the insurrectionists who had committed murder during the uprising against Rome. As the crowd came up and began to present its petition for him to release a prisoner, Pilate anticipated them: "Do you want me to release the King of the Jews to you?" Pilate knew by this time that it was through sheer spite that the high priests had turned Jesus over to him.

11-12 But the high priests by then had worked up the crowd to ask for the release of Barabbas. Pilate came back, "So what do I do with this man you call King of the Jews?"

13 They yelled, "Nail him to a cross!"

14   Pilate objected, "But for what crime?"
But they yelled all the louder, "Nail him to a cross!"

15   Pilate gave the crowd what it wanted, set Barabbas free and turned Jesus over for whipping and crucifixion.

16-20   The soldiers took Jesus into the palace (called Praetorium) and called together the entire brigade. They dressed him up in purple and put a crown plaited from a thornbush on his head. Then they began their mockery: "Bravo, King of the Jews!" They banged on his head with a club, spit on him, and knelt down in mock worship. After they had had their fun, they took off the purple cape and put his own clothes back on him. Then they marched out to nail him to the cross.

THE CRUCIFIXION

21   There was a man walking by, coming from work, Simon from Cyrene, the father of Alexander and Rufus. They made him carry Jesus' cross.

22-24   The soldiers brought Jesus to Golgotha, meaning "Skull Hill." They offered him a mild painkiller (wine mixed with myrrh), but he wouldn't take it. And they nailed him to the cross. They divided up his clothes and threw dice to see who would get them.

25-30   They nailed him up at nine o'clock in the morning. The charge against him — THE KING OF THE JEWS — was printed on a poster. Along with him, they crucified two criminals, one to his right, the other to his left. People passing along the road jeered, shaking their heads in mock lament: "You bragged that you could tear down the Temple and then rebuild it in three days — so show us your stuff! Save yourself! If you're really God's Son, come down from that cross!"

31-32   The high priests, along with the religion scholars, were right there mixing it up with the rest of them, having a great time poking fun at him: "He saved others — but he can't save himself! Messiah, is he? King of Israel? Then let him climb down from that cross. We'll all become believers then!" Even the men crucified alongside him joined in the mockery.

33-34   At noon the sky became extremely dark. The darkness lasted three hours. At three o'clock, Jesus groaned out of the depths, crying loudly, "*Eloi, Eloi, lama sabachthani?*" which means, "My God, my God, why have you abandoned me?"

35-36   Some of the bystanders who heard him said, "Listen, he's calling for Elijah." Someone ran off, soaked a sponge in sour wine, put it on a stick, and gave it to him to drink, saying, "Let's see if Elijah comes to take him down."

37-39   But Jesus, with a loud cry, gave his last breath. At that moment the Temple curtain ripped right down the middle. When the Roman captain standing guard in front of him saw that he had quit breathing, he said, "This has to be the Son of God!"

TAKEN TO A TOMB

40-41   There were women watching from a distance, among them Mary Magdalene, Mary the mother of the younger James and Joses, and Salome. When Jesus was in Galilee, these women followed and served him, and had come up with him to Jerusalem.

42-45   Late in the afternoon, since it was the Day of Preparation (that is, Sabbath eve), Joseph of Arimathea, a highly respected member of the Jewish

Council, came. He was one who lived expectantly, on the lookout for the kingdom of God. Working up his courage, he went to Pilate and asked for Jesus' body. Pilate questioned whether he could be dead that soon and called for the captain to verify that he was really dead. Assured by the captain, he gave Joseph the corpse.

46-47 Having already purchased a linen shroud, Joseph took him down, wrapped him in the shroud, placed him in a tomb that had been cut into the rock, and rolled a large stone across the opening. Mary Magdalene and Mary, mother of Joses, watched the burial.

The Resurrection

1-3 **16** When the Sabbath was over, Mary Magdalene, Mary the mother of James, and Salome bought spices so they could embalm him. Very early on Sunday morning, as the sun rose, they went to the tomb. They worried out loud to each other, "Who will roll back the stone from the tomb for us?"

4-5 Then they looked up, saw that it had been rolled back—it was a huge stone—and walked right in. They saw a young man sitting on the right side, dressed all in white. They were completely taken aback, astonished.

6-7 He said, "Don't be afraid. I know you're looking for Jesus the Nazarene, the One they nailed on the cross. He's been raised up; he's here no longer. You can see for yourselves that the place is empty. Now—on your way. Tell his disciples and Peter that he is going on ahead of you to Galilee. You'll see him there, exactly as he said."

8 They got out as fast as they could, beside themselves, their heads swimming. Stunned, they said nothing to anyone.

9-11 [After rising from the dead, Jesus appeared early on Sunday morning to Mary Magdalene, whom he had delivered from seven demons. She went to his former companions, now weeping and carrying on, and told them. When they heard her report that she had seen him alive and well, they didn't believe her.

12-13 Later he appeared, but in a different form, to two of them out walking in the countryside. They went back and told the rest, but they weren't believed either.

14-16 Still later, as the Eleven were eating supper, he appeared and took them to task most severely for their stubborn unbelief, refusing to believe those who had seen him raised up. Then he said, "Go into the world. Go everywhere and announce the Message of God's good news to one and all. Whoever believes and is baptized is saved; whoever refuses to believe is damned.

17-18 "These are some of the signs that will accompany believers: They will throw out demons in my name, they will speak in new tongues, they will take snakes in their hands, they will drink poison and not be hurt, they will lay hands on the sick and make them well."

19-20 Then the Master Jesus, after briefing them, was taken up to heaven, and he sat down beside God in the place of honor. And the disciples went everywhere preaching, the Master working right with them, validating the Message with indisputable evidence.]

Note: Mark 16:9-20 [the portion in brackets] is contained only in later manuscripts.

LUKE

Most of us, most of the time, feel left out — misfits. We don't belong. Others seem to be so confident, so sure of themselves, "insiders" who know the ropes, old hands in a club from which we are excluded.

One of the ways we have of responding to this is to form our own club, or join one that will have us. Here is at least one place where we are "in" and the others "out." The clubs range from informal to formal in gatherings that are variously political, social, cultural, and economic. But the one thing they have in common is the principle of exclusion. Identity or worth is achieved by excluding all but the chosen. The terrible price we pay for keeping all those other people out so that we can savor the sweetness of being insiders is a reduction of reality, a shrinkage of life.

Nowhere is this price more terrible than when it is paid in the cause of religion. But religion has a long history of doing just that, of reducing the huge mysteries of God to the respectability of club rules, of shrinking the vast human community to a "membership." But with God there are no outsiders.

Luke is a most vigorous champion of the outsider. An outsider himself, the only Gentile in an all-Jewish cast of New Testament writers, he shows how Jesus includes those who typically were treated as outsiders by the religious establishment of the day: women, common laborers (sheepherders), the racially different (Samaritans), the poor. He will not countenance religion as a club. As Luke tells the story, all of us who have found ourselves on the outside looking in on life with no hope of gaining entrance (and who of us hasn't felt it?) now find the doors wide open, found and welcomed by God in Jesus.

LUKE

1-4 **1** So many others have tried their hand at putting together a story of the wonderful harvest of Scripture and history that took place among us, using reports handed down by the original eyewitnesses who served this Word with their very lives. Since I have investigated all the reports in close detail, starting from the story's beginning, I decided to write it all out for you, most honorable Theophilus, so you can know beyond the shadow of a doubt the reliability of what you were taught.

A CHILDLESS COUPLE CONCEIVES

5-7 During the rule of Herod, King of Judea, there was a priest assigned service in the regiment of Abijah. His name was Zachariah. His wife was descended from the daughters of Aaron. Her name was Elizabeth. Together they lived honorably before God, careful in keeping to the ways of the commandments and enjoying a clear conscience before God. But they were childless because Elizabeth could never conceive, and now they were quite old.

8-12 It so happened that as Zachariah was carrying out his priestly duties before God, working the shift assigned to his regiment, it came his one turn in life to enter the sanctuary of God and burn incense. The congregation was gathered and praying outside the Temple at the hour of the incense offering. Unannounced, an angel of God appeared just to the right of the altar of incense. Zachariah was paralyzed in fear.

13-15 But the angel reassured him, "Don't fear, Zachariah. Your prayer has been heard. Elizabeth, your wife, will bear a son by you. You are to name him John. You're going to leap like a gazelle for joy, and not only you — many will delight in his birth. He'll achieve great stature with God.

15-17 "He'll drink neither wine nor beer. He'll be filled with the Holy Spirit from the moment he leaves his mother's womb. He will turn many sons and daughters of Israel back to their God. He will herald God's arrival in the style and strength of Elijah, soften the hearts of parents to children, and kindle devout understanding among hardened skeptics — he'll get the people ready for God."

18 Zachariah said to the angel, "Do you expect me to believe this? I'm an old man and my wife is an old woman."

19-20 But the angel said, "I am Gabriel, the sentinel of God, sent especially to bring you this glad news. But because you won't believe me, you'll be unable to say a word until the day of your son's birth. Every word I've spoken to you will come true on time — *God's* time."

21-22 Meanwhile, the congregation waiting for Zachariah was getting restless, wondering what was keeping him so long in the sanctuary. When he came out and couldn't speak, they knew he had seen a vision. He continued speechless and had to use sign language with the people.

23-25 When the course of his priestly assignment was completed, he went back home. It wasn't long before his wife, Elizabeth, conceived. She went off by herself for five months, relishing her pregnancy. "So, this is how God acts to remedy my unfortunate condition!" she said.

A VIRGIN CONCEIVES

26-28 In the sixth month of Elizabeth's pregnancy, God sent the angel Gabriel to the Galilean village of Nazareth to a virgin engaged to be married to a man descended from David. His name was Joseph, and the virgin's name, Mary. Upon entering, Gabriel greeted her:

> Good morning!
> You're beautiful with God's beauty,
> Beautiful inside and out!
> God be with you.

29-33 She was thoroughly shaken, wondering what was behind a greeting like that. But the angel assured her, "Mary, you have nothing to fear. God has a surprise for you: You will become pregnant and give birth to a son and call his name Jesus.

> He will be great,
>   be called 'Son of the Highest.'
> The Lord God will give him
>   the throne of his father David;
> He will rule Jacob's house forever—
>   no end, ever, to his kingdom."

34 Mary said to the angel, "But how? I've never slept with a man."

35 The angel answered,

> The Holy Spirit will come upon you,
>   the power of the Highest hover over you;
> Therefore, the child you bring to birth
>   will be called Holy, Son of God.

36-38 "And did you know that your cousin Elizabeth conceived a son, old as she is? Everyone called her barren, and here she is six months pregnant! Nothing, you see, is impossible with God."

And Mary said,

> Yes, I see it all now:
>   I'm the Lord's maid, ready to serve.
> Let it be with me
>   just as you say.

Then the angel left her.

BLESSED AMONG WOMEN

39-45 Mary didn't waste a minute. She got up and traveled to a town in Judah in the hill country, straight to Zachariah's house, and greeted Elizabeth. When Elizabeth heard Mary's greeting, the baby in her womb leaped. She was filled with the Holy Spirit, and sang out exuberantly,

You're so blessed among women,
  and the babe in your womb, also blessed!
And why am I so blessed that
  the mother of my Lord visits me?
The moment the sound of your
  greeting entered my ears,
The babe in my womb
  skipped like a lamb for sheer joy.
Blessed woman, who believed what God said,
  believed every word would come true!

46-55   And Mary said,

I'm bursting with God-news;
  I'm dancing the song of my Savior God.
God took one good look at me, and look what happened —
  I'm the most fortunate woman on earth!
What God has done for me will never be forgotten,
  the God whose very name is holy, set apart from all others.
His mercy flows in wave after wave
  on those who are in awe before him.
He bared his arm and showed his strength,
  scattered the bluffing braggarts.
He knocked tyrants off their high horses,
  pulled victims out of the mud.
The starving poor sat down to a banquet;
  the callous rich were left out in the cold.
He embraced his chosen child, Israel;
  he remembered and piled on the mercies, piled them high.
It's exactly what he promised,
  beginning with Abraham and right up to now.

56   Mary stayed with Elizabeth for three months and then went back to her own home.

THE BIRTH OF JOHN

57-58   When Elizabeth was full-term in her pregnancy, she bore a son. Her neighbors and relatives, seeing that God had overwhelmed her with mercy, celebrated with her.

59-60   On the eighth day, they came to circumcise the child and were calling him Zachariah after his father. But his mother intervened: "No. He is to be called John."

61-62   "But," they said, "no one in your family is named that." They used sign language to ask Zachariah what he wanted him named.

63-64   Asking for a tablet, Zachariah wrote, "His name is to be John." That took everyone by surprise. Surprise followed surprise — Zachariah's mouth was now open, his tongue loose, and he was talking, praising God!

65-66   A deep, reverential fear settled over the neighborhood, and in all that Judean hill country people talked about nothing else. Everyone who heard about it took it to heart, wondering, "What will become of this child? Clearly, God has his hand in this."

67-79   Then Zachariah was filled with the Holy Spirit and prophesied,

> Blessed be the Lord, the God of Israel;
>> he came and set his people free.
> He set the power of salvation in the center of our lives,
>> and in the very house of David his servant,
> Just as he promised long ago
>> through the preaching of his holy prophets:
> Deliverance from our enemies
>> and every hateful hand;
> Mercy to our fathers,
>> as he remembers to do what he said he'd do,
> What he swore to our father Abraham —
>> a clean rescue from the enemy camp,
> So we can worship him without a care in the world,
>> made holy before him as long as we live.
>
> And you, my child, "Prophet of the Highest,"
>> will go ahead of the Master to prepare his ways,
> Present the offer of salvation to his people,
>> the forgiveness of their sins.
> Through the heartfelt mercies of our God,
>> God's Sunrise will break in upon us,
> Shining on those in the darkness,
>> those sitting in the shadow of death,
> Then showing us the way, one foot at a time,
>> down the path of peace.

80   The child grew up, healthy and spirited. He lived out in the desert until the day he made his prophetic debut in Israel.

THE BIRTH OF JESUS

1-5   2 About that time Caesar Augustus ordered a census to be taken throughout the Empire. This was the first census when Quirinius was governor of Syria. Everyone had to travel to his own ancestral home-town to be accounted for. So Joseph went from the Galilean town of Nazareth up to Bethlehem in Judah, David's town, for the census. As a descendant of David, he had to go there. He went with Mary, his fiancée, who was pregnant.

6-7   While they were there, the time came for her to give birth. She gave birth to a son, her firstborn. She wrapped him in a blanket and laid him in a manger, because there was no room in the hostel.

AN EVENT FOR EVERYONE

8-12   There were sheepherders camping in the neighborhood. They had set night watches over their sheep. Suddenly, God's angel stood among them and God's glory blazed around them. They were terrified. The angel said, "Don't be afraid. I'm here to announce a great and joyful event that is meant for everybody, worldwide: A Savior has just been born in David's town, a Savior who is Messiah and Master. This is what you're to look for: a baby wrapped in a blanket and lying in a manger."

13-14   At once the angel was joined by a huge angelic choir singing God's praises:

> Glory to God in the heavenly heights,
> Peace to all men and women on earth who please him.

15-18   As the angel choir withdrew into heaven, the sheepherders talked it over. "Let's get over to Bethlehem as fast as we can and see for ourselves what God has revealed to us." They left, running, and found Mary and Joseph, and the baby lying in the manger. Seeing was believing. They told everyone they met what the angels had said about this child. All who heard the sheepherders were impressed.

19-20   Mary kept all these things to herself, holding them dear, deep within herself. The sheepherders returned and let loose, glorifying and praising God for everything they had heard and seen. It turned out exactly the way they'd been told!

BLESSINGS

21   When the eighth day arrived, the day of circumcision, the child was named Jesus, the name given by the angel before he was conceived.

22-24   Then when the days stipulated by Moses for purification were complete, they took him up to Jerusalem to offer him to God as commanded in God's Law: "Every male who opens the womb shall be a holy offering to God," and also to sacrifice the "pair of doves or two young pigeons" prescribed in God's Law.

25-32   In Jerusalem at the time, there was a man, Simeon by name, a good man, a man who lived in the prayerful expectancy of help for Israel. And the Holy Spirit was on him. The Holy Spirit had shown him that he would see the Messiah of God before he died. Led by the Spirit, he entered the Temple. As the parents of the child Jesus brought him in to carry out the rituals of the Law, Simeon took him into his arms and blessed God:

> God, you can now release your servant;
>   release me in peace as you promised.
> With my own eyes I've seen your salvation;
>   it's now out in the open for everyone to see:
> A God-revealing light to the non-Jewish nations,
>   and of glory for your people Israel.

33-35   Jesus' father and mother were speechless with surprise at these words. Simeon went on to bless them, and said to Mary his mother,

> This child marks both the failure and
>   the recovery of many in Israel,
> A figure misunderstood and contradicted—
>   the pain of a sword-thrust through you—
> But the rejection will force honesty,
>   as God reveals who they really are.

36-38   Anna the prophetess was also there, a daughter of Phanuel from the tribe of Asher. She was by now a very old woman. She had been married seven years and a widow for eighty-four. She never left the Temple area, worshiping night and day with her fastings and prayers. At the very time Simeon was praying, she showed up, broke into an anthem of praise to God, and talked about the child to all who were waiting expectantly for the freeing of Jerusalem.

39-40 When they finished everything required by God in the Law, they returned to Galilee and their own town, Nazareth. There the child grew strong in body and wise in spirit. And the grace of God was on him.

THEY FOUND HIM IN THE TEMPLE

41-45 Every year Jesus' parents traveled to Jerusalem for the Feast of Passover. When he was twelve years old, they went up as they always did for the Feast. When it was over and they left for home, the child Jesus stayed behind in Jerusalem, but his parents didn't know it. Thinking he was somewhere in the company of pilgrims, they journeyed for a whole day and then began looking for him among relatives and neighbors. When they didn't find him, they went back to Jerusalem looking for him.

46-48 The next day they found him in the Temple seated among the teachers, listening to them and asking questions. The teachers were all quite taken with him, impressed with the sharpness of his answers. But his parents were not impressed; they were upset and hurt.

His mother said, "Young man, why have you done this to us? Your father and I have been half out of our minds looking for you."

49-50 He said, "Why were you looking for me? Didn't you know that I had to be here, dealing with the things of my Father?" But they had no idea what he was talking about.

51-52 So he went back to Nazareth with them, and lived obediently with them. His mother held these things dearly, deep within herself. And Jesus matured, growing up in both body and spirit, blessed by both God and people.

A BAPTISM OF LIFE-CHANGE

1-6 **3** In the fifteenth year of the rule of Caesar Tiberius — it was while Pontius Pilate was governor of Judea; Herod, ruler of Galilee; his brother Philip, ruler of Iturea and Trachonitis; Lysanias, ruler of Abilene; during the Chief-Priesthood of Annas and Caiaphas — John, Zachariah's son, out in the desert at the time, received a message from God. He went all through the country around the Jordan River preaching a baptism of life-change leading to forgiveness of sins, as described in the words of Isaiah the prophet:

> Thunder in the desert!
> "Prepare God's arrival!
> Make the road smooth and straight!
> Every ditch will be filled in,
> Every bump smoothed out,
> The detours straightened out,
> All the ruts paved over.
> Everyone will be there to see
> The parade of God's salvation."

7-9   When crowds of people came out for baptism because it was the popular thing to do, John exploded: "Brood of snakes! What do you think you're doing slithering down here to the river? Do you think a little water on your snakeskins is going to deflect God's judgment? It's your *life* that must change, not your skin. And don't think you can pull rank by claiming Abraham as 'father.' Being a child of Abraham is neither here nor there — children of Abraham are a dime a dozen. God can make children from stones if he wants. What counts is your life. Is it green and blossoming? Because if it's deadwood, it goes on the fire."

10   The crowd asked him, "Then what are we supposed to do?"

11   "If you have two coats, give one away," he said. "Do the same with your food."

12   Tax men also came to be baptized and said, "Teacher, what should we do?"

13   He told them, "No more extortion — collect only what is required by law."

14   Soldiers asked him, "And what should we do?"

    He told them, "No shakedowns, no blackmail — and be content with your rations."

15   The interest of the people by now was building. They were all beginning to wonder, "Could this John be the Messiah?"

16-17   But John intervened: "I'm baptizing you here in the river. The main character in this drama, to whom I'm a mere stagehand, will ignite the kingdom life, a fire, the Holy Spirit within you, changing you from the inside out. He's going to clean house — make a clean sweep of your lives. He'll place everything true in its proper place before God; everything false he'll put out with the trash to be burned."

18-20   There was a lot more of this — words that gave strength to the people, words that put heart in them. The Message! But Herod, the ruler, stung by John's rebuke in the matter of Herodias, his brother Philip's wife, capped his long string of evil deeds with this outrage: He put John in jail.

21-22   After all the people were baptized, Jesus was baptized. As he was praying, the sky opened up and the Holy Spirit, like a dove descending, came down on him. And along with the Spirit, a voice: "You are my Son, chosen and marked by my love, pride of my life."

Son of Adam, Son of God

23-38   When Jesus entered public life he was about thirty years old, the son (in public perception) of Joseph, who was —

    son of Heli,
    son of Matthat,
    son of Levi,
    son of Melki,
    son of Jannai,
    son of Joseph,
    son of Mattathias,
    son of Amos,
    son of Nahum,
    son of Esli,
    son of Naggai,

son of Maath,
son of Mattathias,
son of Semein,
son of Josech,
son of Joda,
son of Joanan,
son of Rhesa,
son of Zerubbabel,
son of Shealtiel,
son of Neri,
son of Melchi,
son of Addi,
son of Cosam,
son of Elmadam,
son of Er,
son of Joshua,
son of Eliezer,
son of Jorim,
son of Matthat,
son of Levi,
son of Simeon,
son of Judah,
son of Joseph,
son of Jonam,
son of Eliakim,
son of Melea,
son of Menna,
son of Mattatha,
son of Nathan,
son of David,
son of Jesse,
son of Obed,
son of Boaz,
son of Salmon,
son of Nahshon,
son of Amminadab,
son of Admin,
son of Arni,
son of Hezron,
son of Perez,
son of Judah,
son of Jacob,
son of Isaac,
son of Abraham,
son of Terah,
son of Nahor,
son of Serug,
son of Reu,
son of Peleg,
son of Eber,
son of Shelah,
son of Kenan,

son of Arphaxad,
son of Shem,
son of Noah,
son of Lamech,
son of Methuselah,
son of Enoch,
son of Jared,
son of Mahalaleel,
son of Kenan,
son of Enos,
son of Seth,
son of Adam,
son of God.

TESTED BY THE DEVIL

1-2 Now Jesus, full of the Holy Spirit, left the Jordan and was led by the Spirit into the wild. For forty wilderness days and nights he was tested by the Devil. He ate nothing during those days, and when the time was up he was hungry.

3 The Devil, playing on his hunger, gave the first test: "Since you're God's Son, command this stone to turn into a loaf of bread."

4 Jesus answered by quoting Deuteronomy: "It takes more than bread to really live."

5-7 For the second test he led him up and spread out all the kingdoms of the earth on display at once. Then the Devil said, "They're yours in all their splendor to serve your pleasure. I'm in charge of them all and can turn them over to whomever I wish. Worship me and they're yours, the whole works."

8 Jesus refused, again backing his refusal with Deuteronomy: "Worship the Lord your God and only the Lord your God. Serve him with absolute single-heartedness."

9-11 For the third test the Devil took him to Jerusalem and put him on top of the Temple. He said, "If you are God's Son, jump. It's written, isn't it, that 'he has placed you in the care of angels to protect you; they will catch you; you won't so much as stub your toe on a stone'?"

12 "Yes," said Jesus, "and it's also written, 'Don't you dare tempt the Lord your God.'"

13 That completed the testing. The Devil retreated temporarily, lying in wait for another opportunity.

TO SET THE BURDENED FREE

14-15 Jesus returned to Galilee powerful in the Spirit. News that he was back spread through the countryside. He taught in their meeting places to everyone's acclaim and pleasure.

16-21 He came to Nazareth where he had been reared. As he always did on the Sabbath, he went to the meeting place. When he stood up to read, he was handed the scroll of the prophet Isaiah. Unrolling the scroll, he found the place where it was written,

God's Spirit is on me;
    he's chosen me to preach the Message of good news to
        the poor,

Sent me to announce pardon to prisoners and
recovery of sight to the blind,
To set the burdened and battered free,
to announce, "This is God's year to act!"

He rolled up the scroll, handed it back to the assistant, and sat down. Every eye in the place was on him, intent. Then he started in, "You've just heard Scripture make history. It came true just now in this place."

22   All who were there, watching and listening, were surprised at how well he spoke. But they also said, "Isn't this Joseph's son, the one we've known since he was a youngster?"

23-27   He answered, "I suppose you're going to quote the proverb, 'Doctor, go heal yourself. Do here in your hometown what we heard you did in Capernaum.' Well, let me tell you something: No prophet is ever welcomed in his hometown. Isn't it a fact that there were many widows in Israel at the time of Elijah during that three and a half years of drought when famine devastated the land, but the only widow to whom Elijah was sent was in Sarepta in Sidon? And there were many lepers in Israel at the time of the prophet Elisha but the only one cleansed was Naaman the Syrian."

28-30   That set everyone in the meeting place seething with anger. They threw him out, banishing him from the village, then took him to a mountain cliff at the edge of the village to throw him to his doom, but he gave them the slip and was on his way.

31-32   He went down to Capernaum, a village in Galilee. He was teaching the people on the Sabbath. They were surprised and impressed—his teaching was so forthright, so confident, so authoritative, not the quibbling and quoting they were used to.

33-34   In the meeting place that day there was a man demonically disturbed. He screamed, "Ho! What business do you have here with us, Jesus? Nazarene! I know what you're up to. You're the Holy One of God and you've come to destroy us!"

35   Jesus shut him up: "Quiet! Get out of him!" The demonic spirit threw the man down in front of them all and left. The demon didn't hurt him.

36-37   That set everyone back on their heels, whispering and wondering, "What's going on here? Someone whose words make things happen? Someone who orders demonic spirits to get out and they go?" Jesus was the talk of the town.

He Healed Them All

38-39   He left the meeting place and went to Simon's house. Simon's mother-in-law was running a high fever and they asked him to do something for her. He stood over her, told the fever to leave—and it left. Before they knew it, she was up getting dinner for them.

40-41   When the sun went down, everyone who had anyone sick with some ailment or other brought them to him. One by one he placed his hands on them and healed them. Demons left in droves, screaming, "Son of God! You're the Son of God!" But he shut them up, refusing to let them speak because they knew too much, knew him to be the Messiah.

42-44   He left the next day for open country. But the crowds went looking and, when they found him, clung to him so he couldn't go on. He told them, "Don't you realize that there are yet other villages where I have to tell the Message of God's kingdom, that this is the work God sent me to do?" Meanwhile he continued preaching in the meeting places of Galilee.

PUSH OUT INTO DEEP WATER

1-3   5 Once when he was standing on the shore of Lake Gennesaret, the crowd was pushing in on him to better hear the Word of God. He noticed two boats tied up. The fishermen had just left them and were out scrubbing their nets. He climbed into the boat that was Simon's and asked him to put out a little from the shore. Sitting there, using the boat for a pulpit, he taught the crowd.

4   When he finished teaching, he said to Simon, "Push out into deep water and let your nets out for a catch."

5-7   Simon said, "Master, we've been fishing hard all night and haven't caught even a minnow. But if you say so, I'll let out the nets." It was no sooner said than done — a huge haul of fish, straining the nets past capacity. They waved to their partners in the other boat to come help them. They filled both boats, nearly swamping them with the catch.

8-10 Simon Peter, when he saw it, fell to his knees before Jesus. "Master, leave. I'm a sinner and can't handle this holiness. Leave me to myself." When they pulled in that catch of fish, awe overwhelmed Simon and everyone with him. It was the same with James and John, Zebedee's sons, coworkers with Simon.

10-11 Jesus said to Simon, "There is nothing to fear. From now on you'll be fishing for men and women." They pulled their boats up on the beach, left them, nets and all, and followed him.

INVITATION TO A CHANGED LIFE

12   One day in one of the villages there was a man covered with leprosy. When he saw Jesus he fell down before him in prayer and said, "If you want to, you can cleanse me."

13   Jesus put out his hand, touched him, and said, "I want to. Be clean." Then and there his skin was smooth, the leprosy gone.

14-16 Jesus instructed him, "Don't talk about this all over town. Just quietly present your healed self to the priest, along with the offering ordered by Moses. Your cleansed and obedient life, not your words, will bear witness to what I have done." But the man couldn't keep it to himself, and the word got out. Soon a large crowd of people had gathered to listen and be healed of their ailments. As often as possible Jesus withdrew to out-of-the-way places for prayer.

17   One day as he was teaching, Pharisees and religion teachers were sitting around. They had come from nearly every village in Galilee and Judea, even as far away as Jerusalem, to be there. The healing power of God was on him.

18-20 Some men arrived carrying a paraplegic on a stretcher. They were looking for a way to get into the house and set him before Jesus. When they couldn't find a way in because of the crowd, they went up on the roof, removed some tiles, and let him down in the middle of everyone, right in front of Jesus. Impressed by their bold belief, he said, "Friend, I forgive your sins."

21   That set the religion scholars and Pharisees buzzing. "Who does he think he is? That's blasphemous talk! God and only God can forgive sins."

22-26 Jesus knew exactly what they were thinking and said, "Why all this gossipy whispering? Which is simpler: to say 'I forgive your sins,' or to say 'Get up and start walking'? Well, just so it's clear that I'm the Son of Man and authorized to do either, or both. . . ." He now spoke directly to the paraplegic: "Get up. Take your bedroll and go home." Without a moment's hesitation, he did it—got up, took his blanket, and left for home, giving glory to God all the way. The people rubbed their eyes, incredulous—and then also gave glory to God. Awestruck, they said, "We've never seen anything like that!"

27-28 After this he went out and saw a man named Levi at his work collecting taxes. Jesus said, "Come along with me." And he did—walked away from everything and went with him.

29-30 Levi gave a large dinner at his home for Jesus. Everybody was there, tax men and other disreputable characters as guests at the dinner. The Pharisees and their religion scholars came to his disciples greatly offended. "What is he doing eating and drinking with crooks and 'sinners'?"

31-32 Jesus heard about it and spoke up, "Who needs a doctor: the healthy or the sick? I'm here inviting outsiders, not insiders—an invitation to a changed life, changed inside and out."

33 They asked him, "John's disciples are well-known for keeping fasts and saying prayers. Also the Pharisees. But you seem to spend most of your time at parties. Why?"

34-35 Jesus said, "When you're celebrating a wedding, you don't skimp on the cake and wine. You feast. Later you may need to pull in your belt, but this isn't the time. As long as the bride and groom are with you, you have a good time. When the groom is gone, the fasting can begin. No one throws cold water on a friendly bonfire. This is Kingdom Come!

36-39 "No one cuts up a fine silk scarf to patch old work clothes; you want fabrics that match. And you don't put wine in old, cracked bottles; you get strong, clean bottles for your fresh vintage wine. And no one who has ever tasted fine aged wine prefers unaged wine."

IN CHARGE OF THE SABBATH

1-2 On a certain Sabbath Jesus was walking through a field of ripe grain. His disciples were pulling off heads of grain, rubbing them in their hands to get rid of the chaff, and eating them. Some Pharisees said, "Why are you doing that, breaking a Sabbath rule?"

3-4 But Jesus stood up for them. "Have you never read what David and those with him did when they were hungry? How he entered the sanctuary and ate fresh bread off the altar, bread that no one but priests were allowed to eat? He also handed it out to his companions."

5 Then he said, "The Son of Man is no slave to the Sabbath; he's in charge."

6-8 On another Sabbath he went to the meeting place and taught. There was a man there with a crippled right hand. The religion scholars and Pharisees had their eye on Jesus to see if he would heal the man, hoping to catch him in a Sabbath infraction. He knew what they were up to and spoke to the man with the crippled hand: "Get up and stand here before us." He did.

9 Then Jesus addressed them, "Let me ask you something: What kind of action suits the Sabbath best? Doing good or doing evil? Helping people or leaving them helpless?"

10-11 He looked around, looked each one in the eye. He said to the man, "Hold out your hand." He held it out — it was as good as new! They were beside themselves with anger, and started plotting how they might get even with him.

THE TWELVE APOSTLES

12-16 At about that same time he climbed a mountain to pray. He was there all night in prayer before God. The next day he summoned his disciples; from them he selected twelve he designated as apostles:

Simon, whom he named Peter,
Andrew, his brother,
James,
John,
Philip,
Bartholomew,
Matthew,
Thomas,
James, son of Alphaeus,
Simon, called the Zealot,
Judas, son of James,
Judas Iscariot, who betrayed him.

YOU'RE BLESSED

17-21 Coming down off the mountain with them, he stood on a plain surrounded by disciples, and was soon joined by a huge congregation from all over Judea and Jerusalem, even from the seaside towns of Tyre and Sidon. They had come both to hear him and to be cured of their ailments. Those disturbed by evil spirits were healed. Everyone was trying to touch him — so much energy surging from him, so many people healed! Then he spoke:

You're blessed when you've lost it all.
God's kingdom is there for the finding.

You're blessed when you're ravenously hungry.
Then you're ready for the Messianic meal.

You're blessed when the tears flow freely.
Joy comes with the morning.

22-23 "Count yourself blessed every time someone cuts you down or throws you out, every time someone smears or blackens your name to discredit me. What it means is that the truth is too close for comfort and that that person is uncomfortable. You can be glad when that happens — skip like a lamb, if you like! — for even though they don't like it, I do . . . and all heaven applauds. And know that you are in good company; my preachers and witnesses have always been treated like this.

GIVE AWAY YOUR LIFE

24 But it's trouble ahead if you think you have it made.
What you have is all you'll ever get.

25   And it's trouble ahead if you're satisfied with yourself.
Your *self* will not satisfy you for long.

And it's trouble ahead if you think life's all fun and games.
There's suffering to be met, and you're going to meet it.

26   "There's trouble ahead when you live only for the approval of others, saying what flatters them, doing what indulges them. Popularity contests are not truth contests — look how many scoundrel preachers were approved by your ancestors! Your task is to be true, not popular.

27-30   "To you who are ready for the truth, I say this: Love your enemies. Let them bring out the best in you, not the worst. When someone gives you a hard time, respond with the energies of prayer for that person. If someone slaps you in the face, stand there and take it. If someone grabs your shirt, giftwrap your best coat and make a present of it. If someone takes unfair advantage of you, use the occasion to practice the servant life. No more tit-for-tat stuff. Live generously.

31-34   "Here is a simple rule of thumb for behavior: Ask yourself what you want people to do for you; then grab the initiative and do it for *them*! If you only love the lovable, do you expect a pat on the back? Run-of-the-mill sinners do that. If you only help those who help you, do you expect a medal? Garden-variety sinners do that. If you only give for what you hope to get out of it, do you think that's charity? The stingiest of pawnbrokers does that.

35-36   "I tell you, love your enemies. Help and give without expecting a return. You'll never — I promise — regret it. Live out this God-created identity the way our Father lives toward us, generously and graciously, even when we're at our worst. Our Father is kind; you be kind.

37-38   "Don't pick on people, jump on their failures, criticize their faults — unless, of course, you want the same treatment. Don't condemn those who are down; that hardness can boomerang. Be easy on people; you'll find life a lot easier. Give away your life; you'll find life given back, but not merely given back — given back with bonus and blessing. Giving, not getting, is the way. Generosity begets generosity."

39-40   He quoted a proverb: "'Can a blind man guide a blind man?' Wouldn't they both end up in the ditch? An apprentice doesn't lecture the master. The point is to be careful who you follow as your teacher.

41-42   "It's easy to see a smudge on your neighbor's face and be oblivious to the ugly sneer on your own. Do you have the nerve to say, 'Let me wash your face for you,' when your own face is distorted by contempt? It's this I-know-better-than-you mentality again, playing a holier-than-thou part instead of just living your own part. Wipe that ugly sneer off your own face and you might be fit to offer a washcloth to your neighbor.

WORK THE WORDS INTO YOUR LIFE

43-45   "You don't get wormy apples off a healthy tree, nor good apples off a diseased tree. The health of the apple tells the health of the tree. You must begin with your own life-giving lives. It's who you are, not what you say and do, that counts. Your true being brims over into true words and deeds.

46-47   "Why are you so polite with me, always saying 'Yes, sir,' and 'That's right, sir,' but never doing a thing I tell you? These words I speak to you are not mere additions to your life, homeowner improvements to your standard of living. They are foundation words, words to build a life on.

48-49   "If you work the words into your life, you are like a smart carpenter who dug deep and laid the foundation of his house on bedrock. When the river burst its banks and crashed against the house, nothing could shake it; it was built to last. But if you just use my words in Bible studies and don't work them into your life, you are like a dumb carpenter who built a house but skipped the foundation. When the swollen river came crashing in, it collapsed like a house of cards. It was a total loss."

A PLACE OF HOLY MYSTERY

1-5   7 When he finished speaking to the people, he entered Capernaum. A Roman captain there had a servant who was on his deathbed. He prized him highly and didn't want to lose him. When he heard Jesus was back, he sent leaders from the Jewish community asking him to come and heal his servant. They came to Jesus and urged him to do it, saying, "He deserves this. He loves our people. He even built our meeting place."

6-8   Jesus went with them. When he was still quite far from the house, the captain sent friends to tell him, "Master, you don't have to go to all this trouble. I'm not that good a person, you know. I'd be embarrassed for you to come to my house, even embarrassed to come to you in person. Just give the order and my servant will get well. I'm a man under orders; I also give orders. I tell one soldier, 'Go,' and he goes; another, 'Come,' and he comes; my slave, 'Do this,' and he does it."

9-10   Taken aback, Jesus addressed the accompanying crowd: "I've yet to come across this kind of simple trust anywhere in Israel, the very people who are supposed to know about God and how he works." When the messengers got back home, they found the servant up and well.

11-15   Not long after that, Jesus went to the village Nain. His disciples were with him, along with quite a large crowd. As they approached the village gate, they met a funeral procession — a woman's only son was being carried out for burial. And the mother was a widow. When Jesus saw her, his heart broke. He said to her, "Don't cry." Then he went over and touched the coffin. The pallbearers stopped. He said, "Young man, I tell you: Get up." The dead son sat up and began talking. Jesus presented him to his mother.

16-17   They all realized they were in a place of holy mystery, that God was at work among them. They were quietly worshipful — and then noisily grateful, calling out among themselves, "God is back, looking to the needs of his people!" The news of Jesus spread all through the country.

IS THIS WHAT YOU WERE EXPECTING?

18-19   John's disciples reported back to him the news of all these events taking place. He sent two of them to the Master to ask the question, "Are you the One we've been expecting, or are we still waiting?"

20   The men showed up before Jesus and said, "John the Baptizer sent us to ask you, 'Are you the One we've been expecting, or are we still waiting?'"

21-23   In the next two or three hours Jesus healed many from diseases, distress, and evil spirits. To many of the blind he gave the gift of sight. Then he gave his answer: "Go back and tell John what you have just seen and heard:

The blind see,
The lame walk,

Lepers are cleansed,
The deaf hear,
The dead are raised,
The wretched of the earth
    have God's salvation hospitality extended to them.

"Is this what you were expecting? Then count yourselves fortunate!"

24-27   After John's messengers left to make their report, Jesus said more about John to the crowd of people. "What did you expect when you went out to see him in the wild? A weekend camper? Hardly. What then? A sheik in silk pajamas? Not in the wilderness, not by a long shot. What then? A messenger from God? That's right, a messenger! Probably the greatest messenger you'll ever hear. He is the messenger Malachi announced when he wrote,

I'm sending my messenger on ahead
To make the road smooth for you.

28-30   "Let me lay it out for you as plainly as I can: No one in history sur-passes John the Baptizer, but in the kingdom he prepared you for, the lowli-est person is ahead of him. The ordinary and disreputable people who heard John, by being baptized by him into the kingdom, are the clearest evidence; the Pharisees and religious officials would have nothing to do with such a baptism, wouldn't think of giving up their place in line to their inferiors.

31-35   "How can I account for the people of this generation? They're like spoiled children complaining to their parents, 'We wanted to skip rope and you were always too tired; we wanted to talk but you were always too busy.' John the Baptizer came fasting and you called him crazy. The Son of Man came feasting and you called him a lush. Opinion polls don't count for much, do they? The proof of the pudding is in the eating."

ANOINTING HIS FEET

36-39   One of the Pharisees asked him over for a meal. He went to the Pharisee's house and sat down at the dinner table. Just then a woman of the village, the town harlot, having learned that Jesus was a guest in the home of the Pharisee, came with a bottle of very expensive perfume and stood at his feet, weeping, raining tears on his feet. Letting down her hair, she dried his feet, kissed them, and anointed them with the perfume. When the Pharisee who had invited him saw this, he said to himself, "If this man was the prophet I thought he was, he would have known what kind of woman this is who is falling all over him."

40   Jesus said to him, "Simon, I have something to tell you."
    "Oh? Tell me."

41-42   "Two men were in debt to a banker. One owed five hundred silver pieces, the other fifty. Neither of them could pay up, and so the banker can-celed both debts. Which of the two would be more grateful?"

43-47   Simon answered, "I suppose the one who was forgiven the most."
    "That's right," said Jesus. Then turning to the woman, but speaking to Simon, he said, "Do you see this woman? I came to your home; you provided no water for my feet, but she rained tears on my feet and dried them with her hair. You gave me no greeting, but from the time I arrived she hasn't quit kissing my feet. You provided nothing for freshening up, but

she has soothed my feet with perfume. Impressive, isn't it? She was forgiven many, many sins, and so she is very, very grateful. If the forgiveness is minimal, the gratitude is minimal."

48 Then he spoke to her: "I forgive your sins."

49 That set the dinner guests talking behind his back: "Who does he think he is, forgiving sins!"

50 He ignored them and said to the woman, "Your faith has saved you. Go in peace."

1-3 8 He continued according to plan, traveled to town after town, village after village, preaching God's kingdom, spreading the Message. The Twelve were with him. There were also some women in their company who had been healed of various evil afflictions and illnesses: Mary, the one called Magdalene, from whom seven demons had gone out; Joanna, wife of Chuza, Herod's manager; and Susanna — along with many others who used their considerable means to provide for the company.

THE STORY OF THE SEEDS

4-8 As they went from town to town, a lot of people joined in and traveled along. He addressed them, using this story: "A farmer went out to sow his seed. Some of it fell on the road; it was tramped down and the birds ate it. Other seed fell in the gravel; it sprouted, but withered because it didn't have good roots. Other seed fell in the weeds; the weeds grew with it and strangled it. Other seed fell in rich earth and produced a bumper crop.

"Are you listening to this? Really listening?"

9 His disciples asked, "Why did you tell this story?"

10 He said, "You've been given insight into God's kingdom — you know how it works. There are others who need stories. But even with stories some of them aren't going to get it:

Their eyes are open but don't see a thing,
Their ears are open but don't hear a thing.

11-12 "This story is about some of those people. The seed is the Word of God. The seeds on the road are those who hear the Word, but no sooner do they hear it than the Devil snatches it from them so they won't believe and be saved.

13 "The seeds in the gravel are those who hear with enthusiasm, but the enthusiasm doesn't go very deep. It's only another fad, and the moment there's trouble it's gone.

14 "And the seed that fell in the weeds — well, these are the ones who hear, but then the seed is crowded out and nothing comes of it as they go about their lives worrying about tomorrow, making money, and having fun.

15 "But the seed in the good earth — these are the good-hearts who seize the Word and hold on no matter what, sticking with it until there's a harvest.

MISERS OF WHAT YOU HEAR

16-18 "No one lights a lamp and then covers it with a washtub or shoves it under the bed. No, you set it up on a lamp stand so those who enter the room can see their way. We're not keeping secrets; we're telling them. We're not hiding things; we're bringing *everything* out into the open. So be careful that you don't become misers of what you hear. Generosity begets generosity. Stinginess impoverishes."

19-20   His mother and brothers showed up but couldn't get through to him because of the crowd. He was given the message, "Your mother and brothers are standing outside wanting to see you."

21   He replied, "My mother and brothers are the ones who hear and do God's Word. Obedience is thicker than blood."

22-24   One day he and his disciples got in a boat. "Let's cross the lake," he said. And off they went. It was smooth sailing, and he fell asleep. A terrific storm came up suddenly on the lake. Water poured in, and they were about to capsize. They woke Jesus: "Master, Master, we're going to drown!"

Getting to his feet, he told the wind, "Silence!" and the waves, "Quiet down!" They did it. The lake became smooth as glass.

25   Then he said to his disciples, "Why can't you trust me?"

They were in absolute awe, staggered and stammering, "Who is this, anyway? He calls out to the winds and sea, and they do what he tells them!"

THE MADMAN AND THE PIGS

26-29   They sailed on to the country of the Gerasenes, directly opposite Galilee. As he stepped out onto land, a madman from town met him; he was a victim of demons. He hadn't worn clothes for a long time, nor lived at home; he lived in the cemetery. When he saw Jesus he screamed, fell before him, and bellowed, "What business do you have messing with me? You're Jesus, Son of the High God, but don't give me a hard time!" (The man said this because Jesus had started to order the unclean spirit out of him.) Time after time the demon threw the man into convulsions. He had been placed under constant guard and tied with chains and shackles, but crazed and driven wild by the demon, he would shatter the bonds.

30-31   Jesus asked him, "What is your name?"

"Mob. My name is Mob," he said, because many demons afflicted him. And they begged Jesus desperately not to order them to the bottomless pit.

32-33   A large herd of pigs was browsing and rooting on a nearby hill. The demons begged Jesus to order them into the pigs. He gave the order. It was even worse for the pigs than for the man. Crazed, they stampeded over a cliff into the lake and drowned.

34-36   Those tending the pigs, scared to death, bolted and told their story in town and country. People went out to see what had happened. They came to Jesus and found the man from whom the demons had been sent, sitting there at Jesus' feet, wearing decent clothes and making sense. It was a holy moment, and for a short time they were more reverent than curious. Then those who had seen it happen told how the demoniac had been saved.

37-39   Later, a great many people from the Gerasene countryside got together and asked Jesus to leave — too much change, too fast, and they were scared. So Jesus got back in the boat and set off. The man whom he had delivered from the demons asked to go with him, but he sent him back, saying, "Go home and tell everything God did in you." So he went back and preached all over town everything Jesus had done in him.

HIS TOUCH

40-42   On his return, Jesus was welcomed by a crowd. They were all there expecting him. A man came up, Jairus by name. He was president of the meeting place. He fell at Jesus' feet and begged him to come to his home because his twelve-year-old daughter, his only child, was dying. Jesus went with him, making his way through the pushing, jostling crowd.

43-45   In the crowd that day there was a woman who for twelve years had been afflicted with hemorrhages. She had spent every penny she had on doctors but not one had been able to help her. She slipped in from behind and touched the edge of Jesus' robe. At that very moment her hemorrhaging stopped. Jesus said, "Who touched me?"

When no one stepped forward, Peter said, "But Master, we've got crowds of people on our hands. Dozens have touched you."

46   Jesus insisted, "Someone touched me. I felt power discharging from me."

47   When the woman realized that she couldn't remain hidden, she knelt trembling before him. In front of all the people, she blurted out her story — why she touched him and how at that same moment she was healed.

48   Jesus said, "Daughter, you took a risk trusting me, and now you're healed and whole. Live well, live blessed!"

49   While he was still talking, someone from the leader's house came up and told him, "Your daughter died. No need now to bother the Teacher."

50-51   Jesus overheard and said, "Don't be upset. Just trust me and everything will be all right." Going into the house, he wouldn't let anyone enter with him except Peter, John, James, and the child's parents.

52-53   Everyone was crying and carrying on over her. Jesus said, "Don't cry. She didn't die; she's sleeping." They laughed at him. They knew she was dead.

54-56   Then Jesus, gripping her hand, called, "My dear child, get up." She was up in an instant, up and breathing again! He told them to give her something to eat. Her parents were ecstatic, but Jesus warned them to keep quiet. "Don't tell a soul what happened in this room."

KEEP IT SIMPLE

1-5   Jesus now called the Twelve and gave them authority and power to deal with all the demons and cure diseases. He commissioned them to preach the news of God's kingdom and heal the sick. He said, "Don't load yourselves up with equipment. Keep it simple; *you* are the equipment. And no luxury inns — get a modest place and be content there until you leave. If you're not welcomed, leave town. Don't make a scene. Shrug your shoulders and move on."

6   Commissioned, they left. They traveled from town to town telling the latest news of God, the Message, and curing people everywhere they went.

7-9   Herod, the ruler, heard of these goings on and didn't know what to think. There were people saying John had come back from the dead, others that Elijah had appeared, still others that some prophet of long ago had shown up. Herod said, "But I killed John — took off his head. So who is this that I keep hearing about?" Curious, he looked for a chance to see him in action.

10-11   The apostles returned and reported on what they had done. Jesus took them away, off by themselves, near the town called Bethsaida. But the crowds got wind of it and followed. Jesus graciously welcomed them and talked to them about the kingdom of God. Those who needed healing, he healed.

BREAD AND FISH FOR FIVE THOUSAND

12 As the day declined, the Twelve said, "Dismiss the crowd so they can go to the farms or villages around here and get a room for the night and a bite to eat. We're out in the middle of nowhere."

13-14 "You feed them," Jesus said.

They said, "We couldn't scrape up more than five loaves of bread and a couple of fish — unless, of course, you want us to go to town ourselves and buy food for everybody." (There were more than five thousand people in the crowd.)

14-17 But he went ahead and directed his disciples, "Sit them down in groups of about fifty." They did what he said, and soon had everyone seated. He took the five loaves and two fish, lifted his face to heaven in prayer, blessed, broke, and gave the bread and fish to the disciples to hand out to the crowd. After the people had all eaten their fill, twelve baskets of leftovers were gathered up.

DON'T RUN FROM SUFFERING

18 One time when Jesus was off praying by himself, his disciples nearby, he asked them, "What are the crowds saying about me, about who I am?"

19 They said, "John the Baptizer. Others say Elijah. Still others say that one of the prophets from long ago has come back."

20-21 He then asked, "And you — what are you saying about me? Who am I?"

Peter answered, "The Messiah of God." Jesus then warned them to keep it quiet. They were to tell no one what Peter had said.

22 He went on, "It is necessary that the Son of Man proceed to an ordeal of suffering, be tried and found guilty by the religious leaders, high priests, and religion scholars, be killed, and on the third day be raised up alive."

23-27 Then he told them what they could expect for themselves: "Anyone who intends to come with me has to let me lead. You're not in the driver's seat — I am. Don't run from suffering; embrace it. Follow me and I'll show you how. Self-help is no help at all. Self-sacrifice is the way, *my* way, to finding yourself, your true self. What good would it do to get everything you want and lose you, the real you? If any of you is embarrassed with me and the way I'm leading you, know that the Son of Man will be far more embarrassed with you when he arrives in all his splendor in company with the Father and the holy angels. This isn't, you realize, pie in the sky by and by. Some who have taken their stand right here are going to see it happen, see with their own eyes the kingdom of God."

JESUS IN HIS GLORY

28-31 About eight days after saying this, he climbed the mountain to pray, taking Peter, John, and James along. While he was in prayer, the appearance of his face changed and his clothes became blinding white. At once two men were there talking with him. They turned out to be Moses and Elijah — and what a glorious appearance they made! They talked over his exodus, the one Jesus was about to complete in Jerusalem.

32-33 Meanwhile, Peter and those with him were slumped over in sleep. When they came to, rubbing their eyes, they saw Jesus in his glory and the two men standing with him. When Moses and Elijah had left, Peter said to Jesus, "Master, this is a great moment! Let's build three memorials: one for you, one for Moses, and one for Elijah." He blurted this out without thinking.

34-35 While he was babbling on like this, a light-radiant cloud enveloped them. As they found themselves buried in the cloud, they became deeply aware of God. Then there was a voice out of the cloud: "This is my Son, the Chosen! Listen to him."

36 When the sound of the voice died away, they saw Jesus there alone. They were speechless. And they continued speechless, said not one thing to anyone during those days of what they had seen.

37-40 When they came down off the mountain the next day, a big crowd was there to meet them. A man called from out of the crowd, "Please, please, Teacher, take a look at my son. He's my only child. Often a spirit seizes him. Suddenly he's screaming, thrown into convulsions, his mouth foaming. And then it beats him black-and-blue before it leaves. I asked your disciples to deliver him but they couldn't."

41 Jesus said, "What a generation! No sense of God! No focus to your lives! How many times do I have to go over these things? How much longer do I have to put up with this? Bring your son here."

42-43 While he was coming, the demon slammed him to the ground and threw him into convulsions. Jesus stepped in, ordered the vile spirit gone, healed the boy, and handed him back to his father. They all shook their heads in wonder, astonished at God's greatness, God's majestic greatness.

YOUR BUSINESS IS LIFE

43-44 While they continued to stand around exclaiming over all the things he was doing, Jesus said to his disciples, "Treasure and ponder each of these next words: The Son of Man is about to be betrayed into human hands."

45 They didn't get what he was saying. It was like he was speaking a foreign language and they couldn't make heads or tails of it. But they were embarrassed to ask him what he meant.

46-48 They started arguing over which of them would be most famous. When Jesus realized how much this mattered to them, he brought a child to his side. "Whoever accepts this child as if the child were me, accepts me," he said. "And whoever accepts me, accepts the One who sent me. You become great by accepting, not asserting. Your spirit, not your size, makes the difference."

49 John spoke up, "Master, we saw a man using your name to expel demons and we stopped him because he wasn't of our group."

50 Jesus said, "Don't stop him. If he's not an enemy, he's an ally."

51-54 When it came close to the time for his Ascension, he gathered up his courage and steeled himself for the journey to Jerusalem. He sent messengers on ahead. They came to a Samaritan village to make arrangements for his hospitality. But when the Samaritans learned that his destination was Jerusalem, they refused hospitality. When the disciples James and John learned of it, they said, "Master, do you want us to call a bolt of lightning down out of the sky and incinerate them?"

55-56 Jesus turned on them: "Of course not!" And they traveled on to another village.

57   On the road someone asked if he could go along. "I'll go with you, wherever," he said.

58   Jesus was curt: "Are you ready to rough it? We're not staying in the best inns, you know."

    Jesus said to another, "Follow me."

59   He said, "Certainly, but first excuse me for a couple of days, please. I have to make arrangements for my father's funeral."

60   Jesus refused. "First things first. Your business is life, not death. And life is urgent: Announce God's kingdom!"

61   Then another said, "I'm ready to follow you, Master, but first excuse me while I get things straightened out at home."

62   Jesus said, "No procrastination. No backward looks. You can't put God's kingdom off till tomorrow. Seize the day."

LAMBS IN A WOLF PACK

1-2   **10** Later the Master selected seventy and sent them ahead of him in pairs to every town and place where he intended to go. He gave them this charge:

"What a huge harvest! And how few the harvest hands. So on your knees; ask the God of the Harvest to send harvest hands.

3   "On your way! But be careful—this is hazardous work. You're like lambs in a wolf pack.

4   "Travel light. Comb and toothbrush and no extra luggage.

"Don't loiter and make small talk with everyone you meet along the way.

5-6   "When you enter a home, greet the family, 'Peace.' If your greeting is received, then it's a good place to stay. But if it's not received, take it back and get out. Don't impose yourself.

7   "Stay at one home, taking your meals there, for a worker deserves three square meals. Don't move from house to house, looking for the best cook in town.

8-9   "When you enter a town and are received, eat what they set before you, heal anyone who is sick, and tell them, 'God's kingdom is right on your doorstep!'

10-12   "When you enter a town and are not received, go out in the street and say, 'The only thing we got from you is the dirt on our feet, and we're giving it back. Did you have any idea that God's kingdom was right on your doorstep?' Sodom will have it better on Judgment Day than the town that rejects you.

13-14   "Doom, Chorazin! Doom, Bethsaida! If Tyre and Sidon had been given half the chances given you, they'd have been on their knees long ago, repenting and crying for mercy. Tyre and Sidon will have it easy on Judgment Day compared to you.

15   "And you, Capernaum! Do you think you're about to be promoted to heaven? Think again. You're on a mudslide to hell.

16   "The one who listens to you, listens to me. The one who rejects you, rejects me. And rejecting me is the same as rejecting God, who sent me."

17   The seventy came back triumphant. "Master, even the demons danced to your tune!"

18-20   Jesus said, "I know. I saw Satan fall, a bolt of lightning out of the sky. See what I've given you? Safe passage as you walk on snakes and scorpions, and protection from every assault of the Enemy. No one can put a hand on you. All the same, the great triumph is not in your authority over evil, but in God's authority over you and presence with you. Not what you do for God but what God does for you — that's the agenda for rejoicing."

21 At that, Jesus rejoiced, exuberant in the Holy Spirit. "I thank you, Father, Master of heaven and earth, that you hid these things from the know-it-alls and showed them to these innocent newcomers. Yes, Father, it pleased you to do it this way.

22 "I've been given it all by my Father! Only the Father knows who the Son is and only the Son knows who the Father is. The Son can introduce the Father to anyone he wants to."

23-24 He then turned in a private aside to his disciples. "Fortunate the eyes that see what you're seeing! There are plenty of prophets and kings who would have given their right arm to see what you are seeing but never got so much as a glimpse, to hear what you are hearing but never got so much as a whisper."

DEFINING "NEIGHBOR"

25 Just then a religion scholar stood up with a question to test Jesus. "Teacher, what do I need to do to get eternal life?"

26 He answered, "What's written in God's Law? How do you interpret it?"

27 He said, "That you love the Lord your God with all your passion and prayer and muscle and intelligence — and that you love your neighbor as well as you do yourself."

28 "Good answer!" said Jesus. "Do it and you'll live."

29 Looking for a loophole, he asked, "And just how would you define 'neighbor'?"

30-32 Jesus answered by telling a story. "There was once a man traveling from Jerusalem to Jericho. On the way he was attacked by robbers. They took his clothes, beat him up, and went off leaving him half-dead. Luckily, a priest was on his way down the same road, but when he saw him he angled across to the other side. Then a Levite religious man showed up; he also avoided the injured man.

33-35 "A Samaritan traveling the road came on him. When he saw the man's condition, his heart went out to him. He gave him first aid, disinfecting and bandaging his wounds. Then he lifted him onto his donkey, led him to an inn, and made him comfortable. In the morning he took out two silver coins and gave them to the innkeeper, saying, 'Take good care of him. If it costs any more, put it on my bill — I'll pay you on my way back.'

36 "What do you think? Which of the three became a neighbor to the man attacked by robbers?"

37 "The one who treated him kindly," the religion scholar responded.

Jesus said, "Go and do the same."

MARY AND MARTHA

38-40 As they continued their travel, Jesus entered a village. A woman by the name of Martha welcomed him and made him feel quite at home. She had a sister, Mary, who sat before the Master, hanging on every word he said. But Martha was pulled away by all she had to do in the kitchen. Later, she stepped in, interrupting them. "Master, don't you care that my sister has abandoned the kitchen to me? Tell her to lend me a hand."

41-42 The Master said, "Martha, dear Martha, you're fussing far too much and getting yourself worked up over nothing. One thing only is essential, and Mary has chosen it — it's the main course, and won't be taken from her."

ASK FOR WHAT YOU NEED

1 **11** One day he was praying in a certain place. When he finished, one of his disciples said, "Master, teach us to pray just as John taught his disciples."

2-4 So he said, "When you pray, say,

Father,
Reveal who you are.
Set the world right.
Keep us alive with three square meals.
Keep us forgiven with you and forgiving others.
Keep us safe from ourselves and the Devil."

5-6 Then he said, "Imagine what would happen if you went to a friend in the middle of the night and said, 'Friend, lend me three loaves of bread. An old friend traveling through just showed up, and I don't have a thing on hand.'

7 "The friend answers from his bed, 'Don't bother me. The door's locked; my children are all down for the night; I can't get up to give you anything.'

8 "But let me tell you, even if he won't get up because he's a friend, if you stand your ground, knocking and waking all the neighbors, he'll finally get up and get you whatever you need.

9 "Here's what I'm saying:

Ask and you'll get;
Seek and you'll find;
Knock and the door will open.

10-13 "Don't bargain with God. Be direct. Ask for what you need. This is not a cat-and-mouse, hide-and-seek game we're in. If your little boy asks for a serving of fish, do you scare him with a live snake on his plate? If your little girl asks for an egg, do you trick her with a spider? As bad as you are, you wouldn't think of such a thing — you're at least decent to your own children. And don't you think the Father who conceived you in love will give the Holy Spirit when you ask him?"

NO NEUTRAL GROUND

14-16 Jesus delivered a man from a demon that had kept him speechless. The demon gone, the man started talking a blue streak, taking the crowd by complete surprise. But some from the crowd were cynical. "Black magic," they said. "Some devil trick he's pulled from his sleeve." Others were skeptical, waiting around for him to prove himself with a spectacular miracle.

17-20 Jesus knew what they were thinking and said, "Any country in civil war for very long is wasted. A constantly squabbling family falls to pieces. If Satan cancels Satan, is there any Satan left? You accuse me of ganging up with the Devil, the prince of demons, to cast out demons, but if you're slinging devil mud at me, calling me a devil who kicks out devils, doesn't the same mud stick to your own exorcists? But if it's *God's* finger I'm pointing that sends the demons on their way, then God's kingdom is here for sure.

21-22   "When a strong man, armed to the teeth, stands guard in his front yard, his property is safe and sound. But what if a stronger man comes along with superior weapons? Then he's beaten at his own game, the arsenal that gave him such confidence hauled off, and his precious possessions plundered.

23   "This is war, and there is no neutral ground. If you're not on my side, you're the enemy; if you're not helping, you're making things worse.

24-26   "When a corrupting spirit is expelled from someone, it drifts along through the desert looking for an oasis, some unsuspecting soul it can bedevil. When it doesn't find anyone, it says, 'I'll go back to my old haunt.' On return, it finds the person swept and dusted, but vacant. It then runs out and rounds up seven other spirits dirtier than itself and they all move in, whooping it up. That person ends up far worse than if he'd never gotten cleaned up in the first place."

27   While he was saying these things, some woman lifted her voice above the murmur of the crowd: "Blessed the womb that carried you, and the breasts at which you nursed!"

28   Jesus commented, "Even more blessed are those who hear God's Word and guard it with their lives!"

Keep Your Eyes Open

29-30   As the crowd swelled, he took a fresh tack: "The mood of this age is all wrong. Everybody's looking for proof, but you're looking for the wrong kind. All you're looking for is something to titillate your curiosity, satisfy your lust for miracles. But the only proof you're going to get is the Jonah-proof given to the Ninevites, which looks like no proof at all. What Jonah was to Nineveh, the Son of Man is to this age.

31-32   "On Judgment Day the Ninevites will stand up and give evidence that will condemn this generation, because when Jonah preached to them they changed their lives. A far greater preacher than Jonah is here, and you squabble about 'proofs.' On Judgment Day the Queen of Sheba will come forward and bring evidence that condemns this generation, because she traveled from a far corner of the earth to listen to wise Solomon. Wisdom far greater than Solomon's is right in front of you, and you quibble over 'evidence.'

33-36   "No one lights a lamp, then hides it in a drawer. It's put on a lamp stand so those entering the room have light to see where they're going. Your eye is a lamp, lighting up your whole body. If you live wide-eyed in wonder and belief, your body fills up with light. If you live squinty-eyed in greed and distrust, your body is a dank cellar. Keep your eyes open, your lamp burning, so you don't get musty and murky. Keep your life as well-lighted as your best-lighted room."

Frauds!

37-41   When he finished that talk, a Pharisee asked him to dinner. He entered his house and sat right down at the table. The Pharisee was shocked and somewhat offended when he saw that Jesus didn't wash up before the meal. But the Master said to him, "I know you Pharisees burnish the surface of your cups and plates so they sparkle in the sun, but I also know your insides are maggoty with greed and secret evil. Stupid Pharisees! Didn't the One who made the outside also make the inside? Turn both your pockets and your hearts inside out and give generously to the poor; then your *lives* will be clean, not just your dishes and your hands.

42   "I've had it with you! You're hopeless, you Pharisees! Frauds! You keep meticulous account books, tithing on every nickel and dime you get, but manage to find loopholes for getting around basic matters of justice and God's love. Careful bookkeeping is commendable, but the basics are required.

43-44   "You're hopeless, you Pharisees! Frauds! You love sitting at the head table at church dinners, love preening yourselves in the radiance of public flattery. Frauds! You're just like unmarked graves: People walk over that nice, grassy surface, never suspecting the rot and corruption that is six feet under."

45   One of the religion scholars spoke up: "Teacher, do you realize that in saying these things you're insulting us?"

46   He said, "Yes, and I can be even more explicit. You're hopeless, you religion scholars! You load people down with rules and regulations, nearly breaking their backs, but never lift even a finger to help.

47-51   "You're hopeless! You build tombs for the prophets your ancestors killed. The tombs you build are monuments to your murdering ancestors more than to the murdered prophets. That accounts for God's Wisdom saying, 'I will send them prophets and apostles, but they'll kill them and run them off.' What it means is that every drop of righteous blood ever spilled from the time earth began until now, from the blood of Abel to the blood of Zechariah, who was struck down between altar and sanctuary, is on your heads. Yes, it's on the bill of this generation and this generation will pay.

52   "You're hopeless, you religion scholars! You took the key of knowledge, but instead of unlocking doors, you locked them. You won't go in yourself, and won't let anyone else in either."

53-54   As soon as Jesus left the table, the religion scholars and Pharisees went into a rage. They went over and over everything he said, plotting how they could trap him in something from his own mouth.

Can't Hide Behind a Religious Mask

1-3   **12** By this time the crowd, unwieldy and stepping on each other's toes, numbered into the thousands. But Jesus' primary concern was his disciples. He said to them, "Watch yourselves carefully so you don't get contaminated with Pharisee yeast, Pharisee phoniness. You can't keep your true self hidden forever; before long you'll be exposed. You can't hide behind a religious mask forever; sooner or later the mask will slip and your true face will be known. You can't whisper one thing in private and preach the opposite in public; the day's coming when those whispers will be repeated all over town.

4-5   "I'm speaking to you as dear friends. Don't be bluffed into silence or insincerity by the threats of religious bullies. True, they can kill you, but *then* what can they do? There's nothing they can do to your soul, your core being. Save your fear for God, who holds your entire life — body and soul — in his hands.

6-7   "What's the price of two or three pet canaries? Some loose change,

right? But God never overlooks a single one. And he pays even greater attention to you, down to the last detail—even numbering the hairs on your
head! So don't be intimidated by all this bully talk. You're worth more than
a million canaries.

8-9   "Stand up for me among the people you meet and the Son of Man will
stand up for you before all God's angels. But if you pretend you don't know
me, do you think I'll defend you before God's angels?

10   "If you bad-mouth the Son of Man out of misunderstanding or ignorance, that can be overlooked. But if you're knowingly attacking God himself, taking aim at the Holy Spirit, that won't be overlooked.

11-12   "When they drag you into their meeting places, or into police courts
and before judges, don't worry about defending yourselves—what you'll say
or how you'll say it. The right words will be there. The Holy Spirit will give
you the right words when the time comes."

The Story of the Greedy Farmer

13   Someone out of the crowd said, "Teacher, order my brother to give me a
fair share of the family inheritance."

14   He replied, "Mister, what makes you think it's any of my business to be
a judge or mediator for you?"

15   Speaking to the people, he went on, "Take care! Protect yourself against the least bit of greed. Life is not defined by what you have,
even when you have a lot."

16-19   Then he told them this story: "The farm of a certain rich man produced
a terrific crop. He talked to himself: 'What can I do? My barn isn't big
enough for this harvest.' Then he said, 'Here's what I'll do: I'll tear down
my barns and build bigger ones. Then I'll gather in all my grain and goods,
and I'll say to myself, Self, you've done well! You've got it made and can now
retire. Take it easy and have the time of your life!'

20   "Just then God showed up and said, 'Fool! Tonight you die. And your
barnful of goods—who gets it?'

21   "That's what happens when you fill your barn with Self and not with
God."

Steep Yourself in God-Reality

22-24   He continued this subject with his disciples. "Don't fuss about what's
on the table at mealtimes or if the clothes in your closet are in fashion. There
is far more to your inner life than the food you put in your stomach, more to
your outer appearance than the clothes you hang on your body. Look at the
ravens, free and unfettered, not tied down to a job description, carefree in the
care of God. And you count far more.

25-28   "Has anyone by fussing before the mirror ever gotten taller by so much
as an inch? If fussing can't even do that, why fuss at all? Walk into the fields
and look at the wildflowers. They don't fuss with their appearance—but have
you ever seen color and design quite like it? The ten best-dressed men and
women in the country look shabby alongside them. If God gives such attention to the wildflowers, most of them never even seen, don't you think he'll
attend to you, take pride in you, do his best for you?

29-32   "What I'm trying to do here is get you to relax, not be so preoccupied
with *getting* so you can respond to God's *giving*. People who don't know
God and the way he works fuss over these things, but you know both God

and how he works. Steep yourself in God-reality, God-initiative, God-provisions. You'll find all your everyday human concerns will be met. Don't be afraid of missing out. You're my dearest friends! The Father wants to give you the very kingdom itself.

33-34   "Be generous. Give to the poor. Get yourselves a bank that can't go bankrupt, a bank in heaven far from bankrobbers, safe from embezzlers, a bank you can bank on. It's obvious, isn't it? The place where your treasure is, is the place you will most want to be, and end up being.

When the Master Shows Up

35-38   "Keep your shirts on; keep the lights on! Be like house servants waiting for their master to come back from his honeymoon, awake and ready to open the door when he arrives and knocks. Lucky the servants whom the master finds on watch! He'll put on an apron, sit them at the table, and serve them a meal, sharing his wedding feast with them. It doesn't matter what time of the night he arrives; they're awake—and so blessed!

39-40   "You know that if the house owner had known what night the burglar was coming, he wouldn't have stayed out late and left the place unlocked. So don't you be slovenly and careless. Just when you don't expect him, the Son of Man will show up."

41   Peter said, "Master, are you telling this story just for us? Or is it for everybody?"

42-46   The Master said, "Let me ask you: Who is the dependable manager, full of common sense, that the master puts in charge of his staff to feed them well and on time? He is a blessed man if when the master shows up he's doing his job. But if he says to himself, 'The master is certainly taking his time,' begins maltreating the servants and maids, throws parties for his friends, and gets drunk, the master will walk in when he least expects it, give him the thrashing of his life, and put him back in the kitchen peeling potatoes.

47-48   "The servant who knows what his master wants and ignores it, or insolently does whatever he pleases, will be thoroughly thrashed. But if he does a poor job through ignorance, he'll get off with a slap on the hand. Great gifts mean great responsibilities; greater gifts, greater responsibilities!

To Start a Fire

49-53   "I've come to start a fire on this earth—how I wish it were blazing right now! I've come to change everything, turn everything rightside up—how I long for it to be finished! Do you think I came to smooth things over and make everything nice? Not so. I've come to disrupt and confront! From now on, when you find five in a house, it will be—

Three against two,
    and two against three;
Father against son,
    and son against father;
Mother against daughter,
    and daughter against mother;
Mother-in-law against bride,
    and bride against mother-in-law."

54-56   Then he turned to the crowd: "When you see clouds coming in from the west, you say, 'Storm's coming' — and you're right. And when the wind comes out of the south, you say, 'This'll be a hot one' — and you're right. Frauds! You know how to tell a change in the weather, so don't tell me you can't tell a change in the season, the God-season we're in right now.

57-59   "You don't have to be a genius to understand these things. Just use your common sense, the kind you'd use if, while being taken to court, you decided to settle up with your accuser on the way, knowing that if the case went to the judge you'd probably go to jail and pay every last penny of the fine. That's the kind of decision I'm asking you to make."

UNLESS YOU TURN TO GOD

1-5   **13** About that time some people came up and told him about the Galileans Pilate had killed while they were at worship, mixing their blood with the blood of the sacrifices on the altar. Jesus responded, "Do you think those murdered Galileans were worse sinners than all other Galileans? Not at all. Unless you turn to God, you, too, will die. And those eighteen in Jerusalem the other day, the ones crushed and killed when the Tower of Siloam collapsed and fell on them, do you think they were worse citizens than all other Jerusalemites? Not at all. Unless you turn to God, you, too, will die."

6-7   Then he told them a story: "A man had an apple tree planted in his front yard. He came to it expecting to find apples, but there weren't any. He said to his gardener, 'What's going on here? For three years now I've come to this tree expecting apples and not one apple have I found. Chop it down! Why waste good ground with it any longer?'

8-9   "The gardener said, 'Let's give it another year. I'll dig around it and fertilize, and maybe it will produce next year; if it doesn't, then chop it down.'"

HEALING ON THE SABBATH

10-13   He was teaching in one of the meeting places on the Sabbath. There was a woman present, so twisted and bent over with arthritis that she couldn't even look up. She had been afflicted with this for eighteen years. When Jesus saw her, he called her over. "Woman, you're free!" He laid hands on her and suddenly she was standing straight and tall, giving glory to God.

14   The meeting-place president, furious because Jesus had healed on the Sabbath, said to the congregation, "Six days have been defined as work days. Come on one of the six if you want to be healed, but not on the seventh, the Sabbath."

15-16   But Jesus shot back, "You frauds! Each Sabbath every one of you regularly unties your cow or donkey from its stall, leads it out for water, and thinks nothing of it. So why isn't it all right for me to untie this daughter of Abraham and lead her from the stall where Satan has had her tied these eighteen years?"

17   When he put it that way, his critics were left looking quite silly and red-faced. The congregation was delighted and cheered him on.

THE WAY TO GOD

18-19   Then he said, "How can I picture God's kingdom for you? What kind of story can I use? It's like a pine nut that a man plants in his front yard.

It grows into a huge pine tree with thick branches, and eagles build nests in it."

20-21 He tried again. "How can I picture God's kingdom? It's like yeast that a woman works into enough dough for three loaves of bread—and waits while the dough rises."

22 He went on teaching from town to village, village to town, but keeping on a steady course toward Jerusalem.

23-25 A bystander said, "Master, will only a few be saved?"

He said, "Whether few or many is none of your business. Put your mind on your life with God. The way to life—to God!—is vigorous and requires your total attention. A lot of you are going to assume that you'll sit down to God's salvation banquet just because you've been hanging around the neighborhood all your lives. Well, one day you're going to be banging on the door, wanting to get in, but you'll find the door locked and the Master saying, 'Sorry, you're not on my guest list.'

26-27 "You'll protest, 'But we've known you all our lives!' only to be interrupted with his abrupt, 'Your kind of knowing can hardly be called knowing. You don't know the first thing about me.'

28-30 "That's when you'll find yourselves out in the cold, strangers to grace. You'll watch Abraham, Isaac, Jacob, and all the prophets march into God's kingdom. You'll watch outsiders stream in from east, west, north, and south and sit down at the table of God's kingdom. And all the time you'll be outside looking in—and wondering what happened. This is the Great Reversal: the last in line put at the head of the line, and the so-called first ending up last."

31 Just then some Pharisees came up and said, "Run for your life! Herod's on the hunt. He's out to kill you!"

32-35 Jesus said, "Tell that fox that I've no time for him right now. Today and tomorrow I'm busy clearing out the demons and healing the sick; the third day I'm wrapping things up. Besides, it's not proper for a prophet to come to a bad end outside Jerusalem.

> Jerusalem, Jerusalem, killer of prophets,
>   abuser of the messengers of God!
> How often I've longed to gather your children,
>   gather your children like a hen,
> Her brood safe under her wings—
>   but you refused and turned away!
> And now it's too late: You won't see me again
>   until the day you say,
>   'Blessed is he
>   who comes in
>   the name of God.'"

1-3 **14** One time when Jesus went for a Sabbath meal with one of the top leaders of the Pharisees, all the guests had their eyes on him, watching his every move. Right before him there was a man hugely swollen in his joints. So Jesus asked the religion scholars and Pharisees present, "Is it permitted to heal on the Sabbath? Yes or no?"

4-6 They were silent. So he took the man, healed him, and sent him on his way. Then he said, "Is there anyone here who, if a child or animal fell down a well, wouldn't rush to pull him out immediately, not asking whether or not it was the Sabbath?" They were stumped. There was nothing they could say to that.

INVITE THE MISFITS

7-9 He went on to tell a story to the guests around the table. Noticing how each had tried to elbow into the place of honor, he said, "When someone invites you to dinner, don't take the place of honor. Somebody more important than you might have been invited by the host. Then he'll come and call out in front of everybody, 'You're in the wrong place. The place of honor belongs to this man.' Red-faced, you'll have to make your way to the very last table, the only place left.

10-11 "When you're invited to dinner, go and sit at the last place. Then when the host comes he may very well say, 'Friend, come up to the front.' That will give the dinner guests something to talk about! What I'm saying is, If you walk around with your nose in the air, you're going to end up flat on your face. But if you're content to be simply yourself, you will become more than yourself."

12-14 Then he turned to the host. "The next time you put on a dinner, don't just invite your friends and family and rich neighbors, the kind of people who will return the favor. Invite some people who never get invited out, the misfits from the wrong side of the tracks. You'll be—and experience—a blessing. They won't be able to return the favor, but the favor will be returned—oh, how it will be returned!—at the resurrection of God's people."

THE STORY OF THE DINNER PARTY

15 That triggered a response from one of the guests: "How fortunate the one who gets to eat dinner in God's kingdom!"

16-17 Jesus followed up. "Yes. For there was once a man who threw a great dinner party and invited many. When it was time for dinner, he sent out his servant to the invited guests, saying, 'Come on in; the food's on the table.'

18 "Then they all began to beg off, one after another making excuses. The first said, 'I bought a piece of property and need to look it over. Send my regrets.'

19 "Another said, 'I just bought five teams of oxen, and I really need to check them out. Send my regrets.'

20 "And yet another said, 'I just got married and need to get home to my wife.'

21 "The servant went back and told the master what had happened. He was outraged and told the servant, 'Quickly, get out into the city streets and alleys. Collect all who look like they need a square meal, all the misfits and homeless and wretched you can lay your hands on, and bring them here.'

22 "The servant reported back, 'Master, I did what you commanded—and there's still room.'

23-24 "The master said, 'Then go to the country roads. Whoever you find, drag them in. I want my house full! Let me tell you, not one of those originally invited is going to get so much as a bite at my dinner party.'"

Figure the Cost

25-27 One day when large groups of people were walking along with him, Jesus turned and told them, "Anyone who comes to me but refuses to let go of father, mother, spouse, children, brothers, sisters — yes, even one's own self! — can't be my disciple. Anyone who won't shoulder his own cross and follow behind me can't be my disciple.

28-30 "Is there anyone here who, planning to build a new house, doesn't first sit down and figure the cost so you'll know if you can complete it? If you only get the foundation laid and then run out of money, you're going to look pretty foolish. Everyone passing by will poke fun at you: 'He started something he couldn't finish.'

31-32 "Or can you imagine a king going into battle against another king without first deciding whether it is possible with his ten thousand troops to face the twenty thousand troops of the other? And if he decides he can't, won't he send an emissary and work out a truce?

33 "Simply put, if you're not willing to take what is dearest to you, whether plans or people, and kiss it good-bye, you can't be my disciple.

34 "Salt is excellent. But if the salt goes flat, it's useless, good for nothing.
"Are you listening to this? Really listening?"

The Story of the Lost Sheep

1-3 By this time a lot of men and women of doubtful reputation were hanging around Jesus, listening intently. The Pharisees and religion scholars were not pleased, not at all pleased. They growled, "He takes in sinners and eats meals with them, treating them like old friends." Their grumbling triggered this story.

4-7 "Suppose one of you had a hundred sheep and lost one. Wouldn't you leave the ninety-nine in the wilderness and go after the lost one until you found it? When found, you can be sure you would put it across your shoulders, rejoicing, and when you got home call in your friends and neighbors, saying, 'Celebrate with me! I've found my lost sheep!' Count on it — there's more joy in heaven over one sinner's rescued life than over ninety-nine good people in no need of rescue.

The Story of the Lost Coin

8-10 "Or imagine a woman who has ten coins and loses one. Won't she light a lamp and scour the house, looking in every nook and cranny until she finds it? And when she finds it you can be sure she'll call her friends and neighbors: 'Celebrate with me! I found my lost coin!' Count on it — that's the kind of party God's angels throw every time one lost soul turns to God."

The Story of the Lost Son

11-12 Then he said, "There was once a man who had two sons. The younger said to his father, 'Father, I want right now what's coming to me.'

12-16 "So the father divided the property between them. It wasn't long before the younger son packed his bags and left for a distant country. There, undisciplined and dissipated, he wasted everything he had. After he had gone through all his money, there was a bad famine all through that country and he began to hurt. He signed on with a citizen there who assigned him to his fields to slop the pigs. He was so hungry he would have eaten the corncobs in the pig slop, but no one would give him any.

17-20 "That brought him to his senses. He said, 'All those farmhands working for my father sit down to three meals a day, and here I am starving to death. I'm going back to my father. I'll say to him, Father, I've sinned against God, I've sinned before you; I don't deserve to be called your son. Take me on as a hired hand.' He got right up and went home to his father.

20-21 "When he was still a long way off, his father saw him. His heart pounding, he ran out, embraced him, and kissed him. The son started his speech: 'Father, I've sinned against God, I've sinned before you; I don't deserve to be called your son ever again.'

22-24 "But the father wasn't listening. He was calling to the servants, 'Quick. Bring a clean set of clothes and dress him. Put the family ring on his finger and sandals on his feet. Then get a grain-fed heifer and roast it. We're going to feast! We're going to have a wonderful time! My son is here — given up for dead and now alive! Given up for lost and now found!' And they began to have a wonderful time.

25-27 "All this time his older son was out in the field. When the day's work was done he came in. As he approached the house, he heard the music and dancing. Calling over one of the houseboys, he asked what was going on. He told him, 'Your brother came home. Your father has ordered a feast — barbecued beef! — because he has him home safe and sound.'

28-30 "The older brother stalked off in an angry sulk and refused to join in. His father came out and tried to talk to him, but he wouldn't listen. The son said, 'Look how many years I've stayed here serving you, never giving you one moment of grief, but have you ever thrown a party for me and my friends? Then this son of yours who has thrown away your money on whores shows up and you go all out with a feast!'

31-32 "His father said, 'Son, you don't understand. You're with me all the time, and everything that is mine is yours — but this is a wonderful time, and we had to celebrate. This brother of yours was dead, and he's alive! He was lost, and he's found!'"

THE STORY OF THE CROOKED MANAGER

1-2 16 Jesus said to his disciples, "There was once a rich man who had a manager. He got reports that the manager had been taking advantage of his position by running up huge personal expenses. So he called him in and said, 'What's this I hear about you? You're fired. And I want a complete audit of your books.'

3-4 "The manager said to himself, 'What am I going to do? I've lost my job as manager. I'm not strong enough for a laboring job, and I'm too proud to beg. . . . Ah, I've got a plan. Here's what I'll do . . . then when I'm turned out into the street, people will take me into their houses.'

5 "Then he went at it. One after another, he called in the people who were in debt to his master. He said to the first, 'How much do you owe my master?'

6 "He replied, 'A hundred jugs of olive oil.'

"The manager said, 'Here, take your bill, sit down here — quick now — write fifty.'

7 "To the next he said, 'And you, what do you owe?'

"He answered, 'A hundred sacks of wheat.'

"He said, 'Take your bill, write in eighty.'

8-9 "Now here's a surprise: The master praised the crooked manager! And why? Because he knew how to look after himself. Streetwise people are smarter in this regard than law-abiding citizens. They are on constant alert, looking for angles, surviving by their wits. I want you to be smart in the same way—but for what is *right*—using every adversity to stimulate you to creative survival, to concentrate your attention on the bare essentials, so you'll live, really live, and not complacently just get by on good behavior."

GOD SEES BEHIND APPEARANCES

10-13 Jesus went on to make these comments:

> If you're honest in small things,
>   you'll be honest in big things;
> If you're a crook in small things,
>   you'll be a crook in big things.
> If you're not honest in small jobs,
>   who will put you in charge of the store?
> No worker can serve two bosses:
>   He'll either hate the first and love the second
> Or adore the first and despise the second.
>   You can't serve both God and the Bank.

14-18 When the Pharisees, a money-obsessed bunch, heard him say these things, they rolled their eyes, dismissing him as hopelessly out of touch. So Jesus spoke to them: "You are masters at making yourselves look good in front of others, but God knows what's behind the appearance.

> What society sees and calls monumental,
>   God sees through and calls monstrous.
> God's Law and the Prophets climaxed in John;
> Now it's all kingdom of God—the glad news
>   and compelling invitation to every man and woman.
> The sky will disintegrate and the earth dissolve
>   before a single letter of God's Law wears out.
> Using the legalities of divorce
>   as a cover for lust is adultery;
> Using the legalities of marriage
>   as a cover for lust is adultery.

THE RICH MAN AND LAZARUS

19-21 "There once was a rich man, expensively dressed in the latest fashions, wasting his days in conspicuous consumption. A poor man named Lazarus, covered with sores, had been dumped on his doorstep. All he lived for was to get a meal from scraps off the rich man's table. His best friends were the dogs who came and licked his sores.

22-24 "Then he died, this poor man, and was taken up by the angels to the lap of Abraham. The rich man also died and was buried. In hell and in torment, he looked up and saw Abraham in the distance and Lazarus in his lap. He called out, 'Father Abraham, mercy! Have mercy! Send Lazarus to dip his finger in water to cool my tongue. I'm in agony in this fire.'

25-26 "But Abraham said, 'Child, remember that in your lifetime you got the good things and Lazarus the bad things. It's not like that here. Here he's consoled and you're tormented. Besides, in all these matters there is a huge chasm set between us so that no one can go from us to you even if he wanted to, nor can anyone cross over from you to us.'

27-28 "The rich man said, 'Then let me ask you, Father: Send him to the house of my father where I have five brothers, so he can tell them the score and warn them so they won't end up here in this place of torment.'

29 "Abraham answered, 'They have Moses and the Prophets to tell them the score. Let them listen to them.'

30 "'I know, Father Abraham,' he said, 'but they're not listening. If someone came back to them from the dead, they would change their ways.'

31 "Abraham replied, 'If they won't listen to Moses and the Prophets, they're not going to be convinced by someone who rises from the dead.'"

A KERNEL OF FAITH

1-2 **17** He said to his disciples, "Hard trials and temptations are bound to come, but too bad for whoever brings them on! Better to wear a millstone necklace and take a swim in the deep blue sea than give even one of these dear little ones a hard time!

3-4 "Be alert. If you see your friend going wrong, correct him. If he responds, forgive him. Even if it's personal against you and repeated seven times through the day, and seven times he says, 'I'm sorry, I won't do it again,' forgive him."

5 The apostles came up and said to the Master, "Give us more faith."

6 But the Master said, "You don't need *more* faith. There is no 'more' or 'less' in faith. If you have a bare kernel of faith, say the size of a poppy seed, you could say to this sycamore tree, 'Go jump in the lake,' and it would do it.

7-10 "Suppose one of you has a servant who comes in from plowing the field or tending the sheep. Would you take his coat, set the table, and say, 'Sit down and eat'? Wouldn't you be more likely to say, 'Prepare dinner; change your clothes and wait table for me until I've finished my coffee; then go to the kitchen and have your supper'? Does the servant get special thanks for doing what's expected of him? It's the same with you. When you've done everything expected of you, be matter-of-fact and say, 'The work is done. What we were told to do, we did.'"

11-13 It happened that as he made his way toward Jerusalem, he crossed over the border between Samaria and Galilee. As he entered a village, ten men, all lepers, met him. They kept their distance but raised their voices, calling out, "Jesus, Master, have mercy on us!"

14-16 Taking a good look at them, he said, "Go, show yourselves to the priests." They went, and while still on their way, became clean. One of them, when he realized that he was healed, turned around and came back, shouting his gratitude, glorifying God. He kneeled at Jesus' feet, so grateful. He couldn't thank him enough — and he was a Samaritan.

17-19 Jesus said, "Were not ten healed? Where are the nine? Can none be found to come back and give glory to God except this outsider?" Then he said to him, "Get up. On your way. Your faith has healed and saved you."

WHEN THE SON OF MAN ARRIVES

20-21 Jesus, grilled by the Pharisees on when the kingdom of God would come, answered, "The kingdom of God doesn't come by counting the days on the calendar. Nor when someone says, 'Look here!' or, 'There it is!' And why? Because God's kingdom is already among you."

22-24 He went on to say to his disciples, "The days are coming when you are going to be desperately homesick for just a glimpse of one of the days of the Son of Man, and you won't see a thing. And they'll say to you, 'Look over there!' or, 'Look here!' Don't fall for any of that nonsense. The arrival of the Son of Man is not something you go out to see. He simply comes.

24-25 "You know how the whole sky lights up from a single flash of lightning? That's how it will be on the Day of the Son of Man. But first it's necessary that he suffer many things and be turned down by the people of today.

26-27 "The time of the Son of Man will be just like the time of Noah — everyone carrying on as usual, having a good time right up to the day Noah boarded the ship. They suspected nothing until the flood hit and swept everything away.

28-30 "It was the same in the time of Lot — the people carrying on, having a good time, business as usual right up to the day Lot walked out of Sodom and a firestorm swept down and burned everything to a crisp. That's how it will be — sudden, total — when the Son of Man is revealed.

31-33 "When the Day arrives and you're out working in the yard, don't run into the house to get anything. And if you're out in the field, don't go back and get your coat. Remember what happened to Lot's wife! If you grasp and cling to life on your terms, you'll lose it, but if you let that life go, you'll get life on God's terms.

34-35 "On that Day, two men will be in the same boat fishing — one taken, the other left. Two women will be working in the same kitchen — one taken, the other left."

37 Trying to take all this in, the disciples said, "Master, where?"

He told them, "Watch for the circling of the vultures. They'll spot the corpse first. The action will begin around my dead body."

THE STORY OF THE PERSISTENT WIDOW

1-3 **18** Jesus told them a story showing that it was necessary for them to pray consistently and never quit. He said, "There was once a judge in some city who never gave God a thought and cared nothing for people. A widow in that city kept after him: 'My rights are being violated. Protect me!'

4-5 "He never gave her the time of day. But after this went on and on he said to himself, 'I care nothing what God thinks, even less what people think. But because this widow won't quit badgering me, I'd better do something and see that she gets justice — otherwise I'm going to end up beaten black-and-blue by her pounding.'"

6-8 Then the Master said, "Do you hear what that judge, corrupt as he is, is saying? So what makes you think God won't step in and work justice for his chosen people, who continue to cry out for help? Won't he stick up for them? I assure you, he will. He will not drag his feet. But how much of that kind of persistent faith will the Son of Man find on the earth when he returns?"

THE STORY OF THE TAX MAN AND THE PHARISEE

9-12 He told his next story to some who were complacently pleased with themselves over their moral performance and looked down their noses at the common people: "Two men went up to the Temple to pray, one a Pharisee, the other a tax man. The Pharisee posed and prayed like this: 'Oh, God, I thank you that I am not like other people—robbers, crooks, adulterers, or, heaven forbid, like this tax man. I fast twice a week and tithe on all my income.'

13 "Meanwhile the tax man, slumped in the shadows, his face in his hands, not daring to look up, said, 'God, give mercy. Forgive me, a sinner.'"

14 Jesus commented, "This tax man, not the other, went home made right with God. If you walk around with your nose in the air, you're going to end up flat on your face, but if you're content to be simply yourself, you will become more than yourself."

15-17 People brought babies to Jesus, hoping he might touch them. When the disciples saw it, they shooed them off. Jesus called them back. "Let these children alone. Don't get between them and me. These children are the kingdom's pride and joy. Mark this: Unless you accept God's kingdom in the simplicity of a child, you'll never get in."

THE RICH OFFICIAL

18 One day one of the local officials asked him, "Good Teacher, what must I do to deserve eternal life?"

19-20 Jesus said, "Why are you calling me good? No one is good—only God. You know the commandments, don't you? No illicit sex, no killing, no stealing, no lying, honor your father and mother."

21 He said, "I've kept them all for as long as I can remember."

22 When Jesus heard that, he said, "Then there's only one thing left to do: Sell everything you own and give it away to the poor. You will have riches in heaven. Then come, follow me."

23 This was the last thing the official expected to hear. He was very rich and became terribly sad. He was holding on tight to a lot of things and not about to let them go.

24-25 Seeing his reaction, Jesus said, "Do you have any idea how difficult it is for people who have it all to enter God's kingdom? I'd say it's easier to thread a camel through a needle's eye than get a rich person into God's kingdom."

26 "Then who has any chance at all?" the others asked.

27 "No chance at all," Jesus said, "if you think you can pull it off by yourself. Every chance in the world if you trust God to do it."

28 Peter tried to regain some initiative: "We left everything we owned and followed you, didn't we?"

29-30 "Yes," said Jesus, "and you won't regret it. No one who has sacrificed home, spouse, brothers and sisters, parents, children—whatever—will lose out. It will all come back multiplied many times over in your lifetime. And then the bonus of eternal life!"

I Want to See Again

31-34 Then Jesus took the Twelve off to the side and said, "Listen carefully. We're on our way up to Jerusalem. Everything written in the Prophets about the Son of Man will take place. He will be handed over to the Romans, jeered at, made sport of, and spit on. Then, after giving him the third degree, they will kill him. In three days he will rise, alive." But they didn't get it, could make neither heads nor tails of what he was talking about.

35-37 He came to the outskirts of Jericho. A blind man was sitting beside the road asking for handouts. When he heard the rustle of the crowd, he asked what was going on. They told him, "Jesus the Nazarene is going by."

38 He yelled, "Jesus! Son of David! Mercy, have mercy on me!"

39 Those ahead of Jesus told the man to shut up, but he only yelled all the louder, "Son of David! Mercy, have mercy on me!"

40 Jesus stopped and ordered him to be brought over. When he had come near, Jesus asked, "What do you want from me?"

41 He said, "Master, I want to see again."

42-43 Jesus said, "Go ahead — see again! Your faith has saved and healed you!" The healing was instant: He looked up, seeing — and then followed Jesus, glorifying God. Everyone in the street joined in, shouting praise to God.

Zacchaeus

1-4 Then Jesus entered and walked through Jericho. There was a man there, his name Zacchaeus, the head tax man and quite rich. He wanted desperately to see Jesus, but the crowd was in his way — he was a short man and couldn't see over the crowd. So he ran on ahead and climbed up in a sycamore tree so he could see Jesus when he came by.

5-7 When Jesus got to the tree, he looked up and said, "Zacchaeus, hurry down. Today is my day to be a guest in your home." Zacchaeus scrambled out of the tree, hardly believing his good luck, delighted to take Jesus home with him. Everyone who saw the incident was indignant and grumped, "What business does he have getting cozy with this crook?"

8 Zacchaeus just stood there, a little stunned. He stammered apologetically, "Master, I give away half my income to the poor — and if I'm caught cheating, I pay four times the damages."

9-10 Jesus said, "Today is salvation day in this home! Here he is: Zacchaeus, son of Abraham! For the Son of Man came to find and restore the lost."

The Story About Investment

11 While he had their attention, and because they were getting close to Jerusalem by this time and expectation was building that God's kingdom would appear any minute, he told this story:

12-13 "There was once a man descended from a royal house who needed to make a long trip back to headquarters to get authorization for his rule and then return. But first he called ten servants together, gave them each a sum of money, and instructed them, 'Operate with this until I return.'

14 "But the citizens there hated him. So they sent a commission with a signed petition to oppose his rule: 'We don't want this man to rule us.'

15 "When he came back bringing the authorization of his rule, he called those ten servants to whom he had given the money to find out how they had done.

16   "The first said, 'Master, I doubled your money.'

17   "He said, 'Good servant! Great work! Because you've been trustworthy in this small job, I'm making you governor of ten towns.'

18   "The second said, 'Master, I made a fifty percent profit on your money.'

19   "He said, 'I'm putting you in charge of five towns.'

20-21   "The next servant said, 'Master, here's your money safe and sound. I kept it hidden in the cellar. To tell you the truth, I was a little afraid. I know you have high standards and hate sloppiness, and don't suffer fools gladly.'

22-23   "He said, 'You're right that I don't suffer fools gladly—and you've acted the fool! Why didn't you at least invest the money in securities so I would have gotten a little interest on it?'

24   "Then he said to those standing there, 'Take the money from him and give it to the servant who doubled my stake.'

25   "They said, 'But Master, he already has double . . .'

26   "He said, 'That's what I mean: Risk your life and get more than you ever dreamed of. Play it safe and end up holding the bag.

27   "'As for these enemies of mine who petitioned against my rule, clear them out of here. I don't want to see their faces around here again.'"

GOD'S PERSONAL VISIT

28-31   After saying these things, Jesus headed straight up to Jerusalem. When he got near Bethphage and Bethany at the mountain called Olives, he sent off two of the disciples with instructions: "Go to the village across from you. As soon as you enter, you'll find a colt tethered, one that has never been ridden. Untie it and bring it. If anyone says anything, asks, 'What are you doing?' say, 'His Master needs him.'"

32-33   The two left and found it just as he said. As they were untying the colt, its owners said, "What are you doing untying the colt?"

34   They said, "His Master needs him."

35-36   They brought the colt to Jesus. Then, throwing their coats on its back, they helped Jesus get on. As he rode, the people gave him a grand welcome, throwing their coats on the street.

37-38   Right at the crest, where Mount Olives begins its descent, the whole crowd of disciples burst into enthusiastic praise over all the mighty works they had witnessed:

> Blessed is he who comes,
>   the king in God's name!
> All's well in heaven!
>   Glory in the high places!

39   Some Pharisees from the crowd told him, "Teacher, get your disciples under control!"

40   But he said, "If they kept quiet, the stones would do it for them, shouting praise."

41-44   When the city came into view, he wept over it. "If you had only recognized this day, and everything that was good for you! But now it's too late. In the days ahead your enemies are going to bring up their heavy artillery and surround you, pressing in from every side. They'll smash you and your babies on the pavement. Not one stone will be left intact. All this because you didn't recognize and welcome God's personal visit."

45-46 Going into the Temple he began to throw out everyone who had set up shop, selling everything and anything. He said, "It's written in Scripture,

My house is a house of prayer;
You have turned it into a religious bazaar."

47-48 From then on he taught each day in the Temple. The high priests, religion scholars, and the leaders of the people were trying their best to find a way to get rid of him. But with the people hanging on every word he spoke, they couldn't come up with anything.

1-2 **20** One day he was teaching the people in the Temple, proclaiming the Message. The high priests, religion scholars, and leaders confronted him and demanded, "Show us your credentials. Who authorized you to speak and act like this?"

3-4 Jesus answered, "First, let me ask you a question: About the baptism of John — who authorized it, heaven or humans?"

5-7 They were on the spot, and knew it. They pulled back into a huddle and whispered, "If we say 'heaven,' he'll ask us why we didn't believe him; if we say 'humans,' the people will tear us limb from limb, convinced as they are that John was God's prophet." They agreed to concede that round to Jesus and said they didn't know.

8 Jesus said, "Then neither will I answer your question."

THE STORY OF CORRUPT FARMHANDS

9-12 Jesus told another story to the people: "A man planted a vineyard. He handed it over to farmhands and went off on a trip. He was gone a long time. In time he sent a servant back to the farmhands to collect the profits, but they beat him up and sent him off empty-handed. He decided to try again and sent another servant. That one they beat black-and-blue, and sent him off empty-handed. He tried a third time. They worked that servant over from head to foot and dumped him in the street.

13 "Then the owner of the vineyard said, 'I know what I'll do: I'll send my beloved son. They're bound to respect my son.'

14-15 "But when the farmhands saw him coming, they quickly put their heads together. 'This is our chance — this is the heir! Let's kill him and have it all to ourselves.' They killed him and threw him over the fence.

15-16 "What do you think the owner of the vineyard will do? Right. He'll come and clean house. Then he'll assign the care of the vineyard to others."

Those who were listening said, "Oh, no! He'd never do that!"

17-18 But Jesus didn't back down. "Why, then, do you think this was written:

That stone the masons threw out —
It's now the cornerstone!?

"Anyone falling over that stone will break every bone in his body; if the stone falls on anyone, it will be a total smashup."

19 The religion scholars and high priests wanted to lynch him on the spot, but they were intimidated by public opinion. They knew the story was about them.

PAYING TAXES

20-22   Watching for a chance to get him, they sent spies who posed as honest inquirers, hoping to trick him into saying something that would get him in trouble with the law. So they asked him, "Teacher, we know that you're honest and straightforward when you teach, that you don't pander to anyone but teach the way of God accurately. Tell us: Is it lawful to pay taxes to Caesar or not?"

23-24   He knew they were laying for him and said, "Show me a coin. Now, this engraving, who does it look like and what does it say?"

25   "Caesar," they said.

Jesus said, "Then give Caesar what is his and give God what is his."

26   Try as they might, they couldn't trap him into saying anything incriminating. His answer caught them off guard and left them speechless.

ALL INTIMACIES WILL BE WITH GOD

27-33   Some Sadducees came up. This is the Jewish party that denies any possibility of resurrection. They asked, "Teacher, Moses wrote us that if a man dies and leaves a wife but no child, his brother is obligated to take the widow to wife and get her with child. Well, there once were seven brothers. The first took a wife. He died childless. The second married her and died, then the third, and eventually all seven had their turn, but no child. After all that, the wife died. That wife, now—in the resurrection whose wife is she? All seven married her."

34-38   Jesus said, "Marriage is a major preoccupation here, but not there. Those who are included in the resurrection of the dead will no longer be concerned with marriage nor, of course, with death. They will have better things to think about, if you can believe it. All ecstasies and intimacies then will be with God. Even Moses exclaimed about resurrection at the burning bush, saying, 'God: God of Abraham, God of Isaac, God of Jacob!' God isn't the God of dead men, but of the living. To him all are alive."

39-40   Some of the religion scholars said, "Teacher, that's a great answer!" For a while, anyway, no one dared put questions to him.

41-44   Then he put a question to them: "How is it that they say that the Messiah is David's son? In the Book of Psalms, David clearly says,

> God said to my Master,
> "Sit here at my right hand
>   until I put your enemies under your feet."

"David here designates the Messiah as 'my Master'—so how can the Messiah also be his 'son'?"

45-47   With everybody listening, Jesus spoke to his disciples. "Watch out for the religion scholars. They love to walk around in academic gowns, preen in the radiance of public flattery, bask in prominent positions, sit at the head table at every church function. And all the time they are exploiting the weak and helpless. The longer their prayers, the worse they get. But they'll pay for it in the end."

21 1-4 Just then he looked up and saw the rich people dropping offerings in the collection plate. Then he saw a poor widow put in two pennies. He said, "The plain truth is that this widow has given by far the largest offering today. All these others made offerings that they'll never miss; she gave extravagantly what she couldn't afford — she gave her all!"

WATCH OUT FOR DOOMSDAY DECEIVERS

5-6 One day people were standing around talking about the Temple, remarking how beautiful it was, the splendor of its stonework and memorial gifts. Jesus said, "All this you're admiring so much — the time is coming when every stone in that building will end up in a heap of rubble."

7 They asked him, "Teacher, when is this going to happen? What clue will we get that it's about to take place?"

8-9 He said, "Watch out for the doomsday deceivers. Many leaders are going to show up with forged identities claiming, 'I'm the One,' or, 'The end is near.' Don't fall for any of that. When you hear of wars and uprisings, keep your head and don't panic. This is routine history and no sign of the end."

10-11 He went on, "Nation will fight nation and ruler fight ruler, over and over. Huge earthquakes will occur in various places. There will be famines. You'll think at times that the very sky is falling.

12-15 "But before any of this happens, they'll arrest you, hunt you down, and drag you to court and jail. It will go from bad to worse, dog-eat-dog, everyone at your throat because you carry my name. You'll end up on the witness stand, called to testify. Make up your mind right now not to worry about it. I'll give you the words and wisdom that will reduce all your accusers to stammers and stutters.

16-19 "You'll even be turned in by parents, brothers, relatives, and friends. Some of you will be killed. There's no telling who will hate you because of me. Even so, every detail of your body and soul — even the hairs of your head! — is in my care; nothing of you will be lost. Staying with it — that's what is required. Stay with it to the end. You won't be sorry; you'll be saved.

VENGEANCE DAY

20-24 "When you see soldiers camped all around Jerusalem, then you'll know that she is about to be devastated. If you're living in Judea at the time, run for the hills. If you're in the city, get out quickly. If you're out in the fields, don't go home to get your coat. This is Vengeance Day — everything written about it will come to a head. Pregnant and nursing mothers will have it especially hard. Incredible misery! Torrential rage! People dropping like flies; people dragged off to prisons; Jerusalem under the boot of barbarians until the nations finish what was given them to do.

25-26 "It will seem like all hell has broken loose — sun, moon, stars, earth, sea, in an uproar and everyone all over the world in a panic, the wind knocked out of them by the threat of doom, the powers-that-be quaking.

27-28 "And then — then! — they'll see the Son of Man welcomed in grand style — a glorious welcome! When all this starts to happen, up on your feet. Stand tall with your heads high. Help is on the way!"

29-33 He told them a story. "Look at a fig tree. Any tree for that matter. When the leaves begin to show, one look tells you that summer is right around the corner. The same here — when you see these things happen, you know God's kingdom is about here. Don't brush this off: I'm not just saying this for some future generation, but for this one, too — these things will happen. Sky and earth will wear out; my words won't wear out.

34-36 "But be on your guard. Don't let the sharp edge of your expectation get dulled by parties and drinking and shopping. Otherwise, that Day is going to take you by complete surprise, spring on you suddenly like a trap, for it's going to come on everyone, everywhere, at once. So, whatever you do, don't go to sleep at the switch. Pray constantly that you will have the strength and wits to make it through everything that's coming and end up on your feet before the Son of Man."

37-38 He spent his days in the Temple teaching, but his nights out on the mountain called Olives. All the people were up at the crack of dawn to come to the Temple and listen to him.

THE PASSOVER MEAL

1-2 *22* The Feast of Unleavened Bread, also called Passover, drew near. The high priests and religion scholars were looking for a way to do away with Jesus but, fearful of the people, they were also looking for a way to cover their tracks.

3-6 That's when Satan entered Judas, the one called Iscariot. He was one of the Twelve. Leaving the others, he conferred with the high priests and the Temple guards about how he might betray Jesus to them. They couldn't believe their good luck and agreed to pay him well. He gave them his word and started looking for a way to betray Jesus, but out of sight of the crowd.

7-8 The Day of Unleavened Bread came, the day the Passover lamb was butchered. Jesus sent Peter and John off, saying, "Go prepare the Passover for us so we can eat it together."

9 They said, "Where do you want us to do this?"

10-12 He said, "Keep your eyes open as you enter the city. A man carrying a water jug will meet you. Follow him home. Then speak with the owner of the house: The Teacher wants to know, 'Where is the guest room where I can eat the Passover meal with my disciples?' He will show you a spacious second-story room, swept and ready. Prepare the meal there."

13 They left, found everything just as he told them, and prepared the Passover meal.

14-16 When it was time, he sat down, all the apostles with him, and said, "You've no idea how much I have looked forward to eating this Passover meal with you before I enter my time of suffering. It's the last one I'll eat until we all eat it together in the kingdom of God."

17-18 Taking the cup, he blessed it, then said, "Take this and pass it among you. As for me, I'll not drink wine again until the kingdom of God arrives."

19 Taking bread, he blessed it, broke it, and gave it to them, saying, "This is my body, given for you. Eat it in my memory."

20 He did the same with the cup after supper, saying, "This cup is the new covenant written in my blood, blood poured out for you.

21-22 "Do you realize that the hand of the one who is betraying me is at this moment on this table? It's true that the Son of Man is going down a path already marked out — no surprises there. But for the one who turns him in, turns traitor to the Son of Man, this is doomsday."

23 They immediately became suspicious of each other and began quizzing one another, wondering who might be about to do this.

GET READY FOR TROUBLE

24-26   Within minutes they were bickering over who of them would end up the greatest. But Jesus intervened: "Kings like to throw their weight around and people in authority like to give themselves fancy titles. It's not going to be that way with you. Let the senior among you become like the junior; let the leader act the part of the servant.

27-30   "Who would you rather be: the one who eats the dinner or the one who serves the dinner? You'd rather eat and be served, right? But I've taken my place among you as the one who serves. And you've stuck with me through thick and thin. Now I confer on you the royal authority my Father conferred on me so you can eat and drink at my table in my kingdom and be strengthened as you take up responsibilities among the congregations of God's people.

31-32   "Simon, stay on your toes. Satan has tried his best to separate all of you from me, like chaff from wheat. Simon, I've prayed for you in particular that you not give in or give out. When you have come through the time of testing, turn to your companions and give them a fresh start."

33   Peter said, "Master, I'm ready for anything with you. I'd go to jail for you. I'd *die* for you!"

34   Jesus said, "I'm sorry to have to tell you this, Peter, but before the rooster crows you will have three times denied that you know me."

35   Then Jesus said, "When I sent you out and told you to travel light, to take only the bare necessities, did you get along all right?"

"Certainly," they said, "we got along just fine."

36-37   He said, "This is different. Get ready for trouble. Look to what you'll need; there are difficult times ahead. Pawn your coat and get a sword. What was written in Scripture, 'He was lumped in with the criminals,' gets its final meaning in me. Everything written about me is now coming to a conclusion."

38   They said, "Look, Master, two swords!"

But he said, "Enough of that; no more sword talk!"

A DARK NIGHT

39-40   Leaving there, he went, as he so often did, to Mount Olives. The disciples followed him. When they arrived at the place, he said, "Pray that you don't give in to temptation."

41-44   He pulled away from them about a stone's throw, knelt down, and prayed, "Father, remove this cup from me. But please, not what I want. What do *you* want?" At once an angel from heaven was at his side, strengthening him. He prayed on all the harder. Sweat, wrung from him like drops of blood, poured off his face.

45-46   He got up from prayer, went back to the disciples and found them asleep, drugged by grief. He said, "What business do you have sleeping? Get up. Pray so you won't give in to temptation."

47-48   No sooner were the words out of his mouth than a crowd showed up, Judas, the one from the Twelve, in the lead. He came right up to Jesus to kiss him. Jesus said, "Judas, you would betray the Son of Man with a kiss?"

49-50   When those with him saw what was happening, they said, "Master, shall we fight?" One of them took a swing at the Chief Priest's servant and cut off his right ear.

51 Jesus said, "Let them be. Even in this." Then, touching the servant's ear, he healed him.

52-53 Jesus spoke to those who had come — high priests, Temple police, religion leaders: "What is this, jumping me with swords and clubs as if I were a dangerous criminal? Day after day I've been with you in the Temple and you've not so much as lifted a hand against me. But do it your way — it's a dark night, a dark hour."

A ROOSTER CROWED

54-56 Arresting Jesus, they marched him off and took him into the house of the Chief Priest. Peter followed, but at a safe distance. In the middle of the courtyard some people had started a fire and were sitting around it, trying to keep warm. One of the serving maids sitting at the fire noticed him, then took a second look and said, "This man was with him!"

57 He denied it, "Woman, I don't even know him."

58 A short time later, someone else noticed him and said, "You're one of them."

But Peter denied it: "Man, I am not."

59 About an hour later, someone else spoke up, really adamant: "He's got to have been with him! He's got 'Galilean' written all over him."

60-62 Peter said, "Man, I don't know what you're talking about." At that very moment, the last word hardly off his lips, a rooster crowed. Just then, the Master turned and looked at Peter. Peter remembered what the Master had said to him: "Before the rooster crows, you will deny me three times." He went out and cried and cried and cried.

SLAPPING HIM AROUND

63-65 The men in charge of Jesus began poking fun at him, slapping him around. They put a blindfold on him and taunted, "Who hit you that time?" They were having a grand time with him.

66-67 When it was morning, the religious leaders of the people and the high priests and scholars all got together and brought him before their High Council. They said, "Are you the Messiah?"

67-69 He answered, "If I said yes, you wouldn't believe me. If I asked what you meant by your question, you wouldn't answer me. So here's what I have to say: From here on the Son of Man takes his place at God's right hand, the place of power."

70 They all said, "So you admit your claim to be the Son of God?"

"You're the ones who keep saying it," he said.

71 But they had made up their minds, "Why do we need any more evidence? We've all heard him as good as say it himself."

PILATE

1-2 **23** Then they all took Jesus to Pilate and began to bring up charges against him. They said, "We found this man undermining our law and order, forbidding taxes to be paid to Caesar, setting himself up as Messiah-King."

3 Pilate asked him, "Is this true that you're 'King of the Jews'?"

"Those are your words, not mine," Jesus replied.

4 Pilate told the high priests and the accompanying crowd, "I find nothing wrong here. He seems harmless enough to me."

5 But they were vehement. "He's stirring up unrest among the people with his teaching, disturbing the peace everywhere, starting in Galilee and now all through Judea. He's a dangerous man, endangering the peace."

6-7 When Pilate heard that, he asked, "So, he's a Galilean?" Realizing that he properly came under Herod's jurisdiction, he passed the buck to Herod, who just happened to be in Jerusalem for a few days.

8-10 Herod was delighted when Jesus showed up. He had wanted for a long time to see him, he'd heard so much about him. He hoped to see him do something spectacular. He peppered him with questions. Jesus didn't answer — not one word. But the high priests and religion scholars were right there, saying their piece, strident and shrill in their accusations.

11-12 Mightily offended, Herod turned on Jesus. His soldiers joined in, taunting and jeering. Then they dressed him up in an elaborate king costume and sent him back to Pilate. That day Herod and Pilate became thick as thieves. Always before they had kept their distance.

13-16 Then Pilate called in the high priests, rulers, and the others and said, "You brought this man to me as a disturber of the peace. I examined him in front of all of you and found there was nothing to your charge. And neither did Herod, for he has sent him back here with a clean bill of health. It's clear that he's done nothing wrong, let alone anything deserving death. I'm going to warn him to watch his step and let him go."

18-20 At that, the crowd went wild: "Kill him! Give us Barabbas!" (Barabbas had been thrown in prison for starting a riot in the city and for murder.) Pilate still wanted to let Jesus go, and so spoke out again.

21 But they kept shouting back, "Crucify! Crucify him!"

22 He tried a third time. "But for what crime? I've found nothing in him deserving death. I'm going to warn him to watch his step and let him go."

23-25 But they kept at it, a shouting mob, demanding that he be crucified. And finally they shouted him down. Pilate caved in and gave them what they wanted. He released the man thrown in prison for rioting and murder, and gave them Jesus to do whatever they wanted.

SKULL HILL

26-31 As they led him off, they made Simon, a man from Cyrene who happened to be coming in from the countryside, carry the cross behind Jesus. A huge crowd of people followed, along with women weeping and carrying on. At one point Jesus turned to the women and said, "Daughters of Jerusalem, don't cry for me. Cry for yourselves and for your children. The time is coming when they'll say, 'Lucky the women who never conceived! Lucky the wombs that never gave birth! Lucky the breasts that never gave milk!' Then they'll start calling to the mountains, 'Fall down on us!' calling to the hills, 'Cover us up!' If people do these things to a live, green tree, can you imagine what they'll do with deadwood?"

32 Two others, both criminals, were taken along with him for execution.

33 When they got to the place called Skull Hill, they crucified him, along with the criminals, one on his right, the other on his left.

34-35 Jesus prayed, "Father, forgive them; they don't know what they're doing."
Dividing up his clothes, they threw dice for them. The people stood there staring at Jesus, and the ringleaders made faces, taunting, "He saved others. Let's see him save himself! The Messiah of God — ha! The Chosen — ha!"

36-37 The soldiers also came up and poked fun at him, making a game of it. They toasted him with sour wine: "So you're King of the Jews! Save yourself!"

38 Printed over him was a sign: THIS IS THE KING OF THE JEWS.

39 One of the criminals hanging alongside cursed him: "Some Messiah you are! Save yourself! Save us!"

40-41 But the other one made him shut up: "Have you no fear of God? You're getting the same as him. We deserve this, but not him — he did nothing to deserve this."

42 Then he said, "Jesus, remember me when you enter your kingdom."

43 He said, "Don't worry, I will. Today you will join me in paradise."

44-46 By now it was noon. The whole earth became dark, the darkness lasting three hours — a total blackout. The Temple curtain split right down the middle. Jesus called loudly, "Father, I place my life in your hands!" Then he breathed his last.

47 When the captain there saw what happened, he honored God: "This man was innocent! A good man, and innocent!"

48-49 All who had come around as spectators to watch the show, when they saw what actually happened, were overcome with grief and headed home. Those who knew Jesus well, along with the women who had followed him from Galilee, stood at a respectful distance and kept vigil.

50-54 There was a man by the name of Joseph, a member of the Jewish High Council, a man of good heart and good character. He had not gone along with the plans and actions of the council. His hometown was the Jewish village of Arimathea. He lived in alert expectation of the kingdom of God. He went to Pilate and asked for the body of Jesus. Taking him down, he wrapped him in a linen shroud and placed him in a tomb chiseled into the rock, a tomb never yet used. It was the day before Sabbath, the Sabbath just about to begin.

55-56 The women who had been companions of Jesus from Galilee followed along. They saw the tomb where Jesus' body was placed. Then they went back to prepare burial spices and perfumes. They rested quietly on the Sabbath, as commanded.

LOOKING FOR THE LIVING ONE IN A CEMETERY

1-3 At the crack of dawn on Sunday, the women came to the tomb carrying the burial spices they had prepared. They found the entrance stone rolled back from the tomb, so they walked in. But once inside, they couldn't find the body of the Master Jesus.

4-8 They were puzzled, wondering what to make of this. Then, out of nowhere it seemed, two men, light cascading over them, stood there. The women were awestruck and bowed down in worship. The men said, "Why are you looking for the Living One in a cemetery? He is not here, but raised up. Remember how he told you when you were still back in Galilee that he had to be handed over to sinners, be killed on a cross, and in three days rise up?" Then they remembered Jesus' words.

9-11 They left the tomb and broke the news of all this to the Eleven and the rest. Mary Magdalene, Joanna, Mary the mother of James, and the other women with them kept telling these things to the apostles, but the apostles didn't believe a word of it, thought they were making it all up.

12 But Peter jumped to his feet and ran to the tomb. He stooped to look in and saw a few grave clothes, that's all. He walked away puzzled, shaking his head.

THE ROAD TO EMMAUS

13-16 That same day two of them were walking to the village Emmaus, about seven miles out of Jerusalem. They were deep in conversation, going over all these things that had happened. In the middle of their talk and questions, Jesus came up and walked along with them. But they were not able to recognize who he was.

17-18 He asked, "What's this you're discussing so intently as you walk along?"

They just stood there, long-faced, like they had lost their best friend. Then one of them, his name was Cleopas, said, "Are you the only one in Jerusalem who hasn't heard what's happened during the last few days?"

19-24 He said, "What has happened?"

They said, "The things that happened to Jesus the Nazarene. He was a man of God, a prophet, dynamic in work and word, blessed by both God and all the people. Then our high priests and leaders betrayed him, got him sentenced to death, and crucified him. And we had our hopes up that he was the One, the One about to deliver Israel. And it is now the third day since it happened. But now some of our women have completely confused us. Early this morning they were at the tomb and couldn't find his body. They came back with the story that they had seen a vision of angels who said he was alive. Some of our friends went off to the tomb to check and found it empty just as the women said, but they didn't see Jesus."

25-27 Then he said to them, "So thick-headed! So slow-hearted! Why can't you simply believe all that the prophets said? Don't you see that these things had to happen, that the Messiah had to suffer and only then enter into his glory?" Then he started at the beginning, with the Books of Moses, and went on through all the Prophets, pointing out everything in the Scriptures that referred to him.

28-31 They came to the edge of the village where they were headed. He acted as if he were going on but they pressed him: "Stay and have supper with us. It's nearly evening; the day is done." So he went in with them. And here is what happened: He sat down at the table with them. Taking the bread, he blessed and broke and gave it to them. At that moment, open-eyed, wide-eyed, they recognized him. And then he disappeared.

32 Back and forth they talked. "Didn't we feel on fire as he conversed with us on the road, as he opened up the Scriptures for us?"

A GHOST DOESN'T HAVE MUSCLE AND BONE

33-34 They didn't waste a minute. They were up and on their way back to Jerusalem. They found the Eleven and their friends gathered together, talking away: "It's really happened! The Master has been raised up — Simon saw him!"

35 Then the two went over everything that happened on the road and how they recognized him when he broke the bread.

36-41 While they were saying all this, Jesus appeared to them and said, "Peace be with you." They thought they were seeing a ghost and were scared half to death. He continued with them, "Don't be upset, and don't let all these doubting questions take over. Look at my hands; look at my feet — it's really me. Touch me. Look me over from head to toe. A ghost doesn't have muscle and bone like this." As he said this, he showed them his hands and feet. They still couldn't believe what they were seeing. It was too much; it seemed too good to be true.

41-43 He asked, "Do you have any food here?" They gave him a piece of leftover fish they had cooked. He took it and ate it right before their eyes.

YOU'RE THE WITNESSES

44 Then he said, "Everything I told you while I was with you comes to this: All the things written about me in the Law of Moses, in the Prophets, and in the Psalms have to be fulfilled."

45-49 He went on to open their understanding of the Word of God, showing them how to read their Bibles this way. He said, "You can see now how it is written that the Messiah suffers, rises from the dead on the third day, and then a total life-change through the forgiveness of sins is proclaimed in his name to all nations — starting from here, from Jerusalem! You're the first to hear and see it. You're the witnesses. What comes next is very important: I am sending what my Father promised to you, so stay here in the city until he arrives, until you're equipped with power from on high."

50-51 He then led them out of the city over to Bethany. Raising his hands he blessed them, and while blessing them, took his leave, being carried up to heaven.

52-53 And they were on their knees, worshiping him. They returned to Jerusalem bursting with joy. They spent all their time in the Temple praising God. Yes.

JOHN

In Genesis, the first book of the Bible, God is presented as speaking the creation into existence. God speaks the word and it happens: heaven and earth, ocean and stream, trees and grass, birds and fish, animals and humans. Everything, seen and unseen, called into being by God's spoken word.

In deliberate parallel to the opening words of Genesis, John presents God as speaking salvation into existence. This time God's word takes on human form and enters history in the person of Jesus. Jesus speaks the word and it happens: forgiveness and judgment, healing and illumination, mercy and grace, joy and love, freedom and resurrection. Everything broken and fallen, sinful and diseased, called into salvation by God's spoken word.

For, somewhere along the line things went wrong (Genesis tells that story, too) and are in desperate need of fixing. The fixing is all accomplished by speaking—God speaking salvation into being in the person of Jesus. Jesus, in this account, not only speaks the word of God; he *is* the Word of God.

Keeping company with these words, we begin to realize that our words are more important than we ever supposed. Saying "I believe," for instance, marks the difference between life and death. Our words accrue dignity and gravity in conversations with Jesus. For Jesus doesn't impose salvation as a solution; he *narrates* salvation into being through leisurely conversation, intimate personal relationships, compassionate responses, passionate prayer, and—putting it all together—a sacrificial death. We don't casually walk away from words like that.

JOHN

THE LIFE-LIGHT

1-2 The Word was first,
        the Word present to God,
     God present to the Word.
     The Word was God,
        in readiness for God from day one.

3-5 Everything was created through him;
        nothing — not one thing! —
        came into being without him.
     What came into existence was Life,
        and the Life was Light to live by.
     The Life-Light blazed out of the darkness;
        the darkness couldn't put it out.

6-8 There once was a man, his name John, sent by God to point out the way
     to the Life-Light. He came to show everyone where to look, who to believe in.
     John was not himself the Light; he was there to show the way to the Light.

9-13 The Life-Light was the real thing:
        Every person entering Life
        he brings into Light.
      He was in the world,
        the world was there through him,
        and yet the world didn't even notice.
      He came to his own people,
        but they didn't want him.
      But whoever did want him,
        who believed he was who he claimed
        and would do what he said,
      He made to be their true selves,
        their child-of-God selves.
      These are the God-begotten,
        not blood-begotten,
        not flesh-begotten,
        not sex-begotten.

14 The Word became flesh and blood,
        and moved into the neighborhood.
    We saw the glory with our own eyes,
        the one-of-a-kind glory,
        like Father, like Son,
    Generous inside and out,
        true from start to finish.

15 John pointed him out and called, "This is the One! The One I told
    you was coming after me but in fact was ahead of me. He has always been

ahead of me, has always had the first word."

16-18
We all live off his generous bounty,
   gift after gift after gift.
We got the basics from Moses,
   and then this exuberant giving and receiving,
This endless knowing and understanding —
   all this came through Jesus, the Messiah.
No one has ever seen God,
   not so much as a glimpse.
This one-of-a-kind God-Expression,
   who exists at the very heart of the Father,
   has made him plain as day.

THUNDER IN THE DESERT

19-20
When Jews from Jerusalem sent a group of priests and officials to ask John who he was, he was completely honest. He didn't evade the question. He told the plain truth: "I am not the Messiah."

21
They pressed him, "Who, then? Elijah?"

"I am not."

"The Prophet?"

"No."

22
Exasperated, they said, "Who, then? We need an answer for those who sent us. Tell us something — anything! — about yourself."

23
"I'm thunder in the desert: 'Make the road straight for God!' I'm doing what the prophet Isaiah preached."

24-25
Those sent to question him were from the Pharisee party. Now they had a question of their own: "If you're neither the Messiah, nor Elijah, nor the Prophet, why do you baptize?"

26-27
John answered, "I only baptize using water. A person you don't recognize has taken his stand in your midst. He comes after me, but he is not in second place to me. I'm not even worthy to hold his coat for him."

28
These conversations took place in Bethany on the other side of the Jordan, where John was baptizing at the time.

THE GOD-REVEALER

29-31
The very next day John saw Jesus coming toward him and yelled out, "Here he is, God's Passover Lamb! He forgives the sins of the world! This is the man I've been talking about, 'the One who comes after me but is really ahead of me.' I knew nothing about who he was — only this: that my task has been to get Israel ready to recognize him as the God-Revealer. That is why I came here baptizing with water, giving you a good bath and scrubbing sins from your life so you can get a fresh start with God."

32-34
John clinched his witness with this: "I watched the Spirit, like a dove flying down out of the sky, making himself at home in him. I repeat, I know nothing about him except this: The One who authorized me to baptize with water told me, 'The One on whom you see the Spirit come down and stay, this One will baptize with the Holy Spirit.' That's exactly what I saw happen, and I'm telling you, there's no question about it: *This* is the Son of God."

COME, SEE FOR YOURSELF

35-36 The next day John was back at his post with two disciples, who were watching. He looked up, saw Jesus walking nearby, and said, "Here he is, God's Passover Lamb."

37-38 The two disciples heard him and went after Jesus. Jesus looked over his shoulder and said to them, "What are you after?"

They said, "Rabbi" (which means "Teacher"), "where are you staying?"

39 He replied, "Come along and see for yourself."

They came, saw where he was living, and ended up staying with him for the day. It was late afternoon when this happened.

40-42 Andrew, Simon Peter's brother, was one of the two who heard John's witness and followed Jesus. The first thing he did after finding where Jesus lived was find his own brother, Simon, telling him, "We've found the Messiah" (that is, "Christ"). He immediately led him to Jesus.

Jesus took one look up and said, "You're John's son, Simon? From now on your name is Cephas" (or Peter, which means "Rock").

43-44 The next day Jesus decided to go to Galilee. When he got there, he ran across Philip and said, "Come, follow me." (Philip's hometown was Bethsaida, the same as Andrew and Peter.)

45-46 Philip went and found Nathanael and told him, "We've found the One Moses wrote of in the Law, the One preached by the prophets. It's *Jesus*, Joseph's son, the one from Nazareth!" Nathanael said, "Nazareth? You've got to be kidding."

But Philip said, "Come, see for yourself."

47 When Jesus saw him coming he said, "There's a real Israelite, not a false bone in his body."

48 Nathanael said, "Where did you get that idea? You don't know me."

Jesus answered, "One day, long before Philip called you here, I saw you under the fig tree."

49 Nathanael exclaimed, "Rabbi! You are the Son of God, the King of Israel!"

50-51 Jesus said, "You've become a believer simply because I say I saw you one day sitting under the fig tree? You haven't seen anything yet! Before this is over you're going to see heaven open and God's angels descending to the Son of Man and ascending again."

FROM WATER TO WINE

1-3 Three days later there was a wedding in the village of Cana in Galilee. Jesus' mother was there. Jesus and his disciples were guests also. When they started running low on wine at the wedding banquet, Jesus' mother told him, "They're just about out of wine."

4 Jesus said, "Is that any of our business, Mother—yours or mine? This isn't my time. Don't push me."

5 She went ahead anyway, telling the servants, "Whatever he tells you, do it."

6-7 Six stoneware water pots were there, used by the Jews for ritual washings. Each held twenty to thirty gallons. Jesus ordered the servants, "Fill the pots with water." And they filled them to the brim.

8 "Now fill your pitchers and take them to the host," Jesus said, and they did.

9-10 When the host tasted the water that had become wine (he didn't know what had just happened but the servants, of course, knew), he called out to the bridegroom, "Everybody I know begins with their finest wines and after the guests have had their fill brings in the cheap stuff. But you've saved the best till now!"

11 This act in Cana of Galilee was the first sign Jesus gave, the first glimpse of his glory. And his disciples believed in him.

12 After this he went down to Capernaum along with his mother, brothers, and disciples, and stayed several days.

TEAR DOWN THIS TEMPLE . . .

13-14 When the Passover Feast, celebrated each spring by the Jews, was about to take place, Jesus traveled up to Jerusalem. He found the Temple teeming with people selling cattle and sheep and doves. The loan sharks were also there in full strength.

15-17 Jesus put together a whip out of strips of leather and chased them out of the Temple, stampeding the sheep and cattle, upending the tables of the loan sharks, spilling coins left and right. He told the dove merchants, "Get your things out of here! Stop turning my Father's house into a shopping mall!" That's when his disciples remembered the Scripture, "Zeal for your house consumes me."

18-19 But the Jews were upset. They asked, "What credentials can you present to justify this?" Jesus answered, "Tear down this Temple and in three days I'll put it back together."

20-22 They were indignant: "It took forty-six years to build this Temple, and you're going to rebuild it in three days?" But Jesus was talking about his body as the Temple. Later, after he was raised from the dead, his disciples remembered he had said this. They then put two and two together and believed both what was written in Scripture and what Jesus had said.

23-25 During the time he was in Jerusalem, those days of the Passover Feast, many people noticed the signs he was displaying and, seeing they pointed straight to God, entrusted their lives to him. But Jesus didn't entrust his life to them. He knew them inside and out, knew how untrustworthy they were. He didn't need any help in seeing right through them.

BORN FROM ABOVE

1-2 There was a man of the Pharisee sect, Nicodemus, a prominent leader among the Jews. Late one night he visited Jesus and said, "Rabbi, we all know you're a teacher straight from God. No one could do all the God-pointing, God-revealing acts you do if God weren't in on it."

3 Jesus said, "You're absolutely right. Take it from me: Unless a person is born from above, it's not possible to see what I'm pointing to—to God's kingdom."

4 "How can anyone," said Nicodemus, "be born who has already been born and grown up? You can't re-enter your mother's womb and be born again. What are you saying with this 'born-from-above' talk?"

5-6 Jesus said, "You're not listening. Let me say it again. Unless a person submits to this original creation—the 'wind-hovering-over-the-water' creation, the invisible moving the visible, a baptism into a new life—it's not possible to enter God's kingdom. When you look at a baby, it's just that: a body you can look at and touch. But the person who takes shape within is formed by something you can't see and touch — the Spirit — and becomes a living spirit.

7-8 "So don't be so surprised when I tell you that you have to be 'born from above' — out of this world, so to speak. You know well enough how the wind blows this way and that. You hear it rustling through the trees, but you have no idea where it comes from or where it's headed next. That's the way it is with everyone 'born from above' by the wind of God, the Spirit of God."

9 Nicodemus asked, "What do you mean by this? How does this happen?"

10-12 Jesus said, "You're a respected teacher of Israel and you don't know these basics? Listen carefully. I'm speaking sober truth to you. I speak only of what I know by experience; I give witness only to what I have seen with my own eyes. There is nothing secondhand here, no hearsay. Yet instead of facing the evidence and accepting it, you procrastinate with questions. If I tell you things that are plain as the hand before your face and you don't believe me, what use is there in telling you of things you can't see, the things of God?

13-15 "No one has ever gone up into the presence of God except the One who came down from that Presence, the Son of Man. In the same way that Moses lifted the serpent in the desert so people could have something to see and then believe, it is necessary for the Son of Man to be lifted up — and everyone who looks up to him, trusting and expectant, will gain a real life, eternal life.

16-18 "This is how much God loved the world: He gave his Son, his one and only Son. And this is why: so that no one need be destroyed; by believing in him, anyone can have a whole and lasting life. God didn't go to all the trouble of sending his Son merely to point an accusing finger, telling the world how bad it was. He came to help, to put the world right again. Anyone who trusts in him is acquitted; anyone who refuses to trust him has long since been under the death sentence without knowing it. And why? Because of that person's failure to believe in the one-of-a-kind Son of God when introduced to him.

19-21 "This is the crisis we're in: God-light streamed into the world, but men and women everywhere ran for the darkness. They went for the darkness because they were not really interested in pleasing God. Everyone who makes a practice of doing evil, addicted to denial and illusion, hates God-light and won't come near it, fearing a painful exposure. But anyone working and living in truth and reality welcomes God-light so the work can be seen for the God-work it is."

THE BRIDEGROOM'S FRIEND

22-26 After this conversation, Jesus went on with his disciples into the Judean countryside and relaxed with them there. He was also baptizing. At the same time, John was baptizing over at Aenon near Salim, where water was abundant. This was before John was thrown into jail. John's disciples got into an argument with the establishment Jews over the nature of baptism. They came to John and said, "Rabbi, you know the one who was with you on the other side of the Jordan? The one you authorized with your witness? Well, he's now competing with us. He's baptizing, too, and everyone's going to him instead of us."

27-29 John answered, "It's not possible for a person to succeed — I'm talking about *eternal* success — without heaven's help. You yourselves were there when I made it public that I was not the Messiah but simply the one sent ahead of him to get things ready. The one who gets the bride is, by definition, the bridegroom. And the bridegroom's friend, his 'best man' — that's me — in place at his side where he can hear every word, is genuinely happy. How could he be jealous when he knows that the wedding is finished and the marriage is off to a good start?

29-30 "That's why my cup is running over. This is the assigned moment for him to move into the center, while I slip off to the sidelines.

31-33 "The One who comes from above is head and shoulders over other messengers from God. The earthborn is earthbound and speaks earth language; the heavenborn is in a league of his own. He sets out the evidence of what he saw and heard in heaven. No one wants to deal with these facts. But anyone who examines this evidence will come to stake his life on this: that God himself is the truth.

34-36 "The One that God sent speaks God's words. And don't think he rations out the Spirit in bits and pieces. The Father loves the Son extravagantly. He turned everything over to him so he could give it away — a lavish distribution of gifts. That is why whoever accepts and trusts the Son gets in on everything, life complete and forever! And that is also why the person who avoids and distrusts the Son is in the dark and doesn't see life. All he experiences of God is darkness, and an angry darkness at that."

The Woman at the Well

1-3 Jesus realized that the Pharisees were keeping count of the baptisms that he and John performed (although his disciples, not Jesus, did the actual baptizing). They had posted the score that Jesus was ahead, turning him and John into rivals in the eyes of the people. So Jesus left the Judean countryside and went back to Galilee.

4-6 To get there, he had to pass through Samaria. He came into Sychar, a Samaritan village that bordered the field Jacob had given his son Joseph. Jacob's well was still there. Jesus, worn out by the trip, sat down at the well. It was noon.

7-8 A woman, a Samaritan, came to draw water. Jesus said, "Would you give me a drink of water?" (His disciples had gone to the village to buy food for lunch.)

9 The Samaritan woman, taken aback, asked, "How come you, a Jew, are asking me, a Samaritan woman, for a drink?" (Jews in those days wouldn't be caught dead talking to Samaritans.)

10 Jesus answered, "If you knew the generosity of God and who I am, you would be asking *me* for a drink, and I would give you fresh, living water."

11-12 The woman said, "Sir, you don't even have a bucket to draw with, and this well is deep. So how are you going to get this 'living water'? Are you a better man than our ancestor Jacob, who dug this well and drank from it, he and his sons and livestock, and passed it down to us?"

13-14 Jesus said, "Everyone who drinks this water will get thirsty again and again. Anyone who drinks the water I give will never thirst — not ever. The water I give will be an artesian spring within, gushing fountains of endless life."

15 The woman said, "Sir, give me this water so I won't ever get thirsty, won't ever have to come back to this well again!"

16 He said, "Go call your husband and then come back."

17-18   "I have no husband," she said.

"That's nicely put: 'I have no husband.' You've had five husbands, and the man you're living with now isn't even your husband. You spoke the truth there, sure enough."

19-20   "Oh, so you're a prophet! Well, tell me this: Our ancestors worshiped God at this mountain, but you Jews insist that Jerusalem is the only place for worship, right?"

21-23   "Believe me, woman, the time is coming when you Samaritans will worship the Father neither here at this mountain nor there in Jerusalem. You worship guessing in the dark; we Jews worship in the clear light of day. God's way of salvation is made available through the Jews. But the time is coming—it has, in fact, come—when what you're called will not matter and where you go to worship will not matter.

23-24   "It's who you are and the way you live that count before God. Your worship must engage your spirit in the pursuit of truth. That's the kind of people the Father is out looking for: those who are simply and honestly *themselves* before him in their worship. God is sheer being itself—Spirit. Those who worship him must do it out of their very being, their spirits, their true selves, in adoration."

25   The woman said, "I don't know about that. I do know that the Messiah is coming. When he arrives, we'll get the whole story."

26   "I am he," said Jesus. "You don't have to wait any longer or look any further."

27   Just then his disciples came back. They were shocked. They couldn't believe he was talking with that kind of a woman. No one said what they were all thinking, but their faces showed it.

28-30   The woman took the hint and left. In her confusion she left her water pot. Back in the village she told the people, "Come see a man who knew all about the things I did, who knows me inside and out. Do you think this could be the Messiah?" And they went out to see for themselves.

It's Harvest Time

31   In the meantime, the disciples pressed him, "Rabbi, eat. Aren't you going to eat?"

32   He told them, "I have food to eat you know nothing about."

33   The disciples were puzzled. "Who could have brought him food?"

34-35   Jesus said, "The food that keeps me going is that I do the will of the One who sent me, finishing the work he started. As you look around right now, wouldn't you say that in about four months it will be time to harvest? Well, I'm telling you to open your eyes and take a good look at what's right in front of you. These Samaritan fields are ripe. It's harvest time!

36-38   "The Harvester isn't waiting. He's taking his pay, gathering in this grain that's ripe for eternal life. Now the Sower is arm in arm with the Harvester, triumphant. That's the truth of the saying, 'This one sows, that one harvests.' I sent you to harvest a field you never worked. Without lifting a finger, you have walked in on a field worked long and hard by others."

39-42   Many of the Samaritans from that village committed themselves to him because of the woman's witness: "He knew all about the things I did. He knows me inside and out!" They asked him to stay on, so Jesus stayed two days. A lot more people entrusted their lives to him when they heard what he had to say. They said to the woman, "We're no longer taking this on your say-so. We've heard it for ourselves and know it for sure. He's the Savior of the world!"

43-45 After the two days he left for Galilee. Now, Jesus knew well from experience that a prophet is not respected in the place where he grew up. So when he arrived in Galilee, the Galileans welcomed him, but only because they were impressed with what he had done in Jerusalem during the Passover Feast, not that they really had a clue about who he was or what he was up to.

46-48 Now he was back in Cana of Galilee, the place where he made the water into wine. Meanwhile in Capernaum, there was a certain official from the king's court whose son was sick. When he heard that Jesus had come from Judea to Galilee, he went and asked that he come down and heal his son, who was on the brink of death. Jesus put him off: "Unless you people are dazzled by a miracle, you refuse to believe."

49 But the court official wouldn't be put off. "Come down! It's life or death for my son."

50-51 Jesus simply replied, "Go home. Your son lives."

The man believed the bare word Jesus spoke and headed home. On his way back, his servants intercepted him and announced, "Your son lives!"

52-53 He asked them what time he began to get better. They said, "The fever broke yesterday afternoon at one o'clock." The father knew that that was the very moment Jesus had said, "Your son lives."

53-54 That clinched it. Not only he but his entire household believed. This was now the second sign Jesus gave after having come from Judea into Galilee.

EVEN ON THE SABBATH

1-6 5 Soon another Feast came around and Jesus was back in Jerusalem. Near the Sheep Gate in Jerusalem there was a pool, in Hebrew called *Bethesda*, with five alcoves. Hundreds of sick people — blind, crippled, paralyzed — were in these alcoves. One man had been an invalid there for thirty-eight years. When Jesus saw him stretched out by the pool and knew how long he had been there, he said, "Do you want to get well?"

7 The sick man said, "Sir, when the water is stirred, I don't have anybody to put me in the pool. By the time I get there, somebody else is already in."

8-9 Jesus said, "Get up, take your bedroll, start walking." The man was healed on the spot. He picked up his bedroll and walked off.

9-10 That day happened to be the Sabbath. The Jews stopped the healed man and said, "It's the Sabbath. You can't carry your bedroll around. It's against the rules."

11 But he told them, "The man who made me well told me to. He said, 'Take your bedroll and start walking.'"

12-13 They asked, "Who gave you the order to take it up and start walking?" But the healed man didn't know, for Jesus had slipped away into the crowd.

14 A little later Jesus found him in the Temple and said, "You look wonderful! You're well! Don't return to a sinning life or something worse might happen."

15-16 The man went back and told the Jews that it was Jesus who had made him well. That is why the Jews were out to get Jesus — because he did this kind of thing on the Sabbath.

17 But Jesus defended himself. "My Father is working straight through, even on the Sabbath. So am I."

18 That really set them off. The Jews were now not only out to expose him; they were out to *kill* him. Not only was he breaking the Sabbath, but he was calling God his own Father, putting himself on a level with God.

WHAT THE FATHER DOES, THE SON DOES

19-20 So Jesus explained himself at length. "I'm telling you this straight. The Son can't independently do a thing, only what he sees the Father doing. What the Father does, the Son does. The Father loves the Son and includes him in everything he is doing.

20-23 "But you haven't seen the half of it yet, for in the same way that the Father raises the dead and creates life, so does the Son. The Son gives life to anyone he chooses. Neither he nor the Father shuts anyone out. The Father handed all authority to judge over to the Son so that the Son will be honored equally with the Father. Anyone who dishonors the Son, dishonors the Father, for it was the Father's decision to put the Son in the place of honor.

24 "It's urgent that you listen carefully to this: Anyone here who believes what I am saying right now and aligns himself with the Father, who has in fact put me in charge, has at this very moment the real, lasting life and is no longer condemned to be an outsider. This person has taken a giant step from the world of the dead to the world of the living.

25-27 "It's urgent that you get this right: The time has arrived—I mean right now!—when dead men and women will hear the voice of the Son of God and, hearing, will come alive. Just as the Father has life in himself, he has conferred on the Son life in himself. And he has given him the authority, simply because he is the Son of Man, to decide and carry out matters of Judgment.

28-29 "Don't act so surprised at all this. The time is coming when everyone dead and buried will hear his voice. Those who have lived the right way will walk out into a resurrection Life; those who have lived the wrong way, into a resurrection Judgment.

30-33 "I can't do a solitary thing on my own: I listen, then I decide. You can trust my decision because I'm not out to get my own way but only to carry out orders. If I were simply speaking on my own account, it would be an empty, self-serving witness. But an independent witness confirms me, the most reliable Witness of all. Furthermore, you all saw and heard John, and he gave expert and reliable testimony about me, didn't he?

34-38 "But my purpose is not to get your vote, and not to appeal to mere human testimony. I'm speaking to you this way so that you will be saved. John was a torch, blazing and bright, and you were glad enough to dance for an hour or so in his bright light. But the witness that really confirms me far exceeds John's witness. It's the work the Father gave me to complete. These very tasks, as I go about completing them, confirm that the Father, in fact, sent me. The Father who sent me, confirmed me. And you missed it. You never heard his voice, you never saw his appearance. There is nothing left in your memory of his Message because you do not take his Messenger seriously.

39-40 "You have your heads in your Bibles constantly because you think you'll find eternal life there. But you miss the forest for the trees. These Scriptures are all about *me*! And here I am, standing right before you, and you aren't willing to receive from me the life you say you want.

41-44 "I'm not interested in crowd approval. And do you know why? Because I know you and your crowds. I know that love, especially God's love, is not on your working agenda. I came with the authority of my Father, and you either dismiss me or avoid me. If another came, acting self-important, you would welcome him with open arms. How do you expect to get anywhere with God when you spend all your time jockeying for position with each other, ranking your rivals and ignoring God?

45-47 "But don't think I'm going to accuse you before my Father. Moses, in whom you put so much stock, is your accuser. If you believed, really believed, what Moses said, you would believe me. He wrote of me. If you won't take seriously what *he* wrote, how can I expect you to take seriously what *I* speak?"

BREAD AND FISH FOR ALL

1-4 6 After this, Jesus went across the Sea of Galilee (some call it Tiberias). A huge crowd followed him, attracted by the miracles they had seen him do among the sick. When he got to the other side, he climbed a hill and sat down, surrounded by his disciples. It was nearly time for the Feast of Passover, kept annually by the Jews.

5-6 When Jesus looked out and saw that a large crowd had arrived, he said to Philip, "Where can we buy bread to feed these people?" He said this to stretch Philip's faith. He already knew what he was going to do.

7 Philip answered, "Two hundred silver pieces wouldn't be enough to buy bread for each person to get a piece."

8-9 One of the disciples — it was Andrew, brother to Simon Peter — said, "There's a little boy here who has five barley loaves and two fish. But that's a drop in the bucket for a crowd like this."

10-11 Jesus said, "Make the people sit down." There was a nice carpet of green grass in this place. They sat down, about five thousand of them. Then Jesus took the bread and, having given thanks, gave it to those who were seated. He did the same with the fish. All ate as much as they wanted.

12-13 When the people had eaten their fill, he said to his disciples, "Gather the leftovers so nothing is wasted." They went to work and filled twelve large baskets with leftovers from the five barley loaves.

14-15 The people realized that God was at work among them in what Jesus had just done. They said, "This is the Prophet for sure, God's Prophet right here in Galilee!" Jesus saw that in their enthusiasm, they were about to grab him and make him king, so he slipped off and went back up the mountain to be by himself.

16-21 In the evening his disciples went down to the sea, got in the boat, and headed back across the water to Capernaum. It had grown quite dark and Jesus had not yet returned. A huge wind blew up, churning the sea. They were maybe three or four miles out when they saw Jesus walking on the sea, quite near the boat. They were scared senseless, but he reassured them, "It's me. It's all right. Don't be afraid." So they took him on board. In no time they reached land — the exact spot they were headed to.

22-24 The next day the crowd that was left behind realized that there had been only one boat, and that Jesus had not gotten into it with his disciples. They had seen them go off without him. By now boats from Tiberias had pulled up near where they had eaten the bread blessed by the Master. So when the crowd realized he was gone and wasn't coming back, they piled into the Tiberias boats and headed for Capernaum, looking for Jesus.

25   When they found him back across the sea, they said, "Rabbi, when did you get here?"

26   Jesus answered, "You've come looking for me not because you saw God in my actions but because I fed you, filled your stomachs — and for free.

The Bread of Life

27   "Don't waste your energy striving for perishable food like that. Work for the food that sticks with you, food that nourishes your lasting life, food the Son of Man provides. He and what he does are guaranteed by God the Father to last."

28   To that they said, "Well, what do we do then to get in on God's works?"

29   Jesus said, "Throw your lot in with the One that God has sent. That kind of a commitment gets you in on God's works."

30-31   They waffled: "Why don't you give us a clue about who you are, just a hint of what's going on? When we see what's up, we'll commit ourselves. Show us what you can do. Moses fed our ancestors with bread in the desert. It says so in the Scriptures: 'He gave them bread from heaven to eat.'"

32-33   Jesus responded, "The real significance of that Scripture is not that Moses gave you bread from heaven but that my Father is right now offering you bread from heaven, the *real* bread. The Bread of God came down out of heaven and is giving life to the world."

34   They jumped at that: "Master, give us this bread, now and forever!"

35-38   Jesus said, "I am the Bread of Life. The person who aligns with me hungers no more and thirsts no more, ever. I have told you this explicitly because even though you have seen me in action, you don't really believe me. Every person the Father gives me eventually comes running to me. And once that person is with me, I hold on and don't let go. I came down from heaven not to follow my own whim but to accomplish the will of the One who sent me.

39-40   "This, in a nutshell, is that will: that everything handed over to me by the Father be completed — not a single detail missed — and at the wrap-up of time I have everything and everyone put together, upright and whole. This is what my Father wants: that anyone who sees the Son and trusts who he is and what he does and then aligns with him will enter *real* life, *eternal* life. My part is to put them on their feet alive and whole at the completion of time."

41-42   At this, because he said, "I am the Bread that came down from heaven," the Jews started arguing over him: "Isn't this the son of Joseph? Don't we know his father? Don't we know his mother? How can he now say, 'I came down out of heaven' and expect anyone to believe him?"

43-46   Jesus said, "Don't bicker among yourselves over me. You're not in charge here. The Father who sent me is in charge. He draws people to me — that's the only way you'll ever come. Only then do I do my work, putting people together, setting them on their feet, ready for the End. This is what the prophets meant when they wrote, 'And then they will all be personally taught by God.' Anyone who has spent any time at all listening to the Father, really listening and therefore learning, comes to me to be taught person-ally — to see it with his own eyes, hear it with his own ears, from me, since I have it firsthand from the Father. No one has seen the Father except the One who has his Being alongside the Father — and you can see *me.*

47-51 "I'm telling you the most solemn and sober truth now: Whoever believes in me has real life, eternal life. I am the Bread of Life. Your ancestors ate the manna bread in the desert and died. But now here is Bread that truly comes down out of heaven. Anyone eating this Bread will not die, ever. I am the Bread — living Bread! — who came down out of heaven. Anyone who eats this Bread will live — and forever! The Bread that I present to the world so that it can eat and live is myself, this flesh-and-blood self."

52 At this, the Jews started fighting among themselves: "How can this man serve up his flesh for a meal?"

53-58 But Jesus didn't give an inch. "Only insofar as you eat and drink flesh and blood, the flesh and blood of the Son of Man, do you have life within you. The one who brings a hearty appetite to this eating and drinking has eternal life and will be fit and ready for the Final Day. My flesh is real food and my blood is real drink. By eating my flesh and drinking my blood you enter into me and I into you. In the same way that the fully alive Father sent me here and I live because of him, so the one who makes a meal of me lives because of me. This is the Bread from heaven. Your ancestors ate bread and later died. Whoever eats this Bread will live always."

59 He said these things while teaching in the meeting place in Capernaum.

Too Tough to Swallow

60 Many among his disciples heard this and said, "This is tough teaching, too tough to swallow."

61-65 Jesus sensed that his disciples were having a hard time with this and said, "Does this throw you completely? What would happen if you saw the Son of Man ascending to where he came from? The Spirit can make life. Sheer muscle and willpower don't make anything happen. Every word I've spoken to you is a Spirit-word, and so it is life-making. But some of you are resisting, refusing to have any part in this." (Jesus knew from the start that some weren't going to risk themselves with him. He knew also who would betray him.) He went on to say, "This is why I told you earlier that no one is capable of coming to me on his own. You get to me only as a gift from the Father."

66-67 After this a lot of his disciples left. They no longer wanted to be associated with him. Then Jesus gave the Twelve their chance: "Do you also want to leave?"

68-69 Peter replied, "Master, to whom would we go? You have the words of real life, eternal life. We've already committed ourselves, confident that you are the Holy One of God."

70-71 Jesus responded, "Haven't I handpicked you, the Twelve? Still, one of you is a devil!" He was referring to Judas, son of Simon Iscariot. This man — one from the Twelve! — was even then getting ready to betray him.

1-2 Later Jesus was going about his business in Galilee. He didn't want to travel in Judea because the Jews there were looking for a chance to kill him. It was near the time of Tabernacles, a feast observed annually by the Jews.

3-5 His brothers said, "Why don't you leave here and go up to the Feast so your disciples can get a good look at the works you do? No one who intends to be publicly known does everything behind the scenes. If you're serious about what you are doing, come out in the open and show the world." His brothers were pushing him like this because they didn't believe in him either.

6-8 Jesus came back at them, "Don't crowd me. This isn't my time. It's your time — it's *always* your time; you have nothing to lose. The world has nothing against you, but it's up in arms against me. It's against me because I expose the evil behind its pretensions. You go ahead, go up to the Feast. Don't wait for me. I'm not ready. It's not the right time for me."

9-11 He said this and stayed on in Galilee. But later, after his family had gone up to the Feast, he also went. But he kept out of the way, careful not to draw attention to himself. The Jews were already out looking for him, asking around, "Where is that man?"

12-13 There was a lot of contentious talk about him circulating through the crowds. Some were saying, "He's a good man." But others said, "Not so. He's selling snake oil." This kind of talk went on in guarded whispers because of the intimidating Jewish leaders.

Could It Be the Messiah?

14-15 With the Feast already half over, Jesus showed up in the Temple, teaching. The Jews were impressed, but puzzled: "How does he know so much without being schooled?"

16-19 Jesus said, "I didn't make this up. What I teach comes from the One who sent me. Anyone who wants to do his will can test this teaching and know whether it's from God or whether I'm making it up. A person making things up tries to make himself look good. But someone trying to honor the one who sent him sticks to the facts and doesn't tamper with reality. It was Moses, wasn't it, who gave you God's Law? But none of you are living it. So why are you trying to kill me?"

20 The crowd said, "You're crazy! Who's trying to kill you? You're demon-possessed."

21-24 Jesus said, "I did one miraculous thing a few months ago, and you're still standing around getting all upset, wondering what I'm up to. Moses prescribed circumcision — originally it came not from Moses but from his ancestors — and so you circumcise a man, dealing with one part of his body, even if it's the Sabbath. You do this in order to preserve one item in the Law of Moses. So why are you upset with me because I made a man's whole body well on the Sabbath? Don't be nitpickers; use your head — and heart! — to discern what is right, to test what is authentically right."

25-27 That's when some of the people of Jerusalem said, "Isn't this the one they were out to kill? And here he is out in the open, saying whatever he pleases, and no one is stopping him. Could it be that the rulers know that he is, in fact, the Messiah? And yet we know where this man came from. The Messiah is going to come out of nowhere. Nobody is going to know where he comes from."

28-29 That provoked Jesus, who was teaching in the Temple, to cry out, "Yes, you think you know me and where I'm from, but that's not where I'm from. I didn't set myself up in business. My true origin is in the One who sent me, and you don't know him at all. I come from him — that's how I know him. He sent me here."

30-31 They were looking for a way to arrest him, but not a hand was laid on him because it wasn't yet God's time. Many from the crowd committed themselves in faith to him, saying, "Will the Messiah, when he comes, provide better or more convincing evidence than this?"

32-34 The Pharisees, alarmed at this seditious undertow going through the crowd, teamed up with the high priests and sent their police to arrest him. Jesus rebuffed them: "I am with you only a short time. Then I go on to the One who sent me. You will look for me, but you won't find me. Where I am, you can't come."

35-36 The Jews put their heads together. "Where do you think he is going that we won't be able to find him? Do you think he is about to travel to the Greek world to teach the Jews? What is he talking about, anyway: 'You will look for me, but you won't find me,' and 'Where I am, you can't come'?"

37-39 On the final and climactic day of the Feast, Jesus took his stand. He cried out, "If anyone thirsts, let him come to me and drink. Rivers of living water will brim and spill out of the depths of anyone who believes in me this way, just as the Scripture says." (He said this in regard to the Spirit, whom those who believed in him were about to receive. The Spirit had not yet been given because Jesus had not yet been glorified.)

40-44 Those in the crowd who heard these words were saying, "This has to be the Prophet." Others said, "He is the Messiah!" But others were saying, "The Messiah doesn't come from Galilee, does he? Don't the Scriptures tell us that the Messiah comes from David's line and from Bethlehem, David's village?" So there was a split in the crowd over him. Some went so far as wanting to arrest him, but no one laid a hand on him.

45 That's when the Temple police reported back to the high priests and Pharisees, who demanded, "Why didn't you bring him with you?"

46 The police answered, "Have you heard the way he talks? We've never heard anyone speak like this man."

47-49 The Pharisees said, "Are you carried away like the rest of the rabble? You don't see any of the leaders believing in him, do you? Or any from the Pharisees? It's only this crowd, ignorant of God's Law, that is taken in by him — and damned."

50-51 Nicodemus, the man who had come to Jesus earlier and was both a ruler and a Pharisee, spoke up. "Does our Law decide about a man's guilt without first listening to him and finding out what he is doing?"

52-53 But they cut him off. "Are you also campaigning for the Galilean? Examine the evidence. See if any prophet ever comes from Galilee."

Then they all went home.

To Throw the Stone

1-2 Jesus went across to Mount Olives, but he was soon back in the Temple again. Swarms of people came to him. He sat down and taught them.

3-6 The religion scholars and Pharisees led in a woman who had been caught in an act of adultery. They stood her in plain sight of everyone and said, "Teacher, this woman was caught red-handed in the act of adultery. Moses, in the Law, gives orders to stone such persons. What do you say?" They were trying to trap him into saying something incriminating so they could bring charges against him.

6-8 Jesus bent down and wrote with his finger in the dirt. They kept at him, badgering him. He straightened up and said, "The sinless one among you, go first: Throw the stone." Bending down again, he wrote some more in the dirt.

9-10 Hearing that, they walked away, one after another, beginning with the oldest. The woman was left alone. Jesus stood up and spoke to her. "Woman, where are they? Does no one condemn you?"

11 "No one, Master."

"Neither do I," said Jesus. "Go on your way. From now on, don't sin."

You're Missing God in All This

12 Jesus once again addressed them: "I am the world's Light. No one who follows me stumbles around in the darkness. I provide plenty of light to live in."

13 The Pharisees objected, "All we have is your word on this. We need more than this to go on."

14-18 Jesus replied, "You're right that you only have my word. But you can depend on it being true. I know where I've come from and where I go next. You don't know where I'm from or where I'm headed. You decide according to what you can see and touch. I don't make judgments like that. But even if I did, my judgment would be true because I wouldn't make it out of the narrowness of my experience but in the largeness of the One who sent me, the Father. That fulfills the conditions set down in God's Law: that you can count on the testimony of two witnesses. And that is what you have: You have my word and you have the word of the Father who sent me."

19 They said, "Where is this so-called Father of yours?"

Jesus said, "You're looking right at me and you don't see me. How do you expect to see the Father? If you knew me, you would at the same time know the Father."

20 He gave this speech in the Treasury while teaching in the Temple. No one arrested him because his time wasn't yet up.

21 Then he went over the same ground again. "I'm leaving and you are going to look for me, but you're missing God in this and are headed for a dead end. There is no way you can come with me."

22 The Jews said, "So, is he going to kill himself? Is that what he means by 'You can't come with me'?"

23-24 Jesus said, "You're tied down to the mundane; I'm in touch with what is beyond your horizons. You live in terms of what you see and touch. I'm living on other terms. I told you that you were missing God in all this. You're at a dead end. If you won't believe I am who I say I am, you're at the dead end of sins. You're missing God in your lives."

25-26 They said to him, "Just who are you anyway?"

Jesus said, "What I've said from the start. I have so many things to say that concern you, judgments to make that affect you, but if you don't accept the trustworthiness of the One who commanded my words and acts, none of it matters. That is who you are questioning — not me but the One who sent me."

27-29 They still didn't get it, didn't realize that he was referring to the Father. So Jesus tried again. "When you raise up the Son of Man, then you will know who I am — that I'm not making this up, but speaking only what the Father taught me. The One who sent me stays with me. He doesn't abandon me. He sees how much joy I take in pleasing him."

30 When he put it in these terms, many people decided to believe.

IF THE SON SETS YOU FREE

31-32 Then Jesus turned to the Jews who had claimed to believe in him. "If you stick with this, living out what I tell you, you are my disciples for sure. Then you will experience for yourselves the truth, and the truth will free you."

33 Surprised, they said, "But we're descendants of Abraham. We've never been slaves to anyone. How can you say, 'The truth will free you'?"

34-38 Jesus said, "I tell you most solemnly that anyone who chooses a life of sin is trapped in a dead-end life and is, in fact, a slave. A slave is a transient, who can't come and go at will. The Son, though, has an established position, the run of the house. So if the Son sets you free, you are free through and through. I know you are Abraham's descendants. But I also know that you are trying to kill me because my message hasn't yet penetrated your thick skulls. I'm talking about things I have seen while keeping company with the Father, and you just go on doing what you have heard from your father."

39-41 They were indignant. "Our father is Abraham!"

Jesus said, "If you were Abraham's children, you would have been doing the things Abraham did. And yet here you are trying to kill me, a man who has spoken to you the truth he got straight from God! Abraham never did that sort of thing. You persist in repeating the works of your father."

They said, "We're not bastards. We have a legitimate father: the one and only God."

42-47 "If God were your father," said Jesus, "you would love me, for I came from God and arrived here. I didn't come on my own. He sent me. Why can't you understand one word I say? Here's why: You can't handle it. You're from your father, the Devil, and all you want to do is please him. He was a killer from the very start. He couldn't stand the truth because there wasn't a shred of truth in him. When the Liar speaks, he makes it up out of his lying nature and fills the world with lies. I arrive on the scene, tell you the plain truth, and you refuse to have a thing to do with me. Can any one of you convict me of a single misleading word, a single sinful act? But if I'm telling the truth, why don't you believe me? Anyone on God's side listens to God's words. This is why you're not listening—because you're not on God's side."

I AM WHO I AM

48 The Jews then said, "That clinches it. We were right all along when we called you a Samaritan and said you were crazy—demon-possessed!"

49-51 Jesus said, "I'm not crazy. I simply honor my Father, while you dishonor me. I am not trying to get anything for myself. God intends something gloriously grand here and is making the decisions that will bring it about. I say this with absolute confidence. If you practice what I'm telling you, you'll never have to look death in the face."

52-53 At this point the Jews said, "Now we *know* you're crazy. Abraham died. The prophets died. And you show up saying, 'If you practice what I'm telling you, you'll never have to face death, not even a taste.' Are you greater than Abraham, who died? And the prophets died! Who do you think you are!"

54-56 Jesus said, "If I turned the spotlight on myself, it wouldn't amount to anything. But my Father, the same One you say is your Father, put me here at this time and place of splendor. You haven't recognized him in this. But I have. If I, in false modesty, said I didn't know what was going on, I would be as much of a liar as you are. But I do know, and I am doing what he says. Abraham—your 'father'—with jubilant faith looked down the corridors of history and saw my day coming. He saw it and cheered."

57 The Jews said, "You're not even fifty years old—and Abraham saw you?"

58 "Believe me," said Jesus, "*I am who I am* long before Abraham was anything."

59 That did it—pushed them over the edge. They picked up rocks to throw at him. But Jesus slipped away, getting out of the Temple.

True Blindness

1-2 Walking down the street, Jesus saw a man blind from birth. His disciples asked, "Rabbi, who sinned: this man or his parents, causing him to be born blind?"

3-5 Jesus said, "You're asking the wrong question. You're looking for someone to blame. There is no such cause-effect here. Look instead for what God can do. We need to be energetically at work for the One who sent me here, working while the sun shines. When night falls, the workday is over. For as long as I am in the world, there is plenty of light. I am the world's Light."

6-7 He said this and then spit in the dust, made a clay paste with the saliva, rubbed the paste on the blind man's eyes, and said, "Go, wash at the Pool of Siloam" (Siloam means "Sent"). The man went and washed—and saw.

8 Soon the town was buzzing. His relatives and those who year after year had seen him as a blind man begging were saying, "Why, isn't this the man we knew, who sat here and begged?"

9 Others said, "It's him all right!"

But others objected, "It's not the same man at all. It just looks like him."

He said, "It's me, the very one."

10 They said, "How did your eyes get opened?"

11 "A man named Jesus made a paste and rubbed it on my eyes and told me, 'Go to Siloam and wash.' I did what he said. When I washed, I saw."

12 "So where is he?"

"I don't know."

13-15 They marched the man to the Pharisees. This day when Jesus made the paste and healed his blindness was the Sabbath. The Pharisees grilled him again on how he had come to see. He said, "He put a clay paste on my eyes, and I washed, and now I see."

16 Some of the Pharisees said, "Obviously, this man can't be from God. He doesn't keep the Sabbath."

Others countered, "How can a bad man do miraculous, God-revealing things like this?" There was a split in their ranks.

17 They came back at the blind man, "You're the expert. He opened *your* eyes. What do you say about him?"

He said, "He is a prophet."

18-19 The Jews didn't believe it, didn't believe the man was blind to begin with. So they called the parents of the man now bright-eyed with sight. They asked them, "Is this your son, the one you say was born blind? So how is it that he now sees?"

20-23 His parents said, "We know he is our son, and we know he was born blind. But we don't know how he came to see—haven't a clue about who opened his eyes. Why don't you ask him? He's a grown man and can speak for himself." (His parents were talking like this because they were intimidated by the Jewish leaders, who had already decided that anyone who took a stand that this was the Messiah would be kicked out of the meeting place. That's why his parents said, "Ask him. He's a grown man.")

24   They called the man back a second time — the man who had been blind — and told him, "Give credit to God. We know this man is an impostor."

25   He replied, "I know nothing about that one way or the other. But I know one thing for sure: I was blind . . . I now see."

26   They said, "What did he do to you? How did he open your eyes?"

27   "I've told you over and over and you haven't listened. Why do you want to hear it again? Are you so eager to become his disciples?"

28-29   With that they jumped all over him. "*You* might be a disciple of that man, but we're disciples of Moses. We know for sure that God spoke to Moses, but we have no idea where this man even comes from."

30-33   The man replied, "This is amazing! You claim to know nothing about him, but the fact is, he opened my eyes! It's well known that God isn't at the beck and call of sinners, but listens carefully to anyone who lives in reverence and does his will. That someone opened the eyes of a man born blind has never been heard of — ever. If this man didn't come from God, he wouldn't be able to do anything."

34   They said, "You're nothing but dirt! How dare you take that tone with us!" Then they threw him out in the street.

35   Jesus heard that they had thrown him out, and went and found him. He asked him, "Do you believe in the Son of Man?"

36   The man said, "Point him out to me, sir, so that I can believe in him."

37   Jesus said, "You're looking right at him. Don't you recognize my voice?"

38   "Master, I believe," the man said, and worshiped him.

39   Jesus then said, "I came into the world to bring everything into the clear light of day, making all the distinctions clear, so that those who have never seen will see, and those who have made a great pretense of seeing will be exposed as blind."

40   Some Pharisees overheard him and said, "Does that mean you're calling us blind?"

41   Jesus said, "If you were really blind, you would be blameless, but since you claim to see everything so well, you're accountable for every fault and failure."

He Calls His Sheep by Name

1-5   **10** "Let me set this before you as plainly as I can. If a person climbs over or through the fence of a sheep pen instead of going through the gate, you know he's up to no good — a sheep rustler! The shepherd walks right up to the gate. The gatekeeper opens the gate to him and the sheep recognize his voice. He calls his own sheep by name and leads them out. When he gets them all out, he leads them and they follow because they are familiar with his voice. They won't follow a stranger's voice but will scatter because they aren't used to the sound of it."

6-10   Jesus told this simple story, but they had no idea what he was talking about. So he tried again. "I'll be explicit, then. I am the Gate for the sheep. All those others are up to no good — sheep stealers, every one of them. But the sheep didn't listen to them. I am the Gate. Anyone who goes through me will be cared for — will freely go in and out, and find pasture. A thief is only there to steal and kill and destroy. I came so they can have real and eternal life, more and better life than they ever dreamed of.

11-13 "I am the Good Shepherd. The Good Shepherd puts the sheep before himself, sacrifices himself if necessary. A hired man is not a real shepherd. The sheep mean nothing to him. He sees a wolf come and runs for it, leaving the sheep to be ravaged and scattered by the wolf. He's only in it for the money. The sheep don't matter to him.

14-18 "I am the Good Shepherd. I know my own sheep and my own sheep know me. In the same way, the Father knows me and I know the Father. I put the sheep before myself, sacrificing myself if necessary. You need to know that I have other sheep in addition to those in this pen. I need to gather and bring them, too. They'll also recognize my voice. Then it will be one flock, one Shepherd. This is why the Father loves me: because I freely lay down my life. And so I am free to take it up again. No one takes it from me. I lay it down of my own free will. I have the right to lay it down; I also have the right to take it up again. I received this authority personally from my Father."

19-21 This kind of talk caused another split in the Jewish ranks. A lot of them were saying, "He's crazy, a maniac — out of his head completely. Why bother listening to him?" But others weren't so sure: "These aren't the words of a crazy man. Can a 'maniac' open blind eyes?"

22-24 They were celebrating Hanukkah just then in Jerusalem. It was winter. Jesus was strolling in the Temple across Solomon's Porch. The Jews, circling him, said, "How long are you going to keep us guessing? If you're the Messiah, tell us straight out."

25-30 Jesus answered, "I told you, but you don't believe. Everything I have done has been authorized by my Father, actions that speak louder than words. You don't believe because you're not my sheep. My sheep recognize my voice. I know them, and they follow me. I give them real and eternal life. They are protected from the Destroyer for good. No one can steal them from out of my hand. The Father who put them under my care is so much greater than the Destroyer and Thief. No one could ever get them away from him. I and the Father are one heart and mind."

31-32 Again the Jews picked up rocks to throw at him. Jesus said, "I have made a present to you from the Father of a great many good actions. For which of these acts do you stone me?"

33 The Jews said, "We're not stoning you for anything good you did, but for what you said — this blasphemy of calling yourself God."

34-38 Jesus said, "I'm only quoting your inspired Scriptures, where God said, 'I tell you — you are gods.' If God called your ancestors 'gods' — and Scripture doesn't lie — why do you yell, 'Blasphemer! Blasphemer!' at the unique One the Father consecrated and sent into the world, just because I said, 'I am the Son of God'? If I don't do the things my Father does, well and good; don't believe me. But if I am doing them, put aside for a moment what you hear me say about myself and just take the evidence of the actions that are right before your eyes. Then perhaps things will come together for you, and you'll see that not only are we doing the same thing, we *are* the same — Father and Son. He is in me; I am in him."

39-42 They tried yet again to arrest him, but he slipped through their fingers.

He went back across the Jordan to the place where John first baptized, and stayed there. A lot of people followed him over. They were saying, "John did no miracles, but everything he said about this man has come true." Many believed in him then and there.

The Death of Lazarus

1-3   **11** A man was sick, Lazarus of Bethany, the town of Mary and her sister Martha. This was the same Mary who massaged the Lord's feet with aromatic oils and then wiped them with her hair. It was her brother Lazarus who was sick. So the sisters sent word to Jesus, "Master, the one you love so very much is sick."

4   When Jesus got the message, he said, "This sickness is not fatal. It will become an occasion to show God's glory by glorifying God's Son."

5-7   Jesus loved Martha and her sister and Lazarus, but oddly, when he heard that Lazarus was sick, he stayed on where he was for two more days. After the two days, he said to his disciples, "Let's go back to Judea."

8   They said, "Rabbi, you can't do that. The Jews are out to kill you, and you're going back?"

9-10   Jesus replied, "Are there not twelve hours of daylight? Anyone who walks in daylight doesn't stumble because there's plenty of light from the sun. Walking at night, he might very well stumble because he can't see where he's going."

11   He said these things, and then announced, "Our friend Lazarus has fallen asleep. I'm going to wake him up."

12-13   The disciples said, "Master, if he's gone to sleep, he'll get a good rest and wake up feeling fine." Jesus was talking about death, while his disciples thought he was talking about taking a nap.

14-15   Then Jesus became explicit: "Lazarus died. And I am glad for your sakes that I wasn't there. You're about to be given new grounds for believing. Now let's go to him."

16   That's when Thomas, the one called the Twin, said to his companions, "Come along. We might as well die with him."

17-20   When Jesus finally got there, he found Lazarus already four days dead. Bethany was near Jerusalem, only a couple of miles away, and many of the Jews were visiting Martha and Mary, sympathizing with them over their brother. Martha heard Jesus was coming and went out to meet him. Mary remained in the house.

21-22   Martha said, "Master, if you'd been here, my brother wouldn't have died. Even now, I know that whatever you ask God he will give you."

23   Jesus said, "Your brother will be raised up."

24   Martha replied, "I know that he will be raised up in the resurrection at the end of time."

25-26   "You don't have to wait for the End. I am, right now, Resurrection and Life. The one who believes in me, even though he or she dies, will live. And everyone who lives believing in me does not ultimately die at all. Do you believe this?"

27   "Yes, Master. All along I have believed that you are the Messiah, the Son of God who comes into the world."

28   After saying this, she went to her sister Mary and whispered in her ear, "The Teacher is here and is asking for you."

29-32   The moment she heard that, she jumped up and ran out to him. Jesus had not yet entered the town but was still at the place where Martha had met him. When her sympathizing Jewish friends saw Mary run off, they followed her, thinking she was on her way to the tomb to weep there. Mary came to where Jesus was waiting and fell at his feet, saying, "Master, if only you had been here, my brother would not have died."

33-34 When Jesus saw her sobbing and the Jews with her sobbing, a deep anger welled up within him. He said, "Where did you put him?"

34-35 "Master, come and see," they said. Now Jesus wept.

36 The Jews said, "Look how deeply he loved him."

37 Others among them said, "Well, if he loved him so much, why didn't he do something to keep him from dying? After all, he opened the eyes of a blind man."

38-39 Then Jesus, the anger again welling up within him, arrived at the tomb. It was a simple cave in the hillside with a slab of stone laid against it. Jesus said, "Remove the stone."

The sister of the dead man, Martha, said, "Master, by this time there's a stench. He's been dead four days!"

40 Jesus looked her in the eye. "Didn't I tell you that if you believed, you would see the glory of God?"

41-42 Then, to the others, "Go ahead, take away the stone." They removed the stone. Jesus raised his eyes to heaven and prayed, "Father, I'm grateful that you have listened to me. I know you always do listen, but on account of this crowd standing here I've spoken so that they might believe that you sent me."

43-44 Then he shouted, "Lazarus, come out!" And he came out, a cadaver, wrapped from head to toe, and with a kerchief over his face.

Jesus told them, "Unwrap him and let him loose."

THE MAN WHO CREATES GOD-SIGNS

45-48 That was a turnaround for many of the Jews who were with Mary. They saw what Jesus did, and believed in him. But some went back to the Pharisees and told on Jesus. The high priests and Pharisees called a meeting of the Jewish ruling body. "What do we do now?" they asked. "This man keeps on doing things, creating God-signs. If we let him go on, pretty soon everyone will be believing in him and the Romans will come and remove what little power and privilege we still have."

49-52 Then one of them — it was Caiaphas, the designated Chief Priest that year — spoke up, "Don't you know anything? Can't you see that it's to our advantage that one man dies for the people rather than the whole nation be destroyed?" He didn't say this of his own accord, but as Chief Priest that year he unwittingly prophesied that Jesus was about to die sacrificially for the nation, and not only for the nation but so that all God's exile-scattered children might be gathered together into one people.

53-54 From that day on, they plotted to kill him. So Jesus no longer went out in public among the Jews. He withdrew into the country bordering the desert to a town called Ephraim and secluded himself there with his disciples.

55-56 The Jewish Passover was coming up. Crowds of people were making their way from the country up to Jerusalem to get themselves ready for the Feast. They were curious about Jesus. There was a lot of talk of him among those standing around in the Temple: "What do you think? Do you think he'll show up at the Feast or not?"

57   Meanwhile, the high priests and Pharisees gave out the word that anyone getting wind of him should inform them. They were all set to arrest him.

ANOINTING HIS FEET

1-3   **12** Six days before Passover, Jesus entered Bethany where Lazarus, so recently raised from the dead, was living. Lazarus and his sisters invited Jesus to dinner at their home. Martha served. Lazarus was one of those sitting at the table with them. Mary came in with a jar of very expensive aromatic oils, anointed and massaged Jesus' feet, and then wiped them with her hair. The fragrance of the oils filled the house.

4-6   Judas Iscariot, one of his disciples, even then getting ready to betray him, said, "Why wasn't this oil sold and the money given to the poor? It would have easily brought three hundred silver pieces." He said this not because he cared two cents about the poor but because he was a thief. He was in charge of their common funds, but also embezzled them.

7-8   Jesus said, "Let her alone. She's anticipating and honoring the day of my burial. You always have the poor with you. You don't always have me."

9-11   Word got out among the Jews that he was back in town. The people came to take a look, not only at Jesus but also at Lazarus, who had been raised from the dead. So the high priests plotted to kill Lazarus because so many of the Jews were going over and believing in Jesus on account of him.

SEE HOW YOUR KING COMES

12-15   The next day the huge crowd that had arrived for the Feast heard that Jesus was entering Jerusalem. They broke off palm branches and went out to meet him. And they cheered:

> Hosanna!
> Blessed is he who comes in God's name!
> Yes! The King of Israel!

Jesus got a young donkey and rode it, just as the Scripture has it:

> No fear, Daughter Zion:
>   See how your king comes,
>   riding a donkey's colt.

16   The disciples didn't notice the fulfillment of many Scriptures at the time, but after Jesus was glorified, they remembered that what was written about him matched what was done to him.

17-19   The crowd that had been with him when he called Lazarus from the tomb, raising him from the dead, was there giving eyewitness accounts. It was because they had spread the word of this latest God-sign that the crowd swelled to a welcoming parade. The Pharisees took one look and threw up their hands: "It's out of control. The world's in a stampede after him."

A GRAIN OF WHEAT MUST DIE

20-21   There were some Greeks in town who had come up to worship at the Feast. They approached Philip, who was from Bethsaida in Galilee: "Sir, we want to see Jesus. Can you help us?"

22-23 Philip went and told Andrew. Andrew and Philip together told Jesus. Jesus answered, "Time's up. The time has come for the Son of Man to be glorified.

24-25 "Listen carefully: Unless a grain of wheat is buried in the ground, dead to the world, it is never any more than a grain of wheat. But if it is buried, it sprouts and reproduces itself many times over. In the same way, anyone who holds on to life just as it is destroys that life. But if you let it go, reckless in your love, you'll have it forever, real and eternal.

26 "If any of you wants to serve me, then follow me. Then you'll be where I am, ready to serve at a moment's notice. The Father will honor and reward anyone who serves me.

27-28 "Right now I am storm-tossed. And what am I going to say? 'Father, get me out of this'? No, this is why I came in the first place. I'll say, 'Father, put your glory on display.'"

A voice came out of the sky: "I have glorified it, and I'll glorify it again."

29 The listening crowd said, "Thunder!"

Others said, "An angel spoke to him!"

30-33 Jesus said, "The voice didn't come for me but for you. At this moment the world is in crisis. Now Satan, the ruler of this world, will be thrown out. And I, as I am lifted up from the earth, will attract everyone to me and gather them around me." He put it this way to show how he was going to be put to death.

34 Voices from the crowd answered, "We heard from God's Law that the Messiah lasts forever. How can it be necessary, as you put it, that the Son of Man 'be lifted up'? Who is this 'Son of Man'?"

35-36 Jesus said, "For a brief time still, the light is among you. Walk by the light you have so darkness doesn't destroy you. If you walk in darkness, you don't know where you're going. As you have the light, believe in the light. Then the light will be within you, and shining through your lives. You'll be children of light."

THEIR EYES ARE BLINDED

36-40 Jesus said all this, and then went into hiding. All these God-signs he had given them and they still didn't get it, still wouldn't trust him. This proved that the prophet Isaiah was right:

God, who believed what we preached?
Who recognized God's arm, outstretched and ready to act?

First they wouldn't believe, then they *couldn't* — again, just as Isaiah said:

Their eyes are blinded,
    their hearts are hardened,
So that they wouldn't see with their eyes
    and perceive with their hearts,
And turn to me, God,
    so I could heal them.

41 Isaiah said these things after he got a glimpse of God's cascading brightness that would pour through the Messiah.

42-43 On the other hand, a considerable number from the ranks of the leaders did believe. But because of the Pharisees, they didn't come out in the open with it. They were afraid of getting kicked out of the meeting place. When push came to shove they cared more for human approval than for God's glory.

44-46 Jesus summed it all up when he cried out, "Whoever believes in me, believes not just in me but in the One who sent me. Whoever looks at me is looking, in fact, at the One who sent me. I am Light that has come into the world so that all who believe in me won't have to stay any longer in the dark.

47-50 "If anyone hears what I am saying and doesn't take it seriously, I don't reject him. I didn't come to reject the world; I came to save the world. But you need to know that whoever puts me off, refusing to take in what I'm saying, is willfully choosing rejection. The Word, the Word-made-flesh that I have spoken and that I am, *that* Word and no other is the last word. I'm not making any of this up on my own. The Father who sent me gave me orders, told me what to say and how to say it. And I know exactly what his command produces: real and eternal life. That's all I have to say. What the Father told me, I tell you."

WASHING HIS DISCIPLES' FEET

1-2 13 Just before the Passover Feast, Jesus knew that the time had come to leave this world to go to the Father. Having loved his dear companions, he continued to love them right to the end. It was suppertime. The Devil by now had Judas, son of Simon the Iscariot, firmly in his grip, all set for the betrayal.

3-6 Jesus knew that the Father had put him in complete charge of everything, that he came from God and was on his way back to God. So he got up from the supper table, set aside his robe, and put on an apron. Then he poured water into a basin and began to wash the feet of the disciples, drying them with his apron. When he got to Simon Peter, Peter said, "Master, *you* wash *my* feet?"

7 Jesus answered, "You don't understand now what I'm doing, but it will be clear enough to you later."

8 Peter persisted, "You're not going to wash my feet — ever!"

Jesus said, "If I don't wash you, you can't be part of what I'm doing."

9 "Master!" said Peter. "Not only my feet, then. Wash my hands! Wash my head!"

10-12 Jesus said, "If you've had a bath in the morning, you only need your feet washed now and you're clean from head to toe. My concern, you understand, is holiness, not hygiene. So now you're clean. But not every one of you." (He knew who was betraying him. That's why he said, "Not every one of you.") After he had finished washing their feet, he took his robe, put it back on, and went back to his place at the table.

12-17 Then he said, "Do you understand what I have done to you? You address me as 'Teacher' and 'Master,' and rightly so. That is what I am. So if I, the Master and Teacher, washed your feet, you must now wash each other's feet. I've laid down a pattern for you. What I've done, you do. I'm only pointing out the obvious. A servant is not ranked above his master; an employee doesn't give orders to the employer. If you understand what I'm telling you, act like it — and live a blessed life.

THE ONE WHO ATE BREAD AT MY TABLE

18-20 "I'm not including all of you in this. I know precisely whom I've selected, so as not to interfere with the fulfillment of this Scripture:

The one who ate bread at my table
Turned on his heel against me.

"I'm telling you all this ahead of time so that when it happens you will believe that I am who I say I am. Make sure you get this right: Receiving someone I send is the same as receiving me, just as receiving me is the same as receiving the One who sent me."

21 After he said these things, Jesus became visibly upset, and then he told them why. "One of you is going to betray me."

22-25 The disciples looked around at one another, wondering who on earth he was talking about. One of the disciples, the one Jesus loved dearly, was reclining against him, his head on his shoulder. Peter motioned to him to ask who Jesus might be talking about. So, being the closest, he said, "Master, who?"

26-27 Jesus said, "The one to whom I give this crust of bread after I've dipped it." Then he dipped the crust and gave it to Judas, son of Simon the Iscariot. As soon as the bread was in his hand, Satan entered him.

"What you must do," said Jesus, "do. Do it and get it over with."

28-29 No one around the supper table knew why he said this to him. Some thought that since Judas was their treasurer, Jesus was telling him to buy what they needed for the Feast, or that he should give something to the poor.

30 Judas, with the piece of bread, left. It was night.

A NEW COMMAND

31-32 When he had left, Jesus said, "Now the Son of Man is seen for who he is, and God seen for who he is in him. The moment God is seen in him, God's glory will be on display. In glorifying him, he himself is glorified — glory all around!

33 "Children, I am with you for only a short time longer. You are going to look high and low for me. But just as I told the Jews, I'm telling you: 'Where I go, you are not able to come.'

34-35 "Let me give you a new command: Love one another. In the same way I loved you, you love one another. This is how everyone will recognize that you are my disciples — when they see the love you have for each other."

36 Simon Peter asked, "Master, just where are you going?"

Jesus answered, "You can't now follow me where I'm going. You will follow later."

37 "Master," said Peter, "why can't I follow now? I'll lay down my life for you!"

38 "Really? You'll lay down your life for me? The truth is that before the rooster crows, you'll deny me three times."

THE ROAD

1-4 **14** "Don't let this throw you. You trust God, don't you? Trust me. There is plenty of room for you in my Father's home. If that weren't so, would I have told you that I'm on my way to get a room ready for you? And if I'm on my way to get your room ready, I'll come back and get you so you can live where I live. And you already know the road I'm taking."

5   Thomas said, "Master, we have no idea where you're going. How do you expect us to know the road?"

6-7   Jesus said, "I am the Road, also the Truth, also the Life. No one gets to the Father apart from me. If you really knew me, you would know my Father as well. From now on, you do know him. You've even seen him!"

8   Philip said, "Master, show us the Father; then we'll be content."

9-10   "You've been with me all this time, Philip, and you still don't understand? To see me is to see the Father. So how can you ask, 'Where is the Father?' Don't you believe that I am in the Father and the Father is in me? The words that I speak to you aren't mere words. I don't just make them up on my own. The Father who resides in me crafts each word into a divine act.

11-14   "Believe me: I am in my Father and my Father is in me. If you can't believe that, believe what you see—these works. The person who trusts me will not only do what I'm doing but even greater things, because I, on my way to the Father, am giving you the same work to do that I've been doing. You can count on it. From now on, whatever you request along the lines of who I am and what I am doing, I'll do it. That's how the Father will be seen for who he is in the Son. I mean it. Whatever you request in this way, I'll do.

THE SPIRIT OF TRUTH

15-17   "If you love me, show it by doing what I've told you. I will talk to the Father, and he'll provide you another Friend so that you will always have someone with you. This Friend is the Spirit of Truth. The godless world can't take him in because it doesn't have eyes to see him, doesn't know what to look for. But you know him already because he has been staying with you, and will even be *in* you!

18-20   "I will not leave you orphaned. I'm coming back. In just a little while the world will no longer see me, but you're going to see me because I am alive and you're about to come alive. At that moment you will know absolutely that I'm in my Father, and you're in me, and I'm in you.

21   "The person who knows my commandments and keeps them, that's who loves me. And the person who loves me will be loved by my Father, and I will love him and make myself plain to him."

22   Judas (not Iscariot) said, "Master, why is it that you are about to make yourself plain to us but not to the world?"

23-24   "Because a loveless world," said Jesus, "is a sightless world. If anyone loves me, he will carefully keep my word and my Father will love him—we'll move right into the neighborhood! Not loving me means not keeping my words. The message you are hearing isn't mine. It's the message of the Father who sent me.

25-27   "I'm telling you these things while I'm still living with you. The Friend, the Holy Spirit whom the Father will send at my request, will make everything plain to you. He will remind you of all the things I have told you. I'm leaving you well and whole. That's my parting gift to you. Peace. I don't leave you the way you're used to being left—feeling abandoned, bereft. So don't be upset. Don't be distraught.

28   "You've heard me tell you, 'I'm going away, and I'm coming back.'

If you loved me, you would be glad that I'm on my way to the Father because the Father is the goal and purpose of my life.

29-31 "I've told you this ahead of time, before it happens, so that when it does happen, the confirmation will deepen your belief in me. I'll not be talking with you much more like this because the chief of this godless world is about to attack. But don't worry — he has nothing on me, no claim on me. But so the world might know how thoroughly I love the Father, I am carrying out my Father's instructions right down to the last detail.

"Get up. Let's go. It's time to leave here."

THE VINE AND THE BRANCHES

1-3 **15** "I am the Real Vine and my Father is the Farmer. He cuts off every branch of me that doesn't bear grapes. And every branch that is grape-bearing he prunes back so it will bear even more. You are already pruned back by the message I have spoken.

4 "Live in me. Make your home in me just as I do in you. In the same way that a branch can't bear grapes by itself but only by being joined to the vine, you can't bear fruit unless you are joined with me.

5-8 "I am the Vine, you are the branches. When you're joined with me and I with you, the relation intimate and organic, the harvest is sure to be abundant. Separated, you can't produce a thing. Anyone who separates from me is deadwood, gathered up and thrown on the bonfire. But if you make yourselves at home with me and my words are at home in you, you can be sure that whatever you ask will be listened to and acted upon. This is how my Father shows who he is — when you produce grapes, when you mature as my disciples.

9-10 "I've loved you the way my Father has loved me. Make yourselves at home in my love. If you keep my commands, you'll remain intimately at home in my love. That's what I've done — kept my Father's commands and made myself at home in his love.

11-15 "I've told you these things for a purpose: that my joy might be your joy, and your joy wholly mature. This is my command: Love one another the way I loved you. This is the very best way to love. Put your life on the line for your friends. You are my friends when you do the things I command you. I'm no longer calling you servants because servants don't understand what their master is thinking and planning. No, I've named you friends because I've let you in on everything I've heard from the Father.

16 "You didn't choose me, remember; I chose you, and put you in the world to bear fruit, fruit that won't spoil. As fruit bearers, whatever you ask the Father in relation to me, he gives you.

17 "But remember the root command: Love one another.

HATED BY THE WORLD

18-19 "If you find the godless world is hating you, remember it got its start hating me. If you lived on the world's terms, the world would love you as one of its own. But since I picked you to live on God's terms and no longer on the world's terms, the world is going to hate you.

20 "When that happens, remember this: Servants don't get better treatment than their masters. If they beat on me, they will certainly beat on you. If they did what I told them, they will do what you tell them.

21-25 "They are going to do all these things to you because of the way they treated me, because they don't know the One who sent me. If I hadn't come and told them all this in plain language, it wouldn't be so bad. As it is, they have no excuse. Hate me, hate my Father — it's all the same. If I hadn't done what I have done among them, works no one has *ever* done, they wouldn't be to blame. But they saw the God-signs and hated anyway, both me and my Father. Interesting — they have verified the truth of their own Scriptures where it is written, 'They hated me for no good reason.'

26-27   "When the Friend I plan to send you from the Father comes — the Spirit of Truth issuing from the Father — he will confirm everything about me. You, too, from your side must give your confirming evidence, since you are in this with me from the start."

1-4 **16** "I've told you these things to prepare you for rough times ahead. They are going to throw you out of the meeting places. There will even come a time when anyone who kills you will think he's doing God a favor. They will do these things because they never really understood the Father. I've told you these things so that when the time comes and they start in on you, you'll be well-warned and ready for them.

The Friend Will Come

4-7   "I didn't tell you this earlier because I was with you every day. But now I am on my way to the One who sent me. Not one of you has asked, 'Where are you going?' Instead, the longer I've talked, the sadder you've become. So let me say it again, this truth: It's better for you that I leave. If I don't leave, the Friend won't come. But if I go, I'll send him to you.

8-11   "When he comes, he'll expose the error of the godless world's view of sin, righteousness, and judgment: He'll show them that their refusal to believe in me is their basic sin; that righteousness comes from above, where I am with the Father, out of their sight and control; that judgment takes place as the ruler of this godless world is brought to trial and convicted.

12-15   "I still have many things to tell you, but you can't handle them now. But when the Friend comes, the Spirit of the Truth, he will take you by the hand and guide you into all the truth there is. He won't draw attention to himself, but will make sense out of what is about to happen and, indeed, out of all that I have done and said. He will honor me; he will take from me and deliver it to you. Everything the Father has is also mine. That is why I've said, 'He takes from me and delivers to you.'

16   "In a day or so you're not going to see me, but then in another day or so you will see me."

Joy Like a River Overflowing

17-18   That stirred up a hornet's nest of questions among the disciples: "What's he talking about: 'In a day or so you're not going to see me, but then in another day or so you will see me'? And, 'Because I'm on my way to the Father'? What is this 'day or so'? We don't know what he's talking about."

19-20   Jesus knew they were dying to ask him what he meant, so he said, "Are you trying to figure out among yourselves what I meant when I said, 'In a day or so you're not going to see me, but then in another day or so you will see me'? Then fix this firmly in your minds: You're going to be in deep mourning while the godless world throws a party. You'll be sad, very sad, but your sadness will develop into gladness.

21-23   "When a woman gives birth, she has a hard time, there's no getting around it. But when the baby is born, there is joy in the birth. This new life in the world wipes out memory of the pain. The sadness you have right now is similar to that pain, but the coming joy is also similar. When I see you again, you'll be full of joy, and it will be a joy no one can rob from you. You'll no longer be so full of questions.

23-24   "This is what I want you to do: Ask the Father for whatever is in keeping with the things I've revealed to you. Ask in my name, according to my will, and he'll most certainly give it to you. Your joy will be a river overflowing its banks!

25-28   "I've used figures of speech in telling you these things. Soon I'll drop the figures and tell you about the Father in plain language. Then you can make your requests directly to him in relation to this life I've revealed to you. I won't continue making requests of the Father on your behalf. I won't need to. Because you've gone out on a limb, committed yourselves to love and trust in me, believing I came directly from the Father, the Father loves you directly. First, I left the Father and arrived in the world; now I leave the world and travel to the Father."

29-30   His disciples said, "Finally! You're giving it to us straight, in plain talk—no more figures of speech. Now we know that you know everything—it all comes together in you. You won't have to put up with our questions anymore. We're convinced you came from God."

31-33   Jesus answered them, "Do you finally believe? In fact, you're about to make a run for it—saving your own skins and abandoning me. But I'm not abandoned. The Father is with me. I've told you all this so that trusting me, you will be unshakable and assured, deeply at peace. In this godless world you will continue to experience difficulties. But take heart! I've conquered the world."

JESUS' PRAYER FOR HIS FOLLOWERS

1-5   **17** Jesus said these things. Then, raising his eyes in prayer, he said:

Father, it's time.
Display the bright splendor of your Son
So the Son in turn may show your bright splendor.
You put him in charge of everything human
So he might give real and eternal life to all in his charge.
And this is the real and eternal life:
That they know you,
The one and only true God,
And Jesus Christ, whom you sent.
I glorified you on earth
By completing down to the last detail
What you assigned me to do.
And now, Father, glorify me with your very own splendor,
The very splendor I had in your presence
Before there was a world.

6-12   I spelled out your character in detail
To the men and women you gave me.

They were yours in the first place;
Then you gave them to me,
And they have now done what you said.
They know now, beyond the shadow of a doubt,
That everything you gave me is firsthand from you,
For the message you gave me, I gave them;
And they took it, and were convinced
That I came from you.
They believed that you sent me.
I pray for them.
I'm not praying for the God-rejecting world
But for those you gave me,
For they are yours by right.
Everything mine is yours, and yours mine,
And my life is on display in them.
For I'm no longer going to be visible in the world;
They'll continue in the world
While I return to you.
Holy Father, guard them as they pursue this life
That you conferred as a gift through me,
So they can be one heart and mind
As we are one heart and mind.
As long as I was with them, I guarded them
In the pursuit of the life you gave through me;
I even posted a night watch.
And not one of them got away,
Except for the rebel bent on destruction
(the exception that proved the rule of Scripture).

13-19   Now I'm returning to you.
I'm saying these things in the world's hearing
So my people can experience
My joy completed in them.
I gave them your word;
The godless world hated them because of it,
Because they didn't join the world's ways,
Just as I didn't join the world's ways.
I'm not asking that you take them out of the world
But that you guard them from the Evil One.
They are no more defined by the world
Than I am defined by the world.
Make them holy — consecrated — with the truth;
Your word is consecrating truth.
In the same way that you gave me a mission in the world,
I give them a mission in the world.
I'm consecrating myself for their sakes
So they'll be truth-consecrated in their mission.

20-23
I'm praying not only for them
But also for those who will believe in me
Because of them and their witness about me.
The goal is for all of them to become one heart and mind —
Just as you, Father, are in me and I in you,
So they might be one heart and mind with us.
Then the world might believe that you, in fact, sent me.
The same glory you gave me, I gave them,
So they'll be as unified and together as we are —
I in them and you in me.
Then they'll be mature in this oneness,
And give the godless world evidence
That you've sent me and loved them
In the same way you've loved me.

24-26
Father, I want those you gave me
To be with me, right where I am,
So they can see my glory, the splendor you gave me,
Having loved me
Long before there ever was a world.
Righteous Father, the world has never known you,
But I have known you, and these disciples know
That you sent me on this mission.
I have made your very being known to them —
Who you are and what you do —
And continue to make it known,
So that your love for me
Might be in them
Exactly as I am in them.

SEIZED IN THE GARDEN AT NIGHT

1
18 Jesus, having prayed this prayer, left with his disciples and crossed over the brook Kidron at a place where there was a garden. He and his disciples entered it.

2-4
Judas, his betrayer, knew the place because Jesus and his disciples went there often. So Judas led the way to the garden, and the Roman soldiers and police sent by the high priests and Pharisees followed. They arrived there with lanterns and torches and swords. Jesus, knowing by now everything that was coming down on him, went out and met them. He said, "Who are you after?"

They answered, "Jesus the Nazarene."

5-6
He said, "That's me." The soldiers recoiled, totally taken aback. Judas, his betrayer, stood out like a sore thumb.

7
Jesus asked again, "Who are you after?"

They answered, "Jesus the Nazarene."

8-9
"I told you," said Jesus, "that's me. I'm the one. So if it's me you're after, let these others go." (This validated the words in his prayer, "I didn't lose one of those you gave.")

10
Just then Simon Peter, who was carrying a sword, pulled it from its sheath and struck the Chief Priest's servant, cutting off his right ear.

Malchus was the servant's name.

11 Jesus ordered Peter, "Put back your sword. Do you think for a minute I'm not going to drink this cup the Father gave me?"

12-14 Then the Roman soldiers under their commander, joined by the Jewish police, seized Jesus and tied him up. They took him first to Annas, father-in-law of Caiaphas. Caiaphas was the Chief Priest that year. It was Caiaphas who had advised the Jews that it was to their advantage that one man die for the people.

15-16 Simon Peter and another disciple followed Jesus. That other disciple was known to the Chief Priest, and so he went in with Jesus to the Chief Priest's courtyard. Peter had to stay outside. Then the other disciple went out, spoke to the doorkeeper, and got Peter in.

17 The young woman who was the doorkeeper said to Peter, "Aren't you one of this man's disciples?"

He said, "No, I'm not."

18 The servants and police had made a fire because of the cold and were huddled there warming themselves. Peter stood with them, trying to get warm.

THE INTERROGATION

19-21 Annas interrogated Jesus regarding his disciples and his teaching. Jesus answered, "I've spoken openly in public. I've taught regularly in meeting places and the Temple, where the Jews all come together. Everything has been out in the open. I've said nothing in secret. So why are you treating me like a conspirator? Question those who have been listening to me. They know well what I have said. My teachings have all been aboveboard."

22 When he said this, one of the policemen standing there slapped Jesus across the face, saying, "How dare you speak to the Chief Priest like that!"

23 Jesus replied, "If I've said something wrong, prove it. But if I've spoken the plain truth, why this slapping around?"

24 Then Annas sent him, still tied up, to the Chief Priest Caiaphas.

25 Meanwhile, Simon Peter was back at the fire, still trying to get warm. The others there said to him, "Aren't you one of his disciples?"

He denied it, "Not me."

26 One of the Chief Priest's servants, a relative of the man whose ear Peter had cut off, said, "Didn't I see you in the garden with him?"

27 Again, Peter denied it. Just then a rooster crowed.

THE KING OF THE JEWS

28-29 They led Jesus then from Caiaphas to the Roman governor's palace. It was early morning. They themselves didn't enter the palace because they didn't want to be disqualified from eating the Passover. So Pilate came out to them and spoke. "What charge do you bring against this man?"

30 They said, "If he hadn't been doing something evil, do you think we'd be here bothering you?"

31-32 Pilate said, "You take him. Judge him by *your* law."

The Jews said, "We're not allowed to kill anyone." (This would confirm Jesus' word indicating the way he would die.)

33 Pilate went back into the palace and called for Jesus. He said, "Are you the 'King of the Jews'?"

34 Jesus answered, "Are you saying this on your own, or did others tell

you this about me?"

35   Pilate said, "Do I look like a Jew? Your people and your high priests turned you over to me. What did you do?"

36   "My kingdom," said Jesus, "doesn't consist of what you see around you. If it did, my followers would fight so that I wouldn't be handed over to the Jews. But I'm not that kind of king, not the world's kind of king."

37   Then Pilate said, "So, are you a king or not?"

Jesus answered, "You tell me. Because I am King, I was born and entered the world so that I could witness to the truth. Everyone who cares for truth, who has any feeling for the truth, recognizes my voice."

38-39   Pilate said, "What is truth?"

Then he went back out to the Jews and told them, "I find nothing wrong in this man. It's your custom that I pardon one prisoner at Passover. Do you want me to pardon the 'King of the Jews'?"

40   They shouted back, "Not this one, but Barabbas!" Barabbas was a Jewish freedom fighter.

THE THORN CROWN OF THE KING

1-3   **19** So Pilate took Jesus and had him whipped. The soldiers, having braided a crown from thorns, set it on his head, threw a purple robe over him, and approached him with, "Hail, King of the Jews!" Then they greeted him with slaps in the face.

4-5   Pilate went back out again and said to them, "I present him to you, but I want you to know that I do not find him guilty of any crime." Just then Jesus came out wearing the thorn crown and purple robe.

Pilate announced, "Here he is: the Man."

6   When the high priests and police saw him, they shouted in a frenzy, "Crucify! Crucify!"

Pilate told them, "You take him. You crucify him. I find nothing wrong with him."

7   The Jews answered, "We have a law, and by that law he must die because he claimed to be the Son of God."

8 9   When Pilate heard this, he became even more scared. He went back into the palace and said to Jesus, "Where did you come from?"

Jesus gave no answer.

10   Pilate said, "You won't talk? Don't you know that I have the authority to pardon you, and the authority to—crucify you?"

11   Jesus said, "You haven't a shred of authority over me except what has been given you from heaven. That's why the one who betrayed me to you has committed a far greater fault."

12   At this, Pilate tried his best to pardon him, but the Jews shouted him down: "If you pardon this man, you're no friend of Caesar's. Anyone setting himself up as 'king' defies Caesar."

13-14   When Pilate heard those words, he led Jesus outside. He sat down at the judgment seat in the area designated Stone Court (in Hebrew, *Gabbatha*). It was the preparation day for Passover. The hour was noon. Pilate said to the Jews, "Here is your king."

15   They shouted back, "Kill him! Kill him! Crucify him!"

Pilate said, "I am to crucify your king?"

The high priests answered, "We have no king except Caesar."

16-19   Pilate caved in to their demand. He turned him over to be crucified.

THE CRUCIFIXION

They took Jesus away. Carrying his cross, Jesus went out to the place called Skull Hill (the name in Hebrew is *Golgotha*), where they crucified him, and with him two others, one on each side, Jesus in the middle. Pilate wrote a sign and had it placed on the cross. It read:

JESUS THE NAZARENE
THE KING OF THE JEWS.

20-21 Many of the Jews read the sign because the place where Jesus was crucified was right next to the city. It was written in Hebrew, Latin, and Greek. The Jewish high priests objected. "Don't write," they said to Pilate, "'The King of the Jews.' Make it, 'This man said, "I am the King of the Jews."'"

22 Pilate said, "What I've written, I've written."

23-24 When they crucified him, the Roman soldiers took his clothes and divided them up four ways, to each soldier a fourth. But his robe was seamless, a single piece of weaving, so they said to each other, "Let's not tear it up. Let's throw dice to see who gets it." This confirmed the Scripture that said, "They divided up my clothes among them and threw dice for my coat." (The soldiers validated the Scriptures!)

24-27 While the soldiers were looking after themselves, Jesus' mother, his aunt, Mary the wife of Clopas, and Mary Magdalene stood at the foot of the cross. Jesus saw his mother and the disciple he loved standing near her. He said to his mother, "Woman, here is your son." Then to the disciple, "Here is your mother." From that moment the disciple accepted her as his own mother.

28 Jesus, seeing that everything had been completed so that the Scripture record might also be complete, then said, "I'm thirsty."

29-30 A jug of sour wine was standing by. Someone put a sponge soaked with the wine on a javelin and lifted it to his mouth. After he took the wine, Jesus said, "It's done . . . complete." Bowing his head, he offered up his spirit.

31-34 Then the Jews, since it was the day of Sabbath preparation, and so the bodies wouldn't stay on the crosses over the Sabbath (it was a high holy day that year), petitioned Pilate that their legs be broken to speed death, and the bodies taken down. So the soldiers came and broke the legs of the first man crucified with Jesus, and then the other. When they got to Jesus, they saw that he was already dead, so they didn't break his legs. One of the soldiers stabbed him in the side with his spear. Blood and water gushed out.

35 The eyewitness to these things has presented an accurate report. He saw it himself and is telling the truth so that you, also, will believe.

36-37 These things that happened confirmed the Scripture, "Not a bone in his body was broken," and the other Scripture that reads, "They will stare at the one they pierced."

38 After all this, Joseph of Arimathea (he was a disciple of Jesus, but secretly, because he was intimidated by the Jews) petitioned Pilate to take the body of Jesus. Pilate gave permission. So Joseph came and took the body.

39-42 Nicodemus, who had first come to Jesus at night, came now in broad daylight carrying a mixture of myrrh and aloes, about seventy-five pounds. They took Jesus' body and, following the Jewish burial custom, wrapped it in linen with the spices. There was a garden near the place he was crucified, and in the garden a new tomb in which no one had yet been placed. So, because it was Sabbath preparation for the Jews and the tomb was convenient, they placed Jesus in it.

RESURRECTION!

1-2　　Early in the morning on the first day of the week, while it was still dark, Mary Magdalene came to the tomb and saw that the stone was moved away from the entrance. She ran at once to Simon Peter and the other disciple, the one Jesus loved, breathlessly panting, "They took the Master from the tomb. We don't know where they've put him."

3-10　Peter and the other disciple left immediately for the tomb. They ran, neck and neck. The other disciple got to the tomb first, outrunning Peter. Stooping to look in, he saw the pieces of linen cloth lying there, but he didn't go in. Simon Peter arrived after him, entered the tomb, observed the linen cloths lying there, and the kerchief used to cover his head not lying with the linen cloths but separate, neatly folded by itself. Then the other disciple, the one who had gotten there first, went into the tomb, took one look at the evidence, and believed. No one yet knew from the Scripture that he had to rise from the dead. The disciples then went back home.

11-13　But Mary stood outside the tomb weeping. As she wept, she knelt to look into the tomb and saw two angels sitting there, dressed in white, one at the head, the other at the foot of where Jesus' body had been laid. They said to her, "Woman, why do you weep?"

13-14　"They took my Master," she said, "and I don't know where they put him." After she said this, she turned away and saw Jesus standing there. But she didn't recognize him.

15　Jesus spoke to her, "Woman, why do you weep? Who are you looking for?"

She, thinking that he was the gardener, said, "Mister, if you took him, tell me where you put him so I can care for him."

16　Jesus said, "Mary."

Turning to face him, she said in Hebrew, "*Rabboni!*" meaning "Teacher!"

17　Jesus said, "Don't cling to me, for I have not yet ascended to the Father. Go to my brothers and tell them, 'I ascend to my Father and your Father, my God and your God.'"

18　Mary Magdalene went, telling the news to the disciples: "I saw the Master!" And she told them everything he said to her.

TO BELIEVE

19-20　Later on that day, the disciples had gathered together, but, fearful of the Jews, had locked all the doors in the house. Jesus entered, stood among them, and said, "Peace to you." Then he showed them his hands and side.

20-21　The disciples, seeing the Master with their own eyes, were exuberant. Jesus repeated his greeting: "Peace to you. Just as the Father sent me, I send you."

22-23　Then he took a deep breath and breathed into them. "Receive the Holy Spirit," he said. "If you forgive someone's sins, they're gone for good. If you don't forgive sins, what are you going to do with them?"

24-25 But Thomas, sometimes called the Twin, one of the Twelve, was not with them when Jesus came. The other disciples told him, "We saw the Master."

But he said, "Unless I see the nail holes in his hands, put my finger in the nail holes, and stick my hand in his side, I won't believe it."

26 Eight days later, his disciples were again in the room. This time Thomas was with them. Jesus came through the locked doors, stood among them, and said, "Peace to you."

27 Then he focused his attention on Thomas. "Take your finger and examine my hands. Take your hand and stick it in my side. Don't be unbelieving. Believe."

28 Thomas said, "My Master! My God!"

29 Jesus said, "So, you believe because you've seen with your own eyes. Even better blessings are in store for those who believe without seeing."

30-31 Jesus provided far more God-revealing signs than are written down in this book. These are written down so you will believe that Jesus is the Messiah, the Son of God, and in the act of believing, have real and eternal life in the way he personally revealed it.

FISHING

1-3 After this, Jesus appeared again to the disciples, this time at the Tiberias Sea (the Sea of Galilee). This is how he did it: Simon Peter, Thomas (nicknamed "Twin"), Nathanael from Cana in Galilee, the brothers Zebedee, and two other disciples were together. Simon Peter announced, "I'm going fishing."

3-4 The rest of them replied, "We're going with you." They went out and got in the boat. They caught nothing that night. When the sun came up, Jesus was standing on the beach, but they didn't recognize him.

5 Jesus spoke to them: "Good morning! Did you catch anything for breakfast?"

They answered, "No."

6 He said, "Throw the net off the right side of the boat and see what happens."

They did what he said. All of a sudden there were so many fish in it, they weren't strong enough to pull it in.

7-9 Then the disciple Jesus loved said to Peter, "It's the Master!"

When Simon Peter realized that it was the Master, he threw on some clothes, for he was stripped for work, and dove into the sea. The other disciples came in by boat for they weren't far from land, a hundred yards or so, pulling along the net full of fish. When they got out of the boat, they saw a fire laid, with fish and bread cooking on it.

10-11 Jesus said, "Bring some of the fish you've just caught." Simon Peter joined them and pulled the net to shore — 153 big fish! And even with all those fish, the net didn't rip.

12 Jesus said, "Breakfast is ready." Not one of the disciples dared ask, "Who are you?" They knew it was the Master.

13-14 Jesus then took the bread and gave it to them. He did the same with the fish. This was now the third time Jesus had shown himself alive to the disciples since being raised from the dead.

DO YOU LOVE ME?

15 After breakfast, Jesus said to Simon Peter, "Simon, son of John, do you love me more than these?"

"Yes, Master, you know I love you."

Jesus said, "Feed my lambs."

16 He then asked a second time, "Simon, son of John, do you love me?"

"Yes, Master, you know I love you."

Jesus said, "Shepherd my sheep."

17-19 Then he said it a third time: "Simon, son of John, do you love me?"

Peter was upset that he asked for the third time, "Do you love me?" so he answered, "Master, you know everything there is to know. You've got to know that I love you."

Jesus said, "Feed my sheep. I'm telling you the very truth now: When you were young you dressed yourself and went wherever you wished, but when you get old you'll have to stretch out your hands while someone else dresses you and takes you where you don't want to go." He said this to hint at the kind of death by which Peter would glorify God. And then he commanded, "Follow me."

20-21 Turning his head, Peter noticed the disciple Jesus loved following right behind. When Peter noticed him, he asked Jesus, "Master, what's going to happen to *him*?"

22-23 Jesus said, "If I want him to live until I come again, what's that to you? You — follow me." That is how the rumor got out among the brothers that this disciple wouldn't die. But that is not what Jesus said. He simply said, "If I want him to live until I come again, what's that to you?"

24 This is the same disciple who was eyewitness to all these things and wrote them down. And we all know that his eyewitness account is reliable and accurate.

25 There are so many other things Jesus did. If they were all written down, each of them, one by one, I can't imagine a world big enough to hold such a library of books.

ACTS

Because the story of Jesus is so impressive — God among us! God speaking a language we can understand! God acting in ways that heal and help and save us! — there is a danger that we will be impressed, but only be impressed. As the spectacular dimensions of this story slowly (or suddenly) dawn upon us, we could easily become enthusiastic spectators, and then let it go at that — become admirers of Jesus, generous with our oohs and ahs, and in our better moments inspired to imitate him.

It is Luke's task to prevent that, to prevent us from becoming mere spectators to Jesus, fans of the Message. Of the original quartet of writers on Jesus, Luke alone continues to tell the story as the apostles and disciples live it into the next generation. The remarkable thing is that it continues to be essentially the same story. Luke continues his narration with hardly a break, a pause perhaps to dip his pen in the inkwell, writing in the same style, using the same vocabulary.

The story of Jesus doesn't end with Jesus. It continues in the lives of those who believe in him. The supernatural does not stop with Jesus. Luke makes it clear that these Christians he wrote about were no more spectators of Jesus than Jesus was a spectator of God — they are *in* on the action of God, God acting *in* them, God living *in* them. Which also means, of course, in *us*.

ACTS

TO THE ENDS OF THE WORLD

1-5 Dear Theophilus, in the first volume of this book I wrote on everything that Jesus began to do and teach until the day he said good-bye to the apostles, the ones he had chosen through the Holy Spirit, and was taken up to heaven. After his death, he presented himself alive to them in many different settings over a period of forty days. In face-to-face meetings, he talked to them about things concerning the kingdom of God. As they met and ate meals together, he told them that they were on no account to leave Jerusalem but "must wait for what the Father promised: the promise you heard from me. John baptized in water; you will be baptized in the Holy Spirit. And soon."

6 When they were together for the last time they asked, "Master, are you going to restore the kingdom to Israel now? Is this the time?"

7-8 He told them, "You don't get to know the time. Timing is the Father's business. What you'll get is the Holy Spirit. And when the Holy Spirit comes on you, you will be able to be my witnesses in Jerusalem, all over Judea and Samaria, even to the ends of the world."

9-11 These were his last words. As they watched, he was taken up and disappeared in a cloud. They stood there, staring into the empty sky. Suddenly two men appeared — in white robes! They said, "You Galileans! — why do you just stand here looking up at an empty sky? This very Jesus who was taken up from among you to heaven will come as certainly — and mysteriously — as he left."

RETURNING TO JERUSALEM

12-13 So they left the mountain called Olives and returned to Jerusalem. It was a little over half a mile. They went to the upper room they had been using as a meeting place:

Peter,
John,
James,
Andrew,
Philip,
Thomas,
Bartholomew,
Matthew,
James, son of Alphaeus,
Simon the Zealot,
Judas, son of James.

14 They agreed they were in this for good, completely together in prayer, the women included. Also Jesus' mother, Mary, and his brothers.

REPLACING JUDAS

15-17 During this time, Peter stood up in the company — there were about 120 of them in the room at the time — and said, "Friends, long ago the Holy

Spirit spoke through David regarding Judas, who became the guide to those who arrested Jesus. That Scripture had to be fulfilled, and now has been. Judas was one of us and had his assigned place in this ministry.

18-20   "As you know, he took the evil bribe money and bought a small farm. There he came to a bad end, rupturing his belly and spilling his guts. Everybody in Jerusalem knows this by now; they call the place Murder Meadow. It's exactly what we find written in the Psalms:

> Let his farm become haunted
> So no one can ever live there.

"And also what was written later:

> Let someone else take over his post.

21-22   "Judas must now be replaced. The replacement must come from the company of men who stayed together with us from the time Jesus was baptized by John up to the day of his ascension, designated along with us as a witness to his resurrection."

23-26   They nominated two: Joseph Barsabbas, nicknamed Justus, and Matthias. Then they prayed, "You, O God, know every one of us inside and out. Make plain which of these two men you choose to take the place in this ministry and leadership that Judas threw away in order to go his own way." They then drew straws. Matthias won and was counted in with the eleven apostles.

A Sound Like a Strong Wind

1-4   When the Feast of Pentecost came, they were all together in one place. Without warning there was a sound like a strong wind, gale force—no one could tell where it came from. It filled the whole building. Then, like a wildfire, the Holy Spirit spread through their ranks, and they started speaking in a number of different languages as the Spirit prompted them.

5-11   There were many Jews staying in Jerusalem just then, devout pilgrims from all over the world. When they heard the sound, they came on the run. Then when they heard, one after another, their own mother tongues being spoken, they were thunderstruck. They couldn't for the life of them figure out what was going on, and kept saying, "Aren't these all Galileans? How come we're hearing them talk in our various mother tongues?

> Parthians, Medes, and Elamites;
> Visitors from Mesopotamia, Judea, and Cappadocia,
>   Pontus and Asia, Phrygia and Pamphylia,
>   Egypt and the parts of Libya belonging to Cyrene;
> Immigrants from Rome, both Jews and proselytes;
> Even Cretans and Arabs!

"They're speaking our languages, describing God's mighty works!"

12   Their heads were spinning; they couldn't make head or tail of any of it. They talked back and forth, confused: "What's going on here?"

13   Others joked, "They're drunk on cheap wine."

PETER SPEAKS UP

14-21 That's when Peter stood up and, backed by the other eleven, spoke out with bold urgency: "Fellow Jews, all of you who are visiting Jerusalem, listen carefully and get this story straight. These people aren't drunk as some of you suspect. They haven't had time to get drunk—it's only nine o'clock in the morning. This is what the prophet Joel announced would happen:

"In the Last Days," God says,
"I will pour out my Spirit
    on every kind of people:
Your sons will prophesy,
    also your daughters;
Your young men will see visions,
    your old men dream dreams.
When the time comes,
    I'll pour out my Spirit
On those who serve me, men and women both,
    and they'll prophesy.
I'll set wonders in the sky above
    and signs on the earth below,
Blood and fire and billowing smoke,
    the sun turning black and the moon blood-red,
Before the Day of the Lord arrives,
    the Day tremendous and marvelous;
And whoever calls out for help
    to me, God, will be saved."

22-28 "Fellow Israelites, listen carefully to these words: Jesus the Nazarene, a man thoroughly accredited by God to you—the miracles and wonders and signs that God did through him are common knowledge—this Jesus, following the deliberate and well-thought-out plan of God, was betrayed by men who took the law into their own hands, and was handed over to you. And you pinned him to a cross and killed him. But God untied the death ropes and raised him up. Death was no match for him. David said it all:

I saw God before me for all time.
    Nothing can shake me; he's right by my side.
I'm glad from the inside out, ecstatic;
    I've pitched my tent in the land of hope.
I know you'll never dump me in Hades;
    I'll never even smell the stench of death.
You've got my feet on the life-path,
    with your face shining sun-joy all around.

29-36 "Dear friends, let me be completely frank with you. Our ancestor David is dead and buried—his tomb is in plain sight today. But being also a prophet and knowing that God had solemnly sworn that a descendant of his would rule his kingdom, seeing far ahead, he talked of the resurrection of the Messiah—'no trip to Hades, no stench of death.' This Jesus, God raised up. And every one of us here is a witness to it. Then, raised to the heights at the right hand of God and receiving the promise of the Holy Spirit from the Father, he poured out the Spirit he had just received. That is what you see and hear. For David himself did not ascend to heaven, but he did say,

> God said to my Master, "Sit at my right hand
> Until I make your enemies a stool for resting your feet."

"All Israel, then, know this: There's no longer room for doubt—God made him Master and Messiah, this Jesus whom you killed on a cross."

37   Cut to the quick, those who were there listening asked Peter and the other apostles, "Brothers! Brothers! So now what do we do?"

38-39   Peter said, "Change your life. Turn to God and be baptized, each of you, in the name of Jesus Christ, so your sins are forgiven. Receive the gift of the Holy Spirit. The promise is targeted to you and your children, but also to all who are far away—whomever, in fact, our Master God invites."

40   He went on in this vein for a long time, urging them over and over, "Get out while you can; get out of this sick and stupid culture!"

41-42   That day about three thousand took him at his word, were baptized and were signed up. They committed themselves to the teaching of the apostles, the life together, the common meal, and the prayers.

43-45   Everyone around was in awe—all those wonders and signs done through the apostles! And all the believers lived in a wonderful harmony, holding everything in common. They sold whatever they owned and pooled their resources so that each person's need was met.

46-47   They followed a daily discipline of worship in the Temple followed by meals at home, every meal a celebration, exuberant and joyful, as they praised God. People in general liked what they saw. Every day their number grew as God added those who were saved.

1-5   3 One day at three o'clock in the afternoon, Peter and John were on their way into the Temple for prayer meeting. At the same time there was a man crippled from birth being carried up. Every day he was set down at the Temple gate, the one named Beautiful, to beg from those going into the Temple. When he saw Peter and John about to enter the Temple, he asked for a handout. Peter, with John at his side, looked him straight in the eye and said, "Look here." He looked up, expecting to get something from them.

6-8   Peter said, "I don't have a nickel to my name, but what I do have, I give you: In the name of Jesus Christ of Nazareth, walk!" He grabbed him by the right hand and pulled him up. In an instant his feet and ankles became firm. He jumped to his feet and walked.

8-10   The man went into the Temple with them, walking back and forth, dancing and praising God. Everybody there saw him walking around and praising God. They recognized him as the one who sat begging at the Temple's Gate Beautiful and rubbed their eyes, astonished, scarcely believing what they were seeing.

11   The man threw his arms around Peter and John, ecstatic. All the people ran up to where they were at Solomon's Porch to see it for themselves.

TURN TO FACE GOD

¹²⁻¹⁶ When Peter saw he had a congregation, he addressed the people:

"Oh, Israelites, why does this take you by such complete surprise, and why stare at us as if *our* power or piety made him walk? The God of Abraham and Isaac and Jacob, the God of our ancestors, has glorified his Son Jesus. The very One that Pilate called innocent, you repudiated. You repudiated the Holy One, the Just One, and asked for a murderer in his place. You no sooner killed the Author of Life than God raised him from the dead — and we're the witnesses. Faith in Jesus' name put this man, whose condition you know so well, on his feet — yes, faith and nothing but faith put this man healed and whole right before your eyes.

¹⁷⁻¹⁸ "And now, friends, I know you had no idea what you were doing when you killed Jesus, and neither did your leaders. But God, who through the preaching of all the prophets had said all along that his Messiah would be killed, knew exactly what you were doing and used it to fulfill his plans.

¹⁹⁻²³ "Now it's time to change your ways! Turn to face God so he can wipe away your sins, pour out showers of blessing to refresh you, and send you the Messiah he prepared for you, namely, Jesus. For the time being he must remain out of sight in heaven until everything is restored to order again just the way God, through the preaching of his holy prophets of old, said it would be. Moses, for instance, said, 'Your God will raise up for you a prophet just like me from your family. Listen to every word he speaks to you. Every last living soul who refuses to listen to that prophet will be wiped out from the people.'

²⁴⁻²⁶ "All the prophets from Samuel on down said the same thing, said most emphatically that these days would come. These prophets, along with the covenant God made with your ancestors, are your family tree. God's covenant-word to Abraham provides the text: 'By your offspring all the families of the earth will be blessed.' But you are first in line: God, having raised up his Son, sent him to bless you as you turn, one by one, from your evil ways."

NOTHING TO HIDE

¹⁻⁴ 4 While Peter and John were addressing the people, the priests, the chief of the Temple police, and some Sadducees came up, indignant that these upstart apostles were instructing the people and proclaiming that the resurrection from the dead had taken place in Jesus. They arrested them and threw them in jail until morning, for by now it was late in the evening. But many of those who listened had already believed the Message — in round numbers about five thousand!

⁵⁻⁷ The next day a meeting was called in Jerusalem. The rulers, religious leaders, religion scholars, Annas the Chief Priest, Caiaphas, John, Alexander — everybody who was anybody was there. They stood Peter and John in the middle of the room and grilled them: "Who put you in charge here? What business do you have doing this?"

⁸⁻¹² With that, Peter, full of the Holy Spirit, let loose: "Rulers and leaders of the people, if we have been brought to trial today for helping a sick man, put under investigation regarding this healing, I'll be completely frank with you — we have nothing to hide. By the name of Jesus Christ of Nazareth, the One you killed on a cross, the One God raised from the dead, by means of

ACTS

his name this man stands before you healthy and whole. Jesus is 'the stone you masons threw out, which is now the cornerstone.' Salvation comes no other way; no other name has been or will be given to us by which we can be saved, only this one."

13-14 They couldn't take their eyes off them—Peter and John standing there so confident, so sure of themselves! Their fascination deepened when they realized these two were laymen with no training in Scripture or formal education. They recognized them as companions of Jesus, but with the man right before them, seeing him standing there so upright—so healed!—what could they say against that?

15-17 They sent them out of the room so they could work out a plan. They talked it over: "What can we do with these men? By now it's known all over town that a miracle has occurred, and that they are behind it. There is no way we can refute that. But so that it doesn't go any further, let's silence them with threats so they won't dare to use Jesus' name ever again with anyone."

18-20 They called them back and warned them that they were on no account ever again to speak or teach in the name of Jesus. But Peter and John spoke right back, "Whether it's right in God's eyes to listen to you rather than to God, you decide. As for us, there's no question—we can't keep quiet about what we've seen and heard."

21-22 The religious leaders renewed their threats, but then released them. They couldn't come up with a charge that would stick, that would keep them in jail. The people wouldn't have stood for it—they were all praising God over what had happened. The man who had been miraculously healed was over forty years old.

One Heart, One Mind

23-26 As soon as Peter and John were let go, they went to their friends and told them what the high priests and religious leaders had said. Hearing the report, they lifted their voices in a wonderful harmony in prayer: "Strong God, you made heaven and earth and sea and everything in them. By the Holy Spirit you spoke through the mouth of your servant and our father, David:

> Why the big noise, nations?
> Why the mean plots, peoples?
> Earth's leaders push for position,
> Potentates meet for summit talks,
> The God-deniers, the Messiah-defiers!

27-28 "For in fact they did meet—Herod and Pontius Pilate with nations and peoples, even Israel itself!—met in this very city to plot against your holy Son Jesus, the One you made Messiah, to carry out the plans you long ago set in motion.

29-30 "And now they're at it again! Take care of their threats and give your servants fearless confidence in preaching your Message, as you stretch out your hand to us in healings and miracles and wonders done in the name of your holy servant Jesus."

31 While they were praying, the place where they were meeting trembled and shook. They were all filled with the Holy Spirit and continued to speak

God's Word with fearless confidence.

32-33   The whole congregation of believers was united as one — one heart, one mind! They didn't even claim ownership of their own possessions. No one said, "That's mine; you can't have it." They shared everything. The apostles gave powerful witness to the resurrection of the Master Jesus, and grace was on all of them.

34-35   And so it turned out that not a person among them was needy. Those who owned fields or houses sold them and brought the price of the sale to the apostles and made an offering of it. The apostles then distributed it according to each person's need.

36-37   Joseph, called by the apostles "Barnabas" (which means "Son of Comfort"), a Levite born in Cyprus, sold a field that he owned, brought the money, and made an offering of it to the apostles.

ANANIAS AND SAPPHIRA

1-2   But a man named Ananias — his wife, Sapphira, conniving in this with him — sold a piece of land, secretly kept part of the price for himself, and then brought the rest to the apostles and made an offering of it.

3-4   Peter said, "Ananias, how did Satan get you to lie to the Holy Spirit and secretly keep back part of the price of the field? Before you sold it, it was all yours, and after you sold it, the money was yours to do with as you wished. So what got into you to pull a trick like this? You didn't lie to men but to God."

5-6   Ananias, when he heard those words, fell down dead. That put the fear of God into everyone who heard of it. The younger men went right to work and wrapped him up, then carried him out and buried him.

7-8   Not more than three hours later, his wife, knowing nothing of what had happened, came in. Peter said, "Tell me, were you given this price for your field?"

"Yes," she said, "that price."

9-10   Peter responded, "What's going on here that you connived to conspire against the Spirit of the Master? The men who buried your husband are at the door, and you're next." No sooner were the words out of his mouth than she also fell down, dead. When the young men returned they found her body. They carried her out and buried her beside her husband.

11   By this time the whole church and, in fact, everyone who heard of these things had a healthy respect for God. They knew God was not to be trifled with.

THEY ALL MET REGULARLY

12-16   Through the work of the apostles, many God-signs were set up among the people, many wonderful things done. They all met regularly and in remarkable harmony on the Temple porch named after Solomon. But even though people admired them a lot, outsiders were wary about joining them. On the other hand, those who put their trust in the Master were added right and left, men and women both. They even carried the sick out into the streets and laid them on stretchers and bedrolls, hoping they would be touched by Peter's shadow when he walked by. They came from the villages surrounding Jerusalem, throngs of them, bringing the sick and bedeviled. And they all were healed.

TO OBEY GOD RATHER THAN MEN

17-20 Provoked mightily by all this, the Chief Priest and those on his side, mainly the sect of Sadducees, went into action, arrested the apostles and put them in the town jail. But during the night an angel of God opened the jailhouse door and led them out. He said, "Go to the Temple and take your stand. Tell the people everything there is to say about this Life."

Promptly obedient, they entered the Temple at daybreak and went on with their teaching.

21-23 Meanwhile, the Chief Priest and his cronies convened the High Council, Israel's senate, and sent to the jail to have the prisoners brought in. When the police got there, they couldn't find them anywhere in the jail. They went back and reported, "We found the jail locked tight as a drum and the guards posted at the doors, but when we went inside we didn't find a soul."

24 The chief of the Temple police and the high priests were puzzled. "What's going on here anyway?"

25-26 Just then someone showed up and said, "Did you know that the men you put in jail are back in the Temple teaching the people?" The chief and his police went and got them, but they handled them gently, fearful that the people would riot and turn on them.

27-28 Bringing them back, they stood them before the High Council. The Chief Priest said, "Didn't we give you strict orders not to teach in Jesus' name? And here you have filled Jerusalem with your teaching and are trying your best to blame us for the death of this man."

29-32 Peter and the apostles answered, "It's necessary to obey God rather than men. The God of our ancestors raised up Jesus, the One you killed by hanging him on a cross. God set him on high at his side, Prince and Savior, to give Israel the gift of a changed life and sins forgiven. And we are witnesses to these things. The Holy Spirit, whom God gives to those who obey him, corroborates every detail."

33-37 When they heard that, they were furious and wanted to kill them on the spot. But one of the council members stood up, a Pharisee by the name of Gamaliel, a teacher of God's Law who was honored by everyone. He ordered the men taken out of the room for a short time, then said, "Fellow Israelites, be careful what you do to these men. Not long ago Theudas made something of a splash, claiming to be somebody, and got about four hundred men to join him. He was killed, his followers dispersed, and nothing came of it. A little later, at the time of the census, Judas the Galilean appeared and acquired a following. He also fizzled out and the people following him were scattered to the four winds.

38-39 "So I am telling you: Hands off these men! Let them alone. If this program or this work is merely human, it will fall apart, but if it is of God, there is nothing you can do about it — and you better not be found fighting against God!"

40-42 That convinced them. They called the apostles back in. After giving them a thorough whipping, they warned them not to speak in Jesus' name and sent them off. The apostles went out of the High Council overjoyed because they had been given the honor of being dishonored on account of the Name. Every day they were in the Temple and homes, teaching and preaching Christ Jesus, not letting up for a minute.

THE WORD OF GOD PROSPERED

1-4 During this time, as the disciples were increasing in numbers by leaps and bounds, hard feelings developed among the Greek-speaking believers — "Hellenists" — toward the Hebrew-speaking believers because their widows were being discriminated against in the daily food lines. So the Twelve called a meeting of the disciples. They said, "It wouldn't be right for us to abandon our responsibilities for preaching and teaching the Word of God to help with the care of the poor. So, friends, choose seven men from among you whom everyone trusts, men full of the Holy Spirit and good sense, and we'll assign them this task. Meanwhile, we'll stick to our assigned tasks of prayer and speaking God's Word."

5-6 The congregation thought this was a great idea. They went ahead and chose —

Stephen, a man full of faith and the Holy Spirit,
Philip,
Procorus,
Nicanor,
Timon,
Parmenas,
Nicolas, a convert from Antioch.

Then they presented them to the apostles. Praying, the apostles laid on hands and commissioned them for their task.

7 The Word of God prospered. The number of disciples in Jerusalem increased dramatically. Not least, a great many priests submitted themselves to the faith.

8-10 Stephen, brimming with God's grace and energy, was doing wonderful things among the people, unmistakable signs that God was among them. But then some men from the meeting place whose membership was made up of freed slaves, Cyrenians, Alexandrians, and some others from Cilicia and Asia, went up against him trying to argue him down. But they were no match for his wisdom and spirit when he spoke.

11 So in secret they bribed men to lie: "We heard him cursing Moses and God."

12-14 That stirred up the people, the religious leaders, and religion scholars. They grabbed Stephen and took him before the High Council. They put forward their bribed witnesses to testify: "This man talks nonstop against this Holy Place and God's Law. We even heard him say that Jesus of Nazareth would tear this place down and throw out all the customs Moses gave us."

15 As all those who sat on the High Council looked at Stephen, they found they couldn't take their eyes off him — his face was like the face of an angel!

STEPHEN, FULL OF THE HOLY SPIRIT

1 Then the Chief Priest said, "What do you have to say for yourself?"

2-3 Stephen replied, "Friends, fathers, and brothers, the God of glory appeared to our father Abraham when he was still in Mesopotamia, before the move to Haran, and told him, 'Leave your country and family and go to the land I'll show you.'

4-7   "So he left the country of the Chaldees and moved to Haran. After the death of his father, he immigrated to this country where you now live, but God gave him nothing, not so much as a foothold. He did promise to give the country to him and his son later on, even though Abraham had no son at the time. God let him know that his offspring would move to an alien country where they would be enslaved and brutalized for four hundred years. 'But,' God said, 'I will step in and take care of those slaveholders and bring my people out so they can worship me in this place.'

8   "Then he made a covenant with him and signed it in Abraham's flesh by circumcision. When Abraham had his son Isaac, within eight days he reproduced the sign of circumcision in him. Isaac became father of Jacob, and Jacob father of twelve 'fathers,' each faithfully passing on the covenant sign.

9-10   "But then those 'fathers,' burning up with jealousy, sent Joseph off to Egypt as a slave. God was right there with him, though — he not only rescued him from all his troubles but brought him to the attention of Pharaoh, king of Egypt. He was so impressed with Joseph that he put him in charge of the whole country, including his own personal affairs.

11-15   "Later a famine descended on that entire region, stretching from Egypt to Canaan, bringing terrific hardship. Our hungry fathers looked high and low for food, but the cupboard was bare. Jacob heard there was food in Egypt and sent our fathers to scout it out. Having confirmed the report, they went back to Egypt a second time to get food. On that visit, Joseph revealed his true identity to his brothers and introduced the Jacob family to Pharaoh. Then Joseph sent for his father, Jacob, and everyone else in the family, seventy-five in all. That's how the Jacob family got to Egypt.

15-16   "Jacob died, and our fathers after him. They were taken to Shechem and buried in the tomb for which Abraham paid a good price to the sons of Hamor.

17-19   "When the four hundred years were nearly up, the time God promised Abraham for deliverance, the population of our people in Egypt had become very large. And there was now a king over Egypt who had never heard of Joseph. He exploited our race mercilessly. He went so far as forcing us to abandon our newborn infants, exposing them to the elements to die a cruel death.

20-22   "In just such a time Moses was born, a most beautiful baby. He was hidden at home for three months. When he could be hidden no longer, he was put outside — and immediately rescued by Pharaoh's daughter, who mothered him as her own son. Moses was educated in the best schools in Egypt. He was equally impressive as a thinker and an athlete.

23-26   "When he was forty years old, he wondered how everything was going with his Hebrew kin and went out to look things over. He saw an Egyptian abusing one of them and stepped in, avenging his underdog brother by knocking the Egyptian flat. He thought his brothers would be glad that he was on their side, and even see him as an instrument of God to deliver them. But they didn't see it that way. The next day two of them were fighting and he tried to break it up, told them to shake hands and get along with each other: 'Friends, you are brothers, why are you beating up on each other?'

27-29   "The one who had started the fight said, 'Who put you in charge of us? Are you going to kill me like you killed that Egyptian yesterday?' When

Moses heard that, realizing that the word was out, he ran for his life and lived in exile over in Midian. During the years of exile, two sons were born to him.

30-32 "Forty years later, in the wilderness of Mount Sinai, an angel appeared to him in the guise of flames of a burning bush. Moses, not believing his eyes, went up to take a closer look. He heard God's voice: 'I am the God of your fathers, the God of Abraham, Isaac, and Jacob.' Frightened nearly out of his skin, Moses shut his eyes and turned away.

33-34 "God said, 'Kneel and pray. You are in a holy place, on holy ground. I've seen the agony of my people in Egypt. I've heard their groans. I've come to help them. So get yourself ready; I'm sending you back to Egypt.'

35-39 "This is the same Moses whom they earlier rejected, saying, 'Who put you in charge of us?' This is the Moses that God, using the angel flaming in the burning bush, sent back as ruler and redeemer. He led them out of their slavery. He did wonderful things, setting up God-signs all through Egypt, down at the Red Sea, and out in the wilderness for forty years. This is the Moses who said to his congregation, 'God will raise up a prophet just like me from your descendants.' This is the Moses who stood between the angel speaking at Sinai and your fathers assembled in the wilderness and took the life-giving words given to him and handed them over to us, words our fathers would have nothing to do with.

39-41 "They craved the old Egyptian ways, whining to Aaron, 'Make us gods we can see and follow. This Moses who got us out here miles from nowhere—who knows what's happened to him!' That was the time when they made a calf-idol, brought sacrifices to it, and congratulated each other on the wonderful religious program they had put together.

42-43 "God wasn't at all pleased; but he let them do it their way, worship every new god that came down the pike—and live with the consequences, consequences described by the prophet Amos:

Did you bring me offerings of animals and grains
    those forty wilderness years, O Israel?
Hardly. You were too busy building shrines
    to war gods, to sex goddesses,
Worshiping them with all your might.
    That's why I put you in exile in Babylon.

44-47 "And all this time our ancestors had a tent shrine for true worship, made to the exact specifications God provided Moses. They had it with them as they followed Joshua, when God cleared the land of pagans, and still had it right down to the time of David. David asked God for a permanent place for worship. But Solomon built it.

48-50 "Yet that doesn't mean that Most High God lives in a building made by carpenters and masons. The prophet Isaiah put it well when he wrote,

"Heaven is my throne room;
    I rest my feet on earth.
So what kind of house
    will you build me?" says God.
"Where I can get away and relax?
    It's already built, and I built it."

51-53 "And you continue, so bullheaded! Calluses on your hearts, flaps on your ears! Deliberately ignoring the Holy Spirit, you're just like your ancestors. Was there ever a prophet who didn't get the same treatment? Your ancestors killed anyone who dared talk about the coming of the Just One. And you've kept up the family tradition — traitors and murderers, all of you. You had God's Law handed to you by angels — gift-wrapped! — and you squandered it!"

54-56 At that point they went wild, a rioting mob of catcalls and whistles and invective. But Stephen, full of the Holy Spirit, hardly noticed — he only had eyes for God, whom he saw in all his glory with Jesus standing at his side. He said, "Oh! I see heaven wide open and the Son of Man standing at God's side!"

57-58 Yelling and hissing, the mob drowned him out. Now in full stampede, they dragged him out of town and pelted him with rocks. The ringleaders took off their coats and asked a young man named Saul to watch them.

59-60 As the rocks rained down, Stephen prayed, "Master Jesus, take my life." Then he knelt down, praying loud enough for everyone to hear, "Master, don't blame them for this sin" — his last words. Then he died.

1 Saul was right there, congratulating the killers.

SIMON THE WIZARD

1-2 8 That set off a terrific persecution of the church in Jerusalem. The believers were all scattered throughout Judea and Samaria. All, that is, but the apostles. Good and brave men buried Stephen, giving him a solemn funeral — not many dry eyes that day!

3-8 And Saul just went wild, devastating the church, entering house after house after house, dragging men and women off to jail. Forced to leave home base, the followers of Jesus all became missionaries. Wherever they were scattered, they preached the Message about Jesus. Going down to a Samaritan city, Philip proclaimed the Message of the Messiah. When the people heard what he had to say and saw the miracles, the clear signs of God's action, they hung on his every word. Many who could neither stand nor walk were healed that day. The evil spirits protested loudly as they were sent on their way. And what joy in the city!

9-11 Previous to Philip's arrival, a certain Simon had practiced magic in the city, posing as a famous man and dazzling all the Samaritans with his wizardry. He had them all, from little children to old men, eating out of his hand. They all thought he had supernatural powers, and called him "the Great Wizard." He had been around a long time and everyone was more or less in awe of him.

12-13 But when Philip came to town announcing the news of God's kingdom and proclaiming the name of Jesus Christ, they forgot Simon and were baptized, becoming believers right and left! Even Simon himself believed and was baptized. From that moment he was like Philip's shadow, so fascinated with all the God-signs and miracles that he wouldn't leave Philip's side.

14-17 When the apostles in Jerusalem received the report that Samaria had accepted God's Message, they sent Peter and John down to pray for them to receive the Holy Spirit. Up to this point they had only been baptized in the name of the Master Jesus; the Holy Spirit hadn't yet fallen on them. Then the apostles laid their hands on them and they did receive the Holy Spirit.

18-19   When Simon saw that the apostles by merely laying on hands conferred the Spirit, he pulled out his money, excited, and said, "Sell me your
secret! Show me how you did that! How much do you want? Name your
price!"

20-23   Peter said, "To hell with your money! And you along with it. Why,
that's unthinkable — trying to buy God's gift! You'll never be part of
what God is doing by striking bargains and offering bribes. Change
your ways — and now! Ask the Master to forgive you for trying to use
God to make money. I can see this is an old habit with you; you reek with
money-lust."

24   "Oh!" said Simon, "pray for me! Pray to the Master that nothing like
that will ever happen to me!"

25   And with that, the apostles were on their way, continuing to witness
and spread the Message of God's salvation, preaching in every Samaritan
town they passed through on their return to Jerusalem.

THE ETHIOPIAN EUNUCH

26-28   Later God's angel spoke to Philip: "At noon today I want you to walk over
to that desolate road that goes from Jerusalem down to Gaza." He got up
and went. He met an Ethiopian eunuch coming down the road. The eunuch
had been on a pilgrimage to Jerusalem and was returning to Ethiopia,
where he was minister in charge of all the finances of Candace, queen of the
Ethiopians. He was riding in a chariot and reading the prophet Isaiah.

29-30   The Spirit told Philip, "Climb into the chariot." Running up alongside,
Philip heard the eunuch reading Isaiah and asked, "Do you understand
what you're reading?"

31-33   He answered, "How can I without some help?" and invited Philip into
the chariot with him. The passage he was reading was this:

As a sheep led to slaughter,
    and quiet as a lamb being sheared,
He was silent, saying nothing.
    He was mocked and put down, never got a fair trial.
But who now can count his kin
    since he's been taken from the earth?

34-35   The eunuch said, "Tell me, who is the prophet talking about: himself or some other?" Philip grabbed his chance. Using this passage as his
text, he preached Jesus to him.

36-39   As they continued down the road, they came to a stream of water. The
eunuch said, "Here's water. Why can't I be baptized?" He ordered the
chariot to stop. They both went down to the water, and Philip baptized him
on the spot. When they came up out of the water, the Spirit of God suddenly
took Philip off, and that was the last the eunuch saw of him. But he didn't
mind. He had what he'd come for and went on down the road as happy as
he could be.

40   Philip showed up in Azotus and continued north, preaching the Message
in all the villages along that route until he arrived at Caesarea.

The Blinding of Saul

9 1-2 All this time Saul was breathing down the necks of the Master's disciples, out for the kill. He went to the Chief Priest and got arrest warrants to take to the meeting places in Damascus so that if he found anyone there belonging to the Way, whether men or women, he could arrest them and bring them to Jerusalem.

3-4 He set off. When he got to the outskirts of Damascus, he was suddenly dazed by a blinding flash of light. As he fell to the ground, he heard a voice: "Saul, Saul, why are you out to get me?"

5-6 He said, "Who are you, Master?"

"I am Jesus, the One you're hunting down. I want you to get up and enter the city. In the city you'll be told what to do next."

7-9 His companions stood there dumbstruck—they could hear the sound, but couldn't see anyone—while Saul, picking himself up off the ground, found himself stone-blind. They had to take him by the hand and lead him into Damascus. He continued blind for three days. He ate nothing, drank nothing.

10 There was a disciple in Damascus by the name of Ananias. The Master spoke to him in a vision: "Ananias."

"Yes, Master?" he answered.

11-12 "Get up and go over to Straight Avenue. Ask at the house of Judas for a man from Tarsus. His name is Saul. He's there praying. He has just had a dream in which he saw a man named Ananias enter the house and lay hands on him so he could see again."

13-14 Ananias protested, "Master, you can't be serious. Everybody's talking about this man and the terrible things he's been doing, his reign of terror against your people in Jerusalem! And now he's shown up here with papers from the Chief Priest that give him license to do the same to us."

15-16 But the Master said, "Don't argue! Go! I have picked him as my personal representative to non-Jews and kings and Jews. And now I'm about to show him what he's in for — the hard suffering that goes with this job."

17-19 So Ananias went and found the house, placed his hands on blind Saul, and said, "Brother Saul, the Master sent me, the same Jesus you saw on your way here. He sent me so you could see again and be filled with the Holy Spirit." No sooner were the words out of his mouth than something like scales fell from Saul's eyes—he could see again! He got to his feet, was baptized, and sat down with them to a hearty meal.

Plots Against Saul

19-21 Saul spent a few days getting acquainted with the Damascus disciples, but then went right to work, wasting no time, preaching in the meeting places that this Jesus was the Son of God. They were caught off guard by this and, not at all sure they could trust him, they kept saying, "Isn't this the man who wreaked havoc in Jerusalem among the believers? And didn't he come here to do the same thing—arrest us and drag us off to jail in Jerusalem for sentencing by the high priests?"

22 But their suspicions didn't slow Saul down for even a minute. His momentum was up now and he plowed straight into the opposition, disarming the Damascus Jews and trying to show them that this Jesus was the Messiah.

23-25 After this had gone on quite a long time, some Jews conspired to kill him, but Saul got wind of it. They were watching the city gates around the clock so they could kill him. Then one night the disciples engineered his escape by lowering him over the wall in a basket.

26-27 Back in Jerusalem he tried to join the disciples, but they were all afraid of him. They didn't trust him one bit. Then Barnabas took him under his wing. He introduced him to the apostles and stood up for him, told them how Saul had seen and spoken to the Master on the Damascus Road and how in Damascus itself he had laid his life on the line with his bold preaching in Jesus' name.

28-30 After that he was accepted as one of them, going in and out of Jerusalem with no questions asked, uninhibited as he preached in the Master's name. But then he ran afoul of a group called Hellenists—he had been engaged in a running argument with them—who plotted his murder. When his friends learned of the plot, they got him out of town, took him to Caesarea, and then shipped him off to Tarsus.

31 Things calmed down after that and the church had smooth sailing for a while. All over the country—Judea, Samaria, Galilee—the church grew. They were permeated with a deep sense of reverence for God. The Holy Spirit was with them, strengthening them. They prospered wonderfully.

TABITHA

32-35 Peter went off on a mission to visit all the churches. In the course of his travels he arrived in Lydda and met with the believers there. He came across a man—his name was Aeneas—who had been in bed eight years paralyzed. Peter said, "Aeneas, Jesus Christ heals you. Get up and make your bed!" And he did it—jumped right out of bed. Everybody who lived in Lydda and Sharon saw him walking around and woke up to the fact that God was alive and active among them.

36-37 Down the road a way in Joppa there was a disciple named Tabitha, "Gazelle" in our language. She was well-known for doing good and helping out. During the time Peter was in the area she became sick and died. Her friends prepared her body for burial and put her in a cool room.

38-40 Some of the disciples had heard that Peter was visiting in nearby Lydda and sent two men to ask if he would be so kind as to come over. Peter got right up and went with them. They took him into the room where Tabitha's body was laid out. Her old friends, most of them widows, were in the room mourning. They showed Peter pieces of clothing the Gazelle had made while she was with them. Peter put the widows all out of the room. He knelt and prayed. Then he spoke directly to the body: "Tabitha, get up."

40-41 She opened her eyes. When she saw Peter, she sat up. He took her hand and helped her up. Then he called in the believers and widows, and presented her to them alive.

42-43 When this became known all over Joppa, many put their trust in the Master. Peter stayed on a long time in Joppa as a guest of Simon the Tanner.

PETER'S VISION

1-3 10 There was a man named Cornelius who lived in Caesarea, captain of the Italian Guard stationed there. He was a thoroughly good man. He had led everyone in his house to live worshipfully before God, was always helping people in need, and had the habit of prayer. One day about three o'clock in the afternoon he had a vision. An angel of God, as real as his next-door neighbor, came in and said, "Cornelius."

4-6   Cornelius stared hard, wondering if he was seeing things. Then he said, "What do you want, sir?"

The angel said, "Your prayers and neighborly acts have brought you to God's attention. Here's what you are to do. Send men to Joppa to get Simon, the one everyone calls Peter. He is staying with Simon the Tanner, whose house is down by the sea."

7-8   As soon as the angel was gone, Cornelius called two servants and one particularly devout soldier from the guard. He went over with them in great detail everything that had just happened, and then sent them off to Joppa.

9-13   The next day as the three travelers were approaching the town, Peter went out on the balcony to pray. It was about noon. Peter got hungry and started thinking about lunch. While lunch was being prepared, he fell into a trance. He saw the skies open up. Something that looked like a huge blanket lowered by ropes at its four corners settled on the ground. Every kind of animal and reptile and bird you could think of was on it. Then a voice came: "Go to it, Peter — kill and eat."

14   Peter said, "Oh, no, Lord. I've never so much as tasted food that was not kosher."

15   The voice came a second time: "If God says it's okay, it's okay."

16   This happened three times, and then the blanket was pulled back up into the skies.

17-20   As Peter, puzzled, sat there trying to figure out what it all meant, the men sent by Cornelius showed up at Simon's front door. They called in, asking if there was a Simon, also called Peter, staying there. Peter, lost in thought, didn't hear them, so the Spirit whispered to him, "Three men are knocking at the door looking for you. Get down there and go with them. Don't ask any questions. I sent them to get you."

21   Peter went down and said to the men, "I think I'm the man you're looking for. What's up?"

22-23   They said, "Captain Cornelius, a God-fearing man well-known for his fair play — ask any Jew in this part of the country — was commanded by a holy angel to get you and bring you to his house so he could hear what you had to say." Peter invited them in and made them feel at home.

God Plays No Favorites

23-26   The next morning he got up and went with them. Some of his friends from Joppa went along. A day later they entered Caesarea. Cornelius was expecting them and had his relatives and close friends waiting with him. The minute Peter came through the door, Cornelius was up on his feet greeting him — and then down on his face worshiping him! Peter pulled him up and said, "None of that — I'm a man and only a man, no different from you."

27-29   Talking things over, they went on into the house, where Cornelius introduced Peter to everyone who had come. Peter addressed them, "You know, I'm sure that this is highly irregular. Jews just don't do this — visit and relax with people of another race. But God has just shown me that no race is better than any other. So the minute I was sent for, I came, no questions asked. But now I'd like to know why you sent for me."

30-32   Cornelius said, "Four days ago at about this time, midafternoon, I was home praying. Suddenly there was a man right in front of me, flooding the room with light. He said, 'Cornelius, your daily prayers and neighborly acts have brought you to God's attention. I want you to send to Joppa to get Simon, the one they call Peter. He's staying with Simon the Tanner down by the sea.'

33   "So I did it — I sent for you. And you've been good enough to come. And now we're all here in God's presence, ready to listen to whatever the Master put in your heart to tell us."

34-36   Peter fairly exploded with his good news: "It's God's own truth, nothing could be plainer: God plays no favorites! It makes no difference who you are or where you're from — if you want God and are ready to do as he says, the door is open. The Message he sent to the children of Israel — that through Jesus Christ everything is being put together again — well, he's doing it everywhere, among everyone.

37-38   "You know the story of what happened in Judea. It began in Galilee after John preached a total life-change. Then Jesus arrived from Nazareth, anointed by God with the Holy Spirit, ready for action. He went through the country helping people and healing everyone who was beaten down by the Devil. He was able to do all this because God was with him.

39-43   "And we saw it, saw it all, everything he did in the land of the Jews and in Jerusalem where they killed him, hung him from a cross. But in three days God had him up, alive, and out where he could be seen. Not everyone saw him — he wasn't put on public display. Witnesses had been carefully handpicked by God beforehand — us! We were the ones, there to eat and drink with him after he came back from the dead. He commissioned us to announce this in public, to bear solemn witness that he is in fact the One whom God destined as Judge of the living and dead. But we're not alone in this. Our witness that he is the means to forgiveness of sins is backed up by the witness of all the prophets."

44-46   No sooner were these words out of Peter's mouth than the Holy Spirit came on the listeners. The believing Jews who had come with Peter couldn't believe it, couldn't believe that the gift of the Holy Spirit was poured out on "outsider" non-Jews, but there it was — they heard them speaking in tongues, heard them praising God.

46-48   Then Peter said, "Do I hear any objections to baptizing these friends with water? They've received the Holy Spirit exactly as we did." Hearing no objections, he ordered that they be baptized in the name of Jesus Christ.

     Then they asked Peter to stay on for a few days.

God Has Broken Through

1-3   11 The news traveled fast and in no time the leaders and friends back in Jerusalem heard about it — heard that the non-Jewish "outsiders" were now "in." When Peter got back to Jerusalem, some of his old associates, concerned about circumcision, called him on the carpet: "What do you think you're doing rubbing shoulders with that crowd, eating what is prohibited and ruining our good name?"

4-6   So Peter, starting from the beginning, laid it out for them step-by-step: "Recently I was in the town of Joppa praying. I fell into a trance and saw a vision: Something like a huge blanket, lowered by ropes at its four corners, came down out of heaven and settled on the ground in front of me.

Milling around on the blanket were farm animals, wild animals, reptiles, birds—you name it, it was there. Fascinated, I took it all in.

7-10 "Then I heard a voice: 'Go to it, Peter—kill and eat.' I said, 'Oh, no, Master. I've never so much as tasted food that wasn't kosher.' The voice spoke again: 'If God says it's okay, it's okay.' This happened three times, and then the blanket was pulled back up into the sky.

11-14 "Just then three men showed up at the house where I was staying, sent from Caesarea to get me. The Spirit told me to go with them, no questions asked. So I went with them, I and six friends, to the man who had sent for me. He told us how he had seen an angel right in his own house, real as his next-door neighbor, saying, 'Send to Joppa and get Simon, the one they call Peter. He'll tell you something that will save your life—in fact, you and everyone you care for.'

15-17 "So I started in, talking. Before I'd spoken half a dozen sentences, the Holy Spirit fell on them just as he did on us the first time. I remembered Jesus' words: 'John baptized with water; you will be baptized with the Holy Spirit.' So I ask you: If God gave the same exact gift to them as to us when we believed in the Master Jesus Christ, how could I object to God?"

18 Hearing it all laid out like that, they quieted down. And then, as it sank in, they started praising God. "It's really happened! God has broken through to the other nations, opened them up to Life!"

19-21 Those who had been scattered by the persecution triggered by Stephen's death traveled as far as Phoenicia, Cyprus, and Antioch, but they were still only speaking and dealing with their fellow Jews. Then some of the men from Cyprus and Cyrene who had come to Antioch started talking to Greeks, giving them the Message of the Master Jesus. God was pleased with what they were doing and put his stamp of approval on it—quite a number of the Greeks believed and turned to the Master.

22-24 When the church in Jerusalem got wind of this, they sent Barnabas to Antioch to check on things. As soon as he arrived, he saw that God was behind and in it all. He threw himself in with them, got behind them, urging them to stay with it the rest of their lives. He was a good man that way, enthusiastic and confident in the Holy Spirit's ways. The community grew large and strong in the Master.

25-26 Then Barnabas went on to Tarsus to look for Saul. He found him and brought him back to Antioch. They were there a whole year, meeting with the church and teaching a lot of people. It was in Antioch that the disciples were for the first time called Christians.

27-30 It was about this same time that some prophets came to Antioch from Jerusalem. One of them named Agabus stood up one day and, prompted by the Spirit, warned that a severe famine was about to devastate the country. (The famine eventually came during the rule of Claudius.) So the disciples decided that each of them would send whatever they could to their fellow Christians in Judea to help out. They sent Barnabas and Saul to deliver the collection to the leaders in Jerusalem.

PETER UNDER HEAVY GUARD

1-4 **12** That's when King Herod got it into his head to go after some of the church members. He murdered James, John's brother. When he saw how much it raised his popularity ratings with the Jews, he arrested Peter—all this during Passover Week, mind you—and had him thrown in jail, putting four squads of four soldiers each to guard him. He was planning a public lynching after Passover.

5 All the time that Peter was under heavy guard in the jailhouse, the church prayed for him most strenuously.

6 Then the time came for Herod to bring him out for the kill. That night, even though shackled to two soldiers, one on either side, Peter slept like a baby. And there were guards at the door keeping their eyes on the place. Herod was taking no chances!

7-9 Suddenly there was an angel at his side and light flooding the room. The angel shook Peter and got him up: "Hurry!" The handcuffs fell off his wrists. The angel said, "Get dressed. Put on your shoes." Peter did it. Then, "Grab your coat and let's get out of here." Peter followed him, but didn't believe it was really an angel — he thought he was dreaming.

10-11 Past the first guard and then the second, they came to the iron gate that led into the city. It swung open before them on its own, and they were out on the street, free as the breeze. At the first intersection the angel left him, going his own way. That's when Peter realized it was no dream. "I can't believe it — this really happened! The Master sent his angel and rescued me from Herod's vicious little production and the spectacle the Jewish mob was looking forward to."

12-14 Still shaking his head, amazed, he went to Mary's house, the Mary who was John Mark's mother. The house was packed with praying friends. When he knocked on the door to the courtyard, a young woman named Rhoda came to see who it was. But when she recognized his voice — Peter's voice! — she was so excited and eager to tell everyone Peter was there that she forgot to open the door and left him standing in the street.

15-16 But they wouldn't believe her, dismissing her, dismissing her report. "You're crazy," they said. She stuck by her story, insisting. They still wouldn't believe her and said, "It must be his angel." All this time poor Peter was standing out in the street, knocking away.

16-17 Finally they opened up and saw him — and went wild! Peter put his hands up and calmed them down. He described how the Master had gotten him out of jail, then said, "Tell James and the brothers what's happened." He left them and went off to another place.

18-19 At daybreak the jail was in an uproar. "Where is Peter? What's happened to Peter?" When Herod sent for him and they could neither produce him nor explain why not, he ordered their execution: "Off with their heads!" Fed up with Judea and Jews, he went for a vacation to Caesarea.

THE DEATH OF HEROD

20-22 But things went from bad to worse for Herod. Now people from Tyre and Sidon put him on the warpath. But they got Blastus, King Herod's right-hand man, to put in a good word for them and got a delegation together to iron things out. Because they were dependent on Judea for food supplies, they couldn't afford to let this go on too long. On the day set for their meeting, Herod, robed in pomposity, took his place on the throne and regaled them with a lot of hot air. The people played their part to the hilt and shouted flatteries: "The voice of God! The voice of God!"

23 That was the last straw. God had had enough of Herod's arrogance and sent an angel to strike him down. Herod had given God no credit for anything. Down he went. Rotten to the core, a maggoty old man if there

ever was one, he died.

24 Meanwhile, the ministry of God's Word grew by leaps and bounds.

25 Barnabas and Saul, once they had delivered the relief offering to the church in Jerusalem, went back to Antioch. This time they took John with them, the one they called Mark.

BARNABAS, SAUL, AND DOCTOR KNOW-IT-ALL

1-2 13 The congregation in Antioch was blessed with a number of prophet-preachers and teachers:

Barnabas,
Simon, nicknamed Niger,
Lucius the Cyrenian,
Manaen, an advisor to the ruler Herod,
Saul.

One day as they were worshiping God — they were also fasting as they waited for guidance — the Holy Spirit spoke: "Take Barnabas and Saul and commission them for the work I have called them to do."

3 So they commissioned them. In that circle of intensity and obedience, of fasting and praying, they laid hands on their heads and sent them off.

4-5 Sent off on their new assignment by the Holy Spirit, Barnabas and Saul went down to Seleucia and caught a ship for Cyprus. The first thing they did when they put in at Salamis was preach God's Word in the Jewish meeting places. They had John along to help out as needed.

6-7 They traveled the length of the island, and at Paphos came upon a Jewish wizard who had worked himself into the confidence of the governor, Sergius Paulus, an intelligent man not easily taken in by charlatans. The wizard's name was Bar-Jesus. He was as crooked as a corkscrew.

7-11 The governor invited Barnabas and Saul in, wanting to hear God's Word firsthand from them. But Dr. Know-It-All (that's the wizard's name in plain English) stirred up a ruckus, trying to divert the governor from becoming a believer. But Saul (or Paul), full of the Holy Spirit and looking him straight in the eye, said, "You bag of wind, you parody of a devil — why, you stay up nights inventing schemes to cheat people out of God. But now you've come up against God himself, and your game is up. You're about to go blind — no sunlight for you for a good long stretch." He was plunged immediately into a shadowy mist and stumbled around, begging people to take his hand and show him the way.

12 When the governor saw what happened, he became a believer, full of enthusiasm over what they were saying about the Master.

DON'T TAKE THIS LIGHTLY

13-14 From Paphos, Paul and company put out to sea, sailing on to Perga in Pamphylia. That's where John called it quits and went back to Jerusalem. From Perga the rest of them traveled on to Antioch in Pisidia.

14-15 On the Sabbath they went to the meeting place and took their places. After the reading of the Scriptures — God's Law and the Prophets — the president of the meeting asked them, "Friends, do you have anything you want to say? A word of encouragement, perhaps?"

16-20   Paul stood up, paused and took a deep breath, then said, "Fellow Israelites and friends of God, listen. God took a special interest in our ancestors, pulled our people who were beaten down in Egyptian exile to their feet, and led them out of there in grand style. He took good care of them for nearly forty years in that godforsaken wilderness and then, having wiped out seven enemies who stood in the way, gave them the land of Canaan for their very own — a span in all of about 450 years.

20-22   "Up to the time of Samuel the prophet, God provided judges to lead them. But then they asked for a king, and God gave them Saul, son of Kish, out of the tribe of Benjamin. After Saul had ruled forty years, God removed him from office and put King David in his place, with this commendation: 'I've searched the land and found this David, son of Jesse. He's a man whose heart beats to my heart, a man who will do what I tell him.'

23-25   "From out of David's descendants God produced a Savior for Israel, Jesus, exactly as he promised — but only after John had thoroughly alerted the people to his arrival by preparing them for a total life-change. As John was finishing up his work, he said, 'Did you think I was the One? No, I'm not the One. But the One you've been waiting for all these years is just around the corner, about to appear. And I'm about to disappear.'

26-29   "Dear brothers and sisters, children of Abraham, and friends of God, this message of salvation has been precisely targeted to you. The citizens and rulers in Jerusalem didn't recognize who he was and condemned him to death. They couldn't find a good reason, but demanded that Pilate execute him anyway. They did just what the prophets said they would do, but had no idea they were following to the letter the script of the prophets, even though those same prophets are read every Sabbath in their meeting places.

29-31   "After they had done everything the prophets said they would do, they took him down from the cross and buried him. And then God raised him from death. There is no disputing that — he appeared over and over again many times and places to those who had known him well in the Galilean years, and these same people continue to give witness that he is alive.

32-35   "And we're here today bringing you good news: the Message that what God promised the fathers has come true for the children — for us! He raised Jesus, exactly as described in the second Psalm:

My Son! My very own Son!
Today I celebrate you!

"When he raised him from the dead, he did it for good — no going back to that rot and decay for him. That's why Isaiah said, 'I'll give to all of you David's guaranteed blessings.' So also the psalmist's prayer: 'You'll never let your Holy One see death's rot and decay.'

36-39   "David, of course, having completed the work God set out for him, has been in the grave, dust and ashes, a long time now. But the One God raised up — no dust and ashes for him! I want you to know, my very dear friends, that it is on account of this resurrected Jesus that the forgiveness of your sins can be promised. He accomplishes, in those who believe, everything that the Law of Moses could never make good on. But everyone who believes in this raised-up Jesus is declared good and right and whole before God.

40-41   "Don't take this lightly. You don't want the prophet's sermon to describe you:

Watch out, cynics;
Look hard — watch your world fall to pieces.
I'm doing something right before your eyes
That you won't believe, though it's staring you in the face."

42-43 When the service was over, Paul and Barnabas were invited back to preach again the next Sabbath. As the meeting broke up, a good many Jews and converts to Judaism went along with Paul and Barnabas, who urged them in long conversations to stick with what they'd started, this living in and by God's grace.

44-45 When the next Sabbath came around, practically the whole city showed up to hear the Word of God. Some of the Jews, seeing the crowds, went wild with jealousy and tore into Paul, contradicting everything he was saying, making an ugly scene.

46-47 But Paul and Barnabas didn't back down. Standing their ground they said, "It was required that God's Word be spoken first of all to you, the Jews. But seeing that you want no part of it — you've made it quite clear that you have no taste or inclination for eternal life — the door is open to all the outsiders. And we're on our way through it, following orders, doing what God commanded when he said,

I've set you up
    as light to all nations.
You'll proclaim salvation
    to the four winds and seven seas!"

48-49 When the non-Jewish outsiders heard this, they could hardly believe their good fortune. All who were marked out for *real life* put their trust in God — they honored God's Word by receiving that life. And this Message of salvation spread like wildfire all through the region.

50-52 Some of the Jews convinced the most respected women and leading men of the town that their precious way of life was about to be destroyed. Alarmed, they turned on Paul and Barnabas and forced them to leave. Paul and Barnabas shrugged their shoulders and went on to the next town, Iconium, brimming with joy and the Holy Spirit, two happy disciples.

1-3 **14** When they got to Iconium they went, as they always did, to the meeting place of the Jews and gave their message. The Message convinced both Jews and non-Jews — and not just a few, either. But the unbelieving Jews worked up a whispering campaign against Paul and Barnabas, sowing mistrust and suspicion in the minds of the people in the street. The two apostles were there a long time, speaking freely, openly, and confidently as they presented the clear evidence of God's gifts, God corroborating their work with miracles and wonders.

4-7 But then there was a split in public opinion, some siding with the Jews, some with the apostles. One day, learning that both the Jews and non-Jews had been organized by their leaders to beat them up, they escaped as best they could to the next towns — Lyconia, Lystra, Derbe, and that neighborhood — but then were right back at it again, getting out the Message.

Gods or Men?

8-10   There was a man in Lystra who couldn't walk. He sat there, crippled since the day of his birth. He heard Paul talking, and Paul, looking him in the eye, saw that he was ripe for God's work, ready to believe. So he said, loud enough for everyone to hear, "Up on your feet!" The man was up in a flash—jumped up and walked around as if he'd been walking all his life.

11-13   When the crowd saw what Paul had done, they went wild, calling out in their Lyconian dialect, "The gods have come down! These men are gods!" They called Barnabas "Zeus" and Paul "Hermes" (since Paul did most of the speaking). The priest of the local Zeus shrine got up a parade—bulls and banners and people lined right up to the gates, ready for the ritual of sacrifice.

14-15   When Barnabas and Paul finally realized what was going on, they stopped them. Waving their arms, they interrupted the parade, calling out, "What do you think you're doing! We're not gods! We are men just like you, and we're here to bring you the Message, to persuade you to abandon these silly god-superstitions and embrace God himself, the living God. We don't make God; he makes us, and all of this—sky, earth, sea, and everything in them.

16-18   "In the generations before us, God let all the different nations go their own way. But even then he didn't leave them without a clue, for he made a good creation, poured down rain and gave bumper crops. When your bellies were full and your hearts happy, there was evidence of good beyond your doing." Talking fast and hard like this, they prevented them from carrying out the sacrifice that would have honored them as gods—but just barely.

19-20   Then some Jews from Antioch and Iconium caught up with them and turned the fickle crowd against them. They beat Paul unconscious, dragged him outside the town and left him for dead. But as the disciples gathered around him, he came to and got up. He went back into town and the next day left with Barnabas for Derbe.

Plenty of Hard Times

21-22   After proclaiming the Message in Derbe and establishing a strong core of disciples, they retraced their steps to Lystra, then Iconium, and then Antioch, putting muscle and sinew in the lives of the disciples, urging them to stick with what they had begun to believe and not quit, making it clear to them that it wouldn't be easy: "Anyone signing up for the kingdom of God has to go through plenty of hard times."

23-26   Paul and Barnabas handpicked leaders in each church. After praying— their prayers intensified by fasting—they presented these new leaders to the Master to whom they had entrusted their lives. Working their way back through Pisidia, they came to Pamphylia and preached in Perga. Finally, they made it to Attalia and caught a ship back to Antioch, where it had all started—launched by God's grace and now safely home by God's grace. A good piece of work.

27-28   On arrival, they got the church together and reported on their trip, telling in detail how God had used them to throw the door of faith wide open so people of all nations could come streaming in. Then they settled down for a long, leisurely visit with the disciples.

TO LET OUTSIDERS INSIDE

1-2 It wasn't long before some Jews showed up from Judea insisting that everyone be circumcised: "If you're not circumcised in the Mosaic fashion, you can't be saved." Paul and Barnabas were up on their feet at once in fierce protest. The church decided to resolve the matter by sending Paul, Barnabas, and a few others to put it before the apostles and leaders in Jerusalem.

3 After they were sent off and on their way, they told everyone they met as they traveled through Phoenicia and Samaria about the breakthrough to the non-Jewish outsiders. Everyone who heard the news cheered — it was terrific news!

4-5 When they got to Jerusalem, Paul and Barnabas were graciously received by the whole church, including the apostles and leaders. They reported on their recent journey and how God had used them to open things up to the outsiders. Some Pharisees stood up to say their piece. They had become believers, but continued to hold to the hard party line of the Pharisees. "You have to circumcise the pagan converts," they said. "You must make them keep the Law of Moses."

6-9 The apostles and leaders called a special meeting to consider the matter. The arguments went on and on, back and forth, getting more and more heated. Then Peter took the floor: "Friends, you well know that from early on God made it quite plain that he wanted the pagans to hear the Message of this good news and embrace it — and not in any secondhand or roundabout way, but firsthand, straight from my mouth. And God, who can't be fooled by any pretense on our part but always knows a person's thoughts, gave them the Holy Spirit exactly as he gave him to us. He treated the outsiders exactly as he treated us, beginning at the very center of who they were and working from that center outward, cleaning up their lives as they trusted and believed him.

10-11 "So why are you now trying to out-god God, loading these new believers down with rules that crushed our ancestors and crushed us, too? Don't we believe that we are saved because the Master Jesus amazingly and out of sheer generosity moved to save us just as he did those from beyond our nation? So what are we arguing about?"

12-13 There was dead silence. No one said a word. With the room quiet, Barnabas and Paul reported matter-of-factly on the miracles and wonders God had done among the other nations through their ministry. The silence deepened; you could hear a pin drop.

13-18 James broke the silence. "Friends, listen. Simeon has told us the story of how God at the very outset made sure that racial outsiders were included. This is in perfect agreement with the words of the prophets:

> After this, I'm coming back;
>   I'll rebuild David's ruined house;
> I'll put all the pieces together again;
>   I'll make it look like new
> So outsiders who seek will find,
>   so they'll have a place to come to,
> All the pagan peoples
>   included in what I'm doing.

"God said it and now he's doing it. It's no afterthought; he's always known he would do this.

19-21   "So here is my decision: We're not going to unnecessarily burden non-Jewish people who turn to the Master. We'll write them a letter and tell them, 'Be careful to not get involved in activities connected with idols, to guard the morality of sex and marriage, to not serve food offensive to Jewish Christians — blood, for instance.' This is basic wisdom from Moses, preached and honored for centuries now in city after city as we have met and kept the Sabbath."

22-23   Everyone agreed: apostles, leaders, all the people. They picked Judas (nicknamed Barsabbas) and Silas — they both carried considerable weight in the church — and sent them to Antioch with Paul and Barnabas with this letter:

From the apostles and leaders, your friends, to our friends in Antioch, Syria, and Cilicia:

Hello!

24-27   We heard that some men from our church went to you and said things that confused and upset you. Mind you, they had no authority from us; we didn't send them. We have agreed unanimously to pick representatives and send them to you with our good friends Barnabas and Paul. We picked men we knew you could trust, Judas and Silas — they've looked death in the face time and again for the sake of our Master Jesus Christ. We've sent them to confirm in a face-to-face meeting with you what we've written.

28-29   It seemed to the Holy Spirit and to us that you should not be saddled with any crushing burden, but be responsible only for these bare necessities: Be careful not to get involved in activities connected with idols; avoid serving food offensive to Jewish Christians (blood, for instance); and guard the morality of sex and marriage.

These guidelines are sufficient to keep relations congenial between us. And God be with you!

Barnabas and Paul Go Their Separate Ways

30-33   And so off they went to Antioch. On arrival, they gathered the church and read the letter. The people were greatly relieved and pleased. Judas and Silas, good preachers both of them, strengthened their new friends with many words of courage and hope. Then it was time to go home. They were sent off by their new friends with laughter and embraces all around to report back to those who had sent them.

35   Paul and Barnabas stayed on in Antioch, teaching and preaching the Word of God. But they weren't alone. There were a number of teachers and preachers at that time in Antioch.

36   After a few days of this, Paul said to Barnabas, "Let's go back and visit all our friends in each of the towns where we preached the Word of God. Let's see how they're doing."

37-41   Barnabas wanted to take John along, the John nicknamed Mark. But Paul wouldn't have him; he wasn't about to take along a quitter who, as soon as the going got tough, had jumped ship on them in Pamphylia. Tempers flared, and they ended up going their separate ways: Barnabas took Mark and sailed for Cyprus; Paul chose Silas and, offered up by their friends to the grace of the Master, went to Syria and Cilicia to build up muscle and sinew in those congregations.

A D R E A M G A V E P A U L H I S M A P

1-3   16 Paul came first to Derbe, then Lystra. He found a disciple there by the name of Timothy, son of a devout Jewish mother and Greek father. Friends in Lystra and Iconium all said what a fine young man he was. Paul wanted to recruit him for their mission, but first took him aside and circumcised him so he wouldn't offend the Jews who lived in those parts. They all knew that his father was Greek.

4-5   As they traveled from town to town, they presented the simple guidelines the Jerusalem apostles and leaders had come up with. That turned out to be most helpful. Day after day the congregations became stronger in faith and larger in size.

6-8   They went to Phrygia, and then on through the region of Galatia. Their plan was to turn west into Asia province, but the Holy Spirit blocked that route. So they went to Mysia and tried to go north to Bithynia, but the Spirit of Jesus wouldn't let them go there either. Proceeding on through Mysia, they went down to the seaport Troas.

9-10   That night Paul had a dream: A Macedonian stood on the far shore and called across the sea, "Come over to Macedonia and help us!" The dream gave Paul his map. We went to work at once getting things ready to cross over to Macedonia. All the pieces had come together. We knew now for sure that God had called us to preach the good news to the Europeans.

11-12   Putting out from the harbor at Troas, we made a straight run for Samothrace. The next day we tied up at New City and walked from there to Philippi, the main city in that part of Macedonia and, even more importantly, a Roman colony. We lingered there several days.

13-14   On the Sabbath, we left the city and went down along the river where we had heard there was to be a prayer meeting. We took our place with the women who had gathered there and talked with them. One woman, Lydia, was from Thyatira and a dealer in expensive textiles, known to be a God-fearing woman. As she listened with intensity to what was being said, the Master gave her a trusting heart — and she believed!

15   After she was baptized, along with everyone in her household, she said in a surge of hospitality, "If you're confident that I'm in this with you and believe in the Master truly, come home with me and be my guests." We hesitated, but she wouldn't take no for an answer.

B E A T U P A N D T H R O W N I N J A I L

16-18   One day, on our way to the place of prayer, a slave girl ran into us. She was a psychic and, with her fortunetelling, made a lot of money for the people who owned her. She started following Paul around, calling everyone's attention to us by yelling out, "These men are working for the Most High God. They're laying out the road of salvation for you!" She did this for a number of days until Paul, finally fed up with her, turned and commanded the spirit that possessed her, "Out! In the name of Jesus Christ, get out of her!" And it was gone, just like that.

19-22   When her owners saw that their lucrative little business was suddenly bankrupt, they went after Paul and Silas, roughed them up and dragged them into the market square. Then the police arrested them and pulled them into a court with the accusation, "These men are disturbing the peace — dangerous Jewish agitators subverting our Roman law and order." By this time the crowd had turned into a restless mob out for blood.

22-24 The judges went along with the mob, had Paul and Silas's clothes ripped off and ordered a public beating. After beating them black-and-blue, they threw them into jail, telling the jailkeeper to put them under heavy guard so there would be no chance of escape. He did just that — threw them into the maximum security cell in the jail and clamped leg irons on them.

25-26 Along about midnight, Paul and Silas were at prayer and singing a robust hymn to God. The other prisoners couldn't believe their ears. Then, without warning, a huge earthquake! The jailhouse tottered, every door flew open, all the prisoners were loose.

27-28 Startled from sleep, the jailer saw all the doors swinging loose on their hinges. Assuming that all the prisoners had escaped, he pulled out his sword and was about to do himself in, figuring he was as good as dead anyway, when Paul stopped him: "Don't do that! We're all still here! Nobody's run away!"

29-31 The jailer got a torch and ran inside. Badly shaken, he collapsed in front of Paul and Silas. He led them out of the jail and asked, "Sirs, what do I have to do to be saved, to really live?" They said, "Put your entire trust in the Master Jesus. Then you'll live as you were meant to live — and everyone in your house included!"

32-34 They went on to spell out in detail the story of the Master — the entire family got in on this part. They never did get to bed that night. The jailer made them feel at home, dressed their wounds, and then — he couldn't wait till morning! — was baptized, he and everyone in his family. There in his home, he had food set out for a festive meal. It was a night to remember: He and his entire family had put their trust in God; everyone in the house was in on the celebration.

35-36 At daybreak, the court judges sent officers with the instructions, "Release these men." The jailer gave Paul the message, "The judges sent word that you're free to go on your way. Congratulations! Go in peace!"

37 But Paul wouldn't budge. He told the officers, "They beat us up in public and threw us in jail, Roman citizens in good standing! And now they want to get us out of the way on the sly without anyone knowing? Nothing doing! If they want us out of here, let them come themselves and lead us out in broad daylight."

38-40 When the officers reported this, the judges panicked. They had no idea that Paul and Silas were Roman citizens. They hurried over and apologized, personally escorted them from the jail, and then asked them if they wouldn't please leave the city. Walking out of the jail, Paul and Silas went straight to Lydia's house, saw their friends again, encouraged them in the faith, and only then went on their way.

THESSALONICA

1-3 **17** They took the road south through Amphipolis and Apollonia to Thessalonica, where there was a community of Jews. Paul went to their meeting place, as he usually did when he came to a town, and for three Sabbaths running he preached to them from the Scriptures. He opened up the texts so they understood what they'd been reading all their lives: that the Messiah absolutely *had* to be put to death and raised from the dead — there were no other options — and that "this Jesus I'm introducing you to is that Messiah."

4-5 Some of them were won over and joined ranks with Paul and Silas, among them a great many God-fearing Greeks and a considerable number of women from the aristocracy. But the hard-line Jews became furious over the conversions. Mad with jealousy, they rounded up a bunch of brawlers off the streets and soon had an ugly mob terrorizing the city as they hunted down Paul and Silas.

5-7 They broke into Jason's house, thinking that Paul and Silas were there. When they couldn't find them, they collared Jason and his friends instead and dragged them before the city fathers, yelling hysterically, "These people are out to destroy the world, and now they've shown up on our doorstep, attacking everything we hold dear! And Jason is hiding them, these traitors and turncoats who say Jesus is king and Caesar is nothing!"

8-9 The city fathers and the crowd of people were totally alarmed by what they heard. They made Jason and his friends post heavy bail and let them go while they investigated the charges.

BEREA

10-12 That night, under cover of darkness, their friends got Paul and Silas out of town as fast as they could. They sent them to Berea, where they again met with the Jewish community. They were treated a lot better there than in Thessalonica. The Jews received Paul's message with enthusiasm and met with him daily, examining the Scriptures to see if they supported what he said. A lot of them became believers, including many Greeks who were prominent in the community, women and men of influence.

13-15 But it wasn't long before reports got back to the Thessalonian hard-line Jews that Paul was at it again, preaching the Word of God, this time in Berea. They lost no time responding, and created a mob scene there, too. With the help of his friends, Paul gave them the slip — caught a boat and put out to sea. Silas and Timothy stayed behind. The men who helped Paul escape got him as far as Athens and left him there. Paul sent word back with them to Silas and Timothy: "Come as quickly as you can!"

ATHENS

16 The longer Paul waited in Athens for Silas and Timothy, the angrier he got — all those idols! The city was a junkyard of idols.

17-18 He discussed it with the Jews and other like-minded people at their meeting place. And every day he went out on the streets and talked with anyone who happened along. He got to know some of the Epicurean and Stoic intellectuals pretty well through these conversations. Some of them dismissed him with sarcasm: "What an airhead!" But others, listening to him go on about Jesus and the resurrection, were intrigued: "That's a new slant on the gods. Tell us more."

19-21 These people got together and asked him to make a public presentation over at the Areopagus, where things were a little quieter. They said, "This is a new one on us. We've never heard anything quite like it. Where did you come up with this anyway? Explain it so we can understand." Downtown Athens was a great place for gossip. There were always people hanging around, natives and tourists alike, waiting for the latest tidbit on most anything.

22-23 So Paul took his stand in the open space at the Areopagus and laid it out for them. "It is plain to see that you Athenians take your religion seriously. When I arrived here the other day, I was fascinated with all the shrines I came across. And then I found one inscribed, TO THE GOD NOBODY KNOWS. I'm here to introduce you to this God so you can worship intelligently, know who you're dealing with.

24-29 "The God who made the world and everything in it, this Master of sky and land, doesn't live in custom-made shrines or need the human race to run errands for him, as if he couldn't take care of himself. He makes the creatures; the creatures don't make him. Starting from scratch, he made the entire human race and made the earth hospitable, with plenty of time and space for living so we could seek after God, and not just grope around in the dark but actually *find* him. He doesn't play hide-and-seek with us. He's not remote; he's *near*. We live and move in him, can't get away from him! One of your poets said it well: 'We're the God-created.' Well, if we are the God-created, it doesn't make a lot of sense to think we could hire a sculptor to chisel a god out of stone for *us*, does it?

30-31 "God overlooks it as long as you don't know any better—but that time is past. The unknown is now known, and he's calling for a radical life-change. He has set a day when the entire human race will be judged and everything set right. And he has already appointed the judge, confirming him before everyone by raising him from the dead."

32-34 At the phrase "raising him from the dead," the listeners split: Some laughed at him and walked off making jokes; others said, "Let's do this again. We want to hear more." But that was it for the day, and Paul left. There were still others, it turned out, who were convinced then and there, and stuck with Paul—among them Dionysius the Areopagite and a woman named Damaris.

CORINTH

1-4 **18** After Athens, Paul went to Corinth. That is where he discovered Aquila, a Jew born in Pontus, and his wife, Priscilla. They had just arrived from Italy, part of the general expulsion of Jews from Rome ordered by Claudius. Paul moved in with them, and they worked together at their common trade of tentmaking. But every Sabbath he was at the meeting place, doing his best to convince both Jews and Greeks about Jesus.

5-6 When Silas and Timothy arrived from Macedonia, Paul was able to give all his time to preaching and teaching, doing everything he could to persuade the Jews that Jesus was in fact God's Messiah. But no such luck. All they did was argue contentiously and contradict him at every turn. Totally exasperated, Paul had finally had it with them and gave it up as a bad job. "Have it your way, then," he said. "You've made your bed; now lie in it. From now on I'm spending my time with the other nations."

7-8 He walked out and went to the home of Titius Justus, a God-fearing man who lived right next to the Jews' meeting place. But Paul's efforts with the Jews weren't a total loss, for Crispus, the meeting-place president, put his trust in the Master. His entire family believed with him.

8-11 In the course of listening to Paul, a great many Corinthians believed and were baptized. One night the Master spoke to Paul in a dream: "Keep it up, and don't let anyone intimidate or silence you. No matter what happens, I'm with you and no one is going to be able to hurt you. You have no idea how many people I have on my side in this city." That was all he needed to stick it out. He stayed another year and a half, faithfully teaching the Word of God to the Corinthians.

12-13 But when Gallio was governor of Achaia province, the Jews got up a campaign against Paul, hauled him into court, and filed charges: "This man is seducing people into acts of worship that are illegal."

14-16 Just as Paul was about to defend himself, Gallio interrupted and said to the Jews, "If this was a matter of criminal conduct, I would gladly hear you out. But it sounds to me like one more Jewish squabble, another of your endless hairsplitting quarrels over religion. Take care of it on your own time. I can't be bothered with this nonsense," and he cleared them out of the courtroom.

17 Now the street rabble turned on Sosthenes, the new meeting-place president, and beat him up in plain sight of the court. Gallio didn't raise a finger. He could not have cared less.

EPHESUS

18 Paul stayed a while longer in Corinth, but then it was time to take leave of his friends. Saying his good-byes, he sailed for Syria, Priscilla and Aquila with him. Before boarding the ship in the harbor town of Cenchrea, he had his head shaved as part of a vow he had taken.

19-21 They landed in Ephesus, where Priscilla and Aquila got off and stayed. Paul left the ship briefly to go to the meeting place and preach to the Jews. They wanted him to stay longer, but he said he couldn't. But after saying good-bye, he promised, "I'll be back, God willing."

21-22 From Ephesus he sailed to Caesarea. He greeted the church there, and then went on to Antioch, completing the journey.

23 After spending a considerable time with the Antioch Christians, Paul set off again for Galatia and Phrygia, retracing his old tracks, one town after another, putting fresh heart into the disciples.

24-26 A man named Apollos came to Ephesus. He was a Jew, born in Alexandria, Egypt, and a terrific speaker, eloquent and powerful in his preaching of the Scriptures. He was well-educated in the way of the Master and fiery in his enthusiasm. Apollos was accurate in everything he taught about Jesus up to a point, but he only went as far as the baptism of John. He preached with power in the meeting place. When Priscilla and Aquila heard him, they took him aside and told him the rest of the story.

27-28 When Apollos decided to go on to Achaia province, his Ephesian friends gave their blessing and wrote a letter of recommendation for him, urging the disciples there to welcome him with open arms. The welcome paid off: Apollos turned out to be a great help to those who had become believers through God's immense generosity. He was particularly effective in public debate with the Jews as he brought out proof after convincing proof from the Scriptures that Jesus was in fact God's Messiah.

1-2 19 Now, it happened that while Apollos was away in Corinth, Paul made his way down through the mountains, came to Ephesus, and happened on some disciples there. The first thing he said was, "Did you receive the Holy Spirit when you believed? Did you take God into your mind only, or did you also embrace him with your heart? Did he get inside you?"

"We've never even heard of that — a Holy Spirit? God within us?"

3   "How were you baptized, then?" asked Paul.

"In John's baptism."

4   "That explains it," said Paul. "John preached a baptism of radical life-change so that people would be ready to receive the One coming after him, who turned out to be Jesus. If you've been baptized in John's baptism, you're ready now for the real thing, for Jesus."

5-7   And they were. As soon as they heard of it, they were baptized in the name of the Master Jesus. Paul put his hands on their heads and the Holy Spirit entered them. From that moment on, they were praising God in tongues and talking about God's actions. Altogether there were about twelve people there that day.

8-10   Paul then went straight to the meeting place. He had the run of the place for three months, doing his best to make the things of the kingdom of God real and convincing to them. But then resistance began to form as some of them began spreading evil rumors through the congregation about the Christian way of life. So Paul left, taking the disciples with him, and set up shop in the school of Tyrannus, holding class there daily. He did this for two years, giving everyone in the province of Asia, Jews as well as Greeks, ample opportunity to hear the Message of the Master.

WITCHES CAME OUT OF THE WOODWORK

11-12   God did powerful things through Paul, things quite out of the ordinary. The word got around and people started taking pieces of clothing — handkerchiefs and scarves and the like — that had touched Paul's skin and then touching the sick with them. The touch did it — they were healed and whole.

13-16   Some itinerant Jewish exorcists who happened to be in town at the time tried their hand at what they assumed to be Paul's "game." They pronounced the name of the Master Jesus over victims of evil spirits, saying, "I command you by the Jesus preached by Paul!" The seven sons of a certain Sceva, a Jewish high priest, were trying to do this on a man when the evil spirit talked back: "I know Jesus and I've heard of Paul, but who are you?" Then the possessed man went berserk — jumped the exorcists, beat them up, and tore off their clothes. Naked and bloody, they got away as best they could.

17-20   It was soon news all over Ephesus among both Jews and Greeks. The realization spread that God was in and behind this. Curiosity about Paul developed into reverence for the Master Jesus. Many of those who thus believed came out of the closet and made a clean break with their secret sorceries. All kinds of witches and warlocks came out of the woodwork with their books of spells and incantations and made a huge bonfire of them. Someone estimated their worth at fifty thousand silver coins. In such ways it became evident that the Word of the Master was now sovereign and prevailed in Ephesus.

THE GODDESS ARTEMIS

21-22   After all this had come to a head, Paul decided it was time to move on to Macedonia and Achaia provinces, and from there to Jerusalem. "Then," he said, "I'm off to Rome. I've got to see Rome!" He sent two of his assistants, Timothy and Erastus, on to Macedonia and then stayed for a while and wrapped things up in Asia.

23-26   But before he got away, a huge ruckus occurred over what was now being referred to as "the Way." A certain silversmith, Demetrius, conducted a brisk trade in the manufacture of shrines to the goddess Artemis, employing a number of artisans in his business. He rounded up his workers and others similarly employed and said, "Men, you well know that we have a good thing going here — and you've seen how Paul has barged in and discredited what we're doing by telling people that there's no such thing as a god made with hands. A lot of people are going along with him, not only here in Ephesus but all through Asia province.

27   "Not only is our little business in danger of falling apart, but the temple of our famous goddess Artemis will certainly end up a pile of rubble as her glorious reputation fades to nothing. And this is no mere local matter — the whole world worships our Artemis!"

28-31   That set them off in a frenzy. They ran into the street yelling, "Great Artemis of the Ephesians! Great Artemis of the Ephesians!" They put the whole city in an uproar, stampeding into the stadium, and grabbing two of Paul's associates on the way, the Macedonians Gaius and Aristarchus. Paul wanted to go in, too, but the disciples wouldn't let him. Prominent religious leaders in the city who had become friendly to Paul concurred: "By no means go near that mob!"

32-34   Some were yelling one thing, some another. Most of them had no idea what was going on or why they were there. As the Jews pushed Alexander to the front to try to gain control, different factions clamored to get him on their side. But he brushed them off and quieted the mob with an impressive sweep of his arms. But the moment he opened his mouth and they knew he was a Jew, they shouted him down: "Great Artemis of the Ephesians! Great Artemis of the Ephesians!" — on and on and on, for over two hours.

35-37   Finally, the town clerk got the mob quieted down and said, "Fellow citizens, is there anyone anywhere who doesn't know that our dear city Ephesus is protector of glorious Artemis and her sacred stone image that fell straight out of heaven? Since this is beyond contradiction, you had better get hold of yourselves. This is conduct unworthy of Artemis. These men you've dragged in here have done nothing to harm either our temple or our goddess.

38-41   "So if Demetrius and his guild of artisans have a complaint, they can take it to court and make all the accusations they want. If anything else is bothering you, bring it to the regularly scheduled town meeting and let it be settled there. There is no excuse for what's happened today. We're putting our city in serious danger. Rome, remember, does not look kindly on rioters." With that, he sent them home.

MACEDONIA AND GREECE

1-2   **20** With things back to normal, Paul called the disciples together and encouraged them to keep up the good work in Ephesus. Then, saying his good-byes, he left for Macedonia. Traveling through the country, passing from one gathering to another, he gave constant encouragement, lifting their spirits and charging them with fresh hope.

2-4   Then he came to Greece and stayed on for three months. Just as he was about to sail for Syria, the Jews cooked up a plot against him. So he went the other way, by land back through Macedonia, and gave them the slip. His companions for the journey were Sopater, son of Pyrrhus, from Berea; Aristarchus and Secundus, both Thessalonians; Gaius from Derbe; Timothy; and the two from western Asia, Tychicus and Trophimus.

5-6   They went on ahead and waited for us in Troas. Meanwhile, we stayed in Philippi for Passover Week, and then set sail. Within five days we were again in Troas and stayed a week.

7-9   We met on Sunday to worship and celebrate the Master's Supper. Paul addressed the congregation. Our plan was to leave first thing in the morning, but Paul talked on, way past midnight. We were meeting in a well-lighted upper room. A young man named Eutychus was sitting in an open window. As Paul went on and on, Eutychus fell sound asleep and toppled out the third-story window. When they picked him up, he was dead.

10-12   Paul went down, stretched himself on him, and hugged him hard. "No more crying," he said. "There's life in him yet." Then Paul got up and served the Master's Supper. And went on telling stories of the faith until dawn! On that note, they left — Paul going one way, the congregation another, leading the boy off alive, and full of life themselves.

13-16   In the meantime, the rest of us had gone on ahead to the ship and sailed for Assos, where we planned to pick up Paul. Paul wanted to walk there, and so had made these arrangements earlier. Things went according to plan: We met him in Assos, took him on board, and sailed to Mitylene. The next day we put in opposite Chios, Samos a day later, and then Miletus. Paul had decided to bypass Ephesus so that he wouldn't be held up in Asia province. He was in a hurry to get to Jerusalem in time for the Feast of Pentecost, if at all possible.

On to Jerusalem

17-21   From Miletus he sent to Ephesus for the leaders of the congregation. When they arrived, he said, "You know that from day one of my arrival in Asia I was with you totally — laying my life on the line, serving the Master no matter what, putting up with no end of scheming by Jews who wanted to do me in. I didn't skimp or trim in any way. Every truth and encouragement that could have made a difference to you, you got. I taught you out in public and I taught you in your homes, urging Jews and Greeks alike to a radical life-change before God and an equally radical trust in our Master Jesus.

22-24   "But there is another urgency before me now. I feel compelled to go to Jerusalem. I'm completely in the dark about what will happen when I get there. I do know that it won't be any picnic, for the Holy Spirit has let me know repeatedly and clearly that there are hard times and imprisonment ahead. But that matters little. What matters most to me is to finish what God started: the job the Master Jesus gave me of letting everyone I meet know all about this incredibly extravagant generosity of God.

25-27   "And so this is good-bye. You're not going to see me again, nor I you, you whom I have gone among for so long proclaiming the news of God's inaugurated kingdom. I've done my best for you, given you my all, held back nothing of God's will for you.

28   "Now it's up to you. Be on your toes — both for yourselves and your congregation of sheep. The Holy Spirit has put you in charge of these people — God's people they are — to guard and protect them. God himself thought they were worth dying for.

29-31   "I know that as soon as I'm gone, vicious wolves are going to show up and rip into this flock, men from your very own ranks twisting words so as to seduce disciples into following them instead of Jesus. So stay awake and keep up your guard. Remember those three years I kept at it with you, never letting up, pouring my heart out with you, one after another.

32   "Now I'm turning you over to God, our marvelous God whose gracious Word can make you into what he wants you to be and give you everything you could possibly need in this community of holy friends.

33-35   "I've never, as you so well know, had any taste for wealth or fashion. With these bare hands I took care of my own basic needs and those who worked with me. In everything I've done, I have demonstrated to you how necessary it is to work on behalf of the weak and not exploit them. You'll not likely go wrong here if you keep remembering that our Master said, 'You're far happier giving than getting.'"

36-38   Then Paul went down on his knees, all of them kneeling with him, and prayed. And then a river of tears. Much clinging to Paul, not wanting to let him go. They knew they would never see him again — he had told them quite plainly. The pain cut deep. Then, bravely, they walked him down to the ship.

TYRE AND CAESAREA

1-4   **21** And so, with the tearful good-byes behind us, we were on our way. We made a straight run to Cos, the next day reached Rhodes, and then Patara. There we found a ship going direct to Phoenicia, got on board, and set sail. Cyprus came into view on our left, but was soon out of sight as we kept on course for Syria, and eventually docked in the port of Tyre. While the cargo was being unloaded, we looked up the local disciples and stayed with them seven days. Their message to Paul, from insight given by the Spirit, was "Don't go to Jerusalem."

5-6   When our time was up, they escorted us out of the city to the docks. Everyone came along — men, women, children. They made a farewell party of the occasion! We all kneeled together on the beach and prayed. Then, after another round of saying good-bye, we climbed on board the ship while they drifted back to their homes.

7-9   A short run from Tyre to Ptolemais completed the voyage. We greeted our Christian friends there and stayed with them a day. In the morning we went on to Caesarea and stayed with Philip the Evangelist, one of "the Seven." Philip had four virgin daughters who prophesied.

10-11   After several days of visiting, a prophet from Judea by the name of Agabus came down to see us. He went right up to Paul, took Paul's belt, and, in a dramatic gesture, tied himself up, hands and feet. He said, "This is what the Holy Spirit says: The Jews in Jerusalem are going to tie up the man who owns this belt just like this and hand him over to godless unbelievers."

12-13   When we heard that, we and everyone there that day begged Paul not to be stubborn and persist in going to Jerusalem. But Paul wouldn't budge: "Why all this hysteria? Why do you insist on making a scene and making it even harder for me? You're looking at this backward. The issue in Jerusalem is not what they do to me, whether arrest or murder, but what the Master Jesus does through my obedience. Can't you see that?"

14   We saw that we weren't making even a dent in his resolve, and gave up. "It's in God's hands now," we said. "Master, you handle it."

15-16 It wasn't long before we had our luggage together and were on our way to Jerusalem. Some of the disciples from Caesarea went with us and took us to the home of Mnason, who received us warmly as his guests. A native of Cyprus, he had been among the earliest disciples.

JERUSALEM

17-19 In Jerusalem, our friends, glad to see us, received us with open arms. The first thing next morning, we took Paul to see James. All the church leaders were there. After a time of greeting and small talk, Paul told the story, detail by detail, of what God had done among the non-Jewish people through his ministry. They listened with delight and gave God the glory.

20-21 They had a story to tell, too: "And just look at what's been happening here — thousands upon thousands of God-fearing Jews have become believers in Jesus! But there's also a problem because they are more zealous than ever in observing the laws of Moses. They've been told that you advise believing Jews who live surrounded by unbelieving outsiders to go light on Moses, telling them that they don't need to circumcise their children or keep up the old traditions. This isn't sitting at all well with them.

22-24 "We're worried about what will happen when they discover you're in town. There's bound to be trouble. So here is what we want you to do: There are four men from our company who have taken a vow involving ritual purification, but have no money to pay the expenses. Join these men in their vows and pay their expenses. Then it will become obvious to everyone that there is nothing to the rumors going around about you and that you are in fact scrupulous in your reverence for the laws of Moses.

25 "In asking you to do this, we're not going back on our agreement regarding non-Jews who have become believers. We continue to hold fast to what we wrote in that letter, namely, to be careful not to get involved in activities connected with idols; to avoid serving food offensive to Jewish Christians; to guard the morality of sex and marriage."

26 So Paul did it — took the men, joined them in their vows, and paid their way. The next day he went to the Temple to make it official and stay there until the proper sacrifices had been offered and completed for each of them.

PAUL UNDER ARREST

27-29 When the seven days of their purification were nearly up, some Jews from around Ephesus spotted him in the Temple. At once they turned the place upside-down. They grabbed Paul and started yelling at the top of their lungs, "Help! You Israelites, help! This is the man who is going all over the world telling lies against us and our religion and this place. He's even brought Greeks in here and defiled this holy place." (What had happened was that they had seen Paul and Trophimus, the Ephesian Greek, walking together in the city and had just assumed that he had also taken him to the Temple and shown him around.)

30 Soon the whole city was in an uproar, people running from everywhere to the Temple to get in on the action. They grabbed Paul, dragged him outside, and locked the Temple gates so he couldn't get back in and gain sanctuary.

31-32 As they were trying to kill him, word came to the captain of the guard, "A riot! The whole city's boiling over!" He acted swiftly. His soldiers and centurions ran to the scene at once. As soon as the mob saw the captain and his soldiers, they quit beating Paul.

33-36   The captain came up and put Paul under arrest. He first ordered him handcuffed, and then asked who he was and what he had done. All he got from the crowd were shouts, one yelling this, another that. It was impossible to tell one word from another in the mob hysteria, so the captain ordered Paul taken to the military barracks. But when they got to the Temple steps, the mob became so violent that the soldiers had to carry Paul. As they carried him away, the crowd followed, shouting, "Kill him! Kill him!"

37-38   When they got to the barracks and were about to go in, Paul said to the captain, "Can I say something to you?"

He answered, "Oh, I didn't know you spoke Greek. I thought you were the Egyptian who not long ago started a riot here, and then hid out in the desert with his four thousand thugs."

39   Paul said, "No, I'm a Jew, born in Tarsus. And I'm a citizen still of that influential city. I have a simple request: Let me speak to the crowd."

PAUL TELLS HIS STORY

40   Standing on the barracks steps, Paul turned and held his arms up. A hush fell over the crowd as Paul began to speak. He spoke in Hebrew.

1-2   22 "My dear brothers and fathers, listen carefully to what I have to say before you jump to conclusions about me." When they heard him speaking Hebrew, they grew even quieter. No one wanted to miss a word of this.

2-3   He continued, "I am a good Jew, born in Tarsus in the province of Cilicia, but educated here in Jerusalem under the exacting eye of Rabbi Gamaliel, thoroughly instructed in our religious traditions. And I've always been passionately on God's side, just as you are right now.

4-5   "I went after anyone connected with this 'Way,' went at them hammer and tongs, ready to kill for God. I rounded up men and women right and left and had them thrown in prison. You can ask the Chief Priest or anyone in the High Council to verify this; they all knew me well. Then I went off to our brothers in Damascus, armed with official documents authorizing me to hunt down the followers of Jesus there, arrest them, and bring them back to Jerusalem for sentencing.

6-7   "As I arrived on the outskirts of Damascus about noon, a blinding light blazed out of the skies and I fell to the ground, dazed. I heard a voice: 'Saul, Saul, why are you out to get me?'

8-9   "'Who are you, Master?' I asked.

"He said, 'I am Jesus the Nazarene, the One you're hunting down.' My companions saw the light, but they didn't hear the conversation.

10-11   "Then I said, 'What do I do now, Master?'

"He said, 'Get to your feet and enter Damascus. There you'll be told everything that's been set out for you to do.' And so we entered Damascus, but nothing like the entrance I had planned — I was blind as a bat and my companions had to lead me in by the hand.

12-13   "And that's when I met Ananias, a man with a sterling reputation in observing our laws — the Jewish community in Damascus is unanimous on that score. He came and put his arm on my shoulder. 'Look up,' he said. I looked, and found myself looking right into his eyes — I could see again!

14-16 "Then he said, 'The God of our ancestors has handpicked you to be briefed on his plan of action. You've actually seen the Righteous Innocent and heard him speak. You are to be a key witness to everyone you meet of what you've seen and heard. So what are you waiting for? Get up and get yourself baptized, scrubbed clean of those sins and personally acquainted with God.'

17-18 "Well, it happened just as Ananias said. After I was back in Jerusalem and praying one day in the Temple, lost in the presence of God, I saw him, saw God's Righteous Innocent, and heard him say to me, 'Hurry up! Get out of here as quickly as you can. None of the Jews here in Jerusalem are going to accept what you say about me.'

19-20 "At first I objected: 'Who has better credentials? They all know how obsessed I was with hunting out those who believed in you, beating them up in the meeting places and throwing them in jail. And when your witness Stephen was murdered, I was right there, holding the coats of the murderers and cheering them on. And now they see me totally converted. What better qualification could I have?'

21 "But he said, 'Don't argue. Go. I'm sending you on a long journey to outsider non-Jews.'"

A ROMAN CITIZEN

22-25 The people in the crowd had listened attentively up to this point, but now they broke loose, shouting out, "Kill him! He's an insect! Stomp on him!" They shook their fists. They filled the air with curses. That's when the captain intervened and ordered Paul taken into the barracks. By now the captain was thoroughly exasperated. He decided to interrogate Paul under torture in order to get to the bottom of this, to find out what he had done that provoked this outraged violence. As they spread-eagled him with thongs, getting him ready for the whip, Paul said to the centurion standing there, "Is this legal: torturing a Roman citizen without a fair trial?"

26 When the centurion heard that, he went directly to the captain. "Do you realize what you've done? This man is a Roman citizen!"

27 The captain came back and took charge. "Is what I hear right? You're a Roman citizen?"

Paul said, "I certainly am."

28 The captain was impressed. "I paid a huge sum for my citizenship. How much did it cost you?"

"Nothing," said Paul. "It cost me nothing. I was free from the day of my birth."

29 That put a stop to the interrogation. And it put the fear of God into the captain. He had put a Roman citizen in chains and come within a whisker of putting him under torture!

30 The next day, determined to get to the root of the trouble and know for sure what was behind the Jewish accusation, the captain released Paul and ordered a meeting of the high priests and the High Council to see what they could make of it. Paul was led in and took his place before them.

BEFORE THE HIGH COUNCIL

1-3 **23** Paul surveyed the members of the council with a steady gaze, and then said his piece: "Friends, I've lived with a clear conscience before God all my life, up to this very moment." That set the Chief Priest Ananias off. He ordered his aides to slap Paul in the face. Paul shot back, "God will slap you down! What a fake you are! You sit there and judge me by the Law and then break the Law by ordering me slapped around!"

4 The aides were scandalized: "How dare you talk to God's Chief Priest like that!"

5 Paul acted surprised. "How was I to know he was Chief Priest? He doesn't act like a Chief Priest. You're right, the Scripture does say, 'Don't speak abusively to a ruler of the people.' Sorry."

6 Paul, knowing some of the council was made up of Sadducees and others of Pharisees and how they hated each other, decided to exploit their antagonism: "Friends, I am a stalwart Pharisee from a long line of Pharisees. It's because of my Pharisee convictions — the hope and resurrection of the dead — that I've been hauled into this court."

7-9 The moment he said this, the council split right down the middle, Pharisees and Sadducees going at each other in heated argument. Sadducees have nothing to do with a resurrection or angels or even a spirit. If they can't see it, they don't believe it. Pharisees believe it all. And so a huge and noisy quarrel broke out. Then some of the religion scholars on the Pharisee side shouted down the others: "We don't find anything wrong with this man! And what if a spirit has spoken to him? Or maybe an angel? What if it turns out we're fighting against God?"

10 That was fuel on the fire. The quarrel flamed up and became so violent the captain was afraid they would tear Paul apart, limb from limb. He ordered the soldiers to get him out of there and escort him back to the safety of the barracks.

A Plot Against Paul

11 That night the Master appeared to Paul: "It's going to be all right. Everything is going to turn out for the best. You've been a good witness for me here in Jerusalem. Now you're going to be my witness in Rome!"

12-15 Next day the Jews worked up a plot against Paul. They took a solemn oath that they would neither eat nor drink until they had killed him. Over forty of them ritually bound themselves to this murder pact and presented themselves to the high priests and religious leaders. "We've bound ourselves by a solemn oath to eat nothing until we have killed Paul. But we need your help. Send a request from the council to the captain to bring Paul back so that you can investigate the charges in more detail. We'll do the rest. Before he gets anywhere near you, we'll have killed him. You won't be involved."

16-17 Paul's nephew, his sister's son, overheard them plotting the ambush. He went immediately to the barracks and told Paul. Paul called over one of the centurions and said, "Take this young man to the captain. He has something important to tell him."

18 The centurion brought him to the captain and said, "The prisoner Paul asked me to bring this young man to you. He said he has something urgent to tell you."

19 The captain took him by the arm and led him aside privately. "What is it? What do you have to tell me?"

20-21 Paul's nephew said, "The Jews have worked up a plot against Paul. They're going to ask you to bring Paul to the council first thing in the morning on the pretext that they want to investigate the charges against him in more detail. But it's a trick to get him out of your safekeeping so they can murder him. Right now there are more than forty men lying in ambush for him. They've all taken a vow to neither eat nor drink until they've killed him. The ambush is set—all they're waiting for is for you to send him over."

22 The captain dismissed the nephew with a warning: "Don't breathe a word of this to a soul."

23-24 The captain called up two centurions. "Get two hundred soldiers ready to go immediately to Caesarea. Also seventy cavalry and two hundred light infantry. I want them ready to march by nine o'clock tonight. And you'll need a couple of mules for Paul and his gear. We're going to present this man safe and sound to Governor Felix."

25-30 Then he wrote this letter:

> From Claudius Lysias, to the Most Honorable Governor Felix: Greetings!
>
> I rescued this man from a Jewish mob. They had seized him and were about to kill him when I learned that he was a Roman citizen. So I sent in my soldiers. Wanting to know what he had done wrong, I had him brought before their council. It turned out to be a squabble turned vicious over some of their religious differences, but nothing remotely criminal.
>
> The next thing I knew, they had cooked up a plot to murder him. I decided that for his own safety I'd better get him out of here in a hurry. So I'm sending him to you. I'm informing his accusers that he's now under your jurisdiction.

31-33 The soldiers, following orders, took Paul that same night to safety in Antipatris. In the morning the soldiers returned to their barracks in Jerusalem, sending Paul on to Caesarea under guard of the cavalry. The cavalry entered Caesarea and handed Paul and the letter over to the governor.

34-35 After reading the letter, the governor asked Paul what province he came from and was told "Cilicia." Then he said, "I'll take up your case when your accusers show up." He ordered him locked up for the meantime in King Herod's official quarters.

PAUL STATES HIS DEFENSE

1-4 24 Within five days, the Chief Priest Ananias arrived with a contingent of leaders, along with Tertullus, a trial lawyer. They presented the governor with their case against Paul. When Paul was called before the court, Tertullus spoke for the prosecution: "Most Honorable Felix, we are most grateful in all times and places for your wise and gentle rule. We are much aware that it is because of you and you alone that we enjoy all this peace and gain daily profit from your reforms. I'm not going to tire you out with a long speech. I beg your kind indulgence in listening to me. I'll be quite brief.

5-8 "We've found this man time and again disturbing the peace, stirring up riots against Jews all over the world, the ringleader of a seditious sect called Nazarenes. He's a real bad apple, I must say. We caught him trying to defile our holy Temple and arrested him. You'll be able to verify all these accusations when you examine him yourself."

9 The Jews joined in: "Hear, hear! That's right!"

10-13   The governor motioned to Paul that it was now his turn. Paul said, "I count myself fortunate to be defending myself before you, Governor, knowing how fair-minded you've been in judging us all these years. I've been back in the country only twelve days — you can check out these dates easily enough. I came with the express purpose of worshiping in Jerusalem on Pentecost, and I've been minding my own business the whole time. Nobody can say they saw me arguing in the Temple or working up a crowd in the streets. Not one of their charges can be backed up with evidence or witnesses.

14-15   "But I do freely admit this: In regard to the Way, which they malign as a dead-end street, I serve and worship the very same God served and worshiped by all our ancestors and embrace everything written in all our Scriptures. And I admit to living in hopeful anticipation that God will raise the dead, both the good and the bad. If that's my crime, my accusers are just as guilty as I am.

16-19   "Believe me, I do my level best to keep a clear conscience before God and my neighbors in everything I do. I've been out of the country for a number of years and now I'm back. While I was away, I took up a collection for the poor and brought that with me, along with offerings for the Temple. It was while making those offerings that they found me quietly at my prayers in the Temple. There was no crowd, there was no disturbance. It was some Jews from around Ephesus who started all this trouble. And you'll notice they're not here today. They're cowards, too cowardly to accuse me in front of you.

20-21   "So ask these others what crime they've caught me in. Don't let them hide behind this smooth-talking Tertullus. The only thing they have on me is that one sentence I shouted out in the council: 'It's because I believe in the resurrection that I've been hauled into this court!' Does that sound to you like grounds for a criminal case?"

22-23   Felix shilly-shallied. He knew far more about the Way than he let on, and could have settled the case then and there. But uncertain of his best move politically, he played for time. "When Captain Lysias comes down, I'll decide your case." He gave orders to the centurion to keep Paul in custody, but to more or less give him the run of the place and not prevent his friends from helping him.

24-26   A few days later Felix and his wife, Drusilla, who was Jewish, sent for Paul and listened to him talk about a life of believing in Jesus Christ. As Paul continued to insist on right relations with God and his people, about a life of moral discipline and the coming Judgment, Felix felt things getting a little too close for comfort and dismissed him. "That's enough for today. I'll call you back when it's convenient." At the same time he was secretly hoping that Paul would offer him a substantial bribe. These conversations were repeated frequently.

27   After two years of this, Felix was replaced by Porcius Festus. Still playing up to the Jews and ignoring justice, Felix left Paul in prison.

An Appeal to Caesar

1-3 25 Three days after Festus arrived in Caesarea to take up his duties as governor, he went up to Jerusalem. The high priests and top leaders renewed their vendetta against Paul. They asked Festus if he wouldn't please do them a favor by sending Paul to Jerusalem to respond to their charges. A lie, of course — they had revived their old plot to set an ambush and kill him along the way.

4-5 Festus answered that Caesarea was the proper jurisdiction for Paul, and that he himself was going back there in a few days. "You're perfectly welcome," he said, "to go back with me then and accuse him of whatever you think he's done wrong."

6-7 About eight or ten days later, Festus returned to Caesarea. The next morning he took his place in the courtroom and had Paul brought in. The minute he walked in, the Jews who had come down from Jerusalem were all over him, hurling the most extreme accusations, none of which they could prove.

8 Then Paul took the stand and said simply, "I've done nothing wrong against the Jewish religion, or the Temple, or Caesar. Period."

9 Festus, though, wanted to get on the good side of the Jews and so said, "How would you like to go up to Jerusalem, and let me conduct your trial there?"

10-11 Paul answered, "I'm standing at this moment before Caesar's bar of justice, where I have a perfect right to stand. And I'm going to keep standing here. I've done nothing wrong to the Jews, and you know it as well as I do. If I've committed a crime and deserve death, name the day. I can face it. But if there's nothing to their accusations — and you know there isn't — nobody can force me to go along with their nonsense. We've fooled around here long enough. I appeal to Caesar."

12 Festus huddled with his advisors briefly and then gave his verdict: "You've appealed to Caesar; you'll go to Caesar!"

13-17 A few days later King Agrippa and his wife, Bernice, visited Caesarea to welcome Festus to his new post. After several days, Festus brought up Paul's case to the king. "I have a man on my hands here, a prisoner left by Felix. When I was in Jerusalem, the high priests and Jewish leaders brought a bunch of accusations against him and wanted me to sentence him to death. I told them that wasn't the way we Romans did things. Just because a man is accused, we don't throw him out to the dogs. We make sure the accused has a chance to face his accusers and defend himself of the charges. So when they came down here I got right on the case. I took my place in the courtroom and put the man on the stand.

18-21 "The accusers came at him from all sides, but their accusations turned out to be nothing more than arguments about their religion and a dead man named Jesus, who the prisoner claimed was alive. Since I'm a newcomer here and don't understand everything involved in cases like this, I asked if he'd be willing to go to Jerusalem and be tried there. Paul refused and demanded a hearing before His Majesty in our highest court. So I ordered him returned to custody until I could send him to Caesar in Rome."

22 Agrippa said, "I'd like to see this man and hear his story."

"Good," said Festus. "We'll bring him in first thing in the morning and you'll hear it for yourself."

23 The next day everybody who was anybody in Caesarea found his way to the Great Hall, along with the top military brass. Agrippa and Bernice made a flourishing grand entrance and took their places. Festus then ordered Paul brought in.

24-26 Festus said, "King Agrippa and distinguished guests, take a good look at this man. A bunch of Jews petitioned me first in Jerusalem, and later here, to do away with him. They have been most vehement in demanding his execution. I looked into it and decided that he had committed no crime. He requested a trial before Caesar and I agreed to send him to Rome. But what am I going to write to my master, Caesar? All the charges made by the Jews were fabrications, and I've uncovered nothing else.

26-27 "That's why I've brought him before this company, and especially you, King Agrippa: so we can come up with something in the nature of a charge that will hold water. For it seems to me silly to send a prisoner all that way for a trial and not be able to document what he did wrong."

"I Couldn't Just Walk Away"

1-3 **26** Agrippa spoke directly to Paul: "Go ahead — tell us about yourself."

Paul took the stand and told his story. "I can't think of anyone, King Agrippa, before whom I'd rather be answering all these Jewish accusations than you, knowing how well you are acquainted with Jewish ways and all our family quarrels.

4-8 "From the time of my youth, my life has been lived among my own people in Jerusalem. Practically every Jew in town who watched me grow up — and if they were willing to stick their necks out they'd tell you in person — knows that I lived as a strict Pharisee, the most demanding branch of our religion. It's because I believed it and took it seriously, committed myself heart and soul to what God promised my ancestors — the identical hope, mind you, that the twelve tribes have lived for night and day all these centuries — it's because I have held on to this tested and tried hope that I'm being called on the carpet by the Jews. They should be the ones standing trial here, not me! For the life of me, I can't see why it's a criminal offense to believe that God raises the dead.

9-11 "I admit that I didn't always hold to this position. For a time I thought it was my duty to oppose this Jesus of Nazareth with all my might. Backed with the full authority of the high priests, I threw these believers — I had no idea they were God's people! — into the Jerusalem jail right and left, and whenever it came to a vote, I voted for their execution. I stormed through their meeting places, bullying them into cursing Jesus, a one-man terror obsessed with obliterating these people. And then I started on the towns outside Jerusalem.

12-14 "One day on my way to Damascus, armed as always with papers from the high priests authorizing my action, right in the middle of the day a blaze of light, light outshining the sun, poured out of the sky on me and my companions. Oh, King, it was so bright! We fell flat on our faces. Then I heard a voice in Hebrew: 'Saul, Saul, why are you out to get me? Why do you insist on going against the grain?'

15-16 "I said, 'Who are you, Master?'

"The voice answered, 'I am Jesus, the One you're hunting down like an animal. But now, up on your feet — I have a job for you. I've handpicked you to be a servant and witness to what's happened today, and to what I am going to show you.

17-18 "'I'm sending you off to open the eyes of the outsiders so they can see the difference between dark and light, and choose light, see the difference between Satan and God, and choose God. I'm sending you off to present my offer of sins forgiven, and a place in the family, inviting them into the company of those who begin real living by believing in me.'

19-20 "What could I do, King Agrippa? I couldn't just walk away from a vision like that! I became an obedient believer on the spot. I started preaching this life-change—this radical turn to God and everything it meant in everyday life—right there in Damascus, went on to Jerusalem and the surrounding countryside, and from there to the whole world.

21-23 "It's because of this 'whole world' dimension that the Jews grabbed me in the Temple that day and tried to kill me. They want to keep God for themselves. But God has stood by me, just as he promised, and I'm standing here saying what I've been saying to anyone, whether king or child, who will listen. And everything I'm saying is completely in line with what the prophets and Moses said would happen: One, the Messiah must die; two, raised from the dead, he would be the first rays of God's daylight shining on people far and near, people both godless and God-fearing."

24 That was too much for Festus. He interrupted with a shout: "Paul, you're crazy! You've read too many books, spent too much time staring off into space! Get a grip on yourself, get back in the real world!"

25-27 But Paul stood his ground. "With all respect, Festus, Your Honor, I'm not crazy. I'm both accurate and sane in what I'm saying. The king knows what I'm talking about. I'm sure that nothing of what I've said sounds crazy to him. He's known all about it for a long time. You must realize that this wasn't done behind the scenes. You believe the prophets, don't you, King Agrippa? Don't answer that—I know you believe."

28 But Agrippa did answer: "Keep this up much longer and you'll make a Christian out of me!"

29 Paul, still in chains, said, "That's what I'm praying for, whether now or later, and not only you but everyone listening today, to become like me—except, of course, for this prison jewelry!"

30-31 The king and the governor, along with Bernice and their advisors, got up and went into the next room to talk over what they had heard. They quickly agreed on Paul's innocence, saying, "There's nothing in this man deserving prison, let alone death."

32 Agrippa told Festus, "He could be set free right now if he hadn't requested the hearing before Caesar."

A STORM AT SEA

1-2 **27** As soon as arrangements were complete for our sailing to Italy, Paul and a few other prisoners were placed under the supervision of a centurion named Julius, a member of an elite guard. We boarded a ship from Adramyttium that was bound for Ephesus and ports west. Aristarchus, a Macedonian from Thessalonica, went with us.

3 The next day we put in at Sidon. Julius treated Paul most decently—let him get off the ship and enjoy the hospitality of his friends there.

4-8 Out to sea again, we sailed north under the protection of the northeast shore of Cyprus because winds out of the west were against us, and then along the coast westward to the port of Myra. There the centurion found an Egyptian ship headed for Italy and transferred us on board. We ran into bad weather and found it impossible to stay on course. After much difficulty, we finally made it to the southern coast of the island of Crete and docked at

Good Harbor (appropriate name!).

9-10   By this time we had lost a lot of time. We had passed the autumn equinox, so it would be stormy weather from now on through the winter, too dangerous for sailing. Paul warned, "I see only disaster ahead for cargo and ship — to say nothing of our lives! — if we put out to sea now."

12,11   But it was not the best harbor for staying the winter. Phoenix, a few miles further on, was more suitable. The centurion set Paul's warning aside and let the ship captain and the shipowner talk him into trying for the next harbor.

13-15   When a gentle southerly breeze came up, they weighed anchor, thinking it would be smooth sailing. But they were no sooner out to sea than a gale-force wind, the infamous nor'easter, struck. They lost all control of the ship. It was a cork in the storm.

16-17   We came under the lee of the small island named Clauda, and managed to get a lifeboat ready and reef the sails. But rocky shoals prevented us from getting close. We only managed to avoid them by throwing out drift anchors.

18-20   Next day, out on the high seas again and badly damaged now by the storm, we dumped the cargo overboard. The third day the sailors lightened the ship further by throwing off all the tackle and provisions. It had been many days since we had seen either sun or stars. Wind and waves were battering us unmercifully, and we lost all hope of rescue.

21-22   With our appetite for both food and life long gone, Paul took his place in our midst and said, "Friends, you really should have listened to me back in Crete. We could have avoided all this trouble and trial. But there's no need to dwell on that now. From now on, things are looking up! I can assure you that there'll not be a single drowning among us, although I can't say as much for the ship — the ship itself is doomed.

23-26   "Last night God's angel stood at my side, an angel of this God I serve, saying to me, 'Don't give up, Paul. You're going to stand before Caesar yet — and everyone sailing with you is also going to make it.' So, dear friends, take heart. I believe God will do exactly what he told me. But we're going to shipwreck on some island or other."

27-29   On the fourteenth night, adrift somewhere on the Adriatic Sea, at about midnight the sailors sensed that we were approaching land. Sounding, they measured a depth of 120 feet, and shortly after that ninety feet. Afraid that we were about to run aground, they threw out four anchors and prayed for daylight.

30-32   Some of the sailors tried to jump ship. They let down the lifeboat, pretending they were going to set out more anchors from the bow. Paul saw through their guise and told the centurion and his soldiers, "If these sailors don't stay with the ship, we're all going down." So the soldiers cut the lines to the lifeboat and let it drift off.

33-34   With dawn about to break, Paul called everyone together and proposed breakfast: "This is the fourteenth day we've gone without food. None of us has felt like eating! But I urge you to eat something now. You'll need strength for the rescue ahead. You're going to come out of this without even a scratch!"

35-38   He broke the bread, gave thanks to God, passed it around, and they all ate heartily — 276 of us, all told! With the meal finished and everyone full, the ship was further lightened by dumping the grain overboard.

39-41 At daybreak, no one recognized the land—but then they did notice a bay with a nice beach. They decided to try to run the ship up on the beach. They cut the anchors, loosed the tiller, raised the sail, and ran before the wind toward the beach. But we didn't make it. Still far from shore, we hit a reef and the ship began to break up.

42-44 The soldiers decided to kill the prisoners so none could escape by swimming, but the centurion, determined to save Paul, stopped them. He gave orders for anyone who could swim to dive in and go for it, and for the rest to grab a plank. Everyone made it to shore safely.

1-2 28 Once everyone was accounted for and we realized we had all made it, we learned that we were on the island of Malta. The natives went out of their way to be friendly to us. The day was rainy and cold and we were already soaked to the bone, but they built a huge bonfire and gathered us around it.

3-6 Paul pitched in and helped. He had gathered up a bundle of sticks, but when he put it on the fire, a venomous snake, roused from its torpor by the heat, struck his hand and held on. Seeing the snake hanging from Paul's hand like that, the natives jumped to the conclusion that he was a murderer getting his just deserts. Paul shook the snake off into the fire, none the worse for wear. They kept expecting him to drop dead, but when it was obvious he wasn't going to, they jumped to the conclusion that he was a god!

7-9 The head man in that part of the island was Publius. He took us into his home as his guests, drying us out and putting us up in fine style for the next three days. Publius's father was sick at the time, down with a high fever and dysentery. Paul went to the old man's room, and when he laid hands on him and prayed, the man was healed. Word of the healing got around fast, and soon everyone on the island who was sick came and got healed.

ROME

10-11 We spent a wonderful three months on Malta. They treated us royally, took care of all our needs and outfitted us for the rest of the journey. When an Egyptian ship that had wintered there in the harbor prepared to leave for Italy, we got on board. The ship had a carved Gemini for its figurehead: "the Heavenly Twins."

12-14 We put in at Syracuse for three days and then went up the coast to Rhegium. Two days later, with the wind out of the south, we sailed into the Bay of Naples. We found Christian friends there and stayed with them for a week.

14-16 And then we came to Rome. Friends in Rome heard we were on the way and came out to meet us. One group got as far as Appian Court; another group met us at Three Taverns—emotion-packed meetings, as you can well imagine. Paul, brimming over with praise, led us in prayers of thanksgiving. When we actually entered Rome, they let Paul live in his own private quarters with a soldier who had been assigned to guard him.

17-20 Three days later, Paul called the Jewish leaders together for a meeting at his house. He said, "The Jews in Jerusalem arrested me on trumped-up charges, and I was taken into custody by the Romans. I assure you that I did absolutely nothing against Jewish laws or Jewish customs. After the Romans investigated the charges and found there was nothing to them, they wanted to set me free, but the Jews objected so fiercely that I was forced to appeal to Caesar. I did this not to accuse them of any wrongdoing or to get our people in trouble with Rome. We've had enough trouble through the years that way. I did it *for* Israel. I asked you to come and listen to me today to make it clear that I'm on Israel's side, not against her. I'm a hostage here for hope, not doom."

21-22 They said, "Nobody wrote warning us about you. And no one has shown up saying anything bad about you. But we would like very much to hear more. The only thing we know about this Christian sect is that nobody seems to have anything good to say about it."

23 They agreed on a time. When the day arrived, they came back to his home with a number of their friends. Paul talked to them all day, from morning to evening, explaining everything involved in the kingdom of God, and trying to persuade them all about Jesus by pointing out what Moses and the prophets had written about him.

24-27 Some of them were persuaded by what he said, but others refused to believe a word of it. When the unbelievers got cantankerous and started bickering with each other, Paul interrupted: "I have just one more thing to say to you. The Holy Spirit sure knew what he was talking about when he addressed our ancestors through Isaiah the prophet:

Go to this people and tell them this:
"You're going to listen with your ears,
    but you won't hear a word;
You're going to stare with your eyes,
    but you won't see a thing.
These people are blockheads!
They stick their fingers in their ears
    so they won't have to listen;
They screw their eyes shut
    so they won't have to look,
    so they won't have to deal with me face-to-face
    and let me heal them."

28 "You've had your chance. The non-Jewish outsiders are next on the list. And believe me, they're going to receive it with open arms!"

30-31 Paul lived for two years in his rented house. He welcomed everyone who came to visit. He urgently presented all matters of the kingdom of God. He explained everything about Jesus Christ. His door was always open.

ROMANS

The event that split history into "before" and "after" and changed the world took place about thirty years before Paul wrote this letter. The event — the life, death, and resurrection of Jesus — took place in a remote corner of the extensive Roman Empire: the province of Judea in Palestine. Hardly anyone noticed, certainly no one in busy and powerful Rome.

And when this letter arrived in Rome, hardly anyone read it, certainly no one of influence. There was much to read in Rome — imperial decrees, exquisite poetry, finely crafted moral philosophy — and much of it was world-class. And yet in no time, as such things go, this letter left all those other writings in the dust. Paul's letter to the Romans has had a far larger impact on its readers than the volumes of all those Roman writers put together.

The quick rise of this letter to a peak of influence is extraordinary, written as it was by an obscure Roman citizen without connections. But when we read it for ourselves, we begin to realize that it is the letter itself that is truly extraordinary, and that no obscurity in writer or readers could have kept it obscure for long.

The letter to the Romans is a piece of exuberant and passionate thinking. This is the glorious life of the mind enlisted in the service of God. Paul takes the well-witnessed and devoutly believed fact of the life, death, and resurrection of Jesus of Nazareth and thinks through its implications. How does it happen that in the death and resurrection of Jesus, world history took a new direction, and at the same moment the life of every man, woman, and child on the planet was eternally affected? What is God up to? What does it *mean* that Jesus "saves"? What's behind all this, and where is it going?

These are the questions that drive Paul's thinking. Paul's mind is supple and capacious. He takes logic and argument, poetry and imagination, Scripture and prayer, creation and history and experience, and weaves them into this letter that has become the premier document of Christian theology.

ROMANS

1 I, Paul, am a devoted slave of Jesus Christ on assignment, authorized as an apostle to proclaim God's words and acts. I write this letter to all the believers in Rome, God's friends.

2-7 The sacred writings contain preliminary reports by the prophets on God's Son. His descent from David roots him in history; his unique identity as Son of God was shown by the Spirit when Jesus was raised from the dead, setting him apart as the Messiah, our Master. Through him we received both the generous gift of his life and the urgent task of passing it on to others who receive it by entering into obedient trust in Jesus. You are who you are through this gift and call of Jesus Christ! And I greet you now with all the generosity of God our Father and our Master Jesus, the Messiah.

8-12 I thank God through Jesus for every one of you. That's first. People everywhere keep telling me about your lives of faith, and every time I hear them, I thank him. And God, whom I so love to worship and serve by spreading the good news of his Son — the Message! — knows that every time I think of you in my prayers, which is practically all the time, I ask him to clear the way for me to come and see you. The longer this waiting goes on, the deeper the ache. I so want to be there to deliver God's gift in person and watch you grow stronger right before my eyes! But don't think I'm not expecting to get something out of this, too! You have as much to give me as I do to you.

13-15 Please don't misinterpret my failure to visit you, friends. You have no idea how many times I've made plans for Rome. I've been determined to get some personal enjoyment out of God's work among you, as I have in so many other non-Jewish towns and communities. But something has always come up and prevented it. Everyone I meet — it matters little whether they're mannered or rude, smart or simple — deepens my sense of interdependence and obligation. And that's why I can't wait to get to you in Rome, preaching this wonderful good news of God.

16-17 It's news I'm most proud to proclaim, this extraordinary Message of God's powerful plan to rescue everyone who trusts him, starting with Jews and then right on to everyone else! God's way of putting people right shows up in the acts of faith, confirming what Scripture has said all along: "The person in right standing before God by trusting him really lives."

IGNORING GOD LEADS TO A DOWNWARD SPIRAL

18-23 But God's angry displeasure erupts as acts of human mistrust and wrongdoing and lying accumulate, as people try to put a shroud over truth. But the basic reality of God is plain enough. Open your eyes and there it is! By taking a long and thoughtful look at what God has created, people have always been able to see what their eyes as such can't see: eternal power, for instance, and the mystery of his divine being. So nobody has a good excuse. What happened was this: People knew God perfectly well, but when they didn't treat him like God, refusing to worship him, they trivialized themselves into silliness and confusion so that there was neither sense nor direction left in their lives. They pretended to know it all, but were illiterate regarding life. They traded the glory of God who holds the whole world in his hands for cheap figurines you can buy at any roadside stand.

24-25 So God said, in effect, "If that's what you want, that's what you get." It wasn't long before they were living in a pigpen, smeared with filth, filthy inside and out. And all this because they traded the true God for a fake god, and worshiped the god they made instead of the God who made them — the God we bless, the God who blesses *us*. Oh, yes!

26-27 Worse followed. Refusing to know God, they soon didn't know how to be human either — women didn't know how to be women, men didn't know how to be men. Sexually confused, they abused and defiled one another, women with women, men with men — all lust, no love. And then they paid for it, oh, how they paid for it — emptied of God and love, godless and loveless wretches.

28-32 Since they didn't bother to acknowledge God, God quit bothering them and let them run loose. And then all hell broke loose: rampant evil, grabbing and grasping, vicious backstabbing. They made life hell on earth with their envy, wanton killing, bickering, and cheating. Look at them: mean-spirited, venomous, fork-tongued God-bashers. Bullies, swaggerers, insufferable windbags! They keep inventing new ways of wrecking lives. They ditch their parents when they get in the way. Stupid, slimy, cruel, cold-blooded. And it's not as if they don't know better. They know perfectly well they're spitting in God's face. And they don't care — worse, they hand out prizes to those who do the worst things best!

God Is Kind, but Not Soft

1-2 2 Those people are on a dark spiral downward. But if you think that leaves you on the high ground where you can point your finger at others, think again. Every time you criticize someone, you condemn yourself. It takes one to know one. Judgmental criticism of others is a well-known way of escaping detection in your own crimes and misdemeanors. But God isn't so easily diverted. He sees right through all such smoke screens and holds you to what *you've* done.

3-4 You didn't think, did you, that just by pointing your finger at others you would distract God from seeing all your misdoings and from coming down on you hard? Or did you think that because he's such a nice God, he'd let you off the hook? Better think this one through from the beginning. God is kind, but he's not soft. In kindness he takes us firmly by the hand and leads us into a radical life-change.

5-8 You're not getting by with anything. Every refusal and avoidance of God adds fuel to the fire. The day is coming when it's going to blaze hot and high, God's fiery and righteous judgment. Make no mistake: In the end you get what's coming to you — *Real Life* for those who work on God's side, but to those who insist on getting their own way and take the path of least resistance, *Fire!*

9-11 If you go against the grain, you get splinters, regardless of which neighborhood you're from, what your parents taught you, what schools you attended. But if you embrace the way God does things, there are wonderful payoffs, again without regard to where you are from or how you were brought up. Being a Jew won't give you an automatic stamp of approval. God pays no attention to what others say (or what you think) about you. He makes up his own mind.

12-13 If you sin without knowing what you're doing, God takes that into account. But if you sin knowing full well what you're doing, that's a different story entirely. Merely hearing God's law is a waste of your time if you don't do what he commands. Doing, not hearing, is what makes the difference with God.

14-16   When outsiders who have never heard of God's law follow it more or less by instinct, they confirm its truth by their obedience. They show that God's law is not something alien, imposed on us from without, but woven into the very fabric of our creation. There is something deep within them that echoes God's yes and no, right and wrong. Their response to God's yes and no will become public knowledge on the day God makes his final decision about every man and woman. The Message from God that I proclaim through Jesus Christ takes into account all these differences.

Religion Can't Save You

17-24   If you're brought up Jewish, don't assume that you can lean back in the arms of your religion and take it easy, feeling smug because you're an insider to God's revelation, a connoisseur of the best things of God, informed on the latest doctrines! I have a special word of caution for you who are sure that you have it all together yourselves and, because you know God's revealed Word inside and out, feel qualified to guide others through their blind alleys and dark nights and confused emotions to God. While you are guiding others, who is going to guide you? I'm quite serious. While preaching "Don't steal!" are you going to rob people blind? Who would suspect you? The same with adultery. The same with idolatry. You can get by with almost anything if you front it with eloquent talk about God and his law. The line from Scripture, "It's because of you Jews that the outsiders are down on God," shows it's an old problem that isn't going to go away.

25-29   Circumcision, the surgical ritual that marks you as a Jew, is great if you live in accord with God's law. But if you don't, it's worse than not being circumcised. The reverse is also true: The uncircumcised who keep God's ways are as good as the circumcised — in fact, better. Better to keep God's law uncircumcised than break it circumcised. Don't you see: It's not the cut of a knife that makes a Jew. You become a Jew by who you *are*. It's the mark of God on your heart, not of a knife on your skin, that makes a Jew. And recognition comes from God, not legalistic critics.

1-2   **3** So what difference does it make who's a Jew and who isn't, who has been trained in God's ways and who hasn't? As it turns out, it makes a lot of difference — but not the difference so many have assumed.

2-6   First, there's the matter of being put in charge of writing down and caring for God's revelation, these Holy Scriptures. So, what if, in the course of doing that, some of those Jews abandoned their post? God didn't abandon them. Do you think their faithlessness cancels out his faithfulness? Not on your life! Depend on it: God keeps his word even when the whole world is lying through its teeth. Scripture says the same:

> Your words stand fast and true;
> Rejection doesn't faze you.

But if our wrongdoing only underlines and confirms God's rightdoing, shouldn't we be commended for helping out? Since our bad words don't even make a dent in his good words, isn't it wrong of God to back us to the wall and hold us to our word? These questions come up. The answer to such questions is *no*, a most emphatic *No!* How else would things ever get straightened out if *God* didn't do the straightening?

7-8   It's simply perverse to say, "If my lies serve to show off God's truth all the more gloriously, why blame me? I'm doing God a favor." Some people are actually trying to put such words in our mouths, claiming that we go around saying, "The more evil we do, the more good God does, so let's just do it!" That's pure slander, as I'm sure you'll agree.

WE'RE ALL IN THE SAME SINKING BOAT

9-20   So where does that put us? Do we Jews get a better break than the others? Not really. Basically, all of us, whether insiders or outsiders, start out in identical conditions, which is to say that we all start out as sinners. Scripture leaves no doubt about it:

> There's nobody living right, not even one,
>   nobody who knows the score, nobody alert for God.
> They've all taken the wrong turn;
>   they've all wandered down blind alleys.
> No one's living right;
>   I can't find a single one.
> Their throats are gaping graves,
>   their tongues slick as mudslides.
> Every word they speak is tinged with poison.
>   They open their mouths and pollute the air.
> They race for the honor of sinner-of-the-year,
>   litter the land with heartbreak and ruin,
> Don't know the first thing about living with others.
>   They never give God the time of day.

This makes it clear, doesn't it, that whatever is written in these Scriptures is not what God says *about others* but *to us* to whom these Scriptures were addressed in the first place! And it's clear enough, isn't it, that we're sinners, every one of us, in the same sinking boat with everybody else? Our involvement with God's revelation doesn't put us right with God. What it does is force us to face our complicity in everyone else's sin.

GOD HAS SET THINGS RIGHT

21-24   But in our time something new has been added. What Moses and the prophets witnessed to all those years has happened. The God-setting-things-right that we read about has become Jesus-setting-things-right for us. And not only for us, but for everyone who believes in him. For there is no difference between us and them in this. Since we've compiled this long and sorry record as sinners (both us and them) and proved that we are utterly incapable of living the glorious lives God wills for us, God did it for us. Out of sheer generosity he put us in right standing with himself. A pure gift. He got us out of the mess we're in and restored us to where he always wanted us to be. And he did it by means of Jesus Christ.

25-26   God sacrificed Jesus on the altar of the world to clear that world of sin. Having faith in him sets us in the clear. God decided on this course of action in full view of the public — to set the world in the clear with himself through the sacrifice of Jesus, finally taking care of the sins he had so patiently endured. This is not only clear, but it's *now* — this is current history! God sets things right. He also makes it possible for us to live in his rightness.

27-28 So where does that leave our proud Jewish insider claims and counter-claims? Canceled? Yes, canceled. What we've learned is this: God does not respond to what *we* do; we respond to what *God* does. We've finally figured it out. Our lives get in step with God and all others by letting him set the pace, not by proudly or anxiously trying to run the parade.

29-30 And where does that leave our proud Jewish claim of having a corner on God? Also canceled. God is the God of outsider non-Jews as well as insider Jews. How could it be otherwise since there is only one God? God sets right all who welcome his action and enter into it, both those who follow our religious system and those who have never heard of our religion.

31 But by shifting our focus from what *we* do to what *God* does, don't we cancel out all our careful keeping of the rules and ways God commanded? Not at all. What happens, in fact, is that by putting that entire way of life in its proper place, we confirm it.

TRUSTING GOD

1-3 4 So how do we fit what we know of Abraham, our first father in the faith, into this new way of looking at things? If Abraham, by what he *did* for God, got God to approve him, he could certainly have taken credit for it. But the story we're given is a God-story, not an Abraham-story. What we read in Scripture is, "Abraham entered into what God was doing for him, and *that* was the turning point. He trusted God to set him right instead of trying to be right on his own."

4-5 If you're a hard worker and do a good job, you deserve your pay; we don't call your wages a gift. But if you see that the job is too big for you, that it's something only *God* can do, and you trust him to do it — you could never do it for yourself no matter how hard and long you worked — well, that trusting-him-to-do-it is what gets you set right with God, *by* God. Sheer gift.

6-9 David confirms this way of looking at it, saying that the one who trusts God to do the putting-everything-right without insisting on having a say in it is one fortunate man:

Fortunate those whose crimes are carted off,
　　whose sins are wiped clean from the slate.
Fortunate the person against
　　whom the Lord does not keep score.

Do you think for a minute that this blessing is only pronounced over those of us who keep our religious ways and are circumcised? Or do you think it possible that the blessing could be given to those who never even heard of our ways, who were never brought up in the disciplines of God? We all agree, don't we, that it was by embracing what God did for him that Abraham was declared fit before God?

10-11 Now *think*: Was that declaration made before or after he was marked by the covenant rite of circumcision? That's right, *before* he was marked. That means that he underwent circumcision as evidence and confirmation of what God had done long before to bring him into this acceptable standing with himself, an act of God he had embraced with his whole life.

12 And it means further that Abraham is father of *all* people who embrace what God does for them while they are still on the "outs" with God, as yet unidentified as God's, in an "uncircumcised" condition. It is precisely these people in this condition who are called "set right by God and with God"! Abraham is also, of course, father of those who have undergone the religious rite of circumcision *not* just because of the ritual but because they were willing to live in the risky faith-embrace of God's action for them, the way Abraham lived long before he was marked by circumcision.

13-15 That famous promise God gave Abraham — that he and his children would possess the earth — was not given because of something Abraham did or would do. It was based on God's decision to put everything together for him, which Abraham then entered when he believed. If those who get what God gives them only get it by doing everything they are told to do and filling out all the right forms properly signed, that eliminates personal trust completely and turns the promise into an ironclad *contract*! That's not a holy promise; that's a business deal. A contract drawn up by a hard-nosed lawyer and with plenty of fine print only makes sure that you will never be able to collect. But if there is no contract in the first place, simply a *promise* — and God's promise at that — you can't break it.

16 This is why the fulfillment of God's promise depends entirely on trusting God and his way, and then simply embracing him and what he does. God's promise arrives as pure gift. That's the only way everyone can be sure to get in on it, those who keep the religious traditions *and* those who have never heard of them. For Abraham is father of us all. He is not our racial father — that's reading the story backward. He is our *faith* father.

17-18 We call Abraham "father" not because he got God's attention by living like a saint, but because God made something out of Abraham when he was a nobody. Isn't that what we've always read in Scripture, God saying to Abraham, "I set you up as father of many peoples"? Abraham was first named "father" and then *became* a father because he dared to trust God to do what only God could do: raise the dead to life, with a word make something out of nothing. When everything was hopeless, Abraham believed anyway, deciding to live not on the basis of what he saw he *couldn't* do but on what God said he *would* do. And so he was made father of a multitude of peoples. God himself said to him, "You're going to have a big family, Abraham!"

19-25 Abraham didn't focus on his own impotence and say, "It's hopeless. This hundred-year-old body could never father a child." Nor did he survey Sarah's decades of infertility and give up. He didn't tiptoe around God's promise asking cautiously skeptical questions. He plunged into the promise and came up strong, ready for God, sure that God would make good on what he had said. That's why it is said, "Abraham was declared fit before God by trusting God to set him right." But it's not just Abraham; it's also us! The same thing gets said about us when we embrace and believe the One who brought Jesus to life when the conditions were equally hopeless. The sacrificed Jesus made us fit for God, set us *right with God*.

DEVELOPING PATIENCE

1-2 **5** By entering through faith into what God has always wanted to do for us — set us right with him, make us fit for him — we have it all together with God because of our Master Jesus. And that's not all:

We throw open our doors to God and discover at the same moment that he has already thrown open his door to us. We find ourselves standing where we always hoped we might stand — out in the wide open spaces of God's grace and glory, standing tall and shouting our praise.

3-5 There's more to come: We continue to shout our praise even when we're hemmed in with troubles, because we know how troubles can develop passionate patience in us, and how that patience in turn forges the tempered steel of virtue, keeping us alert for whatever God will do next. In alert expectancy such as this, we're never left feeling shortchanged. Quite the contrary — we can't round up enough containers to hold everything God generously pours into our lives through the Holy Spirit!

6-8 Christ arrives right on time to make this happen. He didn't, and doesn't, wait for us to get ready. He presented himself for this sacrificial death when we were far too weak and rebellious to do anything to get ourselves ready. And even if we hadn't been so weak, we wouldn't have known what to do anyway. We can understand someone dying for a person worth dying for, and we can understand how someone good and noble could inspire us to selfless sacrifice. But God put his love on the line for us by offering his Son in sacrificial death while we were of no use whatever to him.

9-11 Now that we are set right with God by means of this sacrificial death, the consummate blood sacrifice, there is no longer a question of being at odds with God in any way. If, when we were at our worst, we were put on friendly terms with God by the sacrificial death of his Son, now that we're at our best, just think of how our lives will expand and deepen by means of his resurrection life! Now that we have actually received this amazing friendship with God, we are no longer content to simply say it in plodding prose. We sing and shout our praises to God through Jesus, the Messiah!

The Death-Dealing Sin, the Life-Giving Gift

12-14 You know the story of how Adam landed us in the dilemma we're in — first sin, then death, and no one exempt from either sin or death. That sin disturbed relations with God in everything and everyone, but the extent of the disturbance was not clear until God spelled it out in detail to Moses. So death, this huge abyss separating us from God, dominated the landscape from Adam to Moses. Even those who didn't sin precisely as Adam did by disobeying a specific command of God still had to experience this termination of life, this separation from God. But Adam, who got us into this, also points ahead to the One who will get us out of it.

15-17 Yet the rescuing gift is not exactly parallel to the death-dealing sin. If one man's sin put crowds of people at the dead-end abyss of separation from God, just think what God's gift poured through one man, Jesus Christ, will do! There's no comparison between that death-dealing sin and this generous, life-giving gift. The verdict on that one sin was the death sentence; the verdict on the many sins that followed was this wonderful life sentence. If death got the upper hand through one man's wrongdoing, can you imagine the breathtaking recovery life makes, sovereign life, in those who grasp with both hands this wildly extravagant life-gift, this grand setting-everything-right, that the one man Jesus Christ provides?

18-19 Here it is in a nutshell: Just as one person did it wrong and got us in all this trouble with sin and death, another person did it right and got us out of it. But more than just getting us out of trouble, he got us into life! One man said no to God and put many people in the wrong; one man said yes to God and put many in the right.

20-21 All that passing laws against sin did was produce more lawbreakers. But sin didn't, and doesn't, have a chance in competition with the aggressive forgiveness we call *grace*. When it's sin versus grace, grace wins hands down. All sin can do is threaten us with death, and that's the end of it. Grace, because God is putting everything together again through the Messiah, invites us into life — a life that goes on and on and on, world without end.

When Death Becomes Life

1-3 So what do we do? Keep on sinning so God can keep on forgiving? I should hope not! If we've left the country where sin is sovereign, how can we still live in our old house there? Or didn't you realize we packed up and left there for good? That is what happened in baptism. When we went under the water, we left the old country of sin behind; when we came up out of the water, we entered into the new country of grace — a new life in a new land!

3-5 That's what baptism into the life of Jesus means. When we are lowered into the water, it is like the burial of Jesus; when we are raised up out of the water, it is like the resurrection of Jesus. Each of us is raised into a light-filled world by our Father so that we can see where we're going in our new grace-sovereign country.

6-11 Could it be any clearer? Our old way of life was nailed to the cross with Christ, a decisive end to that sin-miserable life — no longer at sin's every beck and call! What we believe is this: If we get included in Christ's sin-conquering death, we also get included in his life-saving resurrection. We know that when Jesus was raised from the dead it was a signal of the end of death-as-the-end. Never again will death have the last word. When Jesus died, he took sin down with him, but alive he brings God down to us. From now on, think of it this way: Sin speaks a dead language that means nothing to you; God speaks your mother tongue, and you hang on every word. You are dead to sin and alive to God. That's what Jesus did.

12-14 That means you must not give sin a vote in the way you conduct your lives. Don't give it the time of day. Don't even run little errands that are connected with that old way of life. Throw yourselves wholeheartedly and full-time — remember, you've been raised from the dead! — into God's way of doing things. Sin can't tell you how to live. After all, you're not living under that old tyranny any longer. You're living in the freedom of God.

What Is True Freedom?

15-18 So, since we're out from under the old tyranny, does that mean we can live any old way we want? Since we're free in the freedom of God, can we do anything that comes to mind? Hardly. You know well enough from your own experience that there are some acts of so-called freedom that destroy freedom. Offer yourselves to sin, for instance, and it's your last free act. But offer yourselves to the ways of God and the freedom never quits. All your lives you've let sin tell you what to do. But thank God you've started listening to a new master, one whose commands set you free to live openly in *his* freedom!

19 I'm using this freedom language because it's easy to picture. You can readily recall, can't you, how at one time the more you did just what you

felt like doing — not caring about others, not caring about God — the worse your life became and the less freedom you had? And how much different is it now as you live in God's freedom, your lives healed and expansive in holiness?

20-21   As long as you did what you felt like doing, ignoring God, you didn't have to bother with right thinking or right living, or right *anything* for that matter. But do you call that a free life? What did you get out of it? Nothing you're proud of now. Where did it get you? A dead end.

22-23   But now that you've found you don't have to listen to sin tell you what to do, and have discovered the delight of listening to God telling you, what a surprise! A whole, healed, put-together life right now, with more and more of life on the way! Work hard for sin your whole life and your pension is death. But God's gift is *real life*, eternal life, delivered by Jesus, our Master.

Torn Between One Way and Another

1-3   7 You shouldn't have any trouble understanding this, friends, for you know all the ins and outs of the law — how it works and how its power touches only the living. For instance, a wife is legally tied to her husband while he lives, but if he dies, she's free. If she lives with another man while her husband is living, she's obviously an adulteress. But if he dies, she is quite free to marry another man in good conscience, with no one's disapproval.

4-6   So, my friends, this is something like what has taken place with you. When Christ died he took that entire rule-dominated way of life down with him and left it in the tomb, leaving you free to "marry" a resurrection life and bear "offspring" of faith for God. For as long as we lived that old way of life, doing whatever we felt we could get away with, sin was calling most of the shots as the old law code hemmed us in. And this made us all the more rebellious. In the end, all we had to show for it was miscarriages and stillbirths. But now that we're no longer shackled to that domineering mate of sin, and out from under all those oppressive regulations and fine print, we're free to live a new life in the freedom of God.

7   But I can hear you say, "If the law code was as bad as all that, it's no better than sin itself." That's certainly not true. The law code had a perfectly legitimate function. Without its clear guidelines for right and wrong, moral behavior would be mostly guesswork. Apart from the succinct, surgical command, "You shall not covet," I could have dressed covetousness up to look like a virtue and ruined my life with it.

8-12   Don't you remember how it was? I do, perfectly well. The law code started out as an excellent piece of work. What happened, though, was that sin found a way to pervert the command into a temptation, making a piece of "forbidden fruit" out of it. The law code, instead of being used to guide me, was used to seduce me. Without all the paraphernalia of the law code, sin looked pretty dull and lifeless, and I went along without paying much attention to it. But once sin got its hands on the law code and decked itself out in all that finery, I was fooled, and fell for it. The very command that was supposed to guide me into life was cleverly used to trip me up, throwing me headlong. So sin was plenty alive, and I was stone dead. But the law code itself is God's good and common sense, each command sane and holy counsel.

13   I can already hear your next question: "Does that mean I can't even trust what is good [that is, the law]? Is good just as dangerous as evil?" No

again! Sin simply did what sin is so famous for doing: using the good as a
cover to tempt me to do what would finally destroy me. By hiding within
God's good commandment, sin did far more mischief than it could ever
have accomplished on its own.

14-16 I can anticipate the response that is coming: "I know that all God's commands are spiritual, but I'm not. Isn't this also your experience?" Yes. I'm
full of myself — after all, I've spent a long time in sin's prison. What I don't
understand about myself is that I decide one way, but then I act another,
doing things I absolutely despise. So if I can't be trusted to figure out what
is best for myself and then do it, it becomes obvious that God's command
is necessary.

17-20 But I need something *more*! For if I know the law but still can't keep it,
and if the power of sin within me keeps sabotaging my best intentions, I
obviously need help! I realize that I don't have what it takes. I can will it,
but I can't *do* it. I decide to do good, but I don't *really* do it; I decide not to
do bad, but then I do it anyway. My decisions, such as they are, don't result
in actions. Something has gone wrong deep within me and gets the better
of me every time.

21-23 It happens so regularly that it's predictable. The moment I decide to
do good, sin is there to trip me up. I truly delight in God's commands,
but it's pretty obvious that not all of me joins in that delight. Parts of me
covertly rebel, and just when I least expect it, they take charge.

24 I've tried everything and nothing helps. I'm at the end of my rope. Is
there no one who can do anything for me? Isn't that the real question?

25 The answer, thank God, is that Jesus Christ can and does. He acted
to set things right in this life of contradictions where I want to serve God
with all my heart and mind, but am pulled by the influence of sin to do
something totally different.

THE SOLUTION IS LIFE ON GOD'S TERMS

1-2 With the arrival of Jesus, the Messiah, that fateful dilemma is
resolved. Those who enter into Christ's being-here-for-us no longer
have to live under a continuous, low-lying black cloud. A new power
is in operation. The Spirit of life in Christ, like a strong wind, has magnifi-
cently cleared the air, freeing you from a fated lifetime of brutal tyranny at
the hands of sin and death.

3-4 God went for the jugular when he sent his own Son. He didn't deal with
the problem as something remote and unimportant. In his Son, Jesus, he
personally took on the human condition, entered the disordered mess of
struggling humanity in order to set it right once and for all. The law code,
weakened as it always was by fractured human nature, could never have
done that.

The law always ended up being used as a Band-Aid on sin instead of a
deep healing of it. And now what the law code asked for but we couldn't
deliver is accomplished as we, instead of redoubling our own efforts, simply
embrace what the Spirit is doing in us.

5-8 Those who think they can do it on their own end up obsessed with
measuring their own moral muscle but never get around to exercising it in
real life. Those who trust God's action in them find that God's Spirit is in
them — living and breathing God! Obsession with self in these matters is a
dead end; attention to God leads us out into the open, into a spacious, free

life. Focusing on the self is the opposite of focusing on God. Anyone completely absorbed in self ignores God, ends up thinking more about self than God. That person ignores who God is and what he is doing. And God isn't pleased at being ignored.

9-11   But if God himself has taken up residence in your life, you can hardly be thinking more of yourself than of him. Anyone, of course, who has not welcomed this invisible but clearly present God, the Spirit of Christ, won't know what we're talking about. But for you who welcome him, in whom he dwells — even though you still experience all the limitations of sin — you yourself experience life on God's terms. It stands to reason, doesn't it, that if the alive-and-present God who raised Jesus from the dead moves into your life, he'll do the same thing in you that he did in Jesus, bringing you alive to himself? When God lives and breathes in you (and he does, as surely as he did in Jesus), you are delivered from that dead life. With his Spirit living in you, your body will be as alive as Christ's!

12-14   So don't you see that we don't owe this old do-it-yourself life one red cent. There's nothing in it for us, nothing at all. The best thing to do is give it a decent burial and get on with your new life. God's Spirit beckons. There are things to do and places to go!

15-17   This resurrection life you received from God is not a timid, grave-tending life. It's adventurously expectant, greeting God with a childlike "What's next, Papa?" God's Spirit touches our spirits and confirms who we really are. We know who he is, and we know who we are: Father and children. And we know we are going to get what's coming to us — an unbelievable inheritance! We go through exactly what Christ goes through. If we go through the hard times with him, then we're certainly going to go through the good times with him!

18-21   That's why I don't think there's any comparison between the present hard times and the coming good times. The created world itself can hardly wait for what's coming next. Everything in creation is being more or less held back. God reins it in until both creation and all the creatures are ready and can be released at the same moment into the glorious times ahead. Meanwhile, the joyful anticipation deepens.

22-25   All around us we observe a pregnant creation. The difficult times of pain throughout the world are simply birth pangs. But it's not only around us; it's *within* us. The Spirit of God is arousing us within. We're also feeling the birth pangs. These sterile and barren bodies of ours are yearning for full deliverance. That is why waiting does not diminish us, any more than waiting diminishes a pregnant mother. We are enlarged in the waiting. We, of course, don't see what is enlarging us. But the longer we wait, the larger we become, and the more joyful our expectancy.

26-28   Meanwhile, the moment we get tired in the waiting, God's Spirit is right alongside helping us along. If we don't know how or what to pray, it doesn't matter. He does our praying in and for us, making prayer out of our wordless sighs, our aching groans. He knows us far better than we know ourselves, knows our pregnant condition, and keeps us present before God. That's why we can be so sure that every detail in our lives of love for God is worked into something good.

29-30   God knew what he was doing from the very beginning. He decided from the outset to shape the lives of those who love him along the same lines as the life of his Son. The Son stands first in the line of humanity he restored. We see the original and intended shape of our lives there in him. After God made that decision of what his children should be like, he followed it up by calling people by name. After he called them by name, he set them on a solid basis with himself. And then, after getting them established, he stayed with them to the end, gloriously completing what he had begun.

31-39 So, what do you think? With God on our side like this, how can we lose? If God didn't hesitate to put everything on the line for us, embracing our condition and exposing himself to the worst by sending his own Son, is there anything else he wouldn't gladly and freely do for us? And who would dare tangle with God by messing with one of God's chosen? Who would dare even to point a finger? The One who died for us — who was raised to life for us! — is in the presence of God at this very moment sticking up for us. Do you think anyone is going to be able to drive a wedge between us and Christ's love for us? There is no way! Not trouble, not hard times, not hatred, not hunger, not homelessness, not bullying threats, not backstabbing, not even the worst sins listed in Scripture:

They kill us in cold blood because they hate you.
We're sitting ducks; they pick us off one by one.

None of this fazes us because Jesus loves us. I'm absolutely convinced that nothing — nothing living or dead, angelic or demonic, today or tomorrow, high or low, thinkable or unthinkable — absolutely *nothing* can get between us and God's love because of the way that Jesus our Master has embraced us.

GOD IS CALLING HIS PEOPLE

1-5 **9** At the same time, you need to know that I carry with me at all times a huge sorrow. It's an enormous pain deep within me, and I'm never free of it. I'm not exaggerating — Christ and the Holy Spirit are my witnesses. It's the Israelites . . . If there were any way I could be cursed by the Messiah so they could be blessed by him, I'd do it in a minute. They're my family. I grew up with them. They had everything going for them — family, glory, covenants, revelation, worship, promises, to say nothing of being the race that produced the Messiah, the Christ, who is God over everything, always. Oh, yes!

6-9 Don't suppose for a moment, though, that God's Word has malfunctioned in some way or other. The problem goes back a long way. From the outset, not all Israelites of the flesh were Israelites of the spirit. It wasn't Abraham's sperm that gave identity here, but God's *promise*. Remember how it was put: "Your family will be defined by Isaac"? That means that Israelite identity was never racially determined by sexual transmission, but it was *God*-determined by promise. Remember that promise, "When I come back next year at this time, Sarah will have a son"?

10-13 And that's not the only time. To Rebecca, also, a promise was made that took priority over genetics. When she became pregnant by our one-of-a-kind ancestor, Isaac, and her babies were still innocent in the womb — incapable of good or bad — she received a special assurance from God. What God did in this case made it perfectly plain that his purpose is not a hit-or-miss thing dependent on what we do or don't do, but a sure thing determined by his decision, flowing steadily from his initiative. God told Rebecca, "The firstborn of your twins will take second place." Later that was turned into a stark epigram: "I loved Jacob; I hated Esau."

14-18 Is that grounds for complaining that God is unfair? Not so fast, please. God told Moses, "*I'm* in charge of mercy. *I'm* in charge of compassion." Compassion doesn't originate in our bleeding hearts or moral sweat, but in God's mercy. The same point was made when God said to Pharaoh, "I picked you as a bit player in this drama of my salvation power." All we're saying is that God has the first word, initiating the action in which we play our part for good or ill.

19 Are you going to object, "So how can God blame us for anything since he's in charge of everything? If the big decisions are already made, what say do we have in it?"

20-33 Who in the world do you think you are to second-guess God? Do you for one moment suppose any of us knows enough to call God into question? Clay doesn't talk back to the fingers that mold it, saying, "Why did you shape me like this?" Isn't it obvious that a potter has a perfect right to shape one lump of clay into a vase for holding flowers and another into a pot for cooking beans? If God needs one style of pottery especially designed to show his angry displeasure and another style carefully crafted to show his glorious goodness, isn't that all right? Either or both happens to Jews, but it also happens to the other people. Hosea put it well:

> I'll call nobodies and make them somebodies;
>   I'll call the unloved and make them beloved.
> In the place where they yelled out, "You're nobody!"
>   they're calling you "God's living children."

Isaiah maintained this same emphasis:

> If each grain of sand on the seashore were numbered
>   and the sum labeled "chosen of God,"
> They'd be numbers still, not names;
>   salvation comes by personal selection.
> God doesn't count us; he calls us by name.
>   Arithmetic is not his focus.

Isaiah had looked ahead and spoken the truth:

> If our powerful God
>   had not provided us a legacy of living children,
> We would have ended up like ghost towns,
>   like Sodom and Gomorrah.

How can we sum this up? All those people who didn't seem interested in what God was doing actually *embraced* what God was doing as he straightened out their lives. And Israel, who seemed so interested in reading and talking about what God was doing, missed it. How could they miss it? Because instead of trusting God, *they* took over. They were absorbed in what they themselves were doing. They were so absorbed in their "God projects" that they didn't notice God right in front of them, like a huge rock in the middle of the road. And so they stumbled into him and went sprawling.

Isaiah (again!) gives us the metaphor for pulling this together:

> Careful! I've put a huge stone on the road to Mount Zion,
>   a stone you can't get around.
> But the stone is me! If you're looking for me,
>   you'll find me on the way, not in the way.

ISRAEL REDUCED TO RELIGION

1-3   1 O Believe me, friends, all I want for Israel is what's best for Israel: salvation, nothing less. I want it with all my heart and pray to God for it all the time. I readily admit that the Jews are impressively energetic regarding God — but they are doing everything exactly backward. They don't seem to realize that this comprehensive setting-things-right that is salvation is *God's* business, and a most flourishing business it is. Right across the street they set up their own salvation shops and noisily hawk their wares. After all these years of refusing to really deal with God on his terms, insisting instead on making their own deals, they have nothing to show for it.

4-10   The earlier revelation was intended simply to get us ready for the Messiah, who then puts everything right for those who trust him to do it. Moses wrote that anyone who insists on using the law code to live right before God soon discovers it's not so easy — every detail of life regulated by fine print! But trusting God to shape the right living in us is a different story — no precarious climb up to heaven to recruit the Messiah, no dangerous descent into hell to rescue the Messiah. So what exactly was Moses saying?

> The word that saves is right here,
>   as near as the tongue in your mouth,
>   as close as the heart in your chest.

It's the word of faith that welcomes God to go to work and set things right for us. This is the core of our preaching. Say the welcoming word to God — "Jesus is my Master" — embracing, body and soul, God's work of doing in us what he did in raising Jesus from the dead. That's it. You're not "doing" anything; you're simply calling out to God, trusting him to do it for you. That's salvation. With your whole being you embrace God setting things right, and then you say it, right out loud: "God has set everything right between him and me!"

11-13   Scripture reassures us, "No one who trusts God like this — heart and soul — will ever regret it." It's exactly the same no matter what a person's religious background may be: the same God for all of us, acting the same incredibly generous way to everyone who calls out for help. "Everyone who calls, 'Help, God!' gets help."

14-17   But how can people call for help if they don't know who to trust? And how can they know who to trust if they haven't heard of the One who can be trusted? And how can they hear if nobody tells them? And how is anyone going to tell them, unless someone is sent to do it? That's why Scripture exclaims,

> A sight to take your breath away!
> Grand processions of people
>   telling all the good things of God!

But not everybody is ready for this, ready to see and hear and act. Isaiah asked what we all ask at one time or another: "Does anyone care, God? Is anyone listening and believing a word of it?" The point is: Before you trust, you have to listen. But unless Christ's Word is preached, there's nothing to listen to.

18-21   But haven't there been plenty of opportunities for Israel to listen and understand what's going on? *Plenty*, I'd say.

> Preachers' voices have gone 'round the world,
> Their message to earth's seven seas.

So the big question is, Why didn't Israel understand that she had no corner on this message? Moses had it right when he predicted,

> When you see God reach out to those
>   you consider your inferiors — outsiders! —
>   you'll become insanely jealous.
> When you see God reach out to people
>   you think are religiously stupid,
>   you'll throw temper tantrums.

Isaiah dared to speak out these words of God:
>   People found and welcomed me
>   who never so much as looked for me.
>   And I found and welcomed people
>   who had never even asked about me.

Then he capped it with a damning indictment:
>   Day after day after day,
>   I beckoned Israel with open arms,
>   And got nothing for my trouble
>   but cold shoulders and icy stares.

The Loyal Minority

1-2   **11** Does this mean, then, that God is so fed up with Israel that he'll have nothing more to do with them? Hardly. Remember that I, the one writing these things, am an Israelite, a descendant of Abraham out of the tribe of Benjamin. You can't get much more Semitic than that! So we're not talking about repudiation. God has been too long involved with Israel, has too much invested, to simply wash his hands of them.

2-6   Do you remember that time Elijah was agonizing over this same Israel and cried out in prayer?

> God, they murdered your prophets,
> They trashed your altars;
> I'm the only one left and now they're after me!

And do you remember God's answer?
>   I still have seven thousand who haven't quit,
>   Seven thousand who are loyal to the finish.

It's the same today. There's a fiercely loyal minority still — not many, perhaps, but probably more than you think. They're holding on, not because of what they think they're going to get out of it, but because they're convinced of God's grace and purpose in choosing them. If they were only thinking of their own immediate self-interest, they would have left long ago.

7-10 And then what happened? Well, when Israel tried to be right with God on her own, pursuing her own self-interest, she didn't succeed. The chosen ones of God were those who let God pursue his interest in them, and as a result received his stamp of legitimacy. The "self-interest Israel" became thick-skinned toward God. Moses and Isaiah both commented on this:

Fed up with their quarrelsome, self-centered ways,
    God blurred their eyes and dulled their ears,
Shut them in on themselves in a hall of mirrors,
    and they're there to this day.

David was upset about the same thing:
    I hope they get sick eating self-serving meals,
        break a leg walking their self-serving ways.
    I hope they go blind staring in their mirrors,
        get ulcers from playing at god.

PRUNING AND GRAFTING BRANCHES

11-12 The next question is, "Are they down for the count? Are they out of this for good?" And the answer is a clear-cut *No*. Ironically when they walked out, they left the door open and the outsiders walked in. But the next thing you know, the Jews were starting to wonder if perhaps they had walked out on a good thing. Now, if their leaving triggered this worldwide coming of non-Jewish outsiders to God's kingdom, just imagine the effect of their coming back! What a homecoming!

13-15 But I don't want to go on about them. It's you, the outsiders, that I'm concerned with now. Because my personal assignment is focused on the so-called outsiders, I make as much of this as I can when I'm among my Israelite kin, the so-called *insiders*, hoping they'll realize what they're missing and want to get in on what God is doing. If their falling out initiated this worldwide coming together, their recovery is going to set off something even better: mass homecoming! If the first thing the Jews did, even though it was wrong for them, turned out for your good, just think what's going to happen when they get it right!

16-18 Behind and underneath all this there is a holy, God-planted, God-tended root. If the primary root of the tree is holy, there's bound to be some holy fruit. Some of the tree's branches were pruned and you wild olive shoots were grafted in. Yet the fact that you are now fed by that rich and holy root gives you no cause to crow over the pruned branches. Remember, you aren't feeding the root; the root is feeding you.

19-20 It's certainly possible to say, "Other branches were pruned so that *I* could be grafted in!" Well and good. But they were pruned because they were deadwood, no longer connected by belief and commitment to the root. The only reason you're on the tree is because your graft "took" when you believed, and because you're connected to that belief-nurturing root. So don't get cocky and strut your branch. Be humbly mindful of the root that keeps you lithe and green.

21-22   If God didn't think twice about taking pruning shears to the natural branches, why would he hesitate over you? He wouldn't give it a second thought. Make sure you stay alert to these qualities of gentle kindness and ruthless severity that exist side by side in God — ruthless with the deadwood, gentle with the grafted shoot. But don't presume on this gentleness. The moment you become deadwood, you're out of there.

23-24   And don't get to feeling superior to those pruned branches down on the ground. If they don't persist in remaining deadwood, they could very well get grafted back in. God can do that. He can perform miracle grafts. Why, if he could graft *you* — branches cut from a tree out in the wild — into an orchard tree, he certainly isn't going to have any trouble grafting branches back into the tree they grew from in the first place. Just be glad you're in the tree, and hope for the best for the others.

A COMPLETE ISRAEL

25-29   I want to lay all this out on the table as clearly as I can, friends. This is complicated. It would be easy to misinterpret what's going on and arrogantly assume that you're royalty and they're just rabble, out on their ears for good. But that's not it at all. This hardness on the part of insider Israel toward God is temporary. Its effect is to open things up to all the outsiders so that we end up with a full house. Before it's all over, there will be a complete Israel. As it is written,

> A champion will stride down from the mountain of Zion;
>   he'll clean house in Jacob.
> And this is my commitment to my people:
>   removal of their sins.

From your point of view as you hear and embrace the good news of the Message, it looks like the Jews are God's enemies. But looked at from the long-range perspective of God's overall purpose, they remain God's oldest friends. God's gifts and God's call are under full warranty — never canceled, never rescinded.

30-32   There was a time not so long ago when you were on the outs with God. But then the Jews slammed the door on him and things opened up for you. Now *they* are on the outs. But with the door held wide open for you, they have a way back in. In one way or another, God makes sure that we all experience what it means to be outside so that he can personally open the door and welcome us back in.

33-36   Have you ever come on anything quite like this extravagant generosity of God, this deep, deep wisdom? It's way over our heads. We'll never figure it out.

> Is there anyone around who can explain God?
> Anyone smart enough to tell him what to do?
> Anyone who has done him such a huge favor
>   that God has to ask his advice?
>
> Everything comes from him;
> Everything happens through him;

Everything ends up in him.
Always glory! Always praise!
Yes. Yes. Yes.

PLACE YOUR LIFE BEFORE GOD

¹⁻² **12** So here's what I want you to do, God helping you: Take your everyday, ordinary life—your sleeping, eating, going-to-work, and walking-around life—and place it before God as an offering. Embracing what God does for you is the best thing you can do for him. Don't become so well-adjusted to your culture that you fit into it without even thinking. Instead, fix your attention on God. You'll be changed from the inside out. Readily recognize what he wants from you, and quickly respond to it. Unlike the culture around you, always dragging you down to its level of immaturity, God brings the best out of you, develops well-formed maturity in you.

³ I'm speaking to you out of deep gratitude for all that God has given me, and especially as I have responsibilities in relation to you. Living then, as every one of you does, in pure grace, it's important that you not misinterpret yourselves as people who are bringing this goodness to God. No, God brings it all to you. The only accurate way to understand ourselves is by what God is and by what he does for us, not by what we are and what we do for him.

⁴⁻⁶ In this way we are like the various parts of a human body. Each part gets its meaning from the body as a whole, not the other way around. The body we're talking about is Christ's body of chosen people. Each of us finds our meaning and function as a part of his body. But as a chopped-off finger or cut-off toe we wouldn't amount to much, would we? So since we find ourselves fashioned into all these excellently formed and marvelously functioning parts in Christ's body, let's just go ahead and be what we were made to be, without enviously or pridefully comparing ourselves with each other, or trying to be something we aren't.

⁶⁻⁸ If you preach, just preach God's Message, nothing else; if you help, just help, don't take over; if you teach, stick to your teaching; if you give encouraging guidance, be careful that you don't get bossy; if you're put in charge, don't manipulate; if you're called to give aid to people in distress, keep your eyes open and be quick to respond; if you work with the disadvantaged, don't let yourself get irritated with them or depressed by them. Keep a smile on your face.

⁹⁻¹⁰ Love from the center of who you are; don't fake it. Run for dear life from evil; hold on for dear life to good. Be good friends who love deeply; practice playing second fiddle.

¹¹⁻¹³ Don't burn out; keep yourselves fueled and aflame. Be alert servants of the Master, cheerfully expectant. Don't quit in hard times; pray all the harder. Help needy Christians; be inventive in hospitality.

¹⁴⁻¹⁶ Bless your enemies; no cursing under your breath. Laugh with your happy friends when they're happy; share tears when they're down. Get along with each other; don't be stuck-up. Make friends with nobodies; don't be the great somebody.

¹⁷⁻¹⁹ Don't hit back; discover beauty in everyone. If you've got it in you, get along with everybody. Don't insist on getting even; that's not for you to do. "I'll do the judging," says God. "I'll take care of it."

20-21   Our Scriptures tell us that if you see your enemy hungry, go buy that person lunch, or if he's thirsty, get him a drink. Your generosity will surprise him with goodness. Don't let evil get the best of you; get the best of evil by doing good.

To Be a Responsible Citizen

1-3   **13** Be a good citizen. All governments are under God. Insofar as there is peace and order, it's God's order. So live responsibly as a citizen. If you're irresponsible to the state, then you're irresponsible with God, and God will hold you responsible. Duly constituted authorities are only a threat if you're trying to get by with something. Decent citizens should have nothing to fear.

3-5   Do you want to be on good terms with the government? Be a responsible citizen and you'll get on just fine, the government working to your advantage. But if you're breaking the rules right and left, watch out. The police aren't there just to be admired in their uniforms. God also has an interest in keeping order, and he uses them to do it. That's why you must live responsibly — not just to avoid punishment but also because it's the right way to live.

6-7   That's also why you pay taxes — so that an orderly way of life can be maintained. Fulfill your obligations as a citizen. Pay your taxes, pay your bills, respect your leaders.

8-10   Don't run up debts, except for the huge debt of love you owe each other. When you love others, you complete what the law has been after all along. The law code — don't sleep with another person's spouse, don't take someone's life, don't take what isn't yours, don't always be wanting what you don't have, and any other "don't" you can think of — finally adds up to this: Love other people as well as you do yourself. You can't go wrong when you love others. When you add up everything in the law code, the sum total is *love.*

11-14   But make sure that you don't get so absorbed and exhausted in taking care of all your day-by-day obligations that you lose track of the time and doze off, oblivious to God. The night is about over, dawn is about to break. Be up and awake to what God is doing! God is putting the finishing touches on the salvation work he began when we first believed. We can't afford to waste a minute, must not squander these precious daylight hours in frivolity and indulgence, in sleeping around and dissipation, in bickering and grabbing everything in sight. Get out of bed and get dressed! Don't loiter and linger, waiting until the very last minute. Dress yourselves in Christ, and be up and about!

Cultivating Good Relationships

1   **14** Welcome with open arms fellow believers who don't see things the way you do. And don't jump all over them every time they do or say something you don't agree with — even when it seems that they are strong on opinions but weak in the faith department. Remember, they have their own history to deal with. Treat them gently.

2-4   For instance, a person who has been around for a while might well be convinced that he can eat anything on the table, while another, with a different background, might assume he should only be a vegetarian and eat accordingly. But since both are guests at Christ's table, wouldn't it be terribly rude if they fell to criticizing what the other ate or didn't eat? God, after all, invited them both to the table. Do you have any business crossing people off the guest list or interfering with God's welcome? If there are corrections to be made or manners to be learned, God can handle that without your help.

5 Or, say, one person thinks that some days should be set aside as holy and another thinks that each day is pretty much like any other. There are good reasons either way. So, each person is free to follow the convictions of conscience.

6-9 What's important in all this is that if you keep a holy day, keep it for *God's* sake; if you eat meat, eat it to the glory of God and thank God for prime rib; if you're a vegetarian, eat vegetables to the glory of God and thank God for broccoli. None of us are permitted to insist on our own way in these matters. It's *God* we are answerable to — all the way from life to death and everything in between — not each other. That's why Jesus lived and died and then lived again: so that he could be our Master across the entire range of life and death, and free us from the petty tyrannies of each other.

10-12 So where does that leave you when you criticize a brother? And where does that leave you when you condescend to a sister? I'd say it leaves you looking pretty silly — or worse. Eventually, we're all going to end up kneeling side by side in the place of judgment, facing God. Your critical and condescending ways aren't going to improve your position there one bit. Read it for yourself in Scripture:

> "As I live and breathe," God says,
>   "every knee will bow before me;
> Every tongue will tell the honest truth
>   that I and only I am God."

So tend to your knitting. You've got your hands full just taking care of your own life before God.

13-14 Forget about deciding what's right for each other. Here's what you need to be concerned about: that you don't get in the way of someone else, making life more difficult than it already is. I'm convinced — Jesus convinced me! — that everything as it is in itself is holy. We, of course, by the way we treat it or talk about it, can contaminate it.

15-16 If you confuse others by making a big issue over what they eat or don't eat, you're no longer a companion with them in love, are you? These, remember, are persons for whom Christ died. Would you risk sending them to hell over an item in their diet? Don't you dare let a piece of God-blessed food become an occasion of soul-poisoning!

17-18 God's kingdom isn't a matter of what you put in your stomach, for goodness' sake. It's what God does with your life as he sets it right, puts it together, and completes it with joy. Your task is to single-mindedly serve Christ. Do that and you'll kill two birds with one stone: pleasing the God above you and proving your worth to the people around you.

19-21 So let's agree to use all our energy in getting along with each other. Help others with encouraging words; don't drag them down by finding fault. You're certainly not going to permit an argument over what is served or not served at supper to wreck God's work among you, are you? I said it

before and I'll say it again: All food is good, but it can turn bad if you use
it badly, if you use it to trip others up and send them sprawling. When you
sit down to a meal, your primary concern should not be to feed your own
face but to share the life of Jesus. So be sensitive and courteous to the others
who are eating. Don't eat or say or do things that might interfere with the
free exchange of love.

22-23   Cultivate your own relationship with God, but don't impose it on
others. You're fortunate if your behavior and your belief are coherent. But
if you're not sure, if you notice that you are acting in ways inconsistent
with what you believe — some days trying to impose your opinions on
others, other days just trying to please them — then you know that you're
out of line. If the way you live isn't consistent with what you believe, then
it's wrong.

1-2   **15** Those of us who are strong and able in the faith need to step
in and lend a hand to those who falter, and not just do what is
most convenient for us. Strength is for service, not status. Each
one of us needs to look after the good of the people around us, asking ourselves, "How can I help?"

3-6   That's exactly what Jesus did. He didn't make it easy for himself by
avoiding people's troubles, but waded right in and helped out. "I took on the
troubles of the troubled," is the way Scripture puts it. Even if it was written
in Scripture long ago, you can be sure it's written for *us*. God wants the
combination of his steady, constant calling and warm, personal counsel in
Scripture to come to characterize *us*, keeping us alert for whatever he will
do next. May our dependably steady and warmly personal God develop
maturity in you so that you get along with each other as well as Jesus gets
along with us all. Then we'll be a choir — not our voices only, but our very
lives singing in harmony in a stunning anthem to the God and Father of
our Master Jesus!

7-13   So reach out and welcome one another to God's glory. Jesus did it;
now *you* do it! Jesus, staying true to God's purposes, reached out in a special
way to the Jewish insiders so that the old ancestral promises would come
true for them. As a result, the non-Jewish outsiders have been able to experience mercy and to show appreciation to God. Just think of all the Scriptures
that will come true in what we do! For instance:

> Then I'll join outsiders in a hymn-sing;
> I'll sing to your name!

And this one:
> Outsiders and insiders, rejoice together!

And again:
> People of all nations, celebrate God!
> All colors and races, give hearty praise!

And Isaiah's word:
> There's the root of our ancestor Jesse,
>   breaking through the earth and growing tree tall,
> Tall enough for everyone everywhere to see and take hope!

Oh! May the God of green hope fill you up with joy, fill you up with peace, so that your believing lives, filled with the life-giving energy of the Holy Spirit, will brim over with hope!

※

14-16 Personally, I've been completely satisfied with who you are and what you are doing. You seem to me to be well-motivated and well-instructed, quite capable of guiding and advising one another. So, my dear friends, don't take my rather bold and blunt language as criticism. It's not criticism. I'm simply underlining how very much I need your help in carrying out this highly focused assignment God gave me, this priestly and gospel work of serving the spiritual needs of the non-Jewish outsiders so they can be presented as an acceptable offering to God, made whole and holy by God's Holy Spirit.

17-21 Looking back over what has been accomplished and what I have observed, I must say I am most pleased — in the context of Jesus, I'd even say *proud*, but only in that context. I have no interest in giving you a chatty account of my adventures, only the wondrously powerful and transformingly present words and deeds of Christ in me that triggered a believing response among the outsiders. In such ways I have trailblazed a preaching of the Message of Jesus all the way from Jerusalem far into northwestern Greece. This has all been pioneer work, bringing the Message only into those places where Jesus was not yet known and worshiped. My text has been,

> Those who were never told of him —
>   they'll see him!
> Those who've never heard of him —
>   they'll get the message!

※

22-24 And that's why it has taken me so long to finally get around to coming to you. But now that there is no more pioneering work to be done in these parts, and since I have looked forward to seeing you for many years, I'm planning my visit. I'm headed for Spain, and expect to stop off on the way to enjoy a good visit with you, and eventually have you send me off with God's blessing.

25-29 First, though, I'm going to Jerusalem to deliver a relief offering to the followers of Jesus there. The Greeks — all the way from the Macedonians in the north to the Achaians in the south — decided they wanted to take up a collection for the poor among the believers in Jerusalem. They were happy to do this, but it was also their duty. Seeing that they got in on all the spiritual gifts that flowed out of the Jerusalem community so generously, it is only right that they do what they can to relieve their poverty. As soon as I have done this — personally handed over this "fruit basket" — I'm off to Spain, with a stopover with you in Rome. My hope is that my visit with you is going to be one of Christ's more extravagant blessings.

30-33 I have one request, dear friends: Pray for me. Pray strenuously with and for me — to God the Father, through the power of our Master Jesus, through the love of the Spirit — that I will be delivered from the lions' den of unbelievers in Judea. Pray also that my relief offering to the Jerusalem believers will be accepted in the spirit in which it is given. Then, God willing, I'll be on my way to you with a light and eager heart, looking forward to being refreshed by your company. God's peace be with all of you. Oh, yes!

❋

1-2   **16** Be sure to welcome our friend Phoebe in the way of the Master, with all the generous hospitality we Christians are famous for. I heartily endorse both her and her work. She's a key representative of the church at Cenchrea. Help her out in whatever she asks. She deserves anything you can do for her. She's helped many a person, including me.

3-5   Say hello to Priscilla and Aquila, who have worked hand in hand with me in serving Jesus. They once put their lives on the line for me. And I'm not the only one grateful to them. All the non-Jewish gatherings of believers also owe them plenty, to say nothing of the church that meets in their house.

Hello to my dear friend Epenetus. He was the very first follower of Jesus in the province of Asia.

6   Hello to Mary. What a worker she has turned out to be!

7   Hello to my cousins Andronicus and Junias. We once shared a jail cell. They were believers in Christ before I was. Both of them are outstanding leaders.

8   Hello to Ampliatus, my good friend in the family of God.

9   Hello to Urbanus, our companion in Christ's work, and my good friend Stachys.

10   Hello to Apelles, a tried-and-true veteran in following Christ.

Hello to the family of Aristobulus.

11   Hello to my cousin Herodion.

Hello to those who belong to the Lord from the family of Narcissus.

12   Hello to Tryphena and Tryphosa—such diligent women in serving the Master.

Hello to Persis, a dear friend and hard worker in Christ.

13   Hello to Rufus—a good choice by the Master!—and his mother. She has also been a dear mother to me.

14   Hello to Asyncritus, Phlegon, Hermes, Patrobas, Hermas, and also to all of their families.

15   Hello to Philologus, Julia, Nereus and his sister, and Olympas—and all the followers of Jesus who live with them.

16   Holy embraces all around! All the churches of Christ send their warmest greetings!

17-18   One final word of counsel, friends. Keep a sharp eye out for those who take bits and pieces of the teaching that you learned and then use them to make trouble. Give these people a wide berth. They have no intention of living for our Master Christ. They're only in this for what they can get out of it, and aren't above using pious sweet talk to dupe unsuspecting innocents.

19-20   And so while there has never been any question about your honesty in these matters—I couldn't be more proud of you!—I want you also to be smart, making sure every "good" thing is the *real* thing. Don't be gullible in regard to smooth-talking evil. Stay alert like this, and before you know it the God of peace will come down on Satan with both feet, stomping him into the dirt. Enjoy the best of Jesus!

21   And here are some more greetings from our end. Timothy, my partner

in this work, Lucius, and my cousins Jason and Sosipater all said to tell you hello.

22   I, Tertius, who wrote this letter at Paul's dictation, send you my personal greetings.

23   Gaius, who is host here to both me and the whole church, wants to be remembered to you.

    Erastus, the city treasurer, and our good friend Quartus send their greetings.

25-26   All of our praise rises to the One who is strong enough to make *you* strong, exactly as preached in Jesus Christ, precisely as revealed in the mystery kept secret for so long but now an open book through the prophetic Scriptures. All the nations of the world can now know the truth and be brought into obedient belief, carrying out the orders of God, who got all this started, down to the very last letter.

27   All our praise is focused through Jesus on this incomparably wise God! Yes!

1 Corinthians

When people become Christians, they don't at the same moment become nice. This always comes as something of a surprise. Conversion to Christ and his ways doesn't automatically furnish a person with impeccable manners and suitable morals.

The people of Corinth had a reputation in the ancient world as an unruly, hard-drinking, sexually promiscuous bunch of people. When Paul arrived with the Message and many of them became believers in Jesus, they brought their reputations with them right into the church.

Paul spent a year and a half with them as their pastor, going over the Message of the "good news" in detail, showing them how to live out this new life of salvation and holiness as a community of believers. Then he went on his way to other towns and churches.

Sometime later Paul received a report from one of the Corinthian families that in his absence things had more or less fallen apart. He also received a letter from Corinth asking for help. Factions had developed, morals were in disrepair, worship had degenerated into a selfish grabbing for the supernatural. It was the kind of thing that might have been expected from Corinthians!

Paul's first letter to the Corinthians is a classic of pastoral response: affectionate, firm, clear, and unswerving in the conviction that God among them, revealed in Jesus and present in his Holy Spirit, continued to be the central issue in their lives, regardless of how much of a mess they had made of things. Paul doesn't disown them as brother and sister Christians, doesn't throw them out because of their bad behavior, and doesn't fly into a tirade over their irresponsible ways. He takes it all more or less in stride, but also takes them by the hand and goes over all the old ground again, directing them in how to work all the glorious details of God's saving love into their love for one another.

1 CORINTHIANS

1-2 **1** I, Paul, have been called and sent by Jesus, the Messiah, according to God's plan, along with my friend Sosthenes. I send this letter to you in God's church at Corinth, believers cleaned up by Jesus and set apart for a God-filled life. I include in my greeting all who call out to Jesus, wherever they live. He's their Master as well as ours!

3 May all the gifts and benefits that come from God our Father, and the Master, Jesus Christ, be yours.

4-6 Every time I think of you — and I think of you often! — I thank God for your lives of free and open access to God, given by Jesus. There's no end to what has happened in you — it's beyond speech, beyond knowledge. The evidence of Christ has been clearly verified in your lives.

7-9 Just think — you don't need a thing, you've got it all! All God's gifts are right in front of you as you wait expectantly for our Master Jesus to arrive on the scene for the Finale. And not only that, but God himself is right alongside to keep you steady and on track until things are all wrapped up by Jesus. God, who got you started in this spiritual adventure, shares with us the life of his Son and our Master Jesus. He will never give up on you. Never forget that.

THE CROSS: THE IRONY OF GOD'S WISDOM

10 I have a serious concern to bring up with you, my friends, using the authority of Jesus, our Master. I'll put it as urgently as I can: You *must* get along with each other. You must learn to be considerate of one another, cultivating a life in common.

11-12 I bring this up because some from Chloe's family brought a most disturbing report to my attention — that you're fighting among yourselves! I'll tell you exactly what I was told: You're all picking sides, going around saying, "I'm on Paul's side," or "I'm for Apollos," or "Peter is my man," or "I'm in the Messiah group."

13-16 I ask you, "Has the Messiah been chopped up in little pieces so we can each have a relic all our own? Was Paul crucified for you? Was a single one of you baptized in Paul's name?" I was not involved with any of your baptisms — except for Crispus and Gaius — and on getting this report, I'm sure glad I wasn't. At least no one can go around saying he was baptized in my name. (Come to think of it, I also baptized Stephanas's family, but as far as I can recall, that's it.)

17 God didn't send me out to collect a following for myself, but to preach the Message of what he has done, collecting a following for him. And he didn't send me to do it with a lot of fancy rhetoric of my own, lest the powerful action at the center — Christ on the Cross — be trivialized into mere words.

18-21 The Message that points to Christ on the Cross seems like sheer silliness to those hellbent on destruction, but for those on the way of salvation it makes perfect sense. This is the way God works, and most powerfully as it turns out. It's written,

> I'll turn conventional wisdom on its head,
> I'll expose so-called experts as crackpots.

So where can you find someone truly wise, truly educated, truly intelligent in this day and age? Hasn't God exposed it all as pretentious nonsense? Since the world in all its fancy wisdom never had a clue when it came to knowing God, God in his wisdom took delight in using what the world considered dumb — *preaching*, of all things! — to bring those who trust him into the way of salvation.

22-25   While Jews clamor for miraculous demonstrations and Greeks go in for philosophical wisdom, we go right on proclaiming Christ, the Crucified. Jews treat this like an *anti*-miracle — and Greeks pass it off as absurd. But to us who are personally called by God himself — both Jews and Greeks — Christ is God's ultimate miracle and wisdom all wrapped up in one. Human wisdom is so tinny, so impotent, next to the seeming absurdity of God. Human strength can't begin to compete with God's "weakness."

26-31   Take a good look, friends, at who you were when you got called into this life. I don't see many of "the brightest and the best" among you, not many influential, not many from high-society families. Isn't it obvious that God deliberately chose men and women that the culture overlooks and exploits and abuses, chose these "nobodies" to expose the hollow pretensions of the "somebodies"? That makes it quite clear that none of you can get by with blowing your own horn before God. Everything that we have — right thinking and right living, a clean slate and a fresh start — comes from God by way of Jesus Christ. That's why we have the saying, "If you're going to blow a horn, blow a trumpet for God."

1-2   2 You'll remember, friends, that when I first came to you to let you in on God's master stroke, I didn't try to impress you with polished speeches and the latest philosophy. I deliberately kept it plain and simple: first Jesus and who he is; then Jesus and what he did — Jesus crucified.

3-5   I was unsure of how to go about this, and felt totally inadequate — I was scared to death, if you want the truth of it — and so nothing I said could have impressed you or anyone else. But the Message came through anyway. God's Spirit and God's power did it, which made it clear that your life of faith is a response to God's power, not to some fancy mental or emotional footwork by me or anyone else.

6-10   We, of course, have plenty of wisdom to pass on to you once you get your feet on firm spiritual ground, but it's not popular wisdom, the fashionable wisdom of high-priced experts that will be out-of-date in a year or so. God's wisdom is something mysterious that goes deep into the interior of his purposes. You don't find it lying around on the surface. It's not the latest message, but more like the oldest — what God determined as the way to bring out his best in us, long before we ever arrived on the scene. The experts of our day haven't a clue about what this eternal plan is. If they had, they wouldn't have killed the Master of the God-designed life on a cross. That's why we have this Scripture text:

> No one's ever seen or heard anything like this,
> Never so much as imagined anything quite like it —
> What God has arranged for those who love him.

But *you've* seen and heard it because God by his Spirit has brought it all out into the open before you.

10-13 The Spirit, not content to flit around on the surface, dives into the depths of God, and brings out what God planned all along. Who ever knows what you're thinking and planning except you yourself? The same with God—except that he not only knows what he's thinking, but he lets *us* in on it. God offers a full report on the gifts of life and salvation that he is giving us. We don't have to rely on the world's guesses and opinions. We didn't learn this by reading books or going to school; we learned it from God, who taught us person-to-person through Jesus, and we're passing it on to you in the same firsthand, personal way.

14-16 The unspiritual self, just as it is by nature, can't receive the gifts of God's Spirit. There's no capacity for them. They seem like so much silliness. Spirit can be known only by spirit—God's Spirit and our spirits in open communion. Spiritually alive, we have access to everything God's Spirit is doing, and can't be judged by unspiritual critics. Isaiah's question, "Is there anyone around who knows God's Spirit, anyone who knows what he is doing?" has been answered: Christ knows, and we have Christ's Spirit.

1-4 3 But for right now, friends, I'm completely frustrated by your unspiritual dealings with each other and with God. You're acting like infants in relation to Christ, capable of nothing much more than nursing at the breast. Well, then, I'll nurse you since you don't seem capable of anything more. As long as you grab for what makes you feel good or makes you look important, are you really much different than a babe at the breast, content only when everything's going your way? When one of you says, "I'm on Paul's side," and another says, "I'm for Apollos," aren't you being totally infantile?

5-9 Who do you think Paul is, anyway? Or Apollos, for that matter? Servants, both of us—servants who waited on you as you gradually learned to entrust your lives to our mutual Master. We each carried out our servant assignment. I planted the seed, Apollos watered the plants, but *God* made you grow. It's not the one who plants or the one who waters who is at the center of this process but God, who makes things grow. Planting and watering are menial servant jobs at minimum wages. What makes them worth doing is the God we are serving. You happen to be God's field in which we are working.

9-15 Or, to put it another way, you are God's house. Using the gift God gave me as a good architect, I designed blueprints; Apollos is putting up the walls. Let each carpenter who comes on the job take care to build on the foundation! Remember, there is only one foundation, the one already laid: Jesus Christ. Take particular care in picking out your building materials. Eventually there is going to be an inspection. If you use cheap or inferior materials, you'll be found out. The inspection will be thorough and rigorous. You won't get by with a thing. If your work passes inspection, fine; if it doesn't, your part of the building will be torn out and started over. But *you* won't be torn out; you'll survive—but just barely.

16-17 You realize, don't you, that you are the temple of God, and God himself is present in you? No one will get by with vandalizing God's temple, you can be sure of that. God's temple is sacred—and you, remember, *are* the temple.

18-20　　Don't fool yourself. Don't think that you can be wise merely by being up-to-date with the times. Be God's fool—that's the path to true wisdom. What the world calls smart, God calls stupid. It's written in Scripture,

> He exposes the chicanery of the chic.
> The Master sees through the smoke screens
> 　　of the know-it-alls.

21-23　　I don't want to hear any of you bragging about yourself or anyone else. Everything is already yours as a gift—Paul, Apollos, Peter, the world, life, death, the present, the future—all of it is yours, and you are privileged to be in union with Christ, who is in union with God.

1-4　　**4** Don't imagine us leaders to be something we aren't. We are servants of Christ, not his masters. We are guides into God's most sublime secrets, not security guards posted to protect them. The requirements for a good guide are reliability and accurate knowledge. It matters very little to me what you think of me, even less where I rank in popular opinion. I don't even rank myself. Comparisons in these matters are pointless. I'm not aware of anything that would disqualify me from being a good guide for you, but that doesn't mean much. The *Master* makes that judgment.

5　　So don't get ahead of the Master and jump to conclusions with your judgments before all the evidence is in. When he comes, he will bring out in the open and place in evidence all kinds of things we never even dreamed of—inner motives and purposes and prayers. Only then will any one of us get to hear the "Well done!" of God.

6　　All I'm doing right now, friends, is showing how these things pertain to Apollos and me so that you will learn restraint and not rush into making judgments without knowing all the facts. It's important to look at things from God's point of view. I would rather not see you inflating or deflating reputations based on mere hearsay.

7-8　　For who do you know that really knows *you*, knows your heart? And even if they did, is there anything they would discover in you that you could take credit for? Isn't everything you *have* and everything you *are* sheer gifts from God? So what's the point of all this comparing and competing? You already have all you need. You already have more access to God than you can handle. Without bringing either Apollos or me into it, you're sitting on top of the world—at least God's world—and we're right there, sitting alongside you!

9-13　　It seems to me that God has put us who bear his Message on stage in a theater in which no one wants to buy a ticket. We're something everyone stands around and stares at, like an accident in the street. We're the Messiah's misfits. You might be sure of yourselves, but we live in the midst of frailties and uncertainties. You might be well-thought-of by others, but we're mostly kicked around. Much of the time we don't have enough to eat, we wear patched and threadbare clothes, we get doors slammed in our faces, and we pick up odd jobs anywhere we can to eke out a living. When they call us names, we say, "God bless you." When they spread rumors about *us*, we put in a good word for *them*. We're treated like garbage, potato peelings from the culture's kitchen. And it's not getting any better.

14-16   I'm not writing all this as a neighborhood scold just to make you feel rotten. I'm writing as a father to you, my children. I love you and want you to grow up well, not spoiled. There are a lot of people around who can't wait to tell you what you've done wrong, but there aren't many fathers willing to take the time and effort to help you grow up. It was as Jesus helped me proclaim God's Message to you that I became your father. I'm not, you know, asking you to do anything I'm not already doing myself.

17   This is why I sent Timothy to you earlier. He is also my dear son, and true to the Master. He will refresh your memory on the instructions I regularly give all the churches on the way of Christ.

18-20   I know there are some among you who are so full of themselves they never listen to anyone, let alone me. They don't think I'll ever show up in person. But I'll be there sooner than you think, God willing, and then we'll see if they're full of anything but hot air. God's Way is not a matter of mere talk; it's an empowered life.

21   So how should I prepare to come to you? As a severe disciplinarian who makes you toe the mark? Or as a good friend and counselor who wants to share heart-to-heart with you? You decide.

THE MYSTERY OF SEX

1-2   **5** I also received a report of scandalous sex within your church family, a kind that wouldn't be tolerated even outside the church: One of your men is sleeping with his stepmother. And you're so above it all that it doesn't even faze you! Shouldn't this break your hearts? Shouldn't it bring you to your knees in tears? Shouldn't this person and his conduct be confronted and dealt with?

3-5   I'll tell you what I would do. Even though I'm not there in person, consider me right there with you, because I can fully see what's going on. I'm telling you that this is wrong. You must not simply look the other way and hope it goes away on its own. Bring it out in the open and deal with it in the authority of Jesus our Master. Assemble the community — I'll be present in spirit with you and our Master Jesus will be present in power. Hold this man's conduct up to public scrutiny. Let him defend it if he can! But if he can't, then out with him! It will be totally devastating to him, of course, and embarrassing to you. But better devastation and embarrassment than damnation. You want him on his feet and forgiven before the Master on the Day of Judgment.

6-8   Your flip and callous arrogance in these things bothers me. You pass it off as a small thing, but it's anything but that. Yeast, too, is a "small thing," but it works its way through a whole batch of bread dough pretty fast. So get rid of this "yeast." Our true identity is flat and plain, not puffed up with the wrong kind of ingredient. The Messiah, our Passover Lamb, has already been sacrificed for the Passover meal, and we are the Unraised Bread part of the Feast. So let's live out our part in the Feast, not as raised bread swollen with the yeast of evil, but as flat bread — simple, genuine, unpretentious.

9-13   I wrote you in my earlier letter that you shouldn't make yourselves at home among the sexually promiscuous. I didn't mean that you should have nothing at all to do with outsiders of that sort. Or with crooks, whether blue- or white-collar. Or with spiritual phonies, for that matter. You'd have to leave the world entirely to do that! But I *am* saying that you shouldn't act as if everything is just fine when a friend who claims to be a Christian is promiscuous or crooked, is flip with God or rude to friends, gets drunk or becomes greedy and predatory. You can't just go along with this, treating it as acceptable behavior. I'm not responsible for what the *outsiders* do, but don't we have some responsibility for those within our community of believers? God decides on the outsiders, but we need to decide when our brothers and sisters are out of line and, if necessary, clean house.

1-4
6 And how dare you take each other to court! When you think you have been wronged, does it make any sense to go before a court that knows nothing of God's ways instead of a family of Christians? The day is coming when the world is going to stand before a jury made up of followers of Jesus. If someday you are going to rule on the world's fate, wouldn't it be a good idea to practice on some of these smaller cases? Why, we're even going to judge angels! So why not these everyday affairs? As these disagreements and wrongs surface, why would you ever entrust them to the judgment of people you don't trust in any other way?

5-6
I say this as bluntly as I can to wake you up to the stupidity of what you're doing. Is it possible that there isn't one levelheaded person among you who can make fair decisions when disagreements and disputes come up? I don't believe it. And here you are taking each other to court before people who don't even believe in God! How can they render justice if they don't believe in the *God* of justice?

7-8
These court cases are an ugly blot on your community. Wouldn't it be far better to just take it, to let yourselves be wronged and forget it? All you're doing is providing fuel for more wrong, more injustice, bringing more hurt to the people of your own spiritual family.

9-11
Don't you realize that this is not the way to live? Unjust people who don't care about God will not be joining in his kingdom. Those who use and abuse each other, use and abuse sex, use and abuse the earth and everything in it, don't qualify as citizens in God's kingdom. A number of you know from experience what I'm talking about, for not so long ago you were on that list. Since then, you've been cleaned up and given a fresh start by Jesus, our Master, our Messiah, and by our God present in us, the Spirit.

12
Just because something is technically legal doesn't mean that it's spiritually appropriate. If I went around doing whatever I thought I could get by with, I'd be a slave to my whims.

13
You know the old saying, "First you eat to live, and then you live to eat"? Well, it may be true that the body is only a temporary thing, but that's no excuse for stuffing your body with food, or indulging it with sex. Since the Master honors you with a body, honor him with your body!

14-15
God honored the Master's body by raising it from the grave. He'll treat yours with the same resurrection power. Until that time, remember that your bodies are created with the same dignity as the Master's body. You wouldn't take the Master's body off to a whorehouse, would you? I should hope not.

16-20
There's more to sex than mere skin on skin. Sex is as much spiritual mystery as physical fact. As written in Scripture, "The two become one." Since we want to become spiritually one with the Master, we must not pursue the kind of sex that avoids commitment and intimacy, leaving us more lonely than ever — the kind of sex that can never "become one." There is a sense in which sexual sins are different from all others. In sexual sin we

violate the sacredness of our own bodies, these bodies that were made for God-given and God-modeled love, for "becoming one" with another. Or didn't you realize that your body is a sacred place, the place of the Holy Spirit? Don't you see that you can't live however you please, squandering what God paid such a high price for? The physical part of you is not some piece of property belonging to the spiritual part of you. God owns the whole works. So let people see God in and through your body.

TO BE MARRIED, TO BE SINGLE . . .

1 7 Now, getting down to the questions you asked in your letter to me. First, Is it a good thing to have sexual relations?

2-6 Certainly — but only within a certain context. It's good for a man to have a wife, and for a woman to have a husband. Sexual drives are strong, but marriage is strong enough to contain them and provide for a balanced and fulfilling sexual life in a world of sexual disorder. The marriage bed must be a place of mutuality — the husband seeking to satisfy his wife, the wife seeking to satisfy her husband. Marriage is not a place to "stand up for your rights." Marriage is a decision to serve the other, whether in bed or out. Abstaining from sex is permissible for a period of time if you both agree to it, and if it's for the purposes of prayer and fasting — but only for such times. Then come back together again. Satan has an ingenious way of tempting us when we least expect it. I'm not, understand, commanding these periods of abstinence — only providing my best counsel if you should choose them.

7 Sometimes I wish everyone were single like me — a simpler life in many ways! But celibacy is not for everyone any more than marriage is. God gives the gift of the single life to some, the gift of the married life to others.

8-9 I do, though, tell the unmarried and widows that singleness might well be the best thing for them, as it has been for me. But if they can't manage their desires and emotions, they should by all means go ahead and get married. The difficulties of marriage are preferable by far to a sexually tortured life as a single.

10-11 And if you are married, stay married. This is the Master's command, not mine. If a wife should leave her husband, she must either remain single or else come back and make things right with him. And a husband has no right to get rid of his wife.

12-14 For the rest of you who are in mixed marriages — Christian married to non-Christian — we have no explicit command from the Master. So this is what you must do. If you are a man with a wife who is not a believer but who still wants to live with you, hold on to her. If you are a woman with a husband who is not a believer but he wants to live with you, hold on to him. The unbelieving husband shares to an extent in the holiness of his wife, and the unbelieving wife is likewise touched by the holiness of her husband. Otherwise, your children would be left out; as it is, they also are included in the spiritual purposes of God.

15-16 On the other hand, if the unbelieving spouse walks out, you've got to let him or her go. You don't have to hold on desperately. God has called us to make the best of it, as peacefully as we can. You never know, wife: The way you handle this might bring your husband not only back to you but to God. You never know, husband: The way you handle this might bring your wife not only back to you but to God.

17   And don't be wishing you were someplace else or with someone else. Where you are right now is God's place for you. Live and obey and love and believe right there. God, not your marital status, defines your life. Don't think I'm being harder on you than on the others. I give this same counsel in all the churches.

18-19   Were you Jewish at the time God called you? Don't try to remove the evidence. Were you non-Jewish at the time of your call? Don't become a Jew. Being Jewish isn't the point. The really important thing is obeying God's call, following his commands.

20-22   Stay where you were when God called your name. Were you a slave? Slavery is no roadblock to obeying and believing. I don't mean you're stuck and can't leave. If you have a chance at freedom, go ahead and take it. I'm simply trying to point out that under your new Master you're going to experience a marvelous freedom you would never have dreamed of. On the other hand, if you were free when Christ called you, you'll experience a delightful "enslavement to God" you would never have dreamed of.

23-24   All of you, slave and free both, were once held hostage in a sinful society. Then a huge sum was paid out for your ransom. So please don't, out of old habit, slip back into being or doing what everyone else tells you. Friends, stay where you were called to be. God is there. Hold the high ground with him at your side.

25-28   The Master did not give explicit direction regarding virgins, but as one much experienced in the mercy of the Master and loyal to him all the way, you can trust my counsel. Because of the current pressures on us from all sides, I think it would probably be best to stay just as you are. Are you married? Stay married. Are you unmarried? Don't get married. But there's certainly no sin in getting married, whether you're a virgin or not. All I am saying is that when you marry, you take on additional stress in an already stressful time, and I want to spare you if possible.

29-31   I do want to point out, friends, that time is of the essence. There is no time to waste, so don't complicate your lives unnecessarily. Keep it simple — in marriage, grief, joy, whatever. Even in ordinary things — your daily routines of shopping, and so on. Deal as sparingly as possible with the things the world thrusts on you. This world as you see it is on its way out.

32-35   I want you to live as free of complications as possible. When you're unmarried, you're free to concentrate on simply pleasing the Master. Marriage involves you in all the nuts and bolts of domestic life and in wanting to please your spouse, leading to so many more demands on your attention. The time and energy that married people spend on caring for and nurturing each other, the unmarried can spend in becoming whole and holy instruments of God. I'm trying to be helpful and make it as easy as possible for you, not make things harder. All I want is for you to be able to develop a way of life in which you can spend plenty of time together with the Master without a lot of distractions.

36-38   If a man has a woman friend to whom he is loyal but never intended to marry, having decided to serve God as a "single," and then changes his mind, deciding he should marry her, he should go ahead and marry. It's no sin; it's not even a "step down" from celibacy, as some say. On the other hand, if a man is comfortable in his decision for a single life in service to God and it's entirely his own conviction and not imposed on him by others, he ought to stick with it. Marriage is spiritually and morally right and not inferior to singleness in any way, although as I indicated earlier, because of the times we live in, I do have pastoral reasons for encouraging singleness.

39-40   A wife must stay with her husband as long as he lives. If he dies, she is free to marry anyone she chooses. She will, of course, want to marry a believer and have the blessing of the Master. By now you know that I think she'll be better off staying single. The Master, in my opinion, thinks so, too.

FREEDOM WITH RESPONSIBILITY

1-3   The question keeps coming up regarding meat that has been offered up to an idol: Should you attend meals where such meat is served, or not? We sometimes tend to think we know all we need to know to answer these kinds of questions — *but* sometimes our humble hearts can help us more than our proud minds. We never really know enough until we recognize that God alone knows it all.

4-6   Some people say, quite rightly, that idols have no actual existence, that there's nothing to them, that there is no God other than our one God, that no matter how many of these so-called gods are named and worshiped they still don't add up to anything but a tall story. They say — again, quite rightly — that there is only one God the Father, that everything comes from him, and that he wants us to live for him. Also, they say that there is only one Master — Jesus the Messiah — and that everything is for his sake, including us. Yes. It's true.

7   In strict logic, then, nothing happened to the meat when it was offered up to an idol. It's just like any other meat. I know that, and you know that. But knowing isn't everything. If it becomes everything, some people end up as know-it-alls who treat others as know-nothings. Real knowledge isn't that insensitive.

    We need to be sensitive to the fact that we're not all at the same level of understanding in this. Some of you have spent your entire lives eating "idol meat," and are sure that there's something bad in the meat that then becomes something bad inside of you. An imagination and conscience shaped under those conditions isn't going to change overnight.

8-9   But fortunately God doesn't grade us on our diet. We're neither commended when we clean our plate nor reprimanded when we just can't stomach it. But God *does* care when you use your freedom carelessly in a way that leads a fellow believer still vulnerable to those old associations to be thrown off track.

10   For instance, say you flaunt your freedom by going to a banquet thrown in honor of idols, where the main course is meat sacrificed to idols. Isn't there great danger if someone still struggling over this issue, someone who looks up to you as knowledgeable and mature, sees you go into that banquet? The danger is that he will become terribly confused — maybe even to the point of getting mixed up himself in what his conscience tells him is wrong.

11-13   Christ gave up his life for that person. Wouldn't you at least be willing to give up going to dinner for him — because, as you say, it doesn't really make any difference? But it *does* make a difference if you hurt your friend terribly, risking his eternal ruin! When you hurt your friend, you hurt Christ. A free meal here and there isn't worth it at the cost of even one of these "weak ones." So, never go to these idol-tainted meals if there's any chance it will trip up one of your brothers or sisters.

9 **1-2** And don't tell me that I have no authority to write like this. I'm perfectly free to do this — isn't that obvious? Haven't I been given a job to do? Wasn't I commissioned to this work in a face-to-face meeting with Jesus, our Master? Aren't you yourselves proof of the good work that I've done for the Master? Even if no one else admits the authority of my commission, *you* can't deny it. Why, my work with you is living proof of my authority!

3-7 I'm not shy in standing up to my critics. We who are on missionary assignments for God have a right to decent accommodations, and we have a right to support for us and our families. You don't seem to have raised questions with the other apostles and our Master's brothers and Peter in these matters. So, why me? Is it just Barnabas and I who have to go it alone and pay our own way? Are soldiers self-employed? Are gardeners forbidden to eat vegetables from their own gardens? Don't milkmaids get to drink their fill from the pail?

8-12 I'm not just sounding off because I'm irritated. This is all written in the scriptural law. Moses wrote, "Don't muzzle an ox to keep it from eating the grain when it's threshing." Do you think Moses' primary concern was the care of farm animals? Don't you think his concern extends to us? Of course. Farmers plow and thresh expecting something when the crop comes in. So if we have planted spiritual seed among you, is it out of line to expect a meal or two from you? Others demand plenty from you in these ways. Don't we who have never demanded deserve even more?

12-14 But we're not going to start demanding now what we've always had a perfect right to. Our decision all along has been to put up with anything rather than to get in the way or detract from the Message of Christ. All I'm concerned with right now is that you not use our decision to take advantage of others, depriving them of what is rightly theirs. You know, don't you, that it's always been taken for granted that those who work in the Temple live off the proceeds of the Temple, and that those who offer sacrifices at the altar eat their meals from what has been sacrificed? Along the same lines, the Master directed that those who spread the Message be supported by those who believe the Message.

15-18 Still, I want it made clear that I've never gotten anything out of this for myself, and that I'm not writing now to get something. I'd rather die than give anyone ammunition to discredit me or impugn my motives. If I proclaim the Message, it's not to get something out of it for myself. I'm *compelled* to do it, and doomed if I don't! If this was my own idea of just another way to make a living, I'd expect some pay. But since it's *not* my idea but something solemnly entrusted to me, why would I expect to get paid? So am I getting anything out of it? Yes, as a matter of fact: the pleasure of proclaiming the Message at no cost to you. You don't even have to pay my expenses!

19-23 Even though I am free of the demands and expectations of everyone, I have voluntarily become a servant to any and all in order to reach a wide range of people: religious, nonreligious, meticulous moralists, loose-living immoralists, the defeated, the demoralized — whoever. I didn't take on their way of life. I kept my bearings in Christ — but I entered their world and tried to experience things from their point of view. I've become just about every sort of servant there is in my attempts to lead those I meet into a God-saved life. I did all this because of the Message. I didn't just want to talk about it; I wanted to be *in* on it!

24-25 You've all been to the stadium and seen the athletes race. Everyone runs; one wins. Run to win. All good athletes train hard. They do it for a gold medal that tarnishes and fades. You're after one that's gold eternally.

26-27 I don't know about you, but I'm running hard for the finish line. I'm giving it everything I've got. No sloppy living for me! I'm staying alert and in top condition. I'm not going to get caught napping, telling everyone else all about it and then missing out myself.

1-5 **10** Remember our history, friends, and be warned. All our ancestors were led by the providential Cloud and taken miraculously through the Sea. They went through the waters, in a baptism like ours, as Moses led them from enslaving death to salvation life. They all ate and drank identical food and drink, meals provided daily by God. They drank from the Rock, God's fountain for them that stayed with them wherever they were. And the Rock was Christ. But just experiencing God's wonder and grace didn't seem to mean much — most of them were defeated by temptation during the hard times in the desert, and God was not pleased.

6-10 The same thing could happen to us. We must be on guard so that we never get caught up in wanting our own way as they did. And we must not turn our religion into a circus as they did — "First the people partied, then they threw a dance." We must not be sexually promiscuous — they paid for that, remember, with 23,000 deaths in one day! We must never try to get Christ to serve us instead of us serving him; they tried it, and God launched an epidemic of poisonous snakes. We must be careful not to stir up discontent; discontent destroyed them.

11-12 These are all warning markers — DANGER! — in our history books, written down so that we don't repeat their mistakes. Our positions in the story are parallel — they at the beginning, we at the end — and we are just as capable of messing it up as they were. Don't be so naive and self-confident. You're not exempt. You could fall flat on your face as easily as anyone else. Forget about self-confidence; it's useless. Cultivate God-confidence.

13 No test or temptation that comes your way is beyond the course of what others have had to face. All you need to remember is that God will never let you down; he'll never let you be pushed past your limit; he'll always be there to help you come through it.

14 So, my very dear friends, when you see people reducing God to something they can use or control, get out of their company as fast as you can.

15-18 I assume I'm addressing believers now who are mature. Draw your own conclusions: When we drink the cup of blessing, aren't we taking into ourselves the blood, the very life, of Christ? And isn't it the same with the loaf of bread we break and eat? Don't we take into ourselves the body, the very life, of Christ? Because there is one loaf, our many-ness becomes oneness — Christ doesn't become fragmented in us. Rather, we become unified in him. We don't reduce Christ to what we are; he raises us to what he is. That's basically what happened even in old Israel — those who ate the sacrifices offered on God's altar entered into God's action at the altar.

19-22 Do you see the difference? Sacrifices offered to idols are offered to nothing, for what's the idol but a nothing? Or worse than nothing, a minus, a demon! I don't want you to become part of something that reduces you to less than yourself. And you can't have it both ways, banqueting with the Master one day and slumming with demons the next. Besides, the Master won't put up with it. He wants *us* — all or nothing. Do you think you can get off with anything less?

23-24   Looking at it one way, you could say, "Anything goes. Because of God's immense generosity and grace, we don't have to dissect and scrutinize every action to see if it will pass muster." But the point is not to just get by. We want to live well, but our foremost efforts should be to help *others* live well.

25-28   With that as a base to work from, common sense can take you the rest of the way. Eat anything sold at the butcher shop, for instance; you don't have to run an "idolatry test" on every item. "The earth," after all, "is God's, and everything in it." That "everything" certainly includes the leg of lamb in the butcher shop. If a nonbeliever invites you to dinner and you feel like going, go ahead and enjoy yourself; eat everything placed before you. It would be both bad manners and bad spirituality to cross-examine your host on the ethical purity of each course as it is served. On the other hand, if he goes out of his way to tell you that this or that was sacrificed to god or goddess so-and-so, you should pass. Even though you may be indifferent as to where it came from, he isn't, and you don't want to send mixed messages to him about who *you* are worshiping.

29-30   But, except for these special cases, I'm not going to walk around on eggshells worrying about what small-minded people might say; I'm going to stride free and easy, knowing what our large-minded Master has already said. If I eat what is served to me, grateful to God for what is on the table, how can I worry about what someone will say? I thanked God for it and he blessed it!

31-33   So eat your meals heartily, not worrying about what others say about you — you're eating to God's glory, after all, not to please them. As a matter of fact, do everything that way, heartily and freely to God's glory. At the same time, don't be callous in your exercise of freedom, thoughtlessly stepping on the toes of those who aren't as free as you are. I try my best to be considerate of everyone's feelings in all these matters; I hope you will be, too.

To Honor God

1-2   It pleases me that you continue to remember and honor me by keeping up the traditions of the faith I taught you. All actual authority stems from Christ.

3-9   In a marriage relationship, there is authority from Christ to husband, and from husband to wife. The authority of Christ is the authority of God. Any man who speaks with God or about God in a way that shows a lack of respect for the authority of Christ, dishonors Christ. In the same way, a wife who speaks with God in a way that shows a lack of respect for the authority of her husband, dishonors her husband. Worse, she dishonors herself — an ugly sight, like a woman with her head shaved. This is basically the origin of these customs we have of women wearing head coverings in worship, while men take their hats off. By these symbolic acts, men and women, who far too often butt heads with each other, submit their "heads" to the Head: God.

10-12   Don't, by the way, read too much into the differences here between men and women. Neither man nor woman can go it alone or claim priority. Man was created first, as a beautiful shining reflection of God — that is true. But the head on a woman's body clearly outshines in beauty the head of her "head," her husband. The first woman came from man, true — but ever since then, every man comes from a woman! And since virtually everything comes from God anyway, let's quit going through these "who's first" routines.

13-16   Don't you agree there is something naturally powerful in the symbolism — a woman, her beautiful hair reminiscent of angels, praying in adoration; a man, his head bared in reverence, praying in submission? I hope you're not going to be argumentative about this. All God's churches see it this way; I don't want you standing out as an exception.

17-19   Regarding this next item, I'm not at all pleased. I am getting the picture that when you meet together it brings out your worst side instead of your best! First, I get this report on your divisiveness, competing with and criticizing each other. I'm reluctant to believe it, but there it is. The best that can be said for it is that the testing process will bring truth into the open and confirm it.

20-22   And then I find that you bring your divisions to worship — you come together, and instead of eating the Lord's Supper, you bring in a lot of food from the outside and make pigs of yourselves. Some are left out, and go home hungry. Others have to be carried out, too drunk to walk. I can't believe it! Don't you have your own homes to eat and drink in? Why would you stoop to desecrating God's church? Why would you actually shame God's poor? I never would have believed you would stoop to this. And I'm not going to stand by and say nothing.

23-26   Let me go over with you again exactly what goes on in the Lord's Supper and why it is so centrally important. I received my instructions from the Master himself and passed them on to you. The Master, Jesus, on the night of his betrayal, took bread. Having given thanks, he broke it and said,

This is my body, broken for you.
Do this to remember me.

After supper, he did the same thing with the cup:
This cup is my blood, my new covenant with you.
Each time you drink this cup, remember me.

What you must solemnly realize is that every time you eat this bread and every time you drink this cup, you reenact in your words and actions the death of the Master. You will be drawn back to this meal again and again until the Master returns. You must never let familiarity breed contempt.

27-28   Anyone who eats the bread or drinks the cup of the Master irreverently is like part of the crowd that jeered and spit on him at his death. Is that the kind of "remembrance" you want to be part of? Examine your motives, test your heart, come to this meal in holy awe.

29-32   If you give no thought (or worse, don't care) about the broken body of the Master when you eat and drink, you're running the risk of serious consequences. That's why so many of you even now are listless and sick, and others have gone to an early grave. If we get this straight now, we won't have to be straightened out later on. Better to be confronted by the Master now than to face a fiery confrontation later.

³³⁻³⁴ So, my friends, when you come together to the Lord's Table, be reverent and courteous with one another. If you're so hungry that you can't wait to be served, go home and get a sandwich. But by no means risk turning this Meal into an eating and drinking binge or a family squabble. It is a spiritual meal—a love feast.

The other things you asked about, I'll respond to in person when I make my next visit.

SPIRITUAL GIFTS

¹⁻³ 12 What I want to talk about now is the various ways God's Spirit gets worked into our lives. This is complex and often misunderstood, but I want you to be informed and knowledgeable. Remember how you were when you didn't know God, led from one phony god to another, never knowing what you were doing, just doing it because everybody else did it? It's different in this life. God wants us to use our intelligence, to seek to understand as well as we can. For instance, by using your heads, you know perfectly well that the Spirit of God would never prompt anyone to say "Jesus be damned!" Nor would anyone be inclined to say "Jesus is Master!" without the insight of the Holy Spirit.

⁴⁻¹¹ God's various gifts are handed out everywhere; but they all originate in God's Spirit. God's various ministries are carried out everywhere; but they all originate in God's Spirit. God's various expressions of power are in action everywhere; but God himself is behind it all. Each person is given something to do that shows who God is: Everyone gets in on it, everyone benefits. All kinds of things are handed out by the Spirit, and to all kinds of people! The variety is wonderful:

wise counsel
clear understanding
simple trust
healing the sick
miraculous acts
proclamation
distinguishing between spirits
tongues
interpretation of tongues.

All these gifts have a common origin, but are handed out one by one by the one Spirit of God. He decides who gets what, and when.

¹²⁻¹³ You can easily enough see how this kind of thing works by looking no further than your own body. Your body has many parts—limbs, organs, cells—but no matter how many parts you can name, you're still one body. It's exactly the same with Christ. By means of his one Spirit, we all said good-bye to our partial and piecemeal lives. We each used to independently call our own shots, but then we entered into a large and integrated life in which *he* has the final say in everything. (This is what we proclaimed in word and action when we were baptized.) Each of us is now a part of his resurrection body, refreshed and sustained at one fountain—his Spirit—where we all come to drink. The old labels we once used to identify ourselves—labels like Jew or Greek, slave or

free — are no longer useful. We need something larger, more comprehensive.

14-18   I want you to think about how all this makes you more significant, not less. A body isn't just a single part blown up into something huge. It's all the different-but-similar parts arranged and functioning together. If Foot said, "I'm not elegant like Hand, embellished with rings; I guess I don't belong to this body," would that make it so? If Ear said, "I'm not beautiful like Eye, limpid and expressive; I don't deserve a place on the head," would you want to remove it from the body? If the body was all eye, how could it hear? If all ear, how could it smell? As it is, we see that God has carefully placed each part of the body right where he wanted it.

19-24   But I also want you to think about how this keeps your significance from getting blown up into self-importance. For no matter how significant you are, it is only because of what you are a *part* of. An enormous eye or a gigantic hand wouldn't be a body, but a monster. What we have is one body with many parts, each its proper size and in its proper place. No part is important on its own. Can you imagine Eye telling Hand, "Get lost; I don't need you"? Or, Head telling Foot, "You're fired; your job has been phased out"? As a matter of fact, in practice it works the other way — the "lower" the part, the more basic, and therefore necessary. You can live without an eye, for instance, but not without a stomach. When it's a part of your own body you are concerned with, it makes *no* difference whether the part is visible or clothed, higher or lower. You give it dignity and honor just as it is, without comparisons. If anything, you have more concern for the lower parts than the higher. If you had to choose, wouldn't you prefer good digestion to full-bodied hair?

25-26   The way God designed our bodies is a model for understanding our lives together as a church: every part dependent on every other part, the parts we mention and the parts we don't, the parts we see and the parts we don't. If one part hurts, every other part is involved in the hurt, and in the healing. If one part flourishes, every other part enters into the exuberance.

27-31   You are Christ's body — that's who you are! You must never forget this. Only as you accept your part of that body does your "part" mean anything. You're familiar with some of the parts that God has formed in his church, which is his "body":

apostles
prophets
teachers
miracle workers
healers
helpers
organizers
those who pray in tongues.

But it's obvious by now, isn't it, that Christ's church is a complete Body and not a gigantic, unidimensional Part? It's not all Apostle, not all Prophet, not all Miracle Worker, not all Healer, not all Prayer in Tongues, not all Interpreter of Tongues. And yet some of you keep competing for so-called "important" parts.

But now I want to lay out a far better way for you.

THE WAY OF LOVE

1 **13** If I speak with human eloquence and angelic ecstasy but don't love, I'm nothing but the creaking of a rusty gate.

2 If I speak God's Word with power, revealing all his mysteries and making everything plain as day, and if I have faith that says to a mountain, "Jump," and it jumps, but I don't love, I'm nothing.

3-7 If I give everything I own to the poor and even go to the stake to be burned as a martyr, but I don't love, I've gotten nowhere. So, no matter what I say, what I believe, and what I do, I'm bankrupt without love.

> Love never gives up.
> Love cares more for others than for self.
> Love doesn't want what it doesn't have.
> Love doesn't strut,
> Doesn't have a swelled head,
> Doesn't force itself on others,
> Isn't always "me first,"
> Doesn't fly off the handle,
> Doesn't keep score of the sins of others,
> Doesn't revel when others grovel,
> Takes pleasure in the flowering of truth,
> Puts up with anything,
> Trusts God always,
> Always looks for the best,
> Never looks back,
> But keeps going to the end.

8-10 Love never dies. Inspired speech will be over some day; praying in tongues will end; understanding will reach its limit. We know only a portion of the truth, and what we say about God is always incomplete. But when the Complete arrives, our incompletes will be canceled.

11 When I was an infant at my mother's breast, I gurgled and cooed like any infant. When I grew up, I left those infant ways for good.

12 We don't yet see things clearly. We're squinting in a fog, peering through a mist. But it won't be long before the weather clears and the sun shines bright! We'll see it all then, see it all as clearly as God sees us, knowing him directly just as he knows us!

13 But for right now, until that completeness, we have three things to do to lead us toward that consummation: Trust steadily in God, hope unswervingly, love extravagantly. And the best of the three is love.

PRAYER LANGUAGE

1-3 **14** Go after a life of love as if your life depended on it—because it does. Give yourselves to the gifts God gives you. Most of all, try to proclaim his truth. If you praise him in the private language of tongues, God understands you but no one else does, for you are sharing intimacies just between you and him. But when you proclaim his truth in everyday speech, you're letting *others* in on the truth so that they can grow and be strong and experience his presence with you.

4-5 The one who prays using a private "prayer language" certainly gets a lot out of it, but proclaiming God's truth to the church in its common language brings the whole church into growth and strength. I want all of you to develop intimacies with God in prayer, but please don't stop with that. Go on and proclaim his clear truth to others. It's more important that everyone have access to the knowledge and love of God in language everyone understands than that you go off and cultivate God's presence in a mysterious prayer language — unless, of course, there is someone who can interpret what you are saying for the benefit of all.

6-8 Think, friends: If I come to you and all I do is pray privately to God in a way only he can understand, what are you going to get out of that? If I don't address you plainly with some insight or truth or proclamation or teaching, what help am I to you? If musical instruments — flutes, say, or harps — aren't played so that each note is distinct and in tune, how will anyone be able to catch the melody and enjoy the music? If the trumpet call can't be distinguished, will anyone show up for the battle?

9-12 So if you speak in a way no one can understand, what's the point of opening your mouth? There are many languages in the world and they all mean something to someone. But if I don't understand the language, it's not going to do me much good. It's no different with you. Since you're so eager to participate in what God is doing, why don't you concentrate on doing what helps everyone in the church?

13-17 So, when you pray in your private prayer language, don't hoard the experience for yourself. Pray for the insight and ability to bring others into that intimacy. If I pray in tongues, my spirit prays but my mind lies fallow, and all that intelligence is wasted. So what's the solution? The answer is simple enough. Do both. I should be spiritually free and expressive as I pray, but I should also be thoughtful and mindful as I pray. I should sing with my spirit, and sing with my mind. If you give a blessing using your private prayer language, which no one else understands, how can some outsider who has just shown up and has no idea what's going on know when to say "Amen"? Your blessing might be beautiful, but you have very effectively cut that person out of it.

18-19 I'm grateful to God for the gift of praying in tongues that he gives us for praising him, which leads to wonderful intimacies we enjoy with him. I enter into this as much or more than any of you. But when I'm in a church assembled for worship, I'd rather say five words that everyone can understand and learn from than say ten thousand that sound to others like gibberish.

20-25 To be perfectly frank, I'm getting exasperated with your infantile thinking. How long before you grow up and use your head — your *adult* head? It's all right to have a childlike unfamiliarity with evil; a simple *no* is all that's needed there. But there's far more to saying *yes* to something. Only mature and well-exercised intelligence can save you from falling into gullibility. It's written in Scripture that God said,

> In strange tongues
>   and from the mouths of strangers
> I will preach to this people,
>   but they'll neither listen nor believe.

So where does it get you, all this speaking in tongues no one understands? It doesn't help believers, and it only gives unbelievers something to gawk at. Plain truth-speaking, on the other hand, goes straight to the heart of believers and doesn't get in the way of unbelievers. If you come together as a congregation and some unbelieving outsiders walk in on you as you're all praying in tongues, unintelligible to each other and to them, won't they assume you've taken leave of your senses and get out of there as fast as they can? But if some unbelieving outsiders walk in on a service where people are speaking out God's truth, the plain words will bring them up against the truth and probe their hearts. Before you know it, they're going to be on their faces before God, recognizing that God is among you.

26-33   So here's what I want you to do. When you gather for worship, each one of you be prepared with something that will be useful for all: Sing a hymn, teach a lesson, tell a story, lead a prayer, provide an insight. If prayers are offered in tongues, two or three's the limit, and then only if someone is present who can interpret what you're saying. Otherwise, keep it between God and yourself. And no more than two or three speakers at a meeting, with the rest of you listening and taking it to heart. Take your turn, no one person taking over. Then each speaker gets a chance to say something special from God, and you all learn from each other. If you choose to speak, you're also responsible for how and when you speak. When we worship the right way, God doesn't stir us up into confusion; he brings us into harmony. This goes for all the churches — no exceptions.

34-36   Wives must not disrupt worship, talking when they should be listening, asking questions that could more appropriately be asked of their husbands at home. God's Book of the law guides our manners and customs here. Wives have no license to use the time of worship for unwarranted speaking. Do you — both women *and* men — imagine that you're a sacred oracle determining what's right and wrong? Do you think everything revolves around you?

37-38   If any one of you thinks God has something for you to say or has inspired you to do something, pay close attention to what I have written. This is the way the Master wants it. If you won't play by these rules, God can't use you. Sorry.

39-40   Three things, then, to sum this up: When you speak forth God's truth, speak your heart out. Don't tell people how they should or shouldn't pray when they're praying in tongues that you don't understand. Be courteous and considerate in everything.

RESURRECTION

1-2   **15** Friends, let me go over the Message with you one final time — this Message that I proclaimed and that you made your own; this Message on which you took your stand and by which your life has been saved. (I'm assuming, now, that your belief was the real thing and not a passing fancy, that you're in this for good and holding fast.)

3-9   The first thing I did was place before you what was placed so emphatically before me: that the Messiah died for our sins, exactly as Scripture tells it; that he was buried; that he was raised from death on the third day, again exactly as Scripture says; that he presented himself alive to Peter, then to his closest followers, and later to more than five hundred of his followers all at the same time, most of them still around (although a few have since died); that he then spent time with James and the rest of those he commissioned to represent him; and that he finally presented himself alive to *me*. It was fitting that I bring up the rear. I don't deserve to be included in that inner circle, as you well know, having spent all those early years trying my best to stamp God's church right out of existence.

10-11 But because God was so gracious, so very generous, here I am. And I'm not about to let his grace go to waste. Haven't I worked hard trying to do more than any of the others? Even then, my work didn't amount to all that much. It was God giving me the work to do, God giving me the energy to do it. So whether you heard it from me or from those others, it's all the same: We spoke God's truth and you entrusted your lives.

12-15 Now, let me ask you something profound yet troubling. If you became believers because you trusted the proclamation that Christ is alive, risen from the dead, how can you let people say that there is no such thing as a resurrection? If there's no resurrection, there's no living Christ. And face it — if there's no resurrection for Christ, everything we've told you is smoke and mirrors, and everything you've staked your life on is smoke and mirrors. Not only that, but we would be guilty of telling a string of barefaced lies about God, all these affidavits we passed on to you verifying that God raised up Christ — sheer fabrications, if there's no resurrection.

16-20 If corpses can't be raised, then Christ wasn't, because he was indeed dead. And if Christ weren't raised, then all you're doing is wandering about in the dark, as lost as ever. It's even worse for those who died hoping in Christ and resurrection, because they're already in their graves. If all we get out of Christ is a little inspiration for a few short years, we're a pretty sorry lot. But the truth is that Christ *has* been raised up, the first in a long legacy of those who are going to leave the cemeteries.

21-28 There is a nice symmetry in this: Death initially came by a man, and resurrection from death came by a man. Everybody dies in Adam; everybody comes alive in Christ. But we have to wait our turn: Christ is first, then those with him at his Coming, the grand consummation when, after crushing the opposition, he hands over his kingdom to God the Father. He won't let up until the last enemy is down — and the very last enemy is death! As the psalmist said, "He laid them low, one and all; he walked all over them." When Scripture says that "he walked all over them," it's obvious that he couldn't at the same time be walked on. When everything and everyone is finally under God's rule, the Son will step down, taking his place with everyone else, showing that God's rule is absolutely comprehensive — a perfect ending!

29 Why do you think people offer themselves to be baptized for those already in the grave? If there's no chance of resurrection for a corpse, if God's power stops at the cemetery gates, why do we keep doing things that suggest he's going to clean the place out someday, pulling everyone up on their feet alive?

30-33 And why do you think I keep risking my neck in this dangerous work? I look death in the face practically every day I live. Do you think I'd do this if I wasn't convinced of your resurrection and mine as guaranteed by the resurrected Messiah Jesus? Do you think I was just trying to act heroic when I fought the wild beasts at Ephesus, hoping it wouldn't be the end of me? Not on your life! It's resurrection, resurrection, always resurrection, that undergirds what I do and say, the way I live. If there's no resurrection, "We eat, we drink, the next day we die," and that's all there is to it. But don't fool yourselves. Don't let yourselves be poisoned by this anti-resurrection loose talk. "Bad company ruins good manners."

34   Think straight. Awaken to the holiness of life. No more playing fast and loose with resurrection facts. Ignorance of God is a luxury you can't afford in times like these. Aren't you embarrassed that you've let this kind of thing go on as long as you have?

35-38   Some skeptic is sure to ask, "Show me how resurrection works. Give me a diagram; draw me a picture. What does this 'resurrection body' look like?" If you look at this question closely, you realize how absurd it is. There are no diagrams for this kind of thing. We do have a parallel experience in gardening. You plant a "dead" seed; soon there is a flourishing plant. There is no visual likeness between seed and plant. You could never guess what a tomato would look like by looking at a tomato seed. What we plant in the soil and what grows out of it don't look anything alike. The dead body that we bury in the ground and the resurrection body that comes from it will be dramatically different.

39-41   You will notice that the variety of bodies is stunning. Just as there are different kinds of seeds, there are different kinds of bodies — humans, animals, birds, fish — each unprecedented in its form. You get a hint at the diversity of resurrection glory by looking at the diversity of bodies not only on earth but in the skies — sun, moon, stars — all these varieties of beauty and brightness. And we're only looking at pre-resurrection "seeds" — who can imagine what the resurrection "plants" will be like!

42-44   This image of planting a dead seed and raising a live plant is a mere sketch at best, but perhaps it will help in approaching the mystery of the resurrection body — but only if you keep in mind that when we're raised, we're raised for *good*, alive forever! The corpse that's planted is no beauty, but when it's raised, it's glorious. Put in the ground weak, it comes up powerful. The seed sown is natural; the seed grown is supernatural — same seed, same body, but what a difference from when it goes down in physical mortality to when it is raised up in spiritual immortality!

45-49   We follow this sequence in Scripture: The First Adam received life, the Last Adam is a life-giving Spirit. Physical life comes first, then spiritual — a firm base shaped from the earth, a final completion coming out of heaven. The First Man was made out of earth, and people since then are earthy; the Second Man was made out of heaven, and people now can be heavenly. In the same way that we've worked from our earthy origins, let's embrace our heavenly ends.

50   I need to emphasize, friends, that our natural, earthy lives don't in themselves lead us by their very nature into the kingdom of God. Their very "nature" is to die, so how could they "naturally" end up in the Life kingdom?

51-57   But let me tell you something wonderful, a mystery I'll probably never fully understand. We're not all going to die — *but* we are all going to be changed. You hear a blast to end all blasts from a trumpet, and in the time that you look up and blink your eyes — it's over. On signal from that trumpet from heaven, the dead will be up and out of their graves, beyond the reach of death, never to die again. At the same moment and in the same way, we'll all be changed. In the resurrection scheme of things, this has to happen: everything perishable taken off the shelves and replaced by the imperishable, this mortal replaced by the immortal. Then the saying will come true:

Death swallowed by triumphant Life!
Who got the last word, oh, Death?
Oh, Death, who's afraid of you now?

It was sin that made death so frightening and law-code guilt that gave sin its leverage, its destructive power. But now in a single victorious stroke of Life, all three — sin, guilt, death — are gone, the gift of our Master, Jesus Christ. Thank God!

58   With all this going for us, my dear, dear friends, stand your ground. And don't hold back. Throw yourselves into the work of the Master, confident that nothing you do for him is a waste of time or effort.

COMING TO SEE YOU

1-4   Regarding the relief offering for poor Christians that is being collected, you get the same instructions I gave the churches in Galatia. Every Sunday each of you make an offering and put it in safekeeping. Be as generous as you can. When I get there you'll have it ready, and I won't have to make a special appeal. Then after I arrive, I'll write letters authorizing whomever you delegate, and send them off to Jerusalem to deliver your gift. If you think it best that I go along, I'll be glad to travel with them.

5-9   I plan to visit you after passing through northern Greece. I won't be staying long there, but maybe I can stay awhile with you — maybe even spend the winter? Then you could give me a good send-off, wherever I may be headed next. I don't want to just drop by in between other "primary" destinations. I want a good, long, leisurely visit. If the Master agrees, we'll have it! For the present, I'm staying right here in Ephesus. A huge door of opportunity for good work has opened up here. (There is also mushrooming opposition.)

10-11   If Timothy shows up, take good care of him. Make him feel completely at home among you. He works so hard for the Master, just as I do. Don't let anyone disparage him. After a while, send him on to me with your blessing. Tell him I'm expecting him, and any friends he has with him.

12   About our friend Apollos, I've done my best to get him to pay you a visit, but haven't talked him into it yet. He doesn't think this is the right time. But there will be a "right time."

13-14   Keep your eyes open, hold tight to your convictions, give it all you've got, be resolute, and love without stopping.

15-16   Would you do me a favor, friends, and give special recognition to the family of Stephanas? You know, they were among the first converts in Greece, and they've put themselves out, serving Christians ever since then. I want you to honor and look up to people like that: companions and workers who show us how to do it, giving us something to aspire to.

17-18   I want you to know how delighted I am to have Stephanas, Fortunatus, and Achaicus here with me. They partially make up for your absence! They've refreshed me by keeping me in touch with you. Be proud that you have people like this among you.

19   The churches here in western Asia send greetings.

Aquila, Priscilla, and the church that meets in their house say hello.

20   All the friends here say hello.

Pass the greetings around with holy embraces!

21   And I, Paul — in my own handwriting! — send you my regards.

22   If anyone won't love the Master, throw him out. Make room for the Master!

23   Our Master Jesus has his arms wide open for you.

24   And I love all of you in the Messiah, in Jesus.

2 CORINTHIANS

The Corinthian Christians gave their founding pastor, Paul, more trouble than all his other churches put together. No sooner did Paul get one problem straightened out in Corinth than three more appeared.

For anyone operating under the naive presumption that joining a Christian church is a good way to meet all the best people and cultivate smooth social relations, a reading of Paul's Corinthian correspondence is the prescribed cure. But however much trouble the Corinthians were to each other and to Paul, they prove to be a cornucopia of blessings to us, for they triggered some of Paul's most profound and vigorous writing.

The provocation for Paul's second letter to the Christians in Corinth was an attack on his leadership. In his first letter, though he wrote most kindly and sympathetically, he didn't mince words. He wrote with the confident authority of a pastor who understands the ways God's salvation works and the kind of community that comes into being as a result. At least some of what he wrote to them was hard to hear and hard to take.

So they bucked his authority — accused him of inconsistencies, impugned his motives, questioned his credentials. They didn't argue with what he had written; they simply denied his right to tell them what to do.

And so Paul was forced to defend his leadership. After mopping up a few details left over from the first letter, he confronted the challenge, and in the process probed the very nature of leadership in a community of believers.

Because leadership is necessarily an exercise of authority, it easily shifts into an exercise of power. But the minute it does that, it begins to inflict damage on both the leader and the led. Paul, studying Jesus, had learned a kind of leadership in which he managed to stay out of the way so that the others could deal with God without having to go through him. All who are called to exercise leadership in whatever capacity — parent or coach, pastor or president, teacher or manager — can be grateful to Paul for this letter, and to the Corinthians for provoking it.

2 CORINTHIANS

1-2   I, Paul, have been sent on a special mission by the Messiah, Jesus, planned by God himself. I write this to God's congregation in Corinth, and to believers all over Achaia province. May all the gifts and benefits that come from God our Father and the Master, Jesus Christ, be yours! Timothy, someone you know and trust, joins me in this greeting.

THE RESCUE

3-5   All praise to the God and Father of our Master, Jesus the Messiah! Father of all mercy! God of all healing counsel! He comes alongside us when we go through hard times, and before you know it, he brings us alongside someone else who is going through hard times so that we can be there for that person just as God was there for us. We have plenty of hard times that come from following the Messiah, but no more so than the good times of his healing comfort — we get a full measure of that, too.

6-7   When we suffer for Jesus, it works out for your healing and salvation. If we are treated well, given a helping hand and encouraging word, that also works to your benefit, spurring you on, face forward, unflinching. Your hard times are also our hard times. When we see that you're just as willing to endure the hard times as to enjoy the good times, we know you're going to make it, no doubt about it.

8-11   We don't want you in the dark, friends, about how hard it was when all this came down on us in Asia province. It was so bad we didn't think we were going to make it. We felt like we'd been sent to death row, that it was all over for us. As it turned out, it was the best thing that could have happened. Instead of trusting in our own strength or wits to get out of it, we were forced to trust God totally — not a bad idea since he's the God who raises the dead! And he did it, rescued us from certain doom. *And* he'll do it again, rescuing us as many times as we need rescuing. You and your prayers are part of the rescue operation — I don't want you in the dark about that either. I can see your faces even now, lifted in praise for God's deliverance of us, a rescue in which your prayers played such a crucial part.

12-14   Now that the worst is over, we're pleased we can report that we've come out of this with conscience and faith intact, and can face the world — and even more importantly, face you with our heads held high. But it wasn't by any fancy footwork on our part. It was *God* who kept us focused on him, uncompromised. Don't try to read between the lines or look for hidden meanings in this letter. We're writing plain, unembellished truth, hoping that you'll now see the whole picture as well as you've seen some of the details. We want you to be as proud of us as we are of you when we stand together before our Master Jesus.

15-16   Confident of your welcome, I had originally planned two great visits with you — coming by on my way to Macedonia province, and then again on my return trip. Then we could have had a bon-voyage party as you sent me off to Judea. That was the plan.

17-19   Are you now going to accuse me of being flip with my promises because it didn't work out? Do you think I talk out of both sides of my mouth — a glib *yes* one moment, a glib *no* the next? Well, you're wrong. I try to be as true to my word as God is to his. Our word to you wasn't a careless yes canceled by an indifferent no. How could it be? When Silas and Timothy and I proclaimed the Son of God among you, did you pick up on any yes-and-no, on-again, off-again waffling? Wasn't it a clean, strong Yes?

20-22 Whatever God has promised gets stamped with the Yes of Jesus. In him, this is what we preach and pray, the great Amen, God's Yes and our Yes together, gloriously evident. God affirms us, making us a sure thing in Christ, putting his Yes within us. By his Spirit he has stamped us with his eternal pledge — a sure beginning of what he is destined to complete.

23 Now, are you ready for the real reason I didn't visit you in Corinth? As God is my witness, the only reason I didn't come was to spare you pain. I was being *considerate* of you, not indifferent, not manipulative.

24 We're not in charge of how you live out the faith, looking over your shoulders, suspiciously critical. We're partners, working alongside you, joyfully expectant. I know that you stand by your own faith, not by ours.

1-2 2 That's why I decided not to make another visit that could only be painful to both of us. If by merely showing up I would put you in an embarrassingly painful position, how would you then be free to cheer and refresh me?

3-4 That was my reason for writing a letter instead of coming — so I wouldn't have to spend a miserable time disappointing the very friends I had looked forward to cheering me up. I was convinced at the time I wrote it that what was best for me was also best for you. As it turned out, there was pain enough just in writing that letter, more tears than ink on the parchment. But I didn't write it to cause pain; I wrote it so you would know how much I care — oh, more than care — *love* you!

5-8 Now, regarding the one who started all this — the person in question who caused all this pain — I want you to know that I am not the one injured in this as much as, with a few exceptions, all of you. So I don't want to come down too hard. What the majority of you agreed to as punishment is punishment enough. Now is the time to forgive this man and help him back on his feet. If all you do is pour on the guilt, you could very well drown him in it. My counsel now is to pour on the love.

9-11 The focus of my letter wasn't on punishing the offender but on getting you to take responsibility for the health of the church. So if you forgive him, I forgive him. Don't think I'm carrying around a list of personal grudges. The fact is that I'm joining in with *your* forgiveness, as Christ is with us, guiding us. After all, we don't want to unwittingly give Satan an opening for yet more mischief — we're not oblivious to his sly ways!

AN OPEN DOOR

12-14 When I arrived in Troas to proclaim the Message of the Messiah, I found the place wide open: God had opened the door; all I had to do was walk through it. But when I didn't find Titus waiting for me with news of your condition, I couldn't relax. Worried about you, I left and came on to Macedonia province looking for Titus and a reassuring word on you. And I got it, thank God!

14-16 In the Messiah, in Christ, God leads us from place to place in one perpetual victory parade. Through us, he brings knowledge of Christ. Everywhere we go, people breathe in the exquisite fragrance. Because of Christ, we give off a sweet scent rising to God, which is recognized by those on the way of salvation — an aroma redolent with life. But those on the way to destruction treat us more like the stench from a rotting corpse.

16-17   This is a terrific responsibility. Is anyone competent to take it on? No — but at least we don't take God's Word, water it down, and then take it to the streets to sell it cheap. We stand in Christ's presence when we speak; God looks us in the face. We get what we say straight from God and say it as honestly as we can.

1-3   **3** Does it sound like we're patting ourselves on the back, insisting on our credentials, asserting our authority? Well, we're not. Neither do we need letters of endorsement, either to you or from you. You yourselves are all the endorsement we need. Your very lives are a letter that anyone can read by just looking at you. Christ himself wrote it — not with ink, but with God's living Spirit; not chiseled into stone, but carved into human lives — and we publish it.

4-6   We couldn't be more sure of ourselves in this — that *you*, written by Christ himself for God, are our letter of recommendation. We wouldn't think of writing this kind of letter about ourselves. Only God can write such a letter. His letter authorizes us to help carry out this new plan of action. The plan wasn't written out with ink on paper, with pages and pages of legal footnotes, killing your spirit. It's written with Spirit on spirit, his life on our lives!

LIFTING THE VEIL

7-8   The Government of Death, its constitution chiseled on stone tablets, had a dazzling inaugural. Moses' face as he delivered the tablets was so bright that day (even though it would fade soon enough) that the people of Israel could no more look right at him than stare into the sun. How much more dazzling, then, the Government of Living Spirit?

9-11   If the Government of Condemnation was impressive, how about this Government of Affirmation? Bright as that old government was, it would look downright dull alongside this new one. If that makeshift arrangement impressed us, how much more this brightly shining government installed for eternity?

12-15   With that kind of hope to excite us, nothing holds us back. Unlike Moses, we have nothing to hide. Everything is out in the open with us. He wore a veil so the children of Israel wouldn't notice that the glory was fading away — and they *didn't* notice. They didn't notice it then and they don't notice it now, don't notice that there's nothing left behind that veil. Even today when the proclamations of that old, bankrupt government are read out, they can't see through it. Only Christ can get rid of the veil so they can see for themselves that there's nothing there.

16-18   Whenever, though, they turn to face God as Moses did, God removes the veil and there they are — face-to-face! They suddenly recognize that God is a living, personal presence, not a piece of chiseled stone. And when God is personally present, a living Spirit, that old, constricting legislation is recognized as obsolete. We're free of it! All of us! Nothing between us and God, our faces shining with the brightness of his face. And so we are transfigured much like the Messiah, our lives gradually becoming brighter and more beautiful as God enters our lives and we become like him.

TRIAL AND TORTURE

1-2   4 Since God has so generously let us in on what he is doing, we're not about to throw up our hands and walk off the job just because we run into occasional hard times. We refuse to wear masks and play games. We don't maneuver and manipulate behind the scenes. And we don't twist God's Word to suit ourselves. Rather, we keep everything we do and say out in the open, the whole truth on display, so that those who want to can see and judge for themselves in the presence of God.

3-4   If our Message is obscure to anyone, it's not because we're holding back in any way. No, it's because these other people are looking or going the wrong way and refuse to give it serious attention. All they have eyes for is the fashionable god of darkness. They think he can give them what they want, and that they won't have to bother believing a Truth they can't see. They're stone-blind to the dayspring brightness of the Message that shines with Christ, who gives us the best picture of God we'll ever get.

5-6   Remember, our Message is not about ourselves; we're proclaiming Jesus Christ, the Master. All we are is messengers, errand runners from Jesus for you. It started when God said, "Light up the darkness!" and our lives filled up with light as we saw and understood God in the face of Christ, all bright and beautiful.

7-12   If you only look at *us*, you might well miss the brightness. We carry this precious Message around in the unadorned clay pots of our ordinary lives. That's to prevent anyone from confusing God's incomparable power with us. As it is, there's not much chance of that. You know for yourselves that we're not much to look at. We've been surrounded and battered by troubles, but we're not demoralized; we're not sure what to do, but we know that God knows what to do; we've been spiritually terrorized, but God hasn't left our side; we've been thrown down, but we haven't broken. What they did to Jesus, they do to us — trial and torture, mockery and murder; what Jesus did among them, he does in us — he lives! Our lives are at constant risk for Jesus' sake, which makes Jesus' life all the more evident in us. While we're going through the worst, you're getting in on the best!

13-15   We're not keeping this quiet, not on your life. Just like the psalmist who wrote, "I believed it, so I said it," we say what we believe. And what we believe is that the One who raised up the Master Jesus will just as certainly raise us up with you, alive. Every detail works to your advantage and to God's glory: more and more grace, more and more people, more and more praise!

16-18   So we're not giving up. How could we! Even though on the outside it often looks like things are falling apart on us, on the inside, where God is making new life, not a day goes by without his unfolding grace. These hard times are small potatoes compared to the coming good times, the lavish celebration prepared for us. There's far more here than meets the eye. The things we see now are here today, gone tomorrow. But the things we can't see now will last forever.

1-5   5 For instance, we know that when these bodies of ours are taken down like tents and folded away, they will be replaced by resurrection bodies in heaven — God-made, not handmade — and we'll never have to relocate our "tents" again. Sometimes we can hardly wait to move — and so we cry out in frustration. Compared to what's coming, living conditions around here seem like a stopover in an unfurnished shack, and we're tired of it! We've been given a glimpse of the real thing, our true home, our resurrection bodies! The Spirit of God whets our appetite by giving us a taste of what's ahead. He puts a little of heaven in our hearts so that we'll never settle for less.

6-8   That's why we live with such good cheer. You won't see us drooping our heads or dragging our feet! Cramped conditions here don't get us down. They only remind us of the spacious living conditions ahead. It's what we trust in but don't yet see that keeps us going. Do you suppose a few ruts in the road or rocks in the path are going to stop us? When the time comes, we'll be plenty ready to exchange exile for homecoming.

9-10   But neither exile nor homecoming is the main thing. Cheerfully pleasing God is the main thing, and that's what we aim to do, regardless of our conditions. Sooner or later we'll all have to face God, regardless of our conditions. We will appear before Christ and take what's coming to us as a result of our actions, either good or bad.

11-14   *That* keeps us vigilant, you can be sure. It's no light thing to know that we'll all one day stand in that place of Judgment. That's why we work urgently with everyone we meet to get them ready to face God. God alone knows how well we do this, but I hope you realize how much and deeply we care. We're not saying this to make ourselves look good to you. We just thought it would make you feel good, proud even, that we're on your side and not just nice to your face as so many people are. If I acted crazy, I did it for God; if I acted overly serious, I did it for you. Christ's love has moved me to such extremes. His love has the first and last word in everything we do.

A New Life

14-15   Our firm decision is to work from this focused center: One man died for everyone. That puts everyone in the same boat. He included everyone in his death so that everyone could also be included in his life, a resurrection life, a far better life than people ever lived on their own.

16-20   Because of this decision we don't evaluate people by what they have or how they look. We looked at the Messiah that way once and got it all wrong, as you know. We certainly don't look at him that way anymore. Now we look inside, and what we see is that anyone united with the Messiah gets a fresh start, is created new. The old life is gone; a new life burgeons! Look at it! All this comes from the God who settled the relationship between us and him, and then called us to settle our relationships with each other. God put the world square with himself through the Messiah, giving the world a fresh start by offering forgiveness of sins. God has given us the task of telling everyone what he is doing. We're Christ's representatives. God uses us to persuade men and women to drop their differences and enter into God's work of making things right between them. We're speaking for Christ himself now: Become friends with God; he's already a friend with you.

21   How? you ask. In Christ. God put the wrong on him who never did anything wrong, so we could be put right with God.

Staying at Our Post

1-10   6 Companions as we are in this work with you, we beg you, please don't squander one bit of this marvelous life God has given us. God reminds us,

I heard your call in the nick of time;
The day you needed me, I was there to help.

Well, now is the right time to listen, the day to be helped. Don't put it off; don't frustrate God's work by showing up late, throwing a question mark over everything we're doing. Our work as God's servants gets validated — or not — in the details. People are watching us as we stay at our post, alertly, unswervingly . . . in hard times, tough times, bad times; when we're beaten up, jailed, and mobbed; working hard, working late, working without eating; with pure heart, clear head, steady hand; in gentleness, holiness, and honest love; when we're telling the truth, and when God's showing his power; when we're doing our best setting things right; when we're praised, and when we're blamed; slandered, and honored; true to our word, though distrusted; ignored by the world, but recognized by God; terrifically alive, though rumored to be dead; beaten within an inch of our lives, but refusing to die; immersed in tears, yet always filled with deep joy; living on handouts, yet enriching many; having nothing, having it all.

11-13 Dear, dear Corinthians, I can't tell you how much I long for you to enter this wide-open, spacious life. We didn't fence you in. The smallness you feel comes from within you. Your lives aren't small, but you're living them in a small way. I'm speaking as plainly as I can and with great affection. Open up your lives. Live openly and expansively!

14-18 Don't become partners with those who reject God. How can you make a partnership out of right and wrong? That's not partnership; that's war. Is light best friends with dark? Does Christ go strolling with the Devil? Do trust and mistrust hold hands? Who would think of setting up pagan idols in God's holy Temple? But that is exactly what we are, each of us a temple in whom God lives. God himself put it this way:

"I'll live in them, move into them;
    I'll be their God and they'll be my people.
So leave the corruption and compromise;
    leave it for good," says God.
"Don't link up with those who will pollute you.
    I want you all for myself.
I'll be a Father to you;
    you'll be sons and daughters to me."
The Word of the Master, God.

1 With promises like this to pull us on, dear friends, let's make a clean break with everything that defiles or distracts us, both within and without. Let's make our entire lives fit and holy temples for the worship of God.

MORE PASSIONATE, MORE RESPONSIBLE

2-4 Trust us. We've never hurt a soul, never exploited or taken advantage of anyone. Don't think I'm finding fault with you. I told you earlier that I'm with you all the way, no matter what. I have, in fact, the greatest confidence in you. If only you knew how proud I am of you! I am overwhelmed with joy despite all our troubles.

5-7   When we arrived in Macedonia province, we couldn't settle down. The fights in the church and the fears in our hearts kept us on pins and needles. We couldn't relax because we didn't know how it would turn out. Then the God who lifts up the downcast lifted our heads and our hearts with the arrival of Titus. We were glad just to see him, but the true reassurance came in what he told us about you: how much you cared, how much you grieved, how concerned you were for me. I went from worry to tranquility in no time!

8-9   I know I distressed you greatly with my letter. Although I felt awful at the time, I don't feel at all bad now that I see how it turned out. The letter upset you, but only for a while. Now I'm glad — not that you were upset, but that you were jarred into turning things around. You let the distress bring you to God, not drive you from him. The result was all gain, no loss.

10   Distress that drives us to God does that. It turns us around. It gets us back in the way of salvation. We never regret that kind of pain. But those who let distress drive them away from God are full of regrets, end up on a deathbed of regrets.

11-13   And now, isn't it wonderful all the ways in which this distress has goaded you closer to God? You're more alive, more concerned, more sensitive, more reverent, more human, more passionate, more responsible. Looked at from any angle, you've come out of this with purity of heart. And that is what I was hoping for in the first place when I wrote the letter. My primary concern was not for the one who did the wrong or even the one wronged, but for you — that you would realize and act upon the deep, deep ties between us before God. That's what happened — and we felt just great.

13-16   And then, when we saw how Titus felt — his exuberance over your response — our joy doubled. It was wonderful to see how revived and refreshed he was by everything you did. If I went out on a limb in telling Titus how great I thought you were, you didn't cut off that limb. As it turned out, I hadn't exaggerated one bit. Titus saw for himself that everything I had said about you was true. He can't quit talking about it, going over again and again the story of your prompt obedience, and the dignity and sensitivity of your hospitality. He was quite overwhelmed by it all! And I couldn't be more pleased — I'm so confident and proud of you.

THE OFFERING

1-4   **8** Now, friends, I want to report on the surprising and generous ways in which God is working in the churches in Macedonia province. Fierce troubles came down on the people of those churches, pushing them to the very limit. The trial exposed their true colors: They were incredibly happy, though desperately poor. The pressure triggered something totally unexpected: an outpouring of pure and generous gifts. I was there and saw it for myself. They gave offerings of whatever they could — far more than they could afford! — pleading for the privilege of helping out in the relief of poor Christians.

5-7   This was totally spontaneous, entirely their own idea, and caught us completely off guard. What explains it was that they had first given themselves unreservedly to God and to us. The other giving simply flowed out of the purposes of God working in their lives. That's what prompted us to ask Titus to bring the relief offering to your attention, so that what was so well begun could be finished up. You do so well in so many things — you trust God, you're articulate, you're insightful, you're passionate, you love us — now, do your best in this, too.

8-9   I'm not trying to order you around against your will. But by bringing in the Macedonians' enthusiasm as a stimulus to your love, I am hoping to bring the best out of you. You are familiar with the generosity of our Master, Jesus Christ. Rich as he was, he gave it all away for us — in one stroke he became poor and we became rich.

10-20   So here's what I think: The best thing you can do right now is to finish what you started last year and not let those good intentions grow stale. Your heart's been in the right place all along. You've got what it takes to finish it up, so go to it. Once the commitment is clear, you do what you can, not what you can't. The heart regulates the hands. This isn't so others can take it easy while you sweat it out. No, you're shoulder to shoulder with them all the way, your surplus matching their deficit, their surplus matching your deficit. In the end you come out even. As it is written,

Nothing left over to the one with the most,
Nothing lacking to the one with the least.

I thank God for giving Titus the same devoted concern for you that I have. He was most considerate of how we felt, but his eagerness to go to you and help out with this relief offering is his own idea. We're sending a companion along with him, someone very popular in the churches for his preaching of the Message. But there's far more to him than popularity. He's rock-solid trustworthy. The churches handpicked him to go with us as we travel about doing this work of sharing God's gifts to honor God as well as we can, taking every precaution against scandal.

20-22   We don't want anyone suspecting us of taking one penny of this money for ourselves. We're being as careful in our reputation with the public as in our reputation with God. That's why we're sending another trusted friend along. He's proved his dependability many times over, and carries on as energetically as the day he started. He's heard much about you, and liked what he's heard — so much so that he can't wait to get there.

23-24   I don't need to say anything further about Titus. We've been close associates in this work of serving you for a long time. The brothers who travel with him are delegates from churches, a real credit to Christ. Show them what you're made of, the love I've been talking up in the churches. Let them see it for themselves!

1-2   **9** If I wrote any more on this relief offering for the poor Christians, I'd be repeating myself. I know you're on board and ready to go. I've been bragging about you all through Macedonia province, telling them, "Achaia province has been ready to go on this since last year." Your enthusiasm by now has spread to most of them.

3-5   Now I'm sending the brothers to make sure you're ready, as I said you would be, so my bragging won't turn out to be just so much hot air. If some Macedonians and I happened to drop in on you and found you weren't prepared, we'd all be pretty red-faced — you and us — for acting so sure of ourselves. So to make sure there will be no slipup, I've recruited these brothers as an advance team to get you and your promised offering all ready before I get there. I want you to have all the time you need to make this offering in your own way. I don't want anything forced or hurried at the last minute.

6-7   Remember: A stingy planter gets a stingy crop; a lavish planter gets a lavish crop. I want each of you to take plenty of time to think it over, and make up your own mind what you will give. That will protect you against sob stories and arm-twisting. God loves it when the giver delights in the giving.

8-11   God can pour on the blessings in astonishing ways so that you're ready for anything and everything, more than just ready to do what needs to be done. As one psalmist puts it,

> He throws caution to the winds,
> giving to the needy in reckless abandon.
> His right-living, right-giving ways
> never run out, never wear out.

This most generous God who gives seed to the farmer that becomes bread for your meals is more than extravagant with you. He gives you something you can then give away, which grows into full-formed lives, robust in God, wealthy in every way, so that you can be generous in every way, producing with us great praise to God.

12-15   Carrying out this social relief work involves far more than helping meet the bare needs of poor Christians. It also produces abundant and bountiful thanksgivings to God. This relief offering is a prod to live at your very best, showing your gratitude to God by being openly obedient to the plain meaning of the Message of Christ. You show your gratitude through your generous offerings to your needy brothers and sisters, and really toward everyone. Meanwhile, moved by the extravagance of God in your lives, they'll respond by praying for you in passionate intercession for whatever you need. Thank God for this gift, his gift. No language can praise it enough!

TEARING DOWN BARRIERS

1-2   **10** And now a personal but most urgent matter; I write in the gentle but firm spirit of Christ. I hear that I'm being painted as cringing and wishy-washy when I'm with you, but harsh and demanding when at a safe distance writing letters. Please don't force me to take a hard line when I'm present with you. Don't think that I'll hesitate a single minute to stand up to those who say I'm an unprincipled opportunist. Then they'll have to eat their words.

3-6   The world is unprincipled. It's dog-eat-dog out there! The world doesn't fight fair. But we don't live or fight our battles that way — never have and never will. The tools of our trade aren't for marketing or manipulation, but they are for demolishing that entire massively corrupt culture. We use our powerful God-tools for smashing warped philosophies, tearing down barriers erected against the truth of God, fitting every loose thought and emotion and impulse into the structure of life shaped by Christ. Our tools are ready at hand for clearing the ground of every obstruction and building lives of obedience into maturity.

7-8   You stare and stare at the obvious, but you can't see the forest for the trees. If you're looking for a clear example of someone on Christ's side, why do you so quickly cut me out? Believe me, I am quite sure of my standing with Christ. You may think I overstate the authority he gave me, but I'm not backing off. Every bit of my commitment is for the purpose of building you up, after all, not tearing you down.

9-11 And what's this talk about me bullying you with my letters? "His letters are brawny and potent, but in person he's a weakling and mumbles when he talks." Such talk won't survive scrutiny. What we write when away, we do when present. We're the exact same people, absent or present, in letter or in person.

12 We're not, understand, putting ourselves in a league with those who boast that they're our superiors. We wouldn't dare do that. But in all this comparing and grading and competing, they quite miss the point.

13-14 We aren't making outrageous claims here. We're sticking to the limits of what God has set for us. But there can be no question that those limits reach to and include you. We're not moving into someone else's "territory." We were already there with you, weren't we? We were the first ones to get there with the Message of Christ, right? So how can there be any question of overstepping our bounds by writing or visiting you?

15-18 We're not barging in on the rightful work of others, interfering with their ministries, demanding a place in the sun with them. What we're hoping for is that as your lives grow in faith, you'll play a part within our expanding work. And we'll all still be within the limits God sets as we proclaim the Message in countries beyond Corinth. But we have no intention of moving in on what others have done and taking credit for it. "If you want to claim credit, claim it for God." What you say about yourself means nothing in God's work. It's what God says about you that makes the difference.

PSEUDO-SERVANTS OF GOD

1-3 **11** Will you put up with a little foolish aside from me? Please, just for a moment. The thing that has me so upset is that I care about you so much—this is the passion of God burning inside me! I promised your hand in marriage to Christ, presented you as a pure virgin to her husband. And now I'm afraid that exactly as the Snake seduced Eve with his smooth patter, you are being lured away from the simple purity of your love for Christ.

4-6 It seems that if someone shows up preaching quite another Jesus than we preached—different spirit, different message—you put up with him quite nicely. But if you put up with these big-shot "apostles," why can't you put up with simple me? I'm as good as they are. It's true that I don't have their voice, haven't mastered that smooth eloquence that impresses you so much. But when I do open my mouth, I at least know what I'm talking about. We haven't kept anything back. We let you in on everything.

7-12 I wonder, did I make a bad mistake in proclaiming God's Message to you without asking for something in return, serving you free of charge so that you wouldn't be inconvenienced by me? It turns out that the other churches paid my way so that you could have a free ride. Not once during the time I lived among you did anyone have to lift a finger to help me out. My needs were always supplied by the believers from Macedonia province. I was careful never to be a burden to you, and I never will be, you can count on it. With Christ as my witness, it's a point of honor with me, and I'm not going to keep it quiet just to protect you from what the neighbors will think.

It's not that I don't love you; God knows I do. I'm just trying to keep things open and honest between us.

12-15   And I'm not changing my position on this. I'd die before taking your money. I'm giving nobody grounds for lumping me in with those money-grubbing "preachers," vaunting themselves as something special. They're a sorry bunch — pseudo-apostles, lying preachers, crooked workers — posing as Christ's agents but sham to the core. And no wonder! Satan does it all the time, dressing up as a beautiful angel of light. So it shouldn't surprise us when his servants masquerade as servants of God. But they're not getting by with anything. They'll pay for it in the end.

Many a Long and Lonely Night

16-21   Let me come back to where I started — and don't hold it against me if I continue to sound a little foolish. Or if you'd rather, just accept that I am a fool and let me rant on a little. I didn't learn this kind of talk from Christ. Oh, no, it's a bad habit I picked up from the three-ring preachers that are so popular these days. Since you sit there in the judgment seat observing all these shenanigans, you can afford to humor an occasional fool who happens along. You have such admirable tolerance for impostors who rob your freedom, rip you off, steal you blind, put you down — even slap your face! I shouldn't admit it to you, but our stomachs aren't strong enough to tolerate that kind of stuff.

21-23   Since you admire the egomaniacs of the pulpit so much (remember, this is your old friend, the fool, talking), let me try my hand at it. Do they brag of being Hebrews, Israelites, the pure race of Abraham? I'm their match. Are they servants of Christ? I can go them one better. (I can't believe I'm saying these things. It's crazy to talk this way! But I started, and I'm going to finish.)

23-27   I've worked much harder, been jailed more often, beaten up more times than I can count, and at death's door time after time. I've been flogged five times with the Jews' thirty-nine lashes, beaten by Roman rods three times, pummeled with rocks once. I've been shipwrecked three times, and immersed in the open sea for a night and a day. In hard traveling year in and year out, I've had to ford rivers, fend off robbers, struggle with friends, struggle with foes. I've been at risk in the city, at risk in the country, endangered by desert sun and sea storm, and betrayed by those I thought were my brothers. I've known drudgery and hard labor, many a long and lonely night without sleep, many a missed meal, blasted by the cold, naked to the weather.

28-29   And that's not the half of it, when you throw in the daily pressures and anxieties of all the churches. When someone gets to the end of his rope, I feel the desperation in my bones. When someone is duped into sin, an angry fire burns in my gut.

30-33   If I have to "brag" about myself, I'll brag about the humiliations that make me like Jesus. The eternal and blessed God and Father of our Master Jesus knows I'm not lying. Remember the time I was in Damascus and the governor of King Aretas posted guards at the city gates to arrest me? I crawled through a window in the wall, was let down in a basket, and had to run for my life.

STRENGTH FROM WEAKNESS

¹⁻⁵ **12** You've forced me to talk this way, and I do it against my better judgment. But now that we're at it, I may as well bring up the matter of visions and revelations that God gave me. For instance, I know a man who, fourteen years ago, was seized by Christ and swept in ecstasy to the heights of heaven. I really don't know if this took place in the body or out of it; only God knows. I also know that this man was hijacked into paradise — again, whether in or out of the body, I don't know; God knows. There he heard the unspeakable spoken, but was forbidden to tell what he heard. This is the man I want to talk about. But about myself, I'm not saying another word apart from the humiliations.

⁶ If I had a mind to brag a little, I could probably do it without looking ridiculous, and I'd still be speaking plain truth all the way. But I'll spare you. I don't want anyone imagining me as anything other than the fool you'd encounter if you saw me on the street or heard me talk.

⁷⁻¹⁰ Because of the extravagance of those revelations, and so I wouldn't get a big head, I was given the gift of a handicap to keep me in constant touch with my limitations. Satan's angel did his best to get me down; what he in fact did was push me to my knees. No danger then of walking around high and mighty! At first I didn't think of it as a gift, and begged God to remove it. Three times I did that, and then he told me,

My grace is enough; it's all you need.
My strength comes into its own in your weakness.

Once I heard that, I was glad to let it happen. I quit focusing on the handicap and began appreciating the gift. It was a case of Christ's strength moving in on my weakness. Now I take limitations in stride, and with good cheer, these limitations that cut me down to size — abuse, accidents, opposition, bad breaks. I just let Christ take over! And so the weaker I get, the stronger I become.

¹¹⁻¹³ Well, now I've done it! I've made a complete fool of myself by going on like this. But it's not all my fault; you put me up to it. You should have been doing this for me, sticking up for me and commending me instead of making me do it for myself. You know from personal experience that even if I'm a nobody, a nothing, I wasn't second-rate compared to those big-shot apostles you're so taken with. All the signs that mark a true apostle were in evidence while I was with you through both good times and bad: signs of portent, signs of wonder, signs of power. Did you get less of me or of God than any of the other churches? The only thing you got less of was less responsibility for my upkeep. Well, I'm sorry. Forgive me for depriving you.

¹⁴⁻¹⁵ Everything is in readiness now for this, my third visit to you. But don't worry about it; you won't have to put yourselves out. I'll be no more of a bother to you this time than on the other visits. I have no interest in what you have — only in you. Children shouldn't have to look out for their parents; parents look out for the children. I'd be most happy to empty my pockets, even mortgage my life, for your good. So how does it happen that the more I love you, the less I'm loved?

16-18   And why is it that I keep coming across these whiffs of gossip about how my self-support was a front behind which I worked an elaborate scam? Where's the evidence? Did I cheat or trick you through anyone I sent? I asked Titus to visit, and sent some brothers along. Did they swindle you out of anything? And haven't we always been just as aboveboard, just as honest?

19   I hope you don't think that all along we've been making our defense before you, the jury. You're not the jury; God is the jury — God revealed in Christ — and we make our case before him. And we've gone to all the trouble of supporting ourselves so that we won't be in the way or get in the way of your growing up.

20-21   I do admit that I have fears that when I come you'll disappoint me and I'll disappoint you, and in frustration with each other everything will fall to pieces — quarrels, jealousy, flaring tempers, taking sides, angry words, vicious rumors, swelled heads, and general bedlam. I don't look forward to a second humiliation by God among you, compounded by hot tears over that crowd that keeps sinning over and over in the same old ways, who refuse to turn away from the pigsty of evil, sexual disorder, and indecency in which they wallow.

HE'S ALIVE NOW!

1-4   **13** Well, this is my third visit coming up. Remember the Scripture that says, "A matter becomes clear after two or three witnesses give evidence"? On my second visit I warned that bunch that keeps sinning over and over in the same old ways that when I came back I wouldn't go easy on them. Now, preparing for the third, I'm saying it again from a distance. If you haven't changed your ways by the time I get there, look out. You who have been demanding proof that Christ speaks through me will get more than you bargained for. You'll get the full force of Christ, don't think you won't. He was sheer weakness and humiliation when he was killed on the cross, but oh, he's alive now — in the mighty power of God! We weren't much to look at, either, when we were humiliated among you, but when we deal with you this next time, we'll be alive in Christ, strengthened by God.

5-9   Test yourselves to make sure you are solid in the faith. Don't drift along taking everything for granted. Give yourselves regular checkups. You need firsthand evidence, not mere hearsay, that Jesus Christ is in you. Test it out. If you fail the test, do something about it. I hope the test won't show that we have failed. But if it comes to that, we'd rather the test showed our failure than yours. We're rooting for the truth to win out in you. We couldn't possibly do otherwise.

We don't just put up with our limitations; we celebrate them, and then go on to celebrate every strength, every triumph of the truth in you. We pray hard that it will all come together in your lives.

10   I'm writing this to you now so that when I come I won't have to say another word on the subject. The authority the Master gave me is for putting people together, not taking them apart. I want to get on with it, and not have to spend time on reprimands.

11-13 And that's about it, friends. Be cheerful. Keep things in good repair. Keep your spirits up. Think in harmony. Be agreeable. Do all that, and the God of love and peace will be with you for sure. Greet one another with a holy embrace. All the brothers and sisters here say hello.

14 The amazing grace of the Master, Jesus Christ, the extravagant love of God, the intimate friendship of the Holy Spirit, be with all of you.

GALATIANS

When men and women get their hands on religion, one of the first things they often do is turn it into an instrument for controlling others, either putting or keeping them "in their place." The history of such religious manipulation and coercion is long and tedious. It is little wonder that people who have only known religion on such terms experience release or escape from it as freedom. The problem is that the freedom turns out to be short-lived.

Paul of Tarsus was doing his diligent best to add yet another chapter to this dreary history when he was converted by Jesus to something radically and entirely different — a free life in God. Through Jesus, Paul learned that God was not an impersonal force to be used to make people behave in certain prescribed ways, but a personal Savior who set us free to live a free life. God did not coerce us from without, but set us free from within.

It was a glorious experience, and Paul set off telling others, introducing and inviting everyone he met into this free life. In his early travels he founded a series of churches in the Roman province of Galatia. A few years later Paul learned that religious leaders of the old school had come into those churches, called his views and authority into question, and were reintroducing the old ways, herding all these freedom-loving Christians back into the corral of religious rules and regulations.

Paul was, of course, furious. He was furious with the old guard for coming in with their strong-arm religious tactics and intimidating the Christians into giving up their free life in Jesus. But he was also furious with the Christians for caving in to the intimidation.

His letter to the Galatian churches helps them, and us, recover the original freedom. It also gives direction in the nature of God's gift of freedom — most necessary guidance, for freedom is a delicate and subtle gift, easily perverted and often squandered.

GALATIANS

1-5 1 I, Paul, and my companions in faith here, send greetings to the Galatian churches. My authority for writing to you does not come from any popular vote of the people, nor does it come through the appointment of some human higher-up. It comes directly from Jesus the Messiah and God the Father, who raised him from the dead. I'm God-commissioned. So I greet you with the great words, grace and peace! We know the meaning of those words because Jesus Christ rescued us from this evil world we're in by offering himself as a sacrifice for our sins. God's plan is that we all experience that rescue. Glory to God forever! Oh, yes!

THE MESSAGE

6-9 I can't believe your fickleness — how easily you have turned traitor to him who called you by the grace of Christ by embracing a variant message! It is not a minor variation, you know; it is completely other, an alien message, a no-message, a lie about God. Those who are provoking this agitation among you are turning the Message of Christ on its head. Let me be blunt: If one of us — even if an angel from heaven! — were to preach something other than what we preached originally, let him be cursed. I said it once; I'll say it again: If anyone, regardless of reputation or credentials, preaches something other than what you received originally, let him be cursed.

10-12 Do you think I speak this strongly in order to manipulate crowds? Or curry favor with God? Or get popular applause? If my goal was popularity, I wouldn't bother being Christ's slave. Know this — I am most emphatic here, friends — this great Message I delivered to you is not mere human optimism. I didn't receive it through the traditions, and I wasn't taught it in some school. I got it straight from God, received the Message directly from Jesus Christ.

13-16 I'm sure that you've heard the story of my earlier life when I lived in the Jewish way. In those days I went all out in persecuting God's church. I was systematically destroying it. I was so enthusiastic about the traditions of my ancestors that I advanced head and shoulders above my peers in my career. Even then God had designs on me. Why, when I was still in my mother's womb he chose and called me out of sheer generosity! Now he has intervened and revealed his Son to me so that I might joyfully tell non-Jews about him.

16-20 Immediately after my calling — without consulting anyone around me and without going up to Jerusalem to confer with those who were apostles long before I was — I got away to Arabia. Later I returned to Damascus, but it was three years before I went up to Jerusalem to compare stories with Peter. I was there only fifteen days — but what days they were! Except for our Master's brother James, I saw no other apostles. (I'm telling you the absolute truth in this.)

21-24 Then I began my ministry in the regions of Syria and Cilicia. After all that time and activity I was still unknown by face among the Christian churches in Judea. There was only this report: "That man who once persecuted us is now preaching the very message he used to try to destroy." Their response was to recognize and worship *God* because of *me!*

WHAT IS CENTRAL?

1-5 2 Fourteen years after that first visit, Barnabas and I went up to Jerusalem and took Titus with us. I went to clarify with them what had been revealed to me. At that time I placed before them exactly what I was preaching to the non-Jews. I did this in private with the leaders, those held in esteem by the church, so that our concern would not become a controversial public issue, marred by ethnic tensions, exposing my years of work to denigration and endangering my present ministry. Significantly, Titus, non-Jewish though he was, was not required to be circumcised. While we were in conference we were infiltrated by spies pretending to be Christians, who slipped in to find out just how free true Christians are. Their ulterior motive was to reduce us to their brand of servitude. We didn't give them the time of day. We were determined to preserve the truth of the Message for you.

6-10 As for those who were considered important in the church, their reputation doesn't concern me. God isn't impressed with mere appearances, and neither am I. And of course these leaders were able to add nothing to the message I had been preaching. It was soon evident that God had entrusted me with the same message to the non-Jews as Peter had been preaching to the Jews. Recognizing that my calling had been given by God, James, Peter, and John — the pillars of the church — shook hands with me and Barnabas, assigning us to a ministry to the non-Jews, while they continued to be responsible for reaching out to the Jews. The only additional thing they asked was that we remember the poor, and I was already eager to do that.

11-13 Later, when Peter came to Antioch, I had a face-to-face confrontation with him because he was clearly out of line. Here's the situation. Earlier, before certain persons had come from James, Peter regularly ate with the non-Jews. But when that conservative group came from Jerusalem, he cautiously pulled back and put as much distance as he could manage between himself and his non-Jewish friends. That's how fearful he was of the conservative Jewish clique that's been pushing the old system of circumcision. Unfortunately, the rest of the Jews in the Antioch church joined in that hypocrisy so that even Barnabas was swept along in the charade.

14 But when I saw that they were not maintaining a steady, straight course according to the Message, I spoke up to Peter in front of them all: "If you, a Jew, live like a non-Jew when you're not being observed by the watchdogs from Jerusalem, what right do you have to require non-Jews to conform to Jewish customs just to make a favorable impression on your old Jerusalem cronies?"

15-16 We Jews know that we have no advantage of birth over "non-Jewish sinners." We know very well that we are not set right with God by rule-keeping but only through personal faith in Jesus Christ. How do we know? We tried it — and we had the best system of rules the world has ever seen! Convinced that no human being can please God by self-improvement, we believed in Jesus as the Messiah so that we might be set right before God by trusting in the Messiah, not by trying to be good.

17-18 Have some of you noticed that we are not yet perfect? (No great surprise, right?) And are you ready to make the accusation that since people like me, who go through Christ in order to get things right with God, aren't perfectly virtuous, Christ must therefore be an accessory to sin? The accusation is frivolous. If I was "trying to be good," I would be rebuilding the same old barn that I tore down. I would be acting as a charlatan.

19-21   What actually took place is this: I tried keeping rules and working my head off to please God, and it didn't work. So I quit being a "law man" so that I could be *God's* man. Christ's life showed me how, and enabled me to do it. I identified myself completely with him. Indeed, I have been crucified with Christ. My ego is no longer central. It is no longer important that I appear righteous before you or have your good opinion, and I am no longer driven to impress God. Christ lives in me. The life you see me living is not "mine," but it is lived by faith in the Son of God, who loved me and gave himself for me. I am not going to go back on that.

21   Is it not clear to you that to go back to that old rule-keeping, peer-pleasing religion would be an abandonment of everything personal and free in my relationship with God? I refuse to do that, to repudiate God's grace. If a living relationship with God could come by rule-keeping, then Christ died unnecessarily.

TRUST IN CHRIST, NOT THE LAW

1   **3** You crazy Galatians! Did someone put a hex on you? Have you taken leave of your senses? Something crazy has happened, for it's obvious that you no longer have the crucified Jesus in clear focus in your lives. His sacrifice on the cross was certainly set before you clearly enough.

2-4   Let me put this question to you: How did your new life begin? Was it by working your heads off to please God? Or was it by responding to God's Message to you? Are you going to continue this craziness? For only crazy people would think they could complete by their own efforts what was begun by God. If you weren't smart enough or strong enough to begin it, how do you suppose you could perfect it? Did you go through this whole painful learning process for nothing? It is not yet a total loss, but it certainly will be if you keep this up!

5-6   Answer this question: Does the God who lavishly provides you with his own presence, his Holy Spirit, working things in your lives you could never do for yourselves, does he do these things because of your strenuous moral striving *or* because you trust him to do them in you? Don't these things happen among you just as they happened with Abraham? He believed God, and that act of belief was turned into a life that was right with God.

7-8   Is it not obvious to you that persons who put their trust in Christ (not persons who put their trust in the law!) are like Abraham: children of faith? It was all laid out beforehand in Scripture that God would set things right with non-Jews by *faith*. Scripture anticipated this in the promise to Abraham: "All nations will be blessed in you."

9-10   So those now who live by faith are blessed along with Abraham, who lived by faith—this is no new doctrine! And that means that anyone who tries to live by his own effort, independent of God, is doomed to failure. Scripture backs this up: "Utterly cursed is every person who fails to carry out every detail written in the Book of the law."

11-12   The obvious impossibility of carrying out such a moral program should make it plain that no one can sustain a relationship with God that way. The person who lives in right relationship with God does it by embracing what God arranges for him. Doing things for God is the opposite of entering into what God does for you. Habakkuk had it right: "The person who believes God, is set right by God — and that's the real life." Rule-keeping does not naturally evolve into living by faith, but only perpetuates itself in more and more rule-keeping, a fact observed in Scripture: "The one who does these things [rule-keeping] continues to live by them."

13-14 Christ redeemed us from that self-defeating, cursed life by absorbing it completely into himself. Do you remember the Scripture that says, "Cursed is everyone who hangs on a tree"? That is what happened when Jesus was nailed to the cross: He became a curse, and at the same time dissolved the curse. And now, because of that, the air is cleared and we can see that Abraham's blessing is present and available for non-Jews, too. We are *all* able to receive God's life, his Spirit, in and with us by believing — just the way Abraham received it.

15-18 Friends, let me give you an example from everyday affairs of the free life I am talking about. Once a person's will has been ratified, no one else can annul it or add to it. Now, the promises were made to Abraham and to his descendant. You will observe that Scripture, in the careful language of a legal document, does not say "to descendants," referring to everybody in general, but "to your descendant" (the noun, note, is singular), referring to Christ. This is the way I interpret this: A will, earlier ratified by God, is not annulled by an addendum attached 430 years later, thereby negating the promise of the will. No, this addendum, with its instructions and regulations, has nothing to do with the promised inheritance in the will.

18-20 What is the point, then, of the law, the attached addendum? It was a thoughtful addition to the original covenant promises made to Abraham. The purpose of the law was to keep a sinful people in the way of salvation until Christ (the descendant) came, inheriting the promises and distributing them to us. Obviously this law was not a firsthand encounter with God. It was arranged by angelic messengers through a middleman, Moses. But if there is a middleman as there was at Sinai, then the people are not dealing directly with God, are they? But the original promise is the *direct* blessing of God, received by faith.

21-22 If such is the case, is the law, then, an anti-promise, a negation of God's will for us? Not at all. Its purpose was to make obvious to everyone that we are, in ourselves, out of right relationship with God, and therefore to show us the futility of devising some religious system for getting by our own efforts what we can only get by waiting in faith for God to complete his promise. For if any kind of rule-keeping had power to create life in us, we would certainly have gotten it by this time.

23-24 Until the time when we were mature enough to respond freely in faith to the living God, we were carefully surrounded and protected by the Mosaic law. The law was like those Greek tutors, with which you are familiar, who escort children to school and protect them from danger or distraction, making sure the children will really get to the place they set out for.

25-27 But now you have arrived at your destination: By faith in Christ you are in direct relationship with God. Your baptism in Christ was not just washing you up for a fresh start. It also involved dressing you in an adult faith wardrobe — Christ's life, the fulfillment of God's original promise.

IN CHRIST'S FAMILY

28-29 In Christ's family there can be no division into Jew and non-Jew, slave and free, male and female. Among us you are all equal. That is, we are all in a common relationship with Jesus Christ. Also, since you are Christ's family, then you are Abraham's famous "descendant," heirs according to the covenant promises.

1-3 Let me show you the implications of this. As long as the heir is a minor, he has no advantage over the slave. Though legally he owns the entire inheritance, he is subject to tutors and administrators until whatever date the father has set for emancipation. That is the way it is with us: When we were minors, we were just like slaves ordered around by simple instructions (the tutors and administrators of this world), with no say in the conduct of our own lives.

4-7 But when the time arrived that was set by God the Father, God sent his Son, born among us of a woman, born under the conditions of the law so that he might redeem those of us who have been kidnapped by the law. Thus we have been set free to experience our rightful heritage. You can tell for sure that you are now fully adopted as his own children because God sent the Spirit of his Son into our lives crying out, "Papa! Father!" Doesn't that privilege of intimate conversation with God make it plain that you are not a slave, but a child? And if you are a child, you're also an heir, with complete access to the inheritance.

8-11 Earlier, before you knew God personally, you were enslaved to so-called gods that had nothing of the divine about them. But now that you know the real God — or rather since God knows you — how can you possibly subject yourselves again to those paper tigers? For that is exactly what you do when you are intimidated into scrupulously observing all the traditions, taboos, and superstitions associated with special days and seasons and years. I am afraid that all my hard work among you has gone up in a puff of smoke!

12-13 My dear friends, what I would really like you to do is try to put yourselves in my shoes to the same extent that I, when I was with you, put myself in yours. You were very sensitive and kind then. You did not come down on me personally. You were well aware that the reason I ended up preaching to you was that I was physically broken, and so, prevented from continuing my journey, I was forced to stop with you. That is how I came to preach to you.

14-16 And don't you remember that even though taking in a sick guest was most troublesome for you, you chose to treat me as well as you would have treated an angel of God — as well as you would have treated Jesus himself if he had visited you? What has happened to the satisfaction you felt at that time? There were some of you then who, if possible, would have given your very eyes to me — that is how deeply you cared! And now have I suddenly become your enemy simply by telling you the truth? I can't believe it.

17 Those heretical teachers go to great lengths to flatter you, but their motives are rotten. They want to shut you out of the free world of God's grace so that you will always depend on them for approval and direction, making them feel important.

18-20 It is a good thing to be ardent in doing good, but not just when I am in your presence. Can't you continue the same concern for both my person and my message when I am away from you that you had when I was with you? Do you know how I feel right now, and will feel until Christ's life becomes visible in your lives? Like a mother in the pain of childbirth. Oh, I keep wishing that I was with you. Then I wouldn't be reduced to this blunt, letter-writing language out of sheer frustration.

21-31 Tell me now, you who have become so enamored with the law: Have you paid close attention to that law? Abraham, remember, had *two* sons: one by the slave woman and one by the free woman. The son of the slave woman was born by human connivance; the son of the free woman was born by God's promise. This illustrates the very thing we are dealing with now. The two births represent two ways of being in relationship with God. One is from Mount Sinai in Arabia. It corresponds with what is now going on in Jerusalem — a slave life, producing slaves as offspring. This is the way of Hagar. In contrast to that, there is an invisible Jerusalem, a free Jerusalem, and she is our mother — this is the way of Sarah. Remember what Isaiah wrote:

> Rejoice, barren woman who bears no children,
>   shout and cry out, woman who has no birth pangs,
> Because the children of the barren woman
>   now surpass the children of the chosen woman.

Isn't it clear, friends, that you, like Isaac, are children of promise? In the days of Hagar and Sarah, the child who came from faithless connivance (Ishmael) harassed the child who came — empowered by the Spirit — from the faithful promise (Isaac). Isn't it clear that the harassment you are now experiencing from the Jerusalem heretics follows that old pattern? There is a Scripture that tells us what to do: "Expel the slave mother with her son, for the slave son will not inherit with the free son." Isn't that conclusive? We are not children of the slave woman, but of the free woman.

THE LIFE OF FREEDOM

1 **5** Christ has set us free to live a free life. So take your stand! Never again let anyone put a harness of slavery on you.

2-3 I am emphatic about this. The moment any one of you submits to circumcision or any other rule-keeping system, at that same moment Christ's hard-won gift of freedom is squandered. I repeat my warning: The person who accepts the ways of circumcision trades all the advantages of the free life in Christ for the obligations of the slave life of the law.

4-6 I suspect you would never intend this, but this is what happens. When you attempt to live by your own religious plans and projects, you are cut off from Christ, you fall out of grace. Meanwhile we expectantly wait for a satisfying relationship with the Spirit. For in Christ, neither our most conscientious religion nor disregard of religion amounts to anything. What matters is something far more interior: faith expressed in love.

7-10 You were running superbly! Who cut in on you, deflecting you from the true course of obedience? This detour doesn't come from the One who called you into the race in the first place. And please don't toss this off as insignificant. It only takes a minute amount of yeast, you know, to permeate an entire loaf of bread. Deep down, the Master has given me confidence that you will not defect. But the one who is upsetting you, whoever he is, will bear the divine judgment.

11-12 As for the rumor that I continue to preach the ways of circumcision (as I did in those pre-Damascus Road days), that is absurd. Why would I still be persecuted, then? If I were preaching that old message, no one would be offended if I mentioned the Cross now and then — it would be so watered-down it wouldn't matter one way or the other. Why don't these agitators, obsessive as they are about circumcision, go all the way and castrate themselves!

13-15 It is absolutely clear that God has called you to a free life. Just make sure that you don't use this freedom as an excuse to do whatever you want to do and destroy your freedom. Rather, use your freedom to serve one another in love; that's how freedom grows. For everything we know about God's Word is summed up in a single sentence: Love others as you love yourself. That's an act of true freedom. If you bite and ravage each other, watch out — in no time at all you will be annihilating each other, and where will your precious freedom be then?

16-18 My counsel is this: Live freely, animated and motivated by God's Spirit. Then you won't feed the compulsions of selfishness. For there is a root of sinful self-interest in us that is at odds with a free spirit, just as the free spirit is incompatible with selfishness. These two ways of life are antithetical, so that you cannot live at times one way and at times another way according to how you feel on any given day. Why don't you choose to be led by the Spirit and so escape the erratic compulsions of a law-dominated existence?

19-21 It is obvious what kind of life develops out of trying to get your own way all the time: repetitive, loveless, cheap sex; a stinking accumulation of mental and emotional garbage; frenzied and joyless grabs for happiness; trinket gods; magic-show religion; paranoid loneliness; cutthroat competition; all-consuming-yet-never-satisfied wants; a brutal temper; an impotence to love or be loved; divided homes and divided lives; small-minded and lopsided pursuits; the vicious habit of depersonalizing everyone into a rival; uncontrolled and uncontrollable addictions; ugly parodies of community. I could go on.

This isn't the first time I have warned you, you know. If you use your freedom this way, you will not inherit God's kingdom.

22-23 But what happens when we live God's way? He brings gifts into our lives, much the same way that fruit appears in an orchard — things like affection for others, exuberance about life, serenity. We develop a willingness to stick with things, a sense of compassion in the heart, and a conviction that a basic holiness permeates things and people. We find ourselves involved in loyal commitments, not needing to force our way in life, able to marshal and direct our energies wisely.

23-24 Legalism is helpless in bringing this about; it only gets in the way. Among those who belong to Christ, everything connected with getting our own way and mindlessly responding to what everyone else calls necessities is killed off for good — crucified.

25-26 Since this is the kind of life we have chosen, the life of the Spirit, let us make sure that we do not just hold it as an idea in our heads or a sentiment in our hearts, but work out its implications in every detail of our lives. That means we will not compare ourselves with each other as if one of us were better and another worse. We have far more interesting things to do with our lives. Each of us is an original.

NOTHING BUT THE CROSS

1-3 6 Live creatively, friends. If someone falls into sin, forgivingly restore him, saving your critical comments for yourself. *You* might be needing forgiveness before the day's out. Stoop down and reach out to those who are oppressed. Share their burdens, and so complete Christ's law. If you think you are too good for that, you are badly deceived.

4-5 Make a careful exploration of who you are and the work you have been given, and then sink yourself into that. Don't be impressed with yourself. Don't compare yourself with others. Each of you must take responsibility for doing the creative best you can with your own life.

6 Be very sure now, you who have been trained to a self-sufficient maturity, that you enter into a generous common life with those who have trained you, sharing all the good things that you have and experience.

7-8 Don't be misled: No one makes a fool of God. What a person plants, he will harvest. The person who plants selfishness, ignoring the needs of others — ignoring God! — harvests a crop of weeds. All he'll have to show for his life is weeds! But the one who plants in response to God, letting God's Spirit do the growth work in him, harvests a crop of real life, eternal life.

9-10 So let's not allow ourselves to get fatigued doing good. At the right time we will harvest a good crop if we don't give up, or quit. Right now, therefore, every time we get the chance, let us work for the benefit of all, starting with the people closest to us in the community of faith.

11-13 Now, in these last sentences, I want to emphasize in the bold scrawls of my personal handwriting the immense importance of what I have written to you. These people who are attempting to force the ways of circumcision on you have only one motive: They want an easy way to look good before others, lacking the courage to live by a faith that shares Christ's suffering and death. All their talk about the law is gas. They *themselves* don't keep the law! And they are highly selective in the laws they *do* observe. They only want you to be circumcised so they can boast of their success in recruiting you to their side. That is contemptible!

14-16 For my part, I am going to boast about nothing but the Cross of our Master, Jesus Christ. Because of that Cross, I have been crucified in relation to the world, set free from the stifling atmosphere of pleasing others and fitting into the little patterns that they dictate. Can't you see the central issue in all this? It is not what you and I do — submit to circumcision, reject circumcision. It is what *God* is doing, and he is creating something totally new, a free life! All who walk by this standard are the true Israel of God — his chosen people. Peace and mercy on them!

17 Quite frankly, I don't want to be bothered anymore by these disputes. I have far more important things to do — the serious living of this faith. I bear in my body scars from my service to Jesus.

18 May what our Master Jesus Christ gives freely be deeply and personally yours, my friends. Oh, yes!

EPHESIANS

What we know about God and what we do for God have a way of getting broken apart in our lives. The moment the organic unity of belief and behavior is damaged in any way, we are incapable of living out the full humanity for which we were created.

Paul's letter to the Ephesians joins together what has been torn apart in our sin-wrecked world. He begins with an exuberant exploration of what Christians believe about God, and then, like a surgeon skillfully setting a compound fracture, "sets" this belief in God into our behavior before God so that the bones — belief and behavior — knit together and heal.

Once our attention is called to it, we notice these fractures all over the place. There is hardly a bone in our bodies that has escaped injury, hardly a relationship in city or job, school or church, family or country, that isn't out of joint or limping in pain. There is much work to be done.

And so Paul goes to work. He ranges widely, from heaven to earth and back again, showing how Jesus, the Messiah, is eternally and tirelessly bringing everything and everyone together. He also shows us that in addition to having this work done in and for us, we are participants in this most urgent work. Now that we know what is going on, that the energy of reconciliation is the dynamo at the heart of the universe, it is imperative that we join in vigorously and perseveringly, convinced that every detail in our lives contributes (or not) to what Paul describes as God's plan worked out by Christ, "a long-range plan in which everything would be brought together and summed up in him, everything in deepest heaven, everything on planet earth."

EPHESIANS

1-2 I, Paul, am under God's plan as an apostle, a special agent of Christ Jesus, writing to you faithful believers in Ephesus. I greet you with the grace and peace poured into our lives by God our Father and our Master, Jesus Christ.

THE GOD OF GLORY

3-6 How blessed is God! And what a blessing he is! He's the Father of our Master, Jesus Christ, and takes us to the high places of blessing in him. Long before he laid down earth's foundations, he had us in mind, had settled on us as the focus of his love, to be made whole and holy by his love. Long, long ago he decided to adopt us into his family through Jesus Christ. (What pleasure he took in planning this!) He wanted us to enter into the celebration of his lavish gift-giving by the hand of his beloved Son.

7-10 Because of the sacrifice of the Messiah, his blood poured out on the altar of the Cross, we're a free people — free of penalties and punishments chalked up by all our misdeeds. And not just barely free, either. *Abundantly* free! He thought of everything, provided for everything we could possibly need, letting us in on the plans he took such delight in making. He set it all out before us in Christ, a long-range plan in which everything would be brought together and summed up in him, everything in deepest heaven, everything on planet earth.

11-12 It's in Christ that we find out who we are and what we are living for. Long before we first heard of Christ and got our hopes up, he had his eye on us, had designs on us for glorious living, part of the overall purpose he is working out in everything and everyone.

13-14 It's in Christ that you, once you heard the truth and believed it (this Message of your salvation), found yourselves home free — signed, sealed, and delivered by the Holy Spirit. This signet from God is the first installment on what's coming, a reminder that we'll get everything God has planned for us, a praising and glorious life.

15-19 That's why, when I heard of the solid trust you have in the Master Jesus and your outpouring of love to all the followers of Jesus, I couldn't stop thanking God for you — every time I prayed, I'd think of you and give thanks. But I do more than thank. I ask — ask the God of our Master, Jesus Christ, the God of glory — to make you intelligent and discerning in knowing him personally, your eyes focused and clear, so that you can see exactly what it is he is calling you to do, grasp the immensity of this glorious way of life he has for his followers, oh, the utter extravagance of his work in us who trust him — endless energy, boundless strength!

20-23 All this energy issues from Christ: God raised him from death and set him on a throne in deep heaven, in charge of running the universe, everything from galaxies to governments, no name and no power exempt from his rule. And not just for the time being, but *forever*. He is in charge of it all, has the final word on everything. At the center of all this, Christ rules the church. The church, you see, is not peripheral to the world; the world is peripheral to the church. The church is Christ's body, in which he speaks and acts, by which he fills everything with his presence.

HE TORE DOWN THE WALL

1-6 It wasn't so long ago that you were mired in that old stagnant life of sin. You let the world, which doesn't know the first thing about living, tell you how to live. You filled your lungs with polluted unbelief, and then exhaled disobedience. We all did it, all of us doing what we felt like doing, when we felt like doing it, all of us in the same boat. It's a wonder God didn't lose his temper and do away with the whole lot of us. Instead, immense in mercy and with an incredible love, he embraced us. He took our sin-dead lives and made us alive in Christ. He did all this on his own, with no help from us! Then he picked us up and set us down in highest heaven in company with Jesus, our Messiah.

7-10 Now God has us where he wants us, with all the time in this world and the next to shower grace and kindness upon us in Christ Jesus. Saving is all his idea, and all his work. All we do is trust him enough to let him do it. It's God's gift from start to finish! We don't play the major role. If we did, we'd probably go around bragging that we'd done the whole thing! No, we neither make nor save ourselves. God does both the making and saving. He creates each of us by Christ Jesus to join him in the work he does, the good work he has gotten ready for us to do, work we had better be doing.

11-13 But don't take any of this for granted. It was only yesterday that you outsiders to God's ways had no idea of any of this, didn't know the first thing about the way God works, hadn't the faintest idea of Christ. You knew nothing of that rich history of God's covenants and promises in Israel, hadn't a clue about what God was doing in the world at large. Now because of Christ — dying that death, shedding that blood — you who were once out of it altogether are in on everything.

14-15 The Messiah has made things up between us so that we're now together on this, both non-Jewish outsiders and Jewish insiders. He tore down the wall we used to keep each other at a distance. He repealed the law code that had become so clogged with fine print and footnotes that it hindered more than it helped. Then he started over. Instead of continuing with two groups of people separated by centuries of animosity and suspicion, he created a new kind of human being, a fresh start for everybody.

16-18 Christ brought us together through his death on the cross. The Cross got us to embrace, and that was the end of the hostility. Christ came and preached peace to you outsiders and peace to us insiders. He treated us as equals, and so made us equals. Through him we both share the same Spirit and have equal access to the Father.

19-22 That's plain enough, isn't it? You're no longer wandering exiles. This kingdom of faith is now your home country. You're no longer strangers or outsiders. You *belong* here, with as much right to the name Christian as anyone. God is building a home. He's using us all — irrespective of how we got here — in what he is building. He used the apostles and prophets for the foundation. Now he's using you, fitting you in brick by brick, stone by stone, with Christ Jesus as the cornerstone that holds all the parts together. We see it taking shape day after day — a holy temple built by God, all of us built into it, a temple in which God is quite at home.

The Secret Plan of God

¹⁻³ 3 This is why I, Paul, am in jail for Christ, having taken up the cause of you outsiders, so-called. I take it that you're familiar with the part I was given in God's plan for including everybody. I got the inside story on this from God himself, as I just wrote you in brief.

⁴⁻⁶ As you read over what I have written to you, you'll be able to see for yourselves into the mystery of Christ. None of our ancestors understood this. Only in our time has it been made clear by God's Spirit through his holy apostles and prophets of this new order. The mystery is that people who have never heard of God and those who have heard of him all their lives (what I've been calling outsiders and insiders) stand on the same ground before God. They get the same offer, same help, same promises in Christ Jesus. The Message is accessible and welcoming to everyone, across the board.

⁷⁻⁸ This is my life work: helping people understand and respond to this Message. It came as a sheer gift to me, a real surprise, God handling all the details. When it came to presenting the Message to people who had no background in God's way, I was the least qualified of any of the available Christians. God saw to it that I was equipped, but you can be sure that it had nothing to do with my natural abilities.

⁸⁻¹⁰ And so here I am, preaching and writing about things that are way over my head, the inexhaustible riches and generosity of Christ. My task is to bring out in the open and make plain what God, who created all this in the first place, has been doing in secret and behind the scenes all along. Through followers of Jesus like yourselves gathered in churches, this extraordinary plan of God is becoming known and talked about even among the angels!

¹¹⁻¹³ All this is proceeding along lines planned all along by God and then executed in Christ Jesus. When we trust in him, we're free to say whatever needs to be said, bold to go wherever we need to go. So don't let my present trouble on your behalf get you down. Be proud!

¹⁴⁻¹⁹ My response is to get down on my knees before the Father, this magnificent Father who parcels out all heaven and earth. I ask him to strengthen you by his Spirit—not a brute strength but a glorious inner strength—that Christ will live in you as you open the door and invite him in. And I ask him that with both feet planted firmly on love, you'll be able to take in with all followers of Jesus the extravagant dimensions of Christ's love. Reach out and experience the breadth! Test its length! Plumb the depths! Rise to the heights! Live full lives, full in the fullness of God.

²⁰⁻²¹ God can do anything, you know—far more than you could ever imagine or guess or request in your wildest dreams! He does it not by pushing us around but by working within us, his Spirit deeply and gently within us.

> Glory to God in the church!
> Glory to God in the Messiah, in Jesus!
> Glory down all the generations!
> Glory through all millennia! Oh, yes!

To Be Mature

1-3 **4** In light of all this, here's what I want you to do. While I'm locked up here, a prisoner for the Master, I want you to get out there and walk—better yet, run!—on the road God called you to travel. I don't want any of you sitting around on your hands. I don't want anyone strolling off, down some path that goes nowhere. And mark that you do this with humility and discipline—not in fits and starts, but steadily, pouring yourselves out for each other in acts of love, alert at noticing differences and quick at mending fences.

4-6 You were all called to travel on the same road and in the same direction, so stay together, both outwardly and inwardly. You have one Master, one faith, one baptism, one God and Father of all, who rules over all, works through all, and is present in all. Everything you are and think and do is permeated with Oneness.

7-13 But that doesn't mean you should all look and speak and act the same. Out of the generosity of Christ, each of us is given his own gift. The text for this is,

He climbed the high mountain,
He captured the enemy and seized the booty,
He handed it all out in gifts to the people.

Is it not true that the One who climbed up also climbed down, down to the valley of earth? And the One who climbed down is the One who climbed back up, up to highest heaven. He handed out gifts above and below, filled heaven with his gifts, filled earth with his gifts. He handed out gifts of apostle, prophet, evangelist, and pastor-teacher to train Christ's followers in skilled servant work, working within Christ's body, the church, until we're all moving rhythmically and easily with each other, efficient and graceful in response to God's Son, fully mature adults, fully developed within and without, fully alive like Christ.

14-16 No prolonged infancies among us, please. We'll not tolerate babes in the woods, small children who are an easy mark for impostors. God wants us to grow up, to know the whole truth and tell it in love—like Christ in everything. We take our lead from Christ, who is the source of everything we do. He keeps us in step with each other. His very breath and blood flow through us, nourishing us so that we will grow up healthy in God, robust in love.

The Old Way Has to Go

17-19 And so I insist—and God backs me up on this—that there be no going along with the crowd, the empty-headed, mindless crowd. They've refused for so long to deal with God that they've lost touch not only with God but with reality itself. They can't think straight anymore. Feeling no pain, they let themselves go in sexual obsession, addicted to every sort of perversion.

20-24 But that's no life for you. You learned Christ! My assumption is that you have paid careful attention to him, been well instructed in the truth precisely as we have it in Jesus. Since, then, we do not have the excuse of ignorance, everything—and I do mean everything—connected with that old way of life has to go. It's rotten through and through. Get rid of it! And then take on an entirely new way of life — a God-fashioned life, a life renewed from the inside and working itself into your conduct as God accurately reproduces his character in you.

25   What this adds up to, then, is this: no more lies, no more pretense. Tell your neighbor the truth. In Christ's body we're all connected to each other, after all. When you lie to others, you end up lying to yourself.

26-27   Go ahead and be angry. You do well to be angry — but don't use your anger as fuel for revenge. And don't stay angry. Don't go to bed angry. Don't give the Devil that kind of foothold in your life.

28   Did you use to make ends meet by stealing? Well, no more! Get an honest job so that you can help others who can't work.

29   Watch the way you talk. Let nothing foul or dirty come out of your mouth. Say only what helps, each word a gift.

30   Don't grieve God. Don't break his heart. His Holy Spirit, moving and breathing in you, is the most intimate part of your life, making you fit for himself. Don't take such a gift for granted.

31-32   Make a clean break with all cutting, backbiting, profane talk. Be gentle with one another, sensitive. Forgive one another as quickly and thoroughly as God in Christ forgave you.

WAKE UP FROM YOUR SLEEP

1-2   **5** Watch what God does, and then you do it, like children who learn proper behavior from their parents. Mostly what God does is love you. Keep company with him and learn a life of love. Observe how Christ loved us. His love was not cautious but extravagant. He didn't love in order to get something from us but to give everything of himself to us. Love like that.

3-4   Don't allow love to turn into lust, setting off a downhill slide into sexual promiscuity, filthy practices, or bullying greed. Though some tongues just love the taste of gossip, those who follow Jesus have better uses for language than that. Don't talk dirty or silly. That kind of talk doesn't fit our style. Thanksgiving is our dialect.

5   You can be sure that using people or religion or things just for what you can get out of them — the usual variations on idolatry — will get you nowhere, and certainly nowhere near the kingdom of Christ, the kingdom of God.

6-7   Don't let yourselves get taken in by religious smooth talk. God gets furious with people who are full of religious sales talk but want nothing to do with him. Don't even hang around people like that.

8-10   You groped your way through that murk once, but no longer. You're out in the open now. The bright light of Christ makes your way plain. So no more stumbling around. Get on with it! The good, the right, the true — these are the actions appropriate for daylight hours. Figure out what will please Christ, and then do it.

11-16   Don't waste your time on useless work, mere busywork, the barren pursuits of darkness. Expose these things for the sham they are. It's a scandal when people waste their lives on things they must do in the darkness where no one will see. Rip the cover off those frauds and see how attractive they look in the light of Christ.

Wake up from your sleep,
Climb out of your coffins;
Christ will show you the light!

So watch your step. Use your head. Make the most of every chance you get. These are desperate times!

17 Don't live carelessly, unthinkingly. Make sure you understand what the Master wants.

18-20 Don't drink too much wine. That cheapens your life. Drink the Spirit of God, huge draughts of him. Sing hymns instead of drinking songs! Sing songs from your heart to Christ. Sing praises over everything, any excuse for a song to God the Father in the name of our Master, Jesus Christ.

RELATIONSHIPS

21 Out of respect for Christ, be courteously reverent to one another.

22-24 Wives, understand and support your husbands in ways that show your support for Christ. The husband provides leadership to his wife the way Christ does to his church, not by domineering but by cherishing. So just as the church submits to Christ as he exercises such leadership, wives should likewise submit to their husbands.

25-28 Husbands, go all out in your love for your wives, exactly as Christ did for the church—a love marked by giving, not getting. Christ's love makes the church whole. His words evoke her beauty. Everything he does and says is designed to bring the best out of her, dressing her in dazzling white silk, radiant with holiness. And that is how husbands ought to love their wives. They're really doing themselves a favor—since they're already "one" in marriage.

29-33 No one abuses his own body, does he? No, he feeds and pampers it. That's how Christ treats us, the church, since we are part of his body. And this is why a man leaves father and mother and cherishes his wife. No longer two, they become "one flesh." This is a huge mystery, and I don't pretend to understand it all. What is clearest to me is the way Christ treats the church. And this provides a good picture of how each husband is to treat his wife, loving himself in loving her, and how each wife is to honor her husband.

1-3 Children, do what your parents tell you. This is only right. "Honor your father and mother" is the first commandment that has a promise attached to it, namely, "so you will live well and have a long life."

4 Fathers, don't exasperate your children by coming down hard on them. Take them by the hand and lead them in the way of the Master.

5-8 Servants, respectfully obey your earthly masters but always with an eye to obeying the *real* master, Christ. Don't just do what you have to do to get by, but work heartily, as Christ's servants doing what God wants you to do. And work with a smile on your face, always keeping in mind that no matter who happens to be giving the orders, you're really serving God. Good work will get you good pay from the Master, regardless of whether you are slave or free.

9 Masters, it's the same with you. No abuse, please, and no threats. You and your servants are both under the same Master in heaven. He makes no distinction between you and them.

A FIGHT TO THE FINISH

10-12 And that about wraps it up. God is strong, and he wants you strong. So take everything the Master has set out for you, well-made weapons of the best materials. And put them to use so you will be able to stand up to everything the Devil throws your way. This is no afternoon athletic contest that we'll walk away from and forget about in a couple of hours. This is for keeps, a life-or-death fight to the finish against the Devil and all his angels.

13-18 Be prepared. You're up against far more than you can handle on your own. Take all the help you can get, every weapon God has issued, so that when it's all over but the shouting you'll still be on your feet. Truth, righteousness, peace, faith, and salvation are more than words. Learn how to apply them. You'll need them throughout your life. God's Word is an *indispensable* weapon. In the same way, prayer is essential in this ongoing warfare. Pray hard and long. Pray for your brothers and sisters. Keep your eyes open. Keep each other's spirits up so that no one falls behind or drops out.

19-20 And don't forget to pray for me. Pray that I'll know what to say and have the courage to say it at the right time, telling the mystery to one and all, the Message that I, jailbird preacher that I am, am responsible for getting out.

21-22 Tychicus, my good friend here, will tell you what I'm doing and how things are going with me. He is certainly a dependable servant of the Master! I've sent him not only to tell you about us but to cheer you on in your faith.

23-24 Good-bye, friends. Love mixed with faith be yours from God the Father and from the Master, Jesus Christ. Pure grace and nothing but grace be with all who love our Master, Jesus Christ.

PHILIPPIANS

This is Paul's happiest letter. And the happiness is infectious. Before we've read a dozen lines, we begin to feel the joy ourselves — the dance of words and the exclamations of delight have a way of getting inside us.

But happiness is not a word we can understand by looking it up in the dictionary. In fact, none of the qualities of the Christian life can be learned out of a book. Something more like apprenticeship is required, being around someone who out of years of devoted discipline shows us, by his or her entire behavior, what it is. Moments of verbal instruction will certainly occur, but mostly an apprentice acquires skill by daily and intimate association with a "master," picking up subtle but absolutely essential things, such as timing and rhythm and "touch."

When we read what Paul wrote to the Christian believers in the city of Philippi, we find ourselves in the company of just such a master. Paul doesn't tell us that we can be happy, or how to be happy. He simply and unmistakably *is* happy. None of his circumstances contribute to his joy: He wrote from a jail cell, his work was under attack by competitors, and after twenty years or so of hard traveling in the service of Jesus, he was tired and would have welcomed some relief.

But circumstances are incidental compared to the life of Jesus, the Messiah, that Paul experiences from the inside. For it is a life that not only happened at a certain point in history, but continues to happen, spilling out into the lives of those who receive him, and then continues to spill out all over the place. Christ is, among much else, the revelation that God cannot be contained or hoarded. It is this "spilling out" quality of Christ's life that accounts for the happiness of Christians, for joy is life in excess, the overflow of what cannot be contained within any one person.

PHILIPPIANS

1-2 Paul and Timothy, both of us committed servants of Christ Jesus, write this letter to all the followers of Jesus in Philippi, pastors and ministers included. We greet you with the grace and peace that comes from God our Father and our Master, Jesus Christ.

A LOVE THAT WILL GROW

3-6 Every time you cross my mind, I break out in exclamations of thanks to God. Each exclamation is a trigger to prayer. I find myself praying for you with a glad heart. I am so pleased that you have continued on in this with us, believing and proclaiming God's Message, from the day you heard it right up to the present. There has never been the slightest doubt in my mind that the God who started this great work in you would keep at it and bring it to a flourishing finish on the very day Christ Jesus appears.

7-8 It's not at all fanciful for me to think this way about you. My prayers and hopes have deep roots in reality. You have, after all, stuck with me all the way from the time I was thrown in jail, put on trial, and came out of it in one piece. All along you have experienced with me the most generous help from God. He knows how much I love and miss you these days. Sometimes I think I feel as strongly about you as Christ does!

9-11 So this is my prayer: that your love will flourish and that you will not only love much but well. Learn to love appropriately. You need to use your head and test your feelings so that your love is sincere and intelligent, not sentimental gush. Live a lover's life, circumspect and exemplary, a life Jesus will be proud of: bountiful in fruits from the soul, making Jesus Christ attractive to all, getting everyone involved in the glory and praise of God.

THEY CAN'T IMPRISON THE MESSAGE

12-14 I want to report to you, friends, that my imprisonment here has had the opposite of its intended effect. Instead of being squelched, the Message has actually prospered. All the soldiers here, and everyone else, too, found out that I'm in jail because of this Messiah. That piqued their curiosity, and now they've learned all about him. Not only that, but most of the followers of Jesus here have become far more sure of themselves in the faith than ever, speaking out fearlessly about God, about the Messiah.

15-17 It's true that some here preach Christ because with me out of the way, they think they'll step right into the spotlight. But the others do it with the best heart in the world. One group is motivated by pure love, knowing that I am here defending the Message, wanting to help. The others, now that I'm out of the picture, are merely greedy, hoping to get something out of it for themselves. Their motives are bad. They see me as their competition, and so the worse it goes for me, the better — they think — for them.

18-21 So how am I to respond? I've decided that I really don't care about their motives, whether mixed, bad, or indifferent. Every time one of them opens his mouth, Christ is proclaimed, so I just cheer them on!

And I'm going to keep that celebration going because I know how it's going to turn out. Through your faithful prayers and the generous response of the Spirit of Jesus Christ, everything he wants to do in and through me will be done. I can hardly wait to continue on my course. I don't expect to be embarrassed in the least. On the contrary, everything happening to me in this jail only serves to make Christ more accurately known, regardless of whether I live or die. They didn't shut me up; they gave me a pulpit! Alive, I'm Christ's messenger; dead, I'm his bounty. Life versus even more life! I can't lose.

22-26   As long as I'm alive in this body, there is good work for me to do. If I had to choose right now, I hardly know which I'd choose. Hard choice! The desire to break camp here and be with Christ is powerful. Some days I can think of nothing better. But most days, because of what you are going through, I am sure that it's better for me to stick it out here. So I plan to be around awhile, companion to you as your growth and joy in this life of trusting God continues. You can start looking forward to a great reunion when I come visit you again. We'll be praising Christ, enjoying each other.

27-30   Meanwhile, live in such a way that you are a credit to the Message of Christ. Let nothing in your conduct hang on whether I come or not. Your conduct must be the same whether I show up to see things for myself or hear of it from a distance. Stand united, singular in vision, contending for people's trust in the Message, the good news, not flinching or dodging in the slightest before the opposition. Your courage and unity will show them what they're up against: defeat for them, victory for you—and both because of God. There's far more to this life than trusting in Christ. There's also suffering for him. And the suffering is as much a gift as the trusting. You're involved in the same kind of struggle you saw me go through, on which you are now getting an updated report in this letter.

HE TOOK ON THE STATUS OF A SLAVE

1-4   2 If you've gotten anything at all out of following Christ, if his love has made any difference in your life, if being in a community of the Spirit means anything to you, if you have a heart, if you *care*— then do me a favor: Agree with each other, love each other, be deep-spirited friends. Don't push your way to the front; don't sweet-talk your way to the top. Put yourself aside, and help others get ahead. Don't be obsessed with getting your own advantage. Forget yourselves long enough to lend a helping hand.

5-8   Think of yourselves the way Christ Jesus thought of himself. He had equal status with God but didn't think so much of himself that he had to cling to the advantages of that status no matter what. Not at all. When the time came, he set aside the privileges of deity and took on the status of a slave, became *human*! Having become human, he stayed human. It was an incredibly humbling process. He didn't claim special privileges. Instead, he lived a selfless, obedient life and then died a selfless, obedient death—and the worst kind of death at that—a crucifixion.

9-11   Because of that obedience, God lifted him high and honored him far beyond anyone or anything, ever, so that all created beings in heaven and on earth—even those long ago dead and buried—will bow in worship before this Jesus Christ, and call out in praise that he is the Master of all, to the glorious honor of God the Father.

REJOICING TOGETHER

12-13   What I'm getting at, friends, is that you should simply keep on doing what you've done from the beginning. When I was living among you, you lived in responsive obedience. Now that I'm separated from you, keep it up. Better yet, redouble your efforts. Be energetic in your life of salvation, reverent and sensitive before God. That energy is *God's* energy, an energy deep within you, God himself willing and working at what will give him the most pleasure.

14-16 Do everything readily and cheerfully—no bickering, no second-guessing allowed! Go out into the world uncorrupted, a breath of fresh air in this squalid and polluted society. Provide people with a glimpse of good living and of the living God. Carry the light-giving Message into the night so I'll have good cause to be proud of you on the day that Christ returns. You'll be living proof that I didn't go to all this work for nothing.

17-18 Even if I am executed here and now, I'll rejoice in being an element in the offering of your faith that you make on Christ's altar, a part of your rejoicing. But turnabout's fair play—you must join me in *my* rejoicing. Whatever you do, don't feel sorry for me.

19-24 I plan (according to Jesus' plan) to send Timothy to you very soon so he can bring back all the news of you he can gather. Oh, how that will do my heart good! I have no one quite like Timothy. He is loyal, and genuinely concerned for you. Most people around here are looking out for themselves, with little concern for the things of Jesus. But you know yourselves that Timothy's the real thing. He's been a devoted son to me as together we've delivered the Message. As soon as I see how things are going to fall out for me here, I plan to send him off. And then I'm hoping and praying to be right on his heels.

25-27 But for right now, I'm dispatching Epaphroditus, my good friend and companion in my work. You sent him to help me out; now I'm sending him to help you out. He has been wanting in the worst way to get back with you. Especially since recovering from the illness you heard about, he's been wanting to get back and reassure you that he is just fine. He nearly died, as you know, but God had mercy on him. And not only on him—he had mercy on me, too. His death would have been one huge grief piled on top of all the others.

28-30 So you can see why I'm so delighted to send him on to you. When you see him again, hale and hearty, how you'll rejoice and how relieved I'll be. Give him a grand welcome, a joyful embrace! People like him deserve the best you can give. Remember the ministry to me that you started but weren't able to complete? Well, in the process of finishing up that work, he put his life on the line and nearly died doing it.

To Know Him Personally

1 **3** And that's about it, friends. Be glad in God!
I don't mind repeating what I have written in earlier letters, and I hope you don't mind hearing it again. Better safe than sorry—so here goes.

2-6 Steer clear of the barking dogs, those religious busybodies, all bark and no bite. All they're interested in is appearances—knife-happy circumcisers, I call them. The *real* believers are the ones the Spirit of God leads to work away at this ministry, filling the air with Christ's praise as we do it. We couldn't carry this off by our own efforts, and we know it—even though we can list what many might think are impressive credentials. You know my pedigree: a legitimate birth, circumcised on the eighth day; an

Israelite from the elite tribe of Benjamin; a strict and devout adherent to God's law; a fiery defender of the purity of my religion, even to the point of persecuting the church; a meticulous observer of everything set down in God's law Book.

7-9 The very credentials these people are waving around as something special, I'm tearing up and throwing out with the trash — along with everything else I used to take credit for. And why? Because of Christ. Yes, all the things I once thought were so important are gone from my life. Compared to the high privilege of knowing Christ Jesus as my Master, firsthand, everything I once thought I had going for me is insignificant — dog dung. I've dumped it all in the trash so that I could embrace Christ and be embraced by him. I didn't want some petty, inferior brand of righteousness that comes from keeping a list of rules when I could get the robust kind that comes from trusting Christ — *God's* righteousness.

10-11 I gave up all that inferior stuff so I could know Christ personally, experience his resurrection power, be a partner in his suffering, and go all the way with him to death itself. If there was any way to get in on the resurrection from the dead, I wanted to do it.

FOCUSED ON THE GOAL

12-14 I'm not saying that I have this all together, that I have it made. But I am well on my way, reaching out for Christ, who has so wondrously reached out for me. Friends, don't get me wrong: By no means do I count myself an expert in all of this, but I've got my eye on the goal, where God is beckoning us onward — to Jesus. I'm off and running, and I'm not turning back.

15-16 So let's keep focused on that goal, those of us who want everything God has for us. If any of you have something else in mind, something less than total commitment, God will clear your blurred vision — you'll see it yet! Now that we're on the right track, let's stay on it.

17-19 Stick with me, friends. Keep track of those you see running this same course, headed for this same goal. There are many out there taking other paths, choosing other goals, and trying to get you to go along with them. I've warned you of them many times; sadly, I'm having to do it again. All they want is easy street. They hate Christ's Cross. But easy street is a dead-end street. Those who live there make their bellies their gods; belches are their praise; all they can think of is their appetites.

20-21 But there's far more to life for us. We're citizens of high heaven! We're waiting the arrival of the Savior, the Master, Jesus Christ, who will transform our earthy bodies into glorious bodies like his own. He'll make us beautiful and whole with the same powerful skill by which he is putting everything as it should be, under and around him.

1 4 My dear, dear friends! I love you so much. I do want the very best for you. You make me feel such joy, fill me with such pride. Don't waver. Stay on track, steady in God.

PRAY ABOUT EVERYTHING

2 I urge Euodia and Syntyche to iron out their differences and make up. God doesn't want his children holding grudges.

3 And, oh, yes, Syzygus, since you're right there to help them work things out, do your best with them. These women worked for the Message

hand in hand with Clement and me, and with the other veterans — worked as hard as any of us. Remember, their names are also in the Book of Life.

4-5   Celebrate God all day, every day. I mean, *revel* in him! Make it as clear as you can to all you meet that you're on their side, working with them and not against them. Help them see that the Master is about to arrive. He could show up any minute!

6-7   Don't fret or worry. Instead of worrying, pray. Let petitions and praises shape your worries into prayers, letting God know your concerns. Before you know it, a sense of God's wholeness, everything coming together for good, will come and settle you down. It's wonderful what happens when Christ displaces worry at the center of your life.

8-9   Summing it all up, friends, I'd say you'll do best by filling your minds and meditating on things true, noble, reputable, authentic, compelling, gracious — the best, not the worst; the beautiful, not the ugly; things to praise, not things to curse. Put into practice what you learned from me, what you heard and saw and realized. Do that, and God, who makes everything work together, will work you into his most excellent harmonies.

CONTENT WHATEVER THE CIRCUMSTANCES

10-14   I'm glad in God, far happier than you would ever guess — happy that you're again showing such strong concern for me. Not that you ever quit praying and thinking about me. You just had no chance to show it. Actually, I don't have a sense of needing anything personally. I've learned by now to be quite content whatever my circumstances. I'm just as happy with little as with much, with much as with little. I've found the recipe for being happy whether full or hungry, hands full or hands empty. Whatever I have, wherever I am, I can make it through anything in the One who makes me who I am. I don't mean that your help didn't mean a lot to me — it did. It was a beautiful thing that you came alongside me in my troubles.

15-17   You Philippians well know, and you can be sure I'll never forget it, that when I first left Macedonia province, venturing out with the Message, not one church helped out in the give-and-take of this work except you. You were the only one. Even while I was in Thessalonica, you helped out — and not only once, but twice. Not that I'm looking for handouts, but I do want you to experience the blessing that issues from generosity.

18-20   And now I have it all — and keep getting more! The gifts you sent with Epaphroditus were more than enough, like a sweet-smelling sacrifice roasting on the altar, filling the air with fragrance, pleasing God no end. You can be sure that God will take care of everything you need, his generosity exceeding even yours in the glory that pours from Jesus. Our God and Father abounds in glory that just pours out into eternity. Yes.

21-22   Give our regards to every follower of Jesus you meet. Our friends here say hello. All the Christians here, especially the believers who work in the palace of Caesar, want to be remembered to you.

23   Receive and experience the amazing grace of the Master, Jesus Christ, deep, deep within yourselves.

COLOSSIANS

Hardly anyone who hears the full story of Jesus and learns the true facts of his life and teaching, crucifixion and resurrection, walks away with a shrug of the shoulders, dismissing him as unimportant. People ignorant of the story or misinformed about it, of course, regularly dismiss him. But with few exceptions, the others know instinctively that they are dealing with a most remarkable greatness.

But it is quite common for those who consider him truly important to include others who seem to be equally important in his company — Buddha, Moses, Socrates, and Muhammad for a historical start, along with some personal favorites. For these people, Jesus is important, but not central; his prestige is considerable, but he is not preeminent.

The Christians in the town of Colosse, or at least some of them, seem to have been taking this line. For them, cosmic forces of one sort or another were getting equal billing with Jesus. Paul writes to them in an attempt to restore Jesus, the Messiah, to the center of their lives.

The way he makes his argument is as significant as the argument he makes. Claims for the uniqueness of Jesus are common enough. But such claims about Jesus are frequently made with an arrogance that is completely incompatible with Jesus himself. Sometimes the claims are enforced with violence.

But Paul, although unswervingly confident in the conviction that Christ occupies the center of creation and salvation without peers, is not arrogant. And he is certainly not violent. He argues from a position of rooted humility. He writes with the energies of most considerate love. He exhibits again what Christians have come to appreciate so much in Paul — the wedding of a brilliant and uncompromising intellect with a heart that is warmly and wonderfully kind.

COLOSSIANS

1-2 I, Paul, have been sent on special assignment by Christ as part of God's master plan. Together with my friend Timothy, I greet the Christians and stalwart followers of Christ who live in Colosse. May everything good from God our Father be yours!

WORKING IN HIS ORCHARD

3-5 Our prayers for you are always spilling over into thanksgivings. We can't quit thanking God our Father and Jesus our Messiah for you! We keep getting reports on your steady faith in Christ, our Jesus, and the love you continuously extend to all Christians. The lines of purpose in your lives never grow slack, tightly tied as they are to your future in heaven, kept taut by hope.

5-8 The Message is as true among you today as when you first heard it. It doesn't diminish or weaken over time. It's the same all over the world. The Message bears fruit and gets larger and stronger, just as it has in you. From the very first day you heard and recognized the truth of what God is doing, you've been hungry for more. It's as vigorous in you now as when you learned it from our friend and close associate Epaphras. He is one reliable worker for Christ! I could always depend on him. He's the one who told us how thoroughly love had been worked into your lives by the Spirit.

9-12 Be assured that from the first day we heard of you, we haven't stopped praying for you, asking God to give you wise minds and spirits attuned to his will, and so acquire a thorough understanding of the ways in which God works. We pray that you'll live well for the Master, making him proud of you as you work hard in his orchard. As you learn more and more how God works, you will learn how to do *your* work. We pray that you'll have the strength to stick it out over the long haul—not the grim strength of gritting your teeth but the glory-strength God gives. It is strength that endures the unendurable and spills over into joy, thanking the Father who makes us strong enough to take part in everything bright and beautiful that he has for us.

13-14 God rescued us from dead-end alleys and dark dungeons. He's set us up in the kingdom of the Son he loves so much, the Son who got us out of the pit we were in, got rid of the sins we were doomed to keep repeating.

CHRIST HOLDS IT ALL TOGETHER

15-18 We look at this Son and see the God who cannot be seen. We look at this Son and see God's original purpose in everything created. For everything, absolutely everything, above and below, visible and invisible, rank after rank after rank of angels—*everything* got started in him and finds its purpose in him. He was there before any of it came into existence and holds it all together right up to this moment. And when it comes to the church, he organizes and holds it together, like a head does a body.

18-20 He was supreme in the beginning and—leading the resurrection parade—he is supreme in the end. From beginning to end he's there, towering far above everything, everyone. So spacious is he, so roomy, that everything of God finds its proper place in him without crowding. Not only that, but all the broken and dislocated pieces of the universe—people and things, animals and atoms — get properly fixed and fit together in vibrant harmonies, all because of his death, his blood that poured down from the cross.

21-23   You yourselves are a case study of what he does. At one time you all had your backs turned to God, thinking rebellious thoughts of him, giving him trouble every chance you got. But now, by giving himself completely at the Cross, actually *dying* for you, Christ brought you over to God's side and put your lives together, whole and holy in his presence. You don't walk away from a gift like that! You stay grounded and steady in that bond of trust, constantly tuned in to the Message, careful not to be distracted or diverted. There is no other Message — just this one. Every creature under heaven gets this same Message. I, Paul, am a messenger of this Message.

24-25   I want you to know how glad I am that it's me sitting here in this jail and not you. There's a lot of suffering to be entered into in this world — the kind of suffering Christ takes on. I welcome the chance to take my share in the church's part of that suffering. When I became a servant in this church, I experienced this suffering as a sheer gift, God's way of helping me serve you, laying out the whole truth.

26-29   This mystery has been kept in the dark for a long time, but now it's out in the open. God wanted everyone, not just Jews, to know this rich and glorious secret inside and out, regardless of their background, regardless of their religious standing. The mystery in a nutshell is just this: Christ is in you, so therefore you can look forward to sharing in God's glory. It's that simple. That is the substance of our Message. We preach *Christ*, warning people not to add to the Message. We teach in a spirit of profound common sense so that we can bring each person to maturity. To be mature is to be basic. Christ! No more, no less. That's what I'm working so hard at day after day, year after year, doing my best with the energy God so generously gives me.

1   2 I want you to realize that I continue to work as hard as I know how for you, and also for the Christians over at Laodicea. Not many of you have met me face-to-face, but that doesn't make any difference. Know that I'm on your side, right alongside you. You're not in this alone.

2-4   I want you woven into a tapestry of love, in touch with everything there is to know of God. Then you will have minds confident and at rest, focused on Christ, God's great mystery. All the richest treasures of wisdom and knowledge are embedded in that mystery and nowhere else. And we've been shown the mystery! I'm telling you this because I don't want anyone leading you off on some wild-goose chase, after other so-called mysteries, or "the Secret."

5   I'm a long way off, true, and you may never lay eyes on me, but believe me, I'm on your side, right beside you. I am delighted to hear of the careful and orderly ways you conduct your affairs, and impressed with the solid substance of your faith in Christ.

FROM THE SHADOWS TO THE SUBSTANCE

6-7   My counsel for you is simple and straightforward: Just go ahead with what you've been given. You received Christ Jesus, the Master; now *live* him. You're deeply rooted in him. You're well constructed upon him. You know your way around the faith. Now do what you've been taught. School's out;

quit studying the subject and start *living* it! And let your living spill over into thanksgiving.

8-10 Watch out for people who try to dazzle you with big words and intellectual double-talk. They want to drag you off into endless arguments that never amount to anything. They spread their ideas through the empty traditions of human beings and the empty superstitions of spirit beings. But that's not the way of Christ. Everything of God gets expressed in him, so you can see and hear him clearly. You don't need a telescope, a microscope, or a horoscope to realize the fullness of Christ, and the emptiness of the universe without him. When you come to him, that fullness comes together for you, too. His power extends over everything.

11-15 Entering into this fullness is not something you figure out or achieve. It's not a matter of being circumcised or keeping a long list of laws. No, you're already *in* — insiders — not through some secretive initiation rite but rather through what Christ has already gone through for you, destroying the power of sin. If it's an initiation ritual you're after, you've already been through it by submitting to baptism. Going under the water was a burial of your old life; coming up out of it was a resurrection, God raising you from the dead as he did Christ. When you were stuck in your old sin-dead life, you were incapable of responding to God. God brought you alive — right along with Christ! Think of it! All sins forgiven, the slate wiped clean, that old arrest warrant canceled and nailed to Christ's cross. He stripped all the spiritual tyrants in the universe of their sham authority at the Cross and marched them naked through the streets.

16-17 So don't put up with anyone pressuring you in details of diet, worship services, or holy days. All those things are mere shadows cast before what was to come; the substance is Christ.

18-19 Don't tolerate people who try to run your life, ordering you to bow and scrape, insisting that you join their obsession with angels and that you seek out visions. They're a lot of hot air, that's all they are. They're completely out of touch with the source of life, Christ, who puts us together in one piece, whose very breath and blood flow through us. He is the Head and we are the body. We can grow up healthy in God only as he nourishes us.

20-23 So, then, if with Christ you've put all that pretentious and infantile religion behind you, why do you let yourselves be bullied by it? "Don't touch this! Don't taste that! Don't go near this!" Do you think things that are here today and gone tomorrow are worth that kind of attention? Such things sound impressive if said in a deep enough voice. They even give the illusion of being pious and humble and ascetic. But they're just another way of showing off, making yourselves look important.

HE IS YOUR LIFE

1-2 **3** So if you're serious about living this new resurrection life with Christ, *act* like it. Pursue the things over which Christ presides. Don't shuffle along, eyes to the ground, absorbed with the things right in front of you. Look up, and be alert to what is going on around Christ — that's where the action is. See things from *his* perspective.

3-4 Your old life is dead. Your new life, which is your *real* life — even though invisible to spectators — is with Christ in God. *He* is your life. When Christ (your real life, remember) shows up again on this earth, you'll show up, too — the real you, the glorious you. Meanwhile, be content with obscurity, like Christ.

5-8 And that means killing off everything connected with that way of death: sexual promiscuity, impurity, lust, doing whatever you feel like whenever you feel like it, and grabbing whatever attracts your fancy. That's a life shaped by things and feelings instead of by God. It's because of this kind of thing that God is about to explode in anger. It wasn't long ago that you were doing all that stuff and not knowing any better. But you know better now, so make sure it's all gone for good: bad temper, irritability, meanness, profanity, dirty talk.

9-11 Don't lie to one another. You're done with that old life. It's like a filthy set of ill-fitting clothes you've stripped off and put in the fire. Now you're dressed in a new wardrobe. Every item of your new way of life is custom-made by the Creator, with his label on it. All the old fashions are now obsolete. Words like Jewish and non-Jewish, religious and irreligious, insider and outsider, uncivilized and uncouth, slave and free, mean nothing. From now on everyone is defined by Christ, everyone is included in Christ.

12-14 So, chosen by God for this new life of love, dress in the wardrobe God picked out for you: compassion, kindness, humility, quiet strength, discipline. Be even-tempered, content with second place, quick to forgive an offense. Forgive as quickly and completely as the Master forgave you. And regardless of what else you put on, wear love. It's your basic, all-purpose garment. Never be without it.

15-17 Let the peace of Christ keep you in tune with each other, in step with each other. None of this going off and doing your own thing. And cultivate thankfulness. Let the Word of Christ — the Message — have the run of the house. Give it plenty of room in your lives. Instruct and direct one another using good common sense. And sing, sing your hearts out to God! Let every detail in your lives — words, actions, whatever — be done in the name of the Master, Jesus, thanking God the Father every step of the way.

18 Wives, understand and support your husbands by submitting to them in ways that honor the Master.

19 Husbands, go all out in love for your wives. Don't take advantage of them.

20 Children, do what your parents tell you. This delights the Master no end.

21 Parents, don't come down too hard on your children or you'll crush their spirits.

22-25 Servants, do what you're told by your earthly masters. And don't just do the minimum that will get you by. Do your best. Work from the heart for your real Master, for God, confident that you'll get paid in full when you come into your inheritance. Keep in mind always that the ultimate Master you're serving is Christ. The sullen servant who does shoddy work will be held responsible. Being a follower of Jesus doesn't cover up bad work.

1 4 And masters, treat your servants considerately. Be fair with them. Don't forget for a minute that you, too, serve a Master — God in heaven.

2-4   Pray diligently. Stay alert, with your eyes wide open in gratitude. Don't forget to pray for us, that God will open doors for telling the mystery of Christ, even while I'm locked up in this jail. Pray that every time I open my mouth I'll be able to make Christ plain as day to them.

5-6   Use your heads as you live and work among outsiders. Don't miss a trick. Make the most of every opportunity. Be gracious in your speech. The goal is to bring out the best in others in a conversation, not put them down, not cut them out.

7-9   My good friend Tychicus will tell you all about me. He's a trusted minister and companion in the service of the Master. I've sent him to you so that you would know how things are with us, and so he could encourage you in your faith. And I've sent Onesimus with him. Onesimus is one of you, and has become such a trusted and dear brother! Together they'll bring you up-to-date on everything that has been going on here.

10-11   Aristarchus, who is in jail here with me, sends greetings; also Mark, cousin of Barnabas (you received a letter regarding him; if he shows up, welcome him); and also Jesus, the one they call Justus. These are the only ones left from the old crowd who have stuck with me in working for God's kingdom. Don't think they haven't been a big help!

12-13   Epaphras, who is one of you, says hello. What a trooper he has been! He's been tireless in his prayers for you, praying that you'll stand firm, mature and confident in everything God wants you to do. I've watched him closely, and can report on how hard he has worked for you and for those in Laodicea and Hierapolis.

14   Luke, good friend and physician, and Demas both send greetings.

15   Say hello to our friends in Laodicea; also to Nympha and the church that meets in her house.

16   After this letter has been read to you, make sure it gets read also in Laodicea. And get the letter that went to Laodicea and have it read to you.

17   And, oh, yes, tell Archippus, "Do your best in the job you received from the Master. Do your very best."

18   I'm signing off in my own handwriting—Paul. Remember to pray for me in this jail. Grace be with you.

1 & 2 THESSALONIANS

The way we conceive the future sculpts the present, gives contour and tone to nearly every action and thought through the day. If our sense of future is weak, we live listlessly. Much emotional and mental illness and most suicides occur among men and women who feel that they "have no future."

The Christian faith has always been characterized by a strong and focused sense of future, with belief in the Second Coming of Jesus as the most distinctive detail. From the day Jesus ascended into heaven, his followers lived in expectancy of his return. He told them he was coming back. They believed he was coming back. They continue to believe it. For Christians, it is the most important thing to know and believe about the future.

The practical effect of this belief is to charge each moment of the present with hope. For if the future is dominated by the coming again of Jesus, there is little room left on the screen for projecting our anxieties and fantasies. It takes the clutter out of our lives. We're far more free to respond spontaneously to the freedom of God.

All the same, the belief can be misconceived so that it results in paralyzing fear for some, shiftless indolence in others. Paul's two letters to the Christians in Thessalonica, among much else, correct such debilitating misconceptions, prodding us to continue to live forward in taut and joyful expectancy for what God will do next in Jesus.

1 THESSALONIANS

1 I, Paul, together here with Silas and Timothy, send greetings to the church at Thessalonica, Christians assembled by God the Father and by the Master, Jesus Christ. God's amazing grace be with you! God's robust peace!

CONVICTIONS OF STEEL

2-5 Every time we think of you, we thank God for you. Day and night you're in our prayers as we call to mind your work of faith, your labor of love, and your patience of hope in following our Master, Jesus Christ, before God our Father. It is clear to us, friends, that God not only loves you very much but also has put his hand on you for something special. When the Message we preached came to you, it wasn't just words. Something happened in you. The Holy Spirit put steel in your convictions.

5-6 You paid careful attention to the way we lived among you, and determined to live that way yourselves. In imitating us, you imitated the Master. Although great trouble accompanied the Word, you were able to take great joy from the Holy Spirit! — taking the trouble with the joy, the joy with the trouble.

7-10 Do you know that all over the provinces of both Macedonia and Achaia believers look up to you? The word has gotten around. Your lives are echoing the Master's Word, not only in the provinces but all over the place. The news of your faith in God is out. We don't even have to say anything anymore — *you're* the message! People come up and tell us how you received us with open arms, how you deserted the dead idols of your old life so you could embrace and serve God, the true God. They marvel at how expectantly you await the arrival of his Son, whom he raised from the dead — Jesus, who rescued us from certain doom.

1-2 So, friends, it's obvious that our visit to you was no waste of time. We had just been given rough treatment in Philippi, as you know, but that didn't slow us down. We were sure of ourselves in God, and went right ahead and said our piece, presenting God's Message to you, defiant of the opposition.

NO HIDDEN AGENDAS

3-5 God tested us thoroughly to make sure we were qualified to be trusted with this Message. Be assured that when we speak to you we're not after crowd approval — only God approval. Since we've been put through that battery of tests, you're guaranteed that both we and the Message are free of error, mixed motives, or hidden agendas. We never used words to butter you up. No one knows that better than you. And God knows we never used words as a smoke screen to take advantage of you.

6-8 Even though we had some standing as Christ's apostles, we never threw our weight around or tried to come across as important, with you or anyone else. We weren't aloof with you. We took you just as you were. We were never patronizing, never condescending, but we cared for you the way a mother cares for her children. We loved you dearly. Not content to just pass on the Message, we wanted to give you our hearts. And we *did*.

9-12 You remember us in those days, friends, working our fingers to the bone, up half the night, moonlighting so you wouldn't have the burden of supporting us while we proclaimed God's Message to you. You saw with your own eyes how discreet and courteous we were among you, with keen sensitivity to you as fellow believers. And God knows we weren't free-loaders! You experienced it all firsthand. With each of you we were like a father with his child, holding your hand, whispering encouragement, showing you step-by-step how to live well before God, who called us into his own kingdom, into this delightful life.

13 And now we look back on all this and thank God, an artesian well of thanks! When you got the Message of God we preached, you didn't pass it off as just one more human opinion, but you took it to heart as God's true word to you, which it is, God himself at work in you believers!

14-16 Friends, do you realize that you followed in the exact footsteps of the churches of God in Judea, those who were the first to follow in the foot-steps of Jesus Christ? You got the same bad treatment from your country-men as they did from theirs, the Jews who killed the Master Jesus (to say nothing of the prophets) and followed it up by running us out of town. They make themselves offensive to God and everyone else by trying to keep us from telling people who've never heard of our God how to be saved. They've made a career of opposing God, and have gotten mighty good at it. But God is fed up, ready to put an end to it.

17-20 Do you have any idea how very homesick we became for you, dear friends? Even though it hadn't been that long and it was only our bodies that were separated from you, not our hearts, we tried our very best to get back to see you. You can't imagine how much we missed you! I, Paul, tried over and over to get back, but Satan stymied us each time. Who do you think we're going to be proud of when our Master Jesus appears if it's not you? You're our pride and joy!

1-2 **3** So when we couldn't stand being separated from you any longer and could find no way to visit you ourselves, we stayed in Athens and sent Timothy to get you up and about, cheering you on so you wouldn't be discouraged by these hard times. He's a brother and companion in the faith, God's man in spreading the Message, preaching Christ.

3-5 Not that the troubles should come as any surprise to you. You've al-ways known that we're in for this kind of thing. It's part of our calling. When we were with you, we made it quite clear that there was trouble ahead. And now that it's happened, you know what it's like. That's why I couldn't quit worrying; I had to know for myself how you were doing in the faith. I didn't want the Tempter getting to you and tearing down everything we had built up together.

6-8 But now that Timothy is back, bringing this terrific report on your faith and love, we feel a lot better. It's especially gratifying to know that you continue to think well of us, and that you want to see us as much as we want to see you! In the middle of our trouble and hard times here, just knowing how you're doing keeps us going. Knowing that your faith is alive keeps us alive.

9-10 What would be an adequate thanksgiving to offer God for all the joy we experience before him because of you? We do what we can, praying away, night and day, asking for the bonus of seeing your faces again and doing what we can to help when your faith falters.

11-13 May God our Father himself and our Master Jesus clear the road to you! And may the Master pour on the love so it fills your lives and splashes over on everyone around you, just as it does from us to you. May you be infused with strength and purity, filled with confidence in the presence of God our Father when our Master Jesus arrives with all his followers.

You're God-Taught

1-3 One final word, friends. We ask you — *urge* is more like it — that you keep on doing what we told you to do to please God, not in a dogged religious plod, but in a living, spirited dance. You know the guidelines we laid out for you from the Master Jesus. God wants you to live a pure life.

Keep yourselves from sexual promiscuity.

4-5 Learn to appreciate and give dignity to your body, not abusing it, as is so common among those who know nothing of God.

6-7 Don't run roughshod over the concerns of your brothers and sisters. Their concerns are God's concerns, and *he* will take care of them. We've warned you about this before. God hasn't invited us into a disorderly, unkempt life but into something holy and beautiful — as beautiful on the inside as the outside.

8 If you disregard this advice, you're not offending your neighbors; you're rejecting God, who is making you a gift of his Holy Spirit.

9-10 Regarding life together and getting along with each other, you don't need me to tell you what to do. You're *God*-taught in these matters. Just love one another! You're already good at it; your friends all over the province of Macedonia are the evidence. Keep it up; get better and better at it.

11-12 Stay calm; mind your own business; do your own job. You've heard all this from us before, but a reminder never hurts. We want you living in a way that will command the respect of outsiders, not lying around sponging off your friends.

The Master's Coming

13-14 And regarding the question, friends, that has come up about what happens to those already dead and buried, we don't want you in the dark any longer. First off, you must not carry on over them like people who have nothing to look forward to, as if the grave were the last word. Since Jesus died and broke loose from the grave, God will most certainly bring back to life those who died in Jesus.

15-18 And then this: We can tell you with complete confidence — we have the Master's word on it — that when the Master comes again to get us, those of us who are still alive will not get a jump on the dead and leave them behind. In actual fact, they'll be ahead of us. The Master himself will give the command. Archangel thunder! God's trumpet blast! He'll come down from heaven and the dead in Christ will rise — they'll go first. Then the rest of us who are still alive at the time will be caught up with them into the clouds to meet the Master. Oh, we'll be walking on air! And then there will be one huge family reunion with the Master. So reassure one another with these words.

1-3 5 I don't think, friends, that I need to deal with the question of when all this is going to happen. You know as well as I that the day of the Master's coming can't be posted on our calendars. He won't call ahead and make an appointment any more than a burglar would. About the time everybody's walking around complacently, congratulating each other — "We've sure got it made! Now we can take it easy!" — suddenly everything will fall apart. It's going to come as suddenly and inescapably as birth pangs to a pregnant woman.

4-8 But friends, you're not in the dark, so how could you be taken off guard by any of this? You're sons of Light, daughters of Day. We live under wide open skies and know where we stand. So let's not sleepwalk through life like those others. Let's keep our eyes open and be smart. People sleep at night and get drunk at night. But not us! Since we're creatures of Day, let's act like it. Walk out into the daylight sober, dressed up in faith, love, and the hope of salvation.

9-11 God didn't set us up for an angry rejection but for salvation by our Master, Jesus Christ. He died for us, a death that triggered life. Whether we're awake with the living or asleep with the dead, we're *alive* with him! So speak encouraging words to one another. Build up hope so you'll all be together in this, no one left out, no one left behind. I know you're already doing this; just keep on doing it.

THE WAY HE WANTS YOU TO LIVE

12-13 And now, friends, we ask you to honor those leaders who work so hard for you, who have been given the responsibility of urging and guiding you along in your obedience. Overwhelm them with appreciation and love!

13-15 Get along among yourselves, each of you doing your part. Our counsel is that you warn the freeloaders to get a move on. Gently encourage the stragglers, and reach out for the exhausted, pulling them to their feet. Be patient with each person, attentive to individual needs. And be careful that when you get on each other's nerves you don't snap at each other. Look for the best in each other, and always do your best to bring it out.

16-18 Be cheerful no matter what; pray all the time; thank God no matter what happens. This is the way God wants you who belong to Christ Jesus to live.

19-22 Don't suppress the Spirit, and don't stifle those who have a word from the Master. On the other hand, don't be gullible. Check out everything, and keep only what's good. Throw out anything tainted with evil.

23-24 May God himself, the God who makes everything holy and whole, make you holy and whole, put you together — spirit, soul, and body — and keep you fit for the coming of our Master, Jesus Christ. The One who called you is completely dependable. If he said it, he'll do it!

25-27 Friends, keep up your prayers for us. Greet all the followers of Jesus there with a holy embrace. And make sure this letter gets read to all the brothers and sisters. Don't leave anyone out.

28 The amazing grace of Jesus Christ be with you!

2 THESSALONIANS

1-2   **1** I, Paul, together with Silas and Timothy, greet the church of the Thessalonian Christians in the name of God our Father and our Master, Jesus Christ. Our God gives you everything you need, makes you everything you're to be.

JUSTICE IS ON THE WAY

3-4   You need to know, friends, that thanking God over and over for you is not only a pleasure; it's a must. We *have* to do it. Your faith is growing phenomenally; your love for each other is developing wonderfully. Why, it's only right that we give thanks. We're so proud of you; you're so steady and determined in your faith despite all the hard times that have come down on you. We tell everyone we meet in the churches all about you.

5-10   All this trouble is a clear sign that God has decided to make you fit for the kingdom. You're suffering now, but justice is on the way. When the Master Jesus appears out of heaven in a blaze of fire with his strong angels, he'll even up the score by settling accounts with those who gave you such a bad time. His coming will be the break we've been waiting for. Those who refuse to know God and refuse to obey the Message will pay for what they've done. Eternal exile from the presence of the Master and his splendid power is their sentence. But on that very same day when he comes, he will be exalted by his followers and celebrated by all who believe — and all because you believed what we told you.

11-12   Because we know that this extraordinary day is just ahead, we pray for you all the time — pray that our God will make you fit for what he's called you to be, pray that he'll fill your good ideas and acts of faith with his own energy so that it all amounts to something. If your life honors the name of Jesus, he will honor you. Grace is behind and through all of this, our God giving himself freely, the Master, Jesus Christ, giving himself freely.

THE ANARCHIST

1-3   **2** Now, friends, read these next words carefully. Slow down and don't go jumping to conclusions regarding the day when our Master, Jesus Christ, will come back and we assemble to welcome him. Don't let anyone shake you up or get you excited over some breathless report or rumored letter from me that the day of the Master's arrival has come and gone. Don't fall for any line like that.

3-5   Before that day comes, a couple of things have to happen. First, the Apostasy. Second, the debut of the Anarchist, a real dog of Satan. He'll defy and then take over every so-called god or altar. Having cleared away the opposition, he'll then set himself up in God's Temple as "God Almighty." Don't you remember me going over all this in detail when I was with you? Are your memories that short?

6-8   You'll also remember that I told you the Anarchist is being held back until just the right time. That doesn't mean that the spirit of anarchy is not now at work. It is, secretly and underground. But the time will come when the Anarchist will no longer be held back, but will be let loose. But don't worry. The Master Jesus will be right on his heels and blow him away. The Master appears and — puff! — the Anarchist is out of there.

9-12   The Anarchist's coming is all Satan's work. All his power and signs and miracles are fake, evil sleight of hand that plays to the gallery of those who hate the truth that could save them. And since they're so obsessed with evil, God rubs their noses in it — gives them what they want. Since they refuse to trust truth, they're banished to their chosen world of lies and illusions.

13-14   Meanwhile, we've got our hands full continually thanking God for you, our good friends — so loved by God! God picked you out as his from the very start. Think of it: included in God's original plan of salvation by the bond of faith in the living truth. This is the life of the Spirit he invited you to through the Message we delivered, in which you get in on the glory of our Master, Jesus Christ.

15-17   So, friends, take a firm stand, feet on the ground and head high. Keep a tight grip on what you were taught, whether in personal conversation or by our letter. May Jesus himself and God our Father, who reached out in love and surprised you with gifts of unending help and confidence, put a fresh heart in you, invigorate your work, enliven your speech.

THOSE WHO ARE LAZY

1-3   **3** One more thing, friends: Pray for us. Pray that the Master's Word will simply take off and race through the country to a ground-swell of response, just as it did among you. And pray that we'll be rescued from these scoundrels who are trying to do us in. I'm finding that not all "believers" are believers. But the Master never lets us down. He'll stick by you and protect you from evil.

4-5   Because of the *Master*, we have great confidence in *you*. We know you're doing everything we told you and will continue doing it. May the Master take you by the hand and lead you along the path of God's love and Christ's endurance.

6-9   Our orders — backed up by the Master, Jesus — are to refuse to have anything to do with those among you who are lazy and refuse to work the way we taught you. Don't permit them to freeload on the rest. We showed you how to pull your weight when we were with you, so get on with it. We didn't sit around on our hands expecting others to take care of us. In fact, we worked our fingers to the bone, up half the night moonlighting so you wouldn't be burdened with taking care of us. And it wasn't because we didn't have a right to your support; we did. We simply wanted to provide an example of diligence, hoping it would prove contagious.

10-13   Don't you remember the rule we had when we lived with you? "If you don't work, you don't eat." And now we're getting reports that a bunch of lazy good-for-nothings are taking advantage of you. This must not be tolerated. We command them to get to work immediately — no excuses, no arguments — and earn their own keep. Friends, don't slack off in doing your duty.

14-15   If anyone refuses to obey our clear command written in this letter, don't let him get by with it. Point out such a person and refuse to subsidize his freeloading. Maybe then he'll think twice. But don't treat him as an enemy. Sit him down and talk about the problem as someone who cares.

16   May the Master of Peace himself give you the gift of getting along with each other at all times, in all ways. May the Master be truly among you!

17   I, Paul, bid you good-bye in my own handwriting. I do this in all my letters, so examine my signature as proof that the letter is genuine.

18   The incredible grace of our Master, Jesus Christ, be with all of you!

1 & 2 TIMOTHY & TITUS

Christians are quite serious in believing that when they gather together for worship and work, God is present and sovereign, really present and absolutely sovereign. God creates and guides, God saves and heals, God corrects and blesses, God calls and judges. With such comprehensive and personal leadership from God, what is the place of *human* leadership?

Quite obviously, it has to be second place. It must not elbow its way to the front, it must not bossily take over. Ego-centered, ego-prominent leadership betrays the Master. The best leadership in spiritual communities formed in the name of Jesus, the Messiah, is inconspicuous, not calling attention to itself but not sacrificing anything in the way of conviction and firmness either.

In his letters to two young associates — Timothy in Ephesus and Titus in Crete — we see Paul encouraging and guiding the development of just such leadership. What he had learned so thoroughly himself, he was now passing on, and showing them, in turn, how to develop a similar leadership in local congregations. This is essential reading because ill-directed and badly formed spiritual leadership causes much damage in souls. Paul in both his life and his letters shows us how to do it right.

1 TIMOTHY

1-2 I, Paul, am an apostle on special assignment for Christ, our living hope. Under God our Savior's command, I'm writing this to you, Timothy, my son in the faith. All the best from our God and Christ be yours!

SELF-APPOINTED EXPERTS ON LIFE

3-4 On my way to the province of Macedonia, I advised you to stay in Ephesus. Well, I haven't changed my mind. Stay right there on top of things so that the teaching stays on track. Apparently some people have been introducing fantasy stories and fanciful family trees that digress into silliness instead of pulling the people back into the center, deepening faith and obedience.

5-7 The whole point of what we're urging is simply *love*—love uncontaminated by self-interest and counterfeit faith, a life open to God. Those who fail to keep to this point soon wander off into cul-de-sacs of gossip. They set themselves up as experts on religious issues, but haven't the remotest idea of what they're holding forth with such imposing eloquence.

8-11 It's true that moral guidance and counsel need to be given, but the way you say it and to whom you say it are as important as what you say. It's obvious, isn't it, that the law code isn't primarily for people who live responsibly, but for the irresponsible, who defy all authority, riding roughshod over God, life, sex, truth, whatever! They are contemptuous of this great Message I've been put in charge of by this great God.

12-14 I'm so grateful to Christ Jesus for making me adequate to do this work. He went out on a limb, you know, in trusting me with this ministry. The only credentials I brought to it were invective and witch hunts and arrogance. But I was treated mercifully because I didn't know what I was doing—didn't know Who I was doing it against! Grace mixed with faith and love poured over me and into me. And all because of Jesus.

15-19 Here's a word you can take to heart and depend on: Jesus Christ came into the world to save sinners. I'm proof—Public Sinner Number One—of someone who could never have made it apart from sheer mercy. And now he shows me off—evidence of his endless patience—to those who are right on the edge of trusting him forever.

> Deep honor and bright glory
> to the King of All Time—
> One God, Immortal, Invisible,
> ever and always. Oh, yes!

I'm passing this work on to you, my son Timothy. The prophetic word that was directed to you prepared us for this. All those prayers are coming together now so you will do this well, fearless in your struggle, keeping a firm grip on your faith and on yourself. After all, this is a fight we're in.

19-20 There are some, you know, who by relaxing their grip and thinking anything goes have made a thorough mess of their faith. Hymenaeus and

Alexander are two of them. I let them wander off to Satan to be taught a lesson or two about not blaspheming.

SIMPLE FAITH AND PLAIN TRUTH

1-3 2 The first thing I want you to do is pray. Pray every way you know how, for everyone you know. Pray especially for rulers and their governments to rule well so we can be quietly about our business of living simply, in humble contemplation. This is the way our Savior God wants us to live.

4-7 He wants not only us but *everyone* saved, you know, everyone to get to know the truth *we've* learned: that there's one God and only one, and one Priest-Mediator between God and us — Jesus, who offered himself in exchange for everyone held captive by sin, to set them all free. Eventually the news is going to get out. This and this only has been my appointed work: getting this news to those who have never heard of God, and explaining how it works by simple faith and plain truth.

8-10 Since prayer is at the bottom of all this, what I want mostly is for men to pray — not shaking angry fists at enemies but raising holy hands to God. And I want women to get in there with the men in humility before God, not primping before a mirror or chasing the latest fashions but doing something beautiful for God and becoming beautiful doing it.

11-15 I don't let women take over and tell the men what to do. They should study to be quiet and obedient along with everyone else. Adam was made first, then Eve; woman was deceived first — our pioneer in sin! — with Adam right on her heels. On the other hand, her childbearing brought about salvation, reversing Eve. But this salvation only comes to those who continue in faith, love, and holiness, gathering it all into maturity. You can depend on this.

LEADERSHIP IN THE CHURCH

1-7 3 If anyone wants to provide leadership in the church, good! But there are preconditions: A leader must be well-thought-of, committed to his wife, cool and collected, accessible, and hospitable. He must know what he's talking about, not be overfond of wine, not pushy but gentle, not thin-skinned, not money-hungry. He must handle his own affairs well, attentive to his own children and having their respect. For if someone is unable to handle his own affairs, how can he take care of God's church? He must not be a new believer, lest the position go to his head and the Devil trip him up. Outsiders must think well of him, or else the Devil will figure out a way to lure him into his trap.

8-13 The same goes for those who want to be servants in the church: serious, not deceitful, not too free with the bottle, not in it for what they can get out of it. They must be reverent before the mystery of the faith, not using their position to try to run things. Let them prove themselves first. If they show they can do it, take them on. No exceptions are to be made for women — same qualifications: serious, dependable, not sharp-tongued, not overfond of wine. Servants in the church are to be committed to their spouses, attentive to their own children, and diligent in looking after their own affairs. Those who do this servant work will come to be highly respected, a real credit to this Jesus-faith.

14-16 I hope to visit you soon, but just in case I'm delayed, I'm writing this letter so you'll know how things ought to go in God's household, this God-alive church, bastion of truth. This Christian life is a great mystery, far exceeding our understanding, but some things are clear enough:

> He appeared in a human body,
>   was proved right by the invisible Spirit,
>   was seen by angels.
> He was proclaimed among all kinds of peoples,
>   believed in all over the world,
>   taken up into heavenly glory.

TEACH WITH YOUR LIFE

1-5 **4** The Spirit makes it clear that as time goes on, some are going to give up on the faith and chase after demonic illusions put forth by professional liars. These liars have lied so well and for so long that they've lost their capacity for truth. They will tell you not to get married. They'll tell you not to eat this or that food — perfectly good food God created to be eaten heartily and with thanksgiving by believers who know better! Everything God created is good, and to be received with thanks. Nothing is to be sneered at and thrown out. God's Word and our prayers make every item in creation holy.

6-10 You've been raised on the Message of the faith and have followed sound teaching. Now pass on this counsel to the followers of Jesus there, and you'll be a good servant of Jesus. Stay clear of silly stories that get dressed up as religion. Exercise daily in God — no spiritual flabbiness, please! Workouts in the gymnasium are useful, but a disciplined life in God is far more so, making you fit both today and forever. You can count on this. Take it to heart. This is why we've thrown ourselves into this venture so totally. We're banking on the living God, Savior of all men and women, especially believers.

11-14 Get the word out. Teach all these things. And don't let anyone put you down because you're young. Teach believers with your life: by word, by demeanor, by love, by faith, by integrity. Stay at your post reading Scripture, giving counsel, teaching. And that special gift of ministry you were given when the leaders of the church laid hands on you and prayed — keep that dusted off and in use.

15-16 Cultivate these things. Immerse yourself in them. The people will all see you mature right before their eyes! Keep a firm grasp on both your character and your teaching. Don't be diverted. Just keep at it. Both you and those who hear you will experience salvation.

THE FAMILY OF FAITH

1-2 **5** Don't be harsh or impatient with an older man. Talk to him as you would your own father, and to the younger men as your brothers. Reverently honor an older woman as you would your mother, and the younger women as sisters.

3-8 Take care of widows who are destitute. If a widow has family members to take care of her, let them learn that religion begins at their own doorstep and that they should pay back with gratitude some of what they have received. This pleases God immensely. You can tell a legitimate widow by the way she has put all her hope in God, praying to him constantly for the needs of others as well as her own. But a widow who exploits people's emotions and pocketbooks — well, there's nothing to her. Tell these things to the people so that they will do the right thing in their extended family. Anyone who neglects to care for family members in need repudiates the faith. That's worse than refusing to believe in the first place.

9-10 Sign some widows up for the special ministry of offering assistance. They will in turn receive support from the church. They must be over sixty, married only once, and have a reputation for helping out with children, strangers, tired Christians, the hurt and troubled.

11-15 Don't put young widows on this list. No sooner will they get on than they'll want to get off, obsessed with wanting to get a husband rather than serving Christ in this way. By breaking their word, they're liable to go from bad to worse, frittering away their days on empty talk, gossip, and trivialities. No, I'd rather the young widows go ahead and get married in the first place, have children, manage their homes, and not give critics any foothold for finding fault. Some of them have already left and gone after Satan.

16 Any Christian woman who has widows in her family is responsible for them. They shouldn't be dumped on the church. The church has its hands full already with widows who need help.

17-18 Give a bonus to leaders who do a good job, especially the ones who work hard at preaching and teaching. Scripture tells us, "Don't muzzle a working ox" and "A worker deserves his pay."

19 Don't listen to a complaint against a leader that isn't backed up by two or three responsible witnesses.

20 If anyone falls into sin, call that person on the carpet. Those who are inclined that way will know right off they can't get by with it.

21-23 God and Jesus and angels all back me up in these instructions. Carry them out without favoritism, without taking sides. Don't appoint people to church leadership positions too hastily. If a person is involved in some serious sins, you don't want to become an unwitting accomplice. In any event, keep a close check on yourself. And don't worry too much about what the critics will say. Go ahead and drink a little wine, for instance; it's good for your digestion, good medicine for what ails you.

24-25 The sins of some people are blatant and march them right into court. The sins of others don't show up until much later. The same with good deeds. Some you see right off, but none are hidden forever.

1-2 **6** Whoever is a slave must make the best of it, giving respect to his master so that outsiders don't blame God and our teaching for his behavior. Slaves with Christian masters all the more so — their masters are really their beloved brothers!

The Lust for Money

2-5 These are the things I want you to teach and preach. If you have leaders there who teach otherwise, who refuse the solid words of our Master Jesus and this godly instruction, tag them for what they are: ignorant windbags who infect the air with germs of envy, controversy, bad-mouthing, suspicious rumors. Eventually there's an epidemic of backstabbing, and truth is but a distant memory. They think religion is a way to make a fast buck.

6-8   A devout life does bring wealth, but it's the rich simplicity of being yourself before God. Since we entered the world penniless and will leave it penniless, if we have bread on the table and shoes on our feet, that's enough.

9-10   But if it's only money these leaders are after, they'll self-destruct in no time. Lust for money brings trouble and nothing but trouble. Going down that path, some lose their footing in the faith completely and live to regret it bitterly ever after.

RUNNING HARD

11-12   But you, Timothy, man of God: Run for your life from all this. Pursue a righteous life — a life of wonder, faith, love, steadiness, courtesy. Run hard and fast in the faith. Seize the eternal life, the life you were called to, the life you so fervently embraced in the presence of so many witnesses.

13-16   I'm charging you before the life-giving God and before Christ, who took his stand before Pontius Pilate and didn't give an inch: Keep this command to the letter, and don't slack off. Our Master, Jesus Christ, is on his way. He'll show up right on time, his arrival guaranteed by the Blessed and Undisputed Ruler, High King, High God. He's the only one death can't touch, his light so bright no one can get close. He's never been seen by human eyes — human eyes can't take him in! Honor to him, and eternal rule! Oh, yes.

17-19   Tell those rich in this world's wealth to quit being so full of themselves and so obsessed with money, which is here today and gone tomorrow. Tell them to go after God, who piles on all the riches we could ever manage — to do good, to be rich in helping others, to be extravagantly generous. If they do that, they'll build a treasury that will last, gaining life that is truly life.

20-21   And oh, my dear Timothy, guard the treasure you were given! Guard it with your life. Avoid the talk-show religion and the practiced confusion of the so-called experts. People caught up in a lot of talk can miss the whole point of faith.

Overwhelming grace keep you!

2 TIMOTHY

1-2 I, Paul, am on special assignment for Christ, carrying out God's plan laid out in the Message of Life by Jesus. I write this to you, Timothy, the son I love so much. All the best from our God and Christ be yours!

TO BE BOLD WITH GOD'S GIFTS

3-4 Every time I say your name in prayer — which is practically all the time — I thank God for you, the God I worship with my whole life in the tradition of my ancestors. I miss you a lot, especially when I remember that last tearful good-bye, and I look forward to a joy-packed reunion.

5-7 That precious memory triggers another: your honest faith — and what a rich faith it is, handed down from your grandmother Lois to your mother Eunice, and now to you! And the special gift of ministry you received when I laid hands on you and prayed — keep that ablaze! God doesn't want us to be shy with his gifts, but bold and loving and sensible.

8-10 So don't be embarrassed to speak up for our Master or for me, his prisoner. Take your share of suffering for the Message along with the rest of us. We can only keep on going, after all, by the power of God, who first saved us and then called us to this holy work. We had nothing to do with it. It was all *his* idea, a gift prepared for us in Jesus long before we knew anything about it. But we know it now. Since the appearance of our Savior, nothing could be plainer: death defeated, life vindicated in a steady blaze of light, all through the work of Jesus.

11-12 This is the Message I've been set apart to proclaim as preacher, emissary, and teacher. It's also the cause of all this trouble I'm in. But I have no regrets. I couldn't be more sure of my ground — the One I've trusted in can take care of what he's trusted me to do right to the end.

13-14 So keep at your work, this faith and love rooted in Christ, exactly as I set it out for you. It's as sound as the day you first heard it from me. Guard this precious thing placed in your custody by the Holy Spirit who works in us.

15-18 I'm sure you know by now that everyone in the province of Asia deserted me, even Phygelus and Hermogenes. But God bless Onesiphorus and his family! Many's the time I've been refreshed in that house. And he wasn't embarrassed a bit that I was in jail. The first thing he did when he got to Rome was look me up. May God on the Last Day treat him as well as he treated me. And then there was all the help he provided in Ephesus — but you know that better than I.

DOING YOUR BEST FOR GOD

1-7 So, my son, throw yourself into this work for Christ. Pass on what you heard from me — the whole congregation saying Amen! — to reliable leaders who are competent to teach others. When the going gets rough, take it on the chin with the rest of us, the way Jesus did. A soldier on duty doesn't get caught up in making deals at the marketplace. He concentrates on carrying out orders. An athlete who refuses to play by the rules will never get anywhere. It's the diligent farmer who gets the produce. Think it over. God will make it all plain.

8-13 Fix this picture firmly in your mind: Jesus, descended from the line

of David, raised from the dead. It's what you've heard from me all along. It's
what I'm sitting in jail for right now—but God's Word isn't in jail! That's
why I stick it out here—so that everyone God calls will get in on the salvation of Christ in all its glory. This is a sure thing:

> If we die with him, we'll live with him;
> If we stick it out with him, we'll rule with him;
> If we turn our backs on him, he'll turn his back on us;
> If we give up on him, he does not give up—
> for there's no way he can be false to himself.

14-18 Repeat these basic essentials over and over to God's people. Warn
them before God against pious nitpicking, which chips away at the faith.
It just wears everyone out. Concentrate on doing your best for God, work
you won't be ashamed of, laying out the truth plain and simple. Stay clear of
pious talk that is only talk. Words are not mere words, you know. If they're
not backed by a godly life, they accumulate as poison in the soul. Hymenaeus
and Philetus are examples, throwing believers off stride and missing the
truth by a mile by saying the resurrection is over and done with.

19 Meanwhile, God's firm foundation is as firm as ever, these sentences engraved on the stones:

GOD KNOWS WHO BELONGS TO HIM.
SPURN EVIL, ALL YOU WHO NAME GOD AS GOD.

20-21 In a well-furnished kitchen there are not only crystal goblets and
silver platters, but waste cans and compost buckets—some containers used
to serve fine meals, others to take out the garbage. Become the kind of con-
tainer God can use to present any and every kind of gift to his guests for
their blessing.

22-26 Run away from infantile indulgence. Run after mature righteousness—faith, love, peace—joining those who are in honest and serious
prayer before God. Refuse to get involved in inane discussions; they always
end up in fights. God's servant must not be argumentative, but a gentle
listener and a teacher who keeps cool, working firmly but patiently with
those who refuse to obey. You never know how or when God might sober
them up with a change of heart and a turning to the truth, enabling them
to escape the Devil's trap, where they are caught and held captive, forced to
run his errands.

DIFFICULT TIMES AHEAD

1-5 **3** Don't be naive. There are difficult times ahead. As the end ap-
proaches, people are going to be self-absorbed, money-hungry, self-
promoting, stuck-up, profane, contemptuous of parents, crude,
coarse, dog-eat-dog, unbending, slanderers, impulsively wild, savage, cynical,
treacherous, ruthless, bloated windbags, addicted to lust, and allergic to God.
They'll make a show of religion, but behind the scenes they're animals. Stay
clear of these people.

6-9 These are the kind of people who smooth-talk themselves into the homes
of unstable and needy women and take advantage of them; women who,
depressed by their sinfulness, take up with every new religious fad that calls

itself "truth." They get exploited every time and never really learn. These men are like those old Egyptian frauds Jannes and Jambres, who challenged Moses. They were rejects from the faith, twisted in their thinking, defying truth itself. But nothing will come of these latest impostors. Everyone will see through them, just as people saw through that Egyptian hoax.

KEEP THE MESSAGE ALIVE

10-13 You've been a good apprentice to me, a part of my teaching, my manner of life, direction, faith, steadiness, love, patience, troubles, sufferings — suffering along with me in all the grief I had to put up with in Antioch, Iconium, and Lystra. And you also well know that God rescued me! Anyone who wants to live all out for Christ is in for a lot of trouble; there's no getting around it. Unscrupulous con men will continue to exploit the faith. They're as deceived as the people they lead astray. As long as they are out there, things can only get worse.

14-17 But don't let it faze you. Stick with what you learned and believed, sure of the integrity of your teachers — why, you took in the sacred Scriptures with your mother's milk! There's nothing like the written Word of God for showing you the way to salvation through faith in Christ Jesus. Every part of Scripture is God-breathed and useful one way or another — showing us truth, exposing our rebellion, correcting our mistakes, training us to live God's way. Through the Word we are put together and shaped up for the tasks God has for us.

1-2 4 I can't impress this on you too strongly. God is looking over your shoulder. Christ himself is the Judge, with the final say on everyone, living and dead. He is about to break into the open with his rule, so proclaim the Message with intensity; keep on your watch. Challenge, warn, and urge your people. Don't ever quit. Just keep it simple.

3-5 You're going to find that there will be times when people will have no stomach for solid teaching, but will fill up on spiritual junk food — catchy opinions that tickle their fancy. They'll turn their backs on truth and chase mirages. But you — keep your eye on what you're doing; accept the hard times along with the good; keep the Message alive; do a thorough job as God's servant.

6-8 You take over. I'm about to die, my life an offering on God's altar. This is the only race worth running. I've run hard right to the finish, believed all the way. All that's left now is the shouting — God's applause! Depend on it, he's an honest judge. He'll do right not only by me, but by everyone eager for his coming.

9-13 Get here as fast as you can. Demas, chasing fads, went off to Thessalonica and left me here. Crescens is in Galatia province, Titus in Dalmatia. Luke is the only one here with me. Bring Mark with you; he'll be my right-hand man since I'm sending Tychicus to Ephesus. Bring the winter coat I left in Troas with Carpus; also the books and parchment notebooks.

14-15 Watch out for Alexander the coppersmith. Fiercely opposed to our Message, he caused no end of trouble. God will give him what he's got coming.

16-18 At my preliminary hearing no one stood by me. They all ran like scared rabbits. But it doesn't matter — the Master stood by me and helped me spread the Message loud and clear to those who had never heard it. I was snatched from the jaws of the lion! God's looking after me, keeping me safe in the kingdom of heaven. All praise to him, praise forever! Oh, yes!

19-20 Say hello to Priscilla and Aquila; also, the family of Onesiphorus. Erastus stayed behind in Corinth. I had to leave Trophimus sick in Miletus.

21 Try hard to get here before winter.

Eubulus, Pudens, Linus, Claudia, and all your friends here send greetings.

22 God be with you. Grace be with you.

TITUS

1-4 **1** I, Paul, am God's slave and Christ's agent for promoting the faith among God's chosen people, getting out the accurate word on God and how to respond rightly to it. My aim is to raise hopes by pointing the way to life without end. This is the life God promised long ago — and he doesn't break promises! And then when the time was ripe, he went public with his truth. I've been entrusted to proclaim this Message by order of our Savior, God himself. Dear Titus, legitimate son in the faith: Receive everything God our Father and Jesus our Savior give you!

A GOOD GRIP ON THE MESSAGE

5-9 I left you in charge in Crete so you could complete what I left half-done. Appoint leaders in every town according to my instructions. As you select them, ask, "Is this man well-thought-of? Is he committed to his wife? Are his children believers? Do they respect him and stay out of trouble?" It's important that a church leader, responsible for the affairs in God's house, be looked up to — not pushy, not short-tempered, not a drunk, not a bully, not money-hungry. He must welcome people, be helpful, wise, fair, reverent, have a good grip on himself, and have a good grip on the Message, knowing how to use the truth to either spur people on in knowledge or stop them in their tracks if they oppose it.

10-16 For there are a lot of rebels out there, full of loose, confusing, and deceiving talk. Those who were brought up religious and ought to know better are the worst. They've got to be shut up. They're disrupting entire families with their teaching, and all for the sake of a fast buck. One of their own prophets said it best:

The Cretans are liars from the womb,
barking dogs, lazy bellies.

He certainly spoke the truth. Get on them right away. Stop that diseased talk of Jewish make-believe and made-up rules so they can recover a robust faith. Everything is clean to the clean-minded; nothing is clean to dirty-minded unbelievers. They leave their dirty fingerprints on every thought and act. They say they know God, but their actions speak louder than their words. They're real creeps, disobedient good-for-nothings.

A GOD-FILLED LIFE

1-6 **2** Your job is to speak out on the things that make for solid doctrine. Guide older men into lives of temperance, dignity, and wisdom, into healthy faith, love, and endurance. Guide older women into lives of reverence so they end up as neither gossips nor drunks, but models of goodness. By looking at them, the younger women will know how to love their husbands and children, be virtuous and pure, keep a good house, be good wives. We don't want anyone looking down on God's Message because of their behavior. Also, guide the young men to live disciplined lives.

7-8 But mostly, show them all this by doing it yourself, incorruptible in your teaching, your words solid and sane. Then anyone who is dead set against us, when he finds nothing weird or misguided, might eventually come around.

9-10   Guide slaves into being loyal workers, a bonus to their masters—no back talk, no petty thievery. Then their good character will shine through their actions, adding luster to the teaching of our Savior God.

11-14   God's readiness to give and forgive is now public. Salvation's available for everyone! We're being shown how to turn our backs on a godless, indulgent life, and how to take on a God-filled, God-honoring life. This new life is starting right now, and is whetting our appetites for the glorious day when our great God and Savior, Jesus Christ, appears. He offered himself as a sacrifice to free us from a dark, rebellious life into this good, pure life, making us a people he can be proud of, energetic in goodness.

15   Tell them all this. Build up their courage, and discipline them if they get out of line. You're in charge. Don't let anyone put you down.

He Put Our Lives Together

1-2   3 Remind the people to respect the government and be law-abiding, always ready to lend a helping hand. No insults, no fights. God's people should be bighearted and courteous.

3-8   It wasn't so long ago that we ourselves were stupid and stubborn, dupes of sin, ordered every which way by our glands, going around with a chip on our shoulder, hated and hating back. But when God, our kind and loving Savior God, stepped in, he saved us from all that. It was all his doing; we had nothing to do with it. He gave us a good bath, and we came out of it new people, washed inside and out by the Holy Spirit. Our Savior Jesus poured out new life so generously. God's gift has restored our relationship with him and given us back our lives. And there's more life to come—an eternity of life! You can count on this.

8-11   I want you to put your foot down. Take a firm stand on these matters so that those who have put their trust in God will concentrate on the essentials that are good for everyone. Stay away from mindless, pointless quarreling over genealogies and fine print in the law code. That gets you nowhere. Warn a quarrelsome person once or twice, but then be done with him. It's obvious that such a person is out of line, rebellious against God. By persisting in divisiveness he cuts himself off.

12-13   As soon as I send either Artemas or Tychicus to you, come immediately and meet me in Nicopolis. I've decided to spend the winter there. Give Zenas the lawyer and Apollos a hearty send-off. Take good care of them.

14   Our people have to learn to be diligent in their work so that all necessities are met (especially among the needy) and they don't end up with nothing to show for their lives.

15   All here want to be remembered to you. Say hello to our friends in the faith. Grace to all of you.

PHILEMON

Every movement we make in response to God has a ripple effect, touching family, neighbors, friends, community. Belief in God alters our language. Love of God affects daily relationships. Hope in God enters into our work. Also their opposites — unbelief, indifference, and despair. None of these movements and responses, beliefs and prayers, gestures and searches, can be confined to the soul. They spill out and make history. If they don't, they are under suspicion of being fantasies at best, hypocrisies at worst.

Christians have always insisted on the historicity of Jesus — an actual birth, a datable death, a witnessed resurrection, locatable towns. There is a parallel historicity in the followers of Jesus. As they take in everything Jesus said and did — all of it a personal revelation of God in time and place — it all gets worked into local history, eventually into world history.

Philemon and Onesimus, the slave owner and slave who figure prominently in this letter from Paul, had no idea that believing in Jesus would involve them in radical social change. But as the two of them were brought together by this letter, it did. And it still does.

PHILEMON

1-3   I, Paul, am a prisoner for the sake of Christ, here with my brother Timothy. I write this letter to you, Philemon, my good friend and companion in this work — also to our sister Apphia, to Archippus, a real trooper, and to the church that meets in your house. God's best to you! Christ's blessings on you!

4-7   Every time your name comes up in my prayers, I say, "Oh, thank you, God!" I keep hearing of the love and faith you have for the Master Jesus, which brims over to other believers. And I keep praying that this faith we hold in common keeps showing up in the good things we do, and that people recognize Christ in all of it. Friend, you have no idea how good your love makes me feel, doubly so when I see your hospitality to fellow believers.

To Call the Slave Your Friend

8-9   In line with all this I have a favor to ask of you. As Christ's ambassador and now a prisoner for him, I wouldn't hesitate to command this if I thought it necessary, but I'd rather make it a personal request.

10-14   While here in jail, I've fathered a child, so to speak. And here he is, hand-carrying this letter — Onesimus! He was useless to you before; now he's useful to both of us. I'm sending him back to you, but it feels like I'm cutting off my right arm in doing so. I wanted in the worst way to keep him here as your stand-in to help out while I'm in jail for the Message. But I didn't want to do anything behind your back, make you do a good deed that you hadn't willingly agreed to.

15-16   Maybe it's all for the best that you lost him for a while. You're getting him back now for good — and no mere slave this time, but a true Christian brother! That's what he was to me — he'll be even more than that to you.

17-20   So if you still consider me a comrade-in-arms, welcome him back as you would me. If he damaged anything or owes you anything, chalk it up to my account. This is my personal signature — Paul — and I stand behind it. (I don't need to remind you, do I, that you owe your very life to me?) Do me this big favor, friend. You'll be doing it for Christ, but it will also do my heart good.

21-22   I know you well enough to know you will. You'll probably go far beyond what I've written. And by the way, get a room ready for me. Because of your prayers, I fully expect to be your guest again.

23-25   Epaphras, my cellmate in the cause of Christ, says hello. Also my coworkers Mark, Aristarchus, Demas, and Luke. All the best to you from the Master, Jesus Christ!

HEBREWS

It seems odd to have to say so, but too much religion is a bad thing. We can't get too much of God, can't get too much faith and obedience, can't get too much love and worship. But *religion* — the well-intentioned efforts we make to "get it all together" for God — can very well get in the way of what God is doing for us. The main and central action is everywhere and always *what God has done, is doing, and will do for us.* Jesus is the revelation of that action. Our main and central task is to live in responsive obedience to God's action revealed in Jesus. Our part in the action is the act of faith.

But more often than not we become impatiently self-important along the way and decide to improve matters with our two cents' worth. We add on, we supplement, we embellish. But instead of improving on the purity and simplicity of Jesus, we dilute the purity, clutter the simplicity. We become fussily religious, or anxiously religious. We get in the way.

That's when it's time to read and pray our way through the letter to the Hebrews again, written for "too religious" Christians, for "Jesus-and" Christians. In the letter, it is Jesus-and-angels, or Jesus-and-Moses, or Jesus-and-priesthood. In our time it is more likely to be Jesus-and-politics, or Jesus-and-education, or even Jesus-and-Buddha. This letter deletes the hyphens, the add-ons. The focus becomes clear and sharp again: God's action in Jesus. And we are free once more for the act of faith, the one human action in which we don't get *in* the way but *on* the Way.

HEBREWS

1-3 Going through a long line of prophets, God has been addressing our ancestors in different ways for centuries. Recently he spoke to us directly through his Son. By his Son, God created the world in the beginning, and it will all belong to the Son at the end. This Son perfectly mirrors God, and is stamped with God's nature. He holds everything together by what he says — powerful words!

THE SON IS HIGHER THAN ANGELS

3-6 After he finished the sacrifice for sins, the Son took his honored place high in the heavens right alongside God, far higher than any angel in rank and rule. Did God ever say to an angel, "You're my Son; today I celebrate you" or "I'm his Father, he's my Son"? When he presents his honored Son to the world, he says, "All angels must worship him."

7 Regarding angels he says,

The messengers are winds,
the servants are tongues of fire.

8-9 But he says to the Son,
You're God, and on the throne for good;
your rule makes everything right.
You love it when things are right;
you hate it when things are wrong.
That is why God, your God,
poured fragrant oil on your head,
Marking you out as king,
far above your dear companions.

10-12 And again to the Son,
You, Master, started it all, laid earth's foundations,
then crafted the stars in the sky.
Earth and sky will wear out, but not you;
they become threadbare like an old coat;
You'll fold them up like a worn-out cloak,
and lay them away on the shelf.
But you'll stay the same, year after year;
you'll never fade, you'll never wear out.

13 And did he ever say anything like this to an angel?
Sit alongside me here on my throne
Until I make your enemies a stool for your feet.

14 Isn't it obvious that all angels are sent to help out with those lined up to receive salvation?

1-4 It's crucial that we keep a firm grip on what we've heard so that we don't drift off. If the old message delivered by the angels was valid and nobody got away with anything, do you think we can risk neglecting this latest message, this magnificent salvation? First of all, it was delivered in person by the Master, then accurately passed on to us by those who heard it from him. All the while God was validating it with gifts through the Holy Spirit, all sorts of signs and miracles, as he saw fit.

THE SALVATION PIONEER

5-9 God didn't put angels in charge of this business of salvation that we're dealing with here. It says in Scripture,

> What is man and woman that you bother with them;
>   why take a second look their way?
> You made them not quite as high as angels,
>   bright with Eden's dawn light;
> Then you put them in charge
>   of your entire handcrafted world.

When God put them in charge of everything, nothing was excluded. But we don't see it yet, don't see everything under human jurisdiction. What we do see is Jesus, made "not quite as high as angels," and then, through the experience of death, crowned so much higher than any angel, with a glory "bright with Eden's dawn light." In that death, by God's grace, he fully experienced death in every person's place.

10-13 It makes good sense that the God who got everything started and keeps everything going now completes the work by making the Salvation Pioneer perfect through suffering as he leads all these people to glory. Since the One who saves and those who are saved have a common origin, Jesus doesn't hesitate to treat them as family, saying,

> I'll tell my good friends, my brothers and sisters, all I know
>   about you;
> I'll join them in worship and praise to you.

Again, he puts himself in the same family circle when he says,
> Even *I* live by placing my trust in God.

And yet again,
> I'm here with the children God gave me.

14-15 Since the children are made of flesh and blood, it's logical that the Savior took on flesh and blood in order to rescue them by his death. By embracing death, taking it into himself, he destroyed the Devil's hold on death and freed all who cower through life, scared to death of death.

16-18 It's obvious, of course, that he didn't go to all this trouble for angels. It was for people like us, children of Abraham. That's why he had to enter into every detail of human life. Then, when he came before God as high priest to get rid of the people's sins, he would have already experienced it all himself — all the pain, all the testing — and would be able to help where help was needed.

THE CENTERPIECE OF ALL WE BELIEVE

1-6   So, my dear Christian friends, companions in following this call to the heights, take a good hard look at Jesus. He's the centerpiece of everything we believe, faithful in everything God gave him to do. Moses was also faithful, but Jesus gets far more honor. A builder is more valuable than a building any day. Every house has a builder, but the Builder behind them all is God. Moses did a good job in God's house, but it was all servant work, getting things ready for what was to come. Christ as Son is in charge of the house.

6-11   Now, if we can only keep a firm grip on this bold confidence, we're the house! That's why the Holy Spirit says,

> Today, please listen;
>   don't turn a deaf ear as in "the bitter uprising,"
>   that time of wilderness testing!
> Even though they watched me at work for forty years,
>   your ancestors refused to let me do it my way;
>   over and over they tried my patience.
> And I was provoked, oh, so provoked!
>   I said, "They'll never keep their minds on God;
>   they refuse to walk down my road."
> Exasperated, I vowed,
>   "They'll never get where they're going,
>   never be able to sit down and rest."

12-14   So watch your step, friends. Make sure there's no evil unbelief lying around that will trip you up and throw you off course, diverting you from the living God. For as long as it's still God's Today, keep each other on your toes so sin doesn't slow down your reflexes. If we can only keep our grip on the sure thing we started out with, we're in this with Christ for the long haul.

These words keep ringing in our ears:

> Today, please listen;
>   don't turn a deaf ear as in the bitter uprising.

15-19   For who were the people who turned a deaf ear? Weren't they the very ones Moses led out of Egypt? And who was God provoked with for forty years? Wasn't it those who turned a deaf ear and ended up corpses in the wilderness? And when he swore that they'd never get where they were going, wasn't he talking to the ones who turned a deaf ear? They never got there because they never listened, never believed.

WHEN THE PROMISES ARE MIXED WITH FAITH

1-3   For as long, then, as that promise of resting in him pulls us on to God's goal for us, we need to be careful that we're not disqualified. We received the same promises as those people in the wilderness, but the promises didn't do them a bit of good because they didn't receive the promises with faith. If we believe, though, we'll experience that state of resting. But not if we don't have faith. Remember that God said,

Exasperated, I vowed,
"They'll never get where they're going,
never be able to sit down and rest."

3-7 God made that vow, even though he'd finished *his* part before the foundation of the world. Somewhere it's written, "God rested the seventh day, having completed his work," but in this other text he says, "They'll never be able to sit down and rest." So this promise has not yet been fulfilled. Those earlier ones never did get to the place of rest because they were disobedient. God keeps renewing the promise and setting the date as *today*, just as he did in David's psalm, centuries later than the original invitation:

Today, please listen,
don't turn a deaf ear . . .

8-11 And so this is still a live promise. It wasn't canceled at the time of Joshua; otherwise, God wouldn't keep renewing the appointment for "today." The promise of "arrival" and "rest" is still there for God's people. God himself is at rest. And at the end of the journey we'll surely rest with God. So let's keep at it and eventually arrive at the place of rest, not drop out through some sort of disobedience.

12-13 God means what he says. What he says goes. His powerful Word is sharp as a surgeon's scalpel, cutting through everything, whether doubt or defense, laying us open to listen and obey. Nothing and no one is impervious to God's Word. We can't get away from it — no matter what.

THE HIGH PRIEST WHO CRIED OUT IN PAIN

14-16 Now that we know what we have — Jesus, this great High Priest with ready access to God — let's not let it slip through our fingers. We don't have a priest who is out of touch with our reality. He's been through weakness and testing, experienced it all — all but the sin. So let's walk right up to him and get what he is so ready to give. Take the mercy, accept the help.

1-3 5 Every high priest selected to represent men and women before God and offer sacrifices for their sins should be able to deal gently with their failings, since he knows what it's like from his own experience. But that also means that he has to offer sacrifices for his own sins as well as the peoples'.

4-6 No one elects himself to this honored position. He's called to it by God, as Aaron was. Neither did Christ presume to set himself up as high priest, but was set apart by the One who said to him, "You're my Son; today I celebrate you!" In another place God declares, "You're a priest forever in the royal order of Melchizedek."

7-10 While he lived on earth, anticipating death, Jesus cried out in pain and wept in sorrow as he offered up priestly prayers to God. Because he honored God, God answered him. Though he was God's Son, he learned trusting-obedience by what he suffered, just as we do. Then, having arrived at the full stature of his maturity and having been announced by God as high priest in the order of Melchizedek, he became the source of eternal salvation to all who believingly obey him.

RE-CRUCIFYING JESUS

¹¹⁻¹⁴ I have a lot more to say about this, but it is hard to get it across to you since you've picked up this bad habit of not listening. By this time you ought to be teachers yourselves, yet here I find you need someone to sit down with you and go over the basics on God again, starting from square one — baby's milk, when you should have been on solid food long ago! Milk is for beginners, inexperienced in God's ways; solid food is for the mature, who have some practice in telling right from wrong.

¹⁻³ 6 So come on, let's leave the preschool fingerpainting exercises on Christ and get on with the grand work of art. Grow up in Christ. The basic foundational truths are in place: turning your back on "salvation by self-help" and turning in trust toward God; baptismal instructions; laying on of hands; resurrection of the dead; eternal judgment. God helping us, we'll stay true to all that. But there's so much more. Let's get on with it!

⁴⁻⁸ Once people have seen the light, gotten a taste of heaven and been part of the work of the Holy Spirit, once they've personally experienced the sheer goodness of God's Word and the powers breaking in on us — if then they turn their backs on it, washing their hands of the whole thing, well, they can't start over as if nothing happened. That's impossible. Why, they've re-crucified Jesus! They've repudiated him in public! Parched ground that soaks up the rain and then produces an abundance of carrots and corn for its gardener gets God's "Well done!" But if it produces weeds and thistles, it's more likely to get cussed out. Fields like that are burned, not harvested.

⁹⁻¹² I'm sure that won't happen to you, friends. I have better things in mind for you — salvation things! God doesn't miss anything. He knows perfectly well all the love you've shown him by helping needy Christians, and that you keep at it. And now I want each of you to extend that same intensity toward a full-bodied hope, and keep at it till the finish. Don't drag your feet. Be like those who stay the course with committed faith and then get everything promised to them.

GOD GAVE HIS WORD

¹³⁻¹⁸ When God made his promise to Abraham, he backed it to the hilt, putting his own reputation on the line. He said, "I promise that I'll bless you with everything I have — bless and bless and bless!" Abraham stuck it out and got everything that had been promised to him. When people make promises, they guarantee them by appeal to some authority above them so that if there is any question that they'll make good on the promise, the authority will back them up. When God wanted to guarantee his promises, he gave his word, a rock-solid guarantee — God *can't* break his word. And because his word cannot change, the promise is likewise unchangeable.

¹⁸⁻²⁰ We who have run for our very lives to God have every reason to grab the promised hope with both hands and never let go. It's an unbreakable spiritual lifeline, reaching past all appearances right to the very presence of God where Jesus, running on ahead of us, has taken up his permanent post as high priest for us, in the order of Melchizedek.

MELCHIZEDEK, PRIEST OF GOD

1-3 **7** **M**elchizedek was king of Salem and priest of the Highest God. He met Abraham, who was returning from "the royal massacre," and gave him his blessing. Abraham in turn gave him a tenth of the spoils. "Melchizedek" means "King of Righteousness." "Salem" means "Peace." So, he is also "King of Peace." Melchizedek towers out of the past — without record of family ties, no account of beginning or end. In this way he is like the Son of God, one huge priestly presence dominating the landscape always.

4-7 You realize just how great Melchizedek is when you see that Father Abraham gave him a tenth of the captured treasure. Priests descended from Levi are commanded by law to collect tithes from the people, even though they are all more or less equals, priests and people, having a common father in Abraham. But this man, a complete outsider, collected tithes from Abraham and blessed him, the one to whom the promises had been given. In acts of blessing, the lesser is blessed by the greater.

8-10 Or look at it this way: We pay our tithes to priests who die, but Abraham paid tithes to a priest who, the Scripture says, "lives." Ultimately you could even say that since Levi descended from Abraham, who paid tithes to Melchizedek, when we pay tithes to the priestly tribe of Levi they end up with Melchizedek.

A PERMANENT PRIESTHOOD

11-14 If the priesthood of Levi and Aaron, which provided the framework for the giving of the law, could really make people perfect, there wouldn't have been need for a new priesthood like that of Melchizedek. But since it didn't get the job done, there was a change of priesthood, which brought with it a radical new kind of law. There is no way of understanding this in terms of the old Levitical priesthood, which is why there is nothing in Jesus' family tree connecting him with that priestly line.

15-19 But the Melchizedek story provides a perfect analogy: Jesus, a priest like Melchizedek, not by genealogical descent but by the sheer force of resurrection life — he lives! — "priest forever in the royal order of Melchizedek." The former way of doing things, a system of commandments that never worked out the way it was supposed to, was set aside; the law brought nothing to maturity. Another way — Jesus! — a way that *does* work, that brings us right into the presence of God, is put in its place.

20-22 The old priesthood of Aaron perpetuated itself automatically, father to son, without explicit confirmation by God. But then God intervened and called this new, permanent priesthood into being with an added promise:

God gave his word;
  he won't take it back:
"You're the permanent priest."

This makes Jesus the guarantee of a far better way between us and God — one that really works! A new covenant.

23-25 Earlier there were a lot of priests, for they died and had to be replaced. But Jesus' priesthood is permanent. He's there from now to eternity to save everyone who comes to God through him, always on the job to speak up for them.

26-28 So now we have a high priest who perfectly fits our needs: completely holy, uncompromised by sin, with authority extending as high as God's presence in heaven itself. Unlike the other high priests, he doesn't have to offer sacrifices for his own sins every day before he can get around to us and our sins. He's done it, once and for all: offered up *himself* as the sacrifice. The law appoints as high priests men who are never able to get the job done right. But this intervening command of God, which came later, appoints the Son, who is absolutely, eternally perfect.

A New Plan with Israel

1-2 In essence, we have just such a high priest: authoritative right alongside God, conducting worship in the one true sanctuary built by God.

3-5 The assigned task of a high priest is to offer both gifts and sacrifices, and it's no different with the priesthood of Jesus. If he were limited to earth, he wouldn't even be a priest. We wouldn't need him since there are plenty of priests who offer the gifts designated in the law. These priests provide only a hint of what goes on in the true sanctuary of heaven, which Moses caught a glimpse of as he was about to set up the tent-shrine. It was then that God said, "Be careful to do it exactly as you saw it on the Mountain."

6-13 But Jesus' priestly work far surpasses what these other priests do, since he's working from a far better plan. If the first plan — the old covenant — had worked out, a second wouldn't have been needed. But we know the first was found wanting, because God said,

> Heads up! The days are coming
>   when I'll set up a new plan
>   for dealing with Israel and Judah.
> I'll throw out the old plan
>   I set up with their ancestors
>   when I led them by the hand out of Egypt.
> They didn't keep their part of the bargain,
>   so I looked away and let it go.
> This new plan I'm making with Israel
>   isn't going to be written on paper,
>   isn't going to be chiseled in stone;
> This time I'm writing out the plan *in* them,
>   carving it on the lining of their hearts.
> I'll be their God,
>   they'll be my people.
> They won't go to school to learn about me,
>   or buy a book called *God in Five Easy Lessons*.
> They'll all get to know me firsthand,
>   the little and the big, the small and the great.
> They'll get to know me by being kindly forgiven,
>   with the slate of their sins forever wiped clean.

By coming up with a new plan, a new covenant between God and his people, God put the old plan on the shelf. And there it stays, gathering dust.

A Visible Parable

1-5   **9** That first plan contained directions for worship, and a specially designed place of worship. A large outer tent was set up. The lampstand, the table, and "the bread of presence" were placed in it. This was called "the Holy Place." Then a curtain was stretched, and behind it a smaller, inside tent set up. This was called "the Holy of Holies." In it were placed the gold incense altar and the gold-covered ark of the covenant containing the gold urn of manna, Aaron's rod that budded, the covenant tablets, and the angel-wing-shadowed mercy seat. But we don't have time to comment on these now.

6-10   After this was set up, the priests went about their duties in the large tent. Only the high priest entered the smaller, inside tent, and then only once a year, offering a blood sacrifice for his own sins and the people's accumulated sins. This was the Holy Spirit's way of showing with a visible parable that as long as the large tent stands, people can't just walk in on God. Under this system, the gifts and sacrifices can't really get to the heart of the matter, can't assuage the conscience of the people, but are limited to matters of ritual and behavior. It's essentially a temporary arrangement until a complete overhaul could be made.

Pointing to the Realities of Heaven

11-15   But when the Messiah arrived, high priest of the superior things of this new covenant, he bypassed the old tent and its trappings in this created world and went straight into heaven's "tent" — the true Holy Place — once and for all. He also bypassed the sacrifices consisting of goat and calf blood, instead using his own blood as the price to set us free once and for all. If that animal blood and the other rituals of purification were effective in cleaning up certain matters of our religion and behavior, think how much more the blood of Christ cleans up our whole lives, inside and out. Through the Spirit, Christ offered himself as an unblemished sacrifice, freeing us from all those dead-end efforts to make ourselves respectable, so that we can live all out for God.

16-17   Like a will that takes effect when someone dies, the new covenant was put into action at Jesus' death. His death marked the transition from the old plan to the new one, canceling the old obligations and accompanying sins, and summoning the heirs to receive the eternal inheritance that was promised them. He brought together God and his people in this new way.

18-22   Even the first plan required a death to set it in motion. After Moses had read out all the terms of the plan of the law — God's "will" — he took the blood of sacrificed animals and, in a solemn ritual, sprinkled the document and the people who were its beneficiaries. And then he attested its validity with the words, "This is the blood of the covenant commanded by God." He did the same thing with the place of worship and its furniture. Moses said to the people, "This is the blood of the covenant God has established with you." Practically everything in a will hinges on a death. That's why blood, the evidence of death, is used so much in our tradition, especially regarding forgiveness of sins.

23-26   That accounts for the prominence of blood and death in all these secondary practices that point to the realities of heaven. It also accounts for why, when the real thing takes place, these animal sacrifices aren't needed anymore, having served their purpose. For Christ didn't enter the earthly version of the Holy Place; he entered the Place Itself, and offered himself to God as the sacrifice for our sins. He doesn't do this every year as the high priests did under the old plan with blood that was not their own; if that had been the case, he would have to sacrifice himself repeatedly throughout the course of history. But instead he sacrificed himself once and for all, summing up all the other sacrifices in this sacrifice of himself, the final solution of sin.

27-28   Everyone has to die once, then face the consequences. Christ's death was also a one-time event, but it was a sacrifice that took care of sins forever. And so, when he next appears, the outcome for those eager to greet him is, precisely, *salvation*.

The Sacrifice of Jesus

1-10   10 The old plan was only a hint of the good things in the new plan. Since that old "law plan" wasn't complete in itself, it couldn't complete those who followed it. No matter how many sacrifices were offered year after year, they never added up to a complete solution. If they had, the worshipers would have gone merrily on their way, no longer dragged down by their sins. But instead of removing awareness of sin, when those animal sacrifices were repeated over and over they actually heightened awareness and guilt. The plain fact is that bull and goat blood can't get rid of sin. That is what is meant by this prophecy, put in the mouth of Christ:

> You don't want sacrifices and offerings year after year;
>   you've prepared a body for me for a sacrifice.
> It's not fragrance and smoke from the altar
>   that whet your appetite.
> So I said, "I'm here to do it your way, O God,
>   the way it's described in your Book."

When he said, "You don't want sacrifices and offerings," he was referring to practices according to the old plan. When he added, "I'm here to do it your way," he set aside the first in order to enact the new plan — God's way — by which we are made fit for God by the once-for-all sacrifice of Jesus.

11-18   Every priest goes to work at the altar each day, offers the same old sacrifices year in, year out, and never makes a dent in the sin problem. As a priest, Christ made a single sacrifice for sins, and that was it! Then he sat down right beside God and waited for his enemies to cave in. It was a perfect sacrifice by a perfect person to perfect some very imperfect people. By that single offering, he did everything that needed to be done for everyone who takes part in the purifying process. The Holy Spirit confirms this:

> This new plan I'm making with Israel
>   isn't going to be written on paper,
>   isn't going to be chiseled in stone;
> This time "I'm writing out the plan *in* them,
>   carving it on the lining of their hearts."

He concludes,
> I'll forever wipe the slate clean of their sins.

Once sins are taken care of for good, there's no longer any need to offer sacrifices for them.

DON'T THROW IT ALL AWAY

19-21 So, friends, we can now — without hesitation — walk right up to God, into "the Holy Place." Jesus has cleared the way by the blood of his sacrifice, acting as our priest before God. The "curtain" into God's presence is his body.

22-25 So let's *do* it — full of belief, confident that we're presentable inside and out. Let's keep a firm grip on the promises that keep us going. He always keeps his word. Let's see how inventive we can be in encouraging love and helping out, not avoiding worshiping together as some do but spurring each other on, especially as we see the big Day approaching.

26-31 If we give up and turn our backs on all we've learned, all we've been given, all the truth we now know, we repudiate Christ's sacrifice and are left on our own to face the Judgment — and a mighty fierce judgment it will be! If the penalty for breaking the law of Moses is physical death, what do you think will happen if you turn on God's Son, spit on the sacrifice that made you whole, and insult this most gracious Spirit? This is no light matter. God has warned us that he'll hold us to account and make us pay. He was quite explicit: "Vengeance is mine, and I won't overlook a thing" and "God will judge his people." Nobody's getting by with anything, believe me.

32-39 Remember those early days after you first saw the light? Those were the hard times! Kicked around in public, targets of every kind of abuse — some days it was you, other days your friends. If some friends went to prison, you stuck by them. If some enemies broke in and seized your goods, you let them go with a smile, knowing they couldn't touch your real treasure. Nothing they did bothered you, nothing set you back. So don't throw it all away now. You were sure of yourselves then. It's *still* a sure thing! But you need to stick it out, staying with God's plan so you'll be there for the promised completion.

> It won't be long now, he's on the way;
> he'll show up most any minute.
> But anyone who is right with me thrives on loyal trust;
> if he cuts and runs, I won't be very happy.

But we're not quitters who lose out. Oh, no! We'll stay with it and survive, trusting all the way.

FAITH IN WHAT WE DON'T SEE

1-2 **11** The fundamental fact of existence is that this trust in God, this faith, is the firm foundation under everything that makes life worth living. It's our handle on what we can't see. The act of faith is what distinguished our ancestors, set them above the crowd.

3 By faith, we see the world called into existence by God's word, what we see created by what we don't see.

4 By an act of faith, Abel brought a better sacrifice to God than Cain. It was what he *believed*, not what he *brought*, that made the difference. That's what God noticed and approved as righteous. After all these centuries, that belief continues to catch our notice.

5-6   By an act of faith, Enoch skipped death completely. "They looked all over and couldn't find him because God had taken him." We know on the basis of reliable testimony that before he was taken "he pleased God." It's impossible to please God apart from faith. And why? Because anyone who wants to approach God must believe both that he exists *and* that he cares enough to respond to those who seek him.

7   By faith, Noah built a ship in the middle of dry land. He was warned about something he couldn't see, and acted on what he was told. The result? His family was saved. His act of faith drew a sharp line between the evil of the unbelieving world and the rightness of the believing world. As a result, Noah became intimate with God.

8-10   By an act of faith, Abraham said yes to God's call to travel to an unknown place that would become his home. When he left he had no idea where he was going. By an act of faith he lived in the country promised him, lived as a stranger camping in tents. Isaac and Jacob did the same, living under the same promise. Abraham did it by keeping his eye on an unseen city with real, eternal foundations — the City designed and built by God.

11-12   By faith, barren Sarah was able to become pregnant, old woman as she was at the time, because she believed the One who made a promise would do what he said. That's how it happened that from one man's dead and shriveled loins there are now people numbering into the millions.

13-16   Each one of these people of faith died not yet having in hand what was promised, but still believing. How did they do it? They saw it way off in the distance, waved their greeting, and accepted the fact that they were transients in this world. People who live this way make it plain that they are looking for their true home. If they were homesick for the old country, they could have gone back any time they wanted. But they were after a far better country than that — *heaven* country. You can see why God is so proud of them, and has a City waiting for them.

17-19   By faith, Abraham, at the time of testing, offered Isaac back to God. Acting in faith, he was as ready to return the promised son, his only son, as he had been to receive him — and this after he had already been told, "Your descendants shall come from Isaac." Abraham figured that if God wanted to, he could raise the dead. In a sense, that's what happened when he received Isaac back, alive from off the altar.

20   By an act of faith, Isaac reached into the future as he blessed Jacob and Esau.

21   By an act of faith, Jacob on his deathbed blessed each of Joseph's sons in turn, blessing them with God's blessing, not his own — as he bowed worshipfully upon his staff.

22   By an act of faith, Joseph, while dying, prophesied the exodus of Israel, and made arrangements for his own burial.

23   By an act of faith, Moses' parents hid him away for three months after his birth. They saw the child's beauty, and they braved the king's decree.

24-28   By faith, Moses, when grown, refused the privileges of the Egyptian royal house. He chose a hard life with God's people rather than an opportunistic soft life of sin with the oppressors. He valued suffering in the Messiah's camp far greater than Egyptian wealth because he was looking ahead, anticipating the payoff. By an act of faith, he turned his heel on

Egypt, indifferent to the king's blind rage. He had his eye on the One no eye can see, and kept right on going. By an act of faith, he kept the Passover Feast and sprinkled Passover blood on each house so that the destroyer of the firstborn wouldn't touch them.

29 By an act of faith, Israel walked through the Red Sea on dry ground. The Egyptians tried it and drowned.

30 By faith, the Israelites marched around the walls of Jericho for seven days, and the walls fell flat.

31 By an act of faith, Rahab, the Jericho harlot, welcomed the spies and escaped the destruction that came on those who refused to trust God.

32-38 I could go on and on, but I've run out of time. There are so many more — Gideon, Barak, Samson, Jephthah, David, Samuel, the prophets. . . . Through acts of faith, they toppled kingdoms, made justice work, took the promises for themselves. They were protected from lions, fires, and sword thrusts, turned disadvantage to advantage, won battles, routed alien armies. Women received their loved ones back from the dead. There were those who, under torture, refused to give in and go free, preferring something better: resurrection. Others braved abuse and whips, and, yes, chains and dungeons. We have stories of those who were stoned, sawed in two, murdered in cold blood; stories of vagrants wandering the earth in animal skins, homeless, friendless, powerless — the world didn't deserve them! — making their way as best they could on the cruel edges of the world.

39-40 Not one of these people, even though their lives of faith were exemplary, got their hands on what was promised. God had a better plan for us: that their faith and our faith would come together to make one completed whole, their lives of faith not complete apart from ours.

DISCIPLINE IN A LONG-DISTANCE RACE

1-3 **12** Do you see what this means — all these pioneers who blazed the way, all these veterans cheering us on? It means we'd better get on with it. Strip down, start running — and never quit! No extra spiritual fat, no parasitic sins. Keep your eyes on *Jesus*, who both began and finished this race we're in. Study how he did it. Because he never lost sight of where he was headed — that exhilarating finish in and with God — he could put up with anything along the way: Cross, shame, whatever. And now he's *there*, in the place of honor, right alongside God. When you find yourselves flagging in your faith, go over that story again, item by item, that long litany of hostility he plowed through. *That* will shoot adrenaline into your souls!

4-11 In this all-out match against sin, others have suffered far worse than you, to say nothing of what Jesus went through — all that bloodshed! So don't feel sorry for yourselves. Or have you forgotten how good parents treat children, and that God regards you as *his* children?

My dear child, don't shrug off God's discipline,
  but don't be crushed by it either.
It's the child he loves that he disciplines;
  the child he embraces, he also corrects.

God is educating you; that's why you must never drop out. He's treating you as dear children. This trouble you're in isn't punishment; it's *training*, the normal experience of children. Only irresponsible parents leave children to fend for themselves. Would you prefer an irresponsible God? We respect our own parents for training and not spoiling us, so why not embrace God's training so we can truly *live*? While we were children, our parents did what *seemed* best to them. But God is doing what *is* best for us, training us to live God's holy best. At the time, discipline isn't much fun. It always feels like it's going against the grain. Later, of course, it pays off handsomely, for it's the well-trained who find themselves mature in their relationship with God.

12-13   So don't sit around on your hands! No more dragging your feet! Clear the path for long-distance runners so no one will trip and fall, so no one will step in a hole and sprain an ankle. Help each other out. And run for it!

14-17   Work at getting along with each other and with God. Otherwise you'll never get so much as a glimpse of God. Make sure no one gets left out of God's generosity. Keep a sharp eye out for weeds of bitter discontent. A thistle or two gone to seed can ruin a whole garden in no time. Watch out for the Esau syndrome: trading away God's lifelong gift in order to satisfy a short-term appetite. You well know how Esau later regretted that impulsive act and wanted God's blessing — but by then it was too late, tears or no tears.

An Unshakable Kingdom

18-21   Unlike your ancestors, you didn't come to Mount Sinai — all that volcanic blaze and earthshaking rumble — to hear God speak. The earsplitting words and soul-shaking message terrified them and they begged him to stop. When they heard the words — "If an animal touches the Mountain, it's as good as dead" — they were afraid to move. Even Moses was terrified.

22-24   No, that's not *your* experience at all. You've come to Mount Zion, the city where the living God resides. The invisible Jerusalem is populated by throngs of festive angels and Christian citizens. It is the city where God is Judge, with judgments that make us just. You've come to Jesus, who presents us with a new covenant, a fresh charter from God. He is the Mediator of this covenant. The murder of Jesus, unlike Abel's — a homicide that cried out for vengeance — became a proclamation of grace.

25-27   So don't turn a deaf ear to these gracious words. If those who ignored earthly warnings didn't get away with it, what will happen to us if we turn our backs on heavenly warnings? His voice that time shook the earth to its foundations; this time — he's told us this quite plainly — he'll also rock the heavens: "One last shaking, from top to bottom, stem to stern." The phrase "one last shaking" means a thorough housecleaning, getting rid of all the historical and religious junk so that the unshakable essentials stand clear and uncluttered.

28-29   Do you see what we've got? An unshakable kingdom! And do you see how thankful we must be? Not only thankful, but brimming with worship, deeply reverent before God. For God is not an indifferent bystander. He's actively cleaning house, torching all that needs to burn, and he won't quit until it's all cleansed. God himself is Fire!

JESUS DOESN'T CHANGE

1-4 **13** Stay on good terms with each other, held together by love. Be ready with a meal or a bed when it's needed. Why, some have extended hospitality to angels without ever knowing it! Regard prisoners as if you were in prison with them. Look on victims of abuse as if what happened to them had happened to you. Honor marriage, and guard the sacredness of sexual intimacy between wife and husband. God draws a firm line against casual and illicit sex.

5-6 Don't be obsessed with getting more material things. Be relaxed with what you have. Since God assured us, "I'll never let you down, never walk off and leave you," we can boldly quote,

> God is there, ready to help;
> I'm fearless no matter what.
> Who or what can get to me?

7-8 Appreciate your pastoral leaders who gave you the Word of God. Take a good look at the way they live, and let their faithfulness instruct you, as well as their truthfulness. There should be a consistency that runs through us all. For Jesus doesn't change — yesterday, today, tomorrow, he's always totally himself.

9 Don't be lured away from him by the latest speculations about him. The grace of Christ is the only good ground for life. Products named after Christ don't seem to do much for those who buy them.

10-12 The altar from which God gives us the gift of himself is not for exploitation by insiders who grab and loot. In the old system, the animals are killed and the bodies disposed of outside the camp. The blood is then brought inside to the altar as a sacrifice for sin. It's the same with Jesus. He was crucified outside the city gates — *that* is where he poured out the sacrificial blood that was brought to God's altar to cleanse his people.

13-15 So let's go outside, where Jesus is, where the action is — not trying to be privileged insiders, but taking our share in the abuse of Jesus. This "insider world" is not our home. We have our eyes peeled for the City about to come. Let's take our place outside with Jesus, no longer pouring out the sacrificial blood of animals but pouring out sacrificial praises from our lips to God in Jesus' name.

16 Make sure you don't take things for granted and go slack in working for the common good; share what you have with others. God takes particular pleasure in acts of worship — a different kind of "sacrifice" — that take place in kitchen and workplace and on the streets.

17 Be responsive to your pastoral leaders. Listen to their counsel. They are alert to the condition of your lives and work under the strict supervision of God. Contribute to the joy of their leadership, not its drudgery. Why would you want to make things harder for them?

18-21 Pray for us. We have no doubts about what we're doing or why, but it's hard going and we need your prayers. All we care about is living well before God. Pray that we may be together soon.

May God, who puts all things together,
  makes all things whole,
Who made a lasting mark through the sacrifice of Jesus,
  the sacrifice of blood that sealed the eternal covenant,
Who led Jesus, our Great Shepherd,
  up and alive from the dead,
Now put you together, provide you
  with everything you need to please him,
Make us into what gives him most pleasure,
  by means of the sacrifice of Jesus, the Messiah.
All glory to Jesus forever and always!
  Oh, yes, yes, yes.

22-23 Friends, please take what I've written most seriously. I've kept this as brief as possible; I haven't piled on a lot of extras. You'll be glad to know that Timothy has been let out of prison. If he leaves soon, I'll come with him and get to see you myself.

24 Say hello to your pastoral leaders and all the congregations. Everyone here in Italy wants to be remembered to you.

25 Grace be with you, every one.

JAMES

When Christian believers gather in churches, everything that can go wrong sooner or later does. Outsiders, on observing this, conclude that there is nothing to the religion business except, perhaps, business — and dishonest business at that. Insiders see it differently. Just as a hospital collects the sick under one roof and labels them as such, the church collects sinners. Many of the people outside the hospital are every bit as sick as the ones inside, but their illnesses are either undiagnosed or disguised. It's similar with sinners outside the church.

So Christian churches are not, as a rule, model communities of good behavior. They are, rather, places where human misbehavior is brought out in the open, faced, and dealt with.

The letter of James shows one of the church's early pastors skillfully going about his work of confronting, diagnosing, and dealing with areas of misbelief and misbehavior that had turned up in congregations committed to his care. Deep and living wisdom is on display here, wisdom both rare and essential. Wisdom is not primarily knowing the truth, although it certainly includes that; it is skill in living. For, what good is a truth if we don't know how to live it? What good is an intention if we can't sustain it?

According to church traditions, James carried the nickname "Old Camel Knees" because of thick calluses built up on his knees from many years of determined prayer. The prayer is foundational to the wisdom. Prayer is *always* foundational to wisdom.

JAMES

1 I, James, am a slave of God and the Master Jesus, writing to the twelve tribes scattered to Kingdom Come: Hello!

FAITH UNDER PRESSURE

2-4 Consider it a sheer gift, friends, when tests and challenges come at you from all sides. You know that under pressure, your faith-life is forced into the open and shows its true colors. So don't try to get out of anything prematurely. Let it do its work so you become mature and well-developed, not deficient in any way.

5-8 If you don't know what you're doing, pray to the Father. He loves to help. You'll get his help, and won't be condescended to when you ask for it. Ask boldly, believingly, without a second thought. People who "worry their prayers" are like wind-whipped waves. Don't think you're going to get anything from the Master that way, adrift at sea, keeping all your options open.

9-11 When down-and-outers get a break, cheer! And when the arrogant rich are brought down to size, cheer! Prosperity is as short-lived as a wildflower, so don't ever count on it. You know that as soon as the sun rises, pouring down its scorching heat, the flower withers. Its petals wilt and, before you know it, that beautiful face is a barren stem. Well, that's a picture of the "prosperous life." At the very moment everyone is looking on in admiration, it fades away to nothing.

12 Anyone who meets a testing challenge head-on and manages to stick it out is mighty fortunate. For such persons loyally in love with God, the reward is life and more life.

13-15 Don't let anyone under pressure to give in to evil say, "God is trying to trip me up." God is impervious to evil, and puts evil in no one's way. The temptation to give in to evil comes from us and only us. We have no one to blame but the leering, seducing flare-up of our own lust. Lust gets pregnant, and has a baby: sin! Sin grows up to adulthood, and becomes a real killer.

16-18 So, my very dear friends, don't get thrown off course. Every desirable and beneficial gift comes out of heaven. The gifts are rivers of light cascading down from the Father of Light. There is nothing deceitful in God, nothing two-faced, nothing fickle. He brought us to life using the true Word, showing us off as the crown of all his creatures.

ACT ON WHAT YOU HEAR

19-21 Post this at all the intersections, dear friends: Lead with your ears, follow up with your tongue, and let anger straggle along in the rear. God's righteousness doesn't grow from human anger. So throw all spoiled virtue and cancerous evil in the garbage. In simple humility, let our gardener, God, landscape you with the Word, making a salvation-garden of your life.

22-24 Don't fool yourself into thinking that you are a listener when you are anything but, letting the Word go in one ear and out the other. *Act* on what you hear! Those who hear and don't act are like those who glance in the mirror, walk away, and two minutes later have no idea who they are, what they look like.

25 But whoever catches a glimpse of the revealed counsel of God—the free

life! — even out of the corner of his eye, and sticks with it, is no distracted scatterbrain but a man or woman of action. That person will find delight and affirmation in the action.

26-27 Anyone who sets himself up as "religious" by talking a good game is self-deceived. This kind of religion is hot air and only hot air. Real religion, the kind that passes muster before God the Father, is this: Reach out to the homeless and loveless in their plight, and guard against corruption from the godless world.

The Royal Rule of Love

1-4 2 My dear friends, don't let public opinion influence how you live out our glorious, Christ-originated faith. If a man enters your church wearing an expensive suit, and a street person wearing rags comes in right after him, and you say to the man in the suit, "Sit here, sir; this is the best seat in the house!" and either ignore the street person or say, "Better sit here in the back row," haven't you segregated God's children and proved that you are judges who can't be trusted?

5-7 Listen, dear friends. Isn't it clear by now that God operates quite differently? He chose the world's down-and-out as the kingdom's first citizens, with full rights and privileges. This kingdom is promised to anyone who loves God. And here you are abusing these same citizens! Isn't it the high and mighty who exploit you, who use the courts to rob you blind? Aren't they the ones who scorn the new name — "Christian" — used in your baptisms?

8-11 You do well when you complete the Royal Rule of the Scriptures: "Love others as you love yourself." But if you play up to these so-called important people, you go against the Rule and stand convicted by it. You can't pick and choose in these things, specializing in keeping one or two things in God's law and ignoring others. The same God who said, "Don't commit adultery," also said, "Don't murder." If you don't commit adultery but go ahead and murder, do you think your non-adultery will cancel out your murder? No, you're a murderer, period.

12-13 Talk and act like a person expecting to be judged by the Rule that sets us free. For if you refuse to act kindly, you can hardly expect to be treated kindly. Kind mercy wins over harsh judgment every time.

Faith in Action

14-17 Dear friends, do you think you'll get anywhere in this if you learn all the right words but never do anything? Does merely talking about faith indicate that a person really has it? For instance, you come upon an old friend dressed in rags and half-starved and say, "Good morning, friend! Be clothed in Christ! Be filled with the Holy Spirit!" and walk off without providing so much as a coat or a cup of soup — where does that get you? Isn't it obvious that God-talk without God-acts is outrageous nonsense?

18 I can already hear one of you agreeing by saying, "Sounds good. You take care of the faith department, I'll handle the works department."

Not so fast. You can no more show me your works apart from your faith than I can show you my faith apart from my works. Faith and works, works and faith, fit together hand in glove.

19-20 Do I hear you professing to believe in the one and only God, but then observe you complacently sitting back as if you had done something wonderful? That's just great. Demons do that, but what good does it do them? Use your heads! Do you suppose for a minute that you can cut faith and works in two and not end up with a corpse on your hands?

21-24 Wasn't our ancestor Abraham "made right with God by works" when he placed his son Isaac on the sacrificial altar? Isn't it obvious that faith and works are yoked partners, that faith expresses itself in works? That the works are "works of faith"? The full meaning of "believe" in the Scripture sentence, "Abraham believed God and was set right with God," includes his action. It's that mesh of believing and acting that got Abraham named "God's friend." Is it not evident that a person is made right with God not by a barren faith but by faith fruitful in works?

25-26 The same with Rahab, the Jericho harlot. Wasn't her action in hiding God's spies and helping them escape — that seamless unity of *believing* and *doing* — what counted with God? The very moment you separate body and spirit, you end up with a corpse. Separate faith and works and you get the same thing: a corpse.

When You Open Your Mouth

1-2 3 Don't be in any rush to become a teacher, my friends. Teaching is highly responsible work. Teachers are held to the strictest standards. And none of us is perfectly qualified. We get it wrong nearly every time we open our mouths. If you could find someone whose speech was perfectly true, you'd have a perfect person, in perfect control of life.

3-5 A bit in the mouth of a horse controls the whole horse. A small rudder on a huge ship in the hands of a skilled captain sets a course in the face of the strongest winds. A word out of your mouth may seem of no account, but it can accomplish nearly anything — or destroy it!

5-6 It only takes a spark, remember, to set off a forest fire. A careless or wrongly placed word out of your mouth can do that. By our speech we can ruin the world, turn harmony to chaos, throw mud on a reputation, send the whole world up in smoke and go up in smoke with it, smoke right from the pit of hell.

7-10 This is scary: You can tame a tiger, but you can't tame a tongue — it's never been done. The tongue runs wild, a wanton killer. With our tongues we bless God our Father; with the same tongues we curse the very men and women he made in his image. Curses and blessings out of the same mouth!

10-12 My friends, this can't go on. A spring doesn't gush fresh water one day and brackish the next, does it? Apple trees don't bear strawberries, do they? Raspberry bushes don't bear apples, do they? You're not going to dip into a polluted mud hole and get a cup of clear, cool water, are you?

Live Well, Live Wisely

13-16 Do you want to be counted wise, to build a reputation for wisdom? Here's what you do: Live well, live wisely, live humbly. It's the way you live, not the way you talk, that counts. Mean-spirited ambition isn't wisdom. Boasting that you are wise isn't wisdom. Twisting the truth to make yourselves sound wise isn't wisdom. It's the furthest thing from wisdom — it's animal cunning, devilish conniving. Whenever you're trying to look better than others or get the better of others, things fall apart and everyone ends up at the others' throats.

17-18 Real wisdom, God's wisdom, begins with a holy life and is characterized by getting along with others. It is gentle and reasonable, overflowing with mercy and blessings, not hot one day and cold the next, not two-faced. You can develop a healthy, robust community that lives right with God and enjoy its results *only* if you do the hard work of getting along with each other, treating each other with dignity and honor.

GET SERIOUS

1-2   4 Where do you think all these appalling wars and quarrels come from? Do you think they just happen? Think again. They come about because you want your own way, and fight for it deep inside yourselves. You lust for what you don't have and are willing to kill to get it. You want what isn't yours and will risk violence to get your hands on it.

2-3   You wouldn't think of just asking God for it, would you? And why not? Because you know you'd be asking for what you have no right to. You're spoiled children, each wanting your own way.

4-6   You're cheating on God. If all you want is your own way, flirting with the world every chance you get, you end up enemies of God and his way. And do you suppose God doesn't care? The proverb has it that "he's a fiercely jealous lover." And what he gives in love is far better than anything else you'll find. It's common knowledge that "God goes against the willful proud; God gives grace to the willing humble."

7-10   So let God work his will in you. Yell a loud *no* to the Devil and watch him scamper. Say a quiet *yes* to God and he'll be there in no time. Quit dabbling in sin. Purify your inner life. Quit playing the field. Hit bottom, and cry your eyes out. The fun and games are over. Get serious, really serious. Get down on your knees before the Master; it's the only way you'll get on your feet.

11-12   Don't bad-mouth each other, friends. It's God's Word, his Message, his Royal Rule, that takes a beating in that kind of talk. You're supposed to be honoring the Message, not writing graffiti all over it. God is in charge of deciding human destiny. Who do you think you are to meddle in the destiny of others?

NOTHING BUT A WISP OF FOG

13-15   And now I have a word for you who brashly announce, "Today — at the latest, tomorrow — we're off to such and such a city for the year. We're going to start a business and make a lot of money." You don't know the first thing about tomorrow. You're nothing but a wisp of fog, catching a brief bit of sun before disappearing. Instead, make it a habit to say, "If the Master wills it and we're still alive, we'll do this or that."

16-17   As it is, you are full of your grandiose selves. All such vaunting self-importance is evil. In fact, if you know the right thing to do and don't do it, that, for you, *is* evil.

DESTROYING YOUR LIFE FROM WITHIN

1-3   5 And a final word to you arrogant rich: Take some lessons in lament. You'll need buckets for the tears when the crash comes upon you. Your money is corrupt and your fine clothes stink. Your greedy luxuries are a cancer in your gut, destroying your life from within. You thought you were piling up wealth. What you've piled up is judgment.

4-6   All the workers you've exploited and cheated cry out for judgment.

The groans of the workers you used and abused are a roar in the ears of the Master Avenger. You've looted the earth and lived it up. But all you'll have to show for it is a fatter than usual corpse. In fact, what you've done is condemn and murder perfectly good persons, who stand there and take it.

7-8 Meanwhile, friends, wait patiently for the Master's Arrival. You see farmers do this all the time, waiting for their valuable crops to mature, patiently letting the rain do its slow but sure work. Be patient like that. Stay steady and strong. The Master could arrive at any time.

9 Friends, don't complain about each other. A far greater complaint could be lodged against you, you know. The Judge is standing just around the corner.

10-11 Take the old prophets as your mentors. They put up with anything, went through everything, and never once quit, all the time honoring God. What a gift life is to those who stay the course! You've heard, of course, of Job's staying power, and you know how God brought it all together for him at the end. That's because God cares, cares right down to the last detail.

12 And since you know that he cares, let your language show it. Don't add words like "I swear to God" to your own words. Don't show your impatience by concocting oaths to hurry up God. Just say yes or no. Just say what is true. That way, your language can't be used against you.

PRAYER TO BE RECKONED WITH

13-15 Are you hurting? Pray. Do you feel great? Sing. Are you sick? Call the church leaders together to pray and anoint you with oil in the name of the Master. Believing-prayer will heal you, and Jesus will put you on your feet. And if you've sinned, you'll be forgiven — healed inside and out.

16-18 Make this your common practice: Confess your sins to each other and pray for each other so that you can live together whole and healed. The prayer of a person living right with God is something powerful to be reckoned with. Elijah, for instance, human just like us, prayed hard that it wouldn't rain, and it didn't — not a drop for three and a half years. Then he prayed that it would rain, and it did. The showers came and everything started growing again.

19-20 My dear friends, if you know people who have wandered off from God's truth, don't write them off. Go after them. Get them back and you will have rescued precious lives from destruction and prevented an epidemic of wandering away from God.

1 & 2 PETER

Peter's concise confession — "You are the Messiah, the Christ" — focused the faith of the disciples on Jesus as God among us, in person, carrying out the eternal work of salvation. Peter seems to have been a natural leader, commanding the respect of his peers by sheer force of personality. In every listing of Jesus' disciples, Peter's name is invariably first.

In the early church, his influence was enormous and acknowledged by all. By virtue of his position, he was easily the most powerful figure in the Christian community. And his energetic preaching, ardent prayer, bold healing, and wise direction confirmed the trust placed in him.

The way Peter handled himself in that position of power is even more impressive than the power itself. He stayed out of the center, didn't "wield" power, maintained a scrupulous subordination to Jesus. Given his charismatic personality and well-deserved position at the head, he could easily have taken over, using the prominence of his association with Jesus to promote himself. That he didn't do it, given the frequency with which spiritual leaders do exactly that, is impressive. Peter is a breath of fresh air.

The two letters Peter wrote exhibit the qualities of Jesus that the Holy Spirit shaped in him: a readiness to embrace suffering rather than prestige, a wisdom developed from experience and not imposed from a book, a humility that lacked nothing in vigor or imagination. From what we know of the early stories of Peter, he had in him all the makings of a bully. That he didn't become a bully (and religious bullies are the worst kind) but rather the boldly confident and humbly self-effacing servant of Jesus Christ that we discern in these letters, is a compelling witness to what he himself describes as "a brand-new life, with everything to live for."

1 PETER

1-2 I, Peter, am an apostle on assignment by Jesus, the Messiah, writing to exiles scattered to the four winds. Not one is missing, not one forgotten. God the Father has his eye on each of you, and has determined by the work of the Spirit to keep you obedient through the sacrifice of Jesus. May everything good from God be yours!

A NEW LIFE

3-5 What a God we have! And how fortunate we are to have him, this Father of our Master Jesus! Because Jesus was raised from the dead, we've been given a brand-new life and have everything to live for, including a future in heaven — and the future starts now! God is keeping careful watch over us and the future. The Day is coming when you'll have it all — life healed and whole.

6-7 I know how great this makes you feel, even though you have to put up with every kind of aggravation in the meantime. Pure gold put in the fire comes out of it *proved* pure; genuine faith put through this suffering comes out *proved* genuine. When Jesus wraps this all up, it's your faith, not your gold, that God will have on display as evidence of his victory.

8-9 You never saw him, yet you love him. You still don't see him, yet you trust him — with laughter and singing. Because you kept on believing, you'll get what you're looking forward to: total salvation.

10-12 The prophets who told us this was coming asked a lot of questions about this gift of life God was preparing. The Messiah's Spirit let them in on some of it — that the Messiah would experience suffering, followed by glory. They clamored to know who and when. All they were told was that they were serving you, you who by orders from heaven have now heard for yourselves — through the Holy Spirit — the Message of those prophecies fulfilled. Do you realize how fortunate you are? Angels would have given anything to be in on this!

A FUTURE IN GOD

13-16 So roll up your sleeves, put your mind in gear, be totally ready to receive the gift that's coming when Jesus arrives. Don't lazily slip back into those old grooves of evil, doing just what you feel like doing. You didn't know any better then; you do now. As obedient children, let yourselves be pulled into a way of life shaped by God's life, a life energetic and blazing with holiness. God said, "I am holy; you be holy."

17 You call out to God for help and he helps — he's a good Father that way. But don't forget, he's also a responsible Father, and won't let you get by with sloppy living.

18-21 Your life is a journey you must travel with a deep consciousness of God. It cost God plenty to get you out of that dead-end, empty-headed life you grew up in. He paid with Christ's sacred blood, you know. He died like an unblemished, sacrificial lamb. And this was no afterthought. Even though it has only lately — at the end of the ages — become public knowledge, God always knew he was going to do this for you. It's because of this sacrificed Messiah, whom God then raised from the dead and glorified, that you trust God, that you know you have a future in God.

22-25 Now that you've cleaned up your lives by following the truth, love one another as if your lives depended on it. Your new life is not like your old life. Your old birth came from mortal sperm; your new birth comes from God's living Word. Just think: a life conceived by God himself! That's why the prophet said,

> The old life is a grass life,
>   its beauty as short-lived as wildflowers;
> Grass dries up, flowers droop,
>   God's Word goes on and on forever.

This is the Word that conceived the new life in you.

1-3 So clean house! Make a clean sweep of malice and pretense, envy and hurtful talk. You've had a taste of God. Now, like infants at the breast, drink deep of God's pure kindness. Then you'll grow up mature and whole in God.

THE STONE

4-8 Welcome to the living Stone, the source of life. The workmen took one look and threw it out; God set it in the place of honor. Present yourselves as building stones for the construction of a sanctuary vibrant with life, in which you'll serve as holy priests offering Christ-approved lives up to God. The Scriptures provide precedent:

> Look! I'm setting a stone in Zion,
>   a cornerstone in the place of honor.
> Whoever trusts in this stone as a foundation
>   will never have cause to regret it.

To you who trust him, he's a Stone to be proud of, but to those who refuse to trust him,

> The stone the workmen threw out
>   is now the chief foundation stone.

For the untrusting it's
>   . . . a stone to trip over,
>   a boulder blocking the way.

They trip and fall because they refuse to obey, just as predicted.

9-10 But you are the ones chosen by God, chosen for the high calling of priestly work, chosen to be a holy people, God's instruments to do his work and speak out for him, to tell others of the night-and-day difference he made for you — from nothing to something, from rejected to accepted.

11-12 Friends, this world is not your home, so don't make yourselves cozy in it. Don't indulge your ego at the expense of your soul. Live an exemplary life among the natives so that your actions will refute their prejudices. Then they'll be won over to God's side and be there to join in the celebration when he arrives.

13-17   Make the Master proud of you by being good citizens. Respect the authorities, whatever their level; they are God's emissaries for keeping order. It is God's will that by doing good, you might cure the ignorance of the fools who think you're a danger to society. Exercise your freedom by serving God, not by breaking the rules. Treat everyone you meet with dignity. Love your spiritual family. Revere God. Respect the government.

The Kind of Life He Lived

18-20   You who are servants, be good servants to your masters — not just to good masters, but also to bad ones. What counts is that you put up with it for God's sake when you're treated badly for no good reason. There's no particular virtue in accepting punishment that you well deserve. But if you're treated badly for good behavior and continue in spite of it to be a good servant, that is what counts with God.

21-25   This is the kind of life you've been invited into, the kind of life Christ lived. He suffered everything that came his way so you would know that it could be done, and also know how to do it, step-by-step.

> He never did one thing wrong,
> Not once said anything amiss.

They called him every name in the book and he said nothing back. He suffered in silence, content to let God set things right. He used his servant body to carry our sins to the Cross so we could be rid of sin, free to live the right way. His wounds became your healing. You were lost sheep with no idea who you were or where you were going. Now you're named and kept for good by the Shepherd of your souls.

Cultivate Inner Beauty

1-4   3 The same goes for you wives: Be good wives to your husbands, responsive to their needs. There are husbands who, indifferent as they are to any words about God, will be captivated by your life of holy beauty. What matters is not your outer appearance — the styling of your hair, the jewelry you wear, the cut of your clothes — but your inner disposition.

4-6   Cultivate inner beauty, the gentle, gracious kind that God delights in. The holy women of old were beautiful before God that way, and were good, loyal wives to their husbands. Sarah, for instance, taking care of Abraham, would address him as "my dear husband." You'll be true daughters of Sarah if you do the same, unanxious and unintimidated.

7   The same goes for you husbands: Be good husbands to your wives. Honor them, delight in them. As women they lack some of your advantages. But in the new life of God's grace, you're equals. Treat your wives, then, as equals so your prayers don't run aground.

Suffering for Doing Good

8-12   Summing up: Be agreeable, be sympathetic, be loving, be compassionate, be humble. That goes for all of you, no exceptions. No retaliation. No sharp-tongued sarcasm. Instead, bless — that's your job, to bless. You'll be a blessing and also get a blessing.

Whoever wants to embrace life
    and see the day fill up with good,
Here's what you do:
    Say nothing evil or hurtful;
Snub evil and cultivate good;
    run after peace for all you're worth.
God looks on all this with approval,
    listening and responding well to what he's asked;
But he turns his back
    on those who do evil things.

13-18   If with heart and soul you're doing good, do you think you can be stopped? Even if you suffer for it, you're still better off. Don't give the opposition a second thought. Through thick and thin, keep your hearts at attention, in adoration before Christ, your Master. Be ready to speak up and tell anyone who asks why you're living the way you are, and always with the utmost courtesy. Keep a clear conscience before God so that when people throw mud at you, none of it will stick. They'll end up realizing that *they're* the ones who need a bath. It's better to suffer for doing good, if that's what God wants, than to be punished for doing bad. That's what Christ did definitively: suffered because of others' sins, the Righteous One for the unrighteous ones. He went through it all — was put to death and then made alive — to bring us to God.

19-22   He went and proclaimed God's salvation to earlier generations who ended up in the prison of judgment because they wouldn't listen. You know, even though God waited patiently all the days that Noah built his ship, only a few were saved then, eight to be exact — saved *from* the water *by* the water. The waters of baptism do that for you, not by washing away dirt from your skin but by presenting you through Jesus' resurrection before God with a clear conscience. Jesus has the last word on everything and everyone, from angels to armies. He's standing right alongside God, and what he says goes.

LEARN TO THINK LIKE HIM

1-2   Since Jesus went through everything you're going through and more, learn to think like him. Think of your sufferings as a weaning from that old sinful habit of always expecting to get your own way. Then you'll be able to live out your days free to pursue what God wants instead of being tyrannized by what you want.

3-5   You've already put in your time in that God-ignorant way of life, partying night after night, a drunken and profligate life. Now it's time to be done with it for good. Of course, your old friends don't understand why you don't join in with the old gang anymore. But you don't have to give an account to them. They're the ones who will be called on the carpet — and before God himself.

6   Listen to the Message. It was preached to those believers who are now dead, and yet even though they died (just as all people must), they will still get in on the *life* that God has given in Jesus.

7-11   Everything in the world is about to be wrapped up, so take nothing for granted. Stay wide-awake in prayer. Most of all, love each other as if your life depended on it. Love makes up for practically anything. Be quick to give a meal to the hungry, a bed to the homeless — cheerfully. Be generous with the different things God gave you, passing them around so all get in on it: if words, let it be God's words; if help, let it be God's hearty help. That way, God's bright presence will be evident in everything through Jesus, and *he'll* get all the credit as the One mighty in everything — encores to the end of time. Oh, yes!

GLORY JUST AROUND THE CORNER

12-13   Friends, when life gets really difficult, don't jump to the conclusion that God isn't on the job. Instead, be glad that you are in the very thick of what Christ experienced. This is a spiritual refining process, with glory just around the corner.

14-16   If you're abused because of Christ, count yourself fortunate. It's the Spirit of God and his glory in you that brought you to the notice of others. If they're on you because you broke the law or disturbed the peace, that's a different matter. But if it's because you're a Christian, don't give it a second thought. Be proud of the distinguished status reflected in that name!

17-19   It's judgment time for God's own family. We're first in line. If it starts with us, think what it's going to be like for those who refuse God's Message!

> If good people barely make it,
> What's in store for the bad?

So if you find life difficult because you're doing what God said, take it in stride. Trust him. He knows what he's doing, and he'll keep on doing it.

HE'LL PROMOTE YOU AT THE RIGHT TIME

1-3   **5** I have a special concern for you church leaders. I know what it's like to be a leader, in on Christ's sufferings as well as the coming glory. Here's my concern: that you care for God's flock with all the diligence of a shepherd. Not because you have to, but because you want to please God. Not calculating what you can get out of it, but acting spontaneously. Not bossily telling others what to do, but tenderly showing them the way.

4-5   When God, who is the best shepherd of all, comes out in the open with his rule, he'll see that you've done it right and commend you lavishly. And you who are younger must follow your leaders. But all of you, leaders and followers alike, are to be down to earth with each other, for —

> God has had it with the proud,
> But takes delight in just plain people.

6-7   So be content with who you are, and don't put on airs. God's strong hand is on you; he'll promote you at the right time. Live carefree before God; he is most careful with you.

HE GETS THE LAST WORD

8-11   Keep a cool head. Stay alert. The Devil is poised to pounce, and would like nothing better than to catch you napping. Keep your guard up. You're not the only ones plunged into these hard times. It's the same with Christians all over the world. So keep a firm grip on the faith. The suffering won't last forever. It won't be long before this generous God who has great plans for us in Christ — eternal and glorious plans they are! — will have you put together and on your feet for good. He gets the last word; yes, he does.

12 I'm sending this brief letter to you by Silas, a most dependable brother. I have the highest regard for him.

I've written as urgently and accurately as I know how. This is God's generous truth; embrace it with both arms!

13-14 The church in exile here with me — but not for a moment forgotten by God — wants to be remembered to you. Mark, who is like a son to me, says hello. Give holy embraces all around! Peace to you — to all who walk in Christ's ways.

2 PETER

1-2 I, Simon Peter, am a servant and apostle of Jesus Christ. I write this to you whose experience with God is as life-changing as ours, all due to our God's straight dealing and the intervention of our God and Savior, Jesus Christ. Grace and peace to you many times over as you deepen in your experience with God and Jesus, our Master.

Don't Put It Off

3-4 Everything that goes into a life of pleasing God has been miraculously given to us by getting to know, personally and intimately, the One who invited us to God. The best invitation we ever received! We were also given absolutely terrific promises to pass on to you — your tickets to participation in the life of God after you turned your back on a world corrupted by lust.

5-9 So don't lose a minute in building on what you've been given, complementing your basic faith with good character, spiritual understanding, alert discipline, passionate patience, reverent wonder, warm friendliness, and generous love, each dimension fitting into and developing the others. With these qualities active and growing in your lives, no grass will grow under your feet, no day will pass without its reward as you mature in your experience of our Master Jesus. Without these qualities you can't see what's right before you, oblivious that your old sinful life has been wiped off the books.

10-11 So, friends, confirm God's invitation to you, his choice of you. Don't put it off; do it now. Do this, and you'll have your life on a firm footing, the streets paved and the way wide open into the eternal kingdom of our Master and Savior, Jesus Christ.

The One Light in a Dark Time

12-15 Because the stakes are so high, even though you're up-to-date on all this truth and practice it inside and out, I'm not going to let up for a minute in calling you to attention before it. This is the post to which I've been assigned — keeping you alert with frequent reminders — and I'm sticking to it as long as I live. I know that I'm to die soon; the Master has made that quite clear to me. And so I am especially eager that you have all this down in black and white so that after I die, you'll have it for ready reference.

16-18 We weren't, you know, just wishing on a star when we laid the facts out before you regarding the powerful return of our Master, Jesus Christ. We were there for the preview! We saw it with our own eyes: Jesus resplendent with light from God the Father as the voice of Majestic Glory spoke: "This is my Son, marked by my love, focus of all my delight." We were there on the holy mountain with him. We heard the voice out of heaven with our very own ears.

19-21 We couldn't be more sure of what we saw and heard — *God's* glory, *God's* voice. The prophetic Word was confirmed to us. You'll do well to keep focusing on it. It's the one light you have in a dark time as you wait for daybreak and the rising of the Morning Star in your hearts. The main thing to keep in mind here is that no prophecy of Scripture is a matter of private opinion. And why? Because it's not something concocted in the human heart. Prophecy resulted when the Holy Spirit prompted men and women to speak God's Word.

LYING RELIGIOUS LEADERS

1-2 **2** But there were also *lying* prophets among the people then, just as there will be lying religious teachers among you. They'll smuggle in destructive divisions, pitting you against each other—biting the hand of the One who gave them a chance to have their lives back! They've put themselves on a fast downhill slide to destruction, but not before they recruit a crowd of mixed-up followers who can't tell right from wrong.

2-3 They give the way of truth a bad name. They're only out for themselves. They'll say anything, *anything*, that sounds good to exploit you. They won't, of course, get by with it. They'll come to a bad end, for God has never just stood by and let that kind of thing go on.

4-5 God didn't let the rebel angels off the hook, but jailed them in hell till Judgment Day. Neither did he let the ancient ungodly world off. He wiped it out with a flood, rescuing only eight people—Noah, the sole voice of righteousness, was one of them.

6-8 God decreed destruction for the cities of Sodom and Gomorrah. A mound of ashes was all that was left—grim warning to anyone bent on an ungodly life. But that good man Lot, driven nearly out of his mind by the sexual filth and perversity, was rescued. Surrounded by moral rot day after day after day, that righteous man was in constant torment.

9 So God knows how to rescue the godly from evil trials. And he knows how to hold the feet of the wicked to the fire until Judgment Day.

PREDATORS ON THE PROWL

10-11 God is especially incensed against these "teachers" who live by lust, addicted to a filthy existence. They despise interference from true authority, preferring to indulge in self-rule. Insolent egotists, they don't hesitate to speak evil against the most splendid of creatures. Even angels, their superiors in every way, wouldn't think of throwing their weight around like that, trying to slander others before God.

12-14 These people are nothing but brute beasts, born in the wild, predators on the prowl. In the very act of bringing down others with their ignorant blasphemies, they themselves will be brought down, losers in the end. Their evil will boomerang on them. They're so despicable and addicted to pleasure that they indulge in wild parties, carousing in broad daylight. They're obsessed with adultery, compulsive in sin, seducing every vulnerable soul they come upon. Their specialty is greed, and they're experts at it. Dead souls!

15-16 They've left the main road and are directionless, having taken the way of Balaam, son of Beor, the prophet who turned profiteer, a connoisseur of evil. But Balaam was stopped in his wayward tracks: A dumb animal spoke in a human voice and prevented the prophet's craziness.

17-19 There's nothing to these people—they're dried-up fountains, storm-scattered clouds, headed for a black hole in hell. They are loudmouths, full of hot air, but still they're dangerous. Men and women who have recently escaped from a deviant life are most susceptible to their brand of seduction. They promise these newcomers freedom, but they themselves are slaves of corruption, for if they're addicted to corruption—and they are—they're *enslaved*.

20-22 If they've escaped from the slum of sin by experiencing our Master and Savior, Jesus Christ, and then slid back into that same old life again, they're worse than if they had never left. Better not to have started out on the straight road to God than to start out and then turn back, repudiating the experience and the holy command. They prove the point of the proverbs, "A dog goes back to its own vomit" and "A scrubbed-up pig heads for the mud."

IN THE LAST DAYS

1-2 **3** My dear friends, this is now the second time I've written to you, both letters reminders to hold your minds in a state of undistracted attention. Keep in mind what the holy prophets said, and the command of our Master and Savior that was passed on by your apostles.

3-4 First off, you need to know that in the last days, mockers are going to have a heyday. Reducing everything to the level of their puny feelings, they'll mock, "So what's happened to the promise of his Coming? Our ancestors are dead and buried, and everything's going on just as it has from the first day of creation. Nothing's changed."

5-7 They conveniently forget that long ago all the galaxies and this very planet were brought into existence out of watery chaos by God's word. Then God's word brought the chaos back in a flood that destroyed the world. The current galaxies and earth are fuel for the final fire. God is poised, ready to speak his word again, ready to give the signal for the judgment and destruction of the desecrating skeptics.

THE DAY THE SKY WILL COLLAPSE

8-9 Don't overlook the obvious here, friends. With God, one day is as good as a thousand years, a thousand years as a day. God isn't late with his promise as some measure lateness. He is restraining himself on account of you, holding back the End because he doesn't want anyone lost. He's giving everyone space and time to change.

10 But when the Day of God's Judgment does come, it will be unannounced, like a thief. The sky will collapse with a thunderous bang, everything disintegrating in a huge conflagration, earth and all its works exposed to the scrutiny of Judgment.

11-13 Since everything here today might well be gone tomorrow, do you see how essential it is to live a holy life? Daily expect the Day of God, eager for its arrival. The galaxies will burn up and the elements melt down that day—but *we'll* hardly notice. We'll be looking the other way, ready for the promised new heavens and the promised new earth, all landscaped with righteousness.

14-16 So, my dear friends, since this is what you have to look forward to, do your very best to be found living at your best, in purity and peace. Interpret our Master's patient restraint for what it is: salvation. Our good brother Paul, who was given much wisdom in these matters, refers to this in all his letters, and has written you essentially the same thing. Some things Paul writes are difficult to understand. Irresponsible people who don't know what they are talking about twist them every which way. They do it to the rest of the Scriptures, too, destroying themselves as they do it.

17-18 But you, friends, are well-warned. Be on guard lest you lose your footing and get swept off your feet by these lawless and loose-talking teachers. Grow in grace and understanding of our Master and Savior, Jesus Christ.

Glory to the Master, now and forever! Yes!

1, 2, & 3 JOHN

The two most difficult things to get straight in life are love and God. More often than not, the mess people make of their lives can be traced to failure or stupidity or meanness in one or both of these areas.

The basic and biblical Christian conviction is that the two subjects are intricately related. If we want to deal with God the right way, we have to learn to love the right way. If we want to love the right way, we have to deal with God the right way. God and love can't be separated.

John's three letters provide wonderfully explicit direction in how this works. Jesus, the Messiah, is the focus: Jesus provides the full and true understanding of God; Jesus shows us the mature working-out of love. In Jesus, God and love are linked accurately, intricately, and indissolubly.

But there are always people around who don't want to be pinned down to the God Jesus reveals, to the love Jesus reveals. They want to make up their own idea of God, make up their own style of love. John was pastor to a church (or churches) disrupted by some of these people. In his letters we see him reestablishing the original and organic unity of God and love that comes to focus and becomes available to us in Jesus Christ.

1 JOHN

1-2 From the very first day, we were there, taking it all in — we heard it with our own ears, saw it with our own eyes, verified it with our own hands. The Word of Life appeared right before our eyes; we saw it happen! And now we're telling you in most sober prose that what we witnessed was, incredibly, this: The infinite Life of God himself took shape before us.

3-4 We saw it, we heard it, and now we're telling you so you can experience it along with us, this experience of communion with the Father and his Son, Jesus Christ. Our motive for writing is simply this: We want you to enjoy this, too. Your joy will double our joy!

WALK IN THE LIGHT

5 This, in essence, is the message we heard from Christ and are passing on to you: God is light, pure light; there's not a trace of darkness in him.

6-7 If we claim that we experience a shared life with him and continue to stumble around in the dark, we're obviously lying through our teeth — we're not *living* what we claim. But if we walk in the light, God himself being the light, we also experience a shared life with one another, as the sacrificed blood of Jesus, God's Son, purges all our sin.

8-10 If we claim that we're free of sin, we're only fooling ourselves. A claim like that is errant nonsense. On the other hand, if we admit our sins — make a clean breast of them — he won't let us down; he'll be true to himself. He'll forgive our sins and purge us of all wrongdoing. If we claim that we've never sinned, we out-and-out contradict God — make a liar out of him. A claim like that only shows off our ignorance of God.

1-2 I write this, dear children, to guide you out of sin. But if anyone does sin, we have a Priest-Friend in the presence of the Father: Jesus Christ, righteous Jesus. When he served as a sacrifice for our sins, he solved the sin problem for good — not only ours, but the whole world's.

THE ONLY WAY TO KNOW WE'RE IN HIM

2-3 Here's how we can be sure that we know God in the right way: Keep his commandments.

4-6 If someone claims, "I know him well!" but doesn't keep his commandments, he's obviously a liar. His life doesn't match his words. But the one who keeps God's word is the person in whom we see God's mature love. This is the only way to be sure we're in God. Anyone who claims to be intimate with God ought to live the same kind of life Jesus lived.

7-8 My dear friends, I'm not writing anything new here. This is the oldest commandment in the book, and you've known it from day one. It's always been implicit in the Message you've heard. On the other hand, perhaps it is new, freshly minted as it is in both Christ and you — the darkness on its way out and the True Light already blazing!

9-11 Anyone who claims to live in God's light and hates a brother or sister is still in the dark. It's the person who loves brother and sister who dwells in God's light and doesn't block the light from others. But whoever hates is still in the dark, stumbles around in the dark, doesn't know which end is up, blinded by the darkness.

LOVING THE WORLD

12-13 I remind you, my dear children: Your sins are forgiven in Jesus' name. You veterans were in on the ground floor, and know the One who started all this; you newcomers have won a big victory over the Evil One.

13-14 And a second reminder, dear children: You know the Father from personal experience. You veterans know the One who started it all; and you newcomers — such vitality and strength! God's word is so steady in you. Your fellowship with God enables you to gain a victory over the Evil One.

15-17 Don't love the world's ways. Don't love the world's goods. Love of the world squeezes out love for the Father. Practically everything that goes on in the world — wanting your own way, wanting everything for yourself, wanting to appear important — has nothing to do with the Father. It just isolates you from him. The world and all its wanting, wanting, wanting is on the way out — but whoever does what God wants is set for eternity.

ANTICHRISTS EVERYWHERE YOU LOOK

18 Children, time is just about up. You heard that Antichrist is coming. Well, they're all over the place, antichrists everywhere you look. That's how we know that we're close to the end.

19 They left us, but they were never really with us. If they had been, they would have stuck it out with us, loyal to the end. In leaving, they showed their true colors, showed they never did belong.

20-21 But you belong. The Holy One anointed you, and you all know it. I haven't been writing this to tell you something you don't know, but to confirm the truth you do know, and to remind you that the truth doesn't breed lies.

22-23 So who is lying here? It's the person who denies that Jesus is the Divine Christ, that's who. This is what makes an antichrist: denying the Father, denying the Son. No one who denies the Son has any part with the Father, but affirming the Son is an embrace of the Father as well.

24-25 Stay with what you heard from the beginning, the original message. Let it sink into your life. If what you heard from the beginning lives deeply in you, you will live deeply in both Son and Father. This is exactly what Christ promised: eternal life, real life!

26-27 I've written to warn you about those who are trying to deceive you. But they're no match for what is embedded deeply within you — Christ's anointing, no less! You don't need any of their so-called teaching. Christ's anointing teaches you the truth on everything you need to know about yourself and him, uncontaminated by a single lie. Live deeply in what you were taught.

LIVE DEEPLY IN CHRIST

28 And now, children, stay with Christ. Live deeply in Christ. Then we'll be ready for him when he appears, ready to receive him with open arms, with no cause for red-faced guilt or lame excuses when he arrives.

29 Once you're convinced that he is right and righteous, you'll recognize that all who practice righteousness are God's true children.

1 **3** What marvelous love the Father has extended to us! Just look at it — we're called children of God! That's who we really are. But that's also why the world doesn't recognize us or take us seriously, because

it has no idea who he is or what he's up to.

2-3 But friends, that's exactly who we are: children of God. And that's only the beginning. Who knows how we'll end up! What we know is that when Christ is openly revealed, we'll see him — and in seeing him, become like him. All of us who look forward to his Coming stay ready, with the glistening purity of Jesus' life as a model for our own.

4-6 All who indulge in a sinful life are dangerously lawless, for sin is a major disruption of God's order. Surely you know that Christ showed up in order to get rid of sin. There is no sin in him, and sin is not part of his program. No one who lives deeply in Christ makes a practice of sin. None of those who do practice sin have taken a good look at Christ. They've got him all backward.

7-8 So, my dear children, don't let anyone divert you from the truth. It's the person who *acts* right who *is* right, just as we see it lived out in our righteous Messiah. Those who make a practice of sin are straight from the Devil, the pioneer in the practice of sin. The Son of God entered the scene to abolish the Devil's ways.

9-10 People conceived and brought into life by God don't make a practice of sin. How could they? God's seed is deep within them, making them who they are. It's not in the nature of the God-begotten to practice and parade sin. Here's how you tell the difference between God's children and the Devil's children: The one who won't practice righteous ways isn't from God, nor is the one who won't love brother or sister. A simple test.

---

11 For this is the original message we heard: We should love each other.

12-13 We must not be like Cain, who joined the Evil One and then killed his brother. And why did he kill him? Because he was deep in the practice of evil, while the acts of his brother were righteous. So don't be surprised, friends, when the world hates you. This has been going on a long time.

14-15 The way we know we've been transferred from death to life is that we love our brothers and sisters. Anyone who doesn't love is as good as dead. Anyone who hates a brother or sister is a murderer, and you know very well that eternal life and murder don't go together.

16-17 This is how we've come to understand and experience love: Christ sacrificed his life for us. This is why we ought to live sacrificially for our fellow believers, and not just be out for ourselves. If you see some brother or sister in need and have the means to do something about it but turn a cold shoulder and do nothing, what happens to God's love? It disappears. And you made it disappear.

WHEN WE PRACTICE REAL LOVE

18-20 My dear children, let's not just talk about love; let's practice real love. This is the only way we'll know we're living truly, living in God's reality. It's also the way to shut down debilitating self-criticism, even when there is something to it. For God is greater than our worried hearts and knows more about us than we do ourselves.

21-24 And friends, once that's taken care of and we're no longer accusing or condemning ourselves, we're bold and free before God! We're able to stretch our hands out and receive what we asked for because we're doing what he said, doing what pleases him. Again, this is God's command: to believe in his personally named Son, Jesus Christ. He told us to love each other, in line with the original command. As we keep his commands, we live deeply and surely in him, and he lives in us. And this is how we experience his deep and abiding presence in us: by the Spirit he gave us.

DON'T BELIEVE EVERYTHING YOU HEAR

1   **4** My dear friends, don't believe everything you hear. Carefully weigh and examine what people tell you. Not everyone who talks about God comes from God. There are a lot of lying preachers loose in the world.

2-3   Here's how you test for the genuine Spirit of God. Everyone who confesses openly his faith in Jesus Christ — the Son of God, who came as an actual flesh-and-blood person — comes from God and belongs to God. And everyone who refuses to confess faith in Jesus has nothing in common with God. This is the spirit of antichrist that you heard was coming. Well, here it is, sooner than we thought!

4-6   My dear children, you come from God and belong to God. You have already won a big victory over those false teachers, for the Spirit in you is far stronger than anything in the world. These people belong to the Christ-denying world. They talk the world's language and the world eats it up. But we come from God and belong to God. Anyone who knows God understands us and listens. The person who has nothing to do with God will, of course, not listen to us. This is another test for telling the Spirit of Truth from the spirit of deception.

GOD IS LOVE

7-10   My beloved friends, let us continue to love each other since love comes from God. Everyone who loves is born of God and experiences a relationship with God. The person who refuses to love doesn't know the first thing about God, because God *is* love — so you can't know him if you don't love. This is how God showed his love for us: God sent his only Son into the world so we might live through him. This is the kind of love we are talking about — not that we once upon a time loved God, but that he loved us and sent his Son as a sacrifice to clear away our sins and the damage they've done to our relationship with God.

11-12   My dear, dear friends, if God loved us like this, we certainly ought to love each other. No one has seen God, ever. But if we love one another, God dwells deeply within us, and his love becomes complete in us — perfect love!

13-16   This is how we know we're living steadily and deeply in him, and he in us: He's given us life from his life, from his very own Spirit. Also, we've seen for ourselves and continue to state openly that the Father sent his Son as Savior of the world. Everyone who confesses that Jesus is God's Son participates continuously in an intimate relationship with God. We know it so well, we've embraced it heart and soul, this love that comes from God.

TO LOVE, TO BE LOVED

17-18   God is love. When we take up permanent residence in a life of love, we live in God and God lives in us. This way, love has the run of the house, becomes at home and mature in us, so that we're free of worry on Judgment Day — our standing in the world is identical with Christ's. There is no room in love for fear. Well-formed love banishes fear. Since fear is crippling, a fearful life — fear of death, fear of judgment — is one not yet fully formed in love.

19 We, though, are going to love — love and be loved. First we were loved, now we love. He loved us first.

20-21 If anyone boasts, "I love God," and goes right on hating his brother or sister, thinking nothing of it, he is a liar. If he won't love the person he can see, how can he love the God he can't see? The command we have from Christ is blunt: Loving God includes loving people. You've got to love both.

1-3 **5** Every person who believes that Jesus is, in fact, the Messiah, is God-begotten. If we love the One who conceives the child, we'll surely love the child who was conceived. The reality test on whether or not we love God's children is this: Do we love God? Do we keep his commands? The proof that we love God comes when we keep his commandments and they are not at all troublesome.

THE POWER THAT BRINGS THE WORLD TO ITS KNEES

4-5 Every God-begotten person conquers the world's ways. The conquering power that brings the world to its knees is our faith. The person who wins out over the world's ways is simply the one who believes Jesus is the Son of God.

6-8 Jesus — the Divine Christ! He experienced a life-giving birth and a death-killing death. Not only birth from the womb, but baptismal birth of his ministry and sacrificial death. And all the while the Spirit is confirming the truth, the reality of God's presence at Jesus' baptism and crucifixion, bringing those occasions alive for us. A triple testimony: the Spirit, the Baptism, the Crucifixion. And the three in perfect agreement.

9-10 If we take human testimony at face value, how much more should we be reassured when God gives testimony as he does here, testifying concerning his Son. Whoever believes in the Son of God inwardly confirms God's testimony. Whoever refuses to believe in effect calls God a liar, refusing to believe God's own testimony regarding his Son.

11-12 This is the testimony in essence: God gave us eternal life; the life is in his Son. So, whoever has the Son, has life; whoever rejects the Son, rejects life.

THE REALITY, NOT THE ILLUSION

13-15 My purpose in writing is simply this: that you who believe in God's Son will know beyond the shadow of a doubt that you have eternal life, the reality and not the illusion. And how bold and free we then become in his presence, freely asking according to his will, sure that he's listening. And if we're confident that he's listening, we know that what we've asked for is as good as ours.

16-17 For instance, if we see a Christian believer sinning (clearly I'm not talking about those who make a practice of sin in a way that is "fatal," leading to eternal death), we ask for God's help and he gladly gives it, gives life to the sinner whose sin is not fatal. There is such a thing as a fatal sin, and I'm not urging you to pray about that. Everything we do wrong is sin, but not all sin is fatal.

18-21 We know that none of the God-begotten makes a practice of sin — fatal sin. The God-begotten are also the God-protected. The Evil One can't lay a hand on them. We know that we are held firm by God; it's only the people of the world who continue in the grip of the Evil One. And we know that the Son of God came so we could recognize and understand the truth of God — what a gift! — and we are living in the Truth itself, in God's Son, Jesus Christ. This Jesus is both True God and Real Life. Dear children, be on guard against all clever facsimiles.

2 JOHN

1-2 My dear congregation, I, your pastor, love you in very truth. And I'm not alone—everyone who knows the Truth that has taken up permanent residence in us loves you.

3 Let grace, mercy, and peace be with us in truth and love from God the Father and from Jesus Christ, Son of the Father!

4-6 I can't tell you how happy I am to learn that many members of your congregation are diligent in living out the Truth, exactly as commanded by the Father. But permit me a reminder, friends, and this is not a new commandment but simply a repetition of our original and basic charter: that we love each other. Love means following his commandments, and his unifying commandment is that you conduct your lives in love. This is the first thing you heard, and nothing has changed.

DON'T WALK OUT ON GOD

7 There are a lot of smooth-talking charlatans loose in the world who refuse to believe that Jesus Christ was truly human, a flesh-and-blood human being. Give them their true title: Deceiver! Antichrist!

8-9 And be very careful around them so you don't lose out on what we've worked so diligently in together; I want you to get every reward you have coming to you. Anyone who gets so progressive in his thinking that he walks out on the teaching of Christ, walks out on God. But whoever stays with the teaching, stays faithful to both the Father and the Son.

10-11 If anyone shows up who doesn't hold to this teaching, don't invite him in and give him the run of the place. That would just give him a platform to perpetuate his evil ways, making you his partner.

12-13 I have a lot more things to tell you, but I'd rather not use paper and ink. I hope to be there soon in person and have a heart-to-heart talk. That will be far more satisfying to both you and me. Everyone here in your sister congregation sends greetings.

3 JOHN

1-4 The Pastor, to my good friend Gaius: How truly I love you! We're the best of friends, and I pray for good fortune in everything you do, and for your good health — that your everyday affairs prosper, as well as your soul! I was most happy when some friends arrived and brought the news that you persist in following the way of Truth. Nothing could make me happier than getting reports that my children continue diligently in the way of Truth!

MODEL THE GOOD

5-8 Dear friend, when you extend hospitality to Christian brothers and sisters, even when they are strangers, you make the faith visible. They've made a full report back to the church here, a message about your love. It's good work you're doing, helping these travelers on their way, hospitality worthy of God himself! They set out under the banner of the Name, and get no help from unbelievers. So they deserve any support we can give them. In providing meals and a bed, we become their companions in spreading the Truth.

9-10 Earlier I wrote something along this line to the church, but Diotrephes, who loves being in charge, denigrates my counsel. If I come, you can be sure I'll hold him to account for spreading vicious rumors about us.

As if that weren't bad enough, he not only refuses hospitality to traveling Christians but tries to stop others from welcoming them. Worse yet, instead of inviting them in he throws them out.

11 Friend, don't go along with evil. Model the good. The person who does good does God's work. The person who does evil falsifies God, doesn't know the first thing about God.

12 Everyone has a good word for Demetrius — the Truth itself stands up for Demetrius! We concur, and you know we don't hand out endorsements lightly.

13-14 I have a lot more things to tell you, but I'd rather not use pen and ink. I hope to be there soon in person and have a heart-to-heart talk.

Peace to you. The friends here say hello. Greet our friends there by name.

JUDE

Our spiritual communities are as susceptible to disease as our physical bodies. But it is easier to detect whatever is wrong in our stomachs and lungs than in our worship and witness. When our physical bodies are sick or damaged, the pain calls our attention to it, and we do something quick. But a dangerous, even deadly, virus in our spiritual communities can go undetected for a long time. As much as we need physicians for our bodies, we have even greater need for diagnosticians and healers of the spirit.

Jude's letter to an early community of Christians is just such diagnosis. It is all the more necessary in that those believers apparently didn't know anything was wrong, or at least not as desperately wrong as Jude points out.

There is far more, of course, to living in Christian community than protecting the faith against assault or subversion. Paranoia is as unhealthy spiritually as it is mentally. The primary Christian posture is, in Jude's words, "keeping your arms open and outstretched, ready for the mercy of our Master, Jesus Christ." All the same, energetic watchfulness is required. Jude's whistle-blowing has prevented many a disaster.

JUDE

1-2 I, Jude, am a slave to Jesus Christ and brother to James, writing to those loved by God the Father, called and kept safe by Jesus Christ. Relax, everything's going to be all right; rest, everything's coming together; open your hearts, love is on the way!

FIGHT WITH ALL YOU HAVE IN YOU

3-4 Dear friends, I've dropped everything to write you about this life of salvation that we have in common. I have to write insisting — begging! — that you fight with everything you have in you for this faith entrusted to us as a gift to guard and cherish. What has happened is that some people have infiltrated our ranks (our Scriptures warned us this would happen), who beneath their pious skin are shameless scoundrels. Their design is to replace the sheer grace of our God with sheer license — which means doing away with Jesus Christ, our one and only Master.

LOST STARS IN OUTER SPACE

5-7 I'm laying this out as clearly as I can, even though you once knew all this well enough and shouldn't need reminding. Here it is in brief: The Master saved a people out of the land of Egypt. Later he destroyed those who defected. And you know the story of the angels who didn't stick to their post, abandoning it for other, darker missions. But they are now chained and jailed in a black hole until the great Judgment Day. Sodom and Gomorrah, which went to sexual rack and ruin along with the surrounding cities that acted just like them, are another example. Burning and burning and never burning up, they serve still as a stock warning.

8 This is exactly the same program of these latest infiltrators: dirty sex, rule and rulers thrown out, glory dragged in the mud.

9-11 The Archangel Michael, who went to the mat with the Devil as they fought over the body of Moses, wouldn't have dared level him with a blasphemous curse, but said simply, "No you don't. *God* will take care of you!" But these people sneer at anything they can't understand, and by doing whatever they feel like doing — living by animal instinct only — they participate in their own destruction. I'm fed up with them! They've gone down Cain's road; they've been sucked into Balaam's error by greed; they're canceled out in Korah's rebellion.

12-13 These people are warts on your love feasts as you worship and eat together. They're giving you a black eye — carousing shamelessly, grabbing anything that isn't nailed down. They're —

> Puffs of smoke pushed by gusts of wind;
>   late autumn trees stripped clean of leaf and fruit,
> Doubly dead, pulled up by the roots;
>   wild ocean waves leaving nothing on the beach
>   but the foam of their shame;
> Lost stars in outer space
>   on their way to the black hole.

14-16   Enoch, the seventh after Adam, prophesied of them: "Look! The Master comes with thousands of holy angels to bring judgment against them all, convicting each person of every defiling act of shameless sacrilege, of every dirty word they have spewed of their pious filth." These are the "grumpers," the bellyachers, grabbing for the biggest piece of the pie, talking big, saying anything they think will get them ahead.

17-19   But remember, dear friends, that the apostles of our Master, Jesus Christ, told us this would happen: "In the last days there will be people who don't take these things seriously anymore. They'll treat them like a joke, and make a religion of their own whims and lusts." These are the ones who split churches, thinking only of themselves. There's nothing to them, no sign of the Spirit!

20-21   But you, dear friends, carefully build yourselves up in this most holy faith by praying in the Holy Spirit, staying right at the center of God's love, keeping your arms open and outstretched, ready for the mercy of our Master, Jesus Christ. This is the unending life, the *real* life!

22-23   Go easy on those who hesitate in the faith. Go after those who take the wrong way. Be tender with sinners, but not soft on sin. The sin itself stinks to high heaven.

24-25   And now to him who can keep you on your feet, standing tall in his bright presence, fresh and celebrating — to our one God, our only Savior, through Jesus Christ, our Master, be glory, majesty, strength, and rule before all time, and now, and to the end of all time. Yes.

REVELATION

The Bible ends with a flourish: vision and song, doom and deliverance, terror and triumph. The rush of color and sound, image and energy, leaves us reeling. But if we persist through the initial confusion and read on, we begin to pick up the rhythms, realize the connections, and find ourselves enlisted as participants in a multidimensional act of Christian worship.

John of Patmos, a pastor of the late first century, has worship on his mind, is preeminently concerned with worship. The vision, which is The Revelation, comes to him while he is at worship on a certain Sunday on the Mediterranean island of Patmos. He is responsible for a circuit of churches on the mainland whose primary task is worship. Worship shapes the human community in response to the living God. If worship is neglected or perverted, our communities fall into chaos or under tyranny.

Our times are not propitious for worship. The times never are. The world is hostile to worship. The Devil hates worship. As The Revelation makes clear, worship must be carried out under conditions decidedly uncongenial to it. Some Christians even get killed because they worship.

John's Revelation is not easy reading. Besides being a pastor, John is a poet, fond of metaphor and symbol, image and allusion, passionate in his desire to bring us into the presence of Jesus believing and adoring. But the demands he makes on our intelligence and imagination are well rewarded, for in keeping company with John, our worship of God will almost certainly deepen in urgency and joy.

REVELATION

1-2 1 A revealing of Jesus, the Messiah. God gave it to make plain to his servants what is about to happen. He published and delivered it by Angel to his servant John. And John told everything he saw: God's Word — the witness of Jesus Christ!

3 How blessed the reader! How blessed the hearers and keepers of these oracle words, all the words written in this book!

Time is just about up.

HIS EYES POURING FIRE-BLAZE

4-7 I, John, am writing this to the seven churches in Asia province: All the best to you from THE GOD WHO IS, THE GOD WHO WAS, AND THE GOD ABOUT TO ARRIVE, and from the Seven Spirits assembled before his throne, and from Jesus Christ — Loyal Witness, Firstborn from the dead, Ruler of all earthly kings.

Glory and strength to Christ, who loves us,
    who blood-washed our sins from our lives,
Who made us a Kingdom, Priests for his Father,
    forever — and yes, he's on his way!
Riding the clouds, he'll be seen by every eye,
    those who mocked and killed him will see him,
People from all nations and all times
    will tear their clothes in lament.
        Oh, Yes.

8 The Master declares, "I'm A to Z. I'm THE GOD WHO IS, THE GOD WHO WAS, AND THE GOD ABOUT TO ARRIVE. I'm the Sovereign-Strong."

9-17 I, John, with you all the way in the trial and the Kingdom and the passion of patience in Jesus, was on the island called Patmos because of God's Word, the witness of Jesus. It was Sunday and I was in the Spirit, praying. I heard a loud voice behind me, trumpet-clear and piercing: "Write what you see into a book. Send it to the seven churches: to Ephesus, Smyrna, Pergamum, Thyatira, Sardis, Philadelphia, Laodicea." I turned and saw the voice.

I saw a gold menorah
    with seven branches,
And in the center, the Son of Man,
    in a robe and gold breastplate,
    hair a blizzard of white,
Eyes pouring fire-blaze,
    both feet furnace-fired bronze,
His voice a cataract,
    right hand holding the Seven Stars,
His mouth a sharp-biting sword,
    his face a perigee sun.

I saw this and fainted dead at his feet. His right hand pulled me upright, his voice reassured me:

17-20 "Don't fear: I am First, I am Last, I'm Alive. I died, but I came to life, and my life is now forever. See these keys in my hand? They open and lock Death's doors, they open and lock Hell's gates. Now write down everything you see: things that are, things about to be. The Seven Stars you saw in my right hand and the seven-branched gold menorah — do you want to know what's behind them? The Seven Stars are the Angels of the seven churches; the menorah's seven branches are the seven churches."

To Ephesus

1 Write this to Ephesus, to the Angel of the church. The One with Seven Stars in his right-fist grip, striding through the golden seven-lights' circle, speaks:

2-3 "I see what you've done, your hard, hard work, your refusal to quit. I know you can't stomach evil, that you weed out apostolic pretenders. I know your persistence, your courage in my cause, that you never wear out.

4-5 "But you walked away from your first love — why? What's going on with you, anyway? Do you have any idea how far you've fallen? A Lucifer fall!

"Turn back! Recover your dear early love. No time to waste, for I'm well on my way to removing your light from the golden circle.

6 "You do have this to your credit: You hate the Nicolaitan business. I hate it, too.

7 "Are your ears awake? Listen. Listen to the Wind Words, the Spirit blowing through the churches. I'm about to call each conqueror to dinner. I'm spreading a banquet of Tree-of-Life fruit, a supper plucked from God's orchard."

To Smyrna

8 Write this to Smyrna, to the Angel of the church. The Beginning and Ending, the First and Final One, the Once Dead and Then Come Alive, speaks:

9 "I can see your pain and poverty — constant pain, dire poverty — but I also see your wealth. And I hear the lie in the claims of those who pretend to be good Jews, who in fact belong to Satan's crowd.

10 "Fear nothing in the things you're about to suffer — but stay on guard! Fear nothing! The Devil is about to throw you in jail for a time of testing — ten days. It won't last forever.

"Don't quit, even if it costs you your life. Stay there believing. I have a Life-Crown sized and ready for you.

11 "Are your ears awake? Listen. Listen to the Wind Words, the Spirit blowing through the churches. Christ-conquerors are safe from Devil-death."

To Pergamum

12 Write this to Pergamum, to the Angel of the church. The One with the sharp-biting sword draws from the sheath of his mouth — out come the sword words:

13 "I see where you live, right under the shadow of Satan's throne. But you continue boldly in my Name; you never once denied my Name, even when

the pressure was worst, when they martyred Antipas, my witness who stayed faithful to me on Satan's turf.

14-15 "But why do you indulge that Balaam crowd? Don't you remember that Balaam was an enemy agent, seducing Balak and sabotaging Israel's holy pilgrimage by throwing unholy parties? And why do you put up with the Nicolaitans, who do the same thing?

16 "Enough! Don't give in to them; I'll be with you soon. I'm fed up and about to cut them to pieces with my sword-sharp words.

17 "Are your ears awake? Listen. Listen to the Wind Words, the Spirit blowing through the churches. I'll give the sacred manna to every conqueror; I'll also give a clear, smooth stone inscribed with your new name, your secret new name."

To Thyatira

18 Write this to Thyatira, to the Angel of the church. God's Son, eyes pouring fire-blaze, standing on feet of furnace-fired bronze, says this:

19 "I see everything you're doing for me. Impressive! The love and the faith, the service and persistence. Yes, very impressive! You get better at it every day.

20-23 "But why do you let that Jezebel who calls herself a prophet mislead my dear servants into Cross-denying, self-indulging religion? I gave her a chance to change her ways, but she has no intention of giving up a career in the god-business. I'm about to lay her low, along with her partners, as they play their sex-and-religion games. The bastard offspring of their idol-whoring I'll kill. Then every church will know that appearances don't impress me. I x-ray every motive and make sure you get what's coming to you.

24-25 "The rest of you Thyatirans, who have nothing to do with this outrage, who scorn this playing around with the Devil that gets paraded as profundity, be assured I'll not make life any harder for you than it already is. Hold on to the truth you have until I get there.

26-28 "Here's the reward I have for every conqueror, everyone who keeps at it, refusing to give up: You'll rule the nations, your Shepherd-King rule as firm as an iron staff, their resistance fragile as clay pots. This was the gift my Father gave me; I pass it along to you — and with it, the Morning Star!

29 "Are your ears awake? Listen. Listen to the Wind Words, the Spirit blowing through the churches."

To Sardis

1 3 Write this to Sardis, to the Angel of the church. The One holding the Seven Spirits of God in one hand, a firm grip on the Seven Stars with the other, speaks:

"I see right through your work. You have a reputation for vigor and zest, but you're dead, stone-dead.

2-3 "Up on your feet! Take a deep breath! Maybe there's life in you yet. But I wouldn't know it by looking at your busywork; nothing of *God's* work has been completed. Your condition is desperate. Think of the gift you once had in your hands, the Message you heard with your ears — grasp it again and turn back to God.

"If you pull the covers back over your head and sleep on, oblivious to God, I'll return when you least expect it, break into your life like a thief in the night.

4 "You still have a few followers of Jesus in Sardis who haven't ruined themselves wallowing in the muck of the world's ways. They'll walk with me on parade! They've proved their worth!

5 "Conquerors will march in the victory parade, their names indelible in the Book of Life. I'll lead them up and present them by name to my Father and his Angels.

6 "Are your ears awake? Listen. Listen to the Wind Words, the Spirit blowing through the churches."

To PHILADELPHIA

7 Write this to Philadelphia, to the Angel of the church. The Holy, the True—David's key in his hand, opening doors no one can lock, locking doors no one can open—speaks:

8 "I see what you've done. Now see what *I've* done. I've opened a door before you that no one can slam shut. You don't have much strength, I know that; you used what you had to keep my Word. You didn't deny me when times were rough.

9 "And watch as I take those who call themselves true believers but are nothing of the kind, pretenders whose true membership is in the club of Satan—watch as I strip off their pretensions and they're forced to acknowledge it's you that I've loved.

10 "Because you kept my Word in passionate patience, I'll keep you safe in the time of testing that will be here soon, and all over the earth, every man, woman, and child put to the test.

11 "I'm on my way; I'll be there soon. Keep a tight grip on what you have so no one distracts you and steals your crown.

12 "I'll make each conqueror a pillar in the sanctuary of my God, a permanent position of honor. Then I'll write names on you, the pillars: the Name of my God, the Name of God's City—the new Jerusalem coming down out of Heaven—and my new Name.

13 "Are your ears awake? Listen. Listen to the Wind Words, the Spirit blowing through the churches."

To LAODICEA

14 Write to Laodicea, to the Angel of the church. God's Yes, the Faithful and Accurate Witness, the First of God's creation, says:

15-17 "I know you inside and out, and find little to my liking. You're not cold, you're not hot—far better to be either cold or hot! You're stale. You're stagnant. You make me want to vomit. You brag, 'I'm rich, I've got it made, I need nothing from anyone,' oblivious that in fact you're a pitiful, blind beggar, threadbare and homeless.

18 "Here's what I want you to do: Buy your gold from me, gold that's been through the refiner's fire. Then you'll be rich. Buy your clothes from me, clothes designed in Heaven. You've gone around half-naked long enough. And buy medicine for your eyes from me so you can see, *really* see.

19 "The people I love, I call to account—prod and correct and guide so that they'll live at their best. Up on your feet, then! About face! Run after God!

20-21 "Look at me. I stand at the door. I knock. If you hear me call and open the door, I'll come right in and sit down to supper with you. Conquerors will sit alongside me at the head table, just as I, having conquered, took

the place of honor at the side of my Father. That's my gift to the conquerors!
22 "Are your ears awake? Listen. Listen to the Wind Words, the Spirit blowing through the churches."

A Door into Heaven

1 4 Then I looked, and, oh! — a door open into Heaven. The trumpet-voice, the first voice in my vision, called out, "Ascend and enter. I'll show you what happens next."

2-6 I was caught up at once in deep worship and, oh! — a Throne set in Heaven with One Seated on the Throne, suffused in gem hues of amber and flame with a nimbus of emerald. Twenty-four thrones circled the Throne, with Twenty-four Elders seated, white-robed, gold-crowned. Lightning flash and thunder crash pulsed from the Throne. Seven fire-blazing torches fronted the Throne (these are the Sevenfold Spirit of God). Before the Throne it was like a clear crystal sea.

6-8 Prowling around the Throne were Four Animals, all eyes. Eyes to look ahead, eyes to look behind. The first Animal like a lion, the second like an ox, the third with a human face, the fourth like an eagle in flight. The Four Animals were winged, each with six wings. They were all eyes, seeing around and within. And they chanted night and day, never taking a break:

Holy, holy, holy
Is God our Master, Sovereign-Strong,
THE WAS, THE IS, THE COMING.

9-11 Every time the Animals gave glory and honor and thanks to the One Seated on the Throne — the age-after-age Living One — the Twenty-four Elders would fall prostrate before the One Seated on the Throne. They worshiped the age-after-age Living One. They threw their crowns at the foot of the Throne, chanting,

Worthy, O Master! Yes, our God!
Take the glory! the honor! the power!
You created it all;
It was created because you wanted it.

The Lion Is a Lamb

1-2 5 I saw a scroll in the right hand of the One Seated on the Throne. It was written on both sides, fastened with seven seals. I also saw a powerful Angel, calling out in a voice like thunder, "Is there anyone who can open the scroll, who can break its seals?"

3 There was no one — no one in Heaven, no one on earth, no one from the underworld — able to break open the scroll and read it.

4-5 I wept and wept and wept that no one was found able to open the scroll, able to read it. One of the Elders said, "Don't weep. Look — the Lion from Tribe Judah, the Root of David's Tree, has conquered. He can open the scroll, can rip through the seven seals."

6-10 So I looked, and there, surrounded by Throne, Animals, and Elders, was a Lamb, slaughtered but standing tall. Seven horns he had, and seven eyes, the Seven Spirits of God sent into all the earth. He came to the One Seated on the Throne and took the scroll from his right hand. The moment he took the scroll, the Four Animals and Twenty-four Elders fell down and worshiped the Lamb. Each had a harp and each had a bowl, a gold bowl filled with incense, the prayers of God's holy people. And they sang a new song:

> Worthy! Take the scroll, open its seals.
> Slain! Paying in blood, you bought men and women,
> Bought them back from all over the earth,
> Bought them back for God.
> Then you made them a Kingdom, Priests for our God,
> Priest-kings to rule over the earth.

11-14   I looked again. I heard a company of Angels around the Throne, the Animals, and the Elders — ten thousand times ten thousand their number, thousand after thousand after thousand in full song:

> The slain Lamb is worthy!
> Take the power, the wealth, the wisdom, the strength!
> Take the honor, the glory, the blessing!

Then I heard every creature in Heaven and earth, in underworld and sea, join in, all voices in all places, singing:

> To the One on the Throne! To the Lamb!
> The blessing, the honor, the glory, the strength,
> For age after age after age.

The Four Animals called out, "Oh, Yes!" The Elders fell to their knees and worshiped.

UNSEALING THE SCROLL

1-2   **6** I watched while the Lamb ripped off the first of the seven seals. I heard one of the Animals roar, "Come out!" I looked — I saw a white horse. Its rider carried a bow and was given a victory garland. He rode off victorious, conquering right and left.

3-4   When the Lamb ripped off the second seal, I heard the second Animal cry, "Come out!" Another horse appeared, this one red. Its rider was off to take peace from the earth, setting people at each other's throats, killing one another. He was given a huge sword.

5-6   When he ripped off the third seal, I heard the third Animal cry, "Come out!" I looked. A black horse this time. Its rider carried a set of scales in his hand. I heard a message (it seemed to issue from the Four Animals): "A quart of wheat for a day's wages, or three quarts of barley, but all the oil and wine you want."

7-8   When he ripped off the fourth seal, I heard the fourth Animal cry, "Come out!" I looked. A colorless horse, sickly pale. Its rider was Death, and Hell was close on its heels. They were given power to destroy a fourth of the earth by war, famine, disease, and wild beasts.

9-11   When he ripped off the fifth seal, I saw the souls of those killed because they had held firm in their witness to the Word of God. They were gathered under the Altar, and cried out in loud prayers, "How long, Strong

God, Holy and True? How long before you step in and avenge our murders?" Then each martyr was given a white robe and told to sit back and wait until the full number of martyrs was filled from among their servant companions and friends in the faith.

12-17   I watched while he ripped off the sixth seal: a bone-jarring earth-quake, sun turned black as ink, moon all bloody, stars falling out of the sky like figs shaken from a tree in a high wind, sky snapped shut like a book, islands and mountains sliding this way and that. And then pandemonium, everyone and his dog running for cover — kings, princes, generals, rich and strong, along with every commoner, slave or free. They hid in mountain caves and rocky dens, calling out to mountains and rocks, "Refuge! Hide us from the One Seated on the Throne and the wrath of the Lamb! The great Day of their wrath has come — who can stand it?"

THE SERVANTS OF GOD

1   *7* Immediately I saw Four Angels standing at the four corners of earth, standing steady with a firm grip on the four winds so no wind would blow on earth or sea, not even rustle a tree.

2-3   Then I saw another Angel rising from where the sun rose, carrying the seal of the Living God. He thundered to the Four Angels assigned the task of hurting earth and sea, "Don't hurt the earth! Don't hurt the sea! Don't so much as hurt a tree until I've sealed the servants of our God on their foreheads!"

4-8   I heard the count of those who were sealed: 144,000! They were sealed out of every Tribe of Israel: 12,000 sealed from Judah, 12,000 from Reuben, 12,000 from Gad, 12,000 from Asher, 12,000 from Naphtali, 12,000 from Manasseh, 12,000 from Simeon, 12,000 from Levi, 12,000 from Issachar, 12,000 from Zebulun, 12,000 from Joseph, 12,000 sealed from Benjamin.

9-12   I looked again. I saw a huge crowd, too huge to count. Everyone was there — all nations and tribes, all races and languages. And they were *stand ing*, dressed in white robes and waving palm branches, standing before the Throne and the Lamb and heartily singing:

Salvation to our God on his Throne!
Salvation to the Lamb!

All who were standing around the Throne — Angels, Elders, Animals — fell on their faces before the Throne and worshiped God, singing:

Oh, Yes!
The blessing and glory and wisdom and thanksgiving,
The honor and power and strength,
To our God forever and ever and ever!
Oh, Yes!

13-14   Just then one of the Elders addressed me: "Who are these dressed in white robes, and where did they come from?" Taken aback, I said, "O Sir, I have no idea — but you must know."

14-17   Then he told me, "These are those who come from the great tribulation, and they've washed their robes, scrubbed them clean in the blood of the Lamb. That's why they're standing before God's Throne. They serve him day and night in his Temple. The One on the Throne will pitch his tent there for them: no more hunger, no more thirst, no more scorching heat. The Lamb on the Throne will shepherd them, will lead them to spring waters of Life. And God will wipe every last tear from their eyes."

1   When the Lamb ripped off the seventh seal, Heaven fell quiet — complete silence for about half an hour.

BLOWING THE TRUMPETS

2-4   I saw the Seven Angels who are always in readiness before God handed seven trumpets. Then another Angel, carrying a gold censer, came and stood at the Altar. He was given a great quantity of incense so that he could offer up the prayers of all the holy people of God on the Golden Altar before the Throne. Smoke billowed up from the incense-laced prayers of the holy ones, rose before God from the hand of the Angel.

5   Then the Angel filled the censer with fire from the Altar and heaved it to earth. It set off thunders, voices, lightnings, and an earthquake.

6-7   The Seven Angels with the trumpets got ready to blow them. At the first trumpet blast, hail and fire mixed with blood were dumped on earth. A third of the earth was scorched, a third of the trees, and every blade of green grass — burned to a crisp.

8-9   The second Angel trumpeted. Something like a huge mountain blazing with fire was flung into the sea. A third of the sea turned to blood, a third of the living sea creatures died, and a third of the ships sank.

10-11   The third Angel trumpeted. A huge Star, blazing like a torch, fell from Heaven, wiping out a third of the rivers and a third of the springs. The Star's name was Wormwood. A third of the water turned bitter, and many people died from the poisoned water.

12   The fourth Angel trumpeted. A third of the sun, a third of the moon, and a third of the stars were hit, blacked out by a third, both day and night in one-third blackout.

13   I looked hard; I heard a lone eagle, flying through Middle-Heaven, crying out ominously, "Doom! Doom! Doom to everyone left on earth! There are three more Angels about to blow their trumpets. Doom is on its way!"

1-2   The fifth Angel trumpeted. I saw a Star plummet from Heaven to earth. The Star was handed a key to the Well of the Abyss. He unlocked the Well of the Abyss — smoke poured out of the Well, billows and billows of smoke, sun and air in blackout from smoke pouring out of the Well.

3-6   Then out of the smoke crawled locusts with the venom of scorpions. They were given their orders: "Don't hurt the grass, don't hurt anything green, don't hurt a single tree — only men and women, and then only those who lack the seal of God on their foreheads." They were ordered to torture but not kill, torture them for five months, the pain like a scorpion sting. When this happens, people are going to prefer death to torture, look for ways to kill themselves. But they won't find a way — death will have gone into hiding.

7-11   The locusts looked like horses ready for war. They had gold crowns, human faces, women's hair, the teeth of lions, and iron breastplates. The sound of their wings was the sound of horse-drawn chariots charging into battle. Their tails were equipped with stings, like scorpion tails. With those tails they were ordered to torture the human race for five months. They had a king over them, the Angel of the Abyss. His name in Hebrew is *Abaddon*, in Greek, *Apollyon* — "Destroyer."

12   The first doom is past. Two dooms yet to come.

13-14   The sixth Angel trumpeted. I heard a voice speaking to the sixth Angel from the horns of the Golden Altar before God: "Let the Four Angels loose, the Angels confined at the great River Euphrates."

15-19   The Four Angels were untied and let loose, Four Angels all prepared for the exact year, month, day, and even hour when they were to kill a third of the human race. The number of the army of horsemen was twice ten thousand times ten thousand. I heard the count and saw both horses and riders in my vision: fiery breastplates on the riders, lion heads on the horses breathing out fire and smoke and brimstone. With these three weapons — fire and smoke and brimstone — they killed a third of the human race. The horses killed with their mouths and tails; their serpentlike tails also had heads that wreaked havoc.

20-21   The remaining men and women who weren't killed by these weapons went on their merry way — didn't change their way of life, didn't quit worshiping demons, didn't quit centering their lives around lumps of gold and silver and brass, hunks of stone and wood that couldn't see or hear or move. There wasn't a sign of a change of heart. They plunged right on in their murderous, occult, promiscuous, and thieving ways.

1-4   I saw another powerful Angel coming down out of Heaven wrapped in a cloud. There was a rainbow over his head, his face was sun-radiant, his legs pillars of fire. He had a small book open in his hand. He placed his right foot on the sea and his left foot on land, then called out thunderously, a lion roar. When he called out, the Seven Thunders called back. When the Seven Thunders spoke, I started to write it all down, but a voice out of Heaven stopped me, saying, "Seal with silence the Seven Thunders; don't write a word."

5-7   Then the Angel I saw astride sea and land lifted his right hand to Heaven and swore by the One Living Forever and Ever, who created Heaven and everything in it, earth and everything in it, sea and everything in it, that time was up — that when the seventh Angel blew his trumpet, which he was about to do, the Mystery of God, all the plans he had revealed to his servants, the prophets, would be completed.

8-11   The voice out of Heaven spoke to me again: "Go, take the book held open in the hand of the Angel astride sea and earth." I went up to the Angel and said, "Give me the little book." He said, "Take it, then eat it. It will taste sweet like honey, but turn sour in your stomach." I took the little book from the Angel's hand and it was sweet honey in my mouth, but when I swallowed, my stomach curdled. Then I was told, "You must go back and prophesy again over many peoples and nations and languages and kings."

1-2 I was given a stick for a measuring rod and told, "Get up and measure God's Temple and Altar and everyone worshiping in it. Exclude the outside court; don't measure it. It's been handed over to non-Jewish outsiders. They'll desecrate the Holy City for forty-two months.

3-6 "Meanwhile, I'll provide my two Witnesses. Dressed in sackcloth, they'll prophesy for 1,260 days. These are the two Olive Trees, the two Lampstands, standing at attention before God on earth. If anyone tries to hurt them, a blast of fire from their mouths will incinerate them — burn them to a crisp just like that. They'll have power to seal the sky so that it doesn't rain for the time of their prophesying, power to turn rivers and springs to blood, power to hit earth with any and every disaster as often as they want.

7-10 "When they've completed their witness, the Beast from the Abyss will emerge and fight them, conquer and kill them, leaving their corpses exposed on the street of the Great City spiritually called Sodom and Egypt, the same City where their Master was crucified. For three and a half days they'll be there — exposed, prevented from getting a decent burial, stared at by the curious from all over the world. Those people will cheer at the spectacle, shouting 'Good riddance!' and calling for a celebration, for these two prophets pricked the conscience of all the people on earth, made it impossible for them to enjoy their sins.

11 "Then, after three and a half days, the Living Spirit of God will enter them — they're on their feet! — and all those gloating spectators will be scared to death."

12-13 I heard a strong voice out of Heaven calling, "Come up here!" and up they went to Heaven, wrapped in a cloud, their enemies watching it all. At that moment there was a gigantic earthquake — a tenth of the city fell to ruin, seven thousand perished in the earthquake, the rest frightened to the core of their being, frightened into giving honor to the God-of-Heaven.

14 The second doom is past, the third doom coming right on its heels.

THE LAST TRUMPET SOUNDS

15-18 The seventh Angel trumpeted. A crescendo of voices in Heaven sang out,

> The kingdom of the world is now
>   the Kingdom of our God and his Messiah!
> He will rule forever and ever!

The Twenty-four Elders seated before God on their thrones fell to their knees, worshiped, and sang,

> We thank you, O God, Sovereign-Strong,
>   WHO IS AND WHO WAS.
> You took your great power
>   and took over — reigned!
> The angry nations now
>   get a taste of *your* anger.

The time has come to judge the dead,
to reward your servants, all prophets and saints,
Reward small and great who fear your Name,
and destroy the destroyers of earth.

19 The doors of God's Temple in Heaven flew open, and the Ark of his Covenant was clearly seen surrounded by flashes of lightning, loud shouts, peals of thunder, an earthquake, and a fierce hailstorm.

THE WOMAN, HER SON, AND THE DRAGON

1-2 12 A great Sign appeared in Heaven: a Woman dressed all in sunlight, standing on the moon, and crowned with Twelve Stars. She was giving birth to a Child and cried out in the pain of childbirth.

3-4 And then another Sign alongside the first: a huge and fiery Dragon! It had seven heads and ten horns, a crown on each of the seven heads. With one flick of its tail it knocked a third of the Stars from the sky and dumped them on earth. The Dragon crouched before the Woman in childbirth, poised to eat up the Child when it came.

5-6 The Woman gave birth to a Son who will shepherd all nations with an iron rod. Her Son was seized and placed safely before God on his Throne. The Woman herself escaped to the desert to a place of safety prepared by God, all comforts provided her for 1,260 days.

7-12 War broke out in Heaven. Michael and his Angels fought the Dragon. The Dragon and his Angels fought back, but were no match for Michael. They were cleared out of Heaven, not a sign of them left. The great Dragon — ancient Serpent, the one called Devil and Satan, the one who led the whole earth astray — thrown out, and all his Angels thrown out with him, thrown down to earth. Then I heard a strong voice out of Heaven saying,

Salvation and power are established!
Kingdom of our God, authority of his Messiah!
The Accuser of our brothers and sisters thrown out,
who accused them day and night before God.
They defeated him through the blood of the Lamb
and the bold word of their witness.
They weren't in love with themselves;
they were willing to die for Christ.
So rejoice, O Heavens, and all who live there,
but doom to earth and sea,
For the Devil's come down on you with both feet;
he's had a great fall;
He's wild and raging with anger;
he hasn't much time and he knows it.

13-17 When the Dragon saw he'd been thrown to earth, he went after the Woman who had given birth to the Man-Child. The Woman was given wings of a great eagle to fly to a place in the desert to be kept in safety and comfort for a time and times and half a time, safe and sound from the Serpent. The Serpent vomited a river of water to swamp and drown her, but earth came to her help, swallowing the water the Dragon spewed from its mouth. Helpless with rage, the Dragon raged at the Woman, then went off to make war with the rest of her children, the children who keep God's commands and hold firm to the witness of Jesus.

The Beast from the Sea

1-2 **13** And the Dragon stood on the shore of the sea. I saw a Beast rising from the sea. It had ten horns and seven heads — on each horn a crown, and each head inscribed with a blasphemous name. The Beast I saw looked like a leopard with bear paws and a lion's mouth. The Dragon turned over its power to it, its throne and great authority.

3-4 One of the Beast's heads looked as if it had been struck a deathblow, and then healed. The whole earth was agog, gaping at the Beast. They worshiped the Dragon who gave the Beast authority, and they worshiped the Beast, exclaiming, "There's never been anything like the Beast! No one would dare go to war with the Beast!"

5-8 The Beast had a loud mouth, boastful and blasphemous. It could do anything it wanted for forty-two months. It yelled blasphemies against God, blasphemed his Name, blasphemed his Church, especially those already dwelling with God in Heaven. It was permitted to make war on God's holy people and conquer them. It held absolute sway over all tribes and peoples, tongues and races. Everyone on earth whose name was not written from the world's foundation in the slaughtered Lamb's Book of Life will worship the Beast.

9-10 Are you listening to this? They've made their bed; now they must lie in it. Anyone marked for prison goes straight to prison; anyone pulling a sword goes down by the sword. Meanwhile, God's holy people passionately and faithfully stand their ground.

The Beast from Under the Ground

11-12 I saw another Beast rising out of the ground. It had two horns like a lamb but sounded like a dragon when it spoke. It was a puppet of the first Beast, made earth and everyone in it worship the first Beast, which had been healed of its deathblow.

13-17 This second Beast worked magical signs, dazzling people by making fire come down from Heaven. It used the magic it got from the Beast to dupe earth dwellers, getting them to make an image of the Beast that received the deathblow and lived. It was able to animate the image of the Beast so that it talked, and then arrange that anyone not worshiping the Beast would be killed. It forced all people, small and great, rich and poor, free and slave, to have a mark on the right hand or forehead. Without the mark of the name of the Beast or the number of its name, it was impossible to buy or sell anything.

18 Solve a riddle: Put your heads together and figure out the meaning of the number of the Beast. It's a human number: 666.

A Perfect Offering

1-2 **14** I saw — it took my breath away! — the Lamb standing on Mount Zion, 144,000 standing there with him, his Name and the Name of his Father inscribed on their foreheads. And I heard a voice out of Heaven, the sound like a cataract, like the crash of thunder.

2-5   And then I heard music, harp music and the harpists singing a new song before the Throne and the Four Animals and the Elders. Only the 144,000 could learn to sing the song. They were bought from earth, lived without compromise, virgin-fresh before God. Wherever the Lamb went, they followed. They were bought from humankind, firstfruits of the harvest for God and the Lamb. Not a false word in their mouths. A perfect offering.

VOICES FROM HEAVEN

6-7   I saw another Angel soaring in Middle-Heaven. He had an Eternal Message to preach to all who were still on earth, every nation and tribe, every tongue and people. He preached in a loud voice, "Fear God and give him glory! His hour of judgment has come! Worship the Maker of Heaven and earth, salt sea and fresh water!"

8   A second Angel followed, calling out, "Ruined, ruined, Great Babylon ruined! She made all the nations drunk on the wine of her whoring!"

9-11   A third Angel followed, shouting, warning, "If anyone worships the Beast and its image and takes the mark on forehead or hand, that person will drink the wine of God's wrath, prepared unmixed in his chalice of anger, and suffer torment from fire and brimstone in the presence of Holy Angels, in the presence of the Lamb. Smoke from their torment will rise age after age. No respite for those who worship the Beast and its image, who take the mark of its name."

12   Meanwhile, the saints stand passionately patient, keeping God's commands, staying faithful to Jesus.

13   I heard a voice out of Heaven, "Write this: Blessed are those who die in the Master from now on; how blessed to die that way!"

"Yes," says the Spirit, "and blessed rest from their hard, hard work. None of what they've done is wasted; God blesses them for it all in the end."

HARVEST TIME

14-16   I looked up, I caught my breath! — a white cloud and one like the Son of Man sitting on it. He wore a gold crown and held a sharp sickle. Another Angel came out of the Temple, shouting to the Cloud-Enthroned, "Swing your sickle and reap. It's harvest time. Earth's harvest is ripe for reaping." The Cloud-Enthroned gave a mighty sweep of his sickle, began harvesting earth in a stroke.

17-18   Then another Angel came out of the Temple in Heaven. He also had a sharp sickle. Yet another Angel, the one in charge of tending the fire, came from the Altar. He thundered to the Angel who held the sharp sickle, "Swing your sharp sickle. Harvest earth's vineyard. The grapes are bursting with ripeness."

19-20   The Angel swung his sickle, harvested earth's vintage, and heaved it into the winepress, the giant winepress of God's wrath. The winepress was outside the City. As the vintage was trodden, blood poured from the winepress as high as a horse's bridle, a river of blood for two hundred miles.

THE SONG OF MOSES, THE SONG OF THE LAMB

1   15 I saw another Sign in Heaven, huge and breathtaking: seven Angels with seven disasters. These are the final disasters, the wrap-up of God's wrath.

2-4 I saw something like a sea made of glass, the glass all shot through with fire. Carrying harps of God, triumphant over the Beast, its image, and the number of its name, the saved ones stood on the sea of glass. They sang the Song of Moses, servant of God; they sang the Song of the Lamb:

> Mighty your acts and marvelous,
>   O God, the Sovereign-Strong!
> Righteous your ways and true,
>   King of the nations!
> Who can fail to fear you, God,
>   give glory to your Name?
> Because you and you only are holy,
>   all nations will come and worship you,
>   because they see your judgments are right.

5-8 Then I saw the doors of the Temple, the Tent of Witness in Heaven, open wide. The Seven Angels carrying the seven disasters came out of the Temple. They were dressed in clean, bright linen and wore gold vests. One of the Four Animals handed the Seven Angels seven gold bowls, brimming with the wrath of God, who lives forever and ever. Smoke from God's glory and power poured out of the Temple. No one was permitted to enter the Temple until the seven disasters of the Seven Angels were finished.

POURING OUT THE SEVEN DISASTERS

1 **16** I heard a shout of command from the Temple to the Seven Angels: "Begin! Pour out the seven bowls of God's wrath on earth!"

2 The first Angel stepped up and poured his bowl out on earth: Loathsome, stinking sores erupted on all who had taken the mark of the Beast and worshiped its image.

3 The second Angel poured his bowl on the sea: The sea coagulated into blood, and everything in it died.

4-7 The third Angel poured his bowl on rivers and springs: The waters turned to blood. I heard the Angel of Waters say,

> Righteous you are, and your judgments are righteous,
>   THE IS, THE WAS, THE HOLY.
> They poured out the blood of saints and prophets
>   so you've given them blood to drink—
>   they've gotten what they deserve!

Just then I heard the Altar chime in,

> Yes, O God, the Sovereign-Strong!
> Your judgments are true and just!

8-9 The fourth Angel poured his bowl on the sun: Fire blazed from the sun and scorched men and women. Burned and blistered, they cursed God's Name, the God behind these disasters. They refused to repent, refused to honor God.

10-11 The fifth Angel poured his bowl on the throne of the Beast: Its kingdom fell into sudden eclipse. Mad with pain, men and women bit and chewed their tongues, cursed the God-of-Heaven for their torment and sores, and refused to repent and change their ways.

12-14   The sixth Angel poured his bowl on the great Euphrates River: It dried up to nothing. The dry riverbed became a fine roadbed for the kings from the East. From the mouths of the Dragon, the Beast, and the False Prophet I saw three foul demons crawl out — they looked like frogs. These are demon spirits performing signs. They're after the kings of the whole world to get them gathered for battle on the Great Day of God, the Sovereign-Strong.

15   "Keep watch! I come unannounced, like a thief. You're blessed if, awake and dressed, you're ready for me. Too bad if you're found running through the streets, naked and ashamed."

16   The frog-demons gathered the kings together at the place called in Hebrew *Armageddon*.

17-21   The seventh Angel poured his bowl into the air: From the Throne in the Temple came a shout, "Done!" followed by lightning flashes and shouts, thunder crashes and a colossal earthquake — a huge and devastating earthquake, never an earthquake like it since time began. The Great City split three ways, the cities of the nations toppled to ruin. Great Babylon had to drink the wine of God's raging anger — God remembered to give her the cup! Every island fled and not a mountain was to be found. Hailstones weighing a ton plummeted, crushing and smashing men and women as they cursed God for the hail, the epic disaster of hail.

Great Babylon, Mother of Whores

1-2   One of the Seven Angels who carried the seven bowls came and invited me, "Come, I'll show you the judgment of the great Whore who sits enthroned over many waters, the Whore with whom the kings of the earth have gone whoring, show you the judgment on earth dwellers drunk on her whorish lust."

3-6   In the Spirit he carried me out in the desert. I saw a woman mounted on a Scarlet Beast. Stuffed with blasphemies, the Beast had seven heads and ten horns. The woman was dressed in purple and scarlet, festooned with gold and gems and pearls. She held a gold chalice in her hand, brimming with defiling obscenities, her foul fornications. A riddle-name was branded on her forehead: GREAT BABYLON, MOTHER OF WHORES AND ABOMINATIONS OF THE EARTH. I could see that the woman was drunk, drunk on the blood of God's holy people, drunk on the blood of the martyrs of Jesus.

6-8   Astonished, I rubbed my eyes. I shook my head in wonder. The Angel said, "Does this surprise you? Let me tell you the riddle of the woman and the Beast she rides, the Beast with seven heads and ten horns. The Beast you saw once was, is no longer, and is about to ascend from the Abyss and head straight for Hell. Earth dwellers whose names weren't written in the Book of Life from the foundation of the world will be dazzled when they see the Beast that once was, is no longer, and is to come.

9-11   "But don't drop your guard. Use your head. The seven heads are seven hills; they are where the woman sits. They are also seven kings: five dead, one living, the other not yet here — and when he does come his time will be brief. The Beast that once was and is no longer is both an eighth and one of the seven — and headed for Hell.

12-14   "The ten horns you saw are ten kings, but they're not yet in power. They will come to power with the Scarlet Beast, but won't last long—a *very* brief reign. These kings will agree to turn over their power and authority to the Beast. They will go to war against the Lamb but the Lamb will defeat them, proof that he is Lord over all lords, King over all kings, and those with him will be the called, chosen, and faithful."

15-18   The Angel continued, "The waters you saw on which the Whore was enthroned are peoples and crowds, nations and languages. And the ten horns you saw, together with the Beast, will turn on the Whore—they'll hate her, violate her, strip her naked, rip her apart with their teeth, then set fire to her. It was God who put the idea in their heads to turn over their rule to the Beast until the words of God are completed. The woman you saw is the great city, tyrannizing the kings of the earth."

Doom to the City of Darkness

1-8   **18** Following this I saw another Angel descend from Heaven. His authority was immense, his glory flooded earth with brightness, his voice thunderous:
Ruined, ruined, Great Babylon, ruined!
    A ghost town for demons is all that's left!
A garrison of carrion spirits,
    garrison of loathsome, carrion birds.
All nations drank the wild wine of her whoring;
    kings of the earth went whoring with her;
    entrepreneurs made millions exploiting her.

Just then I heard another shout out of Heaven:

Get out, my people, as fast as you can,
    so you don't get mixed up in her sins,
    so you don't get caught in her doom.
Her sins stink to high Heaven;
    God has remembered every evil she's done.
Give her back what she's given,
    double what she's doubled in her works,
    double the recipe in the cup she mixed;
Bring her flaunting and wild ways
    to torment and tears.
Because she gloated, "I'm queen over all,
    and no widow, never a tear on my face,"
In one day, disasters will crush her—
    death, heartbreak, and famine—
Then she'll be burned by fire, because God,
    the Strong God who judges her,
    has had enough.

9-10   "The kings of the earth will see the smoke of her burning, and they'll cry and carry on, the kings who went night after night to her brothel. They'll keep their distance for fear they'll get burned, and they'll cry their lament:

Doom, doom, the great city doomed!

City of Babylon, strong city!
In one hour it's over, your judgment come!

11-17 "The traders will cry and carry on because the bottom dropped out of business, no more market for their goods: gold, silver, precious gems, pearls; fabrics of fine linen, purple, silk, scarlet; perfumed wood and vessels of ivory, precious woods, bronze, iron, and marble; cinnamon and spice, incense, myrrh, and frankincense; wine and oil, flour and wheat; cattle, sheep, horses, and chariots. And slaves — their terrible traffic in human lives.

Everything you've lived for, gone!
All delicate and delectable luxury, lost!
Not a scrap, not a thread to be found!

"The traders who made millions off her kept their distance for fear of getting burned, and cried and carried on all the more:

Doom, doom, the great city doomed!
Dressed in the latest fashions,
adorned with the finest jewels,
in one hour such wealth wiped out!

17-19 "All the ship captains and travelers by sea, sailors and toilers of the sea, stood off at a distance and cried their lament when they saw the smoke from her burning: 'Oh, what a city! There was never a city like her!' They threw dust on their heads and cried as if the world had come to an end:

Doom, doom, the great city doomed!
All who owned ships or did business by sea
Got rich on her getting and spending.
And now it's over — wiped out in one hour!

20 "O Heaven, celebrate! And join in, saints, apostles, and prophets! God has judged her; every wrong you suffered from her has been judged."

21-24 A strong Angel reached for a boulder — huge, like a millstone — and heaved it into the sea, saying,

Heaved and sunk, the great city Babylon,
sunk in the sea, not a sign of her ever again.
Silent the music of harpists and singers —
you'll never hear flutes and trumpets again.
Artisans of every kind — gone;
you'll never see their likes again.
The voice of a millstone grinding falls dumb;
you'll never hear that sound again.
The light from lamps, never again;
never again laughter of bride and groom.
Her traders robbed the whole earth blind,
and by black-magic arts deceived the nations.
The only thing left of Babylon is blood —

the blood of saints and prophets,
the murdered and the martyred.

THE SOUND OF HALLELUJAHS

1-3   **19** I heard a sound like massed choirs in Heaven singing,

Hallelujah!
The salvation and glory and power are God's —
    his judgments true, his judgments just.
He judged the great Whore
    who corrupted the earth with her lust.
He avenged on her the blood of his servants.

Then, more singing:
Hallelujah!
The smoke from her burning billows up
    to high Heaven forever and ever and ever.

4   The Twenty-four Elders and the Four Animals fell to their knees and worshiped God on his Throne, praising,

Amen! Yes! Hallelujah!

5   From the Throne came a shout, a command:

Praise our God, all you his servants,
All you who fear him, small and great!

6-8   Then I heard the sound of massed choirs, the sound of a mighty cataract, the sound of strong thunder:

Hallelujah!
The Master reigns,
    our God, the Sovereign-Strong!
Let us celebrate, let us rejoice,
    let us give him the glory!
The Marriage of the Lamb has come;
    his Wife has made herself ready.
She was given a bridal gown
    of bright and shining linen.
The linen is the righteousness of the saints.

9   The Angel said to me, "Write this: 'Blessed are those invited to the Wedding Supper of the Lamb.'" He added, "These are the true words of God!"

10   I fell at his feet to worship him, but he wouldn't let me. "Don't do that," he said. "I'm a servant just like you, and like your brothers and sisters who hold to the witness of Jesus. The witness of Jesus is the spirit of prophecy."

A White Horse and Its Rider

11-16   Then I saw Heaven open wide — and oh! a white horse and its Rider. The Rider, named Faithful and True, judges and makes war in pure righteousness. His eyes are a blaze of fire, on his head many crowns. He has a Name inscribed that's known only to himself. He is dressed in a robe soaked with blood, and he is addressed as "Word of God." The armies of Heaven, mounted on white horses and dressed in dazzling white linen, follow him. A sharp sword comes out of his mouth so he can subdue the nations, then rule them with a rod of iron. He treads the winepress of the raging wrath of God, the Sovereign-Strong. On his robe and thigh is written, KING OF KINGS, LORD OF LORDS.

17-18   I saw an Angel standing in the sun, shouting to all flying birds in Middle-Heaven, "Come to the Great Supper of God! Feast on the flesh of kings and captains and champions, horses and their riders. Eat your fill of them all — free and slave, small and great!"

19-21   I saw the Beast and, assembled with him, earth's kings and their armies, ready to make war against the One on the horse and his army. The Beast was taken, and with him, his puppet, the False Prophet, who used signs to dazzle and deceive those who had taken the mark of the Beast and worshiped his image. They were thrown alive, those two, into Lake Fire and Brimstone. The rest were killed by the sword of the One on the horse, the sword that comes from his mouth. All the birds held a feast on their flesh.

A Thousand Years

1-3   **20** I saw an Angel descending out of Heaven. He carried the key to the Abyss and a chain — a huge chain. He grabbed the Dragon, that old Snake — the very Devil, Satan himself! — chained him up for a thousand years, dumped him into the Abyss, slammed it shut and sealed it tight. No more trouble out of him, deceiving the nations — until the thousand years are up. After that he has to be let loose briefly.

4-6   I saw thrones. Those put in charge of judgment sat on the thrones. I also saw the souls of those beheaded because of their witness to Jesus and the Word of God, who refused to worship either the Beast or his image, refused to take his mark on forehead or hand — they lived and reigned with Christ for a thousand years! The rest of the dead did not live until the thousand years were up. This is the first resurrection — and those involved most blessed, most holy. No second death for them! They're priests of God and Christ; they'll reign with him a thousand years.

7-10   When the thousand years are up, Satan will be let loose from his cell, and will launch again his old work of deceiving the nations, searching out victims in every nook and cranny of earth, even Gog and Magog! He'll talk them into going to war and will gather a huge army, millions strong. They'll stream across the earth, surround and lay siege to the camp of God's holy people, the Beloved City. They'll no sooner get there than fire will pour out of Heaven and burn them up. The Devil who deceived them will be hurled into Lake Fire and Brimstone, joining the Beast and False Prophet, the three in torment around the clock for ages without end.

Judgment

11-15   I saw a Great White Throne and the One Enthroned. Nothing could stand before or against the Presence, nothing in Heaven, nothing on earth.

And then I saw all the dead, great and small, standing there — before the Throne! And books were opened. Then another book was opened: the Book of Life. The dead were judged by what was written in the books, by the way they had lived. Sea released its dead, Death and Hell turned in their dead. Each man and woman was judged by the way he or she had lived. Then Death and Hell were hurled into Lake Fire. This is the second death — Lake Fire. Anyone whose name was not found inscribed in the Book of Life was hurled into Lake Fire.

EVERYTHING NEW

1   **21** I saw Heaven and earth new-created. Gone the first Heaven, gone the first earth, gone the sea.

2   I saw Holy Jerusalem, new-created, descending resplendent out of Heaven, as ready for God as a bride for her husband.

3-5   I heard a voice thunder from the Throne: "Look! Look! God has moved into the neighborhood, making his home with men and women! They're his people, he's their God. He'll wipe every tear from their eyes. Death is gone for good — tears gone, crying gone, pain gone — all the first order of things gone." The Enthroned continued, "Look! I'm making everything new. Write it all down — each word dependable and accurate."

6-8   Then he said, "It's happened. I'm A to Z. I'm the Beginning, I'm the Conclusion. From Water-of-Life Well I give freely to the thirsty. Conquerors inherit all this. I'll be God to them, they'll be sons and daughters to me. But for the rest — the feckless and faithless, degenerates and murderers, sex peddlers and sorcerers, idolaters and all liars — for them it's Lake Fire and Brimstone. Second death!"

THE CITY OF LIGHT

9-12   One of the Seven Angels who had carried the bowls filled with the seven final disasters spoke to me: "Come here. I'll show you the Bride, the Wife of the Lamb." He took me away in the Spirit to an enormous, high mountain and showed me Holy Jerusalem descending out of Heaven from God, resplendent in the bright glory of God.

12-14   The City shimmered like a precious gem, light-filled, pulsing light. She had a wall majestic and high with twelve gates. At each gate stood an Angel, and on the gates were inscribed the names of the Twelve Tribes of the sons of Israel: three gates on the east, three gates on the north, three gates on the south, three gates on the west. The wall was set on twelve foundations, the names of the Twelve Apostles of the Lamb inscribed on them.

15-21   The Angel speaking with me had a gold measuring stick to measure the City, its gates, and its wall. The City was laid out in a perfect square. He measured the City with the measuring stick: twelve thousand stadia, its length, width, and height all equal. Using the standard measure, the Angel measured the thickness of its wall: 144 cubits. The wall was jasper, the color of Glory, and the City was pure gold, translucent as glass. The foundations of the City walls were garnished with every precious gem imaginable: the first foundation jasper, the second sapphire, the third agate, the fourth emerald, the fifth onyx, the sixth carnelian, the seventh chrysolite, the eighth beryl, the ninth topaz, the tenth chrysoprase, the eleventh jacinth, the twelfth amethyst. The twelve gates were twelve pearls, each gate a single pearl.

21-27   The main street of the City was pure gold, translucent as glass. But there was no sign of a Temple, for the Lord God — the Sovereign-Strong — and the Lamb are the Temple. The City doesn't need sun or moon for light. God's Glory is its light, the Lamb its lamp! The nations will walk in its light and earth's kings bring in their splendor. Its gates will never be shut by day, and there won't be any night. They'll bring the glory and honor of the nations into the City. Nothing dirty or defiled will get into the City, and no one who defiles or deceives. Only those whose names are written in the Lamb's Book of Life will get in.

1-5 22 Then the Angel showed me Water-of-Life River, crystal bright. It flowed from the Throne of God and the Lamb, right down the middle of the street. The Tree of Life was planted on each side of the River, producing twelve kinds of fruit, a ripe fruit each month. The leaves of the Tree are for healing the nations. Never again will anything be cursed. The Throne of God and of the Lamb is at the center. His servants will offer God service — worshiping, they'll look on his face, their foreheads mirroring God. Never again will there be any night. No one will need lamplight or sunlight. The shining of God, the Master, is all the light anyone needs. And they will rule with him age after age after age.

DON'T PUT IT AWAY ON THE SHELF

6-7 The Angel said to me, "These are dependable and accurate words, every one. The God and Master of the spirits of the prophets sent his Angel to show his servants what must take place, and soon. And tell them, 'Yes, I'm on my way!' Blessed be the one who keeps the words of the prophecy of this book."

8-9 I, John, saw all these things with my own eyes, heard them with my ears. Immediately when I heard and saw, I fell on my face to worship at the feet of the Angel who laid it all out before me. He objected, "No you don't! I'm a servant just like you and your companions, the prophets, and all who keep the words of this book. Worship God!"

10-11 The Angel continued, "Don't seal the words of the prophecy of this book; don't put it away on the shelf. Time is just about up. Let evildoers do their worst and the dirty-minded go all out in pollution, but let the righteous maintain a straight course and the holy continue on in holiness."

12-13 "Yes, I'm on my way! I'll be there soon! I'm bringing my payroll with me. I'll pay all people in full for their life's work. I'm A to Z, the First and the Final, Beginning and Conclusion.

14-15 "How blessed are those who wash their robes! The Tree of Life is theirs for good, and they'll walk through the gates to the City. But outside for good are the filthy curs: sorcerers, fornicators, murderers, idolaters — all who love and live lies.

16 "I, Jesus, sent my Angel to testify to these things for the churches. I'm the Root and Branch of David, the Bright Morning Star."

17 "Come!" say the Spirit and the Bride.
Whoever hears, echo, "Come!"

Is anyone thirsty? Come!
All who will, come and drink,
Drink freely of the Water of Life!

18-19   I give fair warning to all who hear the words of the prophecy of this book: If you add to the words of this prophecy, God will add to your life the disasters written in this book; if you subtract from the words of the book of this prophecy, God will subtract your part from the Tree of Life and the Holy City that are written in this book.

20   He who testifies to all these things says it again: "I'm on my way! I'll be there soon!"

Yes! Come, Master Jesus!

21   The grace of the Master Jesus be with all of you. Oh, Yes!

PSALMS AND PROVERBS

PSALMS

Most Christians for most of the Christian centuries have learned to pray by praying the Psalms. The Hebrews, with several centuries of a head start on us in matters of prayer and worship, provided us with this prayer book that gives us a language adequate for responding to the God who speaks to us.

The stimulus to paraphrase the Psalms into a contemporary idiom comes from my lifetime of work as a pastor. As a pastor I was charged with, among other things, teaching people to pray, helping them to give voice to the entire experience of being human, and to do it both honestly and thoroughly. I found that it was not as easy as I expected. Getting started is easy enough. The impulse to pray is deep within us, at the very center of our created being, and so practically anything will do to get us started—"Help" and "Thanks!" are our basic prayers. But honesty and thoroughness don't come quite as spontaneously.

Faced with the prospect of conversation with a holy God who speaks worlds into being, it is not surprising that we have trouble. We feel awkward and out of place: "I'm not good enough for this. I'll wait until I clean up my act and prove that I am a decent person." Or we excuse ourselves on the grounds that our vocabulary is inadequate: "Give me a few months — or years! — to practice prayers that are polished enough for such a sacred meeting. Then I won't feel so stuttery and ill at ease."

My usual response when presented with these difficulties is to put the Psalms in a person's hand and say, "Go home and pray these. You've got wrong ideas about prayer; the praying you find in these Psalms will dispel the wrong ideas and introduce you to the real thing." A common response of those who do what I ask is surprise—they don't expect this kind of thing in the Bible. And then I express surprise at their surprise: "Did you think these would be the prayers of *nice* people? Did you think the psalmists' language would be polished and polite?"

Untutored, we tend to think that prayer is what good people do when they are doing their best. It is not. Inexperienced, we suppose that there must be an "insider" language that must be acquired before God takes us seriously in our prayer. There is not. Prayer is elemental, not advanced, language. It is the means by which our language becomes honest, true, and personal in response to God. It is the means by which we get everything in our lives out in the open before God.

But even with the Psalms in their hands and my pastoral

encouragement, people often tell me that they still don't get it. In English translation, the Psalms often sound smooth and polished, sonorous with Elizabethan rhythms and diction. As literature, they are beyond compare. But as *prayer*, as the utterances of men and women passionate for God in moments of anger and praise and lament, these translations miss something. *Grammatically*, they are accurate. The scholarship undergirding the translations is superb and devout. But as *prayers* they are not quite right. The Psalms in Hebrew are earthy and rough. They are not genteel. They are not the prayers of nice people, couched in cultured language.

And so in my pastoral work of teaching people to pray, I started paraphrasing the Psalms into the rhythms and idiom of contemporary English. I wanted to provide men and women access to the immense range and the terrific energies of prayer in the kind of language that is most immediate to them, which also happens to be the language in which these psalm prayers were first expressed and written by David and his successors.

I continue to want to do that, convinced that only as we develop raw honesty and detailed thoroughness in our praying do we become whole, truly human in Jesus Christ, who also prayed the Psalms.

PSALMS

1   How well God must like you —
      you don't hang out at Sin Saloon,
      you don't slink along Dead-End Road,
      you don't go to Smart-Mouth College.

2-3   Instead you thrill to GOD's Word,
      you chew on Scripture day and night.
    You're a tree replanted in Eden,
      bearing fresh fruit every month,
    Never dropping a leaf,
      always in blossom.

4-5   You're not at all like the wicked,
      who are mere windblown dust —
    Without defense in court,
      unfit company for innocent people.

6   GOD charts the road you take.
    The road *they* take is Skid Row.

1-6   Why the big noise, nations?
      Why the mean plots, peoples?
      Earth-leaders push for position,
    Demagogues and delegates meet for summit talks,
    The God-deniers, the Messiah-defiers:
    "Let's get free of God!
    Cast loose from Messiah!"
    Heaven-throned God breaks out laughing.
    At first he's amused at their presumption;
    Then he gets good and angry.
    Furiously, he shuts them up:
    "Don't you know there's a King in Zion? A coronation banquet
    Is spread for him on the holy summit."

7-9   Let me tell you what GOD said next.
    He said, "You're my son,
    And today is your birthday.
    What do you want? Name it:
    Nations as a present? continents as a prize?
    You can command them all to dance for you,
    Or throw them out with tomorrow's trash."

10-12   So, rebel-kings, use your heads;
    Upstart-judges, learn your lesson:
    Worship GOD in adoring embrace,
    Celebrate in trembling awe. Kiss Messiah!

Your very lives are in danger, you know;
His anger is about to explode,
But if you make a run for God — you won't regret it!

A DAVID PSALM, WHEN HE ESCAPED
FOR HIS LIFE FROM ABSALOM, HIS SON

1-2 **3** GOD! Look! Enemies past counting!
Enemies sprouting like mushrooms,
Mobs of them all around me, roaring their mockery:
"Hah! No help for *him* from God!"

3-4 But you, GOD, shield me on all sides;
You ground my feet, you lift my head high;
With all my might I shout up to GOD,
His answers thunder from the holy mountain.

5-6 I stretch myself out. I sleep.
Then I'm up again — rested, tall and steady,
Fearless before the enemy mobs
Coming at me from all sides.

7 Up, GOD! My God, help me!
Slap their faces,
First this cheek, then the other,
Your fist hard in their teeth!

8 Real help comes from GOD.
Your blessing clothes your people!

A DAVID PSALM

1 **4** When I call, give me answers. God, take my side!
Once, in a tight place, you gave me room;
Now I'm in trouble again: grace me! hear me!

2 You rabble — how long do I put up with your scorn?
How long will you lust after lies?
How long will you live crazed by illusion?

3 Look at this: look
Who got picked by GOD!
He listens the split second I call to him.

4-5 Complain if you must, but don't lash out.
Keep your mouth shut, and let your heart do the talking.
Build your case before God and wait for his verdict.

6-7 Why is everyone hungry for *more*? "More, more," they say.
"More, more."
I have God's more-than-enough,
More joy in one ordinary day

7-8   Than they get in all their shopping sprees.
    At day's end I'm ready for sound sleep,
    For you, GOD, have put my life back together.

A DAVID PSALM

1-3   5 Listen, GOD! Please, pay attention!
       Can you make sense of these ramblings,
       my groans and cries?
       King-God, I need your help.
    Every morning
      you'll hear me at it again.
    Every morning
      I lay out the pieces of my life
      on your altar
      and watch for fire to descend.

4-6   You don't socialize with Wicked,
      or invite Evil over as your houseguest.
    Hot-Air-Boaster collapses in front of you;
      you shake your head over Mischief-Maker.
    GOD destroys Lie-Speaker;
      Blood-Thirsty and Truth-Bender disgust you.

7-8   And here I am, your invited guest —
      it's incredible!
    I enter your house; here I am,
      prostrate in your inner sanctum,
    Waiting for directions
      to get me safely through enemy lines.

9-10   Every word they speak is a land mine;
      their lungs breathe out poison gas.
    Their throats are gaping graves,
      their tongues slick as mudslides.
    Pile on the guilt, God!
      Let their so-called wisdom wreck them.
    Kick them out! They've had their chance.

11-12   But you'll welcome us with open arms
      when we run for cover to you.
    Let the party last all night!
      Stand guard over our celebration.
    You are famous, GOD, for welcoming God-seekers,
      for decking us out in delight.

A DAVID PSALM

1-2   6 Please, GOD, no more yelling,
      no more trips to the woodshed.
      Treat me nice for a change;
    I'm so starved for affection.

2-3 Can't you see I'm black-and-blue,
  beat up badly in bones and soul?
God, how long will it take
  for you to let up?

4-5 Break in, God, and break up this fight;
  if you love me at all, get me out of here.
I'm no good to you dead, am I?
  I can't sing in your choir if I'm buried in some tomb!

6-7 I'm tired of all this — so tired. My bed
  has been floating forty days and nights
On the flood of my tears.
  My mattress is soaked, soggy with tears.
The sockets of my eyes are black holes;
  nearly blind, I squint and grope.

8-9 Get out of here, you Devil's crew:
  at last God has heard my sobs.
My requests have all been granted,
  my prayers are answered.

10 Cowards, my enemies disappear.
Disgraced, they turn tail and run.

A David Psalm

1-2 God! God! I am running to you for dear life;
  the chase is wild.
  If they catch me, I'm finished:
ripped to shreds by foes fierce as lions,
dragged into the forest and left
unlooked for, unremembered.

3-5 God, if I've done what they say —
  betrayed my friends,
  ripped off my enemies —
If my hands are really that dirty,
  let them get me, walk all over me,
  leave me flat on my face in the dirt.

6-8 Stand up, God; pit your holy fury
  against my furious enemies.
Wake up, God. My accusers have packed
  the courtroom; it's judgment time.
Take your place on the bench, reach for your gavel,
  throw out the false charges against me.
I'm ready, confident in your verdict:
  "Innocent."

9-11 Close the book on Evil, God,
  but publish your mandate for us.

You get us ready for life:
    you probe for our soft spots,
    you knock off our rough edges.
And I'm feeling so fit, so safe:
    made right, kept right.
God in solemn honor does things right,
    but his nerves are sandpapered raw.

11-13 Nobody gets by with anything.
    God is already in action —
Sword honed on his whetstone,
    bow strung, arrow on the string,
Lethal weapons in hand,
    each arrow a flaming missile.

14 Look at that guy!
    He had sex with sin,
    he's pregnant with evil.
Oh, look! He's having
    the baby — a Lie-Baby!

15-16 See that man shoveling day after day,
    digging, then concealing, his man-trap
    down that lonely stretch of road?
Go back and look again — you'll see him in it headfirst,
    legs waving in the breeze.
That's what happens:
    mischief backfires;
    violence boomerangs.

17 I'm thanking God, who makes things right.
I'm singing the fame of heaven-high GOD.

A DAVID PSALM

1 **8** GOD, brilliant Lord,
    yours is a household name.

2 Nursing infants gurgle choruses about you;
    toddlers shout the songs
That drown out enemy talk,
    and silence atheist babble.

3-4 I look up at your macro-skies, dark and enormous,
    your handmade sky-jewelry,
Moon and stars mounted in their settings.
    Then I look at my micro-self and wonder,
Why do you bother with us?
    Why take a second look our way?

5-8 Yet we've so narrowly missed being gods,
    bright with Eden's dawn light.

You put us in charge of your handcrafted world,
    repeated to us your Genesis-charge,
Made us lords of sheep and cattle,
    even animals out in the wild,
Birds flying and fish swimming,
    whales singing in the ocean deeps.

9   GOD, brilliant Lord,
        your name echoes around the world.

A DAVID PSALM

1-2   I'm thanking you, GOD, from a full heart,
          I'm writing the book on your wonders.
        I'm whistling, laughing, and jumping for joy;
        I'm singing your song, High God.

3-4   The day my enemies turned tail and ran,
        they stumbled on you and fell on their faces.
       You took over and set everything right;
        when I needed you, you were there, taking charge.

5-6   You blow the whistle on godless nations;
        you throw dirty players out of the game,
          wipe their names right off the roster.
       Enemies disappear from the sidelines,
        their reputation trashed,
          their names erased from the halls of fame.

7-8   GOD holds the high center,
        he sees and sets the world's mess right.
       He decides what is right for us earthlings,
        gives people their just deserts.

9-10   GOD's a safe-house for the battered,
        a sanctuary during bad times.
       The moment you arrive, you relax;
        you're never sorry you knocked.

11-12 Sing your songs to Zion-dwelling GOD,
        tell his stories to everyone you meet:
       How he tracks down killers
        yet keeps his eye on us,
          registers every whimper and moan.

13-14 Be kind to me, GOD;
        I've been kicked around long enough.
       Once you've pulled me back
        from the gates of death,
       I'll write the book on Hallelujahs;
        on the corner of Main and First
          I'll hold a street meeting;

I'll be the song leader; we'll fill the air
   with salvation songs.

15-16   They're trapped, those godless countries,
     in the very snares they set,
Their feet all tangled
     in the net they spread.
They have no excuse;
     the way God works is well-known.
The cunning machinery made by the wicked
     has maimed their own hands.

17-20   The wicked bought a one-way
     ticket to hell.
No longer will the poor be nameless —
     no more humiliation for the humble.
Up, GOD! Aren't you fed up with their empty strutting?
     Expose these grand pretensions!
Shake them up, GOD!
     Show them how silly they look.

1-2   **10** GOD, are you avoiding me?
     Where are you when I need you?
     Full of hot air, the wicked
are hot on the trail of the poor.
Trip them up, tangle them up
     in their fine-tuned plots.

3-4   The wicked are windbags,
     the swindlers have foul breath.
The wicked snub GOD,
     their noses stuck high in the air.
Their graffiti are scrawled on the walls:
     "Catch us if you can!" "God is dead."

5-6   They care nothing for what you think;
     if you get in their way, they blow you off.
They live (they think) a charmed life:
     "We can't go wrong. This is our lucky year!"

7-8   They carry a mouthful of hexes,
     their tongues spit venom like adders.
They hide behind ordinary people,
     then pounce on their victims.

9   They mark the luckless,
     then wait like a hunter in a blind;
When the poor wretch wanders too close,
     they stab him in the back.

10-11   The hapless fool is kicked to the ground,

the unlucky victim is brutally axed.
He thinks God has dumped him,
    he's sure that God is indifferent to his plight.

12-13   Time to get up, G OD — get moving.
    The luckless think they're Godforsaken.
They wonder why the wicked scorn God
    and get away with it,
Why the wicked are so cocksure
    they'll never come up for audit.

14   But you know all about it —
    the contempt, the abuse.
I dare to believe that the luckless
    will get lucky someday in you.
You won't let them down:
    orphans won't be orphans forever.

15-16   Break the wicked right arms,
    break all the evil left arms.
Search and destroy
    every sign of crime.
G OD's grace and order wins;
    godlessness loses.

17-18   The victim's faint pulse picks up;
    the hearts of the hopeless pump red blood
    as you put your ear to their lips.
Orphans get parents,
    the homeless get homes.
The reign of terror is over,
    the rule of the gang lords is ended.

A D AVID P SALM

1-3   **11** I've already run for dear life
    straight to the arms of G OD.
    So why would I run away now
when you say,

"Run to the mountains; the evil
    bows are bent, the wicked arrows
Aimed to shoot under cover of darkness
    at every heart open to God.
The bottom's dropped out of the country;
    good people don't have a chance"?

4-6   But G OD hasn't moved to the mountains;
    his holy address hasn't changed.
He's in charge, as always, his eyes
    taking everything in, his eyelids
Unblinking, examining Adam's unruly brood

inside and out, not missing a thing.
He tests the good and the bad alike;
   if anyone cheats, God's outraged.
Fail the test and you're out,
   out in a hail of firestones,
Drinking from a canteen
   filled with hot desert wind.

7   GOD's business is putting things right;
   he loves getting the lines straight,
Setting us straight. Once we're standing tall,
   we can look him straight in the eye.

A DAVID PSALM

1-2   **12** Quick, GOD, I need your helping hand!
   The last decent person just went down,
   All the friends I depended on gone.
Everyone talks in lie language;
Lies slide off their oily lips.
They doubletalk with forked tongues.

3-4   Slice their lips off their faces! Pull
The braggart tongues from their mouths!
I'm tired of hearing, "We can talk anyone into anything!
Our lips manage the world."

5   Into the hovels of the poor,
Into the dark streets where the homeless groan, God speaks:
"I've had enough; I'm on my way
To heal the ache in the heart of the wretched."

6-8   God's words are pure words,
Pure silver words refined seven times
In the fires of his word-kiln,
Pure on earth as well as in heaven.
GOD, keep us safe from their lies,
From the wicked who stalk us with lies,
From the wicked who collect honors
For their wonderful lies.

A DAVID PSALM

1-2   **13** Long enough, GOD —
   you've ignored me long enough.
   I've looked at the back of your head
   long enough. Long enough
I've carried this ton of trouble,
   lived with a stomach full of pain.
Long enough my arrogant enemies
   have looked down their noses at me.

3-4   Take a good look at me, GOD, my God;

I want to look life in the eye,
So no enemy can get the best of me
    or laugh when I fall on my face.

5-6   I've thrown myself headlong into your arms —
        I'm celebrating your rescue.
    I'm singing at the top of my lungs,
        I'm so full of answered prayers.

A D A V I D   P S A L M

1   **14** Bilious and bloated, they gas,
        "God is gone."
    Their words are poison gas,
        fouling the air; they poison
    Rivers and skies;
        thistles are their cash crop.

2   GOD sticks his head out of heaven.
        He looks around.
    He's looking for someone not stupid —
        one man, even, God-expectant,
        just one God-ready woman.

3   He comes up empty. A string
        of zeros. Useless, unshepherded
    Sheep, taking turns pretending
        to be Shepherd.
    The ninety and nine
        follow their fellow.

4   Don't they know anything,
        all these impostors?
    Don't they know
        they can't get away with this —
    Treating people like a fast-food meal
        over which they're too busy to pray?

5-6   Night is coming for them, and nightmares,
        for God takes the side of victims.
    Do you think you can mess
        with the dreams of the poor?
    You can't, for God
        makes their dreams come true.

7   Is there anyone around to save Israel?
        Yes. God is around; GOD turns life around.
    Turned-around Jacob skips rope,
        turned-around Israel sings laughter.

1　15　GOD, who gets invited
　　　　　　to dinner at your place?
　　　　How do we get on your guest list?

2　"Walk straight,
　　　act right,
　　　　　tell the truth.

3-4　"Don't hurt your friend,
　　　don't blame your neighbor;
　　　　　despise the despicable.

5　"Keep your word even when it costs you,
　　　make an honest living,
　　　　　never take a bribe.

"You'll never get
blacklisted
if you live like this."

1-2　16　Keep me safe, O God,
　　　　　　I've run for dear life to you.
　　　　I say to GOD, "Be my Lord!"
　　　Without you, nothing makes sense.

3　And these God-chosen lives all around —
　　　what splendid friends they make!

4　Don't just go shopping for a god.
　　　Gods are not for sale.
　　I swear I'll never treat god-names
　　　like brand-names.

5-6　My choice is you, GOD, first and only.
　　　And now I find I'm *your* choice!
　　You set me up with a house and yard.
　　　And then you made me your heir!

7-8　The wise counsel GOD gives when I'm awake
　　　is confirmed by my sleeping heart.
　　Day and night I'll stick with GOD;
　　　I've got a good thing going and I'm not letting go.

9-10　I'm happy from the inside out,
　　　and from the outside in, I'm firmly formed.
　　You canceled my ticket to hell —
　　　that's not my destination!

11 Now you've got my feet on the life path,
        all radiant from the shining of your face.
    Ever since you took my hand,
        I'm on the right way.

A DAVID PRAYER

1-2 **17** Listen while I build my case, GOD,
            the most honest prayer you'll ever hear.
            Show the world I'm innocent —
    in your heart you know I am.

3   Go ahead, examine me from inside out,
        surprise me in the middle of the night —
    You'll find I'm just what I say I am.
        My words don't run loose.

4-5 I'm not trying to get my way
        in the world's way.
    I'm trying to get *your* way,
        your Word's way.
    I'm staying on your trail;
        I'm putting one foot
    In front of the other.
        I'm not giving up.

6-7 I call to you, God, because I'm sure of an answer.
        So — answer! bend your ear! listen sharp!
    Paint grace-graffiti on the fences;
        take in your frightened children who
    Are running from the neighborhood bullies
        straight to you.

8-9 Keep your eye on me;
        hide me under your cool wing feathers
    From the wicked who are out to get me,
        from mortal enemies closing in.

10-14 Their hearts are hard as nails,
        their mouths blast hot air.
    They are after me, nipping my heels,
        determined to bring me down,
    Lions ready to rip me apart,
        young lions poised to pounce.
    Up, GOD: beard them! break them!
        By your sword, free me from their clutches;
    Barehanded, GOD, break these mortals,
        these flat-earth people who can't think beyond today.

    I'd like to see their bellies
        swollen with famine food,
    The weeds they've sown

harvested and baked into famine bread,
With second helpings for their children
and crusts for their babies to chew on.

15 And me? I plan on looking
you full in the face. When I get up,
I'll see your full stature
and live heaven on earth.

A DAVID SONG, WHICH HE SANG TO GOD AFTER BEING
SAVED FROM ALL HIS ENEMIES AND FROM SAUL

1-2 **18** I love you, GOD —
you make me strong.
GOD is bedrock under my feet,
the castle in which I live,
my rescuing knight.
My God — the high crag
where I run for dear life,
hiding behind the boulders,
safe in the granite hideout.

3 I sing to GOD, the Praise-Lofty,
and find myself safe and saved.

4-5 The hangman's noose was tight at my throat;
devil waters rushed over me.
Hell's ropes cinched me tight;
death traps barred every exit.

6 A hostile world! I call to GOD,
I cry to God to help me.
From his palace he hears my call;
my cry brings me right into his presence —
a private audience!

7-15 Earth wobbles and lurches;
huge mountains shake like leaves,
Quake like aspen leaves
because of his rage.
His nostrils flare, bellowing smoke;
his mouth spits fire.
Tongues of fire dart in and out;
he lowers the sky.
He steps down;
under his feet an abyss opens up.
He's riding a winged creature,
swift on wind-wings.
Now he's wrapped himself
in a trenchcoat of black-cloud darkness.
But his cloud-brightness bursts through,
spraying hailstones and fireballs.

Then GOD thundered out of heaven;
   the High God gave a great shout,
     spraying hailstones and fireballs.
God shoots his arrows — pandemonium!
   He hurls his lightnings — a rout!
The secret sources of ocean are exposed,
   the hidden depths of earth lie uncovered
The moment you roar in protest,
   let loose your hurricane anger.

16-19   But me he caught — reached all the way
     from sky to sea; he pulled me out
Of that ocean of hate, that enemy chaos,
   the void in which I was drowning.
They hit me when I was down,
   but GOD stuck by me.
He stood me up on a wide-open field;
   I stood there saved — surprised to be loved!

20-24   GOD made my life complete
     when I placed all the pieces before him.
When I got my act together,
   he gave me a fresh start.
Now I'm alert to GOD's ways;
   I don't take God for granted.
Every day I review the ways he works;
   I try not to miss a trick.
I feel put back together,
   and I'm watching my step.
GOD rewrote the text of my life
   when I opened the book of my heart to his eyes.

25-27   The good people taste your goodness,
The whole people taste your health,
The true people taste your truth,
The bad ones can't figure you out.
You take the side of the down-and-out,
But the stuck-up you take down a peg.

28-29   Suddenly, GOD, you floodlight my life;
     I'm blazing with glory, God's glory!
I smash the bands of marauders,
   I vault the highest fences.

30   What a God! His road
     stretches straight and smooth.
Every GOD-direction is road-tested.
   Everyone who runs toward him
Makes it.

31-42   Is there any god like GOD?

Are we not at bedrock?
Is not this the God who armed me,
   then aimed me in the right direction?
Now I run like a deer;
   I'm king of the mountain.
He shows me how to fight;
   I can bend a bronze bow!
You protect me with salvation-armor;
   you hold me up with a firm hand,
   caress me with your gentle ways.
You cleared the ground under me
   so my footing was firm.
When I chased my enemies I caught them;
   I didn't let go till they were dead men.
I nailed them; they were down for good;
   then I walked all over them.
You armed me well for this fight,
   you smashed the upstarts.
You made my enemies turn tail,
   and I wiped out the haters.
They cried "uncle"
   but Uncle didn't come;
They yelled for GOD
   and got no for an answer.
I ground them to dust; they gusted in the wind.
   I threw them out, like garbage in the gutter.

43-45   You rescued me from a squabbling people;
   you made me a leader of nations.
People I'd never heard of served me;
   the moment they got wind of me they listened.
The foreign devils gave up; they came
   on their bellies, crawling from their hideouts.

46-48   Live, GOD! Blessings from my Rock,
   my free and freeing God, towering!
This God set things right for me
   and shut up the people who talked back.
He rescued me from enemy anger,
   he pulled me from the grip of upstarts,
He saved me from the bullies.

49-50   That's why I'm thanking you, GOD,
   all over the world.
That's why I'm singing songs
   that rhyme your name.
God's king takes the trophy;
   God's chosen is beloved.
I mean David and all his children —
   always.

A DAVID PSALM

19

1-2 God's glory is on tour in the skies,
        God-craft on exhibit across the horizon.
        Madame Day holds classes every morning,
    Professor Night lectures each evening.

3-4 Their words aren't heard,
        their voices aren't recorded,
    But their silence fills the earth:
        unspoken truth is spoken everywhere.

4-5 God makes a huge dome
        for the sun — a superdome!
    The morning sun's a new husband
        leaping from his honeymoon bed,
    The daybreaking sun an athlete
        racing to the tape.

6 That's how God's Word vaults across the skies
        from sunrise to sunset,
    Melting ice, scorching deserts,
        warming hearts to faith.

7-9 The revelation of GOD is whole
        and pulls our lives together.
    The signposts of GOD are clear
        and point out the right road.
    The life-maps of GOD are right,
        showing the way to joy.
    The directions of GOD are plain
        and easy on the eyes.
    GOD's reputation is twenty-four-carat gold,
        with a lifetime guarantee.
    The decisions of GOD are accurate
        down to the nth degree.

10 God's Word is better than a diamond,
        better than a diamond set between emeralds.
    You'll like it better than strawberries in spring,
        better than red, ripe strawberries.

11-14 There's more: God's Word warns us of danger
        and directs us to hidden treasure.
    Otherwise how will we find our way?
        Or know when we play the fool?
    Clean the slate, God, so we can start the day fresh!
        Keep me from stupid sins,
        from thinking I can take over your work;
    Then I can start this day sun-washed,
        scrubbed clean of the grime of sin.

These are the words in my mouth;
    these are what I chew on and pray.
Accept them when I place them
    on the morning altar,
O God, my Altar-Rock,
    God, Priest-of-My-Altar.

A DAVID PSALM

1-4
20

GOD answer you on the day you crash,
    The name God-of-Jacob put you out of harm's reach,
    Send reinforcements from Holy Hill,
Dispatch from Zion fresh supplies,
Exclaim over your offerings,
Celebrate your sacrifices,
Give you what your heart desires,
Accomplish your plans.

5   When you win, we plan to raise the roof
    and lead the parade with our banners.
May all your wishes come true!

6   That clinches it — help's coming,
    an answer's on the way,
    everything's going to work out.

7-8   See those people polishing their chariots,
    and those others grooming their horses?
    But we're making garlands for GOD our God.
The chariots will rust,
    those horses pull up lame —
    and we'll be on our feet, standing tall.

9   Make the king a winner, GOD;
    the day we call, give us your answer.

A DAVID PSALM

1-7
21

Your strength, GOD, is the king's strength.
    Helped, he's hollering Hosannas.
    You gave him exactly what he wanted;
    you didn't hold back.
You filled his arms with gifts;
    you gave him a right royal welcome.
He wanted a good life; you gave it to him,
    and then made it a *long* life as a bonus.
You lifted him high and bright as a cumulus cloud,
    then dressed him in rainbow colors.
You pile blessings on him;
    you make him glad when you smile.
Is it any wonder the king loves GOD?
    that he's sticking with the Best?

8-12 With a fistful of enemies in one hand
  and a fistful of haters in the other,
You radiate with such brilliance
  that they cringe as before a furnace.
Now the furnace swallows them whole,
  the fire eats them alive!
You purge the earth of their progeny,
  you wipe the slate clean.
All their evil schemes, the plots they cook up,
  have fizzled — every one.
You sent them packing;
  they couldn't face you.

13 Show your strength, GOD, so no one can miss it.
  We are out singing the good news!

A DAVID PSALM

1-2 **22** God, God . . . my God!
  Why did you dump me
  miles from nowhere?
Doubled up with pain, I call to God
  all the day long. No answer. Nothing.
I keep at it all night, tossing and turning.

3-5 And you! Are you indifferent, above it all,
  leaning back on the cushions of Israel's praise?
We know you were there for our parents:
  they cried for your help and you gave it;
  they trusted and lived a good life.

6-8 And here I am, a nothing — an earthworm,
  something to step on, to squash.
Everyone pokes fun at me;
  they make faces at me, they shake their heads:
"Let's see how GOD handles this one;
  since God likes him so much, let *him* help him!"

9-11 And to think you were midwife at my birth,
  setting me at my mother's breasts!
When I left the womb you cradled me;
  since the moment of birth you've been my God.
Then you moved far away
  and trouble moved in next door.
I need a neighbor.

12-13 Herds of bulls come at me,
  the raging bulls stampede,
Horns lowered, nostrils flaring,
  like a herd of buffalo on the move.

14-15 I'm a bucket kicked over and spilled,

every joint in my body has been pulled apart.
My heart is a blob
    of melted wax in my gut.
I'm dry as a bone,
    my tongue black and swollen.
They have laid me out for burial
    in the dirt.

16-18   Now packs of wild dogs come at me;
    thugs gang up on me.
They pin me down hand and foot,
    and lock me in a cage — a bag
Of bones in a cage, stared at
    by every passerby.
They take my wallet and the shirt off my back,
    and then throw dice for my clothes.

19-21   You, GOD — don't put off my rescue!
    Hurry and help me!
Don't let them cut my throat;
    don't let those mongrels devour me.
If you don't show up soon,
    I'm done for — gored by the bulls,
    meat for the lions.

22-24   Here's the story I'll tell my friends when they come to worship,
    and punctuate it with Hallelujahs:
Shout Hallelujah, you God-worshipers;
    give glory, you sons of Jacob;
    adore him, you daughters of Israel.
He has never let you down,
    never looked the other way
    when you were being kicked around.
He has never wandered off to do his own thing;
    he has been right there, listening.

25-26   Here in this great gathering for worship
    I have discovered this praise-life.
And I'll do what I promised right here
    in front of the God-worshipers.
Down-and-outers sit at GOD's table
    and eat their fill.
Everyone on the hunt for God
    is here, praising him.
"Live it up, from head to toe.
    Don't ever quit!"

27-28   From the four corners of the earth
    people are coming to their senses,
    are running back to GOD.
Long-lost families

are falling on their faces before him.
GOD has taken charge;
   from now on he has the last word.

29 All the power-mongers are before him
      — worshiping!
All the poor and powerless, too
      — worshiping!
Along with those who never got it together
      — worshiping!

30-31 Our children and their children
      will get in on this
As the word is passed along
      from parent to child.
Babies not yet conceived
      will hear the good news —
      that God does what he says.

A DAVID PSALM

1-3 **23** GOD, my shepherd!
      I don't need a thing.
      You have bedded me down in lush meadows,
   you find me quiet pools to drink from.
True to your word,
      you let me catch my breath
      and send me in the right direction.

4 Even when the way goes through
      Death Valley,
I'm not afraid
      when you walk at my side.
Your trusty shepherd's crook
      makes me feel secure.

5 You serve me a six-course dinner
      right in front of my enemies.
You revive my drooping head;
      my cup brims with blessing.

6 Your beauty and love chase after me
      every day of my life.
I'm back home in the house of GOD
      for the rest of my life.

A DAVID PSALM

1-2 **24** GOD claims Earth and everything in it,
      GOD claims World and all who live on it.
      He built it on Ocean foundations,
   laid it out on River girders.

3-4   Who can climb Mount GOD?
     Who can scale the holy north-face?
   Only the clean-handed,
     only the pure-hearted;
   Men who won't cheat,
     women who won't seduce.

5-6   GOD is at their side;
     with GOD's help they make it.
   This, Jacob, is what happens
     to God-seekers, God-questers.

7   Wake up, you sleepyhead city!
   Wake up, you sleepyhead people!
     King-Glory is ready to enter.

8   Who is this King-Glory?
     GOD, armed
     and battle-ready.

9   Wake up, you sleepyhead city!
   Wake up, you sleepyhead people!
     King-Glory is ready to enter.

10   Who is this King-Glory?
     GOD-of-the-Angel-Armies:
     he is King-Glory.

A DAVID PSALM

1-2   **25** My head is high, GOD, held high;
     I'm looking to you, GOD;
     No hangdog skulking for me.

3   I've thrown in my lot with you;
   You won't embarrass me, will you?
   Or let my enemies get the best of me?

   Don't embarrass any of us
   Who went out on a limb for you.
   It's the traitors who should be humiliated.

4   Show me how you work, GOD;
   School me in your ways.

5   Take me by the hand;
   Lead me down the path of truth.
   You are my Savior, aren't you?

6   Mark the milestones of your mercy and love, GOD;
   Rebuild the ancient landmarks!

7   Forget that I sowed wild oats;
    Mark me with your sign of love.
    Plan only the best for me, GOD!

8   GOD is fair and just;
    He corrects the misdirected,
    Sends them in the right direction.

9   He gives the rejects his hand,
    And leads them step-by-step.

10 From now on every road you travel
    Will take you to GOD.
    Follow the Covenant signs;
    Read the charted directions.

11 Keep up your reputation, GOD;
    Forgive my bad life;
    It's been a very bad life.

12 My question: What are God-worshipers like?
    Your answer: Arrows aimed at God's bull's-eye.

13 They settle down in a promising place;
    Their kids inherit a prosperous farm.

14 God-friendship is for God-worshipers;
    They are the ones he confides in.

15 If I keep my eyes on GOD,
    I won't trip over my own feet.

16 Look at me and help me!
    I'm all alone and in big trouble.

17 My heart and kidneys are fighting each other;
    Call a truce to this civil war.

18 Take a hard look at my life of hard labor,
    Then lift this ton of sin.

19 Do you see how many people
    Have it in for me?
    How viciously they hate me?

20 Keep watch over me and keep me out of trouble;
    Don't let me down when I run to you.

21 Use all your skill to put me together;
    I wait to see your finished product.

22 GOD, give your people a break
From this run of bad luck.

1 26 Clear my name, GOD;
I've kept an honest shop.
I've thrown in my lot with you, GOD, and
I'm not budging.

2 Examine me, GOD, from head to foot,
order your battery of tests.
Make sure I'm fit
inside and out

3 So I never lose
sight of your love,
But keep in step with you,
never missing a beat.

4-5 I don't hang out with tricksters,
I don't pal around with thugs;
I hate that pack of gangsters,
I don't deal with double-dealers.

6-7 I scrub my hands with purest soap,
then join hands with the others in the great circle,
dancing around your altar, GOD,
Singing God-songs at the top of my lungs,
telling God-stories.

8-10 GOD, I love living with you;
your house glows with your glory.
When it's time for spring cleaning,
don't sweep me out with the quacks and crooks,
Men with bags of dirty tricks,
women with purses stuffed with bribe-money.

11-12 You know I've been aboveboard with you;
now be aboveboard with me.
I'm on the level with you, GOD;
I bless you every chance I get.

1 27 Light, space, zest —
that's GOD!
So, with him on my side I'm fearless,
afraid of no one and nothing.

2 When vandal hordes ride down
ready to eat me alive,
Those bullies and toughs
fall flat on their faces.

3 When besieged,
  I'm calm as a baby.
 When all hell breaks loose,
  I'm collected and cool.

4 I'm asking GOD for one thing,
  only one thing:
 To live with him in his house
  my whole life long.
 I'll contemplate his beauty;
  I'll study at his feet.

5 That's the only quiet, secure place
  in a noisy world,
 The perfect getaway,
  far from the buzz of traffic.

6 God holds me head and shoulders
  above all who try to pull me down.
 I'm headed for his place to offer anthems
  that will raise the roof!
 Already I'm singing God-songs;
  I'm making music to GOD.

7-9 Listen, GOD, I'm calling at the top of my lungs:
  "Be good to me! Answer me!"
 When my heart whispered, "Seek God,"
  my whole being replied,
 "I'm seeking him!"
  Don't hide from me now!

9-10 You've always been right there for me;
  don't turn your back on me now.
 Don't throw me out, don't abandon me;
  you've always kept the door open.
 My father and mother walked out and left me,
  but GOD took me in.

11-12 Point me down your highway, GOD;
  direct me along a well-lighted street;
  show my enemies whose side you're on.
 Don't throw me to the dogs,
  those liars who are out to get me,
  filling the air with their threats.

13-14 I'm sure now I'll see God's goodness
  in the exuberant earth.
 Stay with GOD!
  Take heart. Don't quit.
 I'll say it again:
  Stay with GOD.

1 **28** D̲o̲n't turn a deaf ear
 when I call you, GOD.
 If all I get from you is
deafening silence,
I'd be better off
 in the Black Hole.

2 I'm letting you know what I need,
 calling out for help
And lifting my arms
 toward your inner sanctum.

3-4 Don't shove me into
 the same jail cell with those crooks,
With those who are
 full-time employees of evil.
They talk a good line of "peace,"
 then moonlight for the Devil.

Pay them back for what they've done,
 for how bad they've been.
Pay them back for their long hours
 in the Devil's workshop;
Then cap it with a huge bonus.

5 Because they have no idea how God works
 or what he is up to,
God will smash them to smithereens
 and walk away from the ruins.

6-7 Blessed be GOD —
 he heard me praying.
He proved he's on my side;
 I've thrown my lot in with him.

Now I'm jumping for joy,
 and shouting and singing my thanks to him.

8-9 GOD is all strength for his people,
 ample refuge for his chosen leader;
Save your people
 and bless your heritage.
Care for them;
 carry them like a good shepherd.

1-2 **29** Bravo, GOD, bravo!
 Gods and all angels shout, "Encore!"
 In awe before the glory,

    in awe before God's visible power.
Stand at attention!
    Dress your best to honor him!

3   GOD thunders across the waters,
Brilliant, his voice and his face, streaming brightness —
GOD, across the flood waters.

4   GOD's thunder tympanic,
GOD's thunder symphonic.

5   GOD's thunder smashes cedars,
GOD topples the northern cedars.

6   The mountain ranges skip like spring colts,
The high ridges jump like wild kid goats.

7-8   GOD's thunder spits fire.
GOD thunders, the wilderness quakes;
He makes the desert of Kadesh shake.

9   GOD's thunder sets the oak trees dancing
A wild dance, whirling; the pelting rain strips their branches.
We fall to our knees — we call out, "Glory!"

10   Above the floodwaters is GOD's throne
    from which his power flows,
    from which he rules the world.

11   GOD makes his people strong.
GOD gives his people peace.

A DAVID PSALM

1   **30** I give you all the credit, GOD —
    you got me out of that mess,
    you didn't let my foes gloat.

2-3   GOD, my God, I yelled for help
    and you put me together.
GOD, you pulled me out of the grave,
    gave me another chance at life
    when I was down-and-out.

4-5   All you saints! Sing your hearts out to GOD!
    Thank him to his face!
He gets angry once in a while, but across
    a lifetime there is only love.
The nights of crying your eyes out
    give way to days of laughter.

6-7　When things were going great
　　　　I crowed, "I've got it made.
　　I'm GOD's favorite.
　　　　He made me king of the mountain."
　　Then you looked the other way
　　　　and I fell to pieces.

8-10　I called out to you, GOD;
　　　　I laid my case before you:
　　"Can you sell me for a profit when I'm dead?
　　　　auction me off at a cemetery yard sale?
　　When I'm 'dust to dust' my songs
　　　　and stories of you won't sell.
　　So listen! and be kind!
　　　　Help me out of this!"

11-12　You did it: you changed wild lament
　　　　into whirling dance;
　　You ripped off my black mourning band
　　　　and decked me with wildflowers.
　　I'm about to burst with song;
　　　　I can't keep quiet about you.
　　GOD, my God,
　　　　I can't thank you enough.

A DAVID PSALM

1-2　**31** I run to you, GOD; I run for dear life.
　　　　Don't let me down!
　　　　Take me seriously this time!
　　Get down on my level and listen,
　　　　and please — no procrastination!
　　Your granite cave a hiding place,
　　　　your high cliff aerie a place of safety.

3-5　You're my cave to hide in,
　　　　my cliff to climb.
　　Be my safe leader,
　　　　be my true mountain guide.
　　Free me from hidden traps;
　　　　I want to hide in you.
　　I've put my life in your hands.
　　　　You won't drop me,
　　　　you'll never let me down.

6-13　I hate all this silly religion,
　　　　but you, GOD, I trust.
　　I'm leaping and singing in the circle of your love;
　　　　you saw my pain,
　　　　you disarmed my tormentors,
　　You didn't leave me in their clutches
　　　　but gave me room to breathe.

Be kind to me, GOD —
    I'm in deep, deep trouble again.
I've cried my eyes out;
    I feel hollow inside.
My life leaks away, groan by groan;
    my years fade out in sighs.
My troubles have worn me out,
    turned my bones to powder.
To my enemies I'm a monster;
    I'm ridiculed by the neighbors.
My friends are horrified;
    they cross the street to avoid me.
They want to blot me from memory,
    forget me like a corpse in a grave,
    discard me like a broken dish in the trash.
The street-talk gossip has me
    "criminally insane"!
Behind locked doors they plot
    how to ruin me for good.

14-18   Desperate, I throw myself on you:
    you are my God!
Hour by hour I place my days in your hand,
    safe from the hands out to get me.
Warm me, your servant, with a smile;
    save me because you love me.
Don't embarrass me by not showing up;
    I've given you plenty of notice.
Embarrass the wicked, stand them up,
    leave them stupidly shaking their heads
    as they drift down to hell.
Gag those loudmouthed liars
    who heckle me, your follower,
    with jeers and catcalls.

19-22   What a stack of blessing you have piled up
    for those who worship you,
Ready and waiting for all who run to you
    to escape an unkind world.
You hide them safely away
    from the opposition.
As you slam the door on those oily, mocking faces,
    you silence the poisonous gossip.
Blessed GOD!
    His love is the wonder of the world.
Trapped by a siege, I panicked.
    "Out of sight, out of mind," I said.
But you heard me say it,
    you heard and listened.

23 Love GOD, all you saints;
  GOD takes care of all who stay close to him,
  But he pays back in full
    those arrogant enough to go it alone.

24 Be brave. Be strong. Don't give up.
  Expect GOD to get here soon.

A DAVID PSALM

1 32 Count yourself lucky, how happy you must be—
    you get a fresh start,
    your slate's wiped clean.

2 Count yourself lucky—
  GOD holds nothing against you
  and you're holding nothing back from him.

3 When I kept it all inside,
  my bones turned to powder,
  my words became daylong groans.

4 The pressure never let up;
  all the juices of my life dried up.

5 Then I let it all out;
  I said, "I'll make a clean breast of my failures to GOD."

Suddenly the pressure was gone—
  my guilt dissolved,
  my sin disappeared.

6 These things add up. Every one of us needs to pray;
  when all hell breaks loose and the dam bursts
  we'll be on high ground, untouched.

7 GOD's my island hideaway,
  keeps danger far from the shore,
  throws garlands of hosannas around my neck.

8 Let me give you some good advice;
  I'm looking you in the eye
  and giving it to you straight:

9 "Don't be ornery like a horse or mule
  that needs bit and bridle
  to stay on track."

10 God-defiers are always in trouble;
  GOD-affirmers find themselves loved
  every time they turn around.

11 Celebrate GOD.
  Sing together—everyone!
  All you honest hearts, raise the roof!

1-3 **33** Good people, cheer GOD!
      Right-living people sound best when praising.
      Use guitars to reinforce your Hallelujahs!
  Play his praise on a grand piano!
Invent your own new song to him;
  give him a trumpet fanfare.

4-5 For GOD's Word is solid to the core;
  everything he makes is sound inside and out.
He loves it when everything fits,
  when his world is in plumb-line true.
Earth is drenched
  in GOD's affectionate satisfaction.

6-7 The skies were made by GOD's command;
  he breathed the word and the stars popped out.
He scooped Sea into his jug,
  put Ocean in his keg.

8-9 Earth-creatures, bow before GOD;
  world-dwellers—down on your knees!
Here's why: he spoke and there it was,
  in place the moment he said so.

10-12 GOD takes the wind out of Babel pretense,
  he shoots down the world's power-schemes.
GOD's plan for the world stands up,
  all his designs are made to last.
Blessed is the country with GOD for God;
  blessed are the people he's put in his will.

13-15 From high in the skies GOD looks around,
  he sees all Adam's brood.
From where he sits
  he overlooks all us earth-dwellers.
He has shaped each person in turn;
  now he watches everything we do.

16-17 No king succeeds with a big army alone,
  no warrior wins by brute strength.
Horsepower is not the answer;
  no one gets by on muscle alone.

18-19 Watch this: God's eye is on those who respect him,
  the ones who are looking for his love.
He's ready to come to their rescue in bad times;
  in lean times he keeps body and soul together.

20-22 We're depending on GOD;
    he's everything we need.
What's more, our hearts brim with joy
    since we've taken for our own his holy name.
Love us, GOD, with all you've got —
    that's what we're depending on.

A DAVID PSALM, WHEN HE OUTWITTED ABIMELECH AND GOT AWAY

1 **34** I bless GOD every chance I get;
    my lungs expand with his praise.

2 I live and breathe GOD;
    if things aren't going well, hear this and be happy:

3 Join me in spreading the news;
    together let's get the word out.

4 GOD met me more than halfway,
    he freed me from my anxious fears.

5 Look at him; give him your warmest smile.
    Never hide your feelings from him.

6 When I was desperate, I called out,
    and GOD got me out of a tight spot.

7 GOD's angel sets up a circle
    of protection around us while we pray.

8 Open your mouth and taste, open your eyes and see —
    how good GOD is.
Blessed are you who run to him.

9 Worship GOD if you want the best;
    worship opens doors to all his goodness.

10 Young lions on the prowl get hungry,
    but GOD-seekers are full of God.

11 Come, children, listen closely;
    I'll give you a lesson in GOD worship.

12 Who out there has a lust for life?
    Can't wait each day to come upon beauty?

13 Guard your tongue from profanity,
    and no more lying through your teeth.

14 Turn your back on sin; do something good.
    Embrace peace — don't let it get away!

15 GOD keeps an eye on his friends,
his ears pick up every moan and groan.

16 GOD won't put up with rebels;
he'll cull them from the pack.

17 Is anyone crying for help? GOD is listening,
ready to rescue you.

18 If your heart is broken, you'll find GOD right there;
if you're kicked in the gut, he'll help you catch your breath.

19 Disciples so often get into trouble;
still, GOD is there every time.

20 He's your bodyguard, shielding every bone;
not even a finger gets broken.

21 The wicked commit slow suicide;
they waste their lives hating the good.

22 GOD pays for each slave's freedom;
no one who runs to him loses out.

A DAVID PSALM

1-3 **35** Harass these hecklers, GOD,
punch these bullies in the nose.
Grab a weapon, anything at hand;
stand up for me!
Get ready to throw the spear, aim the javelin,
at the people who are out to get me.
Reassure me; let me hear you say,
"I'll save you."

4-8 When those thugs try to knife me in the back,
make them look foolish.
Frustrate all those
who are plotting my downfall.
Make them like cinders in a high wind,
with GOD's angel working the bellows.
Make their road lightless and mud-slick,
with GOD's angel on their tails.
Out of sheer cussedness they set a trap to catch me;
for no good reason they dug a ditch to stop me.
Surprise them with your ambush —
catch them in the very trap they set,
the disaster they planned for me.

9-10 But let me run loose and free,
celebrating GOD's great work,
Every bone in my body laughing, singing, "GOD,
there's no one like you.

You put the down-and-out on their feet
    and protect the unprotected from bullies!"

11-12 Hostile accusers appear out of nowhere,
        they stand up and badger me.
    They pay me back misery for mercy,
        leaving my soul empty.

13-14 When they were sick, I dressed in black;
        instead of eating, I prayed.
    My prayers were like lead in my gut,
        like I'd lost my best friend, my brother.
    I paced, distraught as a motherless child,
        hunched and heavyhearted.

15-16 But when I was down
        they threw a party!
    All the nameless riffraff of the town came
        chanting insults about me.
    Like barbarians desecrating a shrine,
        they destroyed my reputation.

17-18 GOD, how long are you going
        to stand there doing nothing?
    Save me from their brutalities;
        everything I've got is being thrown to the lions.
    I will give you full credit
        when everyone gathers for worship;
    When the people turn out in force
        I will say my Hallelujahs.

19-21 Don't let these liars, my enemies,
        have a party at my expense,
    Those who hate me for no reason,
        winking and rolling their eyes.
    No good is going to come
        from that crowd;
    They spend all their time cooking up gossip
        against those who mind their own business.
    They open their mouths
        in ugly grins,
    Mocking, "Ha-ha, ha-ha, thought you'd get away with it?
        We've caught you hands down!"

22 Don't you see what they're doing, GOD?
        You're not going to let them
    Get by with it, are you? Not going to walk off
        without *doing* something, are you?

23-26 Please get up — wake up! Tend to my case.
        My God, my Lord — my life is on the line.

Do what you think is right, GOD, my God,
　　but don't make me pay for their good time.
Don't let them say to themselves,
　　"Ha-ha, we got what we wanted."
Don't let them say,
　　"We've chewed him up and spit him out."
Let those who are being hilarious
　　at my expense
Be made to look ridiculous.
　　Make them wear donkey's ears;
Pin them with the donkey's tail,
　　who made themselves so high and mighty!

27-28　But those who want
　　　　the best for me,
Let them have the last word — a glad shout! —
　　and say, over and over and over,
"GOD is great — everything works
　　together for good for his servant."
I'll tell the world how great and good you are,
　　I'll shout Hallelujah all day, every day.

A D A V I D P S A L M

1-4　　**36** The God-rebel tunes in to sedition —
　　　　　　all ears, eager to sin.
　　　　　He has no regard for God,
　　he stands insolent before him.
He has smooth-talked himself
　　into believing
That his evil
　　will never be noticed.
Words gutter from his mouth,
　　dishwater dirty.
Can't remember when he
　　did anything decent.
Every time he goes to bed,
　　he fathers another evil plot.
When he's loose on the streets,
　　nobody's safe.
He plays with fire
　　and doesn't care who gets burned.

5-6　　God's love is meteoric,
　　　　his loyalty astronomic,
His purpose titanic,
　　his verdicts oceanic.
Yet in his largeness
　　nothing gets lost;
Not a man, not a mouse,
　　slips through the cracks.

7-9　How exquisite your love, O God!
　　　　How eager we are to run under your wings,
　　　To eat our fill at the banquet you spread
　　　　　as you fill our tankards with Eden spring water.
　　　You're a fountain of cascading light,
　　　　and you open our eyes to light.

10-12　Keep on loving your friends;
　　　　　do your work in welcoming hearts.
　　　Don't let the bullies kick me around,
　　　　the moral midgets slap me down.
　　　Send the upstarts sprawling
　　　　flat on their faces in the mud.

A DAVID PSALM

1-2　**37** Don't bother your head with braggarts
　　　　　or wish you could succeed like the wicked.
　　　　　In no time they'll shrivel like grass clippings
　　　and wilt like cut flowers in the sun.

3-4　Get insurance with GOD and do a good deed,
　　　　settle down and stick to your last.
　　　Keep company with GOD,
　　　　get in on the best.

5-6　Open up before GOD, keep nothing back;
　　　　he'll do whatever needs to be done:
　　　He'll validate your life in the clear light of day
　　　　and stamp you with approval at high noon.

7　Quiet down before GOD,
　　　be prayerful before him.
　　Don't bother with those who climb the ladder,
　　　who elbow their way to the top.

8-9　Bridle your anger, trash your wrath,
　　　　cool your pipes — it only makes things worse.
　　　Before long the crooks will be bankrupt;
　　　　GOD-investors will soon own the store.

10-11　Before you know it, the wicked will have had it;
　　　　　you'll stare at his once famous place and — nothing!
　　　Down-to-earth people will move in and take over,
　　　　relishing a huge bonanza.

12-13　Bad guys have it in for the good guys,
　　　　　obsessed with doing them in.
　　　But GOD isn't losing any sleep; to him
　　　　they're a joke with no punch line.

14-15　Bullies brandish their swords,
　　　　　pull back on their bows with a flourish.

They're out to beat up on the harmless,
 or mug that nice man out walking his dog.
A banana peel lands them flat on their faces —
 slapstick figures in a moral circus.

16-17 Less is more and more is less.
  One righteous will outclass fifty wicked,
For the wicked are moral weaklings
  but the righteous are GOD-strong.

18-19 GOD keeps track of the decent folk;
  what they do won't soon be forgotten.
In hard times, they'll hold their heads high;
  when the shelves are bare, they'll be full.

20 God-despisers have had it;
  GOD's enemies are finished —
Stripped bare like vineyards at harvest time,
  vanished like smoke in thin air.

21-22 Wicked borrows and never returns;
  Righteous gives and gives.
Generous gets it all in the end;
  Stingy is cut off at the pass.

23-24 Stalwart walks in step with GOD;
  his path blazed by GOD, he's happy.
If he stumbles, he's not down for long;
  GOD has a grip on his hand.

25-26 I once was young, now I'm a graybeard —
  not once have I seen an abandoned believer,
  or his kids out roaming the streets.
Every day he's out giving and lending,
  his children making him proud.

27-28 Turn your back on evil,
  work for the good and don't quit.
GOD loves this kind of thing,
  never turns away from his friends.

28-29 Live this way and you've got it made,
  but bad eggs will be tossed out.
The good get planted on good land
  and put down healthy roots.

30-31 Righteous chews on wisdom like a dog on a bone,
  rolls virtue around on his tongue.
His heart pumps God's Word like blood through his veins;
  his feet are as sure as a cat's.

32-33 Wicked sets a watch for Righteous,
        he's out for the kill.
     GOD, alert, is also on watch —
        Wicked won't hurt a hair of his head.

  34 Wait passionately for GOD,
        don't leave the path.
     He'll give you your place in the sun
        while you watch the wicked lose it.

35-36 I saw Wicked bloated like a toad,
        croaking pretentious nonsense.
     The next time I looked there was nothing —
        a punctured bladder, vapid and limp.

37-38 Keep your eye on the healthy soul,
        scrutinize the straight life;
     There's a future
        in strenuous wholeness.
     But the willful will soon be discarded;
        insolent souls are on a dead-end street.

39-40 The spacious, free life is from GOD,
        it's also protected and safe.
     GOD-strengthened, we're delivered from evil —
        when we run to him, he saves us.

A DAVID PSALM

1-2 **38** Take a deep breath, GOD; calm down —
        don't be so hasty with your punishing rod.
        Your sharp-pointed arrows of rebuke draw blood;
     my backside smarts from your caning.

 3-4 I've lost twenty pounds in two months
        because of your accusation.
     My bones are brittle as dry sticks
        because of my sin.
     I'm swamped by my bad behavior,
        collapsed under gunnysacks of guilt.

 5-8 The cuts in my flesh stink and grow maggots
        because I've lived so badly.
     And now I'm flat on my face
        feeling sorry for myself morning to night.
     All my insides are on fire,
        my body is a wreck.
     I'm on my last legs; I've had it —
        my life is a vomit of groans.

9-16 Lord, my longings are sitting in plain sight,
        my groans an old story to you.

My heart's about to break;
    I'm a burned-out case.
Cataracts blind me to God and good;
    old friends avoid me like the plague.
My cousins never visit,
    my neighbors stab me in the back.
My competitors blacken my name,
    devoutly they pray for my ruin.
But I'm deaf and mute to it all,
    ears shut, mouth shut.
I don't hear a word they say,
    don't speak a word in response.
What I do, GOD, is wait for you,
    wait for my Lord, my God — you *will* answer!
I wait and pray so they won't laugh me off,
    won't smugly strut off when I stumble.

17-20   I'm on the edge of losing it —
    the pain in my gut keeps burning.
I'm ready to tell my story of failure,
    I'm no longer smug in my sin.
My enemies are alive and in action,
    a lynch mob after my neck.
I give out good and get back evil
    from God-haters who can't stand a God-lover.

21-22   Don't dump me, GOD;
    my God, don't stand me up.
Hurry and help me;
    I want some wide-open space in my life!

A DAVID PSALM

1-3   **39** I'm determined to watch steps and tongue
    so they won't land me in trouble.
    I decided to hold my tongue
as long as Wicked is in the room.
"Mum's the word," I said, and kept quiet.
    But the longer I kept silence
The worse it got —
    my insides got hotter and hotter.
My thoughts boiled over;
    I spilled my guts.

4-6   "Tell me, what's going on, GOD?
    How long do I have to live?
    Give me the bad news!
You've kept me on pretty short rations;
    my life is string too short to be saved.
Oh! we're all puffs of air.
    Oh! we're all shadows in a campfire.

Oh! we're just spit in the wind.
We make our pile, and then we leave it.

7-11 "What am I doing in the meantime, Lord?
Hoping, that's what I'm doing — hoping
You'll save me from a rebel life,
save me from the contempt of dunces.
I'll say no more, I'll shut my mouth,
since you, Lord, are behind all this.
But I can't take it much longer.
When you put us through the fire
to purge us from our sin,
our dearest idols go up in smoke.
Are we also nothing but smoke?

12-13 "Ah, GOD, listen to my prayer, my
cry — open your ears.
Don't be callous;
just look at these tears of mine.
I'm a stranger here. I don't know my way —
a migrant like my whole family.
Give me a break, cut me some slack
before it's too late and I'm out of here."

A DAVID PSALM

1-3 **40** I waited and waited and waited for GOD.
At last he looked; finally he listened.
He lifted me out of the ditch,
pulled me from deep mud.
He stood me up on a solid rock
to make sure I wouldn't slip.
He taught me how to sing the latest God-song,
a praise-song to our God.
More and more people are seeing this:
they enter the mystery,
abandoning themselves to GOD.

4-5 Blessed are you who give yourselves over to GOD,
turn your backs on the world's "sure thing,"
ignore what the world worships;
The world's a huge stockpile
of GOD-wonders and God-thoughts.
Nothing and no one
comes close to you!
I start talking about you, telling what I know,
and quickly run out of words.
Neither numbers nor words
account for you.

6 Doing something for you, bringing something to you —
that's not what you're after.

Being religious, acting pious —
    that's not what you're asking for.
You've opened my ears
    so I can listen.

7-8 So I answered, "I'm coming.
    I read in your letter what you wrote about me,
And I'm coming to the party
    you're throwing for me."
That's when God's Word entered my life,
    became part of my very being.

9-10 I've preached you to the whole congregation,
    I've kept back nothing, GOD — you know that.
I didn't keep the news of your ways
    a secret, didn't keep it to myself.
I told it all, how dependable you are, how thorough.
    I didn't hold back pieces of love and truth
For myself alone. I told it all,
    let the congregation know the whole story.

11-12 Now GOD, don't hold out on me,
    don't hold back your passion.
Your love and truth
    are all that keeps me together.
When troubles ganged up on me,
    a mob of sins past counting,
I was so swamped by guilt
    I couldn't see my way clear.
More guilt in my heart than hair on my head,
    so heavy the guilt that my heart gave out.

13-15 Soften up, GOD, and intervene;
    hurry and get me some help,
So those who are trying to kidnap my soul
    will be embarrassed and lose face,
So anyone who gets a kick out of making me miserable
    will be heckled and disgraced,
So those who pray for my ruin
    will be booed and jeered without mercy.

16-17 But all who are hunting for you —
    oh, let them sing and be happy.
Let those who know what you're all about
    tell the world you're great and not quitting.
And me? I'm a mess. I'm nothing and have nothing:
    make something of me.
You can do it; you've got what it takes —
    but God, don't put it off.

A DAVID PSALM

41

1-3 Dignify those who are down on their luck;
    you'll feel good — *that's* what GOD does.
GOD looks after us all,
makes us robust with life —
Lucky to be in the land,
    we're free from enemy worries.
Whenever we're sick and in bed,
    GOD becomes our nurse,
    nurses us back to health.

4-7 I said, "GOD, be gracious!
    Put me together again —
    my sins have torn me to pieces."
My enemies are wishing the worst for me;
    they make bets on what day I will die.
If someone comes to see me,
    he mouths empty platitudes,
All the while gathering gossip about me
    to entertain the street-corner crowd.
These "friends" who hate me
    whisper slanders all over town.
They form committees
    to plan misery for me.

8-9 The rumor goes out, "He's got some dirty,
    deadly disease. The doctors
    have given up on him."
Even my best friend, the one I always told everything
    — he ate meals at my house all the time! —
    has bitten my hand.

10 GOD, give grace, get me up on my feet.
    I'll show them a thing or two.

11-12 Meanwhile, I'm sure you're on my side —
    no victory shouts yet from the enemy camp!
You know me inside and out, you hold me together,
    you never fail to stand me tall in your presence
    so I can look you in the eye.

13 Blessed is GOD, Israel's God,
    always, always, always.
    Yes. Yes. Yes.

A PSALM OF THE SONS OF KORAH

42

1-3 A white-tailed deer drinks
    from the creek;
    I want to drink God,
deep draughts of God.

I'm thirsty for God-alive.
I wonder, "Will I ever make it —
    arrive and drink in God's presence?"
I'm on a diet of tears —
    tears for breakfast, tears for supper.
All day long
    people knock at my door,
Pestering,
    "Where is this God of yours?"

4   These are the things I go over and over,
    emptying out the pockets of my life.
I was always at the head of the worshiping crowd,
    right out in front,
Leading them all,
    eager to arrive and worship,
Shouting praises, singing thanksgiving —
    celebrating, all of us, God's feast!

5   Why are you down in the dumps, dear soul?
    Why are you crying the blues?
Fix my eyes on God —
    soon I'll be praising again.
He puts a smile on my face.
    He's my God.

6-8 When my soul is in the dumps, I rehearse
    everything I know of you,
From Jordan depths to Hermon heights,
    including Mount Mizar.
Chaos calls to chaos,
    to the tune of whitewater rapids.
Your breaking surf, your thundering breakers
    crash and crush me.
Then GOD promises to love me all day,
    sing songs all through the night!
    My life is God's prayer.

9-10 Sometimes I ask God, my rock-solid God,
    "Why did you let me down?
Why am I walking around in tears,
    harassed by enemies?"
They're out for the kill, these
    tormentors with their obscenities,
Taunting day after day,
    "Where is this God of yours?"

11 Why are you down in the dumps, dear soul?
    Why are you crying the blues?
Fix my eyes on God —
    soon I'll be praising again.

He puts a smile on my face.
He's my God.

43

1-2

Clear my name, God; stick up for me
against these loveless, immoral people.
Get me out of here, away
from these lying degenerates.
I counted on you, God.
Why did you walk out on me?
Why am I pacing the floor, wringing my hands
over these outrageous people?

3-4

Give me your lantern and compass,
give me a map,
So I can find my way to the sacred mountain,
to the place of your presence,
To enter the place of worship,
meet my exuberant God,
Sing my thanks with a harp,
magnificent God, my God.

5

Why are you down in the dumps, dear soul?
Why are you crying the blues?
Fix my eyes on God—
soon I'll be praising again.
He puts a smile on my face.
He's my God.

A PSALM OF THE SONS OF KORAH

44

1-3

We've been hearing about this, God,
all our lives.
Our fathers told us the stories
their fathers told them,
How single-handedly you weeded out the godless
from the fields and planted us,
How you sent those people packing
but gave us a fresh start.
We didn't fight for this land;
we didn't work for it—it was a gift!
You gave it, smiling as you gave it,
delighting as you gave it.

4-8

You're my King, O God—
command victories for Jacob!
With your help we'll wipe out our enemies,
in your name we'll stomp them to dust.
I don't trust in weapons;
my sword won't save me—
But it's you, you who saved us from the enemy;
you made those who hate us lose face.

All day we parade God's praise —
  we thank you by name over and over.

9-12 But now you've walked off and left us,
      you've disgraced us and won't fight for us.
    You made us turn tail and run;
      those who hate us have cleaned us out.
    You delivered us as sheep to the butcher,
      you scattered us to the four winds.
    You sold your people at a discount —
      you made nothing on the sale.

13-16 You made people on the street,
      urchins, poke fun and call us names.
    You made us a joke among the godless,
      a cheap joke among the rabble.
    Every day I'm up against it,
      my nose rubbed in my shame —
    Gossip and ridicule fill the air,
      people out to get me crowd the street.

17-19 All this came down on us,
      and we've done nothing to deserve it.
    We never betrayed your Covenant: our hearts
      were never false, our feet never left your path.
    Do we deserve torture in a den of jackals?
      or lockup in a black hole?

20-22 If we had forgotten to pray to our God
      or made fools of ourselves with store-bought gods,
    Wouldn't God have figured this out?
      We can't hide things from him.
    No, you decided to make us martyrs,
      lambs assigned for sacrifice each day.

23-26 Get up, God! Are you going to sleep all day?
      Wake up! Don't you care what happens to us?
    Why do you bury your face in the pillow?
      Why pretend things are just fine with us?
    And here we are — flat on our faces in the dirt,
      held down with a boot on our necks.
    Get up and come to our rescue.
      If you love us so much, *Help us!*

A Wedding Song of the Sons of Korah

1 **45** My heart bursts its banks,
        spilling beauty and goodness.
      I pour it out in a poem to the king,
    shaping the river into words:

2-4 "You're the handsomest of men;
    every word from your lips is sheer grace,
    and God has blessed you, blessed you so much.
Strap your sword to your side, warrior!
    Accept praise! Accept due honor!
    Ride majestically! Ride triumphantly!
Ride on the side of truth!
    Ride for the righteous meek!

4-5 "Your instructions are glow-in-the-dark;
    you shoot sharp arrows
Into enemy hearts; the king's
    foes lie down in the dust, beaten.

6-7 "Your throne is God's throne,
    ever and always;
The scepter of your royal rule
    measures right living.
You love the right
    and hate the wrong.
And that is why God, your very own God,
    poured fragrant oil on your head,
Marking you out as king
    from among your dear companions.

8-9 "Your ozone-drenched garments
    are fragrant with mountain breeze.
Chamber music — from the throne room —
    makes you want to dance.
Kings' daughters are maids in your court,
    the Bride glittering with golden jewelry.

10-12 "Now listen, daughter, don't miss a word:
    forget your country, put your home behind you.
Be *here* — the king is wild for you.
    Since he's your lord, adore him.
Wedding gifts pour in from Tyre;
    rich guests shower you with presents."

13-15 (Her wedding dress is dazzling,
    lined with gold by the weavers;
All her dresses and robes
    are woven with gold.
She is led to the king,
    followed by her virgin companions.
A procession of joy and laughter!
    a grand entrance to the king's palace!)

16-17 "Set your mind now on sons —
    don't dote on father and grandfather.

You'll set your sons up as princes
    all over the earth.
I'll make you famous for generations;
    you'll be the talk of the town
    for a long, long time."

A Song of the Sons of Korah

46

1-3   God is a safe place to hide,
      ready to help when we need him.
    We stand fearless at the cliff-edge of doom,
courageous in seastorm and earthquake,
Before the rush and roar of oceans,
    the tremors that shift mountains.

Jacob-wrestling God fights for us,
God-of-Angel-Armies protects us.

4-6   River fountains splash joy, cooling God's city,
    this sacred haunt of the Most High.
God lives here, the streets are safe,
    God at your service from crack of dawn.
Godless nations rant and rave, kings and kingdoms threaten,
    but Earth does anything he says.

7   Jacob-wrestling God fights for us,
    God-of-Angel-Armies protects us.

8-10   Attention, all! See the marvels of God!
    He plants flowers and trees all over the earth,
Bans war from pole to pole,
    breaks all the weapons across his knee.
"Step out of the traffic! Take a long,
    loving look at me, your High God,
    above politics, above everything."

11   Jacob-wrestling God fights for us,
    God-of-Angel-Armies protects us.

A Psalm of the Sons of Korah

47

1-9   Applause, everyone. Bravo, bravissimo!
      Shout God-songs at the top of your lungs!
    God Most High is stunning,
    astride land and ocean.
He crushes hostile people,
    puts nations at our feet.
He set us at the head of the line,
    prize-winning Jacob, his favorite.
Loud cheers as God climbs the mountain,
    a ram's horn blast at the summit.
Sing songs to God, sing out!
    Sing to our King, sing praise!

He's Lord over earth,
    so sing your best songs to God.
God is Lord of godless nations —
    sovereign, he's King of the mountain.
Princes from all over are gathered,
    people of Abraham's God.
The powers of earth are God's —
    he soars over all.

A PSALM OF THE SONS OF KORAH

48

1-3 GOD majestic,
    praise abounds in our God-city!
His sacred mountain,
    breathtaking in its heights — earth's joy.
Zion Mountain looms in the North,
    city of the world-King.
God in his citadel peaks
    impregnable.

4-6 The kings got together,
    they united and came.
They took one look and shook their heads,
    they scattered and ran away.
They doubled up in pain
    like a woman having a baby.

7-8 You smashed the ships of Tarshish
    with a storm out of the East.
We heard about it, then we saw it
    with our eyes —
In GOD's city of Angel Armies,
    in the city our God
Set on firm foundations,
    firm forever.

9-10 We pondered your love-in-action, God,
    waiting in your temple:
Your name, God, evokes a train
    of Hallelujahs wherever
It is spoken, near and far;
    your arms are heaped with goodness-in-action.

11 Be glad, Zion Mountain;
    Dance, Judah's daughters!
    He does what he said he'd do!

12-14 Circle Zion, take her measure,
    count her fortress peaks,
Gaze long at her sloping bulwark,
    climb her citadel heights —
Then you can tell the next generation

detail by detail the story of God,
Our God forever,
who guides us till the end of time.

1-2

49 Listen, everyone, listen —
earth-dwellers, don't miss this.
All you haves
and have-nots,
All together now: listen.

3-4 I set plainspoken wisdom before you,
my heart-seasoned understandings of life.
I fine-tuned my ear to the sayings of the wise,
I solve life's riddle with the help of a harp.

5-6 So why should I fear in bad times,
hemmed in by enemy malice,
Shoved around by bullies,
demeaned by the arrogant rich?

7-9 Really! There's no such thing as self-rescue,
pulling yourself up by your bootstraps.
The cost of rescue is beyond our means,
and even then it doesn't guarantee
Life forever, or insurance
against the Black Hole.

10-11 Anyone can see that the brightest and best die,
wiped out right along with fools and dunces.
They leave all their prowess behind,
move into their new home, The Coffin,
The cemetery their permanent address.
And to think they named counties after themselves!

12 We aren't immortal. We don't last long.
Like our dogs, we age and weaken. And die.

13-15 This is what happens to those who live for the moment,
who only look out for themselves:
Death herds them like sheep straight to hell;
they disappear down the gullet of the grave;
They waste away to nothing —
nothing left but a marker in a cemetery.
But me? God snatches me from the clutch of death,
he reaches down and grabs me.

16-19 So don't be impressed with those who get rich
and pile up fame and fortune.
They can't take it with them;
fame and fortune all get left behind.

Just when they think they've arrived
    and folks praise them because they've made good,
They enter the family burial plot
    where they'll never see sunshine again.

20   We aren't immortal. We don't last long.
        Like our dogs, we age and weaken. And die.

AN ASAPH PSALM

1-3   **50** The God of gods — it's GOD! — speaks out, shouts, "Earth!"
        welcomes the sun in the east,
        farewells the disappearing sun in the west.
From the dazzle of Zion,
    God blazes into view.
Our God makes his entrance,
    he's not shy in his coming.
Starbursts of fireworks precede him.

4-5   He summons heaven and earth as a jury,
        he's taking his people to court:
"Round up my saints who swore
    on the Bible their loyalty to me."

6   The whole cosmos attests to the fairness of this court,
        that here *God* is judge.

7-15   "Are you listening, dear people? I'm getting ready to speak;
        Israel, I'm about ready to bring you to trial.
This is God, your God,
    speaking to you.
I don't find fault with your acts of worship,
    the frequent burnt sacrifices you offer.
But why should I want your blue-ribbon bull,
    or more and more goats from your herds?
Every creature in the forest is mine,
    the wild animals on all the mountains.
I know every mountain bird by name;
    the scampering field mice are my friends.
If I get hungry, do you think I'd tell you?
    All creation and its bounty are mine.
Do you think I feast on venison?
    or drink draughts of goats' blood?
Spread for me a banquet of praise,
    serve High God a feast of kept promises,
And call for help when you're in trouble —
    I'll help you, and you'll honor me."

16-21   Next, God calls up the wicked:

"What are you up to, quoting my laws,
    talking like we are good friends?

You never answer the door when I call;
    you treat my words like garbage.
If you find a thief, you make him your buddy;
    adulterers are your friends of choice.
Your mouth drools filth;
    lying is a serious art form with you.
You stab your own brother in the back,
    rip off your little sister.
I kept a quiet patience while you did these things;
    you thought I went along with your game.
I'm calling you on the carpet, *now*,
    laying your wickedness out in plain sight.

22-23 "Time's up for playing fast and
    loose with me.
I'm ready to pass sentence,
    and there's no help in sight!
It's the praising life that honors me.
    As soon as you set your foot on the Way,
I'll show you my salvation."

A DAVID PSALM, AFTER HE WAS CONFRONTED BY NATHAN
ABOUT THE AFFAIR WITH BATHSHEBA

1-3 **51** Generous in love — God, give grace!
    Huge in mercy — wipe out my bad record.
    Scrub away my guilt,
soak out my sins in your laundry.
I know how bad I've been;
    my sins are staring me down.

4-6 You're the One I've violated, and you've seen
    it all, seen the full extent of my evil.
You have all the facts before you;
    whatever you decide about me is fair.
I've been out of step with you for a long time,
    in the wrong since before I was born.
What you're after is truth from the inside out.
    Enter me, then; conceive a new, true life.

7-15 Soak me in your laundry and I'll come out clean,
    scrub me and I'll have a snow-white life.
Tune me in to foot-tapping songs,
    set these once-broken bones to dancing.
Don't look too close for blemishes,
    give me a clean bill of health.
God, make a fresh start in me,
    shape a Genesis week from the chaos of my life.
Don't throw me out with the trash,
    or fail to breathe holiness in me.
Bring me back from gray exile,
    put a fresh wind in my sails!

Give me a job teaching rebels your ways
  so the lost can find their way home.
Commute my death sentence, God, my salvation God,
  and I'll sing anthems to your life-giving ways.
Unbutton my lips, dear God;
  I'll let loose with your praise.

16-17 Going through the motions doesn't please you,
  a flawless performance is nothing to you.
I learned God-worship
  when my pride was shattered.
Heart-shattered lives ready for love
  don't for a moment escape God's notice.

18-19 Make Zion the place you delight in,
  repair Jerusalem's broken-down walls.
Then you'll get real worship from us,
  acts of worship small and large,
Including all the bulls
  they can heave onto your altar!

A DAVID PSALM, WHEN DOEG THE EDOMITE REPORTED TO SAUL,
"DAVID'S AT AHIMELECH'S HOUSE"

1-4 **52** Why do you brag of evil, "Big Man"?
  God's mercy carries the day.
  You scheme catastrophe;
your tongue cuts razor-sharp,
  artisan in lies.
You love evil more than good,
  you call black white.
You love malicious gossip,
  you foul-mouth.

5 God will tear you limb from limb,
  sweep you up and throw you out,
Pull you up by the roots
  from the land of life.

6-7 Good people will watch and
  worship. They'll laugh in relief:
"Big Man bet on the wrong horse,
  trusted in big money,
  made his living from catastrophe."

8 And I'm an olive tree,
  growing green in God's house.
I trusted in the generous mercy
  of God then and now.

9 I thank you always
  that you went into action.

And I'll stay right here,
  your good name my hope,
  in company with your faithful friends.

A DAVID PSALM

1-2

53

Bilious and bloated, they gas,
    "God is gone."
  It's poison gas —
  they foul themselves, they poison
Rivers and skies;
  thistles are their cash crop.
God sticks his head out of heaven.
  He looks around.
He's looking for someone not stupid —
  one man, even, God-expectant,
  just one God-ready woman.

3 He comes up empty. A string
    of zeros. Useless, unshepherded
Sheep, taking turns pretending
    to be Shepherd.
The ninety and nine
    follow the one.

4 Don't they know anything,
    all these impostors?
Don't they know
    they can't get away with this,
Treating people like a fast-food meal
    over which they're too busy to pray?

5 Night is coming for them, and nightmare —
    a nightmare they'll never wake up from.
God will make hash of these squatters,
    send them packing for good.

6 Is there anyone around to save Israel?
    God turns life around.
Turned-around Jacob skips rope,
    turned-around Israel sings laughter.

A DAVID PSALM, WHEN THE ZIPHITES REPORTED TO SAUL,
"DAVID IS HIDING OUT WITH US"

1-2

54

God, for your sake, help me!
    Use your influence to clear me.
  Listen, God — I'm desperate.
Don't be too busy to hear me.

3 Outlaws are out to get me,
    hit men are trying to kill me.

Nothing will stop them;
    God means nothing to them.

4-5   Oh, look! God's right here helping!
    GOD's on my side,
Evil is looping back on my enemies.
    Don't let up! Finish them off!

6-7   I'm ready now to worship, so ready.
    I thank you, GOD — you're so good.
You got me out of every scrape,
    and I saw my enemies get it.

A DAVID PSALM

1-3   **55** Open your ears, God, to my prayer;
    don't pretend you don't hear me knocking.
    Come close and whisper your answer.
I really need you.
I shudder at the mean voice,
    quail before the evil eye,
As they pile on the guilt,
    stockpile angry slander.

4-8   My insides are turned inside out;
    specters of death have me down.
I shake with fear,
    I shudder from head to foot.
"Who will give me wings," I ask —
    "wings like a dove?"
Get me out of here on dove wings;
    I want some peace and quiet.
I want a walk in the country,
    I want a cabin in the woods.
I'm desperate for a change
    from rage and stormy weather.

9-11   Come down hard, Lord — slit their tongues.
    I'm appalled how they've split the city
Into rival gangs
    prowling the alleys
Day and night spoiling for a fight,
    trash piled in the streets,
Even shopkeepers gouging and cheating
    in broad daylight.

12-14   This isn't the neighborhood bully
    mocking me — I could take that.
This isn't a foreign devil spitting
    invective — I could tune that out.
It's *you*! We grew up together!
    You! My best friend!

Those long hours of leisure as we walked
    arm in arm, God a third party to our conversation.

15   Haul my betrayers off alive to hell — let them
    experience the horror, let them
    feel every desolate detail of a damned life.

16-19   I call to God;
    GOD will help me.
At dusk, dawn, and noon I sigh
    deep sighs — he hears, he rescues.
My life is well and whole, secure
    in the middle of danger
Even while thousands
    are lined up against me.
God hears it all, and from his judge's bench
    puts them in their place.
But, set in their ways, they won't change;
    they pay him no mind.

20-21   And this, my best friend, betrayed his best friends;
    his life betrayed his word.
All my life I've been charmed by his speech,
    never dreaming he'd turn on me.
His words, which were music to my ears,
    turned to daggers in my heart.

22-23   Pile your troubles on GOD's shoulders —
    he'll carry your load, he'll help you out.
He'll never let good people
    topple into ruin.
But you, God, will throw the others
    into a muddy bog,
Cut the lifespan of assassins
    and traitors in half.

And I trust in you.

A DAVID PSALM, WHEN HE WAS CAPTURED
BY THE PHILISTINES IN GATH

1-4   **56** Take my side, God — I'm getting kicked around,
    stomped on every day.
    Not a day goes by
but somebody beats me up;
They make it their duty
    to beat me up.
When I get really afraid
    I come to you in trust.
I'm proud to praise God;
    fearless now, I trust in God.
    What can mere mortals do?

5-6　They don't let up —
　　　they smear my reputation
　　　and huddle to plot my collapse.
　　They gang up,
　　　sneak together through the alleys
　　To take me by surprise,
　　　wait their chance to get me.

7　Pay them back in evil!
　　Get angry, God!
　　Down with these people!

8　You've kept track of my every toss and turn
　　　through the sleepless nights,
　　Each tear entered in your ledger,
　　　each ache written in your book.

9　If my enemies run away,
　　　turn tail when I yell at them,
　　Then I'll know
　　　that God is on my side.

10-11　I'm proud to praise God,
　　　proud to praise GOD.
　　Fearless now, I trust in God;
　　　what can mere mortals do to me?

12-13　God, you did everything you promised,
　　　and I'm thanking you with all my heart.
　　You pulled me from the brink of death,
　　　my feet from the cliff-edge of doom.
　　Now I stroll at leisure with God
　　　in the sunlit fields of life.

A DAVID PSALM, WHEN HE HID IN A CAVE FROM SAUL

1-3　**57** Be good to me, God — and now!
　　　　I've run to you for dear life.
　　　　I'm hiding out under your wings
　　until the hurricane blows over.
　　I call out to High God,
　　　the God who holds me together.
　　He sends orders from heaven and saves me,
　　　he humiliates those who kick me around.
　　God delivers generous love,
　　　he makes good on his word.

4　I find myself in a pride of lions
　　　who are wild for a taste of human flesh;
　　Their teeth are lances and arrows,
　　　their tongues are sharp daggers.

5   Soar high in the skies, O God!
         Cover the whole earth with your glory!

6   They booby-trapped my path;
         I thought I was dead and done for.
     They dug a mantrap to catch me,
         and fell in headlong themselves.

7-8 I'm ready, God, so ready,
         ready from head to toe,
     Ready to sing, ready to raise a tune:
         "Wake up, soul!
     Wake up, harp! wake up, lute!
         Wake up, you sleepyhead sun!"

9-10 I'm thanking you, GOD, out loud in the streets,
         singing your praises in town and country.
     The deeper your love, the higher it goes;
         every cloud is a flag to your faithfulness.

11   Soar high in the skies, O God!
         Cover the whole earth with your glory!

A DAVID PSALM

1-2   **58** Is this any way to run a country?
             Is there an honest politician in the house?
             Behind the scenes you brew cauldrons of evil,
         behind closed doors you make deals with demons.

3-5 The wicked crawl from the wrong side of the cradle;
         their first words out of the womb are lies.
     Poison, lethal rattlesnake poison,
         drips from their forked tongues —
     Deaf to threats, deaf to charm,
         decades of wax built up in their ears.

6-9 God, smash their teeth to bits,
         leave them toothless tigers.
     Let their lives be buckets of water spilled,
         all that's left, a damp stain in the sand.
     Let them be trampled grass
         worn smooth by the traffic.
     Let them dissolve into snail slime,
         be a miscarried fetus that never sees sunlight.
     Before what they cook up is half-done, God,
         throw it out with the garbage!

10-11 The righteous will call up their friends
         when they see the wicked get their reward,
     Serve up their blood in goblets
         as they toast one another,

Everyone cheering, "It's worth it to play by the rules!
God's handing out trophies and tending the earth!"

A DAVID PSALM, WHEN SAUL SET A WATCH ON
DAVID'S HOUSE IN ORDER TO KILL HIM

1-2 **59** My God! Rescue me from my enemies,
      defend me from these mutineers.
      Rescue me from their dirty tricks,
save me from their hit men.

3-4 Desperadoes have ganged up on me,
      they're hiding in ambush for me.
I did nothing to deserve this, GOD,
      crossed no one, wronged no one.
All the same, they're after me,
      determined to get me.

4-5 Wake up and see for yourself! You're GOD,
      GOD-of-Angel-Armies, Israel's God!
Get on the job and take care of these pagans,
      don't be soft on these hard cases.

6-7 They return when the sun goes down,
      They howl like coyotes, ringing the city.
Then suddenly they're all at the gate,
      Snarling invective, drawn daggers in their teeth.
They think they'll never get caught.

8-10 But you, GOD, break out laughing;
      you treat the godless nations like jokes.
Strong God, I'm watching you do it,
      I can always count on you.
God in dependable love shows up on time,
      shows me my enemies in ruin.

11-13 Don't make quick work of them, GOD,
      lest my people forget.
Bring them down in slow motion,
      take them apart piece by piece.
Let all their mean-mouthed arrogance
      catch up with them,
Catch them out and bring them down
      — every muttered curse
      — every barefaced lie.
Finish them off in fine style!
      Finish them off for good!
Then all the world will see
      that God rules well in Jacob,
      everywhere that God's in charge.

14-15
They return when the sun goes down,
They howl like coyotes, ringing the city.
They scavenge for bones,
And bite the hand that feeds them.

16-17
And me? I'm singing your prowess,
shouting at cockcrow your largesse,
For you've been a safe place for me,
a good place to hide.
Strong God, I'm watching you do it,
I can always count on you —
God, my dependable love.

A David Psalm, When He Fought Against
Aram-Naharaim and Aram-Zobah and Joab Killed
Twelve Thousand Edomites at the Valley of Salt

1-2
60
God! you walked off and left us,
kicked our defenses to bits
And stalked off angry.
Come back. Oh please, come back!

You shook earth to the foundations,
ripped open huge crevasses.
Heal the breaks! Everything's
coming apart at the seams.

3-5
You made your people look doom in the face,
then gave us cheap wine to drown our troubles.
Then you planted a flag to rally your people,
an unfurled flag to look to for courage.
Now do something quickly, answer right now,
so the one you love best is saved.

6-8
That's when God spoke in holy splendor,
"Bursting with joy,
I make a present of Shechem,
I hand out Succoth Valley as a gift.
Gilead's in my pocket,
to say nothing of Manasseh.
Ephraim's my hard hat,
Judah my hammer;
Moab's a scrub bucket,
I mop the floor with Moab,
Spit on Edom,
rain fireworks all over Philistia."

9-10
Who will take me to the thick of the fight?
Who'll show me the road to Edom?
You aren't giving up on us, are you, God?
refusing to go out with our troops?

11-12 Give us help for the hard task;
    human help is worthless.
In God we'll do our very best;
    he'll flatten the opposition for good.

A DAVID PSALM

1-2 **61** God, listen to me shout,
    bend an ear to my prayer.
    When I'm far from anywhere,
    down to my last gasp,
I call out, "Guide me
    up High Rock Mountain!"

3-5 You've always given me breathing room,
    a place to get away from it all,
A lifetime pass to your safe-house,
    an open invitation as your guest.
You've always taken me seriously, God,
    made me welcome among those who know and love you.

6-8 Let the days of the king add up
    to years and years of good rule.
Set his throne in the full light of God;
    post Steady Love and Good Faith as lookouts,
And I'll be the poet who sings your glory —
    and live what I sing every day.

A DAVID PSALM

1-2 **62** God, the one and only —
    I'll wait as long as he says.
    Everything I need comes from him,
    so why not?
He's solid rock under my feet,
    breathing room for my soul,
An impregnable castle:
    I'm set for life.

3-4 How long will you gang up on me?
    How long will you run with the bullies?
There's nothing to you, any of you —
    rotten floorboards, worm-eaten rafters,
Anthills plotting to bring down mountains,
    far gone in make-believe.
You talk a good line,
    but every "blessing" breathes a curse.

5-6 God, the one and only —
    I'll wait as long as he says.
Everything I hope for comes from him,
    so why not?
He's solid rock under my feet,

breathing room for my soul,
An impregnable castle:
I'm set for life.

7-8 My help and glory are in God
— granite-strength and safe-harbor-God —
So trust him absolutely, people;
lay your lives on the line for him.
God is a safe place to be.

9 Man as such is smoke,
woman as such, a mirage.
Put them together, they're nothing;
two times nothing is nothing.

10 And a windfall, if it comes —
don't make too much of it.

11 God said this once and for all;
how many times
Have I heard it repeated?
"Strength comes
Straight from God."

12 Love to you, Lord God!
You pay a fair wage for a good day's work!

A DAVID PSALM, WHEN HE WAS OUT IN THE JUDEAN WILDERNESS

1 **63** God — you're my God!
I can't get enough of you!
I've worked up such hunger and thirst for God,
traveling across dry and weary deserts.

2-4 So here I am in the place of worship, eyes open,
drinking in your strength and glory.
In your generous love I am really living at last!
My lips brim praises like fountains.
I bless you every time I take a breath;
My arms wave like banners of praise to you.

5-8 I eat my fill of prime rib and gravy;
I smack my lips. It's time to shout praises!
If I'm sleepless at midnight,
I spend the hours in grateful reflection.
Because you've always stood up for me,
I'm free to run and play.
I hold on to you for dear life,
and you hold me steady as a post.

9-11 Those who are out to get me are marked for doom,
marked for death, bound for hell.

They'll die violent deaths;
jackals will tear them limb from limb.
But the king is glad in God;
his true friends spread the joy,
While small-minded gossips
are gagged for good.

A DAVID PSALM

64

1 Listen and help, O God.
I'm reduced to a whine
And a whimper, obsessed
with feelings of doomsday.

2-6 Don't let them find me —
the conspirators out to get me,
Using their tongues as weapons,
flinging poison words,
poison-tipped arrow-words.
They shoot from ambush,
shoot without warning,
not caring who they hit.
They keep fit doing calisthenics
of evil purpose,
They keep lists of the traps
they've secretly set.
They say to each other,
"No one can catch us,
no one can detect our perfect crime."
The Detective detects the mystery
in the dark of the cellar heart.

7-8 The God of the Arrow shoots!
They double up in pain,
Fall flat on their faces
in full view of the grinning crowd.

9-10 Everyone sees it. God's
work is the talk of the town.
Be glad, good people! Fly to GOD!
Good-hearted people, make praise your habit.

A DAVID PSALM

65

1-2 Silence is praise to you,
Zion-dwelling God,
And also obedience.
You hear the prayer in it all.

2-8 We all arrive at your doorstep sooner
or later, loaded with guilt,
Our sins too much for us —
but you get rid of them once and for all.

Blessed are the chosen! Blessed the guest
    at home in your place!
We expect our fill of good things
    in your house, your heavenly manse.
All your salvation wonders
    are on display in your trophy room.
Earth-Tamer, Ocean-Pourer,
    Mountain-Maker, Hill-Dresser,
Muzzler of sea storm and wave crash,
    of mobs in noisy riot —
Far and wide they'll come to a stop,
    they'll stare in awe, in wonder.
Dawn and dusk take turns
    calling, "Come and worship."

9-13   Oh, visit the earth,
    ask her to join the dance!
Deck her out in spring showers,
    fill the God-River with living water.
Paint the wheat fields golden.
    Creation was made for this!
Drench the plowed fields,
    soak the dirt clods
With rainfall as harrow and rake
    bring her to blossom and fruit.
Snow-crown the peaks with splendor,
    scatter rose petals down your paths,
All through the wild meadows, rose petals.
    Set the hills to dancing,
Dress the canyon walls with live sheep,
    a drape of flax across the valleys.
Let them shout, and shout, and shout!
    Oh, oh, let them sing!

1-4   **66** All together now — applause for God!
    Sing songs to the tune of his glory,
    set glory to the rhythms of his praise.
Say of God, "We've never seen anything like him!"
    When your enemies see you in action,
    they slink off like scolded dogs.
The whole earth falls to its knees —
    it worships you, sings to you,
    can't stop enjoying your name and fame.

5-6   Take a good look at God's wonders —
    they'll take your breath away.
He converted sea to dry land;
    travelers crossed the river on foot.
    Now isn't that cause for a song?

7   Ever sovereign in his high tower, he keeps
        his eye on the godless nations.
    Rebels don't dare
        raise a finger against him.

8-12   Bless our God, O peoples!
           Give him a thunderous welcome!
       Didn't he set us on the road to life?
           Didn't he keep us out of the ditch?
       He trained us first,
           passed us like silver through refining fires,
       Brought us into hardscrabble country,
           pushed us to our very limit,
       Road-tested us inside and out,
           took us to hell and back;
       Finally he brought us
           to this well-watered place.

13-15   I'm bringing my prizes and presents to your house.
            I'm doing what I said I'd do,
        What I solemnly swore I'd do
            that day when I was in so much trouble:
        The choicest cuts of meat
            for the sacrificial meal;
        Even the fragrance
            of roasted lamb is like a meal!
        Or make it an ox
            garnished with goat meat!

16-20   All believers, come here and listen,
            let me tell you what God did for me.
        I called out to him with my mouth,
            my tongue shaped the sounds of music.
        If I had been cozy with evil,
            the Lord would never have listened.
        But he most surely *did* listen,
            he came on the double when he heard my prayer.
        Blessed be God: he didn't turn a deaf ear,
            he stayed with me, loyal in his love.

1-7   **67** God, mark us with grace
               and blessing! Smile!
           The whole country will see how you work,
       all the godless nations see how you save.
       God! Let people thank and enjoy you.
           Let all people thank and enjoy you.
       Let all far-flung people become happy
           and shout their happiness because
       You judge them fair and square,
           you tend the far-flung peoples.
       God! Let people thank and enjoy you.

Let all people thank and enjoy you.
Earth, display your exuberance!
　　You mark us with blessing, O God, our God.
You mark us with blessing, O God.
　　Earth's four corners — honor him!

A Davi d Psalm

1-4

68

Up with God!
　　Down with his enemies!
　　　　Adversaries, run for the hills!
Gone like a puff of smoke,
　　like a blob of wax in the fire —
　　　　one look at God and the wicked vanish.
When the righteous see God in action
　　they'll laugh, they'll sing,
　　　　they'll laugh and sing for joy.
Sing hymns to God;
　　all heaven, sing out;
　　　　clear the way for the coming of Cloud-Rider.
Enjoy God,
　　cheer when you see him!

5-6

Father of orphans,
　　champion of widows,
　　　　is God in his holy house.
God makes homes for the homeless,
　　leads prisoners to freedom,
　　　　but leaves rebels to rot in hell.

7-10

God, when you took the lead with your people,
　　when you marched out into the wild,
Earth shook, sky broke out in a sweat;
　　God was on the march.
Even Sinai trembled at the sight of God on the move,
　　at the sight of Israel's God.
You pour out rain in buckets, O God;
　　thorn and cactus become an oasis
For your people to camp in and enjoy.
　　You set them up in business;
　　　　they went from rags to riches.

11-14

The Lord gave the word;
　　thousands called out the good news:
"Kings of the armies
　　are on the run, on the run!"
While housewives, safe and sound back home,
　　divide up the plunder,
　　　　the plunder of Canaanite silver and gold.
On that day that Shaddai scattered the kings,
　　snow fell on Black Mountain.

15-16   You huge mountains, Bashan mountains,
      mighty mountains, dragon mountains.
  All you mountains not chosen,
      sulk now, and feel sorry for yourselves,
  For this is the mountain God has chosen to live on;
      he'll rule from this mountain forever.

17-18   The chariots of God, twice ten thousand,
      and thousands more besides,
  The Lord in the lead, riding down Sinai —
      straight to the Holy Place!
  You climbed to the High Place, captives in tow,
      your arms full of booty from rebels,
  And now you sit there in state,
      GOD, sovereign GOD!

19-23   Blessed be the Lord —
      day after day he carries us along.
  He's our Savior, our God, oh yes!
      He's God-for-us, he's God-who-saves-us.
  Lord GOD knows all
      death's ins and outs.
  What's more, he made heads roll,
      split the skulls of the enemy
  As he marched out of heaven,
      saying, "I tied up the Dragon in knots,
      put a muzzle on the Deep Blue Sea."
  You can wade through your enemies' blood,
      and your dogs taste of your enemies from your boots.

24-31   See God on parade
      to the sanctuary, my God,
      my King on the march!
  Singers out front, the band behind,
      maidens in the middle with castanets.
  The whole choir blesses God.
      Like a fountain of praise, Israel blesses GOD.
  Look — little Benjamin's out
      front and leading
  Princes of Judah in their royal robes,
      princes of Zebulon, princes of Naphtali.
  Parade your power, O God,
      the power, O God, that made us what we are.
  Your temple, High God, is Jerusalem;
      kings bring gifts to you.
  Rebuke that old crocodile, Egypt,
      with her herd of wild bulls and calves,
  Rapacious in her lust for silver,
      crushing peoples, spoiling for a fight.
  Let Egyptian traders bring blue cloth
      and Cush come running to God, her hands outstretched.

32-34　Sing, O kings of the earth!
　　　　Sing praises to the Lord!
　　There he is: Sky-Rider,
　　　　striding the ancient skies.
　　Listen — he's calling in thunder,
　　　　rumbling, rolling thunder.
　　Call out "Bravo!" to God,
　　　　the High God of Israel.
　　His splendor and strength
　　　　rise huge as thunderheads.

35　A terrible beauty, O God,
　　　　streams from your sanctuary.
　　It's Israel's strong God! He gives
　　　　power and might to his people!
　　O you, his people — bless God!

A D a v i d P s a l m

1　**69** God, God, save me!
　　　　　I'm in over my head,

2　Quicksand under me, swamp water over me;
　　I'm going down for the third time.

3　I'm hoarse from calling for help,
　　Bleary-eyed from searching the sky for God.

4　I've got more enemies than hairs on my head;
　　Sneaks and liars are out to knife me in the back.

　　What I never stole
　　Must I now give back?

5　God, you know every sin I've committed;
　　My life's a wide-open book before you.

6　Don't let those who look to you in hope
　　Be discouraged by what happens to me,
　　Dear Lord! GOD of the armies!

　　Don't let those out looking for you
　　Come to a dead end by following me —
　　Please, dear God of Israel!

7　Because of you I look like an idiot,
　　I walk around ashamed to show my face.

8　My brothers shun me like a bum off the street;
　　My family treats me like an unwanted guest.

9 I love you more than I can say.
Because I'm madly in love with you,
They blame me for everything they dislike about you.

10 When I poured myself out in prayer and fasting,
All it got me was more contempt.

11 When I put on a sad face,
They treated me like a clown.

12 Now drunks and gluttons
Make up drinking songs about me.

13 And me? I pray.
GOD, it's time for a break!

God, answer in love!
Answer with your sure salvation!

14 Rescue me from the swamp,
Don't let me go under for good,

Pull me out of the clutch of the enemy;
This whirlpool is sucking me down.

15 Don't let the swamp be my grave, the Black Hole
Swallow me, its jaws clenched around me.

16 Now answer me, GOD, because you love me;
Let me see your great mercy full-face.

17 Don't look the other way; your servant can't take it.
I'm in trouble. Answer right now!

18 Come close, God; get me out of here.
Rescue me from this deathtrap.

19 You know how they kick me around—
Pin on me the donkey's ears, the dunce's cap.

20 I'm broken by their taunts,
Flat on my face, reduced to a nothing.

I looked in vain for one friendly face. Not one.
I couldn't find one shoulder to cry on.

21 They put poison in my soup,
Vinegar in my drink.

22 Let their supper be bait in a trap that snaps shut;
May their best friends be trappers who'll skin them alive.

23 Make them become blind as bats,
Give them the shakes from morning to night.

24 Let them know what you think of them,
Blast them with your red-hot anger.

25 Burn down their houses,
Leave them desolate with nobody at home.

26 They gossiped about the one you disciplined,
Made up stories about anyone wounded by God.

27 Pile on the guilt,
Don't let them off the hook.

28 Strike their names from the list of the living;
No rock-carved honor for them among the righteous.

29 I'm hurt and in pain;
Give me space for healing, and mountain air.

30 Let me shout God's name with a praising song,
Let me tell his greatness in a prayer of thanks.

31 For GOD, this is better than oxen on the altar,
Far better than blue-ribbon bulls.

32 The poor in spirit see and are glad —
Oh, you God-seekers, take heart!

33 For GOD listens to the poor,
He doesn't walk out on the wretched.

34 You heavens, praise him; praise him, earth;
Also ocean and all things that swim in it.

35 For God is out to help Zion,
Rebuilding the wrecked towns of Judah.

Guess who will live there —
The proud owners of the land?

36 No, the children of his servants will get it,
The lovers of his name will live in it.

A DAVID PRAYER

1-3 God! Please hurry to my rescue!
GOD, come quickly to my side!
Those who are out to get me —
let them fall all over themselves.
Those who relish my downfall —

send them down a blind alley.
Give them a taste of their own medicine,
 those gossips off clucking their tongues.

4 Let those on the hunt for you
 sing and celebrate.
Let all who love your saving way
 say over and over, "God is mighty!"

5 But I've lost it. I'm wasted.
 God — quickly, quickly!
Quick to my side, quick to my rescue!
 GOD, don't lose a minute.

1-3 **71** I run for dear life to GOD,
 I'll never live to regret it.
 Do what you do so well:
get me out of this mess and up on my feet.
Put your ear to the ground and listen,
 give me space for salvation.
Be a guest room where I can retreat;
 you said your door was always open!
You're my salvation — my vast, granite fortress.

4-7 My God, free me from the grip of Wicked,
 from the clutch of Bad and Bully.
You keep me going when times are tough —
 my bedrock, GOD, since my childhood.
I've hung on you from the day of my birth,
 the day you took me from the cradle;
 I'll never run out of praise.
Many gasp in alarm when they see me,
 but you take me in stride.

8-11 Just as each day brims with your beauty,
 my mouth brims with praise.
But don't turn me out to pasture when I'm old
 or put me on the shelf when I can't pull my weight.
My enemies are talking behind my back,
 watching for their chance to knife me.
The gossip is: "God has abandoned him.
 Pounce on him now; no one will help him."

12-16 God, don't just watch from the sidelines.
 Come on! Run to my side!
My accusers — make them lose face.
 Those out to get me — make them look
Like idiots, while I stretch out, reaching for you,
 and daily add praise to praise.
I'll write the book on your righteousness,
 talk up your salvation the livelong day,

never run out of good things to write or say.
I come in the power of the Lord GOD,
    I post signs marking his right-of-way.

17-24
You got me when I was an unformed youth,
    God, and taught me everything I know.
Now I'm telling the world your wonders;
    I'll keep at it until I'm old and gray.
God, don't walk off and leave me
    until I get out the news
Of your strong right arm to this world,
    news of your power to the world yet to come,
Your famous and righteous
    ways, O God.
God, you've done it all!
    Who is quite like you?
You, who made me stare trouble in the face,
    Turn me around;
Now let me look life in the face.
    I've been to the bottom;
Bring me up, streaming with honors;
    turn to me, be tender to me,
And I'll take up the lute and thank you
    to the tune of your faithfulness, God.
I'll make music for you on a harp,
    Holy One of Israel.
When I open up in song to you,
    I let out lungsful of praise,
    my rescued life a song.
All day long I'm chanting
    about you and your righteous ways,
While those who tried to do me in
    slink off looking ashamed.

A SOLOMON PSALM

1-8
72 Give the gift of wise rule to the king, O God,
    the gift of just rule to the crown prince.
May he judge your people rightly,
    be honorable to your meek and lowly.
Let the mountains give exuberant witness;
    shape the hills with the contours of right living.
Please stand up for the poor,
    help the children of the needy,
    come down hard on the cruel tyrants.
Outlast the sun, outlive the moon —
    age after age after age.
Be rainfall on cut grass,
    earth-refreshing rain showers.
Let righteousness burst into blossom
    and peace abound until the moon fades to nothing.

Rule from sea to sea,
from the River to the Rim.

9-14 Foes will fall on their knees before God,
his enemies lick the dust.
Kings remote and legendary will pay homage,
kings rich and resplendent will turn over their wealth.
All kings will fall down and worship,
and godless nations sign up to serve him,
Because he rescues the poor at the first sign of need,
the destitute who have run out of luck.
He opens a place in his heart for the down-and-out,
he restores the wretched of the earth.
He frees them from tyranny and torture —
when they bleed, he bleeds;
when they die, he dies.

15-17 And live! Oh, let him live!
Deck him out in Sheba gold.
Offer prayers unceasing to him,
bless him from morning to night.
Fields of golden grain in the land,
cresting the mountains in wild exuberance,
Cornucopias of praise, praises
springing from the city like grass from the earth.
May he never be forgotten,
his fame shine on like sunshine.
May all godless people enter his circle of blessing
and bless the One who blessed them.

18-20 Blessed GOD, Israel's God,
the one and only wonder-working God!
Blessed always his blazing glory!
All earth brims with his glory.
Yes and Yes and Yes.

AN ASAPH PSALM

1-5 **73** No doubt about it! God is good —
good to good people, good to the good-hearted.
But I nearly missed it,
missed seeing his goodness.
I was looking the other way,
looking up to the people
At the top,
envying the wicked who have it made,
Who have nothing to worry about,
not a care in the whole wide world.

6-10 Pretentious with arrogance,
they wear the latest fashions in violence,
Pampered and overfed,

decked out in silk bows of silliness.
They jeer, using words to kill;
 they bully their way with words.
They're full of hot air,
 loudmouths disturbing the peace.
People actually listen to them — can you believe it?
 Like thirsty puppies, they lap up their words.

11-14 What's going on here? Is God out to lunch?
 Nobody's tending the store.
The wicked get by with everything;
 they have it made, piling up riches.
I've been stupid to play by the rules;
 what has it gotten me?
A long run of bad luck, that's what —
 a slap in the face every time I walk out the door.

15-20 If I'd have given in and talked like this,
 I would have betrayed your dear children.
Still, when I tried to figure it out,
 all I got was a splitting headache . . .
Until I entered the sanctuary of God.
 Then I saw the whole picture:
The slippery road you've put them on,
 with a final crash in a ditch of delusions.
In the blink of an eye, disaster!
 A blind curve in the dark, and — nightmare!
We wake up and rub our eyes. . . . Nothing.
 There's nothing to them. And there never was.

21-24 When I was beleaguered and bitter,
 totally consumed by envy,
I was totally ignorant, a dumb ox
 in your very presence.
I'm still in your presence,
 but you've taken my hand.
You wisely and tenderly lead me,
 and then you bless me.

25-28 You're all I want in heaven!
 You're all I want on earth!
When my skin sags and my bones get brittle,
 GOD is rock-firm and faithful.
Look! Those who left you are falling apart!
 Deserters, they'll never be heard from again.
But I'm in the very presence of God —
 oh, how refreshing it is!
I've made Lord GOD my home.
 God, I'm telling the world what you do!

1 **74** You walked off and left us, and never looked back.
    God, how could you do that?
    We're your very own sheep;
how can you stomp off in anger?

2-3 Refresh your memory of us — you bought us a long time ago.
    Your most precious tribe — you paid a good price for us!
    Your very own Mount Zion — you actually lived here once!
Come and visit the site of disaster,
    see how they've wrecked the sanctuary.

4-8 While your people were at worship, your enemies barged in,
    brawling and scrawling graffiti.
They set fire to the porch;
    axes swinging, they chopped up the woodwork,
Beat down the doors with sledgehammers,
    then split them into kindling.
They burned your holy place to the ground,
    violated the place of worship.
They said to themselves, "We'll wipe them all out,"
    and burned down all the places of worship.

9-17 There's not a sign or symbol of God in sight,
    nor anyone to speak in his name,
    no one who knows what's going on.
How long, God, will barbarians blaspheme,
    enemies curse and get by with it?
Why don't you do something? How long are you going
    to sit there with your hands folded in your lap?
God is my King from the very start;
    he works salvation in the womb of the earth.
With one blow you split the sea in two,
    you made mincemeat of the dragon Tannin.
You lopped off the heads of Leviathan,
    then served them up in a stew for the animals.
With your finger you opened up springs and creeks,
    and dried up the wild floodwaters.
You own the day, you own the night;
    you put stars and sun in place.
You laid out the four corners of earth,
    shaped the seasons of summer and winter.

18-21 Mark and remember, GOD, all the enemy
    taunts, each idiot desecration.
Don't throw your lambs to the wolves;
    after all we've been through, don't forget us.
Remember your promises;
    the city is in darkness, the countryside violent.
Don't leave the victims to rot in the street;
    make them a choir that sings your praises.

22-23　On your feet, O God —
　　　　stand up for yourself!
　　　Do you hear what they're saying about you,
　　　　all the vile obscenities?
　　　Don't tune out their malicious filth,
　　　　the brawling invective that never lets up.

A N A S A P H P S A L M

1　**75** We thank you, God, we thank you —
　　　　your Name is our favorite word;
　　　　your mighty works are all we talk about.

2-4　You say, "I'm calling this meeting to order,
　　　　I'm ready to set things right.
　　　When the earth goes topsy-turvy
　　　　And nobody knows which end is up,
　　　I nail it all down,
　　　　I put everything in place again.
　　　I say to the smart alecks, 'That's enough,'
　　　　to the bullies, 'Not so fast.'"

5-6　Don't raise your fist against High God.
　　　　Don't raise your voice against Rock of Ages.
　　　He's the One from east to west;
　　　　from desert to mountains, he's the One.

7-8　God rules: he brings this one down to his knees,
　　　　pulls that one up on her feet.
　　　GOD has a cup in his hand,
　　　　a bowl of wine, full to the brim.
　　　He draws from it and pours;
　　　　it's drained to the dregs.
　　　Earth's wicked ones drink it all,
　　　　drink it down to the last bitter drop!

9-10　And I'm telling the story of God Eternal,
　　　　singing the praises of Jacob's God.
　　　The fists of the wicked
　　　　are bloody stumps,
　　　The arms of the righteous
　　　　are lofty green branches.

A N A S A P H P S A L M

1-3　**76** God is well-known in Judah;
　　　　in Israel, he's a household name.
　　　　He keeps a house in Salem,
　　　his own suite of rooms in Zion.
　　　That's where, using arrows for kindling,
　　　　he made a bonfire of weapons of war.

4-6   Oh, how bright you shine!
         Outshining their huge piles of loot!
      The warriors were plundered
         and left there impotent.
      And now there's nothing to them,
         nothing to show for their swagger and threats.
      Your sudden roar, God of Jacob,
         knocked the wind out of horse and rider.

7-10 Fierce you are, and fearsome!
         Who can stand up to your rising anger?
      From heaven you thunder judgment;
         earth falls to her knees and holds her breath.
      God stands tall and makes things right,
         he saves all the wretched on earth.
      Instead of smoldering rage — God-praise!
         All that sputtering rage — now a garland for God!

11-12 Do for GOD what you said you'd do —
         he is, after all, your God.
      Let everyone in town bring offerings
         to the One Who Watches our every move.
      Nobody gets by with anything,
         no one plays fast and loose with him.

AN ASAPH PSALM

1   **77** I yell out to my God, I yell with all my might,
         I yell at the top of my lungs. He listens.

2-6   I found myself in trouble and went looking for my Lord;
         my life was an open wound that wouldn't heal.
      When friends said, "Everything will turn out all right,"
         I didn't believe a word they said.
      I remember God — and shake my head.
         I bow my head — then wring my hands.
      I'm awake all night — not a wink of sleep;
         I can't even say what's bothering me.
      I go over the days one by one,
         I ponder the years gone by.
      I strum my lute all through the night,
         wondering how to get my life together.

7-10 Will the Lord walk off and leave us for good?
         Will he never smile again?
      Is his love worn threadbare?
         Has his salvation promise burned out?
      Has God forgotten his manners?
         Has he angrily stalked off and left us?
      "Just my luck," I said. "The High God goes out of business
         just the moment I need him."

11-12   Once again I'll go over what GOD has done,
              lay out on the table the ancient wonders;
         I'll ponder all the things you've accomplished,
              and give a long, loving look at your acts.

13-15   O God! Your way is holy!
              No god is great like God!
         You're the God who makes things happen;
              you showed everyone what you can do —
         You pulled your people out of the worst kind of trouble,
              rescued the children of Jacob and Joseph.

16-19   Ocean saw you in action, God,
              saw you and trembled with fear;
              Deep Ocean was scared to death.
         Clouds belched buckets of rain,
              Sky exploded with thunder,
              your arrows flashing this way and that.
         From Whirlwind came your thundering voice,
              Lightning exposed the world,
              Earth reeled and rocked.
         You strode right through Ocean,
              walked straight through roaring Ocean,
              but nobody saw you come or go.

20   Hidden in the hands of Moses and Aaron,
         You led your people like a flock of sheep.

AN ASAPH PSALM

1-4   **78** Listen, dear friends, to God's truth,
              bend your ears to what I tell you.
              I'm chewing on the morsel of a proverb;
         I'll let you in on the sweet old truths,
         Stories we heard from our fathers,
              counsel we learned at our mother's knee.
         We're not keeping this to ourselves,
              we're passing it along to the next generation —
         GOD's fame and fortune,
              the marvelous things he has done.

5-8   He planted a witness in Jacob,
              set his Word firmly in Israel,
         Then commanded our parents
              to teach it to their children
         So the next generation would know,
              and all the generations to come —
         Know the truth and tell the stories
              so their children can trust in God,
         Never forget the works of God
              but keep his commands to the letter.
         Heaven forbid they should be like their parents,

bullheaded and bad,
A fickle and faithless bunch
who never stayed true to God.

9-16   The Ephraimites, armed to the teeth,
ran off when the battle began.
They were cowards to God's Covenant,
refused to walk by his Word.
They forgot what he had done —
marvels he'd done right before their eyes.
He performed miracles in plain sight of their parents
in Egypt, out on the fields of Zoan.
He split the Sea and they walked right through it;
he piled the waters to the right and the left.
He led them by day with a cloud,
led them all the night long with a fiery torch.
He split rocks in the wilderness,
gave them all they could drink from underground springs;
He made creeks flow out from sheer rock,
and water pour out like a river.

17-20   All they did was sin even more,
rebel in the desert against the High God.
They tried to get their own way with God,
clamored for favors, for special attention.
They whined like spoiled children,
"Why can't God give us a decent meal in this desert?
Sure, he struck the rock and the water flowed,
creeks cascaded from the rock.
But how about some fresh-baked bread?
How about a nice cut of meat?"

21-31   When GOD heard that, he was furious —
his anger flared against Jacob,
he lost his temper with Israel.
It was clear they didn't believe God,
had no intention of trusting in his help.
But God helped them anyway, commanded the clouds
and gave orders that opened the gates of heaven.
He rained down showers of manna to eat,
he gave them the Bread of Heaven.
They ate the bread of the mighty angels;
he sent them all the food they could eat.
He let East Wind break loose from the skies,
gave a strong push to South Wind.
This time it was birds that rained down —
succulent birds, an abundance of birds.
He aimed them right for the center of their camp;
all round their tents there were birds.
They ate and had their fill;
he handed them everything they craved on a platter.

But their greed knew no bounds;
    they stuffed their mouths with more and more.
Finally, God was fed up, his anger erupted —
    he cut down their brightest and best,
    he laid low Israel's finest young men.

32-37   And — can you believe it? — they kept right on sinning;
    all those wonders and they still wouldn't believe!
So their lives dribbled off to nothing —
    nothing to show for their lives but a ghost town.
When he cut them down, they came running for help;
    they turned and pled for mercy.
They gave witness that God was their rock,
    that High God was their redeemer,
But they didn't mean a word of it;
    they lied through their teeth the whole time.
They could not have cared less about him,
    wanted nothing to do with his Covenant.

38-55   And God? Compassionate!
    Forgave the sin! Didn't destroy!
Over and over he reined in his anger,
    restrained his considerable wrath.
He knew what they were made of;
    he knew there wasn't much to them,
How often in the desert they had spurned him,
    tried his patience in those wilderness years.
Time and again they pushed him to the limit,
    provoked Israel's Holy God.
How quickly they forgot what he'd done,
    forgot their day of rescue from the enemy,
When he did miracles in Egypt,
    wonders on the plain of Zoan.
He turned the River and its streams to blood —
    not a drop of water fit to drink.
He sent flies, which ate them alive,
    and frogs, which bedeviled them.
He turned their harvest over to caterpillars,
    everything they had worked for to the locusts.
He flattened their grapevines with hail;
    a killing frost ruined their orchards.
He pounded their cattle with hail,
    let thunderbolts loose on their herds.
His anger flared,
    a wild firestorm of havoc,
An advance guard of disease-carrying angels
    to clear the ground, preparing the way before him.
He didn't spare those people,
    he let the plague rage through their lives.
He killed all the Egyptian firstborns,
    lusty infants, offspring of Ham's virility.

Then he led his people out like sheep,
    took his flock safely through the wilderness.
He took good care of them; they had nothing to fear.
    The Sea took care of their enemies for good.
He brought them into his holy land,
    this mountain he claimed for his own.
He scattered everyone who got in their way;
    he staked out an inheritance for them —
    the tribes of Israel all had their own places.

56-64   But they kept on giving him a hard time,
    rebelled against God, the High God,
    refused to do anything he told them.
They were worse, if that's possible, than their parents:
    traitors — crooked as a corkscrew.
Their pagan orgies provoked God's anger,
    their obscene idolatries broke his heart.
When God heard their carryings-on, he was furious;
    he posted a huge No over Israel.
He walked off and left Shiloh empty,
    abandoned the shrine where he had met with Israel.
He let his pride and joy go to the dogs,
    turned his back on the pride of his life.
He turned them loose on fields of battle;
    angry, he let them fend for themselves.
Their young men went to war and never came back;
    their young women waited in vain.
Their priests were massacred,
    and their widows never shed a tear.

65-72   Suddenly the Lord was up on his feet
    like someone roused from deep sleep,
    shouting like a drunken warrior.
He hit his enemies hard, sent them running,
    yelping, not daring to look back.
He disqualified Joseph as leader,
    told Ephraim he didn't have what it takes,
And chose the Tribe of Judah instead,
    Mount Zion, which he loves so much.
He built his sanctuary there, resplendent,
    solid and lasting as the earth itself.
Then he chose David, his servant,
    handpicked him from his work in the sheep pens.
One day he was caring for the ewes and their lambs,
    the next day God had him shepherding Jacob,
    his people Israel, his prize possession.
His good heart made him a good shepherd;
    he guided the people wisely and well.

An Asaph Psalm

1-4 **79** God! Barbarians have broken into your home,
 violated your holy temple,
 left Jerusalem a pile of rubble!
They've served up the corpses of your servants
 as carrion food for birds of prey,
Threw the bones of your holy people
 out to the wild animals to gnaw on.
They dumped out their blood
 like buckets of water.
All around Jerusalem, their bodies
 were left to rot, unburied.
We're nothing but a joke to our neighbors,
 graffiti scrawled on the city walls.

5-7 How long do we have to put up with this, GOD?
 Do you have it in for us for good?
 Will your smoldering rage never cool down?
If you're going to be angry, be angry
 with the pagans who care nothing about you,
 or your rival kingdoms who ignore you.
They're the ones who ruined Jacob,
 who wrecked and looted the place where he lived.

8-10 Don't blame us for the sins of our parents.
 Hurry up and help us; we're at the end of our rope.
You're famous for helping; God, give *us* a break.
 Your reputation is on the line.
Pull us out of this mess, forgive us our sins —
 do what you're famous for doing!
Don't let the heathen get by with their sneers:
 "Where's your God? Is he out to lunch?"
Go public and show the godless world
 that they can't kill your servants and get by with it.

11-13 Give groaning prisoners a hearing;
 pardon those on death row from their doom — you can do it!
Give our jeering neighbors what they've got coming to them;
 let their God-taunts boomerang and knock them flat.
Then we, your people, the ones you love and care for,
 will thank you over and over and over.
We'll tell everyone we meet
 how wonderful you are, how praiseworthy you are!

An Asaph Psalm

1-2 **80** Listen, Shepherd, Israel's Shepherd —
 get all your Joseph sheep together.
 Throw beams of light
 from your dazzling throne
So Ephraim, Benjamin, and Manasseh

can see where they're going.
Get out of bed — you've slept long enough!
Come on the run before it's too late.

3 God, come back!
Smile your blessing smile:
That will be our salvation.

4-6 GOD, God-of-the-Angel-Armies,
how long will you smolder like a sleeping volcano
while your people call for fire and brimstone?
You put us on a diet of tears,
bucket after bucket of salty tears to drink.
You make us look ridiculous to our friends;
our enemies poke fun day after day.

7 God-of-the-Angel-Armies, come back!
Smile your blessing smile:
That will be our salvation.

8-18 Remember how you brought a young vine from Egypt,
cleared out the brambles and briers
and planted your very own vineyard?
You prepared the good earth,
you planted her roots deep;
the vineyard filled the land.
Your vine soared high and shaded the mountains,
even dwarfing the giant cedars.
Your vine ranged west to the Sea,
east to the River.
So why do you no longer protect your vine?
Trespassers pick its grapes at will;
Wild pigs crash through and crush it,
and the mice nibble away at what's left.
God-of-the-Angel-Armies, turn our way!
Take a good look at what's happened
and attend to this vine.
Care for what you once tenderly planted —
the vine you raised from a shoot.
And those who dared to set it on fire —
give them a look that will kill!
Then take the hand of your once-favorite child,
the child you raised to adulthood.
We will never turn our back on you;
breathe life into our lungs so we can shout your name!

19 GOD, God-of-the-Angel-Armies, come back!
Smile your blessing smile:
That will be our salvation.

A N A S A P H P S A L M

81

₁₋₅

A song to our strong God!
  a shout to the God of Jacob!
Anthems from the choir, music from the band,
  sweet sounds from lute and harp,
Trumpets and trombones and horns:
  it's festival day, a feast to God!
A day decreed by God,
  solemnly ordered by the God of Jacob.
He commanded Joseph to keep this day
  so we'd never forget what he did in Egypt.

I hear this most gentle whisper from One
I never guessed would speak to me:

₆₋₇

"I took the world off your shoulders,
  freed you from a life of hard labor.
You called to me in your pain;
  I got you out of a bad place.
I answered you from where the thunder hides,
  I proved you at Meribah Fountain.

₈₋₁₀

"Listen, dear ones — get this straight;
  O Israel, don't take this lightly.
Don't take up with strange gods,
  don't worship the latest in gods.
I'm GOD, your God, the very God
  who rescued you from doom in Egypt,
Then fed you all you could eat,
  filled your hungry stomachs.

₁₁₋₁₂

"But my people didn't listen,
  Israel paid no attention;
So I let go of the reins and told them, 'Run!
  Do it your own way!'

₁₃₋₁₆

"Oh, dear people, will you listen to me now?
  Israel, will you follow my map?
I'll make short work of your enemies,
  give your foes the back of my hand.
I'll send the GOD-haters cringing like dogs,
  never to be heard from again.
You'll feast on my fresh-baked bread
  spread with butter and rock-pure honey."

A N A S A P H P S A L M

82

₁

God calls the judges into his courtroom,
  he puts all the judges in the dock.

2-4   "Enough! You've corrupted justice long enough,
     you've let the wicked get away with murder.
   You're here to defend the defenseless,
     to make sure that underdogs get a fair break;
   Your job is to stand up for the powerless,
     and prosecute all those who exploit them."

5   Ignorant judges! Head-in-the-sand judges!
     They haven't a clue to what's going on.
   And now everything's falling apart,
     the world's coming unglued.

6-7   "I commissioned you judges, each one of you,
     deputies of the High God,
   But you've betrayed your commission
     and now you're stripped of your rank, busted."

8   O God, give them their just deserts!
     You've got the whole world in your hands!

A N A S A P H P S A L M

1-5   **83**   G<small>OD</small>, don't shut me out;
     don't give me the silent treatment, O God.
     Your enemies are out there whooping it up,
   the God-haters are living it up;
   They're plotting to do your people in,
     conspiring to rob you of your precious ones.
   "Let's wipe this nation from the face of the earth,"
     they say; "scratch Israel's name off the books."
   And now they're putting their heads together,
     making plans to get rid of you.

6-8   Edom and the Ishmaelites,
     Moab and the Hagrites,
     Gebal and Ammon and Amalek,
     Philistia and the Tyrians,
     And now Assyria has joined up,
     Giving muscle to the gang of Lot.

9-12   Do to them what you did to Midian,
     to Sisera and Jabin at Kishon Brook;
   They came to a bad end at Endor,
     nothing but dung for the garden.
   Cut down their leaders as you did Oreb and Zeeb,
     their princes to nothings like Zebah and Zalmunna,
   With their empty brags, "We're grabbing it all,
     grabbing God's gardens for ourselves."

13-18   My God! I've had it with them!
     Blow them away!
   Tumbleweeds in the desert waste,

charred sticks in the burned-over ground.
Knock the breath right out of them, so they're gasping
    for breath, gasping, "GOD."
Bring them to the end of their rope,
    and leave them there dangling, helpless.
Then they'll learn your name: "GOD,"
    the one and only High God on earth.

A KORAH PSALM

84

1-2   What a beautiful home, GOD-of-the-Angel-Armies!
    I've always longed to live in a place like this,
    Always dreamed of a room in your house,
where I could sing for joy to God-alive!

3-4   Birds find nooks and crannies in your house,
    sparrows and swallows make nests there.
They lay their eggs and raise their young,
    singing their songs in the place where we worship.
GOD-of-the-Angel-Armies! King! God!
    How blessed they are to live and sing there!

5-7   And how blessed all those in whom you live,
    whose lives become roads you travel;
They wind through lonesome valleys, come upon brooks,
    discover cool springs and pools brimming with rain!
God-traveled, these roads curve up the mountain, and
    at the last turn — Zion! God in full view!

8-9   GOD-of-the-Angel-Armies, listen:
    O God of Jacob, open your ears — I'm praying!
Look at our shields, glistening in the sun,
    our faces, shining with your gracious anointing.

10-12   One day spent in your house, this beautiful place of worship,
    beats thousands spent on Greek island beaches.
I'd rather scrub floors in the house of my God
    than be honored as a guest in the palace of sin.
All sunshine and sovereign is GOD,
    generous in gifts and glory.
He doesn't scrimp with his traveling companions.
    It's smooth sailing all the way with GOD-of-the-Angel-Armies.

A KORAH PSALM

85

1-3   GOD, you smiled on your good earth!
    You brought good times back to Jacob!
    You lifted the cloud of guilt from your people,
you put their sins far out of sight.
You took back your sin-provoked threats,
    you cooled your hot, righteous anger.

4-7   Help us again, God of our help;
    don't hold a grudge against us forever.

You aren't going to keep this up, are you?
    scowling and angry, year after year?
Why not help us make a fresh start — a resurrection life?
    Then your people will laugh and sing!
Show us how much you love us, GOD!
    Give us the salvation we need!

8-9   I can't wait to hear what he'll say.
    GOD's about to pronounce his people well,
The holy people he loves so much,
    so they'll never again live like fools.
See how close his salvation is to those who fear him?
    Our country is home base for Glory!

10-13 Love and Truth meet in the street,
    Right Living and Whole Living embrace and kiss!
Truth sprouts green from the ground,
    Right Living pours down from the skies!
Oh yes! GOD gives Goodness and Beauty;
    our land responds with Bounty and Blessing.
Right Living strides out before him,
    and clears a path for his passage.

A DAVID PSALM

1-7   **86** Bend an ear, GOD; answer me.
    I'm one miserable wretch!
    Keep me safe — haven't I lived a good life?
    Help your servant — I'm depending on you!
You're my God; have mercy on me.
    I count on you from morning to night.
Give your servant a happy life;
    I put myself in your hands!
You're well-known as good and forgiving,
    bighearted to all who ask for help.
Pay attention, GOD, to my prayer;
    bend down and listen to my cry for help.
Every time I'm in trouble I call on you,
    confident that you'll answer.

8-10 There's no one quite like you among the gods, O Lord,
    and nothing to compare with your works.
All the nations you made are on their way,
    ready to give honor to you, O Lord,
Ready to put your beauty on display,
    parading your greatness,
And the great things you do —
    God, you're the one, there's no one but you!

11-17 Train me, GOD, to walk straight;
    then I'll follow your true path.
Put me together, one heart and mind;

then, undivided, I'll worship in joyful fear.
From the bottom of my heart I thank you, dear Lord;
    I've never kept secret what you're up to.
You've always been great toward me — what love!
    You snatched me from the brink of disaster!
God, these bullies have reared their heads!
    A gang of thugs is after me —
    and they don't care a thing about you.
But you, O God, are both tender and kind,
    not easily angered, immense in love,
    and you never, never quit.
So look me in the eye and show kindness,
    give your servant the strength to go on,
    save your dear, dear child!
Make a show of how much you love me
    so the bullies who hate me will stand there slack-jawed,
As you, GOD, gently and powerfully
    put me back on my feet.

A KORAH PSALM

87

1-3   He founded Zion on the Holy Mountain —
    and oh, how GOD loves his home!
    Loves it far better than all
the homes of Jacob put together!
God's hometown — oh!
    everyone there is talking about you!

4   I name them off, those among whom I'm famous:
    Egypt and Babylon,
    also Philistia,
    even Tyre, along with Cush.
Word's getting around; they point them out:
    "This one was born again here!"

5   The word's getting out on Zion:
    "Men and women, right and left,
    get born again in her!"

6   GOD registers their names in his book:
    "This one, this one, and this one —
    born again, right here."

7   Singers and dancers give credit to Zion:
    "All my springs are in you!"

A KORAH PRAYER OF HEMAN

88

1-9   GOD, you're my last chance of the day.
    I spend the night on my knees before you.
    Put me on your salvation agenda;
    take notes on the trouble I'm in.
I've had my fill of trouble;

I'm camped on the edge of hell.
I'm written off as a lost cause,
   one more statistic, a hopeless case.
Abandoned as already dead,
   one more body in a stack of corpses,
And not so much as a gravestone —
   I'm a black hole in oblivion.
You've dropped me into a bottomless pit,
   sunk me in a pitch-black abyss.
I'm battered senseless by your rage,
   relentlessly pounded by your waves of anger.
You turned my friends against me,
   made me horrible to them.
I'm caught in a maze and can't find my way out,
   blinded by tears of pain and frustration.

9-12   I call to you, GOD; all day I call.
   I wring my hands, I plead for help.
Are the dead a live audience for your miracles?
   Do ghosts ever join the choirs that praise you?
Does your love make any difference in a graveyard?
   Is your faithful presence noticed in the corridors of hell?
Are your marvelous wonders ever seen in the dark,
   your righteous ways noticed in the Land of No Memory?

13-18   I'm standing my ground, GOD, shouting for help,
   at my prayers every morning, on my knees each daybreak.
Why, GOD, do you turn a deaf ear?
   Why do you make yourself scarce?
For as long as I remember I've been hurting;
   I've taken the worst you can hand out, and I've had it.
Your wildfire anger has blazed through my life;
   I'm bleeding, black-and-blue.
You've attacked me fiercely from every side,
   raining down blows till I'm nearly dead.
You made lover and neighbor alike dump me;
   the only friend I have left is Darkness.

An Ethan Prayer

1-4   **89** Your love, GOD, is my song, and I'll sing it!
   I'm forever telling everyone how faithful you are.
   I'll never quit telling the story of your love —
how you built the cosmos
and guaranteed everything in it.
Your love has always been our lives' foundation,
   your fidelity has been the roof over our world.
You once said, "I joined forces with my chosen leader,
   I pledged my word to my servant, David, saying,
'Everyone descending from you is guaranteed life;
   I'll make your rule as solid and lasting as rock.'"

5-18　GOD! Let the cosmos praise your wonderful ways,
　　　　the choir of holy angels sing anthems to your faithful ways!
　　　Search high and low, scan skies and land,
　　　　you'll find nothing and no one quite like GOD.
　　　The holy angels are in awe before him;
　　　　he looms immense and august over everyone around him.
　　　GOD-of-the-Angel-Armies, who is like you,
　　　　powerful and faithful from every angle?
　　　You put the arrogant ocean in its place
　　　　and calm its waves when they turn unruly.
　　　You gave that old hag Egypt the back of your hand,
　　　　you brushed off your enemies with a flick of your wrist.
　　　You own the cosmos — you made everything in it,
　　　　everything from atom to archangel.
　　　You positioned the North and South Poles;
　　　　the mountains Tabor and Hermon sing duets to you.
　　　With your well-muscled arm and your grip of steel —
　　　　nobody trifles with you!
　　　The Right and Justice are the roots of your rule;
　　　　Love and Truth are its fruits.
　　　Blessed are the people who know the passwords of praise,
　　　　who shout on parade in the bright presence of GOD.
　　　Delighted, they dance all day long; they know
　　　　who you are, what you do — they can't keep it quiet!
　　　Your vibrant beauty has gotten inside us —
　　　　you've been so good to us! We're walking on air!
　　　All we are and have we owe to GOD,
　　　　Holy God of Israel, our King!

19-37　A long time ago you spoke in a vision,
　　　　you spoke to your faithful beloved:
　　　"I've crowned a hero,
　　　　I chose the best I could find;
　　　I found David, my servant,
　　　　poured holy oil on his head,
　　　And I'll keep my hand steadily on him,
　　　　yes, I'll stick with him through thick and thin.
　　　No enemy will get the best of him,
　　　　no scoundrel will do him in.
　　　I'll weed out all who oppose him,
　　　　I'll clean out all who hate him.
　　　I'm with him for good and I'll love him forever;
　　　　I've set him on high — he's riding high!
　　　I've put Ocean in his one hand, River in the other;
　　　　he'll call out, 'Oh, my Father — my God, my Rock of Salvation!'
　　　Yes, I'm setting him apart as the First of the royal line,
　　　　High King over all of earth's kings.
　　　I'll preserve him eternally in my love,
　　　　I'll faithfully do all I so solemnly promised.
　　　I'll guarantee his family tree
　　　　and underwrite his rule.

If his children refuse to do what I tell them,
   if they refuse to walk in the way I show them,
If they spit on the directions I give them
   and tear up the rules I post for them —
I'll rub their faces in the dirt of their rebellion
   and make them face the music.
But I'll never throw them out,
   never abandon or disown them.
Do you think I'd withdraw my holy promise?
   or take back words I'd already spoken?
I've given my word, my whole and holy word;
   do you think I would lie to David?
His family tree is here for good,
   his sovereignty as sure as the sun,
Dependable as the phases of the moon,
   inescapable as weather."

38-51   But GOD, you did walk off and leave us,
   you lost your temper with the one you anointed.
You tore up the promise you made to your servant,
   you stomped his crown in the mud.
You blasted his home to kingdom come,
   reduced his city to a pile of rubble
Picked clean by wayfaring strangers,
   a joke to all the neighbors.
You declared a holiday for all his enemies,
   and they're celebrating for all they're worth.
Angry, you opposed him in battle,
   refused to fight on his side;
You robbed him of his splendor, humiliated this warrior,
   ground his kingly honor in the dirt.
You took the best years of his life
   and left him an impotent, ruined husk.
How long do we put up with this, GOD?
   Are you gone for good? Will you hold this grudge forever?
Remember my sorrow and how short life is.
   Did you create men and women for nothing but this?
We'll see death soon enough. Everyone does.
   And there's no back door out of hell.
So where is the love you're so famous for, Lord?
   What happened to your promise to David?
Take a good look at your servant, dear Lord;
   I'm the butt of the jokes of all nations,
The taunting jokes of your enemies, GOD,
   as they dog the steps of your dear anointed.

    Blessed be GOD forever and always!
      Yes. Oh, yes.

A PRAYER OF MOSES, MAN OF GOD

1-2   **90** God, it seems you've been our home forever;
           long before the mountains were born,
       Long before you brought earth itself to birth,
   from "once upon a time" to "kingdom come" — you are God.

3-11   So don't return us to mud, saying,
           "Back to where you came from!"
       Patience! You've got all the time in the world — whether
           a thousand years or a day, it's all the same to you.
       Are we no more to you than a wispy dream,
           no more than a blade of grass
       That springs up gloriously with the rising sun
           and is cut down without a second thought?
       Your anger is far and away too much for us;
           we're at the end of our rope.
       You keep track of all our sins; every misdeed
           since we were children is entered in your books.
       All we can remember is that frown on your face.
           Is that all we're ever going to get?
       We live for seventy years or so
           (with luck we might make it to eighty),
       And what do we have to show for it? Trouble.
           Toil and trouble and a marker in the graveyard.
       Who can make sense of such rage,
           such anger against the very ones who fear you?

12-17 Oh! Teach us to live well!
           Teach us to live wisely and well!
       Come back, GOD — how long do we have to wait? —
           and treat your servants with kindness for a change.
       Surprise us with love at daybreak;
           then we'll skip and dance all the day long.
       Make up for the bad times with some good times;
           we've seen enough evil to last a lifetime.
       Let your servants see what you're best at —
           the ways you rule and bless your children.
       And let the loveliness of our Lord, our God, rest on us,
           confirming the work that we do.
           Oh, yes. Affirm the work that we do!

1-13   **91** You who sit down in the High God's presence,
           spend the night in Shaddai's shadow,
       Say this: "GOD, you're my refuge.
           I trust in you and I'm safe!"
       That's right — he rescues you from hidden traps,
           shields you from deadly hazards.
       His huge outstretched arms protect you —
           under them you're perfectly safe;
           his arms fend off all harm.

Fear nothing — not wild wolves in the night,
   not flying arrows in the day,
Not disease that prowls through the darkness,
   not disaster that erupts at high noon.
Even though others succumb all around,
    drop like flies right and left,
    no harm will even graze you.
You'll stand untouched, watch it all from a distance,
    watch the wicked turn into corpses.
Yes, because GOD's your refuge,
    the High God your very own home,
Evil can't get close to you,
    harm can't get through the door.
He ordered his angels
    to guard you wherever you go.
If you stumble, they'll catch you;
    their job is to keep you from falling.
You'll walk unharmed among lions and snakes,
    and kick young lions and serpents from the path.

14-16 "If you'll hold on to me for dear life," says GOD,
    "I'll get you out of any trouble.
I'll give you the best of care
    if you'll only get to know and trust me.
Call me and I'll answer, be at your side in bad times;
    I'll rescue you, then throw you a party.
I'll give you a long life,
    give you a long drink of salvation!"

A SABBATH SONG

1-3 **92** What a beautiful thing, GOD, to give thanks,
    to sing an anthem to you, the High God!
    To announce your love each daybreak,
    sing your faithful presence all through the night,
Accompanied by dulcimer and harp,
    the full-bodied music of strings.

4-9 You made me so happy, GOD.
    I saw your work and I shouted for joy.
How magnificent your work, GOD!
    How profound your thoughts!
Dullards never notice what you do;
    fools never do get it.
When the wicked popped up like weeds
    and all the evil men and women took over,
You mowed them down,
    finished them off once and for all.
You, GOD, are High and Eternal.
    Look at your enemies, GOD!
Look at your enemies — ruined!
    Scattered to the winds, all those hirelings of evil!

10-14 But you've made me strong as a charging bison,
    you've honored me with a festive parade.
The sight of my critics going down is still fresh,
    the rout of my malicious detractors.
My ears are filled with the sounds of promise:
    "Good people will prosper like palm trees,
Grow tall like Lebanon cedars;
    transplanted to GOD's courtyard,
They'll grow tall in the presence of God,
    lithe and green, virile still in old age."

15 Such witnesses to upright GOD!
    My Mountain, my huge, holy Mountain!

1-2 **93** GOD is King, robed and ruling,
    GOD is robed and surging with strength.

And yes, the world is firm, immovable,
Your throne ever firm — you're Eternal!

3-4 Sea storms are up, GOD,
Sea storms wild and roaring,
Sea storms with thunderous breakers.

Stronger than wild sea storms,
Mightier than sea-storm breakers,
Mighty GOD rules from High Heaven.

5 What you say goes — it always has.
"Beauty" and "Holy" mark your palace rule,
GOD, to the very end of time.

1-2 **94** GOD, put an end to evil;
    avenging God, show your colors!
Judge of the earth, take your stand;
throw the book at the arrogant.

3-4 GOD, the wicked get away with murder —
    how long will you let this go on?
They brag and boast
    and crow about their crimes!

5-7 They walk all over your people, GOD,
    exploit and abuse your precious people.
They take out anyone who gets in their way;
    if they can't use them, they kill them.
They think, "GOD isn't looking,
    Jacob's God is out to lunch."

8-11 Well, think again, you idiots,
    fools — how long before you get smart?

Do you think Ear-Maker doesn't hear,
    Eye-Shaper doesn't see?
Do you think the trainer of nations doesn't correct,
    the teacher of Adam doesn't know?
GOD knows, all right —
    knows your stupidity,
    sees your shallowness.

12-15   How blessed the man you train, GOD,
    the woman you instruct in your Word,
Providing a circle of quiet within the clamor of evil,
    while a jail is being built for the wicked.
GOD will never walk away from his people,
    never desert his precious people.
Rest assured that justice is on its way
    and every good heart put right.

16-19   Who stood up for me against the wicked?
    Who took my side against evil workers?
If GOD hadn't been there for me,
    I never would have made it.
The minute I said, "I'm slipping, I'm falling,"
    your love, GOD, took hold and held me fast.
When I was upset and beside myself,
    you calmed me down and cheered me up.

20-23   Can Misrule have anything in common with you?
    Can Troublemaker pretend to be on your side?
They ganged up on good people,
    plotted behind the backs of the innocent.
But GOD became my hideout,
    God was my high mountain retreat,
Then boomeranged their evil back on them:
    for their evil ways he wiped them out,
    our GOD cleaned them out for good.

1-2   **95** Come, let's shout praises to GOD,
    raise the roof for the Rock who saved us!
    Let's march into his presence singing praises,
lifting the rafters with our hymns!

3-5   And why? Because GOD is the best,
    High King over all the gods.
In one hand he holds deep caves and caverns,
    in the other hand grasps the high mountains.
He made Ocean — he owns it!
    His hands sculpted Earth!

6-7   So come, let us worship: bow before him,
    on your knees before GOD, who made us!
Oh yes, he's our God,
    and we're the people he pastures, the flock he feeds.

7-11 Drop everything and listen, listen as he speaks:
 "Don't turn a deaf ear as in the Bitter Uprising,
As on the day of the Wilderness Test,
 when your ancestors turned and put *me* to the test.
For forty years they watched me at work among them,
 as over and over they tried my patience.
And I was provoked — oh, was I provoked!
 'Can't they keep their minds on God for five minutes?
 Do they simply refuse to walk down my road?'
Exasperated, I exploded,
 'They'll never get where they're headed,
 never be able to sit down and rest.'"

1-2 **96** Sing GOD a brand-new song!
 Earth and everyone in it, sing!
 Sing to GOD — *worship* GOD!

2-3 Shout the news of his victory from sea to sea,
Take the news of his glory to the lost,
News of his wonders to one and all!

4-5 For GOD is great, and worth a thousand Hallelujahs.
His terrible beauty makes the gods look cheap;
Pagan gods are mere tatters and rags.

5-6 GOD made the heavens —
Royal splendor radiates from him,
A powerful beauty sets him apart.

7 Bravo, GOD, Bravo!
Everyone join in the great shout: Encore!
In awe before the beauty, in awe before the might.

8-9 Bring gifts and celebrate,
Bow before the beauty of GOD,
Then to your knees — everyone worship!

10 Get out the message — GOD Rules!
He put the world on a firm foundation;
He treats everyone fair and square.

11 Let's hear it from Sky,
With Earth joining in,
And a huge round of applause from Sea.

12 Let Wilderness turn cartwheels,
Animals, come dance,
Put every tree of the forest in the choir —

13 An extravaganza before GOD as he comes,
As he comes to set everything right on earth,
Set everything right, treat everyone fair.

97 1 GOD rules: *there's* something to shout over!
On the double, mainlands and islands — celebrate!

2 Bright clouds and storm clouds circle 'round him;
Right and justice anchor his rule.

3 Fire blazes out before him,
Flaming high up the craggy mountains.

4 His lightnings light up the world;
Earth, wide-eyed, trembles in fear.

5 The mountains take one look at GOD
And melt, melt like wax before earth's Lord.

6 The heavens announce that he'll set everything right,
And everyone will see it happen — glorious!

7-8 All who serve handcrafted gods will be sorry —
And they were so proud of their ragamuffin gods!

On your knees, all you gods — worship him!
And Zion, you listen and take heart!

Daughters of Zion, sing your hearts out:
GOD has done it all, has set everything right.

9 You, GOD, are High God of the cosmos,
Far, far higher than any of the gods.

10 GOD loves all who hate evil,
And those who love him he keeps safe,
Snatches them from the grip of the wicked.

11 Light-seeds are planted in the souls of God's people,
Joy-seeds are planted in good heart-soil.

12 So, God's people, shout praise to GOD,
Give thanks to our Holy God!

98 1 Sing to GOD a brand-new song.
He's made a world of wonders!

He rolled up his sleeves,
He set things right.

2 GOD made history with salvation,
He showed the world what he could do.

3 He remembered to love us, a bonus
To his dear family, Israel — indefatigable love.

The whole earth comes to attention.
Look — God's work of salvation!

4 Shout your praises to God, everybody!
Let loose and sing! Strike up the band!

5 Round up an orchestra to play for God,
Add on a hundred-voice choir.

6 Feature trumpets and big trombones,
Fill the air with praises to King God.

7 Let the sea and its fish give a round of applause,
With everything living on earth joining in.

8 Let ocean breakers call out, "Encore!"
And mountains harmonize the finale —

9 A tribute to God when he comes,
When he comes to set the earth right.

He'll straighten out the whole world,
He'll put the world right, and everyone in it.

1-3 ## 99 God rules. On your toes, everybody!
He rules from his angel throne — take notice!
God looms majestic in Zion,
He towers in splendor over all the big names.
Great and terrible your beauty: let everyone praise you!
Holy. Yes, holy.

4-5 Strong King, lover of justice,
You laid things out fair and square;
You set down the foundations in Jacob,
Foundation stones of just and right ways.
Honor God, our God; worship his rule!
Holy. Yes, holy.

6-9 Moses and Aaron were his priests,
Samuel among those who prayed to him.
They prayed to God and he answered them;
He spoke from the pillar of cloud.
And they did what he said; they kept the law he gave them.
And then God, our God, answered them
(But you were never soft on their sins).
Lift high God, our God; worship at his holy mountain.
Holy. Yes, holy is God our God.

A Thanksgiving Psalm

100

1-2 On your feet now — applaud God!
Bring a gift of laughter,
sing yourselves into his presence.

3 Know this: God is God, and God, God.
He made us; we didn't make him.
We're his people, his well-tended sheep.

4 Enter with the password: "Thank you!"
Make yourselves at home, talking praise.
Thank him. Worship him.

5 For God is sheer beauty,
all-generous in love,
loyal always and ever.

A David Psalm

101

1-8 My theme song is God's love and justice,
and I'm singing it right to you, God.
I'm finding my way down the road of right living,
but how long before you show up?
I'm doing the very best I can,
and I'm doing it at home, where it counts.
I refuse to take a second look
at corrupting people and degrading things.
I reject made-in-Canaan gods,
stay clear of contamination.
The crooked in heart keep their distance;
I refuse to shake hands with those who plan evil.
I put a gag on the gossip
who bad-mouths his neighbor;
I can't stand
arrogance.
But I have my eye on salt-of-the-earth people —
they're the ones I want working with me;
Men and women on the straight and narrow —
these are the ones I want at my side.
But no one who traffics in lies
gets a job with me; I have no patience with liars.
I've rounded up all the wicked like cattle
and herded them right out of the country.
I purged God's city
of all who make a business of evil.

A Prayer of One Whose Life Is Falling to Pieces,
and Who Lets God Know Just How Bad It Is

102

1-2 God, listen! Listen to my prayer,
listen to the pain in my cries.
Don't turn your back on me

just when I need you so desperately.
Pay attention! This is a cry for *help*!
And hurry — this can't wait!

3-11　　I'm wasting away to nothing,
I'm burning up with fever.
I'm a ghost of my former self,
half-consumed already by terminal illness.
My jaws ache from gritting my teeth;
I'm nothing but skin and bones.
I'm like a buzzard in the desert,
a crow perched on the rubble.
Insomniac, I twitter away,
mournful as a sparrow in the gutter.
All day long my enemies taunt me,
while others just curse.
They bring in meals — casseroles of ashes!
I draw drink from a barrel of my tears.
And all because of your furious anger;
you swept me up and threw me out.
There's nothing left of me —
a withered weed, swept clean from the path.

12-17　　Yet you, God, are sovereign still,
always and ever sovereign.
You'll get up from your throne and help Zion —
it's time for compassionate help.
Oh, how your servants love this city's rubble
and weep with compassion over its dust!
The godless nations will sit up and take notice
— see your glory, worship your name —
When God rebuilds Zion,
when he shows up in all his glory,
When he attends to the prayer of the wretched.
He won't dismiss their prayer.

18-22　　Write this down for the next generation
so people not yet born will praise God:
"God looked out from his high holy place;
from heaven he surveyed the earth.
He listened to the groans of the doomed,
he opened the doors of their death cells."
Write it so the story can be told in Zion,
so God's praise will be sung in Jerusalem's streets
And wherever people gather together
along with their rulers to worship him.

23-28　　God sovereignly brought me to my knees,
he cut me down in my prime.
"Oh, don't," I prayed, "please don't let me die.
You have more years than you know what to do with!

You laid earth's foundations a long time ago,
and handcrafted the very heavens;
You'll still be around when they're long gone,
threadbare and discarded like an old suit of clothes.
You'll throw them away like a worn-out coat,
but year after year you're as good as new.
Your servants' children will have a good place to live
and their children will be at home with you."

A DAVID PSALM

1-2

103

O my soul, bless GOD.
From head to toe, I'll bless his holy name!
O my soul, bless GOD,
don't forget a single blessing!

3-5

He forgives your sins — every one.
He heals your diseases — every one.
He redeems you from hell — saves your life!
He crowns you with love and mercy — a paradise crown.
He wraps you in goodness — beauty eternal.
He renews your youth — you're always young in his presence.

6-18

GOD makes everything come out right;
he puts victims back on their feet.
He showed Moses how he went about his work,
opened up his plans to all Israel.
GOD is sheer mercy and grace;
not easily angered, he's rich in love.
He doesn't endlessly nag and scold,
nor hold grudges forever.
He doesn't treat us as our sins deserve,
nor pay us back in full for our wrongs.
As high as heaven is over the earth,
so strong is his love to those who fear him.
And as far as sunrise is from sunset,
he has separated us from our sins.
As parents feel for their children,
GOD feels for those who fear him.
He knows us inside and out,
keeps in mind that we're made of mud.
Men and women don't live very long;
like wildflowers they spring up and blossom,
But a storm snuffs them out just as quickly,
leaving nothing to show they were here.
GOD's love, though, is ever and always,
eternally present to all who fear him,
Making everything right for them and their children
as they follow his Covenant ways
and remember to do whatever he said.

19-22   GOD has set his throne in heaven;
      he rules over us all. He's the King!
So bless GOD, you angels,
      ready and able to fly at his bidding,
      quick to hear and do what he says.
Bless GOD, all you armies of angels,
      alert to respond to whatever he wills.
Bless GOD, all creatures, wherever you are —
      everything and everyone made by GOD.

And you, O my soul, bless GOD!

1-14   **104** O my soul, bless GOD!

      GOD, my God, how great you are!
      beautifully, gloriously robed,
Dressed up in sunshine,
      and all heaven stretched out for your tent.
You built your palace on the ocean deeps,
      made a chariot out of clouds and took off on wind-wings.
You commandeered winds as messengers,
      appointed fire and flame as ambassadors.
You set earth on a firm foundation
      so that nothing can shake it, ever.
You blanketed earth with ocean,
      covered the mountains with deep waters;
Then you roared and the water ran away —
      your thunder crash put it to flight.
Mountains pushed up, valleys spread out
      in the places you assigned them.
You set boundaries between earth and sea;
      never again will earth be flooded.
You started the springs and rivers,
      sent them flowing among the hills.
All the wild animals now drink their fill,
      wild donkeys quench their thirst.
Along the riverbanks the birds build nests,
      ravens make their voices heard.
You water the mountains from your heavenly cisterns;
      earth is supplied with plenty of water.
You make grass grow for the livestock,
      hay for the animals that plow the ground.

14-23   Oh yes, God brings grain from the land,
      wine to make people happy,
Their faces glowing with health,
      a people well-fed and hearty.
GOD's trees are well-watered —
      the Lebanon cedars he planted.
Birds build their nests in those trees;
      look — the stork at home in the treetop.

Mountain goats climb about the cliffs;
　　badgers burrow among the rocks.
The moon keeps track of the seasons,
　　the sun is in charge of each day.
When it's dark and night takes over,
　　all the forest creatures come out.
The young lions roar for their prey,
　　clamoring to God for their supper.
When the sun comes up, they vanish,
　　lazily stretched out in their dens.
Meanwhile, men and women go out to work,
　　busy at their jobs until evening.

24-30　What a wildly wonderful world, God!
　　　You made it all, with Wisdom at your side,
　　　made earth overflow with your wonderful creations.
　　Oh, look—the deep, wide sea,
　　　brimming with fish past counting,
　　　sardines and sharks and salmon.
　　Ships plow those waters,
　　　and Leviathan, your pet dragon, romps in them.
　　All the creatures look expectantly to you
　　　to give them their meals on time.
　　You come, and they gather around;
　　　you open your hand and they eat from it.
　　If you turned your back,
　　　they'd die in a minute—
　　Take back your Spirit and they die,
　　　revert to original mud;
　　Send out your Spirit and they spring to life—
　　　the whole countryside in bloom and blossom.

31-32　The glory of God—let it last forever!
　　　Let God enjoy his creation!
　　He takes one look at earth and triggers an earthquake,
　　　points a finger at the mountains, and volcanoes erupt.

33-35　Oh, let me sing to God all my life long,
　　　sing hymns to my God as long as I live!
　　Oh, let my song please him;
　　　I'm so pleased to be singing to God.
　　But clear the ground of sinners—
　　　no more godless men and women!

O my soul, bless God!

1-6　**105** Hallelujah!

　　Thank God! Pray to him by name!
　　　Tell everyone you meet what he has done!
　　Sing him songs, belt out hymns,

translate his wonders into music!
Honor his holy name with Hallelujahs,
    you who seek GOD. Live a happy life!
Keep your eyes open for GOD, watch for his works;
    be alert for signs of his presence.
Remember the world of wonders he has made,
    his miracles, and the verdicts he's rendered—
        O seed of Abraham, his servant,
        O child of Jacob, his chosen.

7-15   He's GOD, our God,
    in charge of the whole earth.
And he remembers, remembers his Covenant—
    for a thousand generations he's been as good as his word.
It's the Covenant he made with Abraham,
    the same oath he swore to Isaac,
The very statute he established with Jacob,
    the eternal Covenant with Israel,
Namely, "I give you the land.
    Canaan is your hill-country inheritance."
When they didn't count for much,
    a mere handful, and strangers at that,
Wandering from country to country,
    drifting from pillar to post,
He permitted no one to abuse them.
    He told kings to keep their hands off:
"Don't you dare lay a hand on my anointed,
    don't hurt a hair on the heads of my prophets."

16-22   Then he called down a famine on the country,
    he broke every last blade of wheat.
But he sent a man on ahead:
    Joseph, sold as a slave.
They put cruel chains on his ankles,
    an iron collar around his neck,
Until God's word came to the Pharaoh,
    and GOD confirmed his promise.
God sent the king to release him.
    The Pharaoh set Joseph free;
He appointed him master of his palace,
    put him in charge of all his business
To personally instruct his princes
    and train his advisors in wisdom.

23-42   Then Israel entered Egypt,
    Jacob immigrated to the Land of Ham.
God gave his people lots of babies;
    soon their numbers alarmed their foes.
He turned the Egyptians against his people;
    they abused and cheated God's servants.
Then he sent his servant Moses,

and Aaron, whom he also chose.
They worked marvels in that spiritual wasteland,
    miracles in the Land of Ham.
He spoke, "Darkness!" and it turned dark —
    they couldn't see what they were doing.
He turned all their water to blood
    so that all their fish died;
He made frogs swarm through the land,
    even into the king's bedroom;
He gave the word and flies swarmed,
    gnats filled the air.
He substituted hail for rain,
    he stabbed their land with lightning;
He wasted their vines and fig trees,
    smashed their groves of trees to splinters;
With a word he brought in locusts,
    millions of locusts, armies of locusts;
They consumed every blade of grass in the country
    and picked the ground clean of produce;
He struck down every firstborn in the land,
    the first fruits of their virile powers.
He led Israel out, their arms filled with loot,
    and not one among his tribes even stumbled.
Egypt was glad to have them go —
    they were scared to death of them.
God spread a cloud to keep them cool through the day
    and a fire to light their way through the night;
They prayed and he brought quail,
    filled them with the bread of heaven;
He opened the rock and water poured out;
    it flowed like a river through that desert —
All because he remembered his Covenant,
    his promise to Abraham, his servant.

43-45   Remember this! He led his people out singing for joy;
    his chosen people marched, singing their hearts out!
He made them a gift of the country they entered,
    helped them seize the wealth of the nations
So they could do everything he told them —
    could follow his instructions to the letter.

Hallelujah!

1-3   **106** Hallelujah!
    Thank GOD! And why?
        Because he's good, because his love lasts.
But who on earth can do it —
    declaim GOD's mighty acts, broadcast all his praises?
You're one happy man when you do what's right,
    one happy woman when you form the habit of justice.

4-5 Remember me, GOD, when you enjoy your people;
    include me when you save them;
I want to see your chosen succeed,
    celebrate with your celebrating nation,
    join the Hallelujahs of your pride and joy!

6-12 We've sinned a lot, both we and our parents;
    We've fallen short, hurt a lot of people.
After our parents left Egypt,
    they took your wonders for granted,
    forgot your great and wonderful love.
They were barely beyond the Red Sea
    when they defied the High God
    — the very place he saved them!
    — the place he revealed his amazing power!
He rebuked the Red Sea so that it dried up on the spot
    — he paraded them right through!
    — no one so much as got wet feet!
He saved them from a life of oppression,
    pried them loose from the grip of the enemy.
Then the waters flowed back on their oppressors;
    there wasn't a single survivor.
Then they believed his words were true
    and broke out in songs of praise.

13-18 But it wasn't long before they forgot the whole thing,
    wouldn't wait to be told what to do.
They only cared about pleasing themselves in that desert,
    provoked God with their insistent demands.
He gave them exactly what they asked for —
    but along with it they got an empty heart.
One day in camp some grew jealous of Moses,
    also of Aaron, holy priest of GOD.
The ground opened and swallowed Dathan,
    then buried Abiram's gang.
Fire flared against that rebel crew
    and torched them to a cinder.

19-22 They cast in metal a bull calf at Horeb
    and worshiped the statue they'd made.
They traded the Glory
    for a cheap piece of sculpture — a grass-chewing bull!
They forgot God, their very own Savior,
    who turned things around in Egypt,
Who created a world of wonders in the Land of Ham,
    who gave that stunning performance at the Red Sea.

23-27 Fed up, God decided to get rid of them —
    and except for Moses, his chosen, he would have.
But Moses stood in the gap and deflected God's anger,
    prevented it from destroying them utterly.

They went on to reject the Blessed Land,
    didn't believe a word of what God promised.
They found fault with the life they had
    and turned a deaf ear to GOD's voice.
Exasperated, God swore
    that he'd lay them low in the desert,
Scattering their children hither and yon,
    strewing them all over the earth.

28-31   Then they linked up with Baal Peor,
    attending funeral banquets and eating idol food.
That made God so angry
    that a plague spread through their ranks;
Phinehas stood up and pled their case
    and the plague was stopped.
This was counted to his credit;
    his descendants will never forget it.

32-33   They angered God again at Meribah Springs;
    this time Moses got mixed up in their evil;
Because they defied GOD yet again,
    Moses exploded and lost his temper.

34-39   They didn't wipe out those godless cultures
    as ordered by GOD;
Instead they intermarried with the heathen,
    and in time became just like them.
They worshiped their idols,
    were caught in the trap of idols.
They sacrificed their sons and daughters
    at the altars of demon gods.
They slit the throats of their babies,
    murdered their infant girls and boys.
They offered their babies to Canaan's gods;
    the blood of their babies stained the land.
Their way of life stank to high heaven;
    they lived like whores.

40-43   And GOD was furious — a wildfire anger;
    he couldn't stand even to look at his people.
He turned them over to the heathen
    so that the people who hated them ruled them.
Their enemies made life hard for them;
    they were tyrannized under that rule.
Over and over God rescued them, but they never learned —
    until finally their sins destroyed them.

44-46   Still, when God saw the trouble they were in
    and heard their cries for help,
He remembered his Covenant with them,
    and, immense with love, took them by the hand.

He poured out his mercy on them
while their captors looked on, amazed.

47 Save us, GOD, our God!
Gather us back out of exile
So we can give thanks to your holy name
and join in the glory when you are praised!

Blessed be GOD, Israel's God!
Bless now, bless always!
Oh! Let everyone say Amen!
Hallelujah!

1-3 **107** Oh, thank GOD — he's so good!
His love never runs out.
All of you set free by GOD, tell the world!
Tell how he freed you from oppression,
Then rounded you up from all over the place,
from the four winds, from the seven seas.

4-9 Some of you wandered for years in the desert,
looking but not finding a good place to live,
Half-starved and parched with thirst,
staggering and stumbling, on the brink of exhaustion.
Then, in your desperate condition, you called out to GOD.
He got you out in the nick of time;
He put your feet on a wonderful road
that took you straight to a good place to live.
So thank GOD for his marvelous love,
for his miracle mercy to the children he loves.
He poured great draughts of water down parched throats;
the starved and hungry got plenty to eat.

10-16 Some of you were locked in a dark cell,
cruelly confined behind bars,
Punished for defying God's Word,
for turning your back on the High God's counsel —
A hard sentence, and your hearts so heavy,
and not a soul in sight to help.
Then you called out to GOD in your desperate condition;
he got you out in the nick of time.
He led you out of your dark, dark cell,
broke open the jail and led you out.
So thank GOD for his marvelous love,
for his miracle mercy to the children he loves;
He shattered the heavy jailhouse doors,
he snapped the prison bars like matchsticks!

17-22 Some of you were sick because you'd lived a bad life,
your bodies feeling the effects of your sin;
You couldn't stand the sight of food,

so miserable you thought you'd be better off dead.
Then you called out to GOD in your desperate condition;
    he got you out in the nick of time.
He spoke the word that healed you,
    that pulled you back from the brink of death.
So thank GOD for his marvelous love,
    for his miracle mercy to the children he loves;
Offer thanksgiving sacrifices,
    tell the world what he's done — sing it out!

23-32   Some of you set sail in big ships;
    you put to sea to do business in faraway ports.
Out at sea you saw GOD in action,
    saw his breathtaking ways with the ocean:
With a word he called up the wind —
    an ocean storm, towering waves!
You shot high in the sky, then the bottom dropped out;
    your hearts were stuck in your throats.
You were spun like a top, you reeled like a drunk,
    you didn't know which end was up.
Then you called out to GOD in your desperate condition;
    he got you out in the nick of time.
He quieted the wind down to a whisper,
    put a muzzle on all the big waves.
And you were so glad when the storm died down,
    and he led you safely back to harbor.
So thank GOD for his marvelous love,
    for his miracle mercy to the children he loves.
Lift high your praises when the people assemble,
    shout Hallelujah when the elders meet!

33-41   GOD turned rivers into wasteland,
    springs of water into sunbaked mud;
Luscious orchards became alkali flats
    because of the evil of the people who lived there.
Then he changed wasteland into fresh pools of water,
    arid earth into springs of water,
Brought in the hungry and settled them there;
    they moved in — what a great place to live!
They sowed the fields, they planted vineyards,
    they reaped a bountiful harvest.
He blessed them and they prospered greatly;
    their herds of cattle never decreased.
But abuse and evil and trouble declined
    as he heaped scorn on princes and sent them away.
He gave the poor a safe place to live,
    treated their clans like well-cared-for sheep.

42-43   Good people see this and are glad;
    bad people are speechless, stopped in their tracks.

If you are really wise, you'll think this over —
   it's time you appreciated GOD's deep love.

108

1-2   I'm ready, God, so ready,
         ready from head to toe.
      Ready to sing,
   ready to raise a God-song:
"Wake, soul! Wake, lute!
   Wake up, you sleepyhead sun!"

3-6   I'm thanking you, GOD, out in the streets,
         singing your praises in town and country.
      The deeper your love, the higher it goes;
         every cloud's a flag to your faithfulness.
      Soar high in the skies, O God!
         Cover the whole earth with your glory!
      And for the sake of the one you love so much,
         reach down and help me — answer me!

7-9   That's when God spoke in holy splendor:
         "Brimming over with joy,
      I make a present of Shechem,
         I hand out Succoth Valley as a gift.
      Gilead's in my pocket,
         to say nothing of Manasseh.
      Ephraim's my hard hat,
         Judah my hammer.
      Moab's a scrub bucket —
         I mop the floor with Moab,
      Spit on Edom,
         rain fireworks all over Philistia."

10-11   Who will take me to the thick of the fight?
           Who'll show me the road to Edom?
        You aren't giving up on us, are you, God?
           refusing to go out with our troops?

12-13   Give us help for the hard task;
           human help is worthless.
        In God we'll do our very best;
           he'll flatten the opposition for good.

109

1-5   My God, don't turn a deaf ear to my hallelujah prayer.
         Liars are pouring out invective on me;
         Their lying tongues are like a pack of dogs out to get me,
      barking their hate, nipping my heels — and for no reason!
   I loved them and now they slander me — yes, me! —
         and treat my prayer like a crime;
   They return my good with evil,
         they return my love with hate.

6-20   Send the Evil One to accuse my accusing judge;
        dispatch Satan to prosecute him.
  When he's judged, let the verdict be "Guilty,"
        and when he prays, let his prayer turn to sin.
  Give him a short life,
        and give his job to somebody else.
  Make orphans of his children,
        dress his wife in widow's weeds;
  Turn his children into begging street urchins,
        evicted from their homes — homeless.
  May the bank foreclose and wipe him out,
        and strangers, like vultures, pick him clean.
  May there be no one around to help him out,
        no one willing to give his orphans a break.
  Chop down his family tree
        so that nobody even remembers his name.
  But erect a memorial to the sin of his father,
        and make sure his mother's name is there, too —
  Their sins recorded forever before GOD,
        but they themselves sunk in oblivion.
  That's all he deserves since he was never once kind,
        hounded the afflicted and heartbroken to their graves.
  Since he loved cursing so much,
        let curses rain down;
  Since he had no taste for blessing,
        let blessings flee far from him.
  He dressed up in curses like a fine suit of clothes;
        he drank curses, took his baths in curses.
  So give him a gift — a costume of curses;
        he can wear curses every day of the week!
  That's what they'll get, those out to get me —
        an avalanche of just deserts from GOD.

21-25   Oh, GOD, my Lord, step in;
        work a miracle for me — you can do it!
  Get me out of here — your love is so great! —
        I'm at the end of my rope, my life in ruins.
  I'm fading away to nothing, passing away,
        my youth gone, old before my time.
  I'm weak from hunger and can hardly stand up,
        my body a rack of skin and bones.
  I'm a joke in poor taste to those who see me;
        they take one look and shake their heads.

26-29   Help me, oh help me, GOD, my God,
        save me through your wonderful love;
  Then they'll know that your hand is in this,
        that you, GOD, have been at work.
  Let them curse all they want;
        you do the blessing.
  Let them be jeered by the crowd when they stand up,

followed by cheers for me, your servant.
Dress my accusers in clothes dirty with shame,
    discarded and humiliating old ragbag clothes.

30-31   My mouth's full of great praise for GOD,
    I'm singing his hallelujahs surrounded by crowds,
For he's always at hand to take the side of the needy,
    to rescue a life from the unjust judge.

A DAVID PRAYER

1-3   ## 110 The word of GOD to my Lord:
    "Sit alongside me here on my throne
    until I make your enemies a stool for your feet."
You were forged a strong scepter by GOD of Zion;
    now rule, though surrounded by enemies!
Your people will freely join you, resplendent in holy armor
    on the great day of your conquest,
Join you at the fresh break of day,
    join you with all the vigor of youth.

4-7   GOD gave his word and he won't take it back:
    you're the permanent priest, the Melchizedek priest.
The Lord stands true at your side,
    crushing kings in his terrible wrath,
Bringing judgment on the nations,
    handing out convictions wholesale,
    crushing opposition across the wide earth.
The King-Maker put his King on the throne;
    the True King rules with head held high!

1-10   ## 111 Hallelujah!
    I give thanks to GOD with everything I've got —
    Wherever good people gather, and in the congregation.
GOD's works are so great, worth
A lifetime of study — endless enjoyment!
Splendor and beauty mark his craft;
His generosity never gives out.
His miracles are his memorial —
This GOD of Grace, this GOD of Love.
He gave food to those who fear him,
He remembered to keep his ancient promise.
He proved to his people that he could do what he said:
Hand them the nations on a platter — a gift!
He manufactures truth and justice;
All his products are guaranteed to last —
Never out-of-date, never obsolete, rust-proof.
All that he makes and does is honest and true:
He paid the ransom for his people,
He ordered his Covenant kept forever.
He's so personal and holy, worthy of our respect.
The good life begins in the fear of GOD —

Do that and you'll know the blessing of GOD.
His Hallelujah lasts forever!

1-10

112

Hallelujah!
Blessed man, blessed woman, who fear GOD,
Who cherish and relish his commandments,
Their children robust on the earth,
And the homes of the upright — how blessed!
Their houses brim with wealth
And a generosity that never runs dry.
Sunrise breaks through the darkness for good people —
God's grace and mercy and justice!
The good person is generous and lends lavishly;
No shuffling or stumbling around for this one,
But a sterling and solid and lasting reputation.
Unfazed by rumor and gossip,
Heart ready, trusting in GOD,
Spirit firm, unperturbed,
Ever blessed, relaxed among enemies,
They lavish gifts on the poor —
A generosity that goes on, and on, and on.
An honored life! A beautiful life!
Someone wicked takes one look and rages,
Blusters away but ends up speechless.
There's nothing to the dreams of the wicked. Nothing.

1-3

113

Hallelujah!
You who serve GOD, praise GOD!
Just to speak his name is praise!
Just to remember GOD is a blessing —
now and tomorrow and always.
From east to west, from dawn to dusk,
keep lifting all your praises to GOD!

4-9

GOD is higher than anything and anyone,
outshining everything you can see in the skies.
Who can compare with GOD, our God,
so majestically enthroned,
Surveying his magnificent
heavens and earth?
He picks up the poor from out of the dirt,
rescues the wretched who've been thrown out with the trash,
Seats them among the honored guests,
a place of honor among the brightest and best.
He gives childless couples a family,
gives them joy as the parents of children.
Hallelujah!

1-8

114

After Israel left Egypt,
the clan of Jacob left those barbarians behind;
Judah became holy land for him,

Israel the place of holy rule.
Sea took one look and ran the other way;
 River Jordan turned around and ran off.
The mountains turned playful and skipped like rams,
 the hills frolicked like spring lambs.
What's wrong with you, Sea, that you ran away?
 and you, River Jordan, that you turned and ran off?
And mountains, why did you skip like rams?
 and you, hills, frolic like spring lambs?
Tremble, Earth! You're in the Lord's presence!
 in the presence of Jacob's God.
He turned the rock into a pool of cool water,
 turned flint into fresh spring water.

1-2 **115** Not for our sake, GOD, no, not for our sake,
 but for your name's sake, show your glory.
 Do it on account of your merciful love,
 do it on account of your faithful ways.
Do it so none of the nations can say,
 "Where now, oh where is their God?"

3-8 Our God is in heaven
 doing whatever he wants to do.
Their gods are metal and wood,
 handmade in a basement shop:
Carved mouths that can't talk,
 painted eyes that can't see,
Tin ears that can't hear,
 molded noses that can't smell,
Hands that can't grasp, feet that can't walk or run,
 throats that never utter a sound.
Those who make them have become just like them,
 have become just like the gods they trust.

9-11 But you, Israel: put your trust in GOD!
 — trust your Helper! trust your Ruler!
Clan of Aaron, trust in GOD!
 — trust your Helper! trust your Ruler!
You who fear GOD, trust in GOD!
 — trust your Helper! trust your Ruler!

12-16 O GOD, remember us and bless us,
 bless the families of Israel and Aaron.
And let GOD bless all who fear GOD —
 bless the small, bless the great.
Oh, let GOD enlarge your families —
 giving growth to you, growth to your children.
May you be blessed by GOD,
 by GOD, who made heaven and earth.
The heaven of heavens is for GOD,
 but he put us in charge of the earth.

17-18   Dead people can't praise GOD —
     not a word to be heard from those buried in the ground.
  But we bless GOD, oh yes —
     we bless him now, we bless him always!
  Hallelujah!

1-6   **116** I love GOD because he listened to me,
     listened as I begged for mercy.
    He listened so intently
     as I laid out my case before him.
  Death stared me in the face,
     hell was hard on my heels.
  Up against it, I didn't know which way to turn;
     then I called out to GOD for help:
  "Please, GOD!" I cried out.
     "Save my life!"
  GOD is gracious — it is he who makes things right,
     our most compassionate God.
  GOD takes the side of the helpless;
     when I was at the end of my rope, he saved me.

7-8   I said to myself, "Relax and rest.
     GOD has showered you with blessings.
    Soul, you've been rescued from death;
    Eye, you've been rescued from tears;
    And you, Foot, were kept from stumbling."

9-11   I'm striding in the presence of GOD,
     alive in the land of the living!
  I stayed faithful, though bedeviled,
     and despite a ton of bad luck,
  Despite giving up on the human race,
     saying, "They're all liars and cheats."

12-19   What can I give back to GOD
     for the blessings he's poured out on me?
  I'll lift high the cup of salvation — a toast to GOD!
     I'll pray in the name of GOD;
  I'll complete what I promised GOD I'd do,
     and I'll do it together with his people.
  When they arrive at the gates of death,
     GOD welcomes those who love him.
  Oh, GOD, here I am, your servant,
     your faithful servant: set me free for your service!
  I'm ready to offer the thanksgiving sacrifice
     and pray in the name of GOD.
  I'll complete what I promised GOD I'd do,
     and I'll do it in company with his people,
  In the place of worship, in GOD's house,
     in Jerusalem, GOD's city.
  Hallelujah!

1-2

117

Praise GOD, everybody!
    Applaud GOD, all people!
    His love has taken over our lives;
GOD's faithful ways are eternal.
    Hallelujah!

1-4

118

Thank GOD because he's good,
    because his love never quits.
    Tell the world, Israel,
    "His love never quits."
And you, clan of Aaron, tell the world,
    "His love never quits."
And you who fear GOD, join in,
    "His love never quits."

5-16

Pushed to the wall, I called to GOD;
    from the wide open spaces, he answered.
GOD's now at my side and I'm not afraid;
    who would dare lay a hand on me?
GOD's my strong champion;
    I flick off my enemies like flies.
Far better to take refuge in GOD
    than trust in people;
Far better to take refuge in GOD
    than trust in celebrities.
Hemmed in by barbarians,
    in GOD's name I rubbed their faces in the dirt;
Hemmed in and with no way out,
    in GOD's name I rubbed their faces in the dirt;
Like swarming bees, like wild prairie fire, they hemmed me in;
    in GOD's name I rubbed their faces in the dirt.
I was right on the cliff-edge, ready to fall,
    when GOD grabbed and held me.
GOD's my strength, he's also my song,
    and now he's my salvation.
Hear the shouts, hear the triumph songs
    in the camp of the saved?
        "The hand of GOD has turned the tide!
        The hand of GOD is raised in victory!
        The hand of GOD has turned the tide!"

17-20

I didn't die. I *lived*!
    And now I'm telling the world what GOD did.
GOD tested me, he pushed me hard,
    but he didn't hand me over to Death.
Swing wide the city gates — the *righteous* gates!
    I'll walk right through and thank GOD!
This Temple Gate belongs to GOD,
    so the victors can enter and praise.

21-25 Thank you for responding to me;
   you've truly become my salvation!
The stone the masons discarded as flawed
   is now the capstone!
This is GOD's work.
   We rub our eyes — we can hardly believe it!
This is the very day GOD acted —
   let's celebrate and be festive!
Salvation now, GOD. Salvation now!
   Oh yes, GOD — a free and full life!

26-29 Blessed are you who enter in GOD's name —
   from GOD's house we bless you!
GOD is God,
   he has bathed us in light.
Festoon the shrine with garlands,
   hang colored banners above the altar!
You're my God, and I thank you.
   O my God, I lift high your praise.
Thank GOD — he's so good.
   His love never quits!

1-8 **119** You're blessed when you stay on course,
   walking steadily on the road revealed by GOD.
   You're blessed when you follow his directions,
   doing your best to find him.
That's right — you don't go off on your own;
   you walk straight along the road he set.
You, GOD, prescribed the right way to live;
   now you expect us to live it.
Oh, that my steps might be steady,
   keeping to the course you set;
Then I'd never have any regrets
   in comparing my life with your counsel.
I thank you for speaking straight from your heart;
   I learn the pattern of your righteous ways.
I'm going to do what you tell me to do;
   don't ever walk off and leave me.

9-16 How can a young person live a clean life?
   By carefully reading the map of your Word.
I'm single-minded in pursuit of you;
   don't let me miss the road signs you've posted.
I've banked your promises in the vault of my heart
   so I won't sin myself bankrupt.
Be blessed, GOD;
   train me in your ways of wise living.
I'll transfer to my lips
   all the counsel that comes from your mouth;
I delight far more in what you tell me about living

than in gathering a pile of riches.
I ponder every morsel of wisdom from you,
    I attentively watch how you've done it.
I relish everything you've told me of life,
    I won't forget a word of it.

17-24   Be generous with me and I'll live a full life;
    not for a minute will I take my eyes off your road.
Open my eyes so I can see
    what you show me of your miracle-wonders.
I'm a stranger in these parts;
    give me clear directions.
My soul is starved and hungry, ravenous! —
    insatiable for your nourishing commands.
And those who think they know so much,
    ignoring everything you tell them — let them have it!
Don't let them mock and humiliate me;
    I've been careful to do just what you said.
While bad neighbors maliciously gossip about me,
    I'm absorbed in pondering your wise counsel.
Yes, your sayings on life are what give me delight;
    I listen to them as to good neighbors!

25-32   I'm feeling terrible — I couldn't feel worse!
    Get me on my feet again. You promised, remember?
When I told my story, you responded;
    train me well in your deep wisdom.
Help me understand these things inside and out
    so I can ponder your miracle-wonders.
My sad life's dilapidated, a falling-down barn;
    build me up again by your Word.
Barricade the road that goes Nowhere;
    grace me with your clear revelation.
I choose the true road to Somewhere,
    I post your road signs at every curve and corner.
I grasp and cling to whatever you tell me;
    GOD, don't let me down!
I'll run the course you lay out for me
    if you'll just show me how.

33-40   GOD, teach me lessons for living
    so I can stay the course.
Give me insight so I can do what you tell me —
    my whole life one long, obedient response.
Guide me down the road of your commandments;
    I love traveling this freeway!
Give me a bent for your words of wisdom,
    and not for piling up loot.

Divert my eyes from toys and trinkets,
   invigorate me on the pilgrim way.
Affirm your promises to me —
   promises made to all who fear you.
Deflect the harsh words of my critics —
   but what you say is always so good.
See how hungry I am for your counsel;
   preserve my life through your righteous ways!

41-48 Let your love, GOD, shape my life
   with salvation, exactly as you promised;
Then I'll be able to stand up to mockery
   because I trusted your Word.
Don't ever deprive me of truth, not ever —
   your commandments are what I depend on.
Oh, I'll guard with my life what you've revealed to me,
   guard it now, guard it ever;
And I'll stride freely through wide open spaces
   as I look for your truth and your wisdom;
Then I'll tell the world what I find,
   speak out boldly in public, unembarrassed.
I cherish your commandments — oh, how I love them! —
   relishing every fragment of your counsel.

49-56 Remember what you said to me, your servant —
   I hang on to these words for dear life!
These words hold me up in bad times;
   yes, your promises rejuvenate me.
The insolent ridicule me without mercy,
   but I don't budge from your revelation.
I watch for your ancient landmark words,
   and know I'm on the right track.
But when I see the wicked ignore your directions,
   I'm beside myself with anger.
I set your instructions to music
   and sing them as I walk this pilgrim way.
I meditate on your name all night, GOD,
   treasuring your revelation, O GOD.
Still, I walk through a rain of derision
   because I live by your Word and counsel.

57-64 Because you have satisfied me, GOD, I promise
   to do everything you say.
I beg you from the bottom of my heart: smile,
   be gracious to me just as you promised.
When I took a long, careful look at your ways,
   I got my feet back on the trail you blazed.
I was up at once, didn't drag my feet,

was quick to follow your orders.
The wicked hemmed me in — there was no way out —
    but not for a minute did I forget your plan for me.
I get up in the middle of the night to thank you;
    your decisions are so right, so true — I can't wait till morning!
I'm a friend and companion of all who fear you,
    of those committed to living by your rules.
Your love, GOD, fills the earth!
    Train me to live by your counsel.

65-72   Be good to your servant, GOD;
    be as good as your Word.
Train me in good common sense;
    I'm thoroughly committed to living your way.
Before I learned to answer you, I wandered all over the place,
    but now I'm in step with your Word.
You are good, and the source of good;
    train me in your goodness.
The godless spread lies about me,
    but I focus my attention on what you are saying;
They're bland as a bucket of lard,
    while I dance to the tune of your revelation.
My troubles turned out all for the best —
    they forced me to learn from your textbook.
Truth from your mouth means more to me
    than striking it rich in a gold mine.

73-80   With your very own hands you formed me;
    now breathe your wisdom over me so I can understand you.
When they see me waiting, expecting your Word,
    those who fear you will take heart and be glad.
I can see now, GOD, that your decisions are right;
    your testing has taught me what's true and right.
Oh, love me — and right now! — hold me tight!
    just the way you promised.
Now comfort me so I can live, really live;
    your revelation is the tune I dance to.
Let the fast-talking tricksters be exposed as frauds;
    they tried to sell me a bill of goods,
    but I kept my mind fixed on your counsel.
Let those who fear you turn to me
    for evidence of your wise guidance.
And let me live whole and holy, soul and body,
    so I can always walk with my head held high.

81-88   I'm homesick — longing for your salvation;
    I'm waiting for your word of hope.
My eyes grow heavy watching for some sign of your promise;

how long must I wait for your comfort?
There's smoke in my eyes — they burn and water,
    but I keep a steady gaze on the instructions you post.
How long do I have to put up with all this?
    How long till you haul my tormentors into court?
The arrogant godless try to throw me off track,
    ignorant as they are of God and his ways.
Everything you command is a sure thing,
    but they harass me with lies. Help!
They've pushed and pushed — they never let up —
    but I haven't relaxed my grip on your counsel.
In your great love revive me
    so I can alertly obey your every word.

89-96   What you say goes, GOD,
    and *stays*, as permanent as the heavens.
Your truth never goes out of fashion;
    it's as up-to-date as the earth when the sun comes up.
Your Word and truth are dependable as ever;
    that's what you ordered — you set the earth going.
If your revelation hadn't delighted me so,
    I would have given up when the hard times came.
But I'll never forget the advice you gave me;
    you saved my life with those wise words.
Save me! I'm all yours.
    I look high and low for your words of wisdom.
The wicked lie in ambush to destroy me,
    but I'm only concerned with your plans for me.
I see the limits to everything human,
    but the horizons can't contain your commands!

97-104   Oh, how I love all you've revealed;
    I reverently ponder it all the day long.
Your commands give me an edge on my enemies;
    they never become obsolete.
I've even become smarter than my teachers
    since I've pondered and absorbed your counsel.
I've become wiser than the wise old sages
    simply by doing what you tell me.
I watch my step, avoiding the ditches and ruts of evil
    so I can spend all my time keeping your Word.
I never make detours from the route you laid out;
    you gave me such good directions.
Your words are so choice, so tasty;
    I prefer them to the best home cooking.
With your instruction, I understand life;
    that's why I hate false propaganda.

105-112 By your words I can see where I'm going;
    they throw a beam of light on my dark path.
I've committed myself and I'll never turn back
    from living by your righteous order.
Everything's falling apart on me, GOD;
    put me together again with your Word.
Festoon me with your finest sayings, GOD;
    teach me your holy rules.
My life is as close as my own hands,
    but I don't forget what you have revealed.
The wicked do their best to throw me off track,
    but I don't swerve an inch from your course.
I inherited your book on living; it's mine forever—
    what a gift! And how happy it makes me!
I concentrate on doing exactly what you say—
    I always have and always will.

113-120 I hate the two-faced,
    but I love your clear-cut revelation.
You're my place of quiet retreat;
    I wait for your Word to renew me.
Get out of my life, evildoers,
    so I can keep my God's commands.
Take my side as you promised; I'll live then for sure.
    Don't disappoint all my grand hopes.
Stick with me and I'll be all right;
    I'll give total allegiance to your definitions of life.
Expose all who drift away from your sayings;
    their casual idolatry is lethal.
You reject earth's wicked as so much rubbish;
    therefore I lovingly embrace everything you say.
I shiver in awe before you;
    your decisions leave me speechless with reverence.

121-128 I stood up for justice and the right;
    don't leave me to the mercy of my oppressors.
Take the side of your servant, good God;
    don't let the godless take advantage of me.
I can't keep my eyes open any longer, waiting for you
    to keep your promise to set everything right.
Let your love dictate how you deal with me;
    teach me from your textbook on life.
I'm your servant—help me understand what that means,
    the inner meaning of your instructions.
It's time to act, GOD;
    they've made a shambles of your revelation!
Yea-Saying God, I love what you command,
    I love it better than gold and gemstones;

Yea-Saying God, I honor everything you tell me,
    I despise every deceitful detour.

129-136 Every word you give me is a miracle word —
    how could I help but obey?
Break open your words, let the light shine out,
    let ordinary people see the meaning.
Mouth open and panting,
    I wanted your commands more than anything.
Turn my way, look kindly on me,
    as you always do to those who personally love you.
Steady my steps with your Word of promise
    so nothing malign gets the better of me.
Rescue me from the grip of bad men and women
    so I can live life your way.
Smile on me, your servant;
    teach me the right way to live.
I cry rivers of tears
    because nobody's living by your book!

137-144 You *are* right and you *do* right, GOD;
    your decisions are right on target.
You rightly instruct us in how to live
    ever faithful to you.
My rivals nearly did me in,
    they persistently ignored your commandments.
Your promise has been tested through and through,
    and I, your servant, love it dearly.
I'm too young to be important,
    but I don't forget what you tell me.
Your righteousness is eternally right,
    your revelation is the only truth.
Even though troubles came down on me hard,
    your commands always gave me delight.
The way you tell me to live is always right;
    help me understand it so I can live to the fullest.

145-152 I call out at the top of my lungs,
    "GOD! Answer! I'll do whatever you say."
I called to you, "Save me
    so I can carry out all your instructions."
I was up before sunrise,
    crying for help, hoping for a word from you.
I stayed awake all night,
    prayerfully pondering your promise.
In your love, listen to me;
    in your justice, GOD, keep me alive.
As those out to get me come closer and closer,

they go farther and farther from the truth you reveal;
But you're the closest of all to me, GOD,
    and all your judgments true.
I've known all along from the evidence of your words
    that you meant them to last forever.

153-160 Take a good look at my trouble, and help me —
    I haven't forgotten your revelation.
Take my side and get me out of this;
    give me back my life, just as you promised.
"Salvation" is only gibberish to the wicked
    because they've never looked it up in your dictionary.
Your mercies, GOD, run into the billions;
    following your guidelines, revive me.
My antagonists are too many to count,
    but I don't swerve from the directions you gave.
I took one look at the quitters and was filled with loathing;
    they walked away from your promises so casually!
Take note of how I love what you tell me;
    out of your life of love, prolong my life.
Your words all add up to the sum total: Truth.
    Your righteous decisions are eternal.

161-168 I've been slandered unmercifully by the politicians,
    but my awe at your words keeps me stable.
I'm ecstatic over what you say,
    like one who strikes it rich.
I hate lies — can't stand them! —
    but I love what you have revealed.
Seven times each day I stop and shout praises
    for the way you keep everything running right.
For those who love what you reveal, everything fits —
    no stumbling around in the dark for them.
I wait expectantly for your salvation;
    GOD, I do what you tell me.
My soul guards and keeps all your instructions —
    oh, how much I love them!
I follow your directions, abide by your counsel;
    my life's an open book before you.

169-176 Let my cry come right into your presence, GOD;
    provide me with the insight that comes only from your Word.
Give my request your personal attention,
    rescue me on the terms of your promise.
Let praise cascade off my lips;
    after all, you've taught me the truth about life!
And let your promises ring from my tongue;
    every order you've given is right.

Put your hand out and steady me
    since I've chosen to live by your counsel.
I'm homesick, GOD, for your salvation;
    I love it when you show yourself!
Invigorate my soul so I can praise you well,
    use your decrees to put iron in my soul.
And should I wander off like a lost sheep — seek me!
    I'll recognize the sound of your voice.

A PILGRIM SONG

1-2 **120** I'm in trouble. I cry to GOD,
    desperate for an answer:
    "Deliver me from the liars, GOD!
They smile so sweetly but lie through their teeth."

3-4 Do you know what's next, can you see what's coming,
    all you barefaced liars?
Pointed arrows and burning coals
    will be your reward.

5-7 I'm doomed to live in Meshech,
    cursed with a home in Kedar,
My whole life lived camping
    among quarreling neighbors.
I'm all for peace, but the minute
    I tell them so, they go to war!

A PILGRIM SONG

1-2 **121** I look up to the mountains;
    does my strength come from mountains?
    No, my strength comes from GOD,
who made heaven, and earth, and mountains.

3-4 He won't let you stumble,
    your Guardian God won't fall asleep.
Not on your life! Israel's
    Guardian will never doze or sleep.

5-6 GOD's your Guardian,
    right at your side to protect you —
Shielding you from sunstroke,
    sheltering you from moonstroke.

7-8 GOD guards you from every evil,
    he guards your very life.
He guards you when you leave and when you return,
    he guards you now, he guards you always.

A P I L G R I M S O N G O F D A V I D

1-2   **122** When they said, "Let's go to the house of GOD,"
        my heart leaped for joy.
        And now we're here, O Jerusalem,
    inside Jerusalem's walls!

3-5   Jerusalem, well-built city,
        built as a place for worship!
    The city to which the tribes ascend,
        all GOD's tribes go up to worship,
    To give thanks to the name of GOD —
        this is what it means to be Israel.
    Thrones for righteous judgment
        are set there, famous David-thrones.

6-9   Pray for Jerusalem's peace!
        Prosperity to all you Jerusalem-lovers!
    Friendly insiders, get along!
        Hostile outsiders, keep your distance!
    For the sake of my family and friends,
        I say it again: live in peace!
    For the sake of the house of our God, GOD,
        I'll do my very best for you.

A P I L G R I M S O N G

1-4   **123** I look to you, heaven-dwelling God,
        look up to you for help.
        Like servants, alert to their master's commands,
    like a maiden attending her lady,
    We're watching and waiting, holding our breath,
        awaiting your word of mercy.
    Mercy, GOD, mercy!
        We've been kicked around long enough,
    Kicked in the teeth by complacent rich men,
        kicked when we're down by arrogant brutes.

A P I L G R I M S O N G O F D A V I D

1-5   **124** If GOD hadn't been for us
        — all together now, Israel, sing out! —
        If GOD hadn't been for us
    when everyone went against us,
    We would have been swallowed alive
        by their violent anger,
    Swept away by the flood of rage,
        drowned in the torrent;
    We would have lost our lives
        in the wild, raging water.

6   Oh, blessed be GOD!
        He didn't go off and leave us.

He didn't abandon us defenseless,
  helpless as a rabbit in a pack of snarling dogs.

7 We've flown free from their fangs,
    free of their traps, free as a bird.
  Their grip is broken;
    we're free as a bird in flight.

8 GOD's strong name is our help,
    the same GOD who made heaven and earth.

A PILGRIM SONG

1-5 **125** Those who trust in GOD
        are like Zion Mountain:
      Nothing can move it, a rock-solid mountain
    you can always depend on.
  Mountains encircle Jerusalem,
    and GOD encircles his people —
    always has and always will.
  The fist of the wicked
    will never violate
  What is due the righteous,
    provoking wrongful violence.
  Be good to your good people, GOD,
    to those whose hearts are right!
  GOD will round up the backsliders,
    corral them with the incorrigibles.
  Peace over Israel!

A PILGRIM SONG

1-3 **126** It seemed like a dream, too good to be true,
        when GOD returned Zion's exiles.
      We laughed, we sang,
    we couldn't believe our good fortune.
  We were the talk of the nations —
    "GOD was wonderful to them!"
  GOD *was* wonderful to us;
    we are one happy people.

4-6 And now, GOD, do it again —
    bring rains to our drought-stricken lives
  So those who planted their crops in despair
    will shout hurrahs at the harvest,
  So those who went off with heavy hearts
    will come home laughing, with armloads of blessing.

A PILGRIM SONG OF SOLOMON

1-2 **127** If GOD doesn't build the house,
        the builders only build shacks.
      If GOD doesn't guard the city,
    the night watchman might as well nap.

It's useless to rise early and go to bed late,
and work your worried fingers to the bone.
Don't you know he enjoys
giving rest to those he loves?

3-5   Don't you see that children are GOD's best gift?
the fruit of the womb his generous legacy?
Like a warrior's fistful of arrows
are the children of a vigorous youth.
Oh, how blessed are you parents,
with your quivers full of children!
Your enemies don't stand a chance against you;
you'll sweep them right off your doorstep.

A PILGRIM SONG

1-2   **128** All you who fear GOD, how blessed you are!
how happily you walk on his smooth straight road!
You worked hard and deserve all you've got coming.
Enjoy the blessing! Revel in the goodness!

3-4   Your wife will bear children as a vine bears grapes,
your household lush as a vineyard,
The children around your table
as fresh and promising as young olive shoots.
Stand in awe of God's Yes.
Oh, how he blesses the one who fears GOD!

5-6   Enjoy the good life in Jerusalem
every day of your life.
And enjoy your grandchildren.
Peace to Israel!

A PILGRIM SONG

1-4   **129** "They've kicked me around ever since I was young"
— this is how Israel tells it —
"They've kicked me around ever since I was young,
but they never could keep me down.
Their plowmen plowed long furrows
up and down my back;
But GOD wouldn't put up with it,
he sticks with us.
Then GOD ripped the harnesses
of the evil plowmen to shreds."

5-8   Oh, let all those who hate Zion
grovel in humiliation;
Let them be like grass in shallow ground
that withers before the harvest,
Before the farmhands can gather it in,
the harvesters get in the crop,

Before the neighbors have a chance to call out,
"Congratulations on your wonderful crop!
We bless you in GOD's name!"

A PILGRIM SONG

1-2 130 Help, GOD — the bottom has fallen out of my life!
Master, hear my cry for help!
Listen hard! Open your ears!
Listen to my cries for mercy.

3-4 If you, GOD, kept records on wrongdoings,
who would stand a chance?
As it turns out, forgiveness is your habit,
and that's why you're worshiped.

5-6 I pray to GOD — my life a prayer —
and wait for what he'll say and do.
My life's on the line before God, my Lord,
waiting and watching till morning,
waiting and watching till morning.

7-8 O Israel, wait and watch for GOD —
with GOD's arrival comes love,
with GOD's arrival comes generous redemption.
No doubt about it — he'll redeem Israel,
buy back Israel from captivity to sin.

A PILGRIM SONG

1 131 GOD, I'm not trying to rule the roost,
I don't want to be king of the mountain.
I haven't meddled where I have no business
or fantasized grandiose plans.

2 I've kept my feet on the ground,
I've cultivated a quiet heart.
Like a baby content in its mother's arms,
my soul is a baby content.

3 Wait, Israel, for GOD. Wait with hope.
Hope now; hope always!

A PILGRIM SONG

1-5 132 O GOD, remember David,
remember all his troubles!
And remember how he promised GOD,
made a vow to the Strong God of Jacob,
"I'm not going home,
and I'm not going to bed,
I'm not going to sleep,
not even take time to rest,
Until I find a home for GOD,
a house for the Strong God of Jacob."

6-7   Remember how we got the news in Ephrathah,
           learned all about it at Jaar Meadows?
       We shouted, "Let's go to the shrine dedication!
           Let's worship at God's own footstool!"

8-10   Up, GOD, enjoy your new place of quiet repose,
           you and your mighty covenant ark;
       Get your priests all dressed up in justice;
           prompt your worshipers to sing this prayer:
       "Honor your servant David;
           don't disdain your anointed one."

11-18 GOD gave David his word,
           he won't back out on this promise:
       "One of your sons
           I will set on your throne;
       If your sons stay true to my Covenant
           and learn to live the way I teach them,
       Their sons will continue the line —
           always a son to sit on your throne.
       Yes — I, GOD, chose Zion,
           the place I wanted for my shrine;
       This will always be my home;
           this is what I want, and I'm here for good.
       I'll shower blessings on the pilgrims who come here,
           and give supper to those who arrive hungry;
       I'll dress my priests in salvation clothes;
           the holy people will sing their hearts out!
       Oh, I'll make the place radiant for David!
           I'll fill it with light for my anointed!
       I'll dress his enemies in dirty rags,
           but I'll make his crown sparkle with splendor."

A PILGRIM SONG OF DAVID

1-3   133 How wonderful, how beautiful,
               when brothers and sisters get along!
             It's like costly anointing oil
       flowing down head and beard,
       Flowing down Aaron's beard,
           flowing down the collar of his priestly robes.
       It's like the dew on Mount Hermon
           flowing down the slopes of Zion.
       Yes, that's where GOD commands the blessing,
           ordains eternal life.

A PILGRIM SONG

1-3   134 Come, bless GOD,
               all you servants of GOD!
             You priests of GOD, posted to the nightwatch
       in GOD's shrine,
       Lift your praising hands to the Holy Place,

and bless GOD.
In turn, may GOD of Zion bless you —
GOD who made heaven and earth!

1-4 **135** Hallelujah!
Praise the name of GOD,
praise the works of GOD.
All you priests on duty in GOD's temple,
serving in the sacred halls of our God,
Shout "Hallelujah!" because GOD's so good,
sing anthems to his beautiful name.
And why? Because GOD chose Jacob,
embraced Israel as a prize possession.

5-12 I, too, give witness to the greatness of GOD,
our Lord, high above all other gods.
He does just as he pleases —
however, wherever, whenever.
He makes the weather — clouds and thunder,
lightning and rain, wind pouring out of the north.
He struck down the Egyptian firstborn,
both human and animal firstborn.
He made Egypt sit up and take notice,
confronted Pharaoh and his servants with miracles.
Yes, he struck down great nations,
he slew mighty kings —
Sihon king of the Amorites, also Og of Bashan —
every last one of the Canaanite kings!
Then he turned their land over to Israel,
a gift of good land to his people.

13-18 GOD, your name is eternal,
GOD, you'll never be out-of-date.
GOD stands up for his people,
GOD holds the hands of his people.
The gods of the godless nations are mere trinkets,
made for quick sale in the markets:
Chiseled mouths that can't talk,
painted eyes that can't see,
Carved ears that can't hear —
dead wood! cold metal!
Those who make and trust them
become like them.

19-21 Family of Israel, bless GOD!
Family of Aaron, bless GOD!
Family of Levi, bless GOD!
You who fear GOD, bless GOD!
Oh, blessed be GOD of Zion,
First Citizen of Jerusalem!
Hallelujah!

136

Thank GOD! He deserves your thanks.
His love never quits.
Thank the God of all gods,
His love never quits.
Thank the Lord of all lords.
His love never quits.

4-22   Thank the miracle-working God,
His love never quits.
The God whose skill formed the cosmos,
His love never quits.
The God who laid out earth on ocean foundations,
His love never quits.
The God who filled the skies with light,
His love never quits.
The sun to watch over the day,
His love never quits.
Moon and stars as guardians of the night,
His love never quits.
The God who struck down the Egyptian firstborn,
His love never quits.
And rescued Israel from Egypt's oppression,
His love never quits.
Took Israel in hand with his powerful hand,
His love never quits.
Split the Red Sea right in half,
His love never quits.
Led Israel right through the middle,
His love never quits.
Dumped Pharaoh and his army in the sea,
His love never quits.
The God who marched his people through the desert,
His love never quits.
Smashed huge kingdoms right and left,
His love never quits.
Struck down the famous kings,
His love never quits.
Struck Sihon the Amorite king,
His love never quits.
Struck Og the Bashanite king,
His love never quits.
Then distributed their land as booty,
His love never quits.
Handed the land over to Israel.
His love never quits.

23-26   God remembered us when we were down,
His love never quits.
Rescued us from the trampling boot,
His love never quits.
Takes care of everyone in time of need.

His love never quits.
Thank God, who did it all!
His love never quits!

1-3 137 Alongside Babylon's rivers
we sat on the banks; we cried and cried,
remembering the good old days in Zion.
Alongside the quaking aspens
we stacked our unplayed harps;
That's where our captors demanded songs,
sarcastic and mocking:
"Sing us a happy Zion song!"

4-6   Oh, how could we ever sing GOD's song
in this wasteland?
If I ever forget you, Jerusalem,
let my fingers wither and fall off like leaves.
Let my tongue swell and turn black
if I fail to remember you,
If I fail, O dear Jerusalem,
to honor you as my greatest.

7-9   GOD, remember those Edomites,
and remember the ruin of Jerusalem,
That day they yelled out,
"Wreck it, smash it to bits!"
And you, Babylonians — ravagers!
A reward to whoever gets back at you
for all you've done to us;
Yes, a reward to the one who grabs your babies
and smashes their heads on the rocks!

A DAVID PSALM

1-3 138 Thank you! Everything in me says "Thank you!"
Angels listen as I sing my thanks.
I kneel in worship facing your holy temple
and say it again: "Thank you!"
Thank you for your love,
thank you for your faithfulness;
Most holy is your name,
most holy is your Word.
The moment I called out, you stepped in;
you made my life large with strength.

4-6   When they hear what you have to say, GOD,
all earth's kings will say "Thank you."
They'll sing of what you've done:
"How great the glory of GOD!"
And here's why: GOD, high above, sees far below;
no matter the distance, he knows everything about us.

7-8
When I walk into the thick of trouble,
keep me alive in the angry turmoil.
With one hand
strike my foes,
With your other hand
save me.
Finish what you started in me, GOD.
Your love is eternal — don't quit on me now.

A DAVID PSALM

1-6
139
GOD, investigate my life;
get all the facts firsthand.
I'm an open book to you;
even from a distance, you know what I'm thinking.
You know when I leave and when I get back;
I'm never out of your sight.
You know everything I'm going to say
before I start the first sentence.
I look behind me and you're there,
then up ahead and you're there, too —
your reassuring presence, coming and going.
This is too much, too wonderful —
I can't take it all in!

7-12
Is there anyplace I can go to avoid your Spirit?
to be out of your sight?
If I climb to the sky, you're there!
If I go underground, you're there!
If I flew on morning's wings
to the far western horizon,
You'd find me in a minute —
you're already there waiting!
Then I said to myself, "Oh, he even sees me in the dark!
At night I'm immersed in the light!"
It's a fact: darkness isn't dark to you;
night and day, darkness and light, they're all the same to you.

13-16
Oh yes, you shaped me first inside, then out;
you formed me in my mother's womb.
I thank you, High God — you're breathtaking!
Body and soul, I am marvelously made!
I worship in adoration — what a creation!
You know me inside and out,
you know every bone in my body;
You know exactly how I was made, bit by bit,
how I was sculpted from nothing into something.
Like an open book, you watched me grow from conception to birth;
all the stages of my life were spread out before you,
The days of my life all prepared
before I'd even lived one day.

17-22　Your thoughts — how rare, how beautiful!
　　　God, I'll never comprehend them!
　　I couldn't even begin to count them —
　　　any more than I could count the sand of the sea.
　　Oh, let me rise in the morning and live always with you!
　　　And please, God, do away with wickedness for good!
　　And you murderers — out of here! —
　　　all the men and women who belittle you, God,
　　　infatuated with cheap god-imitations.
　　See how I hate those who hate you, GOD,
　　　see how I loathe all this godless arrogance;
　　I hate it with pure, unadulterated hatred.
　　　Your enemies are my enemies!

23-24　Investigate my life, O God,
　　　find out everything about me;
　　Cross-examine and test me,
　　　get a clear picture of what I'm about;
　　See for yourself whether I've done anything wrong —
　　　then guide me on the road to eternal life.

A DAVID PSALM

1-5　**140** GOD, get me out of here, away from this evil;
　　　protect me from these vicious people.
　　　All they do is think up new ways to be bad;
　　they spend their days plotting war games.
　　They practice the sharp rhetoric of hate and hurt,
　　　speak venomous words that maim and kill.
　　GOD, keep me out of the clutch of these wicked ones,
　　　protect me from these vicious people;
　　Stuffed with self-importance, they plot ways to trip me up,
　　　determined to bring me down.
　　These crooks invent traps to catch me
　　　and do their best to incriminate me.

6-8　I prayed, "GOD, you're my God!
　　　Listen, GOD! Mercy!
　　GOD, my Lord, Strong Savior,
　　　protect me when the fighting breaks out!
　　Don't let the wicked have their way, GOD,
　　　don't give them an inch!"

9-11　These troublemakers all around me —
　　　let them drown in their own verbal poison.
　　Let God pile hellfire on them,
　　　let him bury them alive in crevasses!
　　These loudmouths —
　　　don't let them be taken seriously;
　　These savages —
　　　let the Devil hunt them down!

12-13 I know that you, GOD, are on the side of victims,
that you care for the rights of the poor.
And I know that the righteous personally thank you,
that good people are secure in your presence.

A DAVID PSALM

1-2 **141** GOD, come close. Come quickly!
Open your ears — it's my voice you're hearing!
Treat my prayer as sweet incense rising;
my raised hands are my evening prayers.

3-7 Post a guard at my mouth, GOD,
set a watch at the door of my lips.
Don't let me so much as dream of evil
or thoughtlessly fall into bad company.
And these people who only do wrong —
don't let them lure me with their sweet talk!
May the Just One set me straight,
may the Kind One correct me,
Don't let sin anoint my head.
I'm praying hard against their evil ways!
Oh, let their leaders be pushed off a high rock cliff;
make them face the music.
Like a rock pulverized by a maul,
let their bones be scattered at the gates of hell.

8-10 But GOD, dear Lord,
I only have eyes for you.
Since I've run for dear life to you,
take good care of me.
Protect me from their evil scheming,
from all their demonic subterfuge.
Let the wicked fall flat on their faces,
while I walk off without a scratch.

A DAVID PRAYER — WHEN HE WAS IN THE CAVE

1-2 **142** I cry out loudly to GOD,
loudly I plead with GOD for mercy.
I spill out all my complaints before him,
and spell out my troubles in detail:

3-7 "As I sink in despair, my spirit ebbing away,
you know how I'm feeling,
Know the danger I'm in,
the traps hidden in my path.
Look right, look left —
there's not a soul who cares what happens!
I'm up against it, with no exit —
bereft, left alone.
I cry out, GOD, call out:
'You're my last chance, my only hope for life!'

Oh listen, please listen;
    I've never been this low.
Rescue me from those who are hunting me down;
    I'm no match for them.
Get me out of this dungeon
    so I can thank you in public.
Your people will form a circle around me
    and you'll bring me showers of blessing!"

A DAVID PSALM

1-2 **143** Listen to this prayer of mine, GOD;
    pay attention to what I'm asking.
    Answer me — you're famous for your answers!
Do what's right for me.
But don't, please don't, haul me into court;
    not a person alive would be acquitted there.

3-6 The enemy hunted me down;
    he kicked me and stomped me within an inch of my life.
He put me in a black hole,
    buried me like a corpse in that dungeon.
I sat there in despair, my spirit draining away,
    my heart heavy, like lead.
I remembered the old days,
    went over all you've done, pondered the ways you've worked,
Stretched out my hands to you,
    as thirsty for you as a desert thirsty for rain.

7-10 Hurry with your answer, GOD!
    I'm nearly at the end of my rope.
Don't turn away; don't ignore me!
    That would be certain death.
If you wake me each morning with the sound of your loving voice,
    I'll go to sleep each night trusting in you.
Point out the road I must travel;
    I'm all ears, all eyes before you.
Save me from my enemies, GOD —
    you're my only hope!
Teach me how to live to please you,
    because you're my God.
Lead me by your blessed Spirit
    into cleared and level pastureland.

11-12 Keep up your reputation, God — give me life!
    In your justice, get me out of this trouble!
In your great love, vanquish my enemies;
    make a clean sweep of those who harass me.
And why? Because I'm your servant.

A DAVID PSALM

1-2 **144** Blessed be GOD, my mountain,
who trains me to fight fair and well.
He's the bedrock on which I stand,
the castle in which I live,
my rescuing knight,
The high crag where I run for dear life,
while he lays my enemies low.

3-4 I wonder why you care, GOD —
why do you bother with us at all?
All we are is a puff of air;
we're like shadows in a campfire.

5-8 Step down out of heaven, GOD;
ignite volcanoes in the hearts of the mountains.
Hurl your lightnings in every direction;
shoot your arrows this way and that.
Reach all the way from sky to sea:
pull me out of the ocean of hate,
out of the grip of those barbarians
Who lie through their teeth,
who shake your hand
then knife you in the back.

9-10 O God, let me sing a new song to you,
let me play it on a twelve-string guitar —
A song to the God who saved the king,
the God who rescued David, his servant.

11 Rescue me from the enemy sword,
release me from the grip of those barbarians
Who lie through their teeth,
who shake your hand
then knife you in the back.

12-14 Make our sons in their prime
like sturdy oak trees,
Our daughters as shapely and bright
as fields of wildflowers.
Fill our barns with great harvest,
fill our fields with huge flocks;
Protect us from invasion and exile —
eliminate the crime in our streets.

15 How blessed the people who have all this!
How blessed the people who have GOD for God!

DAVID'S PRAISE

1 145 I lift you high in praise, my God, O my King!
and I'll bless your name into eternity.

2 I'll bless you every day,
and keep it up from now to eternity.

3 GOD is magnificent; he can never be praised enough.
There are no boundaries to his greatness.

4 Generation after generation stands in awe of your work;
each one tells stories of your mighty acts.

5 Your beauty and splendor have everyone talking;
I compose songs on your wonders.

6 Your marvelous doings are headline news;
I could write a book full of the details of your greatness.

7 The fame of your goodness spreads across the country;
your righteousness is on everyone's lips.

8 GOD is all mercy and grace —
not quick to anger, is rich in love.

9 GOD is good to one and all;
everything he does is suffused with grace.

10-11 Creation and creatures applaud you, GOD;
your holy people bless you.

They talk about the glories of your rule,
they exclaim over your splendor,

12 Letting the world know of your power for good,
the lavish splendor of your kingdom.

13 Your kingdom is a kingdom eternal;
you never get voted out of office.

GOD always does what he says,
and is gracious in everything he does.

14 GOD gives a hand to those down on their luck,
gives a fresh start to those ready to quit.

15 All eyes are on you, expectant;
you give them their meals on time.

16 Generous to a fault,
you lavish your favor on all creatures.

17 Everything GOD does is right—
the trademark on all his works is love.

18 GOD's there, listening for all who pray,
for all who pray and mean it.

19 He does what's best for those who fear him—
hears them call out, and saves them.

20 GOD sticks by all who love him,
but it's all over for those who don't.

21 My mouth is filled with GOD's praise.
Let everything living bless him,
bless his holy name from now to eternity!

1-2 **146** Hallelujah!
O my soul, praise GOD!
All my life long I'll praise GOD,
singing songs to my God as long as I live.

3-9 Don't put your life in the hands of experts
who know nothing of life, of *salvation* life.
Mere humans don't have what it takes;
when they die, their projects die with them.
Instead, get help from the God of Jacob,
put your hope in GOD and know real blessing!
GOD made sky and soil,
sea and all the fish in it.
He always does what he says—
he defends the wronged,
he feeds the hungry.
GOD frees prisoners—
he gives sight to the blind,
he lifts up the fallen.
GOD loves good people, protects strangers,
takes the side of orphans and widows,
but makes short work of the wicked.

10 GOD's in charge—*always.*
Zion's God is God for good!
Hallelujah!

1 **147** Hallelujah!
It's a good thing to sing praise to our God;
praise is beautiful, praise is fitting.

2-6 GOD's the one who rebuilds Jerusalem,
who regathers Israel's scattered exiles.
He heals the heartbroken
and bandages their wounds.

He counts the stars
  and assigns each a name.
Our Lord is great, with limitless strength;
  we'll never comprehend what he knows and does.
GOD puts the fallen on their feet again
  and pushes the wicked into the ditch.

7-11 Sing to GOD a thanksgiving hymn,
  play music on your instruments to God,
Who fills the sky with clouds,
  preparing rain for the earth,
Then turning the mountains green with grass,
  feeding both cattle and crows.
He's not impressed with horsepower;
  the size of our muscles means little to him.
Those who fear GOD get GOD's attention;
  they can depend on his strength.

12-18 Jerusalem, worship GOD!
  Zion, praise your God!
He made your city secure,
  he blessed your children among you.
He keeps the peace at your borders,
  he puts the best bread on your tables.
He launches his promises earthward —
  how swift and sure they come!
He spreads snow like a white fleece,
  he scatters frost like ashes,
He broadcasts hail like birdseed —
  who can survive his winter?
Then he gives the command and it all melts;
  he breathes on winter — suddenly it's spring!

19-20 He speaks the same way to Jacob,
  speaks words that work to Israel.
He never did this to the other nations;
  they never heard such commands.
Hallelujah!

1-5 **148** Hallelujah!
      Praise GOD from heaven,
        praise him from the mountaintops;
Praise him, all you his angels,
  praise him, all you his warriors,
Praise him, sun and moon,
  praise him, you morning stars;
Praise him, high heaven,
  praise him, heavenly rain clouds;
Praise, oh let them praise the name of GOD —
  he spoke the word, and there they were!

6   He set them in place
        from all time to eternity;
    He gave his orders,
        and that's it!

7-12   Praise GOD from earth,
        you sea dragons, you fathomless ocean deeps;
    Fire and hail, snow and ice,
        hurricanes obeying his orders;
    Mountains and all hills,
        apple orchards and cedar forests;
    Wild beasts and herds of cattle,
        snakes, and birds in flight;
    Earth's kings and all races,
        leaders and important people,
    Robust men and women in their prime,
        and yes, graybeards and little children.

13-14   Let them praise the name of GOD—
        it's the only Name worth praising.
    His radiance exceeds anything in earth and sky;
        he's built a monument—his very own people!

    Praise from all who love GOD!
        Israel's children, intimate friends of GOD.
    Hallelujah!

1-4   149 Hallelujah!
        Sing to GOD a brand-new song,
            praise him in the company of all who love him.
    Let all Israel celebrate their Sovereign Creator,
        Zion's children exult in their King.
    Let them praise his name in dance;
        strike up the band and make great music!
    And why? Because GOD delights in his people,
        festoons plain folk with salvation garlands!

5-9   Let true lovers break out in praise,
        sing out from wherever they're sitting,
    Shout the high praises of God,
        brandish their swords in the wild sword-dance—
    A portent of vengeance on the God-defying nations,
        a signal that punishment's coming,
    Their kings chained and hauled off to jail,
        their leaders behind bars for good,
    The judgment on them carried out to the letter
        —and all who love God in the seat of honor!
    Hallelujah!

¹⁻⁶

150

Hallelujah!
Praise God in his holy house of worship,
   praise him under the open skies;
Praise him for his acts of power,
   praise him for his magnificent greatness;
Praise with a blast on the trumpet,
   praise by strumming soft strings;
Praise him with castanets and dance,
   praise him with banjo and flute;
Praise him with cymbals and a big bass drum,
   praise him with fiddles and mandolin.
Let every living, breathing creature praise GOD!
   Hallelujah!

PROVERBS

Many people think that what's written in the Bible has mostly to do with getting people into heaven — getting right with God, saving their eternal souls. It does have to do with that, of course, but not mostly. It is equally concerned with living on this earth — living well, living in robust sanity. In our Scriptures, heaven is not the primary concern, to which earth is a tagalong afterthought. "On earth *as* it is in heaven" is Jesus' prayer.

"Wisdom" is the biblical term for this on-earth-as-it-is-in-heaven everyday living. Wisdom is the art of living skillfully in whatever actual conditions we find ourselves. It has virtually nothing to do with information as such, with knowledge as such. A college degree is no certification of wisdom—nor is it primarily concerned with keeping us out of moral mud puddles, although it does have a profound moral effect upon us.

Wisdom has to do with becoming skillful in honoring our parents and raising our children, handling our money and conducting our sexual lives, going to work and exercising leadership, using words well and treating friends kindly, eating and drinking healthily, cultivating emotions within ourselves and attitudes toward others that make for peace. Threaded through all these items is the insistence that the way we think of and respond to God is the most practical thing we do. In matters of everyday practicality, nothing, absolutely nothing, takes precedence over God.

Proverbs concentrates on these concerns more than any other book in the Bible. Attention to the here and now is everywhere present in the stories and legislation, the prayers and the sermons, that are spread over the thousands of pages of the Bible. Proverbs distills it all into riveting images and aphorisms that keep us connected in holy obedience to the ordinary.

PROVERBS

WISE SAYINGS OF SOLOMON
A MANUAL FOR LIVING

1-6 These are the wise sayings of Solomon,
 David's son, Israel's king —
 Written down so we'll know how to live well and right,
to understand what life means and where it's going;
A manual for living,
 for learning what's right and just and fair;
To teach the inexperienced the ropes
 and give our young people a grasp on reality.
There's something here also for seasoned men and women,
 still a thing or two for the experienced to learn —
Fresh wisdom to probe and penetrate,
 the rhymes and reasons of wise men and women.

START WITH GOD

7 Start with GOD — the first step in learning is bowing down to GOD;
 only fools thumb their noses at such wisdom and learning.

8-19 Pay close attention, friend, to what your father tells you;
 never forget what you learned at your mother's knee.
Wear their counsel like flowers in your hair,
 like rings on your fingers.
Dear friend, if bad companions tempt you,
 don't go along with them.
If they say — "Let's go out and raise some hell.
 Let's beat up some old man, mug some old woman.
Let's pick them clean
 and get them ready for their funerals.
We'll load up on top-quality loot.
 We'll haul it home by the truckload.
Join us for the time of your life!
 With us, it's share and share alike!" —
Oh, friend, don't give them a second look;
 don't listen to them for a minute.
They're racing to a very bad end,
 hurrying to ruin everything they lay hands on.
Nobody robs a bank
 with everyone watching,
Yet that's what these people are doing —
 they're doing themselves in.
When you grab all you can get, that's what happens:
 the more you get, the less you are.

LADY WISDOM

20-21 Lady Wisdom goes out in the street and shouts.
 At the town center she makes her speech.

In the middle of the traffic she takes her stand.
  At the busiest corner she calls out:

22-24 "Simpletons! How long will you wallow in ignorance?
  Cynics! How long will you feed your cynicism?
Idiots! How long will you refuse to learn?
  About face! I can revise your life.
Look, I'm ready to pour out my spirit on you;
  I'm ready to tell you all I know.
As it is, I've called, but you've turned a deaf ear;
  I've reached out to you, but you've ignored me.

25-28 "Since you laugh at my counsel
  and make a joke of my advice,
How can I take you seriously?
  I'll turn the tables and joke about *your* troubles!
What if the roof falls in,
  and your whole life goes to pieces?
What if catastrophe strikes and there's nothing
  to show for your life but rubble and ashes?
You'll need me then. You'll call for me, but don't expect
    an answer.
  No matter how hard you look, you won't find me.

29-33 "Because you hated Knowledge
  and had nothing to do with the Fear-of-God,
Because you wouldn't take my advice
  and brushed aside all my offers to train you,
Well, you've made your bed — now lie in it;
  you wanted your own way — now, how do you like it?
Don't you see what happens, you simpletons, you idiots?
  Carelessness kills; complacency is murder.
First pay attention to me, and then relax.
  Now you can take it easy — you're in good hands."

MAKE INSIGHT YOUR PRIORITY

1-5 2 Good friend, take to heart what I'm telling you;
  collect my counsels and guard them with your life.
Tune your ears to the world of Wisdom;
  set your heart on a life of Understanding.
That's right — if you make Insight your priority,
  and won't take no for an answer,
Searching for it like a prospector panning for gold,
  like an adventurer on a treasure hunt,
Believe me, before you know it Fear-of-God will be yours;
  you'll have come upon the Knowledge of God.

6-8 And here's why: God gives out Wisdom free,
  is plainspoken in Knowledge and Understanding.
He's a rich mine of Common Sense for those who live well,
  a personal bodyguard to the candid and sincere.

He keeps his eye on all who live honestly,
and pays special attention to his loyally committed ones.

9-15 So now you can pick out what's true and fair,
find all the good trails!
Lady Wisdom will be your close friend,
and Brother Knowledge your pleasant companion.
Good Sense will scout ahead for danger,
Insight will keep an eye out for you.
They'll keep you from making wrong turns,
or following the bad directions
Of those who are lost themselves
and can't tell a trail from a tumbleweed,
These losers who make a game of evil
and throw parties to celebrate perversity,
Traveling paths that go nowhere,
wandering in a maze of detours and dead ends.

16-19 Wise friends will rescue you from the Temptress —
that smooth-talking Seductress
Who's faithless to the husband she married years ago,
never gave a second thought to her promises before God.
Her whole way of life is doomed;
every step she takes brings her closer to hell.
No one who joins her company ever comes back,
ever sets foot on the path to real living.

20-22 So — join the company of good men and women,
keep your feet on the tried-and-true paths.
It's the men who walk straight who will settle this land,
the women with integrity who will last here.
The corrupt will lose their lives;
the dishonest will be gone for good.

Don't Assume You Know It All

1-2 3 Good friend, don't forget all I've taught you;
take to heart my commands.
They'll help you live a long, long time,
a long life lived full and well.

3-4 Don't lose your grip on Love and Loyalty.
Tie them around your neck; carve their initials on your heart.
Earn a reputation for living well
in God's eyes and the eyes of the people.

5-12 Trust GOD from the bottom of your heart;
don't try to figure out everything on your own.
Listen for GOD's voice in everything you do, everywhere you go;
he's the one who will keep you on track.
Don't assume that you know it all.
Run to GOD! Run from evil!

Your body will glow with health,
    your very bones will vibrate with life!

Honor GOD with everything you own;
    give him the first and the best.
Your barns will burst,
    your wine vats will brim over.
But don't, dear friend, resent GOD's discipline;
    don't sulk under his loving correction.
It's the child he loves that GOD corrects;
    a father's delight is behind all this.

THE VERY TREE OF LIFE

13-18   You're blessed when you meet Lady Wisdom,
    when you make friends with Madame Insight.
She's worth far more than money in the bank;
    her friendship is better than a big salary.
Her value exceeds all the trappings of wealth;
    nothing you could wish for holds a candle to her.
With one hand she gives long life,
    with the other she confers recognition.
Her manner is beautiful,
    her life wonderfully complete.
She's the very Tree of Life to those who embrace her.
    Hold her tight — and be blessed!

19-20   With Lady Wisdom, GOD formed Earth;
    with Madame Insight, he raised Heaven.
They knew when to signal rivers and springs to the surface,
    and dew to descend from the night skies.

NEVER WALK AWAY

21-26   Dear friend, guard Clear Thinking and Common Sense with your life;
    don't for a minute lose sight of them.
They'll keep your soul alive and well,
    they'll keep you fit and attractive.
You'll travel safely,
    you'll neither tire nor trip.
You'll take afternoon naps without a worry,
    you'll enjoy a good night's sleep.
No need to panic over alarms or surprises,
    or predictions that doomsday's just around the corner,
Because GOD will be right there with you;
    he'll keep you safe and sound.

27-29   Never walk away from someone who deserves help;
    your hand is *God's* hand for that person.
Don't tell your neighbor "Maybe some other time"
    or "Try me tomorrow"
    when the money's right there in your pocket.
Don't figure ways of taking advantage of your neighbor
    when he's sitting there trusting and unsuspecting.

30-32 Don't walk around with a chip on your shoulder,
　　　always spoiling for a fight.
Don't try to be like those who shoulder their way through life.
　　　Why be a bully?
"Why not?" you say. Because GOD can't stand twisted souls.
　　　It's the straightforward who get his respect.

33-35 GOD's curse blights the house of the wicked,
　　　but he blesses the home of the righteous.
He gives proud skeptics a cold shoulder,
　　　but if you're down on your luck, he's right there to help.
Wise living gets rewarded with honor;
　　　stupid living gets the booby prize.

YOUR LIFE IS AT STAKE

1-2 **4** Listen, friends, to some fatherly advice;
　　　sit up and take notice so you'll know how to live.
I'm giving you good counsel;
　　　don't let it go in one ear and out the other.

3-9 When I was a boy at my father's knee,
　　　the pride and joy of my mother,
He would sit me down and drill me:
　　　"Take this to heart. Do what I tell you — live!
Sell everything and buy Wisdom! Forage for Understanding!
　　　Don't forget one word! Don't deviate an inch!
Never walk away from Wisdom — she guards your life;
　　　love her — she keeps her eye on you.
Above all and before all, do this: Get Wisdom!
　　　Write this at the top of your list: Get Understanding!
Throw your arms around her — believe me, you won't regret it;
　　　never let her go — she'll make your life glorious.
She'll garland your life with grace,
　　　she'll festoon your days with beauty."

10-15 Dear friend, take my advice;
　　　it will add years to your life.
I'm writing out clear directions to Wisdom Way,
　　　I'm drawing a map to Righteous Road.
I don't want you ending up in blind alleys,
　　　or wasting time making wrong turns.
Hold tight to good advice; don't relax your grip.
　　　Guard it well — your life is at stake!
Don't take Wicked Bypass;
　　　don't so much as set foot on that road.
Stay clear of it; give it a wide berth.
　　　Make a detour and be on your way.

16-17 Evil people are restless
　　　unless they're making trouble;
They can't get a good night's sleep

unless they've made life miserable for somebody.
Perversity is their food and drink,
    violence their drug of choice.

18-19 The ways of right-living people glow with light;
    the longer they live, the brighter they shine.
But the road of wrongdoing gets darker and darker —
    travelers can't see a thing; they fall flat on their faces.

LEARN IT BY HEART

20-22 Dear friend, listen well to my words;
    tune your ears to my voice.
Keep my message in plain view at all times.
    Concentrate! Learn it by heart!
Those who discover these words live, really live;
    body and soul, they're bursting with health.

23-27 Keep vigilant watch over your heart;
    that's where life starts.
Don't talk out of both sides of your mouth;
    avoid careless banter, white lies, and gossip.
Keep your eyes straight ahead;
    ignore all sideshow distractions.
Watch your step,
    and the road will stretch out smooth before you.
Look neither right nor left;
    leave evil in the dust.

NOTHING BUT SIN AND BONES

1-2 5 Dear friend, pay close attention to this, my wisdom;
    listen very closely to the way I see it.
Then you'll acquire a taste for good sense;
    what I tell you will keep you out of trouble.

3-6 The lips of a seductive woman are oh so sweet,
    her soft words are oh so smooth.
But it won't be long before she's gravel in your mouth,
    a pain in your gut, a wound in your heart.
She's dancing down the primrose path to Death;
    she's headed straight for Hell and taking you with her.
She hasn't a clue about Real Life,
    about who she is or where she's going.

7-14 So, my friend, listen closely;
    don't treat my words casually.
Keep your distance from such a woman;
    absolutely stay out of her neighborhood.
You don't want to squander your wonderful life,
    to waste your precious life among the hardhearted.
Why should you allow strangers to take advantage of you?
    Why be exploited by those who care nothing for you?

You don't want to end your life full of regrets,
   nothing but sin and bones,
Saying, "Oh, why didn't I do what they told me?
   Why did I reject a disciplined life?
Why didn't I listen to my mentors,
   or take my teachers seriously?
My life is ruined!
   I haven't one blessed thing to show for my life!"

NEVER TAKE LOVE FOR GRANTED

15-16 Do you know the saying, "Drink from your own rain barrel,
   draw water from your own spring-fed well"?
It's true. Otherwise, you may one day come home
   and find your barrel empty and your well polluted.

17-20 Your spring water is for you and you only,
   not to be passed around among strangers.
Bless your fresh-flowing fountain!
   Enjoy the wife you married as a young man!
Lovely as an angel, beautiful as a rose —
   don't ever quit taking delight in her body.
   Never take her love for granted!
Why would you trade enduring intimacies for cheap thrills with a whore?
   for dalliance with a promiscuous stranger?

21-23 Mark well that GOD doesn't miss a move you make;
   he's aware of every step you take.
The shadow of your sin will overtake you;
   you'll find yourself stumbling all over yourself in the dark.
Death is the reward of an undisciplined life;
   your foolish decisions trap you in a dead end.

LIKE A DEER FROM THE HUNTER

1-5 Dear friend, if you've gone into hock with your neighbor
   or locked yourself into a deal with a stranger,
If you've impulsively promised the shirt off your back
   and now find yourself shivering out in the cold,
Friend, don't waste a minute, get yourself out of that mess.
   You're in that man's clutches!
   Go, put on a long face; act desperate.
Don't procrastinate —
   there's no time to lose.
Run like a deer from the hunter,
   fly like a bird from the trapper!

A LESSON FROM THE ANT

6-11 You lazy fool, look at an ant.
   Watch it closely; let it teach you a thing or two.
Nobody has to tell it what to do.
   All summer it stores up food;
   at harvest it stockpiles provisions.

So how long are you going to laze around doing nothing?
How long before you get out of bed?
A nap here, a nap there, a day off here, a day off there,
sit back, take it easy — do you know what comes next?
Just this: You can look forward to a dirt-poor life,
poverty your permanent houseguest!

ALWAYS COOKING UP SOMETHING NASTY

12-15 Riffraff and rascals
talk out of both sides of their mouths.
They wink at each other, they shuffle their feet,
they cross their fingers behind their backs.
Their perverse minds are always cooking up something nasty,
always stirring up trouble.
Catastrophe is just around the corner for them,
a total smashup, their lives ruined beyond repair.

SEVEN THINGS GOD HATES

16-19 Here are six things GOD hates,
and one more that he loathes with a passion:

eyes that are arrogant,
a tongue that lies,
hands that murder the innocent,
a heart that hatches evil plots,
feet that race down a wicked track,
a mouth that lies under oath,
a troublemaker in the family.

WARNING ON ADULTERY

20-23 Good friend, follow your father's good advice;
don't wander off from your mother's teachings.
Wrap yourself in them from head to foot;
wear them like a scarf around your neck.
Wherever you walk, they'll guide you;
whenever you rest, they'll guard you;
when you wake up, they'll tell you what's next.
For sound advice is a beacon,
good teaching is a light,
moral discipline is a life path.

24-35 They'll protect you from wanton women,
from the seductive talk of some temptress.
Don't lustfully fantasize on her beauty,
nor be taken in by her bedroom eyes.
You can buy an hour with a whore for a loaf of bread,
but a wanton woman may well eat *you* alive.
Can you build a fire in your lap
and not burn your pants?
Can you walk barefoot on hot coals
and not get blisters?

It's the same when you have sex with your neighbor's wife:
    Touch her and you'll pay for it. No excuses.
Hunger is no excuse
    for a thief to steal;
When he's caught he has to pay it back,
    even if he has to put his whole house in hock.
Adultery is a brainless act,
    soul-destroying, self-destructive;
Expect a bloody nose, a black eye,
    and a reputation ruined for good.
For jealousy detonates rage in a cheated husband;
    wild for revenge, he won't make allowances.
Nothing you say or pay will make it all right;
    neither bribes nor reason will satisfy him.

DRESSED TO SEDUCE

1-5   7 Dear friend, do what I tell you;
    treasure my careful instructions.
    Do what I say and you'll live well.
    My teaching is as precious as your eyesight — guard it!
Write it out on the back of your hands;
    etch it on the chambers of your heart.
Talk to Wisdom as to a sister.
    Treat Insight as your companion.
They'll be with you to fend off the Temptress —
    that smooth-talking, honey-tongued Seductress.

6-12 As I stood at the window of my house
    looking out through the shutters,
Watching the mindless crowd stroll by,
    I spotted a young man without any sense
Arriving at the corner of the street where she lived,
    then turning up the path to her house.
It was dusk, the evening coming on,
    the darkness thickening into night.
Just then, a woman met him —
    she'd been lying in wait for him, dressed to seduce him.
Brazen and brash she was,
    restless and roaming, never at home,
Walking the streets, loitering in the mall,
    hanging out at every corner in town.

13-20 She threw her arms around him and kissed him,
    boldly took his arm and said,
"I've got all the makings for a feast —
    today I made my offerings, my vows are all paid,
So now I've come to find you,
    hoping to catch sight of your face — and here you are!
I've spread fresh, clean sheets on my bed,
    colorful imported linens.
My bed is aromatic with spices

and exotic fragrances.
Come, let's make love all night,
    spend the night in ecstatic lovemaking!
My husband's not home; he's away on business,
    and he won't be back for a month."

21-23   Soon she has him eating out of her hand,
    bewitched by her honeyed speech.
Before you know it, he's trotting behind her,
    like a calf led to the butcher shop,
Like a stag lured into ambush
    and then shot with an arrow,
Like a bird flying into a net
    not knowing that its flying life is over.

24-27   So, friends, listen to me,
    take these words of mine most seriously.
Don't fool around with a woman like that;
    don't even stroll through her neighborhood.
Countless victims come under her spell;
    she's the death of many a poor man.
She runs a halfway house to hell,
    fits you out with a shroud and a coffin.

Lady Wisdom Calls Out

1-11   **8** Do you hear Lady Wisdom calling?
    Can you hear Madame Insight raising her voice?
    She's taken her stand at First and Main,
    at the busiest intersection.
Right in the city square
    where the traffic is thickest, she shouts,
"You — I'm talking to all of you,
    everyone out here on the streets!
Listen, you idiots — learn good sense!
    You blockheads — shape up!
Don't miss a word of this — I'm telling you how to live well,
    I'm telling you how to live at your best.
My mouth chews and savors and relishes truth —
    I can't stand the taste of evil!
You'll only hear true and right words from my mouth;
    not one syllable will be twisted or skewed.
You'll recognize this as true — you with open minds;
    truth-ready minds will see it at once.
Prefer my life-disciplines over chasing after money,
    and God-knowledge over a lucrative career.
For Wisdom is better than all the trappings of wealth;
    nothing you could wish for holds a candle to her.

12-21   "I am Lady Wisdom, and I live next to Sanity;
    Knowledge and Discretion live just down the street.
The Fear-of-God means hating Evil,

whose ways I hate with a passion —
    pride and arrogance and crooked talk.
Good counsel and common sense are my characteristics;
    I am both Insight and the Virtue to live it out.
With my help, leaders rule,
    and lawmakers legislate fairly;
With my help, governors govern,
    along with all in legitimate authority.
I love those who love me;
    those who look for me find me.
Wealth and Glory accompany me —
    also substantial Honor and a Good Name.
My benefits are worth more than a big salary, even a *very* big salary;
    the returns on me exceed any imaginable bonus.
You can find me on Righteous Road — that's where I walk —
    at the intersection of Justice Avenue,
Handing out life to those who love me,
    filling their arms with life — armloads of life!

22-31   "GOD sovereignly made me — the first, the basic —
    before he did anything else.
I was brought into being a long time ago,
    well before Earth got its start.
I arrived on the scene before Ocean,
    yes, even before Springs and Rivers and Lakes.
Before Mountains were sculpted and Hills took shape,
    I was already there, newborn;
Long before GOD stretched out Earth's Horizons,
    and tended to the minute details of Soil and Weather,
And set Sky firmly in place,
    I was there.
When he mapped and gave borders to wild Ocean,
    built the vast vault of Heaven,
    and installed the fountains that fed Ocean,
When he drew a boundary for Sea,
    posted a sign that said NO TRESPASSING,
And then staked out Earth's Foundations,
    I was right there with him, making sure everything fit.
Day after day I was there, with my joyful applause,
    always enjoying his company,
Delighted with the world of things and creatures,
    happily celebrating the human family.

32-36   "So, my dear friends, listen carefully;
    those who embrace these my ways are most blessed.
Mark a life of discipline and live wisely;
    don't squander your precious life.
Blessed the man, blessed the woman, who listens to me,
    awake and ready for me each morning,
    alert and responsive as I start my day's work.
When you find me, you find life, real life,

to say nothing of GOD's good pleasure.
But if you wrong me, you damage your very soul;
    when you reject me, you're flirting with death."

LADY WISDOM GIVES A DINNER PARTY

1-6 9 Lady Wisdom has built and furnished her home;
    it's supported by seven hewn timbers.
    The banquet meal is ready to be served: lamb roasted,
wine poured out, table set with silver and flowers.
Having dismissed her serving maids,
    Lady Wisdom goes to town, stands in a prominent place,
    and invites everyone within sound of her voice:
"Are you confused about life, don't know what's going on?
    Come with me, oh come, have dinner with me!
I've prepared a wonderful spread — fresh-baked bread,
    roast lamb, carefully selected wines.
Leave your impoverished confusion and *live*!
    Walk up the street to a life with meaning."

7-12 If you reason with an arrogant cynic, you'll get slapped in the face;
    confront bad behavior and get a kick in the shins.
So don't waste your time on a scoffer;
    all you'll get for your pains is abuse.
But if you correct those who care about life,
    that's different — they'll love you for it!
Save your breath for the wise — they'll be wiser for it;
    tell good people what you know — they'll profit from it.
Skilled living gets its start in the Fear-of-GOD,
    insight into life from knowing a Holy God.
It's through me, Lady Wisdom, that your life deepens,
    and the years of your life ripen.
Live wisely and wisdom will permeate your life;
    mock life and life will mock you.

MADAME WHORE CALLS OUT, TOO

13-18 Then there's this other woman, Madame Whore —
    brazen, empty-headed, frivolous.
She sits on the front porch
    of her house on Main Street,
And as people walk by minding
    their own business, calls out,
"Are you confused about life, don't know what's going on?
    Steal off with me, I'll show you a good time!
    No one will ever know — I'll give you the time of your life."
But they don't know about all the skeletons in her closet,
    that all her guests end up in hell.

THE WISE SAYINGS OF SOLOMON
AN HONEST LIFE IS IMMORTAL

1
10 Wise son, glad father;
stupid son, sad mother.

2 Ill-gotten gain gets you nowhere;
an honest life is immortal.

3 GOD won't starve an honest soul,
but he frustrates the appetites of the wicked.

4 Sloth makes you poor;
diligence brings wealth.

5 Make hay while the sun shines — that's smart;
go fishing during harvest — that's stupid.

6 Blessings accrue on a good and honest life,
but the mouth of the wicked is a dark cave of abuse.

7 A good and honest life is a blessed memorial;
a wicked life leaves a rotten stench.

8 A wise heart takes orders;
an empty head will come unglued.

9 Honesty lives confident and carefree,
but Shifty is sure to be exposed.

10 An evasive eye is a sign of trouble ahead,
but an open, face-to-face meeting results in peace.

11 The mouth of a good person is a deep, life-giving well,
but the mouth of the wicked is a dark cave of abuse.

12 Hatred starts fights,
but love pulls a quilt over the bickering.

13 You'll find wisdom on the lips of a person of insight,
but the shortsighted needs a slap in the face.

14 The wise accumulate knowledge — a true treasure;
know-it-alls talk too much — a sheer waste.

THE ROAD TO LIFE IS A DISCIPLINED LIFE

15 The wealth of the rich is their bastion;
the poverty of the indigent is their ruin.

16 The wage of a good person is exuberant life;
an evil person ends up with nothing but sin.

17 The road to life is a disciplined life;
  ignore correction and you're lost for good.

18 Liars secretly hoard hatred;
  fools openly spread slander.

19 The more talk, the less truth;
  the wise measure their words.

20 The speech of a good person is worth waiting for;
  the blabber of the wicked is worthless.

21 The talk of a good person is rich fare for many,
  but chatterboxes die of an empty heart.

FEAR-OF-GOD EXPANDS YOUR LIFE

22 GOD's blessing makes life rich;
  nothing we do can improve on God.

23 An empty-head thinks mischief is fun,
  but a mindful person relishes wisdom.

24 The nightmares of the wicked come true;
  what the good people desire, they get.

25 When the storm is over, there's nothing left of the wicked;
  good people, firm on their rock foundation, aren't even fazed.

26 A lazy employee will give you nothing but trouble;
  it's vinegar in the mouth, smoke in the eyes.

27 The Fear-of-GOD expands your life;
  a wicked life is a puny life.

28 The aspirations of good people end in celebration;
  the ambitions of bad people crash.

29 GOD is solid backing to a well-lived life,
  but he calls into question a shabby performance.

30 Good people *last* — they can't be moved;
  the wicked are here today, gone tomorrow.

31 A good person's mouth is a clear fountain of wisdom;
  a foul mouth is a stagnant swamp.

32 The speech of a good person clears the air;
  the words of the wicked pollute it.

WITHOUT GOOD DIRECTION, PEOPLE LOSE THEIR WAY

1 **11** GOD hates cheating in the marketplace;
he loves it when business is aboveboard.

2 The stuck-up fall flat on their faces,
but down-to-earth people stand firm.

3 The integrity of the honest keeps them on track;
the deviousness of crooks brings them to ruin.

4 A thick bankroll is no help when life falls apart,
but a principled life can stand up to the worst.

5 Moral character makes for smooth traveling;
an evil life is a hard life.

6 Good character is the best insurance;
crooks get trapped in their sinful lust.

7 When the wicked die, that's it —
the story's over, end of hope.

8 A good person is saved from much trouble;
a bad person runs straight into it.

9 The loose tongue of the godless spreads destruction;
the common sense of the godly preserves them.

10 When it goes well for good people, the whole town cheers;
when it goes badly for bad people, the town celebrates.

11 When right-living people bless the city, it flourishes;
evil talk turns it into a ghost town in no time.

12 Mean-spirited slander is heartless;
quiet discretion accompanies good sense.

13 A gadabout gossip can't be trusted with a secret,
but someone of integrity won't violate a confidence.

14 Without good direction, people lose their way;
the more wise counsel you follow, the better your chances.

15 Whoever makes deals with strangers is sure to get burned;
if you keep a cool head, you'll avoid rash bargains.

16 A woman of gentle grace gets respect,
but men of rough violence grab for loot.

A God-Shaped Life

17 When you're kind to others, you help yourself;
    when you're cruel to others, you hurt yourself.

18 Bad work gets paid with a bad check;
    good work gets solid pay.

19 Take your stand with God's loyal community and live,
    or chase after phantoms of evil and die.

20 God can't stand deceivers,
    but oh how he relishes integrity.

21 Count on this: The wicked won't get off scot-free,
    and God's loyal people will triumph.

22 Like a gold ring in a pig's snout
    is a beautiful face on an empty head.

23 The desires of good people lead straight to the best,
    but wicked ambition ends in angry frustration.

24 The world of the generous gets larger and larger;
    the world of the stingy gets smaller and smaller.

25 The one who blesses others is abundantly blessed;
    those who help others are helped.

26 Curses on those who drive a hard bargain!
    Blessings on all who play fair and square!

27 The one who seeks good finds delight;
    the student of evil becomes evil.

28 A life devoted to things is a dead life, a stump;
    a God-shaped life is a flourishing tree.

29 Exploit or abuse your family, and end up with a fistful of air;
    common sense tells you it's a stupid way to live.

30 A good life is a fruit-bearing tree;
    a violent life destroys souls.

31 If good people barely make it,
    what's in store for the bad!

If You Love Learning

1 **12** If you love learning, you love the discipline that goes with it —
    how shortsighted to refuse correction!

2   A good person basks in the delight of GOD,
         and he wants nothing to do with devious schemers.

3   You can't find firm footing in a swamp,
         but life rooted in God stands firm.

4   A hearty wife invigorates her husband,
         but a frigid woman is cancer in the bones.

5   The thinking of principled people makes for justice;
         the plots of degenerates corrupt.

6   The words of the wicked kill;
         the speech of the upright saves.

7   Wicked people fall to pieces — there's nothing to them;
         the homes of good people hold together.

8   A person who talks sense is honored;
         airheads are held in contempt.

9   Better to be ordinary and work for a living
         than act important and starve in the process.

10   Good people are good to their animals;
         the "good-hearted" bad people kick and abuse them.

11   The one who stays on the job has food on the table;
         the witless chase whims and fancies.

12   What the wicked construct finally falls into ruin,
         while the roots of the righteous give life, and more life.

WISE PEOPLE TAKE ADVICE

13   The gossip of bad people gets them in trouble;
         the conversation of good people keeps them out of it.

14   Well-spoken words bring satisfaction;
         well-done work has its own reward.

15   Fools are headstrong and do what they like;
         wise people take advice.

16   Fools have short fuses and explode all too quickly;
         the prudent quietly shrug off insults.

17   Truthful witness by a good person clears the air,
         but liars lay down a smoke screen of deceit.

18   Rash language cuts and maims,
         but there is healing in the words of the wise.

19   Truth lasts;
      lies are here today, gone tomorrow.

20   Evil scheming distorts the schemer;
      peace-planning brings joy to the planner.

21   No evil can overwhelm a good person,
      but the wicked have their hands full of it.

22   God can't stomach liars;
      he loves the company of those who keep their word.

23   Prudent people don't flaunt their knowledge;
      talkative fools broadcast their silliness.

24   The diligent find freedom in their work;
      the lazy are oppressed by work.

25   Worry weighs us down;
      a cheerful word picks us up.

26   A good person survives misfortune,
      but a wicked life invites disaster.

27   A lazy life is an empty life,
      but "early to rise" gets the job done.

28   Good men and women travel right into life;
      sin's detours take you straight to hell.

WALK WITH THE WISE

1   **13** Intelligent children listen to their parents;
      foolish children do their own thing.

2   The good acquire a taste for helpful conversation;
      bullies push and shove their way through life.

3   Careful words make for a careful life;
      careless talk may ruin everything.

4   Indolence wants it all and gets nothing;
      the energetic have something to show for their lives.

5   A good person hates false talk;
      a bad person wallows in gibberish.

6   A God-loyal life keeps you on track;
      sin dumps the wicked in the ditch.

7   A pretentious, showy life is an empty life;
      a plain and simple life is a full life.

8   The rich can be sued for everything they have,
      but the poor are free of such threats.

9   The lives of good people are brightly lit streets;
      the lives of the wicked are dark alleys.

10   Arrogant know-it-alls stir up discord,
      but wise men and women listen to each other's counsel.

11   Easy come, easy go,
      but steady diligence pays off.

12   Unrelenting disappointment leaves you heartsick,
      but a sudden good break can turn life around.

13   Ignore the Word and suffer;
      honor God's commands and grow rich.

14   The teaching of the wise is a fountain of life,
      so, no more drinking from death-tainted wells!

15   Sound thinking makes for gracious living,
      but liars walk a rough road.

16   A commonsense person *lives* good sense;
      fools litter the country with silliness.

17   Irresponsible talk makes a real mess of things,
      but a reliable reporter is a healing presence.

18   Refuse discipline and end up homeless;
      embrace correction and live an honored life.

19   Souls who follow their hearts thrive;
      fools bent on evil despise matters of soul.

20   Become wise by walking with the wise;
      hang out with fools and watch your life fall to pieces.

21   Disaster entraps sinners,
      but God-loyal people get a good life.

22   A good life gets passed on to the grandchildren;
      ill-gotten wealth ends up with good people.

23   Banks foreclose on the farms of the poor,
      or else the poor lose their shirts to crooked lawyers.

24   A refusal to correct is a refusal to love;
      love your children by disciplining them.

25   An appetite for good brings much satisfaction,
      but the belly of the wicked always wants more.

A WAY THAT LEADS TO HELL

1   **14** Lady Wisdom builds a lovely home;
      Sir Fool comes along and tears it down brick by brick.

2   An honest life shows respect for GOD;
      a degenerate life is a slap in his face.

3   Frivolous talk provokes a derisive smile;
      wise speech evokes nothing but respect.

4   No cattle, no crops;
      a good harvest requires a strong ox for the plow.

5   A true witness never lies;
      a false witness makes a business of it.

6   Cynics look high and low for wisdom — and never find it;
      the open-minded find it right on their doorstep!

7   Escape quickly from the company of fools;
      they're a waste of your time, a waste of your words.

8   The wisdom of the wise keeps life on track;
      the foolishness of fools lands them in the ditch.

9   The stupid ridicule right and wrong,
      but a moral life is a favored life.

10   The person who shuns the bitter moments of friends
      will be an outsider at their celebrations.

11   Lives of careless wrongdoing are tumbledown shacks;
      holy living builds soaring cathedrals.

12-13   There's a way of life that looks harmless enough;
      look again — it leads straight to hell.
   Sure, those people appear to be having a good time,
      but all that laughter will end in heartbreak.

SIFT AND WEIGH EVERY WORD

14   A mean person gets paid back in meanness,
      a gracious person in grace.

15   The gullible believe anything they're told;
      the prudent sift and weigh every word.

16   The wise watch their steps and avoid evil;
      fools are headstrong and reckless.

17 The hotheaded do things they'll later regret;
   the coldhearted get the cold shoulder.

18 Foolish dreamers live in a world of illusion;
   wise realists plant their feet on the ground.

19 Eventually, evil will pay tribute to good;
   the wicked will respect God-loyal people.

20 An unlucky loser is shunned by all,
   but everyone loves a winner.

21 It's criminal to ignore a neighbor in need,
   but compassion for the poor — what a blessing!

22 Isn't it obvious that conspirators lose out,
   while the thoughtful win love and trust?

23 Hard work always pays off;
   mere talk puts no bread on the table.

24 The wise accumulate wisdom;
   fools get stupider by the day.

25 Souls are saved by truthful witness
   and betrayed by the spread of lies.

26 The Fear-of-GOD builds up confidence,
   and makes a world safe for your children.

27 The Fear-of-GOD is a spring of living water
   so you won't go off drinking from poisoned wells.

28 The mark of a good leader is loyal followers;
   leadership is nothing without a following.

29 Slowness to anger makes for deep understanding;
   a quick-tempered person stockpiles stupidity.

30 A sound mind makes for a robust body,
   but runaway emotions corrode the bones.

31 You insult your Maker when you exploit the powerless;
   when you're kind to the poor, you honor God.

32 The evil of bad people leaves them out in the cold;
   the integrity of good people creates a safe place for living.

33 Lady Wisdom is at home in an understanding heart —
   fools never even get to say hello.

34 God-devotion makes a country strong;
   God-avoidance leaves people weak.

35 Diligent work gets a warm commendation;
   shiftless work earns an angry rebuke.

GOD DOESN'T MISS A THING

1 **15** A gentle response defuses anger,
   but a sharp tongue kindles a temper-fire.

2 Knowledge flows like spring water from the wise;
   fools are leaky faucets, dripping nonsense.

3 GOD doesn't miss a thing —
   he's alert to good and evil alike.

4 Kind words heal and help;
   cutting words wound and maim.

5 Moral dropouts won't listen to their elders;
   welcoming correction is a mark of good sense.

6 The lives of God-loyal people flourish;
   a misspent life is soon bankrupt.

7 Perceptive words spread knowledge;
   fools are hollow — there's nothing to them.

8 GOD can't stand pious poses,
   but he delights in genuine prayers.

9 A life frittered away disgusts GOD;
   he loves those who run straight for the finish line.

10 It's a school of hard knocks for those who leave God's path,
   a dead-end street for those who hate God's rules.

11 Even hell holds no secrets from GOD —
   do you think he can't read human hearts?

LIFE ASCENDS TO THE HEIGHTS

12 Know-it-alls don't like being told what to do;
   they avoid the company of wise men and women.

13 A cheerful heart brings a smile to your face;
   a sad heart makes it hard to get through the day.

14 An intelligent person is always eager to take in more truth;
   fools feed on fast-food fads and fancies.

15 A miserable heart means a miserable life;
a cheerful heart fills the day with song.

16 A simple life in the Fear-of-God
is better than a rich life with a ton of headaches.

17 Better a bread crust shared in love
than a slab of prime rib served in hate.

18 Hot tempers start fights;
a calm, cool spirit keeps the peace.

19 The path of lazy people is overgrown with briers;
the diligent walk down a smooth road.

20 Intelligent children make their parents proud;
lazy students embarrass their parents.

21 The empty-headed treat life as a plaything;
the perceptive grasp its meaning and make a go of it.

22 Refuse good advice and watch your plans fail;
take good counsel and watch them succeed.

23 Congenial conversation — what a pleasure!
The right word at the right time — beautiful!

24 Life ascends to the heights for the thoughtful —
it's a clean about-face from descent into hell.

25 God smashes the pretensions of the arrogant;
he stands with those who have no standing.

26 God can't stand evil scheming,
but he puts words of grace and beauty on display.

27 A greedy and grasping person destroys community;
those who refuse to exploit live and let live.

28 Prayerful answers come from God-loyal people;
the wicked are sewers of abuse.

29 God keeps his distance from the wicked;
he closely attends to the prayers of God-loyal people.

30 A twinkle in the eye means joy in the heart,
and good news makes you feel fit as a fiddle.

31 Listen to good advice if you want to live well,
an honored guest among wise men and women.

32   An undisciplined, self-willed life is puny;
      an obedient, God-willed life is spacious.

33   Fear-of-God is a school in skilled living —
      first you learn humility, then you experience glory.

EVERYTHING WITH A PLACE AND A PURPOSE

1   **16** Mortals make elaborate plans,
      but God has the last word.

2   Humans are satisfied with whatever looks good;
      God probes for what *is* good.

3   Put God in charge of your work,
      then what you've planned will take place.

4   God made everything with a place and purpose;
      even the wicked are included — but for *judgment.*

5   God can't stomach arrogance or pretense;
      believe me, he'll put those upstarts in their place.

6   Guilt is banished through love and truth;
      Fear-of-God deflects evil.

7   When God approves of your life,
      even your enemies will end up shaking your hand.

8   Far better to be right and poor
      than to be wrong and rich.

9   We plan the way we want to live,
      but only God makes us able to live it.

IT PAYS TO TAKE LIFE SERIOUSLY

10   A good leader motivates,
      doesn't mislead, doesn't exploit.

11   God cares about honesty in the workplace;
      your business is his business.

12   Good leaders abhor wrongdoing of all kinds;
      sound leadership has a moral foundation.

13   Good leaders cultivate honest speech;
      they love advisors who tell them the truth.

14   An intemperate leader wreaks havoc in lives;
      you're smart to stay clear of someone like that.

15   Good-tempered leaders invigorate lives;
        they're like spring rain and sunshine.

16   Get wisdom — it's worth more than money;
        choose insight over income every time.

17   The road of right living bypasses evil;
        watch your step and save your life.

18   First pride, then the crash —
        the bigger the ego, the harder the fall.

19   It's better to live humbly among the poor
        than to live it up among the rich and famous.

20   It pays to take life seriously;
        things work out when you trust in GOD.

21   A wise person gets known for insight;
        gracious words add to one's reputation.

22   True intelligence is a spring of fresh water,
        while fools sweat it out the hard way.

23   They make a lot of sense, these wise folks;
        whenever they speak, their reputation increases.

24   Gracious speech is like clover honey —
        good taste to the soul, quick energy for the body.

25   There's a way that looks harmless enough;
        look again — it leads straight to hell.

26   Appetite is an incentive to work;
        hunger makes you work all the harder.

27   Mean people spread mean gossip;
        their words smart and burn.

28   Troublemakers start fights;
        gossips break up friendships.

29   Calloused climbers betray their very own friends;
        they'd stab their own grandmothers in the back.

30   A shifty eye betrays an evil intention;
        a clenched jaw signals trouble ahead.

31   Gray hair is a mark of distinction,
        the award for a God-loyal life.

32   Moderation is better than muscle,
      self-control better than political power.

33   Make your motions and cast your votes,
      but GOD has the final say.

A WHACK ON THE HEAD OF A FOOL

1   **17** A meal of bread and water in contented peace
      is better than a banquet spiced with quarrels.

2   A wise servant takes charge of an unruly child
      and is honored as one of the family.

3   As silver in a crucible and gold in a pan,
      so our lives are assayed by GOD.

4   Evil people relish malicious conversation;
      the ears of liars itch for dirty gossip.

5   Whoever mocks poor people insults their Creator;
      gloating over misfortune is a punishable crime.

6   Old people are distinguished by grandchildren;
      children take pride in their parents.

7   We don't expect eloquence from fools,
      nor do we expect lies from our leaders.

8   Receiving a gift is like getting a rare gemstone;
      any way you look at it, you see beauty refracted.

9   Overlook an offense and bond a friendship;
      fasten on to a slight and — good-bye, friend!

10 A quiet rebuke to a person of good sense
      does more than a whack on the head of a fool.

11 Criminals out looking for nothing but trouble
      won't have to wait long — they'll meet it coming and going!

12 Better to meet a grizzly robbed of her cubs
      than a fool hellbent on folly.

13 Those who return evil for good
      will meet their own evil returning.

14 The start of a quarrel is like a leak in a dam,
      so stop it before it bursts.

15 Whitewashing bad people and throwing mud on good people
      are equally abhorrent to GOD.

16   What's this? Fools out shopping for wisdom!
      They wouldn't recognize it if they saw it!

ONE WHO KNOWS MUCH SAYS LITTLE

17   Friends love through all kinds of weather,
      and families stick together in all kinds of trouble.

18   It's stupid to try to get something for nothing,
      or run up huge bills you can never pay.

19   The person who courts sin marries trouble;
      build a wall, invite a burglar.

20   A bad motive can't achieve a good end;
      double-talk brings you double trouble.

21   Having a fool for a child is misery;
      it's no fun being the parent of a dolt.

22   A cheerful disposition is good for your health;
      gloom and doom leave you bone-tired.

23   The wicked take bribes under the table;
      they show nothing but contempt for justice.

24   The perceptive find wisdom in their own front yard;
      fools look for it everywhere but right here.

25   A surly, stupid child is sheer pain to a father,
      a bitter pill for a mother to swallow.

26   It's wrong to penalize good behavior,
      or make good citizens pay for the crimes of others.

27   The one who knows much says little;
      an understanding person remains calm.

28   Even dunces who keep quiet are thought to be wise;
      as long as they keep their mouths shut, they're smart.

WORDS KILL, WORDS GIVE LIFE

1   **18** Loners who care only for themselves
         spit on the common good.

2   Fools care nothing for thoughtful discourse;
      all they do is run off at the mouth.

3   When wickedness arrives, shame's not far behind;
      contempt for life is contemptible.

4 Many words rush along like rivers in flood,
    but deep wisdom flows up from artesian springs.

5 It's not right to go easy on the guilty,
    or come down hard on the innocent.

6 The words of a fool start fights;
    do him a favor and gag him.

7 Fools are undone by their big mouths;
    their souls are crushed by their words.

8 Listening to gossip is like eating cheap candy;
    do you really want junk like that in your belly?

9 Slack habits and sloppy work
    are as bad as vandalism.

10 GOD's name is a place of protection—
    good people can run there and be safe.

11 The rich think their wealth protects them;
    they imagine themselves safe behind it.

12 Pride first, then the crash,
    but humility is precursor to honor.

13 Answering before listening
    is both stupid and rude.

14 A healthy spirit conquers adversity,
    but what can you do when the spirit is crushed?

15 Wise men and women are always learning,
    always listening for fresh insights.

16 A gift gets attention;
    it buys the attention of eminent people.

17 The first speech in a court case is always convincing—
    until the cross-examination starts!

18 You may have to draw straws
    when faced with a tough decision.

19 Do a favor and win a friend forever;
    nothing can untie that bond.

20 Words satisfy the mind as much as fruit does the stomach;
    good talk is as gratifying as a good harvest.

21 Words kill, words give life;
     they're either poison or fruit — you choose.

22 Find a good spouse, you find a good life —
     and even more: the favor of GOD!

23 The poor speak in soft supplications;
     the rich bark out answers.

24 Friends come and friends go,
     but a true friend sticks by you like family.

IF YOU QUIT LISTENING

1 **19** Better to be poor and honest
           than a rich person no one can trust.

2 Ignorant zeal is worthless;
     haste makes waste.

3 People ruin their lives by their own stupidity,
     so why does GOD always get blamed?

4 Wealth attracts friends as honey draws flies,
     but poor people are avoided like a plague.

5 Perjury won't go unpunished.
     Would you let a liar go free?

6 Lots of people flock around a generous person;
     everyone's a friend to the philanthropist.

7 When you're down on your luck, even your family avoids you —
     yes, even your best friends wish you'd get lost.
   If they see you coming, they look the other way —
     out of sight, out of mind.

8 Grow a wise heart — you'll do yourself a favor;
     keep a clear head — you'll find a good life.

9 The person who tells lies gets caught;
     the person who spreads rumors is ruined.

10 Blockheads shouldn't live on easy street
     any more than workers should give orders to their boss.

11 Smart people know how to hold their tongue;
     their grandeur is to forgive and forget.

12 Mean-tempered leaders are like mad dogs;
     the good-natured are like fresh morning dew.

13 A parent is worn to a frazzle by a stupid child;
  a nagging spouse is a leaky faucet.

14 House and land are handed down from parents,
  but a congenial spouse comes straight from GOD.

15 Life collapses on loafers;
  lazybones go hungry.

16 Keep the rules and keep your life;
  careless living kills.

17 Mercy to the needy is a loan to GOD,
  and GOD pays back those loans in full.

18 Discipline your children while you still have the chance;
  indulging them destroys them.

19 Let angry people endure the backlash of their own anger;
  if you try to make it better, you'll only make it worse.

20 Take good counsel and accept correction —
  that's the way to live wisely and well.

21 We humans keep brainstorming options and plans,
  but GOD's purpose prevails.

22 It's only human to want to make a buck,
  but it's better to be poor than a liar.

23 Fear-of-GOD is life itself,
  a full life, and serene — no nasty surprises.

24 Some people dig a fork into the pie
  but are too lazy to raise it to their mouth.

25 Punish the insolent — make an example of them.
  Who knows? Somebody might learn a good lesson.

26 Kids who lash out against their parents
  are an embarrassment and disgrace.

27 If you quit listening, dear child, and strike off on your own,
  you'll soon be out of your depth.

28 An unprincipled witness desecrates justice;
  the mouths of the wicked spew malice.

29 The irreverent have to learn reverence the hard way;
  only a slap in the face brings fools to attention.

Deep Water in the Heart

1 **W**ine makes you mean, beer makes you quarrelsome —
a staggering drunk is not much fun.

2 Quick-tempered leaders are like mad dogs —
cross them and they bite your head off.

3 It's a mark of good character to avert quarrels,
but fools love to pick fights.

4 A farmer too lazy to plant in the spring
has nothing to harvest in the fall.

5 Knowing what is right is like deep water in the heart;
a wise person draws from the well within.

6 Lots of people claim to be loyal and loving,
but where on earth can you find one?

7 God-loyal people, living honest lives,
make it much easier for their children.

8-9 Leaders who know their business and care
keep a sharp eye out for the shoddy and cheap,
For who among us can be trusted
to be always diligent and honest?

10 Switching price tags and padding the expense account
are two things GOD hates.

11 Young people eventually reveal by their actions
if their motives are on the up and up.

Drinking from the Chalice of Knowledge

12 **E**ars that hear and eyes that see —
we get our basic equipment from GOD!

13 Don't be too fond of sleep; you'll end up in the poorhouse.
Wake up and get up; then there'll be food on the table.

14 The shopper says, "That's junk — I'll take it off your hands,"
then goes off boasting of the bargain.

15 Drinking from the beautiful chalice of knowledge
is better than adorning oneself with gold and rare gems.

16 Hold tight to collateral on any loan to a stranger;
beware of accepting what a transient has pawned.

17 Stolen bread tastes sweet,
   but soon your mouth is full of gravel.

18 Form your purpose by asking for counsel,
   then carry it out using all the help you can get.

19 Gossips can't keep secrets,
   so never confide in blabbermouths.

20 Anyone who curses father and mother
   extinguishes light and exists benighted.

The Very Steps We Take

21 A bonanza at the beginning
   is no guarantee of blessing at the end.

22 Don't ever say, "I'll get you for that!"
   Wait for God; he'll settle the score.

23 God hates cheating in the marketplace;
   rigged scales are an outrage.

24 The very steps we take come from God;
   otherwise how would we know where we're going?

25 An impulsive vow is a trap;
   later you'll wish you could get out of it.

26 After careful scrutiny, a wise leader
   makes a clean sweep of rebels and dolts.

27 God is in charge of human life,
   watching and examining us inside and out.

28 Love and truth form a good leader;
   sound leadership is founded on loving integrity.

29 Youth may be admired for vigor,
   but gray hair gives prestige to old age.

30 A good thrashing purges evil;
   punishment goes deep within us.

God Examines Our Motives

21 1 Good leadership is a channel of water controlled by God;
   he directs it to whatever ends he chooses.

2 We justify our actions by appearances;
   God examines our motives.

3 Clean living before God and justice with our neighbors
mean far more to GOD than religious performance.

4 Arrogance and pride — distinguishing marks in the wicked —
are just plain sin.

5 Careful planning puts you ahead in the long run;
hurry and scurry puts you further behind.

6 Make it to the top by lying and cheating;
get paid with smoke and a promotion — to death!

7 The wicked get buried alive by their loot
because they refuse to use it to help others.

8 Mixed motives twist life into tangles;
pure motives take you straight down the road.

DO YOUR BEST, PREPARE FOR THE WORST

9 Better to live alone in a tumbledown shack
than share a mansion with a nagging spouse.

10 Wicked souls love to make trouble;
they feel nothing for friends and neighbors.

11 Simpletons only learn the hard way,
but the wise learn by listening.

12 A God-loyal person will see right through the wicked
and undo the evil they've planned.

13 If you stop your ears to the cries of the poor,
your cries will go unheard, unanswered.

14 A quietly given gift soothes an irritable person;
a heartfelt present cools a hot temper.

15 Good people celebrate when justice triumphs,
but for the workers of evil it's a bad day.

16 Whoever wanders off the straight and narrow
ends up in a congregation of ghosts.

17 You're addicted to thrills? What an empty life!
The pursuit of pleasure is never satisfied.

18 What a bad person plots against the good, boomerangs;
the plotter gets it in the end.

19 Better to live in a tent in the wild
than with a cross and petulant spouse.

20 Valuables are safe in a wise person's home;
    fools put it all out for yard sales.

21 Whoever goes hunting for what is right and kind
    finds life itself — *glorious* life!

22 One sage entered a whole city of armed soldiers —
    their trusted defenses fell to pieces!

23 Watch your words and hold your tongue;
    you'll save yourself a lot of grief.

24 You know their names — Brash, Impudent, Blasphemer —
    intemperate hotheads, every one.

25 Lazy people finally die of hunger
    because they won't get up and go to work.

26 Sinners are always wanting what they don't have;
    the God-loyal are always giving what they do have.

27 Religious performance by the wicked stinks;
    it's even worse when they use it to get ahead.

28 A lying witness is unconvincing;
    a person who speaks truth is respected.

29 Unscrupulous people fake it a lot;
    honest people are sure of their steps.

30 Nothing clever, nothing conceived, nothing contrived,
    can get the better of GOD.

31 Do your best, prepare for the worst —
    then trust GOD to bring victory.

THE CURE COMES THROUGH DISCIPLINE

1 **22** A sterling reputation is better than striking it rich;
    a gracious spirit is better than money in the bank.

2 The rich and the poor shake hands as equals —
    GOD made them both!

3 A prudent person sees trouble coming and ducks;
    a simpleton walks in blindly and is clobbered.

4 The payoff for meekness and Fear-of-GOD
    is plenty and honor and a satisfying life.

5 The perverse travel a dangerous road, potholed and mud-slick;
    if you know what's good for you, stay clear of it.

6   Point your kids in the right direction —
     when they're old they won't be lost.

7   The poor are always ruled over by the rich,
     so don't borrow and put yourself under their power.

8   Whoever sows sin reaps weeds,
     and bullying anger sputters into nothing.

9   Generous hands are blessed hands
     because they give bread to the poor.

10 Kick out the troublemakers and things will quiet down;
     you need a break from bickering and griping!

11 GOD loves the pure-hearted and well-spoken;
     good leaders also delight in their friendship.

12 GOD guards knowledge with a passion,
     but he'll have nothing to do with deception.

13 The loafer says, "There's a lion on the loose!
     If I go out I'll be eaten alive!"

14 The mouth of a whore is a bottomless pit;
     you'll fall in that pit if you're on the outs with GOD.

15 Young people are prone to foolishness and fads;
     the cure comes through tough-minded discipline.

16 Exploit the poor or glad-hand the rich — whichever,
     you'll end up the poorer for it.

THE THIRTY PRECEPTS OF THE SAGES
DON'T MOVE BACK THE BOUNDARY LINES

17-21   Listen carefully to my wisdom;
         take to heart what I can teach you.
     You'll treasure its sweetness deep within;
         you'll give it bold expression in your speech.
     To make sure your foundation is trust in GOD,
         I'm laying it all out right now just for you.
     I'm giving you thirty sterling principles —
         tested guidelines to live by.
     Believe me — these are truths that work,
         and will keep you accountable
         to those who sent you.

1

22-23   Don't walk on the poor just because they're poor,
         and don't use your position to crush the weak,

Because GOD will come to their defense;
 the life you took, he'll take from you and give back to them.

2

24-25 Don't hang out with angry people;
 don't keep company with hotheads.
Bad temper is contagious —
 don't get infected.

3

26-27 Don't gamble on the pot of gold at the end of the rainbow,
 hocking your house against a lucky chance.
The time will come when you have to pay up;
 you'll be left with nothing but the shirt on your back.

4

28 Don't stealthily move back the boundary lines
 staked out long ago by your ancestors.

5

29 Observe people who are good at their work —
 skilled workers are always in demand and admired;
 they don't take a backseat to anyone.

RESTRAIN YOURSELF

6

1-3 23 When you go out to dinner with an influential person,
  mind your manners:
  Don't gobble your food,
 don't talk with your mouth full.
And don't stuff yourself;
 bridle your appetite.

7

4-5 Don't wear yourself out trying to get rich;
 restrain yourself!
Riches disappear in the blink of an eye;
 wealth sprouts wings
 and flies off into the wild blue yonder.

8

6-8 Don't accept a meal from a tightwad;
 don't expect anything special.
He'll be as stingy with you as he is with himself;
 he'll say, "Eat! Drink!" but won't mean a word of it.
His miserly serving will turn your stomach
 when you realize the meal's a sham.

9

9 Don't bother talking sense to fools;
 they'll only poke fun at your words.

10

10-11 Don't stealthily move back the boundary lines
or cheat orphans out of their property,
For they have a powerful Advocate
who will go to bat for them.

11

12 Give yourselves to disciplined instruction;
open your ears to tested knowledge.

12

13-14 Don't be afraid to correct your young ones;
a spanking won't kill them.
A good spanking, in fact, might save them
from something worse than death.

13

15-16 Dear child, if you become wise,
I'll be one happy parent.
My heart will dance and sing
to the tuneful truth you'll speak.

14

17-18 Don't for a minute envy careless rebels;
soak yourself in the Fear-of-GOD —
That's where your future lies.
Then you won't be left with an armload of nothing.

15

19-21 Oh listen, dear child — become wise;
point your life in the right direction.
Don't drink too much wine and get drunk;
don't eat too much food and get fat.
Drunks and gluttons will end up on skid row,
in a stupor and dressed in rags.

BUY WISDOM, EDUCATION, INSIGHT

16

22-25 Listen with respect to the father who raised you,
and when your mother grows old, don't neglect her.
Buy truth — don't sell it for love or money;
buy wisdom, buy education, buy insight.
Parents rejoice when their children turn out well;
wise children become proud parents.
So make your father happy!
Make your mother proud!

17

26 Dear child, I want your full attention;
please do what I show you.

27-28   A whore is a bottomless pit;
         a loose woman can get you in deep trouble fast.
      She'll take you for all you've got;
         she's worse than a pack of thieves.

18

29-35   Who are the people who are always crying the blues?
         Who do you know who reeks of self-pity?
      Who keeps getting beat up for no reason at all?
         Whose eyes are bleary and bloodshot?
      It's those who spend the night with a bottle,
         for whom drinking is serious business.
      Don't judge wine by its label,
         or its bouquet, or its full-bodied flavor.
      Judge it rather by the hangover it leaves you with —
         the splitting headache, the queasy stomach.
      Do you really prefer seeing double,
         with your speech all slurred,
      Reeling and seasick,
         drunk as a sailor?
      "They hit me," you'll say, "but it didn't hurt;
         they beat on me, but I didn't feel a thing.
      When I'm sober enough to manage it,
         bring me another drink!"

INTELLIGENCE OUTRANKS MUSCLE

19

1-2   **24** Don't envy bad people;
         don't even want to be around them.
      All they think about is causing a disturbance;
      all they talk about is making trouble.

20

3-4   It takes wisdom to build a house,
         and understanding to set it on a firm foundation;
      It takes knowledge to furnish its rooms
         with fine furniture and beautiful draperies.

21

5-6   It's better to be wise than strong;
         intelligence outranks muscle any day.
      Strategic planning is the key to warfare;
         to win, you need a lot of good counsel.

22

7   Wise conversation is way over the head of fools;
      in a serious discussion they haven't a clue.

23

8-9   The person who's always cooking up some evil
         soon gets a reputation as prince of rogues.

Fools incubate sin;
    cynics desecrate beauty.

RESCUE THE PERISHING

24

10 If you fall to pieces in a crisis,
    there wasn't much to you in the first place.

25

11-12 Rescue the perishing;
    don't hesitate to step in and help.
If you say, "Hey, that's none of my business,"
    will that get you off the hook?
Someone is watching you closely, you know —
    Someone not impressed with weak excuses.

26

13-14 Eat honey, dear child — it's good for you —
    and delicacies that melt in your mouth.
Likewise knowledge,
    and wisdom for your soul —
Get that and your future's secured,
    your hope is on solid rock.

27

15-16 Don't interfere with good people's lives;
    don't try to get the best of them.
No matter how many times you trip them up,
    God-loyal people don't stay down long;
Soon they're up on their feet,
    while the wicked end up flat on their faces.

28

17-18 Don't laugh when your enemy falls;
    don't crow over his collapse.
GOD might see, and become very provoked,
    and then take pity on his plight.

29

19-20 Don't bother your head with braggarts
    or wish you could succeed like the wicked.
Those people have no future at all;
    they're headed down a dead-end street.

30

21-22 Fear GOD, dear child — respect your leaders;
    don't be defiant or mutinous.
Without warning your life can turn upside down,
    and who knows how or when it might happen?

MORE SAYINGS OF THE WISE
AN HONEST ANSWER

23 It's wrong, very wrong,
  to go along with injustice.

24-25 Whoever whitewashes the wicked
  gets a black mark in the history books,
But whoever exposes the wicked
  will be thanked and rewarded.

26 An honest answer
  is like a warm hug.

27 First plant your fields;
  then build your barn.

28-29 Don't talk about your neighbors behind their backs —
  no slander or gossip, please.
Don't say to anyone, "I'll get back at you for what you did to me.
  I'll make you pay for what you did!"

30-34 One day I walked by the field of an old lazybones,
  and then passed the vineyard of a lout;
They were overgrown with weeds,
  thick with thistles, all the fences broken down.
I took a long look and pondered what I saw;
  the fields preached me a sermon and I listened:
"A nap here, a nap there, a day off here, a day off there,
  sit back, take it easy — do you know what comes next?
Just this: You can look forward to a dirt-poor life,
  with poverty as your permanent houseguest!"

FURTHER WISE SAYINGS OF SOLOMON
THE RIGHT WORD AT THE RIGHT TIME

1 25 There are also these proverbs of Solomon,
  collected by scribes of Hezekiah, king of Judah.

2 God delights in concealing things;
  scientists delight in discovering things.

3 Like the horizons for breadth and the ocean for depth,
  the understanding of a good leader is broad and deep.

4-5 Remove impurities from the silver
  and the silversmith can craft a fine chalice;
Remove the wicked from leadership
  and authority will be credible and God-honoring.

6-7 Don't work yourself into the spotlight;
  don't push your way into the place of prominence.

It's better to be promoted to a place of honor
    than face humiliation by being demoted.

8   Don't jump to conclusions — there may be
    a perfectly good explanation for what you just saw.

9-10   In the heat of an argument,
    don't betray confidences;
Word is sure to get around,
    and no one will trust you.

11-12   The right word at the right time
    is like a custom-made piece of jewelry,
And a wise friend's timely reprimand
    is like a gold ring slipped on your finger.

13   Reliable friends who do what they say
    are like cool drinks in sweltering heat — refreshing!

14   Like billowing clouds that bring no rain
    is the person who talks big but never produces.

15   Patient persistence pierces through indifference;
    gentle speech breaks down rigid defenses.

A PERSON WITHOUT SELF-CONTROL

16-17   When you're given a box of candy, don't gulp it all down;
    eat too much chocolate and you'll make yourself sick;
And when you find a friend, don't outwear your welcome;
    show up at all hours and he'll soon get fed up.

18   Anyone who tells lies against the neighbors
    in court or on the street is a loose cannon.

19   Trusting a double-crosser when you're in trouble
    is like biting down on an abscessed tooth.

20   Singing light songs to the heavyhearted
    is like pouring salt in their wounds.

21-22   If you see your enemy hungry, go buy him lunch;
    if he's thirsty, bring him a drink.
Your generosity will surprise him with goodness,
    and GOD will look after you.

23   A north wind brings stormy weather,
    and a gossipy tongue stormy looks.

24   Better to live alone in a tumbledown shack
    than share a mansion with a nagging spouse.

25 Like a cool drink of water when you're worn out and weary
  is a letter from a long-lost friend.

26 A good person who gives in to a bad person
  is a muddied spring, a polluted well.

27 It's not smart to stuff yourself with sweets,
  nor is glory piled on glory good for you.

28 A person without self-control
  is like a house with its doors and windows knocked out.

Fools Recycle Silliness

1 26 We no more give honors to fools
   than pray for snow in summer or rain during harvest.

2 You have as little to fear from an undeserved curse
  as from the dart of a wren or the swoop of a swallow.

3 A whip for the racehorse, a tiller for the sailboat —
  and a stick for the back of fools!

4 Don't respond to the stupidity of a fool;
  you'll only look foolish yourself.

5 Answer a fool in simple terms
  so he doesn't get a swelled head.

6 You're only asking for trouble
  when you send a message by a fool.

7 A proverb quoted by fools
  is limp as a wet noodle.

8 Putting a fool in a place of honor
  is like setting a mud brick on a marble column.

9 To ask a moron to quote a proverb
  is like putting a scalpel in the hands of a drunk.

10 Hire a fool or a drunk
  and you shoot yourself in the foot.

11 As a dog eats its own vomit,
  so fools recycle silliness.

12 See that man who thinks he's so smart?
  You can expect far more from a fool than from him.

13 Loafers say, "It's dangerous out there!
  Tigers are prowling the streets!"
  and then pull the covers back over their heads.

14 Just as a door turns on its hinges,
        so a lazybones turns back over in bed.

15 A shiftless sluggard puts his fork in the pie,
        but is too lazy to lift it to his mouth.

LIKE GLAZE ON CRACKED POTTERY

16 Dreamers fantasize their self-importance;
        they think they are smarter
        than a whole college faculty.

17 You grab a mad dog by the ears
        when you butt into a quarrel that's none of your business.

18-19 People who shrug off deliberate deceptions,
        saying, "I didn't mean it, I was only joking,"
    Are worse than careless campers
        who walk away from smoldering campfires.

20 When you run out of wood, the fire goes out;
        when the gossip ends, the quarrel dies down.

21 A quarrelsome person in a dispute
        is like kerosene thrown on a fire.

22 Listening to gossip is like eating cheap candy;
        do you want junk like that in your belly?

23 Smooth talk from an evil heart
        is like glaze on cracked pottery.

24-26 Your enemy shakes hands and greets you like an old friend,
        all the while conniving against you.
    When he speaks warmly to you, don't believe him for a minute;
        he's just waiting for the chance to rip you off.
    No matter how cunningly he conceals his malice,
        eventually his evil will be exposed in public.

27 Malice backfires;
        spite boomerangs.

28 Liars hate their victims;
        flatterers sabotage trust.

YOU DON'T KNOW TOMORROW

1 27 Don't brashly announce what you're going to do tomorrow;
        you don't know the first thing about tomorrow.

2 Don't call attention to yourself;
        let others do that for you.

3 Carrying a log across your shoulders
    while you're hefting a boulder with your arms
Is nothing compared to the burden
    of putting up with a fool.

4 We're blasted by anger and swamped by rage,
    but who can survive jealousy?

5 A spoken reprimand is better
    than approval that's never expressed.

6 The wounds from a lover are worth it;
    kisses from an enemy do you in.

7 When you've stuffed yourself, you refuse dessert;
    when you're starved, you could eat a horse.

8 People who won't settle down, wandering hither and yon,
    are like restless birds, flitting to and fro.

9 Just as lotions and fragrance give sensual delight,
    a sweet friendship refreshes the soul.

10 Don't leave your friends or your parents' friends
    and run home to your family when things get rough;
Better a nearby friend
    than a distant family.

11 Become wise, dear child, and make me happy;
    then nothing the world throws my way will upset me.

12 A prudent person sees trouble coming and ducks;
    a simpleton walks in blindly and is clobbered.

13 Hold tight to collateral on any loan to a stranger;
    be wary of accepting what a transient has pawned.

14 If you wake your friend in the early morning
    by shouting "Rise and shine!"
It will sound to him
    more like a curse than a blessing.

15-16 A nagging spouse is like
    the drip, drip, drip of a leaky faucet;
You can't turn it off,
    and you can't get away from it.

Your Face Mirrors Your Heart

17 You use steel to sharpen steel,
    and one friend sharpens another.

18   If you care for your orchard, you'll enjoy its fruit;
        if you honor your boss, you'll be honored.

19   Just as water mirrors your face,
        so your face mirrors your heart.

20   Hell has a voracious appetite,
        and lust just never quits.

21   The purity of silver and gold is tested
        by putting them in the fire;
    The purity of human hearts is tested
        by giving them a little fame.

22   Pound on a fool all you like —
        you can't pound out foolishness.

23-27   Know your sheep by name;
        carefully attend to your flocks;
    (Don't take them for granted;
        possessions don't last forever, you know.)
    And then, when the crops are in
        and the harvest is stored in the barns,
    You can knit sweaters from lambs' wool,
        and sell your goats for a profit;
    There will be plenty of milk and meat
        to last your family through the winter.

IF YOU DESERT GOD'S LAW

1   **28** The wicked are edgy with guilt, ready to run off
        even when no one's after them;
    Honest people are relaxed and confident,
    bold as lions.

2   When the country is in chaos,
        everybody has a plan to fix it —
    But it takes a leader of real understanding
        to straighten things out.

3   The wicked who oppress the poor
        are like a hailstorm that beats down the harvest.

4   If you desert God's law, you're free to embrace depravity;
        if you love God's law, you fight for it tooth and nail.

5   Justice makes no sense to the evilminded;
        those who seek GOD know it inside and out.

6   It's better to be poor and direct
        than rich and crooked.

7 Practice God's law — get a reputation for wisdom;
  hang out with a loose crowd — embarrass your family.

8 Get as rich as you want
    through cheating and extortion,
  But eventually some friend of the poor
    is going to give it all back to them.

9 God has no use for the prayers
    of the people who won't listen to him.

10 Lead good people down a wrong path
    and you'll come to a bad end;
    do good and you'll be rewarded for it.

11 The rich think they know it all,
    but the poor can see right through them.

12 When good people are promoted, everything is great,
    but when the bad are in charge, watch out!

13 You can't whitewash your sins and get by with it;
    you find mercy by admitting and leaving them.

14 A tenderhearted person lives a blessed life;
    a hardhearted person lives a hard life.

15 Lions roar and bears charge —
    and the wicked lord it over the poor.

16 Among leaders who lack insight, abuse abounds,
    but for one who hates corruption, the future is bright.

17 A murderer haunted by guilt
    is doomed — there's no helping him.

18 Walk straight — live well and be saved;
    a devious life is a doomed life.

Doing Great Harm in Seemingly Harmless Ways

19 Work your garden — you'll end up with plenty of food;
    play and party — you'll end up with an empty plate.

20 Committed and persistent work pays off;
    get-rich-quick schemes are ripoffs.

21 Playing favorites is always a bad thing;
    you can do great harm in seemingly harmless ways.

22 A miser in a hurry to get rich
    doesn't know that he'll end up broke.

23 In the end, serious reprimand is appreciated
  far more than bootlicking flattery.

24 Anyone who robs father and mother
  and says, "So, what's wrong with that?"
  is worse than a pirate.

25 A grasping person stirs up trouble,
  but trust in GOD brings a sense of well-being.

26 If you think you know it all, you're a fool for sure;
  real survivors learn wisdom from others.

27 Be generous to the poor — you'll never go hungry;
  shut your eyes to their needs, and run a gauntlet of curses.

28 When corruption takes over, good people go underground,
  but when the crooks are thrown out, it's safe to come out.

IF PEOPLE CAN'T SEE WHAT GOD IS DOING

1 **29** For people who hate discipline
  and only get more stubborn,
  There'll come a day when life tumbles in and they break,
 but by then it'll be too late to help them.

2 When good people run things, everyone is glad,
  but when the ruler is bad, everyone groans.

3 If you love wisdom, you'll delight your parents,
  but you'll destroy their trust if you run with whores.

4 A leader of good judgment gives stability;
  an exploiting leader leaves a trail of waste.

5 A flattering neighbor is up to no good;
  he's probably planning to take advantage of you.

6 Evil people fall into their own traps;
  good people run the other way, glad to escape.

7 The good-hearted understand what it's like to be poor;
  the hardhearted haven't the faintest idea.

8 A gang of cynics can upset a whole city;
  a group of sages can calm everyone down.

9 A sage trying to work things out with a fool
  gets only scorn and sarcasm for his trouble.

10 Murderers hate honest people;
  moral folks encourage them.

11   A fool lets it all hang out;
     a sage quietly mulls it over.

12   When a leader listens to malicious gossip,
     all the workers get infected with evil.

13   The poor and their abusers have at least something in common:
     they can both *see* — their sight, GOD's gift!

14   Leadership gains authority and respect
     when the voiceless poor are treated fairly.

15   Wise discipline imparts wisdom;
     spoiled adolescents embarrass their parents.

16   When degenerates take charge, crime runs wild,
     but the righteous will eventually observe their collapse.

17   Discipline your children; you'll be glad you did —
     they'll turn out delightful to live with.

18   If people can't see what God is doing,
     they stumble all over themselves;
   But when they attend to what he reveals,
     they are most blessed.

19   It takes more than talk to keep workers in line;
     mere words go in one ear and out the other.

20   Observe the people who always talk before they think —
     even simpletons are better off than they are.

21   If you let people treat you like a doormat,
     you'll be quite forgotten in the end.

22   Angry people stir up a lot of discord;
     the intemperate stir up trouble.

23   Pride lands you flat on your face;
     humility prepares you for honors.

24   Befriend an outlaw
     and become an enemy to yourself.
   When the victims cry out,
     you'll be included in their curses
     if you're a coward to their cause in court.

25   The fear of human opinion disables;
     trusting in GOD protects you from that.

26 Everyone tries to get help from the leader,
  but only GOD will give us justice.

27 Good people can't stand the sight of deliberate evil;
  the wicked can't stand the sight of well-chosen goodness.

THE WORDS OF AGUR BEN YAKEH
GOD? WHO NEEDS HIM?

1-2 **30** The skeptic swore, "There is no God!
  No God! — I can do anything I want!
  I'm more animal than human;
  so-called human intelligence escapes me.

3-4 "I flunked 'wisdom.'
  I see no evidence of a holy God.
  Has anyone ever seen Anyone
    climb into Heaven and take charge?
    grab the winds and control them?
    gather the rains in his bucket?
    stake out the ends of the earth?
  Just tell me his name, tell me the names of his sons.
  Come on now — tell me!"

5-6 The believer replied, "Every promise of God proves true;
  he protects everyone who runs to him for help.
  So don't second-guess him;
  he might take you to task and show up your lies."

7-9 And then he prayed, "God, I'm asking for two things
    before I die; don't refuse me —
  Banish lies from my lips
    and liars from my presence.
  Give me enough food to live on,
    neither too much nor too little.
  If I'm too full, I might get independent,
    saying, 'God? Who needs him?'
  If I'm poor, I might steal
    and dishonor the name of my God."

10 Don't blow the whistle on your fellow workers
    behind their backs;
  They'll accuse you of being underhanded,
    and then *you'll* be the guilty one!

11 Don't curse your father
    or fail to bless your mother.

12 Don't imagine yourself to be quite presentable
    when you haven't had a bath in weeks.

13   Don't be stuck-up
  and think you're better than everyone else.

14   Don't be greedy,
  merciless and cruel as wolves,
Tearing into the poor and feasting on them,
  shredding the needy to pieces only to discard them.

15-16 A leech has twin daughters
  named "Gimme" and "Gimme more."

FOUR INSATIABLES

Three things are never satisfied,
  no, there are four that never say, "That's enough, thank you!" —

  hell,
  a barren womb,
  a parched land,
  a forest fire.

17   An eye that disdains a father
  and despises a mother —
that eye will be plucked out by wild vultures
  and consumed by young eagles.

FOUR MYSTERIES

18-19 Three things amaze me,
  no, four things I'll never understand —

  how an eagle flies so high in the sky,
  how a snake glides over a rock,
  how a ship navigates the ocean,
  why adolescents act the way they do.

20   Here's how a prostitute operates:
  she has sex with her client,
Takes a bath,
  then asks, "Who's next?"

FOUR INTOLERABLES

21-23 Three things are too much for even the earth to bear,
  yes, four things shake its foundations —

  when the janitor becomes the boss,
  when a fool gets rich,
  when a whore is voted "woman of the year,"
  when a "girlfriend" replaces a faithful wife.

FOUR SMALL WONDERS

24-28   There are four small creatures,
     wisest of the wise they are —

     ants — frail as they are,
       get plenty of food in for the winter;
     marmots — vulnerable as they are,
       manage to arrange for rock-solid homes;
     locusts — leaderless insects,
       yet they strip the field like an army regiment;
     lizards — easy enough to catch,
       but they sneak past vigilant palace guards.

FOUR DIGNITARIES

29-31   There are three solemn dignitaries,
     four that are impressive in their bearing —

     a lion, king of the beasts, deferring to none;
     a rooster, proud and strutting;
     a billy goat;
     a head of state in stately procession.

32-33   If you're dumb enough to call attention to yourself
     by offending people and making rude gestures,
Don't be surprised if someone bloodies your nose.
     Churned milk turns into butter;
     riled emotions turn into fist fights.

SPEAK OUT FOR JUSTICE

1   **31** The words of King Lemuel,
     the strong advice his mother gave him:

2-3   "Oh, son of mine, what can you be thinking of!
     Child whom I bore! The son I dedicated to God!
Don't dissipate your virility on fortune-hunting women,
     promiscuous women who shipwreck leaders.

4-7   "Leaders can't afford to make fools of themselves,
     gulping wine and swilling beer,
Lest, hung over, they don't know right from wrong,
     and the people who depend on them are hurt.
Use wine and beer only as sedatives,
     to kill the pain and dull the ache
Of the terminally ill,
     for whom life is a living death.

8-9   "Speak up for the people who have no voice,
     for the rights of all the down-and-outers.

Speak out for justice!
    Stand up for the poor and destitute!"

H Y M N T O A G O O D W I F E

10-31   A good woman is hard to find,
    and worth far more than diamonds.
Her husband trusts her without reserve,
    and never has reason to regret it.
Never spiteful, she treats him generously
    all her life long.
She shops around for the best yarns and cottons,
    and enjoys knitting and sewing.
She's like a trading ship that sails to faraway places
    and brings back exotic surprises.
She's up before dawn, preparing breakfast
    for her family and organizing her day.
She looks over a field and buys it,
    then, with money she's put aside, plants a garden.
First thing in the morning, she dresses for work,
    rolls up her sleeves, eager to get started.
She senses the worth of her work,
    is in no hurry to call it quits for the day.
She's skilled in the crafts of home and hearth,
    diligent in homemaking.
She's quick to assist anyone in need,
    reaches out to help the poor.
She doesn't worry about her family when it snows;
    their winter clothes are all mended and ready to wear.
She makes her own clothing,
    and dresses in colorful linens and silks.
Her husband is greatly respected
    when he deliberates with the city fathers.
She designs gowns and sells them,
    brings the sweaters she knits to the dress shops.
Her clothes are well-made and elegant,
    and she always faces tomorrow with a smile.
When she speaks she has something worthwhile to say,
    and she always says it kindly.
She keeps an eye on everyone in her household,
    and keeps them all busy and productive.
Her children respect and bless her;
    her husband joins in with words of praise:
"Many women have done wonderful things,
    but you've outclassed them all!"
Charm can mislead and beauty soon fades.
    The woman to be admired and praised
    is the woman who lives in the Fear-of-God.
Give her everything she deserves!
    Festoon her life with praises!